Philosophy and Living

This book is dedicated to my classes at the
University of the Third Age
in London

Philosophy and Living

Ralph Blumenau

ia

IMPRINT ACADEMIC

First reprint: January 2003

Published in the UK by Imprint Academic
PO Box 1, Thorverton EX5 5YX, UK

Published in the USA by Imprint Academic
Philosophy Documentation Center
PO Box 7147, Charlottesville, VA 22906-7147, USA

ISBN 0 907845 33 9

A catalogue record for this book is available from the British Library
Library of Congress Card Number: 2002102728

Contents

PART THREE: RENAISSANCE AND REFORMATION

PART FOUR: THE SEVENTEENTH CENTURY

PART FIVE: THE EIGHTEENTH CENTURY

Introduction

There have always been parts of philosophy which have been highly technical and so abstruse that only specialists could understand them. These features have their own importance, but the title of this book is intended to show that it concerns itself mainly with those aspects of philosophy that have influenced people's attitudes towards their lives, towards each other and their society, towards their Gods, and towards the ethical problems that confront them.

I am a historian by profession; I have taught history as a main subject, initially to sixth formers and now to retired people. I should describe myself as an amateur rather than a professional philosopher (as specialists in the subject may swiftly discover) but I have always taught philosophy as an important component of history. Although I have of course grappled with history's technical matters as well as with the wider issues, it is the latter which have always interested me most, and it is not surprising that my classes have also shown the greatest interest in those aspects which touch on contemporary concerns. The students have not always immediately seen the relevance to contemporary issues of problems raised by philosophers in the past. So I have found that it has been helpful for me to have specifically raised this relevance.

This book is the result of that experience. I have selected mainly those aspects of the history of ideas which have something to say to our present preoccupations; and I have proceeded, as I do in my classes, in a chronological fashion. I am interested in all those figures who, in the past, have contributed to shape the thought of their time and of later ages; and I do not draw the sharp distinction that professionals do between philosophers, theologians, scientists, psychologists and even political propagandists. I set out to expound the ideas of a particular thinker; I then invite discussion of the material and especially of how it relates to issues that are still alive today. Over the last five years I have tape-recorded these discussions, and a special feature of this book is that my student's reflections and mine – set in from the margin and in a different type – interrupt the exposition.

Another feature of the book are the many footnotes which refer the reader back to earlier, and forward to later, pages of the book. They are intended to serve the dual purpose of making the references easier to look up and to reinforce the idea that throughout the centuries philosophers have often grappled with the same problems, sometimes coming up with similar approaches and sometimes with radically different ones.

At the same time I have assumed that many readers will not be reading the book from cover to cover, but may read chapters in isolation. This accounts for the occasional repetition of arguments that I hope will not irritate unduly those who read the complete book in a relatively short time.

The topics I have chosen are selective, and the book does not purport to give a comprehensive account of the thinkers with whom I deal.

As a historian, I am well aware that it is dangerous to read present concerns into an interpretation of the past. I dare say that the same danger exists in philosophy: perhaps the thinkers of the past, were they alive today, would be puzzled by what I may have occasionally read into them. But philosophers, like other figures from the past, have no control over the effect their thoughts and actions have in later years. The historian must be interested not only in what an idea meant to a character in the past, but also in how that idea has been interpreted by later generations. I try to be fair to the original context of an idea, but I must admit that what fascinates me most is the potency of some ideas down the ages. If I have unwittingly falsified the former, I must crave the indulgence of the professional philosophers and theologians.

Acknowledgments

Much of this book is based on notes I have made on my reading over several decades, long before I had the idea that I might be writing a book. Although I have a comprehensive list of the books I have read (they are all on my shelves), it never occurred to me to include page references in my notes. I may occasionally have copied phrases or incorporated lines of arguments that came from these books, but it is impossible now to track all of these down. The bibliography at the end of this volume shows the range of authors to whom I have been indebted. If any of them feel that here and there parts of my text are very close to what they have written, I would apologize for any plagiarism they may suspect and ask them to accept that it was wholly unintentional.

I am very grateful to my editor, Keith Sutherland, for the encouragement he has given me throughout, and to Sandra Good and Bryn Williams for their meticulous proof-reading. In addition Bryn Williams has made many substantive comments that have caused me to make numerous changes to my text. Professional and specialist philosophers will undoubtedly find mistakes in this work of an amateur author. For these I must, of course, take full responsibility.

The other debt I am only too glad to acknowledge is to my classes at the University of the Third Age in London. Several of them had asked me to write such a book. Without the incorporation of their comments and the questions they have raised, this volume would have been very much shorter and much of its flavour would have been lost. It is to my students, therefore, that I dedicate the result.

Parts of chapters 13, 27 and 31 first appeared in the quarterly journal *Philosophy Now*: "Free Will and Predestination" in issue No.20 (Spring 1998); "Aesthetics and Absolutes" in issue No. 3 (Spring 1992); and "Kant and the Thing in Itself" in issue No. 31 (Spring, 2001).

PART ONE:
GREECE AND ROME

CHAPTER 1

The Greek Cosmologists

The earliest Western philosophers came from the Greek settlements on the coast of Ionia, what is today the western coast of Turkey. What made them philosophers was that they sensed that behind the ever-changing phenomena of this world there must be something that does not change. They originally thought that there must be some ultimate stuff – what the Greeks called *arche* and the Germans call *Urstoff* – of which everything is made; and they speculated on what this might be. In the sixth century BC they believed that it must be just one *arche*: Thales thought it was Water; Anaximenes thought it was Air; Heraclitus thought it was Fire because it can transform everything into itself. (He also had a more sophisticated idea: that whilst Fire was the ultimate *stuff*, there lay behind it something that was not a stuff at all, but was Reality itself. We will look at that idea more closely presently.) In the following century, the fifth BC, Empedocles, from Agrigento in Southern Italy, thought that material things were probably composed of a combination of more than one stuff: in his work, we come across the Four Elements (Earth, Air, Fire and Water) which combine in various proportions; but even that seemed unduly limited, and finally Democritus, the most famous of a group of philosophers from Thrace who were called Atomists, postulated the existence of innumerable tiny indivisible building blocks which combined and re-combined to make everything that was in this world. They called these building blocks atoms, from the Greek *a* + *tomos*, which means non-divisible. (The soul, too, was composed of atoms. Like the atoms making up the body, they dispersed on death. They did not perish, but recombined to form new souls: there could therefore be no such thing as individual immortality.)

The branch of philosophy which aims to explain how the material universe works is known as "natural philosophy". It was later to separate itself off from the rest of philosophy and call itself "physical science". The word "science" originally simply meant "knowledge". It separated itself off from philosophy when it had developed its own techniques of experimentation and verification. These are largely specific to what we now call science. They are on the whole not the methods applied in thinking about, for example, religion or ethics or aesthetics, which are typically philosophical subjects. But, for many centuries before the so-called "scientific method" was developed, there was no demarcation between philosophy and science. Of course, the demarcation is not absolute today either: there is a branch of philosophy today which is called the Philosophy of Science, though that is philosophical in a way that what was called "natural philosophy" is not. Anyway, for those early centuries, we class thinkers who reflected about the nature of the physical universe among the philosophers.

One may smile at a "natural philosophy" which held there was just one stuff, or even a mere four elements, at the bottom of everything; in Democritus, however, we meet one of many prescientific thinkers who constantly astonish us by their intuitions. After all, they had no microscopes, and it was many centuries later that the existence of these tiny building blocks was actually scientifically demonstrated.

One of the most astonishing aspects of the Greeks was their intuition that the universe was not random. It is true, of course, that they could observe several separate regular phenomena: the cycle of the seasons, the movements of the stars, the processes of birth, growth and decay. Compared with the knowledge that modern man possesses, the Greeks possessed, as it were, only a few fragments of a gigantic jigsaw puzzle. Indeed, they could not even *know* that these fragments, a few of which they had managed to fit together here and there, *were* part of the same jigsaw puzzle. When the Greeks spoke of the universe, they described it as *cosmos*, and the original meaning of that word was Order. The first philosopher who applied the word Order to the Universe was Pythagoras, who, like the Ionian cosmologists lived in the sixth century BC. The belief that there is such an Order, that where there is one Order there must be one Law governing it, and that the more carefully man observed this world, the more he would find that more and more of the pieces would fit together and that the still missing pieces *must* somehow fit in with the overall plan and with the pieces of the jigsaw which we already have – all that was a stupendous and immensely fruitful leap of faith that made them unique in their time. Over the succeeding centuries that intuition, that faith, would be abundantly justified, so much so that it has governed the outlook of western man ever since. The assumption lies at the bottom of all scientific enquiry, which takes it for granted that we can constantly increase the area of the pieces that we have been able to fit together. Of course, a note of caution has been struck from time to time, especially by some religious people who have warned us to be humble and to remember that God moves in mysterious ways which we will never fathom; but even they believe that God *has* a plan, that there *is* a jigsaw, even if it is one that fallible mortals will never get anywhere near to completing.

We must now go back to Heraclitus, who made two further lasting contributions to the way we think today.

The first was that what appear to be opposites or contradictions, like illness and health, are really complementary: they not only need each other in order to define each other, but the tension between them is a necessary aspect of change and development.

The East has a very similar concept in the Yin and the Yang, whose symbol is a circle with a black and a white part like this:

It symbolizes that both parts are needed to make the whole, and the way each colour penetrates into the other's semicircle symbolizes their interdependence and interpenetration.

Heraclitus says, "We must know that war is common to all things, and that strife is justice, and all things come into being and pass away through strife." Opposites are parts of a reality that embraces them both, and within which they are both absorbed. To this Reality he gave the name *Logos,* whose original meaning was Reason; and he also called it the One.

> The positing of the One is of course another form of that affirmation of that *single universal order* to which we have referred earlier. When Heraclitus speaks of "all things passing away through strife", he may have meant this on several levels: it may be the strife of Life and Death, with Death always being the inescapable victor; or it may be defeat in conflict: the weaker will perish and the fittest will survive. But probably we have here the first seeds of the idea which would be most fully developed by Hegel at the beginning of the nineteenth century: that progress is the result of tensions and contradictions between ideas which are then put into practice in the material world. After a while the tensions are resolved, Hegel believed, not by the total defeat of one side, but by a higher synthesis between the two opposing ideas and their concrete materializations. The new synthesis will in due course generate its own opposite, and that new tension will be resolved by a still higher synthesis – and so on, until all tensions are resolved in the Absolute, which is Heraclitus' One. We can surely think of plenty of situations in the history of thought where the earlier stages of this process have taken place. But we will leave examples of this until we come to consider Hegel.

Man's own reason is a weak form of the Reason that governs the universe. It is the fiery element in him, which flickers upwards towards the Universal Reason and merges with it when it departs from the body, leaving the latter as a mere useless combination of earth and water.

> This is another seminal thought, which will affect the religions of the West, and is also found in the religions of the East: that Man is a creature endowed with reason which can grasp, however feebly and partially, something of the Reason that governs the world. Moreover, human reason *strives* to grasp Divine Reason more fully; or, alternatively, the human soul strives to be united with God. Both strivings can only be achieved after death. Before then, we can only see "through a glass darkly". We have here even the idea that the Soul is imprisoned in the body, is only liberated after death and leaves the body behind as the dross that it is.

Heraclitus made a further contribution to the history of thought. His senses told him that there was nothing permanent in the phenomena of this world: everything was constantly changing, was in a permanent state of flux: "You cannot step twice into the same river." This of course fitted in with the idea we have already mentioned: "that all things come into being and pass away through strife". He trusted what his senses told him.

However, two philosophers from Elea, Parmenides and his pupil Zeno, thought not only that our senses deceived us (and we can think of plenty of examples where they do, can't we?), but that in particular they deceive us when they tell us that everything is continually changing. On the contrary, said Parmenides, his *reason* told him that change is impossible. This is how he argued it:

> If anything comes to be, then it comes either out of being or out of not-being. If the former, then it already is – in which case it does not come to be; if the latter, then it is nothing, since out of nothing comes nothing.[1]

Similarly, Zeno's reason told him that if Achilles and a tortoise have a race and if Achilles, because his speed is ten times that of the tortoise, kindly gives the tortoise a hundred metres start, he can never overtake the tortoise: by the time Achilles has covered the hundred metres start, the tortoise has covered ten metres; by the time that Achilles has covered those ten metres, the tortoise is a further metre ahead; by the time he has covered that metre, the tortoise is a tenth of a metre ahead, and so on ad infinitum. The tortoise leads by a smaller and smaller distance, but it always maintains its lead and therefore Achilles can never overtake it!

In another paradox, Zeno argued that at any one moment an arrow occupies a fixed position in space. A split second later it occupies a different fixed position. There is no moment between the two when it does not occupy a fixed position; therefore our perception that the arrow moves in flight must be a delusion.

From these two examples we can see that "reason" can lead one astray quite as badly as can the senses – and indeed how big the distance can be between the senses or reason on the one hand and "common sense" on the other. This has not stopped philosophers arguing for centuries on what exactly the relationship is between reason and the senses. Some philosophers, like Descartes, maintain that reason, properly handled, will never let you down. Others, like Hume, say that all our thoughts are in the last resort based on our sense impressions.

Is it true that reason, properly handled, will never let us down? And is the real tension not so much between reason and the senses – where certain techniques are available to solve the problem – as between reason and the emotions, where the techniques are rather less precise?

1 The formulation is that of Frederick Coplestone.

CHAPTER 2

Pythagoras

Pythagoras (ca.530 BC) also came from Ionia originally, but he differed from his fellow Ionians in that his temperament was basically religious and metaphysical. He and his followers were members of an Orphic cult – so called after Orpheus, whose music was said to have embodied divine mysteries. Even people who know nothing about philosophy will know that Pythagoras was also a great mathematician. What schoolboy has not struggled with Pythagoras' proof that the sum of the square of the hypotenuse of a right-angled triangle is equal to the sum of the squares of the other two sides? [1] Pythagoras also discovered that there are demonstrable mathematical relationships in music: for example, if you pluck two strings of equal thickness and tension, one of which is exactly twice as long as the other, the sound they produce are an exact octave apart. This led him to think that not only music embodies the divine, but that mathematics does also. From such experiences he concluded that "all things are numbers", that numbers, in fact, rather than air, fire, or water, are the *Urstoff* of which the world is made. The contemplation of the beautiful mathematical order in the universe [2] was for him akin to a religious experience.

> Here again we have an example of the uncanny intuition that the ancient Greeks possessed. How he would have rejoiced to know that one day sound waves could be measured and that it would then be found that these have an exact mathematical relationship with the length of the string that is being plucked! The more we have learnt about mathematics, the more wonderful the relationship between numbers and movement, numbers and gravity, numbers and the components of matter turns out to be. It was such relationships that led the twentieth-century scientist and philosopher A.N. Whitehead to exclaim, "God must be a great mathematician".

Pythagoras thought that the mathematics we practise on earth (he was thinking particularly of geometry) can never achieve the absolute purity of mathematical ideals. The pure concept of a line does not allow for it to have any breadth; yet even the thinnest line we draw on paper has to have breadth, just

1 Pythagoras' Theorem is a beautiful example of *deductive* reasoning: you begin with a very few propositions and then draw conclusions from those. The opposite is called *inductive* reasoning: you begin by collecting a number of experiences and work out by experimentation what conclusions you could draw from them. You then test the conclusions to see whether the induction has been correct. Most Greeks favoured deductive over inductive reasoning (Aristotle is a striking exception). That tendency was reinforced by the teaching of Socrates, as we shall see below where we discuss some of the implications of privileging deductive over inductive reasoning.

2 It will be remembered that to describe the universe, Pythagoras used the word *cosmos*, whose original meaning is order.

as even the minutest point we mark on paper has a dimension which it ought not to have. So he drew a distinction between the concept of the Ideal and the Eternal on the one hand, and the imperfections in the way in which we express them here on earth on the other.

Mathematical truths are of course understood through the intellect, through reason; and if the contemplation of the beauty of mathematics results in religious experience, it means that the path to religious truth comes via the intellect and not in the way of the Dionysiacs, by fostering a deliberate abandonment of rational self-control through dance and rhythm and wine until ecstasy (literally "standing outside yourself") is achieved.

> Pythagoras here begins a debate which will run through the centuries. Some think that religion is not incompatible with reason and can indeed by strengthened by reasoning. Others believe that religion requires an emotional surrender to the Divine, and they tend to distrust reasoning as liable to undermine religious belief.

Mathematical relationships in music create harmony; harmony implies a certain balance, and therefore to achieve balance and harmony must be one of the aims of the philosopher. A harmonious life is a happier life not simply because it is more comfortable: it is more comfortable because in it is reflected the divine plan for what life ought to be. Balance in turn implies the injunction that there should be no excesses, that there should be, in Pythagoras' words "moderation in all things" – an injunction that has become famous because it expresses what most people recognize as wisdom.

> What about enthusiasm? The word comes from the Greek for "being possessed by a god". There have always been people who are incapable of allowing themselves to be *possessed* by anything. Can enthusiasm be temperate? "Moderate enthusiasm" seems to be a contradiction in terms. Yet is not a life without enthusiasm, without the capacity to feel intensely, lacking something of value?
>
> Perhaps Pythagoras meant that, even if we *feel* intensely, we should yet always *act* in moderation. But some people think that few causes are advanced with moderation. Does it need a degree of extremism in certain instances to move the world along? Is moderation often an excuse for inactivity and complacency? Or is it, on the contrary, a most difficult virtue to practise in the face of a disagreeable situation?

It was also requisite for good health that the elements within the body should be in proper balance. Empedocles, who lived in the following century, fixed these elements as four: earth, air, fire and water. Later, these were represented in the four humours. If one of these upsets the balance by being present in excess, then the body and the mind suffered from being either choleric (by having too much yellow bile), or sanguine (too much blood), or phlegmatic (too much phlegm) or melancholic (too much black bile).

Pythagoras and his Orphic friends rejected the traditional Greek idea that the souls of the dead have a wraith-like existence in Hades. Instead, they believed that the soul has a chance to ascend to Elysium or Heaven, but only if it has been purified by having been trained to virtue in life. (If it had not been so trained, it would migrate into another body, possibly a lower one like that of an animal.)

It was therefore very important that the soul should be properly cultivated. For this purpose Pythagoras founded a school and a community, consisting of both men and women on a basis of equality. Its members were to lead a life devoted to virtue and high thinking (in which mathematics surely played a part), and to share all their goods in common.

> We shall see later how great an influence the ideas of Pythagoras had on Plato: the necessity for the wise man to train his soul to understand something of the plan behind the universe; the importance of mathematics in this training; the necessity for this purpose to eschew personal property; the equality of men and women in the community of philosophers and the distinction between the perfect and eternal ideas on the one hand and the imperfect and transitory phenomena on the other.
>
> The two men had something else in common: each of them had bad experiences in advising governments: Pythagoras and his community were driven out of Croton, a town in southern Italy which they had tried to govern; and Plato failed to turn Dionysius II, the Tyrant of Syracuse, into a Philosopher King.

CHAPTER 3

Protagoras and the Sophists

As the Greeks extended their acquaintance with, on the one hand, the neighbouring advanced cultures of Persia, Babylon and Egypt and, on the other, the more primitive cultures of the Scythians and the Thracians, they became increasingly aware of the fact that different societies have different values. This led some of them to the conclusion that standards, values and truths are not absolute: they are shaped by each society and, for that matter, may be shaped by different groups or even different individuals within each society - in other words, that standards, values and truths are *relative.* In the words of Protagoras (ca. 481 to 411 BC), "Man is the measure of all things".

In this saying Protagoras not only set "Man" against the gods or against some pure criteria of perfection laid up in Heaven, but also envisaged the possibility that any one man may entertain values which are not those of the society in which he lives. He accepted, however, that most individuals will accept the values of their society. Either they have never thought deeply enough about them to question them, or they think it is best for them as well as for the cohesion of the community that they should not too lightly challenge the codes of belief and behaviour which bind that community together. We must remember that most Greeks took it for granted that men function at their best only when they are integral members of the community, and that if their beliefs or practices were to cut them off too sharply from the community, they would become in some sense less than fully developed human beings. Good citizenship therefore requires certain *norms* of behaviour, an adhesion to society's values even though these are relative and not absolute. So, although Protagoras had written a book showing that he was personally agnostic about the gods, he still thought that *in practice* men should accept the religious codes of their community.

If values and truths do not depend on divine revelation, then they are of course open to argument, and that in turn means that one needs to distinguish between good and bad arguments. Protagoras and his followers, who called themselves sophists (meaning teachers of wisdom)[1] therefore developed the art of rhetoric.Originally this word was not a synonym for what today we also call oratory. It meant skill in using words correctly - defining them precisely in

1 Pythagoras was the first to have described his pursuit as *philosophia*, specifically describing himself as a *lover* of wisdom. He would have considered the name *sophist*, with the implication that its exponents *knew* what wisdom was, presumptuous.

the first place and then devising the rules of logic within which a sound argument is conducted. That, at least, was the idea. In practice, many sophists were thought to teach their pupils how to be able to argue for any cause and on any side, how to make "the weaker appear the better cause" when, for example, lawyers defended their clients in the courts. Plato accused them of doing just that; and in due course the words "rhetoric" and "sophistry" acquired the pejorative connotations they have today.

As we shall see later, Plato had other reasons for disliking the sophists: he believed that truths were absolute, and he thought that the sophists, with their debating skills and their relativism, undermined and corroded truth, morals and traditions.

> The relativism of the sophists still speaks very powerfully to us today, as does the unease that their opponents felt. There have been periods in the history of thought when the sophists' kind of relativism was treated as blasphemy or as heresy. The orthodox members of the three great monotheistic religions which arose in the Middle East – Judaism, Christianity and Islam – have been, and still are, particularly inclined to oppose relativism. Polytheistic religions have been more accommodating, and some Eastern religions especially Hinduism while believing in certain verities, teach that these can be approached in many different ways. Kipling, who had had so much experience of India, wrote, "Many ways hast Thou fashioned, O Lord; and all of them lead to the Light." How far can a contemporary follower of a monotheistic religion accept this?
>
> Between the time when the monotheistic religions established themselves and the eighteenth century, there was very little acceptance of relativism. In the course of the eighteenth century, the hold of religious orthodoxy weakened considerably, and relativism strengthened accordingly. From time to time, as religious orthodoxy declined, secular orthodoxies, both of the Right and of the Left, took their place. Like their religious forerunners, these, too, regarded any questioning as heresies to be rooted out. Liberal societies deplore such intolerance.
>
> There is no doubt that relativism has made enormous strides during the last two centuries, and the question has often been asked by worried citizens whether it has not in fact damaged the fabric of society. Protagoras, as we have seen, believed that individuals only become fully developed human beings as members of a community. The concept of individuals being primary and society only secondary would never have occurred to him or his contemporaries. While they were aware that relativism could in theory undermine communal values, they did not think that this would happen widely in practice. Today, with individualism very much stronger than it was in the time of Protagoras, we are not so sure.
>
> So the question that arises for us is this: if there are *no absolute* values, does that mean that there are *absolutely no* values? If it does not, what basis is there for value systems that do not purport to be absolute ones? We shall repeatedly be coming back to this question.
>
> There is also a contemporary relevance in Plato's concern that the Sophists taught their pupils how to make the weaker appear the better cause, especially in the law courts. Some people feel uneasy that defence lawyers have to put up the strongest case they can for their client, even in cases when it must be reasonably clear to them that their client has in fact committed the offence with which he is charged. We do of course consider it necessary that a defen-

dant is entitled under all circumstances to the best defence possible, and that the defence lawyer is therefore fulfilling an important civic function. Is this a case where two philosophical principles clash?

CHAPTER 4

Socrates

Socrates had all the dialectical skills of a sophist, but, like his pupil Plato, he intensely disliked the relativism in the service of which so many sophists deployed their abilities. We cannot be sure what absolute truths he espoused. Socrates left no written works behind, and the account we have of his views depends to a very large extent on Plato who, in his dialogues, makes Socrates his spokesman. It is difficult to disentangle what might have been the views of the historical Socrates from the opinions attributed to him by Plato but which were really Plato's own. Socrates is reported as being brilliant at asking questions about concepts, definitions, and philosophical positions, but as having been reluctant to give any clear answers himself: "I know that I do not know" is one of the famous sayings attributed to him. The sophists, too, had claimed that they did not know the ultimate truth, but that was because they did not think an ultimate truth existed. Socrates, however, assumed that there *was* such a thing, however difficult it was to reach a full understanding of it. As Professor Myles Burnyeat has put it, at the end of a session with Socrates, "you end up not with a firm answer, but with a much better grasp of the problem than you had before."[1]

Socrates had begun by studying natural philosophy, asking questions about motion, about atomistic theory etc., as the Greek Cosmologists had done. But he soon realized that what really interested him was not an understanding of material facts or of the origin of matter, but questions of values and ends, of ethics and of politics. These, he thought, were much more important.

> This reversal of the priorities of the Cosmologists had a profound influence on European thought for many centuries. With the notable exception of Aristotle, philosophers for the next 1600 years or so were not very interested in the sciences and considered scientific pursuits as an inferior form of intellectual activity. A concern with ethics, religion and politics was the mark of an educated gentleman; experimentation and practical application in science were not. The classical education which the upper classes continued to receive until the early years of this century reinforced this social attitude; and although from the sixteenth and especially the seventeenth century onwards some gentlemen did a little experimental work in laboratories, that did not greatly increase the social status of those who engaged in applied science. The pursuit of Pure Science was somewhat more prestigious – and that, too, is part of the heritage of classical thought which tended to privilege universal principles over particular manifestations of them.

1 Discussion with Bryan Magee in *The Great Philosophers*, p. 16, BBC Books, 1987.

To what extent has this attitude affected the progress of science in Britain? in France? in Germany? in the United States? in Japan? To what extent does the progress of science depend on the cultural climate in the upper classes?

Certainly in our own time our society has paid more and more attention to the applied sciences. Does it still attach the same importance that Socrates did to the pursuit of values and ends? If not, why not? And if not, what have been and are likely to be the consequences?

Socrates (or perhaps it was Plato) believed that the knowledge of values was *innate*: the Soul had possessed it before it entered the human body, but that knowledge was then clouded or hidden. It was the task of the Socratic teacher, by skilful questioning, to bring it out of the clouded state back into consciousness. Socrates compared his task to that of a midwife. (His mother had in fact been a midwife). The teacher of philosophy is literally an educator; the word "educate" originally means "to lead out", "to bring forth".

The knowledge of values, in other words, is not something to *be inculcated in* the student, but is something to be elicited from him. That procedure is of course much more time-consuming, but many educators believe that the best education is one that forces students to work out answers for themselves, perhaps with the help of skilful questioning.

For the questioning one has to rely on the integrity and wisdom of the person who is asking the questions. The Socrates of the Platonic dialogues is often a little like a sheep-dog: by asking questions in a certain way, Socrates does not really leave the answer open, but herds the replies in the direction in which he wants them to go. A clever teacher, like a clever barrister, can abuse the inexperience of his pupils by asking loaded questions which the student does not recognize as such. The answers brought forth by that technique would then be a distortion of the innate knowledge that the pupil is said to possess.

Some educators are not so opposed to the inculcation of values, provided, of course, that they are the "right ones". It does not disturb them that their critics may call that conditioning. They would answer that children, in particular, need to be given a firm framework of values at an early age. The young may not be capable of working values out for themselves and may not even be interested in trying. If asked to do so, they may merely become confused.

In fact, the pupils of Socrates were not children or early adolescents. It was young men whom he invited to work out values for themselves. What they were encouraged to draw out from within themselves for examination were ideas that were not really innate at all, but had been inculcated in them in their earlier years. We will see that the Socrates who is the spokesman for Plato's educational ideas in *The Republic* will himself impose a drastic system of conditioning upon the very young.

Of course only a certain kind of knowledge can be elicited from within – namely the kind that Socrates thought the most important: knowledge about values and ends, ethics and politics. The technique will not be able to elicit *factual* knowledge, like the date of a battle or the composition of a chemical. That must be acquired from an *outside* source, which may be verbal or written or experimental. But we have already seen that Socrates did not consider that kind of knowledge particularly important.

The knowledge of the Good is to be found by the intellect: it is not handed down by the gods. Good is not good because the gods approve of it; the gods approve of it because it is Good.

> Socrates was asking his young men to elucidate for themselves what is good rather than having it handed down by priests. The opponents of Socrates saw this as tantamount to questioning the role of the gods. One of the charges on which Socrates would be condemned to death was that he had not worshipped the gods of Athens. He therefore opened another debate which was to run for centuries: that between the exponents of free enquiry and those of orthodox intolerance.

A true knowledge of values enables one to be virtuous: the more one knows about them, the more virtuous one is. Indeed, Socrates goes as far as to say that knowledge is virtue, and that sin is the result of ignorance. He argues it in this way: a virtuous Soul is a healthy and therefore a happy soul; a vicious soul (which perpetrates vicious acts) is a damaged soul such as noone would want to have. Those who commit vicious acts, therefore, obviously have no knowledge of the damage they are doing to their soul. That harm is usually much more serious than the harm they inflict on their victims: the injury done to them is generally inflicted only on their bodies. Socrates concludes from this that evildoers are more in need of being *taught* where they have gone wrong than of being *punished*.

> What about people who do something which they *know* is wicked?
>
> Socrates believed that in such a case *true* knowledge, which shows that virtue is always ultimately more rational than vice, is being clouded by psychological impulses and weaknesses.
>
> There is a modern parallel to this view: that wrongdoing is a kind of psychological illness for which people are not responsible. What wrongdoers need, so the argument goes, is not punishment but therapy, and the way that therapy works is to make the patient understand the source of his sickness and, by knowing it, enable him to control it.
>
> Socrates agreed with this; the wise man must be aware of his impulses so as to be able to control them, and therefore one of his cardinal rules was that you should "know yourself".
>
> Self-knowledge is of course important, but is it sufficient? What happens if we know that we are poisoned by, say, envy, but find ourselves incapable of controlling it?
>
> Does Socrates attach too much importance to intellectual knowledge as the basis of virtue? What about moral instincts? The forms that moral instincts take in each one of us are, we know, mostly conditioned by our environment, and they may or may not subsequently be refined by intellectual thought. Could this not often be a sounder basis for virtuous behaviour than pure intellect?
>
> And what about the honourable behaviour of many people who are not very bright? Socrates accepted that a person may behave well – he may, for instance, show courage – but he did not regard a courageous individual as *virtuous* unless that person *knew* what courage is. Is there some unacceptable intellectual élitism here?

Socrates was certainly no egalitarian. He particularly disliked the idea that all Athenian citizens are equally capable of making sound judgments on political matters. Pericles, in his famous Funeral Oration (431 BC), had proclaimed: "An Athenian citizen does not neglect the state because he takes care of his own household; and even those of us who are engaged in business have a very fair idea of politics. We alone regard a man who takes no interest in public affairs not as a harmless but as a useless character; and if few of us are originators, we are all sound judges of policy." The Athenians prided themselves on their "happy versatility". But during the lifetime of Socrates, Athens was rent between the democrats who supported the Periclean ideal and the oligarchs. The oligarchs had twice briefly seized power from the democrats; but these were back in power in 403 BC. Among Socrates' pupils were several who supported the oligarchs' ideas and poured scorn on the democrats. Doubtlessly they availed themselves of the arguments of their teacher that knowledge is needed for good government; that knowledge required training, and that therefore it was absurd to believe that all Athenians were "sound judges of policy". We will look at the arguments that supported the élitist idea of politics when we come to Plato. Here it suffices to say that the democrats held Socrates responsible for the views of his oligarchic pupils; he was accused, among other things, of "corrupting the young" with such ideas - and he was condemned to die. In the *Apology*, the famous last speech attributed to him by Plato, Socrates told his grieving friends that he did not fear death: it was either a dreamless sleep or else a happy after-life, but that in any case he died happy because all his life he had pursued the truth. (399 BC)

CHAPTER 5

Plato

Plato was profoundly shocked by the death of his teacher Socrates. It reinforced his opposition to the democratic ideas in the name of which his teacher had been condemned to death. He fled Athens for a while, but returned in 395 BC. Twelve years later, in 387, he founded the Academy in Athens (so named because it was built on a plot of land which was said to have belonged to Academus, a minor character in the legend of Theseus.)

His teaching there has been handed down to us in the form of written "Socratic" dialogues, in most of which his mentor expresses ideas which were either those of Socrates or Plato's own – it is not always easy to tell which are which. As some of them are successively refined or modified in the later dialogues, we may be sure that at that stage they represent not only Plato's elaboration of Socrates but also ideas which Socrates had never taught.

There are thirty-six dialogues which, at some time or other, have been attributed to Plato. Scholars generally reject six of these as unauthentic, are not sure about six more, but accept twenty-four as undisputedly by Plato. For reasons that will become clear presently, perhaps the key dialogue is the *Politeia,* known in English as *The Republic.* The discussion which follows will centre on this work, supplementing its ideas, where appropriate, with material from other dialogues.

The *Polis*

The title *Politeia* tells us that the dialogue is about the *polis*. This word originally meant "community". It came to be applied to what we call a "city state", which, of course, is a community organized in the particular way and for the particular purposes that we now call "political". The populations of the Greek city states were small, and the number of its citizens (free men as distinct from slaves, and men as distinct from women) was very much smaller still. So there was hardly a distinction between what we today call the community and what we call the state. In Athens, the whole public (i.e. all citizens as defined above) had an active share in deciding the affairs of the community. The communal interest was what the Romans would call a *res publica,* a public thing, from which the word *Republic* derives. So the title which is born by Plato's most famous dialogue is not wholly inappropriate: a substantial section of it does deal with what we would call today the community's political organization. But we should never forget the wider and less specifically political resonance that was carried by the word *politeia.*

When, therefore, Aristotle would define man as "a political animal", he would mean that man is by nature a social, communal animal, who can only fulfill himself by living as part of a community. A hermit, for example, was living a life that was deficient, unfulfilled. It was only the community that made man's life meaningful.

All Athenians accepted this idea, and so did Plato. Where he differed from his fellow citizens was that the latter had come to think in the political terms that had been given such a memorable expression by Pericles: that it was one aspect of a citizen's full life to take an active part in communal decision-making, because "if few of us are originators, we are all sound judges of policy".

Behind this lay the idea that a wise decision would emerge from the free discussion of matters in the *agora*, or market place, in Athens, where the citizens would assemble for public debate. Not all citizens could originate brilliant ideas, but they could all judge the ideas expressed by others. Ultimately, the good ideas would drive out the bad.

> This is one of the classic liberal arguments for freedom of speech, memorably advanced in modern history by John Stuart Mill. Is it true? Are not assemblies frequently swayed by the arguments of demagogues who play on their emotions, often very ignoble ones? Of course, the more sophisticated an audience is (and the Athenians thought that they were very sophisticated) the less chance there is of being swayed by emotional arguments. Is *that* true? Are intelligent men in better control of their emotions, or do they sometimes simply find more sophisticated arguments to support their passions?
>
> Are there better arguments than this to support freedom of speech and the right of all people to participate in public affairs – arguments that have to do with dignity, with the right to make mistakes, with the consequences that so often follow when free speech is suppressed?

Inequalities between People

Plato at any rate was sure that most men were unfitted to judge wisely about matters of policy. Men were not equal, either in intelligence or in aptitude. The human soul had three elements: the rational, the courageous and the appetitive. In only a few individuals are these three in harmonious and appropriate balance. Men (and women, too – Plato did not discriminate between the sexes, as we shall see) fall into three categories: the rational, who think primarily with their heads (and can control the other two elements), the courageous, who think primarily with their hearts, and the appetitive who think primarily with their stomachs. In another dialogue Plato says that, in rational people, reason is like a charioteer controlling the courageous and the appetitive, passions. These are likened to two horses that often want to pull the chariot in the wrong or in conflicting directions. If the rational part is not in control, wrong actions result. Plato agreed with Socrates that knowledge is necessary for virtue, but his analogy avoided Socrates' corollary, that sin is the result of ignorance: the rational knowledge is often there; but the rational part is too weak to resist the courageous or appetitive parts of the soul. In such a case, what is needed is training of the will rather than the removal of ignorance. But, as we shall see, Plato thought that only a few are capable of receiving such training. The rest will continue to be dominated by the courageous or appetitive nature.

Plato believed that men and women will be happy only if they do what they are best fitted to do: the rational types are happiest when they engage in intellectual pursuits, the courageous when they serve in the army, and the appetitive when they engage in activities that will enable them to earn a living and thereby to satisfy their bodily needs. Fit square pegs into round holes and you can only create unhappiness, discontentment, tension and injustice.

> The argument has of course been put forward down the ages to justify a rigidly stratified society where everyone knows his place, accepts it contentedly, and does not aspire to improve his social status. Often those arguments have been accepted even by many of those in the lower strata, sometimes because they have been indoctrinated (especially, as Marx would say, by the churches) and sometimes because they are genuinely content or because they accept their limitations. But many in the lower strata have never accepted the argument. They are actually unhappy rather than content in the stratum in which they find themselves; they aspire to being upwardly mobile, whether they are "fit" for it in Platonic terms or not.
>
> Plato, as we will see, devises an educational system that would not leave someone who is "fit" to think primarily with his head to be kept in the same stratum as those who think primarily with their stomachs. But do people who naturally think primarily with their stomachs not also often have aspirations to move outside the sphere that their nature appears to have allotted to them?
>
> It follows that Plato not only challenges the concept of some kind of equality between citizens, but also abandons the concept of "happy versatility", on which the Athenians had prided themselves, in favour of one of specialization. We will return to this aspect presently.

Justice, for Plato, is that state of affairs in which everybody fulfils his or her proper function. It therefore enshrines *inequality*, and not, as we affirm today, equality. A well organized *polis* will ensure that Justice in this Platonic sense prevails – not only for the good of the community, but also for the sake of its citizens.

The *polis* can do this only if it is led by those who know how to rule wisely – only if it is led by philosophers who have become Guardians or Philosopher Kings. Plato knew that even in an ideal society, it would help if those who are to be governed can be encouraged by a myth to accept the rule of the Guardians, and even the Guardians' self-confidence might be boosted by it. He therefore suggested, somewhat shamefacedly, the propagation of the "noble lie" that when God fashioned mankind, he put gold into those who were capable of ruling, silver into the future soldiers, and iron and copper into those destined to be farmers and craftsmen.

> Note how such useful myths would reappear in later centuries in the form of the Divine Right of Kings and the blue blood of the aristocracy!

The Guardians

The Guardians are specially trained for their task. Plato had Socrates ask: to whom would you go to have a pair of shoes made? A shoemaker, of course, because he has been specially trained to make shoes. Likewise, you would go to a doctor if you were sick, because he has been specially trained to deal with illness. Does it not then follow that you should ask a carefully trained specialist to undertake that most difficult and complicated task of guiding the community?

What do we think of the analogy with the shoemaker and the doctor? We will go to a particular shoe-maker so long as we like his shoes – the style, but particularly the comfort. Suppose we complain to the shoemaker about an uncomfortable fit, and he replies: "There is nothing wrong with my shoe. It is expertly crafted; so the trouble must lie with your feet, which are far from perfect!" Now we are not skilled enough to make our own shoes, but we would certainly not patronize that particular shoemaker again, and would choose a different one next time. So with our rulers: we vote them into office because we trust (shall we say) that they will make life more comfortable for us – perhaps lower taxation, good social services, no fear of unemployment. We may not be expert enough to know what has to be done to bring these results about, but if our politicians fail to deliver the goods, we turn them out at the next election and try a different lot of politicians. In other words, we claim that in the last resort it is the governed and not the governors who are the best judges, if not of economic principles, then at least of the effects of economic policy.

Is this a sound riposte to Plato? Might a country be better governed if the government were not forced by popular demand to produce economic policies which seem attractive in the short run but which are actually profoundly damaging in the long run even to those who demand them? We may get lower taxation, but can we then afford a decent system of publicly funded social services? Or alternatively, we may spend heavily on a generous system of social services, but can we then compete in the world effectively enough to prevent unemployment? Would not a government by experts be able to strike a healthy balance between all these competing demands? (Would it, indeed? Would the experts agree on what the proper balance is?)

Besides, does not handing over all decision making to experts – supposing that they really are experts – deprive the citizens of the dignity of being involved, of taking at least some responsibility? Might not people prefer the right to make mistakes – their own mistakes – to being ever so perfectly governed? Is that preference, as Plato would probably have said, quite indefensible on rational grounds because it is merely part of the emotional spasm that you would expect of people who think primarily with their stomachs? We are back with his contention that people are happy if they do only what they are best fitted to do; as we have seen, that is not always true.

The Importance of Education

By far the most important task that falls to the Guardians is to make sure that the educational system in the Republic is right. If it is, Plato believed, nothing else could really go wrong. The educational system first sorts out by a system of tests, spread out for some citizens over the best part of a lifetime, which role in the community they are best fitted for. It then gives them the training that is most appropriate for that role. Because everyone will be happy when they do what they are best fitted to do, there will be no need for force in a well-governed community. The use of force is already a sign that the society has failed, and there is no discussion of it in *The Republic.*

> We must always remember that what Plato is sketching out in *The Republic* is the perfect, the ideal republic. We will consider the importance of the Ideal in Plato's thought presently. For the moment it must be stressed that Plato believed that any *actual* republic must, by the very fact that it is an actual one, fall short of the Ideal. This would be Plato's response to the frequent occasions on which we might criticize him on the ground that he is out of touch with practical realities, with what men and their societies are *really* like.
>
> Towards the end of his life Plato set out how he thought an actual republic should be run (in the dialogue *The Laws*). He wrote this work in a fit of exasperation. Dionysius II, the Tyrant of Syracuse, had invited him to give advice on how he might become a Philosopher King. Plato soon realized how far short of his ideal either Dionysius or his subjects were. So, presumably in exasperation, he sketched *The Laws*, which will be discussed below. For the present, it suffices to say that the use of force plays a very prominent part in that dialogue.

In an ideal community, however, not only will there be no need for any force, there will also be no need to put any restraints on the powers of the Guardians, for that would be a confession of failure in their education. So there is no discussion in *The Republic* on the limits of the Guardians' authority. The assumption is that in an ideal society the Guardians will deal with each occasion on its own merits. They will exercise their wisdom, and, unhampered by laws, customs, precedent or traditions which might restrict their freedom, they will act appropriately. The welfare of the society is entrusted to the judgment of wise men rather than to the letter of wise laws.

> In all societies there is always the temptation to think that "the law is an ass". Often we might wish that judges could be freer to exercise their compassion when sentencing someone who is guilty under the law and whom they must therefore sentence in accordance with that law. A striking example arises when, in societies which have not legalized euthanasia, the sufferings of an incurably ill person are terminated by a loving relative. Many, even those who do not think that killing is wrong under any circumstances, would be opposed to giving a judge the discretion to exercise more compassion than the law permits, as that might encourage unacceptable abuses of euthanasia. Is it necessary, therefore, that the law, and not the opinions of the ruler or the judge, should be paramount? We do, after all, change or modify the law when its terms appear to the public to lead too frequently to unduly harsh (or unduly lenient) sentences. However, we need to remember that in *The Republic* Plato was describing what he thought was an ideal society. The dialogue *The Laws* is so called because, in the *actual* societies for which it is a prescription, Plato makes the laws, and not the Guardians, supreme.

Because the creation of a sound educational system is the most important task of the Guardians, *The Republic* concerns itself much more extensively with education than it does with politics proper.

The Educational System in The Republic

In an ideal world, Plato says, children would be exposed to no influences other than those of an ideal education. Unfortunately, most parents, at least when the ideal republic is set up for the first time, would influence their children in undesirable ways. So the best thing would be to send those parents away from the *polis,* "into the country", so that nothing should interfere with the perfect education their children are about to receive.

> We might think that no upbringing can be perfect that does not involve a close, individual and loving relationship between parents and their children. As we shall see, this is not the only place where Plato expresses his view that family relationships weaken rather than strengthen the ideal citizen. Theoretically, Plato agrees with Socrates that education is about "bringing forth" what the soul already knows; but one cannot avoid the impression, which will be constantly reinforced by what follows, that in practice he is frequently in the business of indoctrination rather than elucidation. In this respect he provides a pattern for all political, religious or social systems that are anxious to monopolize control over education, so that children can be trained to think only along approved lines. Of course, liberals want to train their children to think along liberal lines, so in that sense we are all involved to a greater or lesser extent in inculcating values into the very young. A liberal education, however, aims to train the young to recognize, to consider and – within limits that we look at presently – to respect a variety of points of view. Nothing could be further from Plato's aim; there is only one ideal, which is all too apt to be deformed by an imperfect humanity.

Plato's educational system is devoted to training the body, the soul, the emotions, the character, and the intellect, and we will see presently just how this is done. For the moment we will look at the structure of the system.

Educational Selection

In Plato's ideal state, everyone - male as well as female - is to have the same education up until the age of twenty. At that age there will be the first of a series of tests of their character and intellect. Those who fail at that stage will be those who think primarily with their stomachs; they will not have the qualities required either of soldiers or of philosophers and their function will therefore be to produce the economic wealth of the society. They will, of course, not have to be forced to do this. They will be happy because it is what they are best fitted for. Slavery - a system by which people are forced to work - has no place in Plato's republic.

> One cannot accuse Plato of not taking account of "late developers". Not for him early sifting at the age of "eleven plus". His is a system of selection at twenty plus. This is a considerable improvement, although of course there are always a few people whose true potential emerges even later than by the age of twenty. But compulsory formal education generally has to stop somewhere, and twenty is quite a generous age. We might even think it is too generous, given that many adolescents want to leave school a lot earlier, but then perhaps that is because their educational experience has been less than ideal – and Plato's ideal system would not have that flaw. Certainly, his wealth-producers, although made of baser metals, enjoy a long run of education and are not relegated to "inferior" work without having been equipped with a wide range of practical and intellectual skills.

Those who have survived this first test will have their next at the age of thirty. Those who fail at this stage have the requisite character to be soldiers, but not enough intelligence to be philosophers. The thinking that is centred in their hearts – the seat of courage – is highly developed. They have shown that they can, and are willing to, live without possessing personal property. Indeed, they will not be allowed any so that there is no temptation for them to oppress the society which they are called upon to protect. They will live in military communes.

> This arrangement would have the perhaps surprising result that all soldiers would be at least 30 years old: no young conscripts, no young volunteers. At least they might have a keener idea of what they are letting themselves in for. On the other hand, how would they cope when confronted by a well-trained army of much younger men?

Those who have survived the test at thirty now *begin* a training in philosophy which will last for five years. It is from their ranks that at the age of fifty the Guardians will emerge.

> Plato did not believe in "premature" training in philosophy, fearing that the skills involved can easily be misused by the immature young. Cleverness is not the same as wisdom. Was he right? His is a view often expressed by older people, who remember that when they were young they held and passionately defended philosophical ideas – perhaps a rapidly changing sequence of them – which they no longer hold once they have become "mature". At thirty-five one has left one's youth behind, and relatively few people change their opinions significantly after that age.
>
> To what extent are the philosophies espoused in "maturity" actually sounder than those we may have entertained in our youth? Many people become more conservative as they grow older. They often claim that experience of life has taught them that what sounded idealistic in youth is impracticable, "doesn't work" or "doesn't take human nature into account". On the other hand, young people often claim that the former idealism of their elders has been affected by growing vested interests or by "prudential considerations".
>
> In England, philosophy is hardly ever taught as a full time subject in secondary schools. In France, however, philosophy is a required subject in the *baccalauréat*, the national school leaving exam taken at the age of eighteen. Is this because the English tacitly agree with Plato? Or is it because the English are so wedded to pragmatism that they do not consider philosophy very important at any age and actually distrust it? Would they distrust it if they had been obliged to study it at school?

Training of the Soul, the Body and the Emotions

We now turn to consider the actual content of education in the Platonic republic. Every part of a good education is a training of the soul. The soul, it will be remembered, existed before it had entered the body and survives it, but it has to be properly cultivated while it is in the body. It is, after all, at best clouded and at worst actually deformed. It has the three aspects which correspond to the three parts of man's nature: the rational, the courageous and the appetitive. These three parts ought to be cultivated harmoniously, with the rational part guiding the properly developed courageous and appetitive parts. The soul is therefore well cultivated through the sound training of the body and the emotions, the character and the intellect.[1]

The body is trained through gymnastics. Bad physical education or bad physical habits will harm not only the body, but also the courageous aspect of the Soul, so that the necessary harmony among the three aspects is destroyed.

The emotions are trained through "music", in which Plato included poetry. In this context we will also look at what he has to say about the other arts, like drama, sculpture and painting.

Plato would certainly have rejected the notion of "art for art's sake". Music and poetry had the quite specific purpose of strengthening virtue. Plato was well aware that the arts have an immense influence on our view of life, but he thought that that influence could be harmful as well as beneficial, and he did not wish anyone to be exposed to harmful forces. He proposed, therefore, that music and poetry should be severely censored.

In music, for example, he would allow only Dorian and Phrygian harmonies, which were associated with courage and temperance; the Lydian harmonies, which were used for sorrowful songs, and the Ionian, which were relaxing, were banned. Literature and drama must be improving. They must not show heroes weeping, for this is unmanly, nor gods cavorting or indulging in immoral behaviour, thus setting a bad example. What a bowdlerization of Homer that would require! There is a long list of other aspects of literature which Plato would ban because they tended to corrupt, especially the young.

> Here we recognize the voice of the archetypal censor which has been echoed down the ages by authoritarian figures of the right and of the left. We instantly recall fascist or soviet man, marching stern-faced to stirring music; fascist or soviet literature dealing stereotypically only with approved themes in the approved manner. We may even glimpse the efforts to purge the universities of anyone who expresses views deemed "politically incorrect".
>
> And yet, do we agree with Plato that the arts *matter*? Why do they matter? Is it not because they can elevate the mind, induce lofty thoughts, improve us as human beings? And if that is so, do we agree that the other side of the coin must be that they can also have a malign influence, that they can help to deprave and corrupt? Do we try to protect our young children from art forms that portray violence and cruelty as exciting, pornography as titillating, or unthinking consumerism as the norm? Would we not wish that our adolescent children were not exposed to such material? And even if such material were produced primarily for "responsible" adults and not specifically to appeal to the unformed young, is it possible to erect an effective screen between these age groups? Is all this merely a matter of personal taste and distaste, or is there a wider issue at stake: whether our young people grow up as decent citi-

1 Plato gives two different accounts of what happens to the soul after death. In the *Republic* he follows the teachings of Pythagoras: if a soul is damaged while it is in the body, it is a damaged soul that survives after death and will be reincorporated in a lower form of life. But in the *Timaeus* he suggests that on death the courageous and appetitive parts of the soul cannot exist apart from the body and therefore perish when the body does: only the rational part of the soul survives and will return to a kind of Heaven to dwell with the pure knowledge it had before it entered the body. Sometimes it looks as if Plato believed in the personal immortality of each individual soul; sometimes he seems to suggest that only an undeformed soul can remain in heaven and that a soul whose rational part had been deformed in one body would have to reenter another body, in a clouded form of course, when the attempt to clear away the clouds will have to start all over again.

zens? Perhaps we trust that our own influence as parents may counteract the corruption pumped out unrelentingly by the media, but do we deny that the media have created a culture in which we can scarcely summon the energy to distinguish between what is acceptable and what is unacceptable, let alone to fight back, to face the charge that we are stuffy or old-fashioned? What, it may be asked, is acceptable and what is unacceptable? We know that there is no general agreement on this; so what follows if we can give no definite answers to this question? If we admit that there are no absolute standards, does this imply that there are absolutely no standards that a society can rightfully demand to be met? Does the danger of a narrow-minded censorship such as that which Plato wanted to impose mean that we dare not impose *any* censorship in case that would be the thin end of a wedge which would make it impossible (impossible? or merely very difficult?) to hold the line against undue restrictions on the freedom of speech?

Moreoever, if a line is to be held, who will decide what that line should be? Some people might say that it should be drawn by public opinion as it is expressed through representative bodies like parliaments. If public opinion really does not wish that a firmer line be drawn because it has no great objection to what is being expressed, we simply have to accept that. If public opinion *does* object to what is being expressed, does think it is corrupting but will not draw a line on the principle that there should be no restrictions on freedom of expression, then at the very least it would be desirable to carefully weigh the dangers involved in censorship against the dangers involved in corruption. Frequently in philosophy there are such choices to be made; they are often hard choices, but they should not be evaded.

There was an additional problem for Plato about drama, even if a play conveyed an improving message and showed the triumph of good over evil. The parts of villains would have to be played by actors, and to imitate bad people, even if only on the stage, was itself a corrupting experience for the actor. Plato therefore decided that there should be no drama in his republic – so much for performances of Sophocles and Aeschylus, Euripides and Aristophanes!

Plato's Aesthetics

Plato was critical not only of imitations of evil, but of imitations altogether, because they must always be inferior to what is being imitated. The pleasures to be derived from art are therefore necessarily second-rate pleasures. A work of art is only an imitation of an imitation: the painting of a horse is only an imperfect representation of an actual horse, and an actual horse, as we shall see, is only an imperfect representation of the Ideal of a horse stored up in Heaven. If an artist aims to make a perfect representation, he will necessarily fail. It is even worse if he tries to make something look better than it actually is. He is not even *trying* to be truthful, and that is just as bad as it would be if he tried to paint an ugly thing as accurately as possible. Just as a good actor should not wish to imitate a bad character, so should a good artist not wish to paint anything that is ugly. The artist can't win!

We notice that the sculptors of Plato's time had moved away from the stiff and stylized figures of the Cycladic and Archaic periods. They were increasingly aiming at the realistic portrayal of the human being in repose and in action – a process that was to continue in the Greek and Roman world for several centuries. Their paintings are less successful in achieving realism: it is more difficult to represent a three-dimensional figure in two dimensions than it is in three, and Plato complained that a painting must always fall short of the truth for that reason. The aesthetic of Plato, like that of his contemporaries, took it for granted that the purpose of artists was to make as realistic an image as possible, even if that aim would always elude them.

There was no conception in Plato or his contemporaries that art might not aim for realism at all, for example, that the artist might want to express what he feels rather than reproduce what he sees.

Plato thought that, if there must be art, then it should aspire to reflect the Idea of Beauty. As we shall see later, Plato, like Pythagoras before him, believed that mathematics had a pure and almost sacred beauty, and it is largely by criteria related to mathematics that he judged a work of art: its forms and composition should have proportion and harmony, the work should have purity, and it should bring out a sense of unity underlying any degree of complexity.

It would follow from this theory that the artist should slightly rearrange, say, a landscape, so that the trees, rivers and hills achieved a perfect relationship to each other that they might not have if copied exactly. Is there a contradiction here with Plato's theory that art was not telling the truth if it tried to make something appear more beautiful than it actually was?

Pythagoras and Plato are probably the first in Europe to write about the branch of philosophy known as Aesthetics, though great buildings and sculptures already existed which expressed the mathematical qualities that Plato admired. He did not so much create these criteria as give them a philosophical basis. His writings about them were to be immensely influential in the later history of aesthetics, so much so that the art forms which accept these mathematical qualities as a model to aim at will be called Classical Art. (The original meaning of the Latin "classicus" was "of the highest class or excellence".)

Though classical qualities are most easily found in the visual arts, they can also be found in poetic forms and in drama. Plato had called for purity and unity in a work of beauty, and Aristotle would take this up in his discussion of the aesthetics of drama.

Mathematical qualities are logical and rational, which is why Plato valued them so highly. He also distrusted art because he knew that much of it is produced in a "manic" state, with the "irrational" part of the soul, just as much of it is also designed to appeal to the emotional and therefore "irrational" reactions of the audience.

Repeatedly, we find Plato distrusting and undervaluing the "feeling" and spontaneous side of life.

Training of the Character

Plato goes on to describe how to ensure that the character of the Guardians will be sound. The greatest dangers to their character are the temptations to abuse their power. Plato considers that the greatest of the temptations to which rulers normally succumb are the possibilities to accumulate property and to advance the interests of their own family over the interests of the community. To make sure that they are not corrupted, Plato laid down that the Guardians may not own any property nor would they be allowed to have a family. The Guardians will therefore live in a kind of commune, in which all property will be held collectively. Within the group, which, it will be remembered, includes both male and female Guardians, there are to be no exclusive attachments or preferments. Indeed, mating should be so unrestricted that no man can know that he is the father of any particular child: in that way nepotism will be avoided. Mating in this way is also encouragedbecause Plato believed in Eugenics, and often used analogies from stock breeding. The likelihood was strong that the children born of the couplings within such a carefully trained élite would inherit the characteristics that would enable them, in their turn, to pass the various tests required to become Guardians. This was a strong likelihood, but of course not a certainty: some children might not pass the test, while there was always at least the possibility that children born from soldiers or from workers might qualify to join the ranks of the Guardians.

The idea that property and family attachments prevent total dedication to a cause will be taken up by the Roman Catholic clergy. Monks and friars were to have no individual property; nor were they allowed to have families. The Church of course will go further than Plato, who encouraged the Guardians to procreate because he was not disturbed by the sex act as such. Although Plato believed that the highest form of love did not involve a sexual relationship (hence the term "Platonic relationship" to describe a close but nonsexual friendship), he regarded the sexual act as morally neutral, neither hallowed within marriage nor condemned outside.

That difference apart, the parallels between the thinking of Plato and that of the Roman Catholic Church is striking. Both demand of their élite total dedication to a community. Both feel that property and the family are distractions which prevent the élite from giving its undivided and unbiased service to the cause. Neither condemn property or family as such: it cannot be expected of ordinary people that they should abstain. As Durant puts it: "Communism is not democratic; it is aristocratic: the common soul is incapable of it; only soldiers and philosophers can bear it."[2]

The Protestant churches allow their clergy to marry. Perhaps they realized that St.Paul's saying "it is better to marry than to burn" (I.Cor.vii.9) applies to the clergy as well as to the laity. The clergy, after all, are also only human, and Luther, when still a Catholic, was much troubled by the febrile sexual thoughts he had when living a celibate life. Compulsory celibacy also raises another question: is one a better human being if one devotes oneself so wholly to government, (or, for that matter, to pastoral care) that one makes no commitment in one's own life to normal human relationships. Do we really think we are better led by full-time politicians than by those who want to spend some time with their families, and have some hinterland that makes them realize that politics is not the be-all and end-all of life? Do politicians really understand the lives of the people over whom they rule if they cut themselves off so drastically from what, for most people, are their most significant experiences and relationships?

Moreover, if we have forbidden rulers to have personal property and family interests, have we then removed the most dangerous sources of corruption?

2 W. Durant - *The Story of Civilization*, Book IV, Ch.XXI, iii. 5

An even more sinister temptation may lurk in the background: the love of exercising control, not for ulterior motives which are either worthy (such as benefiting the community) or unworthy (such as feathering your own nest), but simply for its own sake because you enjoy power *per se* and especially the power to control your fellow citizens. The Guardians, by virtue of their education, are convinced that they know best (or, if they are more modest, that they at least know better than the people over whom they rule); they may be intoxicated by the purity of their own vision. Some of the most dangerous ideologues in history, like Robespierre, the "Sea-Green Incorruptible", have been men just like that. To be fair to Plato, Robespierre fell far short of the kind of training Plato would have wished him to have, and we must always remember that when Plato describes his *politeia*, he is describing an Ideal of which actual polities in this world cannot be but imperfect copies. In the real world, for example, monks who were not allowed personal property sometimes accumulated communal property on a gigantic scale, lived extremely comfortably and exacted rents from their estates. In the ideal *politeia* this would not happen.

The whole idea of holding property in common will be exposed to further criticism by Aristotle, and we shall consider his ideas later.

Training of the Intellect to Understand the Ideas

The training that has so far been described – that of the body, the emotions, and the character – is shared by the Guardians and the military alike. The final training, that of the intellect, comes after the military has fallen out by not passing the tests for this last stage. The intellect will be trained by philosophy. Philosophy will bring its students close to understanding the Good, the True, and the Beautiful, and it is here that Plato expounds his most metaphysical ideas.

As we have seen, Plato considered that everything we see or experience in this world is but an imperfect manifestation of an Idea stored up in Heaven. The Greek word for Idea originally meant "shape", or "model" or "pattern". The fact that we now use the word "ideal" for something that we consider perfect is part of the influence that Plato has had on our thinking.

Let us take an example of what he meant: When we see a pony, a race-horse, or a dray-horse we recognize that all of them have the quality or "horse-ness"; and this quality is the Idea of the horse that is laid up in Heaven.[3] Any existing horse is an imperfect reflection of that Idea. If you think that your racehorse is surely the most perfect horse there can be, you are wrong – for one thing, your racehorse may fall sick or lame, may have some other kind of blemish, and will most certainly become decrepit and die. The Idea of the horse (or even what I would like to call the "sub-idea" of a racehorse – the "racehorse-ness" that all racehorses have in common) is permanent, the eternal and unblemished Idea to which all race-horses on this earth aspire, but which they will never achieve.

Let us consider for a moment the idea of aspiration. It is the philosopher's task to discover the Ideas towards which phenomena are aspiring. The perfect form is the *goal* towards which phenomena are striving. The Greek word for "goal" or "end" or "aim" is *telos*; and the understanding of phenomena in terms

3 If a concept or a presence exists only in Heaven but not on earth, it is called "transcendental". If it suffuses existence on this earth it is called "immanent". Plato usually, but not always, implies that the Ideas are transcendental.

of the end towards which they are striving is called "teleological". Teleology describes the nature of something as residing in its fully developed and perfect form. So a teleologist looks at an acorn and says that it is "really" an oak tree. By this he means that if it develops according to its true nature, it will find its perfect fulfilment when it has become an oak tree. Of course he knows that it may never develop into an oak tree – the soil may be unsuitable, or it may be eaten by a squirrel, but the *telos*, the Idea to which it is aspiring, however much it may fall short of achieving it, is its true nature. Plato is a teleologist.

The opposing view is called "mechanistic". This describes phenomena in terms of their origin, not of their goal. It will see the oak tree as "really" an acorn at heart. Metaphorically speaking, the teleologist sees the idea of the perfect oak-tree as a magnet drawing the acorns upwards towards achieving it; the mechanist sees the oak tree as the result of forces pushing the acorn upwards from behind, as it were.

Does this debate have any practical applications? Consider the two statements: "The child is father of the man", and "When I was a child, ... I thought as a child; but when I became a man, I put away childish things" (1.Cor.xiii.2). The first expresses a mechanistic view; it assumes that the adult is essentially formed by early experiences. The second implies teleology: the man – St. Paul – was striving to fulfill himself in accordance with the vision he had experienced on the road to Damascus.

The first is the view of man taken by many psychotherapists; the second, the view of the visionary or idealist.

The teleologist accepts that the *telos* may never be achieved. If he is a Platonist or a Christian, he *knows* that perfection is beyond the achievement of anything merely earthly, such as Man or the institutions he creates. Nevertheless, the awareness of an Ideal, the effort to come as close to achieving it as possible, will extend Man's reach. The teleologist will never accept as a criticism what the mechanistic philosopher will often say: that the Ideal is impractical and that therefore it is a mistake to try to shape this fallible world in accordance with it: "Ah, but a man's reach should exceed his grasp/Or what's a heaven for?"[4]

The theory of Ideas is Plato's answer to the tension between Heraclitus, who had said that everything was in a state of flux, and Parmenides, who had believed that our senses deceive us and that, philosophically speaking, no change is ever possible. In the Idea (later ages will talk about Universals) we have what is permanent; in its manifestations on this earth (which later ages will call Particulars or sometimes Accidentals), we have continual change - partly because the actual horse itself is liable to change, and partly because an actual horse is a blend of the imperfect and possibly shifting combination of *several* Ideas - such as the Idea of "horse-ness" together with the Idea of "brown-ness", the Idea of "swift-ness" and so on. We recognize the everchanging horses we see as horses because they partake of the unchanging Idea of a horse.

I have talked about the "sub-Idea" of a racehorse. There would also be a "sub-Idea" of a dray horse and one of a pony. What these three "sub-Ideas" have in common is that they partake of a higher Idea, of an Idea of which they themselves are inferior versions - and that higher Idea is the Idea of a horse.

4 Robert Browning - *Andrea del Sarto.*

Goodness, Truth and Beauty

Now consider a still purer idea: you have a horse, a book, a wife and a home. These participate separately in the Idea of perfect horse-ness, perfect book-ness, perfect wife-ness, and perfect Home-ness. But these Ideas are "sub-Ideas" of "Perfect-ness" or "Good-ness". The Good is therefore the ultimate Idea in which all lesser Ideas are subsumed. Nothing in this ultimate Idea can be false or it would not be perfect. The Good is therefore the same as the True. For the same reason, nothing in the ultimate Idea can be ugly; and Beauty is therefore the same as Goodness and Truth. Goodness, Truth and Beauty are therefore, so to speak, Plato's Trinity.

> It is interesting how often the idea of a trinity or a triad crops up in Philosophy. We find it in Plato; in Philo of Alexandria; in the Gospel of St John. Kant had an obsession that constantly makes him produce threefold classifications. Hegel's central concept is the triad of thesis-antithesis-synthesis. Philosophers of history detect the three phases of growth, maturity and decline. Is it possible that the idea of three-in-one and one-in-three reflects the earliest experiences of the child? A baby sees itself, its father and its mother so intimately connected in a threesome that separating that family unit out into its component parts is difficult and is perhaps even felt to be painful or – *pace* Freud – dangerous. Is the idea of a trinity therefore embedded in a Jungian collective unconscious?
>
> Might we go still further? In ancient Sanskrit and in classical Greek, verbs have a singular form when they refer to one thing, a dual form when they refer to two things, and a plural form when they refer to more than two. Could this reflect an even earlier, Kleinian, stage of development? Melanie Klein stressed that in the very beginning the father doesn't really come into the picture for the child: there is just itself and its mother's breast. Then the father swims into vision and is perceived as an integral member of the child's world - but not a wholly welcome one, hence the Oedipus complex. If that idea has any validity, then the concept of the threesome belongs to a later stage of development, not only of a civilization but also of the child.

It is the ultimate task of the philosopher to understand these Ideas, and to the extent that he manages this, he has knowledge. Like Socrates, Plato believed that the ordinary unphilosophical man, who lacks the will or the capacity to go beyond what he sees and experiences, can have no grasp of Ideas and has only beliefs, not knowledge. He may behave well, but his good behaviour will be based not on knowledge of the Good but on beliefs, habit or convention. Again like Socrates, Plato believed that virtue is knowledge.

Beauty, Truth and Goodness are special also because they are Ideas that have the most general application. The Idea of a horse, after all, relates only to horses, but the idea of Beauty relates to all beautiful things. The training of a philosopher should increasingly concern itself with the most generalized, the most widely applicable concepts.

Mathematics

If Goodness, Truth and Beauty are the summit which the philosopher will aim to scale, an excellent training not far below the summit is a training in mathematics and in geometry. Plato valued that training because mathematical and geometrical statements are the most abstract, most generalized, and at the same time the most widely applicable statements that can be made and demonstrated. For example: two plus three is five, whether you apply that statement to horses or apples or anything else you like. The angles of all triangles add up to 180° whether the triangles are small or big, scalene, isosceles or equilateral – and so on through statements of greater and greater mathematical complexity.

A training in mathematics is therefore a training in abstracting, from a whole variety of things, general statements that refer to them all. As such, it will prepare the mind for what I have called the summit – to be able to strip away everything that is particular until one is left with a purity that excels even that of mathematics: the purity of the Good, the True and the Beautiful.

So important did Plato consider this training that he had inscribed over the gates of his Academy: "No one without a knowledge of Geometry may enter here."

Needless to say, for Plato, the value of mathematics and geometry lay entirely in the training of the mind, and not at all in equipping students with the capacity to apply this knowledge for mundane professional uses like engineering or mechanics. He is on record as condemning his friend Archytas, credited with inventing the screw, for making such a debasing use of the sacred knowledge of pure mathematics.

> This is another example of the intellectual snobbery that the classically educated classes would perpetuate at the ancient universities of Europe. They, too, valued and taught Pure Mathematics, but looked down on Applied Mathematics. This is why, until very recently, the great developments in Mechanics, for example, almost all took place outside the universities; and we have already seen how the worship of pure mathematics affected Aesthetics in later centuries.

To repeat: Plato thought that a training in mathematics would prepare the intellect for the final ascent to the summit, the achievement of the philosopher's ultimate crown: a deep understanding of the mystical quality of the Good which is also the True and the Beautiful.

God

We cannot be sure what concept, if any, Plato had of God. Sometimes, indeed, he talks about "the gods", but the whole thrust of his thinking is obviously towards a monist concept. He cannot decide whether the Idea of the Good *is* God, whether it has been fashioned by God (which is the suggestion in *The Republic*), or whether, as he implies in the *Timaeus*, God – called there the *demiourgos*,[5] meaning "craftsman" – used already existing Ideas as the patterns for giving shape to an already existing world.

> Anyway, it is easy to see the similarity between Plato's ideas and aspects of monotheistic religions in general and of Christianity in particular. For them, God represents Goodness, Truth and Beauty; for them, too, the goal of imperfect man is to contemplate and try to achieve an understanding of God, though this will never be perfectly achieved in this world. Even what I have called

5 William Blake's "demi-urge"

Plato's Trinity has a resonance in the Trinity of the Christian faith, where the Father, the Son and the Holy Spirit are "Three in One and One in Three."

As we shall see when we come to consider Christian neo-Platonism, the early Christian philosophers were powerfully influenced by Plato. They could only regret that Plato had been so unfortunate as to have been born before the Christian revelation; otherwise he would certainly have been saved and qualified as one of the Fathers of the Church! As it was, they thought that, like Abraham, Moses and other pre-Christians, he had gone not to the damned in Hell, but to Limbo, whence Christ had already rescued him.

Returning to Plato's belief that the philosopher would concentrate on the Ideas rather than on the particulars, one sees again what a gulf there would be between the Philosopher Kings and their subjects. If an ordinary person owns a horse, he is much more likely to be concerned with its apparently shadowy existence than with its eternal model, and he will regard the actual horse in his stable as very much more *real* than the abstraction stored up in Heaven. Plato believed the opposite: that universals are more real. Hence another name for the heirs of Plato in the Middle Ages is "Realists", whilst those who thought that Universals were only *names* which we give to things we perceive to form a group will be called "Nominalists". The heirs of Plato were in the ascendant when these terms were invented, so they appropriated the better name! Had the particularists (who believed that only particulars were real) been in the ascendant, they would probably have claimed the name "realist" for themselves and would have bestowed the name of "nominalists" on their opponents! If we tend to be particularists, which most of us are today, we will find the medieval nomenclature odd or even confusing!

The Immortality of the Soul

Following the ideas of Socrates, Plato repeated that the knowledge of the Ideas is innate: the child is born with a veiled form of that knowledge and does not have to acquire it from outside.

There seem to be some problems here. How can a person have an innate idea of a horse before he has seen several horses? Can an Eskimo child born in the Arctic possibly have an innate idea of a giraffe? If we can understand the relationship between the Idea of a horse and an actual horse, we can also understand that between the Idea of a motor car and an actual motor car: but can the Idea of a motor car be innate in the mind of a medieval peasant?

These questions would strongly suggest that the Nominalists were right: Ideas or Universals are merely names under which we group Particulars. Not only can they not be innate, but they cannot even exist until we have brought them into existence.

Perhaps it is not fair to take such mundane examples as horses, giraffes, and motor cars – though, as Plato frequently uses the example of the horse in his dialogues, we are only doing what he was doing himself.

Is Plato's concept of innate Ideas more convincing if we move away from physical examples of horses to such abstracts as Beauty, Truth and Goodness? Do we have an instinctive – that would be an innate – response to Beauty, Truth and Goodness? Plato says that Ideas which are innate need to be unveiled, developed, matured, refined: so the child's instinctive response to Beauty, Truth and Goodness will initially be crude and possibly erroneous, but it will be present. It can be developed, trained – and, yes, it can be the subject of conditioning or indoctrination.

The reason Plato believed that all Ideas were innate was that they were known and understood by the soul. The soul has dwelt with the Ideas in Heaven before it has entered the body and thus brings the veiled knowledge of the Ideas with it. It continues to exist after the body has perished, for the soul is immortal.

Plato's thoughts about the immortality of the soul evolved as he grew older. We have seen that he believed that the soul had three components: the rational, the courageous and the appetitive. In *The Republic,* Plato said that the necessary harmony between these three components can be damaged by bad physical education or bad bodily habits. In that case, when the body dies, the deformed soul is not fit to return to Heaven, but will enter another, possibly lower body. This is very close to the ideas of Pythagoras. *The Republic* is a work of Plato's middle years.

In the *Timaeus,* which belongs to the works of his old age, Plato thought that the courageous and appetitive aspects of the soul perished with the body. Only the rational part of the soul does not die: it reascends to Heaven to dwell once more with the Ideas before it descends again into another body.

It is easy to see the echoes of Pythagoras and middle-period Plato in Christian theology. It, too, teaches the immortality of the soul; and it, too, believes that only the pure souls dwell in Heaven. The souls whose purity has been compromised in this life are condemned to suffer – not by being reincorporated in lower forms of life, but by being cast into Hell. There are rewards for the pure souls and punishments for the impure souls. Might the psychological motives for such philosophies or theologies be the need to see the righteous or the clever triumph in the next world as a consolation for what they may have had to put up with in this world at the hands of the unrighteous or the ignorant? The older Plato may have thought this rather crude. At any rate, he allowed the intellectual part of every soul to refresh itself again at the source of all Ideas before it returns once more into a body and again presents man with the challenge to unveil the Ideas which at the beginning of his earthly life are veiled. (We find this metaphor again when we speak of "the naked truth".)[5]

Imperfect States

Much of *The Republic* concerns itself with the Idea of a Republic laid up in Heaven, which, almost by definition, is unachievable in the real world. But in that book Plato also gives himself some scope to describe the inferior forms of the model, which do occur in practice.

5 There was, as we shall see, a great revival of Platonism in fifteenth-century Florence. At the same time there was a Christian allegorization of some pagan deities, so that, for instance, Venus, the goddess of love, was taken to symbolize not only Divine Love, but also Truth. In Botticelli's *The Birth of Venus* (1485, Uffizi) we see Venus, or the naked truth, being wafted from the seas towards the earth on which humans dwell. Awaiting her on the shore is a figure holding out a cloak for Venus. On the surface this might be taken for a sign of modesty; but the deeper meaning was the Platonic one: on this earth mankind cannot see the naked truth. The same point was made in Venice in a painting by Titian, called *Sacred and Profane Love* (1515, Borghese): two women sit on either side of a fountain; one is clothed, the other is unclothed. Contrary to what one might expect in our own time, when nakedness is so often associated with lewdness and profanity, it is the unclothed figure who represents sacred love.

In the Ideal Republic, run by Philosopher Kings, the guiding principle would be wisdom. In the real world, the first decline from this perfect model occurs when wisdom is replaced by honour. The Greek word for Honour is *timé*, and Plato calls a republic that takes honour as its guiding principle a Timocracy. In a Timocracy, the Guardians and the soldiers have fallen out, and the state is held together by the military ethos of honour. Plato had Sparta in mind as an example. The rulers of a Timocracy, however, still have the interests of the state at heart, rather than the interests of a narrow military caste.

> Many military dictatorships in Third World countries originally arose because the soldiers overthrew self-serving and corrupt governing cliques in disgust. Often this disgust, and the intention to purify the state for the greater common good, were perfectly genuine. Such patriotic officers may well have intended to set up a Timocracy in Plato's sense. But we know that, unfortunately, the militaryin its turn usually becomes a narrow and self-serving clique. It fails to maintain a Timocracy and degenerates into the next lowest form of government which Plato described.

In the next lowest form, the state will become what Plato calls an Oligarchy, the government of a narrow clique (from the Greek *oligos*, a few, plus *arkhein*, to rule). It may be a clique of soldiers or a clique of wealthy individuals – but they govern only in their own interest and not in that of the community as a whole.

The next stage is likely to be a revolt of the poor, especially if the clique is of the wealthy, and if that is successful, the form of government which results is a Democracy. The word comes from *demos*, the populace (often with the implication that it is a mob), plus *kratos*, power. This form of government prevailed in Plato's Athens. Plato had no love for it; it was the Athenian Democracy which had put his beloved teacher Socrates to death.

The populace is easily manipulated by demagogues (*demos* plus *agein*, to lead) and the society may then finally decline into the form of government Plato thought the worst: a Tyranny, in which the Tyrant (from *turannos*, a despot, and in Greek the word also carried the connotation of "usurper") governs entirely in his own selfish interests rather than in that of the community as a whole.

> Plato here shows an interest in the dynamics of social and political change. It is *degenerative* change, compared with the *progressive* dynamics of change we will find, for example, in Karl Marx's explanation of what happens to societies. One might argue that the reason Plato saw change as degenerative was that he was after all describing imperfect societies. When in *The Republic* he was writing as a philosopher, he had envisaged that what was imperfect would aspire to the perfection embodied in the Idea of the republic and would therefore improve. But when he came to look at states as they actually were, it would seem that he came to the opposite conclusion: imperfect societies have within them the seeds of corruption, and this will lead to them becoming steadily worse rather than better.
>
> His description of the degenerative process, which he may have seen in the Greek city states around him, would do quite well as a description of social change many centuries after his time. One could, for example, describe the original feudal society in France as a Timocracy, as the feudal system was specifically designed for a military purpose. When its military *raison d'être* disappeared, the nobility was felt to have wealth but no sense of social responsi-

bility. The poor rose up in the French Revolution; mob rule and chaos threatened until a weary France turned to Napoleon, who was certainly a usurper and whom many people regarded as a tyrant.

Although Napoleon ruled despotically, it is arguable that, however self-seeking he was, he actually bestowed great benefits on the people of France. A despot can rule wisely and in the interests of the community as a whole. Plato reflected on such a possibility, and in *The Statesman*, a work of his last years, he formulated a six-fold classification of governments, which was later to be made famous by Aristotle.

The Statesman

In *The Statesman* (also known as the *Politicus*), governments are first divided into two groups: good ones in which the rulers submit to the same laws as the ruled, and bad ones in which the rulers are arbitrary and lawless. (Aristotle will classify them into those which take the interests of the whole community into account, and those who govern only in their narrow selfish interest.)

Each group is then divided into three, depending on how many people are actually doing the governing: one, a few, or a majority. So we can construct the following table:

	Good forms	Bad forms
Rule by one	Monarchy	Tyranny
Rule by a few	Aristocracy	Oligarchy
Rule by a majority	Polity	Democracy

Monarchy is *monos*, one or single, plus *arkhein*. The monarch has all the power, but exercises it for the benefit of the whole community. He would be, as it were, a Platonic Philosopher King, and in *The Laws* Plato describes monarchy as the best of all governments. He still thinks that its negative form, Tyranny, is the worst of all.

We already know that Plato considered that people who thought primarily with their hearts or with their stomachs would not be fit to take part in government, because they have no knowledge or training. Therefore, almost by definition, a polity, let alone a democracy, would produce bad government. Were he alive today, it is unlikely that he would consider such universal education as now prevails in Europe and America an adequate qualification for participating in government, even if only by way of voting. However, he would almost certainly think it absurd to have universal suffrage in countries where the bulk of the electorate is actually illiterate.

Aristocracy is *aristos*, "the best", plus *kratein*.

The word was not intended to mean a hereditary cast. We have already seen that Plato's educational system should make it possible for humbly-born men and women to rise to ruling positions if they meet the challenges that the system provides. On the other hand, his advocacy of eugenics suggested that there was a hereditary element in the *capacity* to become a good ruler which, if

> properly fostered, could in fact produce a hereditary ruling class.
>
> We must not over-idealize the eighteenth-century English noble governing class, but we might maintain that, in one respect at least, it was an aristocracy in Plato's sense, namely in that it claimed no exemption from taxation. The French nobles, on the other hand, formed an oligarchy: the wealthiest class used its monopoly of power to exempt itself from the burden of taxation and to dump it all on the rest of the nation.

The difference between Polity and Democracy is essentially this: in a Polity the majority respects the rights of minorities whereas in a Democracy the majority will not take the interests of the minority into account at all. Contrary to what one might perhaps expect from an élitist like Plato, he thought that Democracy was the least bad of the three bad forms of government – at least more people benefited from it than did from a Tyranny.

> It is ironic that, if we accept Plato's nomenclature, the "Popular Democracies" of the former Soviet bloc had a better claim to call themselves democracies than had the liberal democracies of western Europe, who, pedantically speaking, should perhaps have called themselves "polities". Communist governments made no bones about minorities such as the bourgeoisie having any rights that the majority has to respect. A popular democracy was, even in theory, a "dictatorship of the proletariat" or of the masses – exactly what Plato and Aristotle meant by the word democracy. It seems a pity that the word "polity" in Plato's sense has fallen into disuse. It was of course closely linked to the word *polis*, that small and intimate community which mostly disappeared with the collapse of the Greek city states. The word "democracy" was still used in a pejorative way in much seventeenth- and eighteenth-century writing, but when the American and, particularly, the French Revolution proclaimed the Sovereignty of the People, the word "democracy" acquired the hallowed associations in the West which it has retained ever since.

It is a little odd that in *The Statesman*, Plato should have preferred Monarchy to Aristocracy, as the ideal form of government he has held before us in *The Republic* is obviously an Aristocracy. The chronology of Plato's works is not precise, and it is just possible that he wrote *The Statesman* around 367 BC when he was the courtier of a prince. He had been invited by Dion, an elder statesman in Syracuse, to undertake the education of his nephew Dionysius II. The young man had just become the new ruler and seems, at the age of thirty, to have been badly in need of education. Plato was probably quite excited. According to *The Republic*, thirty was just the right age at which to begin a proper philosophical education, and Plato may have hoped to turn his new pupil into a Philosopher King. For a variety of reasons it did not turn out very well. Plato now had some close acquaintance with a real government rather than an ideal one. He discovered (as Voltaire was to discover with Frederick the Great and Catharine the Great) how difficult it is for a ruler to act as a Philosopher King. Even if the ruler were a philosopher, the chances were slim indeed that his people would be easy to rule.

The Laws

The result of all these experiences was one of Plato's last works, *The Laws*. He seems to have felt the obligation to set down how imperfect men in a country ruled by imperfect rulers had best be run, and the result is a grim prescription. In *The Republic* he had written that in the ideal state laws were unnecessary because a truly wise ruler ought not to be fettered by them. Then, in *The Statesman*, he had turned to dealing with real states, and had concluded that even the good forms of government must be subject to law. In that book, he had not gone into any details about what the laws should actually prescribe. This he now proceeded to do.

The state he now envisaged would be agricultural and self-sufficient. It would not be mercantile: Plato disliked the dynamic, innovative and restless mercantile spirit. He looked down on money-making and distrusted the merchant classes for their foreign contacts. He also suspected them of insufficient respect for tradition. He would restrict agricultural wealth: each family was to have the same amount of landed property, and noone was to be allowed to have personal property which was greater than four times the value of his landed property. Agriculture should not develop into what today we call "agro-business" and thereby produce a commercial ethos on the land. The society would therefore have little more than a subsistence economy; it would aim at autarchy; it would be static; enterprise would be stifled and contact with the outside world would be kept to a minimum.

The highest official in that state would be the Minister of Education who would also be in charge of censorship. All the restrictive attitudes that had already been sketched out for the ideal Republic would be turned into law, but this time penalties - ranging from five years imprisonment to death - were laid down for "heresies". The heresies included any purely atomistic and materialistic view of the universe; any idea that the gods are indifferent to man; any stories in mythology which portrayed the gods as behaving badly; anything that was subversive of what Plato considered good citizenship.

> It is sad to see the Plato who had such an elevated and unanthropomorphic idea of the Divine in *The Republic* now stoop to insist that an anthropomorphic image of the gods be taught to the masses. In *The Laws* the gods are not the gods of popular Greek mythology – gods who could cheat and wench, quarrel and seduce. We have already seen how little use Plato had had for these when he wrote *The Republic.* Now the gods are righteous, all-seeing and punitive. Plato wants to teach the people a religion in which he does not himself believe,[5] because he thought that they would behave better if they thought that the gods would observe and punish their bad behaviour. Plato is the forerunner of those who say that they don't believe in God themselves, but that it is good for the masses to be taught to believe in them. Joseph II, the eighteenth-century Habsburg Emperor, was such a person. He was a free thinker himself; and he tolerated any religion in his empire except Deism. Deism is the idea that there must be a God who created the world (for only thus could one explain its marvellous complexity), but that this Deity had no interest in how his creation now behaved. Joseph wanted his subjects to believe in a God who would care and would punish bad behaviour. The Emperor's police could not be everywhere or see everything so God was

5 I think it may be safe to say that. At the end of the last book of the *Republic,* Plato does recount a myth in which, after death, the gods reward the good and punish the bad; but this seems at odds with the purer conception he had of God. I think he saw the myth as another "noble lie" to convey the idea that a corrupted soul will not be fit to returns to Heaven.

called on to make up for these deficiencies! Joseph II, like Plato, was both patronizing and dictatorial in foisting on the people a belief that he was too sophisticated to share.

No wonder that the first volume of Karl Popper's famous book *The Open Society and its Enemies* is dedicated to a sustained attack on Plato as the great enemy of the Open Society. Plato confessed that the society he had described in *The Laws* was only a second best, because the perfect and ideal society is unattainable in this world, but it is not difficult to produce a "second best" which is a good deal more liberal and open than Plato's; even in Plato's ideal state, illiberalism and élitism are strongly present.

This did not trouble the autocratic ruling classes of Europe. They revered Plato, not least because they identified themselves with a Platonic élite. The fact that so much of Plato's metaphysic would be absorbed in Christian theology also caused him to be regarded with enormous respect and veneration. He is more likely to be challenged in our own more liberal, egalitarian and non-metaphysical age. However, he had doughty critics even in his own age, none more doughty than his former pupil Aristotle.

CHAPTER 6

Aristotle

In the *Stanza della Signatura*, one of the great rooms in the Vatican decorated by Rafael, there is a magnificent mural called *The School of Athens* (1512). It shows famous scholars, artists, poets and scientists, mainly from antiquity, grouped around the two central figures, Plato and Aristotle. Plato is pointing with his right hand towards Heaven. He seems to be saying that if you are looking for reality, that is where you must look: for in Heaven dwell the Ideas which have given shape to everything that exists in an imperfect world here down below. Aristotle makes a gesture down towards the earth, as if he were saying that philosophical enquiry should concern itself primarily with the nature of phenomena as they exist down here.

It is something of an oversimplification. Plato, as we have seen, did, towards the end of his life, apply his mind, in *The Statesman* and in *The Laws*, to the world as it actually exists on earth; and Aristotle had something to say about God. This he did mainly in a series of lectures[1] published under the title of *Metaphysics*. (The title is not Aristotle's but that of his first century BC editor, Andronicus of Rhodes. The original meaning of the Greek word *meta* is "after"; and Andronicus simply wanted to convey that this series of lectures followed another series he published under the title *Physics*. *Ta phusika* is Greek for "natural things", and in those lectures Aristotle had addressed himself mainly to what we would now call the Natural Sciences. But Andronicus' title for the lectures about God has led to the word "metaphysics" in common parlance being applied now to those aspects of philosophy which go *beyond* the physical world and deal with religious or transcendant matters. So, because Plato concerned himself primarily with such matters, we think of Plato's philosophy as primarily metaphysical, while we think of Aristotle's as largely empirical (the word comes from the Greek *empeirikos*, meaning "practised") and interested in this world.

Though the polarity which Plato and Aristotle are said to represent is greatly exaggerated, the two men do represent two rather different mindsets, and one might almost say that thinkers divide into Platonists or Aristotelians in much the same way in which Gilbert and Sullivan believed nineteenth-century Englishmen to divide into Liberals or Conservatives.[2]

1 Aristotle wrote at least twenty-seven works in the Platonic dialogue form, but these have all been lost. Most of his work is known to us largely in the form of lecture notes – either his own or those of his students. There seem to have been some 400 sets of these notes. Many of them were also lost, but some forty sets were rediscovered in the 1st century BC and then put together by Andronicus of Rhodes around 60 to 50 BC.

2 "I often think it's comical/How Nature always does contrive/That every boy and every gal/That's born into the world alive/Is either a little Liberal/Or else a little Conservative!" *Iolanthe*.

The earliest works of Aristotle were written when he was still studying at Plato's Academy, and adhered quite closely to Plato's general philosophy. But after his teacher's death in 347 Aristotle left the Academy, and in 335 he founded his own school, the Lyceum.[3] During this period he first began to criticize some of Plato's teachings and then, at the Lyceum, to develop his own interest in empirical work.

Ideas (or Universals) and Particulars

The first target of his new thinking was Plato's doctrine that Ideas or Forms exist beyond the physical world and are pre-formed models which are imperfectly embodied in the phenomena of this world. He recognizes that there is, say, an Idea of whiteness which several white things have in common. Because they really do have it in common, the Ideas themselves are real and help us to understand the world better; but they are not self-subsistent or transcendent. In the sense that they give us a better understanding of the world, we must use our active intellect (the Greek word for this was *nous*) to *induce* the *universal* of whiteness from the particular white things which we observe. Science will never be satisfied with collecting particulars: its whole aim and purpose is to discover what a group of particular things have in common. The very activity of classifying phenomena, which, as we shall see, was a major part of Aristotle's activities, involved and had as its goal the establishment of universals. But the universals are not self-subsistent or transcendent.

The Idea of a horse, then, does not give us any *prior* information about an actual horse. But we do need to know what a horse actually is. Aristotle said that a horse was a *substance*[4] to which several predicates adhered. He considered that there were nine classes of these predicates. In the case of the horse, they might be things like its quality (white); its quantity or size (tall); its relation (faster than a tortoise); its temporary state (tired); its activity (trotting); and its passivity (being ridden).

You also need to discover the *matter* of which the substance is composed, and for Aristotle this was the lower stage out of which the present stage has developed. For example, the horse was previously a foal; before that it was an embryo; before that it was semen and ovum; and if Aristotle had known about genetic material, he would have been delighted to be able to go back that far.

3 Its name came from the god who presided over the grove where the school was built: Apollo Lyceius, or Apollo the Wolf-killer. It was also known as the Peripatetic School, because Aristotle used to lecture while walking up and down in front of his students. Perhaps he thought that his mind functioned better that way. His students tended to take after him: when they were discussing philosophy among themselves, they would stroll up and down in the open air. A later philosophical school had a pillared colonnade or *Stoa* built in front of it for this purpose. Many people have found since then that thoughts may be exchanged most freely when walking, when physical movement and walking side by side help to eliminate shyness or other inhibitions.

4 "Substance" is a Latin-derived translation of the Greek word *ousios*; and for a philosopher it has a more specific meaning than it has in common usage. It means what "stands underneath" or supports the "predicates", "properties", "attributes" or "accidents" (these four words mean much the same thing in this context) that make something recognizable. Unlike the everyday meaning of the word, it does not have to be material: it could, for instance, be a soul, to which predicates like noble or immortal could adhere.

Thus far, then, Aristotle seems to espouse the mechanical rather than the teleological definition of a horse.[5]

He did not know about genes, so he had to find an explanation for why the sperm and ovum of horses eventually turn into horses, while the sperm and ovum of a cat turn into cats. This explanation he found in the *essence* of something, by virtue of which we recognize the colt and the horse as being the same and not two different animals, by which we know that the green leaf in the spring and the brown leaf in the autumn are the same leaf, or by which a ship whose old mast has been replaced by a new one is still the same ship. The essence lies in the potential or *Entelechy* (from *telos*, goal or purpose) in virtue of which a thing is capable (if not impeded) of functioning in ways that are characteristic of its particular type of life activity.

Epistemology

Epistemology is the name given to that branch of philosophy which explores the nature of knowledge.

Socrates and Plato believed that true knowledge was innate - that is, that it existed before we have any experience of things; and we have looked at the difficulties of this concept above.[6] Aristotle, on the other hand, insisted that the senses are the only *source* of our knowledge: "There is nothing in the mind which was not first in the senses." This philosophical attitude is called Empiricism.

We may of course acquire further knowledge by building on the original source: if we can hold the perceptions in our mind, we have memory. This in turn provides us with experience; and from this we get skills or "a sort of knowledge" - what Plato had called mere "belief". Aristotle agreed with Plato that we have *true* knowledge only when we know the cause of the "sort of knowledge" we have had before - that is when we understand the matter, essence, Idea and causes[7] that can be inferred from our sense experience. And we should strive for this understanding *for its own sake*, rather than for practical purposes.

> This reminds us of Plato's contempt for those who applied the noble understanding of mathematics to problems of engineering or mechanics.[8] Someone who applied knowledge for practical purposes had the nature of a mechanic or a slave. It was the mark of a free man that he should develop understanding for its own sake. If he did that he was pursuing the *liberal arts* – the term means, literally, the skills of a free man.
>
> The social attitudes of Aristotle are of course quite unacceptable today. So is the distinction he makes between intellectual and practical activities: many practical activities, ranging from gardening to making model sailing ships, can be pursued for their own sake. But Aristotle's praise of knowledge for its own sake still has its attractions for millions of people of all ages and all social classes who have intellectual (or practical) interests and who spend many hours in studies which have for them no practical use whatever; and it is only philistines who mock such "useless knowledge".

5 See the discussion of teleology and mechanism on p. 33 above.

6 p. 36 above.

7 For Causes, see p. 47 below.

8 see p. 35 above.

> What might be the relevance of this to educational policy? Some educational politicians lay great stress on the need for schools and universities, financed as they are by public money, to equip their students for the "real" world of competitive economic activities. As a result, Greek has practically disappeared from the school syllabus, and Latin is about to go the same way. Modern history (sometimes only *very* modern history) is taught because it is "relevant"; medieval history is neglected because it not considered such. Bit by bit, we are losing touch with our intellectual heritage because it is considered to be of no practical use.
>
> Conversely, the study of French or German can be as rewarding as the study of Greek and Latin; the study of modern history as thought- provoking as that of medieval history; the accurate use of computer language as valuable as the accurate use of English grammar; all can be – and often are – studied for their own sake. If they have practical value in addition, is this not a compelling reason for substituting the one for the other in timetables in which there is not room for everything?

Aristotle says that we acquire true knowledge and understanding through the active intellect or *nous;* and although in some of his lectures Aristotle said that the activities of the mind perish with the body, in one place he follows the Platonic view that, though the mind (which includes nutrition, reproduction, perception and desire – what Plato had called the courageous and appetitive aspects of the soul) perishes, the *nous* does not. The *nous,* he says, is part of the *nous* of God. Not only is it therefore immortal, but through it man can glimpse a part of the *nous* of God and so has a chance to contemplate eternal truths.

By connecting the human intellect to the Divine in this manner, Aristotle retained an important part of Plato's metaphysical teaching, though there is an important difference: in Plato, when the intellect is embodied in a human, it brings with it, in a veiled form, the knowledge that it had acquired when it dwelt with the Divine before its descent. In Aristotle, what descends from the Divine is a *capacity* to understand; but this capacity is without specific content, because, as we have seen, Aristotle did not believe in innate ideas. We shall consider what else Aristotle has to say about the nature of God later in this chapter.

Logic

The active intellect when embodied in human understanding has to be trained to think logically. Aristotle turned Logic into a science and introduced principles which, with some later refinements, would dominate philosophy for centuries. It is too technical a subject for detailed treatment here; but it was Aristotle who created the system of syllogisms. A syllogism looks like this:

> All humans are mortal.
> Socrates is mortal.
> Therefore Socrates is a human.

But does this really follow? Socrates could be the name of my pet dog, which, alas, is mortal also. In that case the syllogism is a fallacious one. The following syllogism is a valid one:

> All humans are mortal.
> Socrates is a human.
> Therefore Socrates is mortal.

The formal logic which Aristotle created devises rules by which we can recognize which kind of syllogism is valid and which is fallacious.

Collecting and Classifying

As we have seen, Aristotle said that we infer universals from particulars. To do this, we need to have a mass of particulars from which to make the inferences. He and his pupils therefore collected factual material in every field, which he then studied, analyzed and subsequently organized and classified into a conceptual framework. He gathered information about the constitutions and customs of various societies in the Near East; about the anatomy and behaviour of animals and plants; about meteorological conditions, and about much else besides. He was a superb observer, especially in the field of biology, and he reflected on what he saw. He noted how lower forms of life are related to higher forms, and he assumed that the higher forms are the aims of nature.

Causes

"Nature does nothing in vain", concluded Aristotle: there is a teleological explanation for everything in the natural world: why ducks have webbed feet, why roots grow downwards etc. There is always a Final End (or cause) which explains why anything is what it is.

Aristotle distinguished between four causes that determine what a thing is. A sculpture, for instance has a material cause (say, the bronze of which it consists), a formal cause (the pattern or form that is in the sculptor's mind), the efficient cause (the sculptor himself), and the final cause (the purpose for which the sculpture is created.) Another example is given by Jostein Gaarder:[9] the material cause of rain is the moisture in the clouds; the formal cause is the nature of the moisture to fall to earth when it has achieved a sufficient condensation; the efficient cause is the cooling that is necessary for the moisture to achieve this condensation; the final cause is to provide water for the plants and creatures on the earth.

> In the case of the sculpture we may accept Aristotle's account of what goes to achieve the final result. In the case of rain, however, whilst we might accept the first three of these causes, we would be distinctly sceptical at the idea that it rains in order for life to exist on earth. We would be more inclined to say that life on earth exists as the result of the conditions which produce rain. Where these and other particular conditions do not exist, as on most planets, life presumably does not exist. One could combine the first three with the final cause as an explanation if one believed that God chose this earth and none of the uninhabited planets as a home for life as we understand it.

God

What Aristotle meant by God was really the natural order. He might almost have agreed with Spinoza's formulation of *Deus sive Nature* (God or Nature).[10]

9 in *Sophie's World*, London 1995.

10 See p. 237 below.

The natural order for Aristotle is governed both by something that set it going (which he called the First Cause) and by something that it will become when it is finally developed (the Final Cause). The world, Aristotle believed, had existed from eternity. As the First Cause God, "the Unmoved Mover", had set it in motion towards the Final Cause.

Aristotle was not the first thinker who presented God as both the First and the Final Cause: the Jewish prophet Isaiah had said the same some four centuries earlier when he has God say "I am the first and the last" (44:6), and four centuries after Aristotle, in the Christian Book of Revelation, God says, "I am Alpha and Omega, the beginning and the ending." So religions in the West give God two essential functions: he is there at the beginning of Creation, and he also sets the goal or *telos* for this Creation. For Aristotle the existence of this goal provided an *explanation* of development and of evolution. For Plato before him and for Judaism and Christianity later, the goal was also a moral and intellectual *challenge*, demanding that human beings should aim to improve themselves by aspiring to the ideals that God put before them, even though they know that the full attainment of these ideals is not possible in this world – for Plato because everything in this world is but a shadow of the Ideals laid up in Heaven, for Judaism and Christianity because of the expulsion from Paradise.

The reason why Aristotle thought the world was coeval with God and was not created by Him is that he thought God could not have that purely abstract quality, uncombined with any Matter, which Aristotle attributed to him if He were directly involved with making something material. The Bible, however, states that God created the world; so, in later centuries when Aristotle was integrated into Jewish and Christian theology, this aspect of his teaching would be something of a stumbling block and would eventually be rejected.

The idea that God is the very First Cause is the most tenacious of all beliefs about God. There are many people who have lost their belief in a God who sets before us spiritual, moral or intellectual goals, but who feel that the world is such an amazing piece of "work" that a creative force or principle must have been responsible for at least setting it going. The advance of scientific knowledge has merely pushed the operation of the first cause further and further back into the past. In the seventeenth century the Anglo-Irish Bishop James Ussher used the information in the Bible to work out that God must have created the world in 4004 BC. Ussher would also have trusted the Bible when it said that God made the plants, the animals and humans separately. But although we now know that the world is many million years older than that and that all life ultimately evolved from a primal soup and subsequently branched out into its multifarious forms, we still would like to know how the primal soup came into being; and if we push the beginning of the universe back to the Big Bang, we want to know what force created the Big Bang in the first place. That force may not be a personal force; it may not be something that demands worship, therefore it may not merit the name of God at all. However, human beings will always try to discover what there was before the earliest stage that they already know about: they will always be searching for a first cause.

Aristotle himself saw God as an impersonal force: he did not believe that this God was an object of worship (Aristotle did not have Plato's mystical temperament). Such knowledge as we have of God does not come to us from faith or revelation but (he believed) from the exercise of our intellect. Aristotle did

> not believe that God loved us, that He could be prayed to, or that He was displeased when anything in the world fell short of the *telos* of perfection which he represented. Aristotle was therefore not what later ages would call a *Theist* – someone who believes that God cares about the way the world behaves and will either punish or reward. Aristotle was an early *Deist.* A Deist believes that the world obeys such intricate laws that there must have been a law-maker; that therefore there is a God who has in the beginning created both the world (or, as Aristotle believed, had at least set it going) and also the laws which it follows, but that there is no evidence that thereafter He takes any further interest in it.

Aristotle's God is so impersonal that one hesitates to describe his position as a religious one. It seems wholly philosophical. The existence of God can, according to Aristotle, be deduced by the intellect with the help of logic, and without the need for revelation or mystical experience. And, as we have seen, such a God is not interested in how human beings behave. Aristotle's Ethics - the branch of philosophy which concerns itself with good behaviour - is therefore not based on divine commandments or on any other religious foundation. Instead, it is based on rather practical considerations, and these very much reflect the codes of a fourth-century Athenian citizen.

Ethics

Two works deal with Aristotle's ideas on Ethics: the *Nichomachean Ethics,* so called because they were edited after Aristotle's death by his son Nichomachus; and the *Eudaemian Ethics.*

"Eudaemonia" literally means "happy spirit", and the second book was given its title because its theme was that the goal of behaviour should be to produce happiness. That is hardly the criterion by which we would judge ethical behaviour today: when we are confronted with an ethical challenge, we are asked to do what is morally right; and this, in the narrow sense at least, often involves our willingness to sacrifice happiness.

> I say "in the narrow sense at least", because, if we do choose to sacrifice happiness, we may gain satisfaction – i.e. another kind of happiness – from having made that choice, and we might feel guilty – i.e. unhappy – if we had acted otherwise. But that is only true of people whose consciences are sufficiently tender. Someone who has no such conscience could do something we consider unethical and could justify it on Aristotelian grounds by saying that what he had done added to his happiness.

We can see, therefore, that the subject of Ethics for Aristotle was not primarily a question of what we would today call morality. Indeed, the original meaning of the Greek word *ethicos* was "customary" rather than "moral". The English word "ethos" still carries the implication of custom. The ethos of a society is its distinctive character or attitude, in which morality, if it figures at all, is only a part.

We consider someone who acts morally a virtuous person; and the Greek word *arete,* which Aristotle commends, is usually translated as "virtue"; so that perhaps Aristotle is concerned with morality in our sense after all. But Jonathan Barnes writes that what *arete* actually means is "excellence", and that it need not be applied to behaviour at all, but could equally be applied, he says, to the qualities of an argument or of an axe.[11] When it is applied to human character, it means an excellent and intelligent appraisal of one's *eudaemonia*. Now the pursuit of happiness requires an intelligent appraisal of what actually makes us happy, not only in the short term but also in the long term. In an individual case, someone who takes heroin because he feels intense happiness after the injection is not making an intelligent appraisal if he forgets the unhappiness of addiction. Also, if we are aiming for the happiness of the society, we will need to be able to make an intelligent rather than a largely emotional assessment of the long-term results that, say, a particular economic policy will actually bring about.

> The idea that what we describe as ethical is (and indeed ought to be) whatever is conducive to intelligently conceived happiness will be developed by many later philosophers from the seventeenth century onwards; and we will discuss it more fully in due course. For the moment, we should note that, because Aristotle shared the belief of his contemporaries that man can only fulfill himself properly as a "political animal", he cannot achieve "real" happiness at the expense of the community, so that there can be no real conflict between the happiness of the individual and that of the community. The distinction between "real" and "actual" (but "unreal") happiness, between one's "real will" and one's "actual will", between one's "real freedom" and one's "actual freedom", comes in very handy for philosophers who don't want to face the conflict that undoubtedly often exists between the happiness of the individual (whether he is a successful crook or a member of an unfairly treated minority) and that of the community.

An intelligent appraisal should tell a person that excess always harms true happiness. Many virtues strike a happy mean between excesses: the virtue of courage, for instance, avoids recklessness on the one hand and cowardice on the other. *Arete* involves moderation in all things: a moderate but not an excessive pursuit of wealth or pleasure, nor, on the other hand, an excessive neglect of these in the name of saintly austerity.

This looks as if Aristotle is having a dig at Plato's Guardians, who were supposed to abstain from everything that might interfere with their single-minded pursuit of Wisdom - could such people really be happy? But Aristotle knew that the cultivation of all the normal virtues of intelligence, moderation, courage, moral uprightness etc. are no guarantee that their practitioners will always be protected from severe suffering or misfortune; and even when they did produce *eudaimonia*, it was happiness "in a secondary degree". Happiness of the purest kind and which will never be affected by misfortunes, lies in *theoria*, the enquiry into and contemplation of eternal and divine truths. In this he agreed with Plato, although Plato, at least in *The Republic*, was far less interested than Aristotle was in praising those moral qualities that led merely to a second-class kind of happiness.[12]

11 Jonathan Barnes, *Aristotle*, O.U.P. 1982, p. 78. For good measure, Jonathan Barnes also tells us that *eudaemonia* is ill-translated as "happiness"; and that a better translation of the word would be "making a success of life". He also says that the Greek word *ethika* really means "matters to do with character".

12 I owe this passage to Anthony Gottlieb's *The Dream of Reason*, pp. 269 to 272.

Because *arete* requires the use of one's rational powers, Aristotle believed, as Plato had done, that it was not possible for the common people to possess it: he considered that the natural inferiority of slaves, or degrading or time-consuming pursuits such as trade, manufacture or husbandry, made it impossible to develop the intellectual faculties properly. Ignorance was a bar to *arete*; in that respect he agreed with Socrates and Plato. The converse, that if you have true knowledge, you have true virtue (as Socrates and Plato had maintained) did not follow for Aristotle. He had the more common sense view that there were many people who were intelligent enough to know what virtue commanded but who deliberately chose another course of action.

How, then, did a man who had an intelligent appraisal of his happiness behave? Essentially, the virtues that Aristotle recognized were civic virtues, those for which a community honours its leading citizens, its politicians, artists and thinkers. Such people, he thought, were the most fully developed human beings and so came closest to the teleological definition of man. It is not possible for slaves or artisans to develop the whole potential of man, any more than an acorn falling on unsuitable soil can become a noble oak tree.

What is notably missing from Aristotle's ethics is any feeling of compassion for the suffering that results from the treatment of slaves, artisans, etc. as inferiors. In fact, he believes that *arete* actually requires pride in one's own qualities and a contempt for inferiors.

> He would not have understood that part of the American Declaration of Independence which proclaimed that all men were created equal (at least in the sight of God) and that among their inalienable rights is the pursuit of happiness. Here, too, he believed with Plato that justice did not call for men to be treated equally in any way whatever. On the contrary: justice must enshrine the fact that men are *not* created equal – but then Plato and Aristotle lived in the fourth century BC and not in the eighteenth century AD.

Questions of equality and inequality relate not only to Ethics but also to Politics; and it is to Aristotle's treatment of Politics, in the book that carries this title, that we must now turn.

Politics

Perhaps the most famous sentence in that book is, "Man is a political animal". We have already seen above [13] that this is a crude translation. What Aristotle meant was that man is an animal that lives in a *polis*, which was both a political and a social community, and that it is a teleological definition of man, meaning that his full development requires him to be a communal or social being rather than, say, a hermit. The *polis*, in another famous sentence, "originates for the sake of life, but continues for the sake of the good life." Or again: "A *polis* is not ... founded for the purpose of men's living together, *but for their living as men ought.*"

> Living in society, the Greeks believed, makes men *better*. This concept is the opposite of the Romantic notion that would be expounded by Rousseau in 1755: that before the development of sophisticated societies, man was a

13 p. 21 above.

> *noble savage* who was subsequently corrupted by them. Aristotle believed that without people banding together in sophisticated communities, life would be almost impossible and would at best be, as Hobbes would memorably describe it: "solitary, nasty, poor, brutish and short."

Because it brings out of man the best that there is in him, the *polis* does more than make life *possible*, it makes life *civilized*. It does that in its purely political manifestation also. For Aristotle, the state is therefore not merely, as *laissez-faire* political theorists from John Locke to John Stuart Mill would claim, a second best; a piece of machinery we have set up whose functions should ideally be limited to maintaining a degree of order and which definitely does not include a remit to make us into better people. Aristotle believed that in its political manifestations, the *polis* is responsible for the health of the whole community, and this justifies the exercise of a lot of authoritarianism. He thought that it had the duty, for example, to decide who might and might not be allowed to marry, to regulate education and many other aspects of the lives of its members.

> We will have few difficulties in accepting that man is such an integral part of a community that life outside it would be almost as dead and meaningless as would be that of a limb severed from the organism of a living body. It becomes more debatable when what Aristotle said about the relationship between the citizen and the *polis* is extended, first from the community to the city-state and then from the city-state to the large modern state. The so-called Organic Theory of the state does exactly that. It claims that only the state gives real meaning to the citizen; that man can only fulfill himself as an integral member of the state; that the individual is as subordinate to the state as a limb is to the body; that he has no rights against that body; and, what is more, that he does not "really" wish to claim such rights because he "really" knows that it is only within the state that he best fulfils himself. The Organic Theory is the opposite of the theory that the State is actually only a machine which has been set up to serve the individuals who constructed it, an association which, like any other association, from a cooperative society to a golf club, has been set up for specific and probably rather limited purposes. If the machine or association were seriously to fail to deliver what was expected of it, we could, in an extreme case, dismantle or dissolve it. That would not be the death of us (as it would be if we destroyed an organism that gave us life).
>
> The Organic Theory is very popular with those who promote the worship of the state, and it is therefore very dangerous, but it need not be harmful. It was after all taken for granted by all Athenians, and their popular assemblies gave full scope to democratic debate and decision making. One can argue that the healthiest democracies are those in which individuals, while exercising their rights as individuals, also have a sense of a "living" community which is something more valuable than a mere aggregation of individuals.

Aristotle did not merely theorize about the nature of the *polis*. He made a careful study of the way societies are actually governed. His students collected the constitutions of 158 states and city-states in the Middle East for him. Unfortunately all but one of them – the constitution of Athens – have been lost; and even the one that remains was only rediscovered in 1890 – in the form of a copy written on the back of a set of accounts that themselves were dated 70 AD! However, Aristotle's *Politics* does contain the fruit of the conclusions he had reached from studying these actual rather than ideal states. To begin with, he classified them into groups, as was his wont when he had collected materials about animals or plants. He followed Plato's six-fold division, which has already been described above,[14] but he then went further, and described how exactly each of these six should preserve themselves and avoid revolutions. He did this in a quite non-judgmental way. A monarchy, aristocracy or polity could learn from him how to prevent the degeneration of these good forms of government into bad ones; but at the same time a tyrant, for example, could profitably turn to this part of the book and study what mistakes to avoid and what methods of crushing his opponents were likely to be counter-productive. In this sense Aristotle anticipated Machiavelli, whose preferred model of a state was actually a republic of public-minded citizens, but who nevertheless provide,d in *The Prince* of 1513, a handbook advising a tyrant what stratagems and devices would best ensure his lasting hold on power. The difference is that, while Machiavelli dedicated *The Prince* to Giulano de Medici in the hope that his own services to the preceding Florentine republic might be forgiven,[15] Aristotle was simply producing an academic study.

Like Machiavelli, however, Aristotle, too, had his preferences. Naturally, he preferred the three good varieties to the three bad ones, but which of the three good ones is best depends in each case on the circumstances of climate, geography, social development etc. In this respect, Aristotle anticipated the thesis to be worked out in some detail by Montesquieu's *L'Esprit des Lois* of 1748.[16] In a large state like the Persian Empire, for example, it would be impossible to gather all the citizens together for decision-making, and therefore a polity would be impracticable. Aristotle thought it was easiest to make a polity work in societies where middle class people are more numerous than either the rich or the poor, both of whom he thought were likely to govern badly.

Where a polity *is* practicable, it seems to have been Aristotle's preferred type. A monarchy or an aristocracy might be fine in theory, but in practice really wise monarchs and enlightened aristocrats are not so easy to find; and even when found, human nature will not readily subordinate itself to them. Nor, under such governments, would men be encouraged to function as the "political animals" that they are, and would therefore be unable to develop their potential the full.

> Is Aristotle's contention right, that there are several types of good government and that a polity (or what today we call liberal democracy) might not necessarily suit every society? He only knew direct democracies – i.e. societies in which every citizen has a direct say in how a city is to be governed; and so he did not seriously consider "representative democracy" – that is, democracy carried out through elected representatives. Representative government and greater ease of communications today make it possible for very large states to be governed in a democratic manner, so that size is no longer quite such a determining factor. It probably remains true, however, that the smaller a democratic society is, the greater is the chance of the individual fulfilling himself as

14 p. 39 above.

15 see p. 179, note 23 above.

16 See p. 352 below.

a political animal in the Aristotelian sense. That is a strong argument for "subsidiarity" – the principle that, in a large democratic state, whatever can best be decided at the local level should be decided there and not at the centre.

If size is perhaps rather less important than Aristotle thought, what about "social development"? Foremost among these must surely be the state of a society's education, and particularly of its civic education. This was very highly developed among the citizens in Aristotle's Athens – though we need to remember that slaves, artisans and women were not included among the Athenian citizens. Do we think that democracy also suits a state if most of its people are uneducated, both in the wider and in the narrower civic sense? And was Aristotle right in the generalization that men will not readily subordinate themselves to monarchs and aristocrats? Have we not seen the propensity, in many societies, of people – not all of them uneducated – to idolize their rulers; to ascribe to them great wisdom whether they have it or not?

Aristotle had great faith in the common sense of a civically educated public. He considered it a better judge of policy than Plato's expertly trained Guardians would have been. "The public are the best judges," he writes; "for some understand one part, some another, and all collectively the whole."

This view rests on faith in the efficacy of reasoned and open-minded discussion. A community might indeed, by such debate, come to a wider understanding than its individual members had before the debate began, and it would be valuable both for the experts and for the wider community to take each other's views into account.

Does the public always make sound judgments? Is it always the best reasoned argument which prevails? Is it not sometimes the case that the arguments which prevail are those which play on our emotions, sometimes on our baser emotions? Demagogues often play on our emotions rather than on our reason. A politically educated public is less subject to being manipulated in this way, but even well-educated people often use their rational faculties to find arguments to support rather than to check their emotions.

No system is free of dangers: there are dangers in relying on experts just as there are in relying on public opinion. But a system relying on public opinion is on balance more consonant with the dignity of human beings than one in which choices are made for them by the so-called experts. As E.M. Forster wrote in 1951, "Two cheers for Democracy: one because it admits variety and Two because it permits criticism. Two cheers are quite enough: there is no occasion to give three."

Aristotle again: "In some particular arts it is not the workman only who is the best judge."

This is the argument about the customer and the shoemaker, which we have already considered when we looked at Plato's advocacy of government by experts.[17]

To Plato's idea that the Guardians should have no individual property but hold it all in common, Aristotle replies, "What is common to many is least taken care of."

17 see p. 24 above.

> The argument rings a bell on every vandalized piece of public property. On the other hand, some societies have a stronger civic spirit than others. Compared with England, Switzerland is comparatively free of litter and graffiti. The Guardians, as representatives of the civic spirit, should have been able to take good care of communal property.

In Plato's ideal republic there would be equal opportunities for men and women. Aristotle, expressing the "common sense" view of his contemporaries, derides the idea: a woman is merely "an unfinished man", passive and receptive rather than active or productive. Her role is therefore to be ruled by men.

Altogether, Aristotle has little patience with the kind of idealism that Plato represented. "We ought to consult the experience of many years," he writes, "which would plainly enough inform us whether such a scheme is useful; for almost all things have already been found out."

> Many commentators have described Aristotle as a complacent conservative, in a sense more conservative than Plato had been. In theory, Plato had combined some conservative ideas with ideas and structures which were radical and thoroughly subversive of Athenian society as it was: his treatment of women being one case in point, his espousal of communism another. Aristotle thought such ideas utopian.[18]
>
> A scheme is described as utopian if it could not possibly be realized by human beings as they actually are. Now some schemes are clearly utopian in that sense. Some people might argue that theoretical communism would fall into that category, because the attachment of human beings *in general* to the accumulation of personal property is so basic that it can never be eradicated and can only be suppressed by force.
>
> All the same we should be very careful before we write off any scheme as utopian, and this for two reasons. First, a scheme which seems to run counter to human nature in one society may actually come to be seen as quite practicable in another society or at a later age. Consider, for example, the position of women. In Aristotle's time, as we have seen, it was considered "natural" that women were inferior; that they might enjoy equality of status was considered "utopian". Now, although we still have a little way to go, it is certainly no longer a utopian idea that woman should have equal rights with men. The second reason, therefore, why we should hesitate before we describe a scheme as "merely utopian" is that an ideal represents an aspiration towards a goal which, although we may never reach it, provides a spur to improvement. Fully blown communism may be an unattainable ideal; but it represents an aspiration which has led many societies to do *something* to curb the unrestrained pursuit of personal gain by exploitation of the weaker members of society.

By believing that almost all useful things had already been found out, Aristotle had shown himself more conservative than Plato. There were, however, some respects in which Plato, too, had been thoroughly conservative. This came out most clearly where Plato had come to consider the way actual states ought to be governed, when, as we have seen, he had shown his mistrust of groups like the merchants, who, he thought, were likely to be disconcertingly innovative.

18 The name "Utopia" was given by Sir Thomas More in the sixteenth century to a society which does not actually exist (is nowhere – from the Greek *ou* = not, plus *topos* = a place) but which is perfect (the Greek *eu* means good).

Aristotle shared Plato's dislike of the trading classes, who were in the ignoble business of making money. The "middle class", which he thought as predominating in a good polity, was for him made up not of merchants but of small land-owners. When the harvest is bad, those who own or work on the land are often forced to borrow money to tide them over from one autumn to the next, and, speaking for all those who make their living from the land, Aristotle particularly excoriated those who took advantage of such necessities by practising usury.

Aristotle's condemnation of usury has echoed down the many centuries which were dominated by the landed classes. The churches condemned it, and to the extent that they were effective, they hampered investment and the development of commerce. But the need for credit was too strong for the church's condemnation of usury to be very effective. When bankers like the Lombards and the Fuggers lent money to borrowers, they claimed that they were levying not usury (defined as the reward for running a risk), but interest (defined as compensation for what was the difference between – *quod inter est* – the lender's wealth before and after the time he has made his loan.) So what Christians did was considered charging acceptable *interest*, whilst when Jews did the same thing it was described as detestable and (of course) "extortionate" *usury* – so much so that the dictionary now defines usury as lending money at an exorbitant rate of interest, while the more general meaning the word had in the time of Aristotle and the theologians (simply lending money) is now described as "obsolete".

Aesthetics

In his work on Science and on Politics, Aristotle appears to be at his most pragmatic, although, as we have seen, the goal of collecting all the particular material was the establishment of useful universals. When he turned to the field of Aesthetics, it is quite clear that he thought that the highest form of art is the one that has as its object universal and general rather than particular themes. That is why Aristotle preferred poetry to history. The best poetry deals with the feelings that all mankind shares; history deals with individual and particular events, and is therefore inferior to poetry.

The great Greek historian Thucydides, who wrote about a century before Aristotle, from ca. 460 to 404, might have met with Aristotle's approval, as he was the first historian who tried to deduce some laws or generalizations from the events he described; but in this respect he had no great successors in antiquity.

Like Plato, Aristotle also believed that a work of art should have proportion, harmony, and wholeness in form and composition. In the *Poetics*, Aristotle dealt with drama, and it is in this work that he formulated what would become known as the dramatic unities. He demanded that a noble work of drama should be concentrated to deal with only one plot (there should be no sub-plot to distract from the main action) and that the action should take place on one day. He did not actually lay down that it should also be confined to one place, but as classical Greek drama generally observed this restriction also, the dramatic unities are generally held to apply to time, place and action.

> Under these rules, Shakespeare's tragedies will hardly qualify as drama, but the classical unities were observed in the plays of Corneille and Racine in seventeenth century France. In the eighteenth century, Voltaire, who inherited the classical tradition, grudgingly admitted that within the unpolished structure of Shakespeare's tragedies there were actually some rather fine passages.

The concentration created by the dramatic unities would make for the most intense impact of a tragedy on the spectator, so that it would produce *catharsis,* a desirable purging and cleansing of the soul. This was an acute psychological description of the state in which an audience leaves a great tragic performance. It also was an implicit repudiation of Plato, whose suspicion of all emotional, as distinct from intellectual, responses to art had been one of the reasons why he had wanted to banish dramatists and actors from the ideal republic.

The Future of Plato and Aristotle

The thoughts of both Plato and Aristotle had sprung out of their experiences of the Greek city states. The independence of the Greek city states was practically destroyed even in Aristotle's lifetime by the armies of Macedon. Philip of Macedon defeated an Athenian army in 338 BC; his eighteen-year-old son Alexander led the Macedonian cavalry. Two years before that battle, Aristotle had ended a three year stint as Alexander's tutor.

The Greek city-states retained a certain degree of autonomy by submitting to Philip and, after Philip's death, to his son Alexander the Great. In an amazingly short time, Alexander created a vast empire, reaching from the Danube to Egypt in the south-west and the frontiers of India in the south-east. Perhaps it was from Aristotle that Alexander had acquired his love and respect for Greek culture which he tried to foster within that empire. The form that culture took in Alexander's time, and later, is now generally known as Hellenism. Yet at the same time he undermined the importance of the *polis* which for Aristotle had been an essential part of that culture, being the sphere within which man could most meaningfully develop himself.

Alexander died the year before Aristotle, and his empire disintegrated. But Macedon continued to overshadow the Greek city states. From time to time between the death of Alexander (323 BC) and the Roman conquest of Greece in 146 BC, they managed fitful periods of independence, but it was a chaotic period and the civic glory of the Athenian *polis,* the self-confidence of its citizens, had gone for ever.

Plato's philosophy, by concentrating on the ideal state laid up in Heaven, had distanced itself from the actual *polis.* As the citizens of the city-states found themselves bewildered by the collapse of the units that had given their life meaning, many of them escaped into mystical religions, and traces of Plato's own mysticism were an ingredient in some of these beliefs before the advent of Christianity. Christianity itself, we have already seen, easily gave its own meaning to many of Plato's ideas about perfection laid up in Heaven. So Plato's reputation and influence revived within a relatively short time after the collapse of the city-states.

Aristotle's fate was different; his political thinking had been much more concrete. His idea that man could only perfect himself by political as well as social involvement with the *polis* seemed to make no sense when the *polis* had disappeared and huge empires allowed active participation to only a very few people. When Christianity appeared, its whole thrust was other-worldly. It was often even hostile to and suspicious of too much study of this world, which it regarded as a distraction from contemplation of and preparation for the next world.

This may explain why such an enormous amount of Aristotle's work was lost for so long. What survived was due to the work of Boethius (*ca.* 480 to *ca.* 524) who, almost alone among the Christian thinkers of antiquity, was as interested in Aristotle as he was in Plato. He translated much of Aristotle's work into Latin (Greek by that time was scarcely known, even among educated people in the western part of what had been the Roman Empire) but most of these texts were lost for centuries. Only his translations of part of what Aristotle had written on Logic and on the Categories were known to, and influential among, medieval theologians.

The rest of Aristotle's work was eventually rediscovered in the eigth century, in the formerly Hellenic lands of the Middle East, which Islam had overrun a hundred years earlier. During that century the Arabs also conquered Spain, and an Islamic version of Aristotelianism began to establish itself there. The Christians later reconquered parts of Spain and through the contact between Islamic and Christian scholars, Aristotle began to make his impact on Christian thought from about the eleventh century onwards. That story will be told more fully in Chapter 15 below.

CHAPTER 7

The Hellenistic Period

We saw in the last chapter that, as people found that the city- states no longer gave a meaning to their lives, some of them escaped into mystical religions. But another more hard-headed response was also possible. The wise man increasingly saw himself less as a social or political animal and instead sought sufficiency within himself. There could not be a more radical rejection of the earlier Greek conception - embodied in the Funeral Oration of Pericles[1] and which found expression in Aristotle - that someone who took no interest in public affairs was a stunted person who had not fulfilled his potential. Even before the death of Aristotle, two schools of philosophy, known as Cynicism and Epicureanism, had expounded the need for self-sufficiency. The earliest proponents of these philosophies were Antisthenes in the case of the Cynics and Aristippus in that of the Epicureans; but it was their disciples, Diogenes and Epicurus respectively, who made a greater impact than the founders, because by their day the collapse of the city-state had given their ideas greater resonance.

Cynicism

Diogenes (who is said to have died in his nineties on the same day as Alexander the Great in 323 BC) said that the wise man will isolate himself from whatever the world can do to harm him. He will live as simply and austerely as possible; if you own nothing, then you are more or less immune to what the world can do to you. "I do not posses," his teacher Antisthenes had said, "in order not to be possessed." Stories told about Diogenes reinforce this point. It is said that he was content to live in a tub, and that he threw away his drinking bowl when he found that he could drink equally well from his cupped hands. He considered the values that society attached to possessions and to conventional ways of living to be so much dross; the wise man will refuse to be bound by them and will be a law unto himself - and Diogenes took pleasure in flouting conventions. He was said to have copulated in public as human beings need no more be ashamed of such a natural act than dogs were. In fact, he called himself the Dog, in Greek *kunos*, from which the word Cynic is derived.[2] It goes without saying

1 see p. 20 above

2 The name also stuck because the cynics were said to sneer at conventions, and someone who sneers turns down his mouth which then resembles the appearance of a dog's mouth. Yet another theory is that Antisthenes had taught at a charitable institution which for some reason was called the Cynosarges or Dogfish.

that Diogenes was no respecter of authority. Another story has Alexander the Great visiting him in his tub and asking him what he could do for him, to which Diogenes is said to have replied, "You can step out of my light".

One wonders what should have attracted Alexander to visit Diogenes, let alone to ask him what he could do for him – until we remember that Alexander was still a very young man. If such an encounter did indeed take place, Alexander may still have been in his early twenties; he may then, like many other young people, have been attracted, or at least fascinated, by an attitude which is today described as "in yer face". One can imagine some rebellious and alienated Greek youths, wearing the Greek equivalent of torn jeans and perhaps matted hair, getting a less churlish reception when they came to "chew the fat" with Diogenes than that which was accorded to the smartly dressed Alexander, who, moreover, represented the kind of authority that Diogenes refused to acknowledge.

We might find modern followers of Diogenes not only among certain young people who defy conventions and lead a relatively austere and yet free-wheeling life-style, but also among some of the people who actually prefer to sleep rough under bridges or in doorways to taking up any offers of accommodation for vagrants in hostels, where they would feel constrained by a social institution.

Of course, some of the ideas of Diogenes can, and indeed do take a very elevated and moral form, such as the espousal of apostolic poverty in pursuit of some spiritual aim. It is, however, hard to detect truly moral or spiritual concerns in Diogenes. His aim is self-sufficiency for its own sake, to keep at bay any claims that his immediate society might make on him. To ward these off, he claimed to be a citizen of the world, yet he does not seem to have had any commitment to his fellow-citizens in a world community. A sense of fellowship and brotherhood among mankind in general – such as some Stoic philosophers will develop later – would involve certain obligations to other human beings which a loner like Diogenes is unlikely to have felt. It is perhaps because his attitude has more of the corrosive than of the idealistic in it that the word cynicism has not unjustly acquired a pejorative association.

Epicureanism

The pejorative association of the word "Epicureanism" is, however, quite unmerited. The word today implies a dedication to luxurious living and especially to the sensual pleasures of gourmet (and presumably expensive) eating and drinking. Epicurus (341 to 271 BC) did aim for a life of pleasure, but he actually ate very simply and the pleasures he sought were infinitely more rewarding than those of the senses. They were the pleasures derived from friendship, from the garden in which he entertained his friends, from his books, and from a calm, temperate and placid lifestyle.

It is true that Aristippus (435 to 356 BC) the founder of what we now call the Epicurean School, said that the keenest pleasures and the keenest pains are physical and sensual, not intellectual or moral[3] - but he, too, was aware that certain mental attitudes contribute towards happiness. He felt, for example, that, while property could make for happiness, one has to be careful that one

3 Socrates had believed the opposite: hurt inflicted on the body by others is so much less significant than the self-inflicted hurt to the soul, resulting from faulty thinking. See p. 19 above.

does not become unduly attached to it, lest one be devastated by losing it, let alone be disturbed by the fear of losing it. Against the self-congratulation of Antisthenes – "I do not possess in order not to be possessed" – Aristippus set up a more moderate version: "I possess, but am not possessed."

> A modern follower of Aristippus, for example, may well have a home with beautiful paintings on the walls, but he will not grieve unduly if he loses them – or articles of so-called "sentimental value" – in a burglary. There must be a question, however, whether one could retain such serenity if it was not paintings that had been stolen but one's entire fortune that had disappeared, so that one was driven by *force majeure* to live rough as Diogenes had done by choice. This would make a life of pleasure, if not totally impossible, at least very much more difficult. Although, as we shall see below, Epicurus believed that one can, and should, train oneself to retain one's equanimity even under extreme conditions of discomfort and of pain. Even so, it seems only sensible to avoid discomfort where we can, rather than court it as the Cynics did.

The reason that discomfort should be avoided was, according to Aristippus and Epicurus, that personal pleasure was the ultimate good, so the aim of life should therefore be to maximize it. This philosophy is known as Hedonism, from the Greek *hedone,* meaning pleasure and it has had many disciples down the ages.

> There are many psychological theories which teach that man *naturally* seeks pleasure and avoids pain, but even philosophers who have accepted this have often said that this is a part of human nature that we must learn to overcome. The *aim* of life must be to do one's duty (which might indeed bring a "superior" happiness, but which was to be clearly distinguished from the happiness that Hedonists talked about). However, in the eighteenth century, following the teaching of the *philosophes*, the *right* of Man to pursue happiness was asserted and was then actually embodied in the preamble of the American Constitution. It would receive perhaps its most thorough exposition in the works of Bentham, who thought that the job of legislators was to aim for "the greatest happiness of the greatest number." All this will be discussed more fully in chapter 36.

Hedonism does not call for an unbridled life of pleasure: wisdom and self-control are necessary if the pleasure is to last. It is only too easy to be short-sighted about it. To take some simple examples, too self-centred a pursuit of pleasure will bring one into conflict with one's fellows, and that can be very unpleasant. If a gourmet over-indulges in the pleasures of the table, he will suffer from indigestion and other health hazards. Epicurus went further; he was suspicious of sexual passion and of love, which so often bring frustration and despair. Temperate friendships, he thought, were much safer. Even from a purely hedonistic point of view, the Epicureans agreed with the older belief, going back beyond Aristotle[4] to Pythagoras,[5] that "moderation in all things" was a good guide to life.

> Pythagoras had valued moderation for metaphysical reasons; balanced behaviour was more in tune with the harmony that was part of the divine plan

4 see p. 50 above.

5 see p. 10 above.

for what life ought to be. The basis of Aristotle's praise of moderation, however, had been much closer to the hedonism of Epicurus, namely, that an intelligent appraisal of happiness should tell a person that excess would harm *eudaemonia*, the happy life.

Even so, Aristotle's vision of a happy and fulfilled life had involved participation in the *polis*, which, it will be remembered, "originated for the sake of life, but was continued for the sake of the *good* life".[5] For Aristotle, the word *polis* had embraced both the social and the political aspect of the city state. By the time of Epicurus, however, the political form of the *polis*, which we call the state, was seen to be different from its social form, which we call community, and Epicurus saw the state as at best a regrettable necessity. He saw its function as being merely to make life *tolerable* for its citizens, to protect them against lawlessness and attack from outside. He did not believe, as Aristotle had, that the state as such could make the lives of its citizens *positively* meaningful. It was up to the individual, not the state, to create the good life, and a State was only tolerable to the extent to which it protected against violence and allowed the pursuit of happiness. Far from believing that an individual can find happiness by engaging in wider social or political activity, Epicurus believed that no wise man will bother himself with either.

Many people profess a contempt for political activity. They despise its necessary compromises and occasional corruption, the tedium of endless committee meetings, the self-righteousness and self-advancement of politicians, the banality of electioneering. But what happens when "wise men" take no part in politics? Do we not then leave the conduct of politics to those who are not wise and may even be scoundrels? Edmund Burke said in the eighteenth century, "The only thing necessary for the triumph of evil is for good men do nothing." We may not claim that our lives are fulfilled by political activity, but do we not have some duty to ourselves and to our community to take an interest in these matters and, if necessary, to involve ourselves in them?

Moreover, do we agree with Epicurus about the very limited functions which the State ought to have? Violence and disorder are not the only threats to the good life. In the last century or so we have also expected the State to provide some protection against poverty – although this was scarcely a concern of earlier centuries.

Some philosophers and theologians have taught that the "best", the "highest", or the "real" pleasures come from the satisfaction we may get from a life which, with all its difficulties and frustrations, has been dedicated to some higher ideal, to improving our society or, if we prefer (as Epicurus would have done) a less generalized concept, to improve the lot of our fellow men. They contrast this "real" happiness with the "actual" happiness that Epicurus extolled, which they considered shallow and self-centred, if not actually selfish. (In fact, Epicurus was very generous in the help he gave to those in need – when they were his friends.) This distinction between "real" and "actual" happiness, "real" and "actual" freedom, is one we shall meet on several occasions in the history of philosophy and theology[6] and we probably accept that there is indeed such a difference. But it is a presumptuous and insulting formulation.

5 see p. 51 above

6 The words "real" and "actual" to describe this distinction were, I think, first coined by Rousseau. See p. 338 below.

> When the philosopher (let alone the politician) tells someone that his "actual" happiness is not his "real" happiness at all, the reply might be: "Who are you to tell me that my happiness is not real? It is real enough to me!" And the formulation can be hypocritical and dangerous when governments, in the name of what the "real" satisfactions of citizenship ought to be, claim the right to trample over the "actual" satisfactions of the citizen. The pleasures of the individual must sometimes yield to the claim of the society, but let these claims rest on a more honest basis than denying "reality" to the former.

Even if the state does more than Epicurus thought it ought to do, he believed that it was sensible to obey its laws as disobedience often entails unpleasant consequences for the rebel, as does defiance of the customs of society. That was, however, the only valid reason that Epicurus could see for obeying any regulation or convention. He did not believe that these reflected any secular or religious moral laws; he believed that no such laws existed. He did not, for example, believe that we had some moral obligation to obey the laws of society because only through the society did we become full human beings. In Aristotle's time, Athenian citizens may have felt an obligation to obey the laws because the citizens themselves had had an input into the making of them and were therefore morally bound to abide by them. In the time of Epicurus, that kind of citizen participation was largely a thing of the past; the laws were imposed by authorities, often foreign ones, that were quite remote from the citizens.

If we want to live pleasantly, we need to live prudently, honourably and justly. This was a matter of common sense and experience, not of reverence for the commands of men or of gods. The attitude of Epicurus to morality was the same as that of the Sophists before him[8] and that of the Sceptics, who were more or less his contemporaries.[9] If there are gods, they do not care about what we do in this world, as for the next world, Epicurus was convinced by the teaching of Democritus that the "soul atoms" disperse after death and therefore there could be no afterlife. For Epicurus, one of the tasks of philosophy is to free the wise man from fear of the gods and of the next life.

> Had Epicurus lived into the age of the monotheistic religions, he would probably have expressed himself even more strongly on this point. The pagan gods were not after all so very frightening. As long as one sacrificed to them and did not kill animals sacred to them, they left one pretty well free to follow one's own devices. It was Christianity in particular, with its notion of eternal Hellfire in the afterlife as punishment for moral transgressors, which put "the fear of God" (as well, it must be admitted, as the love of God) into people's lives. The afterlife for the ancients had nothing to do with rewards or punishments – even the noblest of heroes were thought to wander wraith-like (and generally unhappily) through Hades.

However, for many there is still the fear of death. That, too, Epicurus believed, was an unnecessary fear. "As long as we exist", he said, "death is not there; and when it does come, we no longer exist."

8 see p. 13 above.

9 see p. 65 below.

10 see p. 5 above.

There may of course be pain in dying, but the wise man will have trained himself in coping with physical pain. On the last day of his life, Epicurus wrote in a letter to a friend:

> On this truly happy day of my life, as I am on the point of death, I write this to you. The diseases in my bladder and stomach are pursuing their course, lacking nothing of their usual severity: but against all this is the joy in my heart at the recollection of my conversations with you.

Aristippus, as we have seen, had considered the most intense pleasures and pains to be physical ones; Epicurus attached more importance to mental pleasures and pains. Friendship always meant more to him than a good meal; physical suffering was merely temporary, belonging to the here and now, whereas mental suffering was often caused by memories of the past or by dread of the future.

To control unnecessary fear of death and suffering in order to get as much pleasure out of life as possible requires a degree of effort which is perhaps not given to everybody – that particular wisdom may have to be hard fought for. But, with that exception, a life of wisdom – the wisdom needed for a pleasant existence – is within the reach of everybody and requires no special training. Epicurus would not have agreed with Plato, who believed that wisdom could be achieved only after prolonged and exacting intellectual training. Wisdom is not that difficult, Epicurus thought, it is just common sense. He is a comfortable philosopher, in more senses of the word than one.

> To sum up, though Epicurus distanced himself from society as Diogenes had done, he did it less drastically and less abrasively. Though he claimed that individual happiness, rather than involvement with society, was the supreme aim of life, the happiness he pursued was hardly self-indulgent. He would do much to avoid distress, but when it came, he met it like a Stoic.[11]

Scepticism

Pyrrho (346 to 275), the founder of Scepticism, was a contemporary of Epicurus, and, like Epicurus, he thought that the wise man should aim above all for tranquillity. This is difficult if he challenges the customs of his society, therefore he should, if at all possible, conform to the values of his environment even if he did not necessarily believe in them. Epicurus had given similar advice, on a purely prudential basis. As we have seen above,[12] he believed that, whatever else underpinned the laws and customs of a particular society, it was not some higher moral order that justified the laws and so there is no ethical obligation to obey them.

In Epicureanism, the primary point was hedonistic; the intellectual doubt about a universal moral order was secondary, perhaps almost a rationalization. These priorities seem to be reversed in Scepticism. Pyrrho and the Sceptics are more interested in exploring the intellectual foundations for this doubt; and indeed it was in a thoroughly scholastic institution – Plato's Academy, no less – that this was done. They actually captured the directorship of the Academy in

11 For Stoicism see Chapter 8.

12 p. 63 above .

the person of Arcesilaus (315 to 241 BC), who became its director in 269 BC. Plato, who had died three quarters of a century earlier, would have turned in his grave, because Scepticism stood for everything Socrates and he had fought against. The Sceptics were the intellectual descendants, a century and a half later, of Protagoras and the Sophists, who had claimed that there were no absolute truths, but that "Man was the measure of all things",[13] and Plato, with his concept that all truth was embodied in unchanging Ideas, had found the philosophy of the Sophists wholly subversive. What would have rubbed salt into the wound was that the Sceptics claimed that they were only following Plato's beloved teacher Socrates, for had not Socrates said, "I know that I do not know"?

The word Scepticism comes from a Greek word meaning "to reflect upon", and the Sceptics demonstrated that, when we reflect, we know that we cannot have certain knowledge about anything. Our knowledge cannot be based on sense observation, because that is often ambiguous or contradictory. We cannot rely on our moral intuitions because these obviously differ widely not only between societies but between people within each society; nor can our logic provide certain knowledge, because all logical conclusions are based in the last resort on unprovable axioms. Therefore, as Arcesilaus said, "Nothing is certain: not even that." [14]

When Arcesilaus was criticized on the grounds that it is impossible to lead a life based on such principles, he replied that "life had long since learned to manage with probabilities". We distinguish by experience between greater and lesser probabilities; we can have *nearly* certain knowledge about some things, but absolute certainty can never be achieved.

> A very similar answer was given by David Hume to his critics in the eighteenth century. He admitted that when he lived his normal life outside his study, the radical scepticism he pursued seemed ridiculous. It almost seems as if this book's title – Philosophy and Living – represents two totally different things, and for that reason, many people become impatient with Philosophy. Yet the reflection that there are indeed theoretical limits to the certainty of our knowledge is salutary and humbling in every field. It may be unsettling, but it is also necessary for progress – surely only fools and fanatics think that they can be in possession of absolute truth. Some intelligent people of course believe that there *is* an absolute truth – Plato was one, and so are many believers in God's truth. But if they are wise, they will also recognize that in practice we can never grasp it, and that therefore, in *relation* to the absolute truth, the knowledge which we think we have of it will be partial, will not be the same for everybody, and will in that sense, therefore, be *relative*.
>
> The Sceptics, then, argued that the reason that the wise man should aim for tranquillity rather than truth is that a search for an absolute truth is futile. In the absence of absolute truth, they could see no good reason to jeopardize this tranquillity and make life uncomfortable for themselves by challenging the conventions of society instead of conforming to them, even if they disagreed with them.
>
> They also claimed that the wise man becomes tranquil once he realizes that the search for absolute truths is futile. But they did not seem to register that

13 see p. 13 above.

14 For a discussion of the issues this raises, refer back to p. 14 above.

many people are unsettled by Scepticism. They enjoy tranquillity because they do not *search* for unattainable absolute truths but rather take the validity of their beliefs for granted, and they become distinctly untranquil when their beliefs are undermined by the Sceptics.

One also wonders how far they were prepared to take their readiness to conform to the conventions of their society. Perhaps, in order not to upset his neighbours, a sceptical nonbeliever might refrain from challenging their belief in the gods, and he might even go through the motions of worshipping them. But what if the community's value system demanded, say, that he denounce nonbelievers so that they could be put to death for blasphemy? Does a relativistic attitude to moral questions demand of a Sceptic that he be philosophically nonjudgmental on moral issues? The Sceptics do not seem to have found a sound position which would allow an individual to commit himself whole-heartedly to some values even while he acknowledges that these values are relative, indeed, it is not until the Existentialism of the twentieth century that this problem will be tackled in a credible fashion.[15]

In the process of examining the arguments used by intelligent people to support their beliefs, the Sophists had become very skilled at producing arguments on any side of a question. We have already seen that Plato had considered the willingness of the Sophists to do just that as thoroughly unprincipled and reprehensible. Some Sceptics likewise did not resist the temptation to indulge in such intellectual virtuosity. One of these was Carneades (213 to 129 BC) a later Director of the Academy. He became well known for producing one set of arguments one day only to demolish them with another set the next day (and for never giving any clues about what, if anything, he believed himself.)

In 155 BC he was part of an embassy which Athens sent to Rome. Many Romans at that time still stood in awe of the sophisticated culture of the Greek world, and Carneades was invited to give a series of lectures to the senators. He took this opportunity to exhibit his intellectual virtuosity. In one of his lectures he won applause by eloquently expounding the views of Plato and Aristotle on the necessity of Justice. The following day, he mocked the ideals of Justice as thoroughly impracticable and indeed undesirable, after all, he suggested, Rome could not be expected to return all the territories she had conquered by force. His audience applauded this sentiment also, though some were doubtless puzzled by the contradiction between the two lectures and some were angered by the amorality of it all. Rome was at this time a relatively young, vigorous society, and its elder statesmen wanted to keep it like that. They were unwillingfor the intellectuals of Rome to be infected by the subversive and decadent influence of a sophisticated but declining Athenian culture. Cato the Elder had the embassy sent back to Athens on the grounds that it was a danger to public morals.

Do we detect in Cato's contempt for Athenian sophistication a precursor of fascist contempt for open-minded democratic discussion or communist contempt for bourgeois liberalism? Fascist and communist states both contrasted the "decadence", the "hair-splitting" of the democracies with the expansionary "vigour" of their own societies, where energies were not allowed to become "dissipated" in debate. The raw concentrated forces of such societies seem

15 see Chapter 40 for a fuller discussion of this point.

> hugely successful at certain stages, and then often induce a sense of defeatism in their opponents. Sometimes that defeatism seems justified – after all, Athens was unable to stand up to Rome. But was its "excessive sophistication" the reason for that, or do we have to look for other causes? After all, there are also occasions in history when the more "sophisticated" societies have managed to summon resources that saved them from being overwhelmed. Democratic debate need not weaken a society as long as there is an underlying sense of community and shared basic values. This had been the case at the time when Athens had been at its most powerful.

The Romans at this stage had the civic confidence in their Republic that the Athenians had once had in their *polis*. The Athenians in their decline had turned away from political commitment to doctrines of self-sufficiency and of scepticism. Cynicism, Epicureanism and Scepticism all lacked an outside point of reference. Their value-systems were wholly dependent on the individual. They could therefore easily degenerate into egocentricity, and this has earned the names of these schools their modern derogatory associations.

> Some critics of twentieth-century society blame many of the ills that it suffers on a moral relativism which, it seems to them, in the absence of commonly accepted values and obligations, inevitably leads to a "me-first" society and therefore a dissolution of social coherence. They call for a "moral revival", by which they mean a reassertion of "traditional" values. How could this be done? The critics hope that people will come to realize the damage that self-indulgence has caused, that they will spontaneously return to the "wisdom" of earlier generations, and that they will then reshape those institutional arrangements – social policy as expressed in legislation, tax regimes etc. – which have been shaped by moral relativism and have allowed it to flourish.
>
> That proposal, however, alarms many other people. Even if they were to agree (and many do not) that moral relativism is the cause of social ills, they nevertheless fear that the so-called "reshaping of institutional arrangements" may, in practice, amount to an imposition of one code of morals as well as intolerance towards those who do not agree with it. For example, the critics may say that easy divorce and illegitimate births undermine the family, are bad for children, have a bearing on delinquency etc. They may go on to argue that "institutional arrangements" should correct that situation (e.g. by discriminating against single mothers in housing policy or by making divorce more difficult). But many people would regard this "cure" as worse than the "disease". It would undermine the "gains" achieved over the decades in liberalizing the divorce laws and removing the stigma from illegitimacy.
>
> Would it be a defence against these objections to argue that such rearrangements would be the result of democratic public opinion, just as the original and more permissive "social arrangements" had been some decades ago? Or would the distinction that Plato and Aristotle had made between a Polity and a Democracy[16] be of relevance here?

Against Cynics, Epicureans, and Sceptics, Roman statesmen like Cato upheld a philosophy – whose first exponents had actually come from the Greek world – that moved away from a value-system based on the individual back to one that accepted wider obligations and once again made participation in public affairs a meaningful activity. That philosophy was Stoicism.

16 see pp. 39 and 53 above.

CHAPTER 8

Stoicism

In 301 BC, some 150 years before the visit of Carneades to Rome, Zeno of Citium (335 to 264 BC) had founded a school of philosophy in Athens in a building which was fronted by a colonnade or *stoa*. Like the Sceptics, the Stoics claimed Socrates as their inspiration – not the Socrates who "knew that he did not know", but the Socrates who had lived austerely and had met his death with dignity and fortitude. Socrates had been given the chance to go into exile, and even to propose a lesser penalty than death after his conviction. As he refused to contemplate either, he had been sentenced to death. He had been allowed to end his own life by drinking a cup of hemlock; it could be argued that he had committed suicide, in that he had chosen death rather than a lesser punishment. The Stoics approved of suicide when an honourable or a meaningful life was no longer possible. Dignity, fortitude in the face of death and of lesser disasters – these were among the qualities the Stoics most admired and fostered.

We have seen that Epicurus, too, had thought that the wise man should train himself not to be overwhelmed by pain or by the fear of death, but he had argued this because the absence of such self-control would only make life more miserable when the aim of life, which is happiness, required us to do what we could to reduce avoidable suffering.

The Stoics, like the Cynics and the Epicureans, also aimed to fortify themselves psychologically against adversity by cultivating self-control, but unlike the Cynics, they did not want to do this by withdrawing from society, and unlike the Epicureans, they never thought that pleasure or happiness should be the aim of life. Rather it should be a calm and dignified acceptance of the laws of the universe in all their apparent harshness and arbitrariness. The Stoics reverenced the cosmic order as god-given; if we could understand it, we would realize that what we consider incomprehensible suffering is part of a bigger scheme of things.

> This is close to the philosophy of Optimism, which, in the eighteenth century, Voltaire was mockingly to ascribe to Pangloss in *Candide:* "everything is for the best in the best of all possible worlds". The arguments of the Stoic philosopher Chrysippus (*ca.* 280 to 206 BC) that wars are a useful corrective for overpopulation and that bedbugs are useful because they prevent us from oversleeping would have delighted Pangloss.
>
> There is a more serious point behind this philosophy. Real or perceived overpopulation has often been a cause for war. We have only to think of the need for *Lebensraum* invoked by Hitler and Mussolini to justify their wars. Pain is unpleasant and often fatal, but if we could feel no pain, we would not

> receive the danger signals that warn us when, for example, we come too close to a fire. We may wince whenever we observe Nature being "red in tooth and claw" (and it is not always so), but the wincing usually does us no good, and we need to understand the role of tooth and claw in the maintenance of an ecological balance.

None of this argues against the obligation of human beings to uphold moral standards and to treat each other decently, nor did the Stoics fall short in demanding that they should do so. But we must distinguish between, on the one hand, circumstances that we cannot alter (and these we must accept with dignity), and on the other, those which we can alter, which therefore impose duties on us and require us to make moral choices, to accept responsibility and to be accountable.

> As Spinoza was to say in the seventeenth century, "Freedom is the recognition of necessity". The opposition between Free Will and Determinism is not absolute; some things are determined and we cannot change them, but with regard to others we are free and responsible.
>
> That does not of course solve the philosophical problem completely, for each person must decide for himself where the boundaries are between what we can and what we cannot change. This applies not only to the outside world, but also to ourselves. There is always the danger of complacency, of too easily accepting certain things in the outside world or in ourselves as "given", as something we can do nothing about. To take some extreme examples, one occasionally hears the argument that poverty in some Third World countries is so extreme, so deeply rooted and so widespread that any attempt to alleviate it is simply pointless. Or someone might say, as Zeno's slave is reported to have said, that it was fated that he should steal; he simply had a kleptomaniac personality which he could do nothing about. If we were to accept such arguments, would we not be guilty of what the twentieth-century existentialist Jean-Paul Sartre called "bad faith"?

So we must train ourselves never to let emotions, especially those of sorrow, fear or anger, get the better of us. The Stoic will aim for *apatheia*, the absence of feelings that might disturb his calm acceptance of misfortune. The emotions of love, pity or compassion can be equally dangerous, for these might prevent us from fulfilling our wider duties.

The Greek Stoics and, after a while, the Roman Stoics also, saw these wider duties as extending to the whole of mankind rather than simply to one's own *polis*. We have certain duties to all our fellow-men, even to slaves. Zeno had been twelve years old when Alexander the Great died, and although Alexander's huge empire disintegrated after his death, Zeno was inspired by the vision of a humanity that transcended little local patriotisms.

Some centuries later that vision was again given concrete form in the Roman Empire. Wherever a man lived within its wide boundaries and whatever ethnic group he belonged to, he could proudly boast: "*civis Romanus sum*". Zeno's notion of a brotherhood of man was therefore not just an abstract ethical concept, but was in some sense actually embodied in the culture of late antiquity; it would be strengthened still further with the emergence of Christianity as an idea and that of the universal Church as an institution.

It cannot be said that adherents to Stoic philosophy always lived up to their own high ideals. When Stoicism was introduced to Rome by Panaetius around 140 BC, a philosophy which called upon its citizens to do their duty by the community seemed tailor-made for a vigorous young republic, but the Roman exponents of Stoicism initially gave it quite a narrow focus. A statesman like Cato the Elder, for instance, was so wholeheartedly dedicated to the Roman Republic that his perception of Stoicism precluded any allegiance to a wider community. Cato the Elder had fought in the Second Punic War against Hannibal and had coined the famous slogan that "Carthage must be destroyed". There is no evidence that he saw Carthage as a member of the world community and that, therefore, he had duties and obligations towards Carthage also.

> Compare this with Edith Cavell: "Patriotism is not enough."

This narrower Stoicism also exalted the allegiance to the Republic over any smaller grouping like the family where the two were incompatible. Thus, the Roman Stoics held up the examples of the legendary heroes like Lucius Junius Brutus or the Horatii brothers, who had put members of their own families to death for disloyalty.

> Compare this with E.M. Forster: "If I had to choose between betraying my country and betraying my friend, I hope I would have the guts to betray my country."

Whether the focus was narrow or wide, we can say that with the Stoics the philosophers returned to the obligations man has towards the community. But the spirit in which those obligations were perceived was not quite the same as it had been in the days of the Athenian *polis*. For the Athenian, involvement in the community had been a matter of pleasurable self-fulfilment; for the Roman Stoic it was a stern duty. The statesman Cicero, who was also a philosopher, understood something of the wider concept of the brotherhood of man.

CICERO

The importance of Cicero (106 to 43 BC) was that he turned the Stoic concept of the brotherhood of man into an influential philosophy of law. If there is indeed a world community, then there must be a world law to govern it. Conversely, because all the members of the world community are subject to that world law, they must be at least in some fundamental sense equal, and must enjoy some kind of equality before the law.

Within each state the citizens are also in some sense equal, and the state belongs to and exists for the benefit of everybody in it. Indeed, Cicero described the State as *res publica* and sometimes as *res populi*. These terms are best translated as a "Commonwealth" - something that is there for the common weal (or good) - rather than as a "Republic", which today means government under a president rather than under a hereditary monarch. (Cicero, however, was also an ardent defender of republican government in our sense.)

> It had never occurred to Aristotle that there was any equality between people. He had regarded women and slaves as naturally not equal to men, so he had not envisaged that there could be a law that applied equally to all human beings. There was still slavery in the time of Cicero, and there is no indication

that Cicero condemned it any more than would the fathers of the American Constitution when they proclaimed that "all men are created equal" and yet maintained slavery in their time. But once some kind of equality is admitted in theory, it will eventually be called in evidence in an attack on slavery and other kinds of social injustice.

Behind that world law there must be a moral law to give it legitimacy. That moral law - and Cicero says it reflects the mind of God - he called the *ius naturale;* this must underlie the *ius gentium,* the legal principles which all civilized nations should observe. For example, every civilized nation believes that murder and theft are wrong. Finally, there is the *ius civile,* the particular codes by which any one country is governed. That would include the ways in which murder or theft are punished and detailed regulations about inheritance or about land tenure. These would differ from country to country, but they must not run counter to the *ius naturale*. The legitimacy of the *ius civile* and of the *ius gentium* depends on their conformity to the *ius naturale.* An unjust law, one which does not conform to the overarching moral law, is not a proper law at all.

Cicero was also a patriotic Roman citizen, and there is at least a possible conflict between his exalted vision of a moral law and that other famous dictum of his: *"salus populi suprema lex"* (the welfare of the people is the supreme law). He almost certainly meant no more than that the lawgiver should rule in the interests of the whole people rather than of his own, but too often in history, that saying has been used to justify putting the interests of one's own state above all other obligations, including moral ones.

Roman Law follows the Ciceronian view by beginning with the assumption that jurisprudence is chiefly guided by the principle of *equity.* In order to observe that principle, a degree of flexibility is necessary in framing laws and even judgments in court; excessive legal rigidity may get in the way of the administration of true justice. Of course, that gives the lawmaker great discretion in interpreting just how these principles of equity apply, and gave rise to the maxim of Roman Law: *quod principi placuit legis habet vigorem* – the will of the ruler has the force of law. (Of course there ought to be the Ciceronian reservation – not always observed in practice – which the will of the ruler must not run counter to the principles of natural justice.) From time to time, Roman rulers would find it desirable to remind lawyers of the relatively few simple principles that should govern their decisions; and they would then issue a Code. Such a task was famously undertaken by the Emperor Justinian, whose Digest or Code in AD 533 reduced the three million lines of law to a mere 150,000.

An alternative tradition was embodied in the Anglo-Saxon Common Law, where the main question asked in deciding a case in court was what are the *precedents*. Law, it was felt, was *found*, not *made*. In theory, Roman law, being based on *ius naturale*, was found too, but the flexibility given to the lawmaker to "simplify" it as Justinian had done was felt by the common lawyers to give too much law-making power to the ruler. For one thing, he who makes the rules will consider himself to be above them, and the common lawyers always stressed that the ruler was under the law just as his subjects were, and that the common law was a bastion against absolutism.

In practice, neither system of law could maintain its purity for any length of time. Roman jurists may have been presented by the Emperor Justinian (527 to 565) with a mere 150,000 lines of principles, but as new situations arose, interpretations would pile up as precedents until they were back to millions of lines and then a new Digest might be necessary to clear the decks once more. Likewise, the Common Law courts in England often became so cumbersome that justice was delayed and therefore denied, and then new courts – significantly called Equity Courts – would be set up alongside the common law courts to see that justice was really done. The Equity courts in turn would, like the Roman courts, become cluttered up with their own interpretations before long, and the protests against the delays and expenses of justice echo down all the ages, whichever system is in use.

Cicero was immensely influential, partly because he wrote so beautifully that he was very widely read, not only for what he said but for the way he said it. His style became the model of classical Latin. Curiously, his actual writings disappeared in the twelfth century, not to be rediscovered until the nineteenth, but even if his original works were lost during that interval, many of his most important ideas were not, for he was admired and extensively quoted by St. Augustine (AD 354 to 430) who would add a deeper theological dimension to Cicero's conception of a just state, thus showing again how aspects of Stoicism form a bridge to aspects of Christianity.

The ideas of a later Stoic, Seneca, further reinforce that bridge.

SENECA

The essential difference between Cicero's time and Seneca's was that in Cicero's time Rome was still a Republic, whose citizens could identify themselves with public affairs, with the *res publica,* somewhat in the way in which the Athenians had once been able to identify themselves with the *polis*. It had not been as easy and as natural in Rome as it had been at Athens because Rome was not a city-state, but the centre of a growing empire. However, Roman thinkers had learnt to adjust to this new scale.

By Seneca's time (3 BC toAD 65), the Republic had given way to the Empire. This process had begun when Augustus was elected *Princeps et Imperator* in 30 BC. Though he still maintained the outward forms of the Republic, he had practically autocratic powers, and in the reigns of his successors, the absolute power of the head of state became ever more obvious. It rested so much on control of the army that the military title of General, in Latin *Imperator*, became the most important one, and is translated as Emperor. Some of the Emperors were accorded or claimed divine status, and the more or less representative bodies like the Senate and the Assembly became ever more obsequious.

Under such circumstances, it became as difficult for Roman citizens to participate meaningfully in public life as it had become for the Athenians during the Hellenistic period. The philosophical response to this, however, was not a total withdrawal from the wider society, such as we saw with the Cynics and the Epicureans. Instead, Seneca developed that side of Stoicism which had already envisaged that the community towards which one has obligations is not limited to one's state, but extends to mankind in general. If it is possible to serve one's fellow men by participating in politics, well and good; that is one way in which one may fulfil one's obligations to them, but there are always other ways of service, too, and in a society where political participation is actually impossible, it is to these other ways that our obligations call us. These include, positively; the duty of mercy, kindliness, charity, benevolence and tolerance, and negatively; the avoidance of cruelty, hatred, anger, and harshness towards dependants and social inferiors.[1]

Lucius Annaeus Seneca did in fact serve the state. He was a senator under the Emperors Caligula and Claudius, though he fell foul of both, and was nearly put to death by the one and exiled to Corsica for eight years by the other. He was recalled from exile to become tutor to the young Nero, and when Nero became Emperor in 53 AD, Seneca was his chief minister for the first five years of the reign. During that time he did what he could to live up to his wider obligations to humanity. He tolerated outspoken attacks on him by political enemies when he might have had them killed, he fostered a more humane attitude towards slaves, and it was on his advice that Nero prohibited, at least for a time, gladiatorial combats to the death. As Nero became increasingly vicious, Seneca asked to be relieved of his post and eventually received permission to withdraw from the court altogether and to live on his estates in the Campania. There he wrote his most influential work, the *Epistolae Morales.*

He had every reason to reflect on the nature of the state. If he had ever felt that man might fulfil himself through the state, his experience at Nero's court had taught him otherwise. Now he agreed with Epicurus that the state was a necessary evil to avoid total chaos. Long ago, he thought, there had once been a Golden Age, a State of Nature, when men lived happily together, but a feature of a developing civilization was the growth of private property; this corrupted people and their greed led them to all kinds of violence which only a state could keep under some control.[2]

> Again we see how far away this idea is from Aristotle's view that the state (in his day the *polis*), so far from being a necessary evil, is the only medium in which man can truly fulfil himself.
>
> The idea of some supposed State of Nature which preceded the development of civil society will be a major theme in future philosophy, especially in the seventeenth and eighteenth centuries. Some thinkers, like Rousseau during his first foray into political thought, will follow Seneca's picture of an idyllic past and will see civilization as corrupting. Others, like Hobbes, will see man utterly savage from the beginning. Both groups, however, see the state as a regrettable necessity, and neither holds the Aristotelian view that the function of the state goes far beyond checking the worst in man, and that its proper role is to bring out the best in him.
>
> There is also the difference between those philosophers who, like Seneca, see a Golden Age in the distant past and those who, like Marx, see it beckoning in the future. The former have a pessimistic view of mankind and see it as irretrievably fallen; the latter are optimistic, if not about the present, then at least about a better world to come. Indeed, Marxists and anarchists believe that we shall recover the original Golden Age once the oppression of one class by another has been brought to an end and social harmony has been

1 G.H. Sabine, *History of Political Theory*, p. 177

2 Actually, Seneca himself was immensely rich, but he lived in an extremely Spartan way in the midst of all his wealth even before he donated the greater part of his wealth to Nero for the rebuilding of Rome after the Great Fire.

achieved. The state – always an instrument of oppression – will then no longer be necessary and will "wither away".

There is a third view found in Judaism and Christianity. These, like Seneca, see a Lost Paradise in the past and accept the Fall of Man; at the same time, like Marx, they envisage a blessed future – only they call it not World Communism, but the Kingdom of God. It is to the philosophies of these religions that we must now turn.

CHAPTER 9

Judaism, Christianity and Hellenism

The Explosive Growth of Christianity.

Seneca was born in the same decade as Jesus, and he died within a year of the date which is traditionally taken to be that of the death of St. Paul. It is with St. Paul that Christianity begins to burst out of Judea. Its explosive growth from that time onwards may be explained in a secular way by the fact that it brought together three philosophical and religious strands, each of which had made a great impact in the Mediterranean area.

Senecan Stoicism was one of these. We have already seen how, like Christianity, it taught the brotherhood of Man, had something like the Doctrine of the Fall, and saw property as something that corrupts one's dealings with other people.

Also, during the lifetime of Jesus there was a renewed interest in Plato with the birth of Neo-Platonism. The next chapter will discuss Neo-Platonism in detail, here it suffices to say that it taught a philosophical monotheism and had the concept of One Transcendent and Unknowable God. It is easy to see the connection between this idea and Christianity.

The third and most important strand was Judaism. Christianity was a Jewish sect until the Jewish followers of Jesus were expelled from the synagogues in AD 89. Judaism, too, had burst out of Judea - into Egypt during the third century BC, and into Greece and Rome in the second century BC. It had begun to make converts in those areas, but the scale of the conversion was limited. Although the Jews were firm that there was only the one God and that no other god existed, they nevertheless gave the impression that He was in a special sense the God of the Jews, and that the Jews were God's Chosen People. To join this Chosen People, it was required not only that other gods had to be rejected and that the moral and ritual teaching of Judaism had to be accepted, but also that converts had to undergo circumcision and had to observe the dietary laws. Many gentiles admired monotheism and the moral teaching of the Jews, but some of them regarded circumcision and adherence to the dietary laws not only as a sacrifice they were not prepared to make, but also as a rite of passage into a tribal rather than a universal community. Paul thought of himself as a Jew throughout his life, but he threw open the fellowship of Jesus, in which there is neither Jew nor Gentile, to the uncircumcised and to those who did not follow the dietary laws and so made Christianity open to all.

Of course, there are other differences between Pauline Christianity and Judaism than those that have just been described, most important of all the ascription of divinity to Jesus in the last Epistles (Philippians and Colossians) of Paul, and the differences widened steadily after Paul's death. But the Christians have always accepted the Jewish Bible and they have constantly drawn on the prophesies within it to show that the roots of Christianity lie in Judaism (though this would not stop them from persecuting the Jews for many centuries).

What Christianity has in common with Stoicism and Neo-Platonism helped it enormously to find acceptance in the Hellenistic culture of the Roman Empire, but the most dynamic part of early Christianity (before the divinity of Jesus became part of it) owed a great deal to opening up its Jewish inheritance to the gentile world.

Theology and Philosophy.

Before we turn to some of the basic theological concepts held by Judaism and Christianity, a comment on the relationship between theology and philosophy is called for.

Some writers, following the distinction formulated in the thirteenth century by St Thomas Aquinas, draw a distinction between Theology and Philosophy on the grounds that Theology *begins* with revelation, with unquestioning faith in something that is given - usually a sacred text in which the existence of God is revealed. This approach is sometimes called Dogmatic Theology. Philosophy is defined as the work of human reason alone and does not take revelation as its starting point. A philosopher may come to the conclusion that there must be a God because - to give one of many lines of arguments - the world seems to follow certain laws; there can be no laws without a lawgiver; therefore there must be a God. A philosopher may then identify that God whose existence has been proved by reason with the God of the Bible; and they may then go on to say that we can trust the way in which God has revealed Himself in the Bible about His nature, His purposes, and His commandments. Using reason and logic to arrive at conclusions about religion is sometimes called Natural Theology.

There are, of course, many philosophers - especially from the eighteenth century onwards - who argue philosophically that there must be a God, but who do not identify that God with the God of the Bible. Those philosophers place no faith at all in revelation and they scoff at the leap from Reason, across the gulf of what they consider the nonrational, into faith in Revelation. Those philosophers who, like Philo for Judaism and St Thomas Aquinas for Christianity, do accept revelation, agree that there is such a leap, but they consider this leap necessary and do not scoff at it.

> I think, however, that the distinction between Theology and Philosophy very easily becomes blurred. It is, I think, possible to develop a philosophy of religion while ignoring or actually rejecting theology, but it is not really possible for any theologian to divorce theology from philosophy. Thoughtful believers in revelation as the *primary* source of religious knowledge are confirmed in their belief by what they consider evidence outside revelation for the existence of

God. More importantly, they have to ask themselves questions about this revealed God. How we are to *interpret* what the Bible says about His nature? How do we try to reconcile statements in the Bible that appear to contradict each other? How does God manifest himself in the world, and what is our relationship with Him? Such intellectual enterprises quickly develop into philosophies of religion, and these cannot be discussed unless you are first aware of what the sacred text has laid down. From this point of view alone, it seems to me that theology quickly becomes one part of philosophy, even if its starting point is not philosophical. In a book with the title *Philosophy and Living*, it would make no sense at all to leave out pure theology entirely, because theological beliefs have had such a profound effect on the way in which people actually live and how they understand the world.[1]

The Judaeo-Christian God

Although there are, as we have seen, important points of contact between the more exalted Hellenistic and the Judaeo-Christian ideas, there were also significant differences. The first Judaeo-Christian concept that was radically different from the Hellenistic ideas we have examined in the previous chapters was that of a personal monotheistic deity; a single God who cared about His Creation, who required worship, made demands on His people and in some way rewarded or punished them according to their deserts. The Greeks and Romans either believed in personal polytheism (in which several gods demanded worship, punished violations, or interfered directly in the affairs of men) or, in the case of the great philosophers like Plato or Aristotle, they thought in terms of an impersonal monotheism. Plato's Idea of the Good or even of the Demiurge,[2] Aristotle's First and Final Cause[3] had no personal qualities at all. A philosopher who had some understanding of the perfection they represented might stand in awe of them, but no system of worship was associated with these, there was no idea of any reciprocal relationship between these and human kind, and no idea of rewards or punishments.

Where the Greeks and Romans did believe in gods who demanded to be worshipped, these gods demanded little else. They could be offended if sacrifices were omitted, if animals sacred to them were killed or the priestesses of their temples were violated, but they made no demands on how people should behave towards each other. If people treated each other immorally, that was of no concern to the gods. Indeed, they hardly set a good example by their own behaviour; their quarrels, seductions and deceptions. The Judaeo-Christian God, on the other hand, did make moral demands of His worshippers. His

1 I realize that not everything that shapes the way people behave or see the world merits discussion in a book on philosophy, though here again it is hard to draw a theoretical line. Our behaviour is obviously often ruled by psychological rather than philosophical considerations – fear or hatred of the stranger, for example, or the instinctual need we feel to avoid isolation and loneliness by belonging to a group. But as often as not, people will subsequently underpin such emotional reactions with some kind of philosophical justification, which are sometimes intellectually shoddy, but by no means invariably so. In a theoretical way, perhaps the whole philosophical enterprise is underpinned *in the last resort* by emotional needs, but in practice we have to draw a line somewhere between reasoning and rationalization – even if we do not all draw it in the same place.

2 see p. 35 above

3 see p. 48 above.

prophets constantly demanded social justice between rich and poor. The moral code was laid down by God, not by a secular ruler so the secular ruler was himself subject to it, and any moral offence, by king or subject, against a fellow human being was at the same time an offence against God. In the early books of the Bible, God was still the tribal god of the Jews and the morality He enjoined saw nothing wrong with the slaughter of conquered enemies. With the prophet Isaiah (eighth century BC), God began to be perceived as the God of all mankind who would one day be accepted by all the peoples and not only by the Jews, and whose aim was universal peace and brotherhood. It is this concept which, as we have seen, tied in with the Stoic idea of world citizenship and the moral duties we owe to one another.[4]

Christianity

We cannot get a totally reliable picture of the teaching of the historical Jesus from the Gospels, because the Gospel writers, writing one or two generations after the Crucifixion, had a particular agenda.[5] In any case it was the Gospel writers and St Paul who, between AD 50 and 100, provided the interpretation that presents Christianity as taking further the ideas that have been described in the previous section. The Jesus that emerges from the Gospels also preaches social justice and is a lover of peace, and he is also an obedient subject of Rome.[6] John reports him as saying "My kingdom is not of this world" (18:36) and Mark has him declare that you should render unto Caesar the things that are Caesar's (12:13–17). St Paul will reinforce that message when, in his Epistle to the Romans (13:1) he urges obedience to the powers that be, for the powers that be are ordained of God, and there is no Power but of God.

> This will become a classical statement of the theoretical Christian attitude to government until theories justifying regicide of godless rulers begin to be pronounced at the time of the Counter-Reformation.
>
> Equally important is the implied division between a spiritual and a secular kingdom, which will be worked out by St Augustine.

By proclaiming circumcision and the Jewish dietary laws unnecessary, St Paul gradually turned "Christianity", which for the first two decades was a purely Jewish sect, into a religion that was open to all mankind, to Jew and Gentile alike. The time when God could be the God of all mankind, as Isaiah had hoped, was brought nearer; not because the whole world would accept the Jewish religion, but because those ritual commands which the God of the Jews enjoined on His followers were set aside, and only a belief in the Lord Jesus was necessary for salvation.

Finally the Christians came to proclaim the Divinity of Jesus, and as they were anxious not to abandon monotheism, they would have to develop the

4 see p. 71 above

5 St. Paul and the Gospel writers were anxious to dissociate the Christians from the anti-Roman riots by the Jews of Judea, which began about 4 BC and culminated in the great Jewish Revolt of AD 66 and the destruction of the Temple by the Romans in AD 70. And the Gospels were written at the time when Judaism and Christianity were finally parting company.

6 Some scholars, however, wonder whether the historical Jesus did not have a political agenda to drive the Romans out of Judea.

idea of the Trinity, in which the Father, the Son and the Holy Ghost are all merged into a mystical unity - the exact nature of which will be the cause of much theological debate in the succeeding centuries.[7]

Everything outlined above is theology (and of course only a small part of it) rather than philosophy, but for several centuries both Judaism and Christianity were operating in a cultural environment that was still strongly influenced by Hellenistic philosophy, which presented both a challenge and, to some extent, an influence. The early encounters between these two world views - the Hellenistic and the Judaeo-Christian - are the prototype of later encounters in the Middle Ages and in the Renaissance.

Judaism and Hellenism

Judea was under Hellenistic rule from 332 BC, when it was conquered by Alexander the Great, until 152 BC, when the Maccabeans drove out the Seleucid dynasty. The orthodox Jews were always at odds with Hellenistic culture in every one of its many forms.

One of the glories of Hellenism was the variety of opinions within it; there was no Hellenistic orthodoxy. Hellenistic thinkers had relatively little regard for tradition or for the authority of earlier writings. Hellenistic thought was ever intellectually curious, speculative, forward looking, ever pushing ahead into unexplored territory. By contrast, intellectual curiosity was not a charac-

7 The doctrine of the Trinity was initially the purest theology, but in the eastern half of the Roman Empire there was an interesting attempt to link it to philosophy. The doctrine evolved slowly, from about AD 95 onwards, when it first appears in the the Gospel of St John: "In the beginning was the Word (Logos - to become the Holy Ghost) ... and the Word was God (the Father).... and the Word was made flesh (the Son) and dwelt amongst us." The Spirit of God had always been thought of as an emanation of God, by the Jews (the Hebrew word was "ruach") though the Holy Spirit was *formally* added as part of the Trinity only at a Council at Constantinople in 381. Initially, the debate was about the relationship between the Father and the Son. Around 320, Arius taught that the Son, though pre-exisiting in time, had been created by the Father, and was therefore subordinate to Him. This was challenged by Athanasius, who thought that this doctrine somehow downgraded the divinity of Christ, and he insisted that the Father and the Son were consubstantial and co-eternal - a view that became Christian orthodoxy in 325 at the Council of Nicaea which formulated what was to be known as the Nicene Creed. Consubstantial, yes, but that raised the question about the nature of substance (in Greek *ousia*). Was the substance of the Son the *same* as that of the Father (*homoousion)* or was it of a *similar* substance as that of the Father (*homoiousion*)? In the eighteenth century Gibbon would famously make fun of the bitterness that arose out of the dispute over a mere diphtong. The Council of Nicaea decided for *homoousion*, though the dispute would continue for many years after.

By this time, the ideas of Philo of Alexandria and of Plotinus - see below - were making headway. The ideas of Philo and Plotinus about God originated in philosophy rather than in theology, and three theologians from Cappadocia in what is now Central Turkey gave the doctrine of the Trinity a philosophical justification. The *ousia*, or substance, of God is unknowable. We can get a faint glimpse of the nature of God through what we can understand from the emanations that stream forth from Him rather in the way in which light streams forth from the sun. The whole world and the laws that govern it are part of that emanation, but the most important of these emanations are the Trinity. Creation itself (and therefore the concept of a Creator) is one. We see it as God the Father. The Redemption of the World (and therefore the concept of the Redeemer) is another, we see it as God the Son. The Guidance and Comfort is the third, we see it as God the Holy Spirit. We can understand the Trinity intuitively as God appears to us in all three forms simultaneously, just as the brightness, heat and roundness of the sun appear to us simultaneously; all three are part of what streams forth from God, so that, though they are different, they are both consubstantial and co-eternal. This interpretation of the Trinity is very prominent in Greek Christianity. Karen Armstrong, to whose brilliant pages in *A History of God* I owe the ideas expressed in this footnote, writes that Greek Christians were more ready to rely on intuitive perceptions than were the Latin Christians, who were altogether more literal-minded and therefore had far more intellectual problems than the Greeks with the concept of the Trinity.

teristic of Jewish thought during this period, and speculation had to be kept within very strict bounds. Anything that exceeded these bounds was likely to be forbidden as heretical. Jewish thought was very tradition-bound, always looking back to the authority of Moses as it was interpreted for them by their religious leaders, who, since the Babylonian capitivity had been anxious to isolate the Jews from what they considered the corrupting influences of their surroundings. The Hellenists were very artistic. The Jews were forbidden to make any images. The Hellenists admired the beauty of the human body. The Bible had shown Adam and Eve being ashamed of their nudity. So the Jews found the games which were staged in the gymnasia in Judea offensive, partly because the games were dedicated to pagan gods and partly because the athletes competed in the nude.

When we move from the general climate of Hellenistic culture to Hellenistic philosophy and religion, we find that the Jews could accept neither the polytheism of the masses nor the impersonal monotheism of Plato and Aristotle. True, there was nothing that was actually offensive to the Jews in Platonic and Aristotelian monotheism, it simply did not go far enough in their opinion in moving from an impersonal to a personal God. The ideas of Plato and Aristotle were so profound, so seductive and so richly suggestive that Jewish and Christian thinkers would, in later centuries, try to add their specific religious ideas about God on to the infrastructure of Platonism and Aristotelianism. But that still lay in the future, the first, second and third century AD in the case of Neo-Platonism,[8] and in the case of Aristotle, as far as European thought is concerned, not until the twelfth and thirteenth centuries.[9]

If Plato and Aristotle were not actually offensive to Jewish thought, other Greek philosophies - the relativism of Protagoras, the cynicism of Diogenes, the scepticism of Pyrrho and the hedonism of Epicurus - were all, for obvious reasons, totally rejected by Judaism, and these were probably more pervasive among the generality of the Hellenes than the more profound and more difficult thought of Plato and Aristotle.

By and large, Hellenism was, as we have seen, rather tolerant. All sorts of opinions flourished freely under Hellenistic rule, including Jewish orthodoxy, which was so at odds with the general spirit of Hellenism. At the end, the Seleucid dynasty threw up an uncharacteristically intolerant ruler in Antiochus IV. He attempted to Hellenize Judea by force, and in 167 BC issued a decree "abolishing" the Mosaic Laws and fiercely punishing any who continued to follow it. This led to the revolt of the Maccabees (166 to 164 BC), the expulsion of the Seleucids, the establishment of the Hasmonean dynasty and the victory of Jewish orthodoxy. So seductive did Hellenism remain, however, that only half a century after the expulsion of the Seleucids, the Hasmonean rulers themselves succumbed to it, and thereby provoked a series of revolts led by the Pharisees, the leaders of Jewish fundamentalism. Hellenism continued to dominate Judea under the last Hasmoneans and continued to do so under the next dynasty, the Herodians. These had been installed by the Romans in 39 BC;

8 see Chapter 10 on Philo of Alexandria and Origen, and Chapter 13 on St Augustine.

9 see Chapter 15 on Maimonides and Chapter 16 on Thomas Aquinas. Aristotle had made an impact earlier than this on Muslim thinkers in the Middle East. This, too, will be dealt with in Chapter 15.

Judea was now a Roman client state, and from AD 6 onwards the Romans ruled Judea directly through a resident procurator.

The Roman Empire was, as we have seen, also Hellenistic in culture, and the clash between Judaism and the Romans was therefore a cultural as well as a political conflict. One of the crisis points in this long struggle came when the Emperor Caligula (AD 37 to 41) demanded that he be worshipped as a god and that statues to him should be put up in temples and in synagogues throughout the empire, of which Egypt was by then a part. At that time, twice as many Jews were living in Egypt than in Judea; and in AD 40, the Jews of Alexandria sent a deputation to Rome. They pledged their loyalty to the Empire, but asked to be exempt from having to do something that would violate their religion. This delegation was led by Philo Judaeus, better known as Philo of Alexandria.

CHAPTER 10

Neo-Platonism

PHILO OF ALEXANDRIA

Philo, whose dates are approximately 25 BC to AD 40, was a contemporary of both Jesus and Paul. He was actually an observant Jew, but thought that this was compatible with an attempt to fuse Plato and Judaism. Plato, with his emphasis on the world "above", had been somewhat in abeyance while the Stoics were dominant in the days of the Roman Republic, because, as we have seen,[1] the Stoics were concentrating on the duties they had to this world, to the *res publica.* But as Rome sank from the *res publica* to an increasingly degenerate Empire such as it was under the egregious tyrant Caligula, a philosophy stressing the duty to participate in the state seemed pointless, and a concern, both in religion and philosophy, with the "Other World", such as had been found in Plato, again came into its own. The thinkers who tried to combine both these strands - religion and Platonic philosophy - are known as Neo-Platonists, and Philo was the first of these. His Platonic commentaries on the Bible make up the bulk of his writing.

Philo admired Plato and his followers for grasping that Perfection - the Good, the True, and the Beautiful - are One,[2] but Plato, he thought, fell short in one respect in which the Jews have excelled him. A Platonist would get no further than having some mystical awareness of Perfection, and that awareness was open only to the trained philosopher. The philosopher might, as a result, try to lead a life of goodness, truth and beauty, but not because he is commanded to do so, nor would he have any rituals expressing worship and service. The Jews, on the other hand, have, as a people, chosen to worship and serve this One as God. Judaism, as it were, adds the missing bit to Platonism (just as later the Christians in their turn were to claim that Christianity added the missing bits to Judaism.) In firmly identifying the Platonic Idea of the Good with God, Philo created the fusion of Neo-Platonism.

Philo held that, like Plato's Idea of the Good, God is totally *transcendent* in relation to the created world, meaning that God is wholly outside the world. He does not directly concern Himself with the world, and a philosopher will know that all expressions in the Bible that suggest that He does should be interpreted allegorically, not literally. To say that God carries out actions like creating, loving, judging, punishing, performing miracles etc. is to *anthropomorphize* Him, to limit Him by attributing to Him human qualities. If we use such words

1 p. 72 above.

2 see p. 35 above.

in talking about God, it is because we have no vocabulary that can express His real nature.

> Whether this is in fact an improvement on Plato may be open to question if serving God involves, as it did for an orthodox Jew like Philo, accepting as divinely ordained a whole host of laws (about diet, about circumcision – 613 altogether) which this transcendent and unanthropomorphic God is supposed to have told Moses to pass on to the Jews. It is hardly possible to treat those commandments allegorically. Philo said that observance of such laws has a symbolic meaning; it expresses subjection to the will of God and self-discipline in His service. But is not such an argument more than a little tinged with the anthropomorphism that Philo theoretically rejects? Is this not an example of theology saying one thing (in this case that God issues highly specific commands) and philosophy (that God is entirely transcendent) another?

If God is totally transcendent, how can we understand anything about Him? Plato had agreed that we can probably never fully grasp the Idea of the Good. With training in philosophy we can only reach some intimations of it as we study the imperfect embodiments of Goodness in the particulars around us. Philo believed that we could understand something about the nature of God through *emanations* coming from Him. Emanations are not *sent* by God, they stream forth from Him in the same way as light streams forth from the sun. In the same way, it is in the nature of God that emanations naturally stream forth from Him. The sun does not shed light by an act of will, but because it is in the nature of the sun to shed light, and by the light we understand something of the nature of the sun, which blinds us if we look at it directly. In this world we can see it, as St Paul will say of God,[3] only "through a glass darkly".

There are several of these emanations - Philo called them Powers - which link the transcendent God with the material cosmos. The most important of these Powers Philo called the *Logos*.[4] This Greek term means "Word" or "reason", and for Philo it was that emanation of the Divine Mind which reflected the order that lay behind Nature. Humans can grasp something of that emanation, and so are enabled to have, in the first place, at least some understanding of the order of the universe and, behind that, a glimmering of the Divine. The Logos enables us to see that the universe has a Design, from which human Reason can deduce that there must be a Designer, even if we cannot perceive Him directly. Philo was the first to formulate the so-called "argument from design" as *philosophical proof*, independent of revelation, for the existence of God.

Philo explained that God did not create nature, because that would mean that He was mixed up with nature and could not therefore be totally transcendent. This was an argument that had already been advanced by Aristotle.[5] Instead, said Philo, God is *the order that lies behind* nature, or in other words, is like Plato's Ideas, the perfect blueprint to which all particulars aspire.

As the principle that lies behind nature, the Logos is immaterial, but Philo apostrophizes it in allegorical language. In places he calls it "the first-born son

3 1.Cor.13:12

4 In the so-called Wisdom Literature, the idea of Wisdom seems to foreshadow the concept of the *Logos* as an emanation of God. Chapter 8 of the biblical Book of Proverbs is an early example.

5 see p. 48 above.

of God", "God's chief messenger" etc. Some thirty years after the death of Philo, chapter 1 of the Gospel according to St. John, the most Hellenized of the Gospel writers, identifies the Logos with Jesus, "In the beginning was the Word, and the Word was with God, and the Word was God ... and the Word was made flesh, and dwelt among us."

One might almost say that what St John did was to give flesh to what in Philo had been a poetic and abstract concept. The leaders of orthodox Judaism had already been deeply suspicious of Philo's Hellenism. They were worried that allegorizing passages of the Bible would weaken or destroy the concept of the Jews as the uniquely Chosen People of God. By the time that St John's Gospel was written, the breach between the Jews and the Christians had become final, and the fact that Philo's concept of the Logos was now identified with Jesus, who in turn had been identified with God, was the last straw as far as the acceptability of Philo to the Jews was concerned.[6] Neo-Platonism played no further acknowledged part in Judaism for at least the next thousand years,[7] but the story of Christian Neo-Platonism was about to begin.

Christian Neo-Platonism

Neo-Platonism was really more congenial to Christianity than it was to Judaism, and not only because the Gospel of St John had appropriated the Logos to the person of Jesus in the way that has just been described. Although by the time of Philo the Jews had anticipated that one day the whole world would acknowledge the God of the Jews,[8] they did not think that day had yet dawned. Judaism remained the religion of the Jewish people alone. As we have seen, it had at one time attracted converts from among Gentiles who had found Jewish monotheism, Jewish family life and Jewish morals more impressive than their own Hellenistic culture. Many more - the so-called "bystanders" - would have converted if circumcision and adherence to the dietary laws had not been demanded of them. But once St Paul had set aside these requirements for adherence to the Jewish sect that became Christianity, there was little prospect of Judaism making more converts and being seen as a universal religion.

6 Philo also produced an idea which would influence the Christian idea of the Trinity. One of the stories in the Bible which was allegorized by him is in Genesis 18, in which Abraham is visited at Mamre by the Lord (verse 1) who in verse 2 appears to have turned into three men, commonly taken to be angels. In the first fifteen verses of the chapter there seems to be some confusion about who is speaking, as the verb shifts from singular to plural and back again to singular. Philo says it is "customary to call angels" what he himself calls *Logoi*; angels (like the *Logoi*, messengers of God) are therefore the way that unphilosophically-minded people perceive the emanations of God. But a philosopher may see the three men or angels as the three most important emanations of God: His Power, His Mercy and His Justice. Abraham comes to realize that the three and the One are the same. We have seen in note 7 on p. 81 how the Greek Christians interpret the Trinity as emanations from God, and Philo's interpretation of Genesis 18 is the subject of many icons in Greek and Russian churches, where this "Old Testament Trinity" is revered as a prefiguration of the New Testament Trinity of Father, Son and Holy Ghost.

7 Yet there are some remarkable parallels between Philo's conceptions and the strand of Jewish mysticism known as the Kabbalah. The organized doctrine of the Kabbalah is traced by the *Encyclopaedia Judaica* to the 1st century AD, the time during which Philo was writing. Scholars are not in agreement about the extent to which Philo's influence played a part, but we can observe the following. Kabbalism has the One transcendental deity called the *Ayn Sof.* From this there are emanations called the *Sefiroth*; the loftiest of these emanation is the trinity of Wisdom (*Hokhma*), Understanding (*Binah*) and Knoweldge (*Da'ath*) and one of the *Sefiroth*, the *Shechina*, is something resembling God's spirit dwelling among men.

8 see p. 80 above.

For Christianity, on the other hand, which proclaimed itself as a universal religion, a Roman Empire which embraced so much of the known world in a universal citizenship was a congenial secular environment. Moreover, the culture of that Empire was still largely Hellenistic, and Hellenist thought also tended to emphasize the universal over and against the particular. We talk of the Age of Greece and Rome as "Classical" Antiquity, and one of the connotations of the word "classical" is precisely the emphasis on universalism; on what men have in common rather than on what distinguishes one group from another.

There was already much that Christianity and Plato had in common. There was the belief in the existence of a transcendental reality that was eternal perfection. Both gave primacy to the spiritual over the material. They attached great importance to the tending of the immortal soul by self-examination, by cultivating virtue and by controlling the passions and the appetites, often to the point of asceticism. The goal of human aspirations should be to have the soul assimilated to God when it left the body, and death is therefore a transition to a more abundant life.

> Some of these ideas can be found in Judaism also, especially in later Judaism, but mainstream Judaism had a much more robust interest in this world than had early Christianity. Christian preachers taught that this world is full of vanity, a vale of tears, and that the real life was the life hereafter. The idea of an afterlife existed in Judaism, but was much more shadowy and much less important than in Christianity. The Christian saints concentrate on purifying their own souls in pursuit of their individual salvation. We can find the idea of individual salvation also in Judaism, but when the Jewish Bible talks about salvation, the references are more often to that of the people of Israel as a community. Jewish religious rituals concerned themselves to a much larger extent than Christian rituals with earthly things like the food that could be eaten, or with what could and could not be done on the Sabbath. It was much less ascetic. Christians and Platonists saw the family as a regrettable necessity for those who were not up to celibacy; the most dedicated souls should renounce marriage. The Jews, on the other hand, actually wanted their rabbis to marry. In the two centuries before Christ, only a small number of Jews sought to avoid the corruptions of the world by withdrawing into desert communities, but in Christianity the monastic life would be embraced by men and women in their tens of thousands.

To Platonism proper, Christian Neo-Platonism, often drawing on its Jewish roots, now added a specifically religious character. In other words, the philosophy was strongly tinged with theology. It intensified the sense of the holy and the sacred and it transformed the Absolute and the *Logos* into a more personal deity, which is demanding and judgmental in relation to humanity, is more freely active and purposive in human history than was the transcendental Platonic Absolute, and therefore becomes the supreme intelligence and the supreme ruling will.

ORIGEN

Ammonius Saccas had founded a school of Neo-Platonism in Alexandria in the third century. One of his pupils was Origen (185 to 254), a Christian theologian who has also been described as the first Christian *philosopher*, though, as we have seen, the opening chapter of St John's Gospel seems at least to assume a philosophical and Neo-Platonist concept. Whereas some early Christian thinkers still saw Jesus as a God-inspired prophet arriving at a particular time in History rather than as God Incarnate, Origen saw Him as pure *Logos* who had existed in all time and was co-eternal with God the Father. In a way he turned St John's procedure upside down. St John had taken the abstract idea of the *Logos* and had given it a physical presence by saying that it was made flesh. Origen took the Christ who dwelt among us and turned him into the abstract *Logos*. In this he followed Philo; just as Philo had treated some passages in the Old Testament, like the appearance at Mamre,[9] in an allegorical rather than a literal way, so Origen did the same to some passages in the New Testament – for example, he allegorized the virgin birth as the birth of wisdom. The stories of the Bible are presented more or less literally to simple people, and then one tries perhaps to show them the wider applications of the stories, but Origen believed that intellectuals should be trained to see and understand them as allegories. In Origen's day, Christian theology had not yet acquired the dogmatic orthodoxy that would be clamped upon it at the Council of Nicea in 325. In 400, Pope Anastasius I was to declare Origen's teaching blasphemous.

PLOTINUS

Ammonius Saccas taught at least two generations of philosophers, and in the generation after Origen one of his pupils was Plotinus (204 to 270), the most influential of the Neo-Platonists after Philo. Plotinus was not a Christian, but he forms an important bridge to Christian Neo-Platonism through St Augustine (354 to 430) who would speak of Plato as "the most pure and bright in all philosophy" and of Plotinus as the man "in whom Plato lives again."[10]

In Plotinus we see a further working out of the ideas we have met in Philo. Plotinus begins as Philo had done: God (Plotinus calls Him the One) is totally transcendent. Any qualities we might ascribe to Him are erroneous, not only because that would be to anthropomorphize Him, but also for logical reasons in that any such ascriptions would limit Him. If, for example, we describe Him as Good, then what we call Evil would be outside of Him, and in that case He could not be the all-embracing One. He could not think, will, or act because "thought", "will" and "action" imply distinctions between the thinker and the object of thought, or between the author of willing and acting and the things willed or done. We have no vocabulary, no capacity even to visualize someone or something that is a seamless melding of thinker and thought.

The world is therefore not God's creation, but an emanation from Him. Plotinus, like Philo, used the image of the light that streams from the sun, not because the sun decides to shed light, but because it is the nature of the sun to shed light. The light, Plotinus says, becomes dimmer the further away it is from its source. Closest to the source is the principle that governs the way the world

9 see note 6 on p. 87 above.

10 We know the work of Plotinus through an edition compiled for him by one of his pupils, Porphyry (*ca.* 232 to 301). Its fifty-four chapters were grouped in six sets of nine chapters each – hence the work is known as the *Enneades* (*ennea* being the Greek for "nine").

ought to be. This was what Plato had called the Idea of the Good, what Philo had called the *Logos*, and what Plotinus himself called *Nous* or Spirit. As we move further away from the source of light, the *Nous* is manifested in what Plotinus called the *Psyche* or Soul of any one particular thing. Something that is only one particular thing is obviously not as close to the ultimate source of the emanations as is the *Nous* that governs *all* things. Plotinus' *Psyche* corresponded to what Aristotle had called *entelechy*,[11] the blueprint or goal that governs the way any particular earthly thing will develop if allowed to do so.

Moving still further away from the source, we come to matter. This has been shaped by its *psyche* to a greater or lesser degree. For example, in an ideal climate the matter that makes up a plant is almost wholly shaped by the blueprint, but if the climate is unfavourable, its matter can be shaped only partially by the blueprint and the plant will be stunted. We think of inanimate objects as being wholly material, but that is mistaken; they, too, have an entelechy, though that has never allowed them more than a very little, if any, development. A piece of stone or a piece of slate are not likely to develop into anything further; their entelechy simply consists of being a stone or a piece of slate for the rest of their existence, but it is through their being infused by entelechy that we can tell that the one is a piece of stone and the other a piece of slate.

Finally, furthest away from the source of light, almost in darkness, is raw matter, wholly untouched as yet by any blueprint or entelechy. It is perhaps difficult to imagine what that might be like, as all matter that we know of is already shaped by its organizing principle. But, according to Plotinus, this raw matter in the darkness that the light cannot reach is where evil resides. Light is equated with goodness, absence of light with the absence of goodness, which is what evil is. Note that this evil is nothing positive, it is simply the absence of good.

> The view, that evil is merely the absence of good, differs from Manicheism, which was taught by Plotinus' contemporary Mani (216 to 274). Good and Evil are separate, essentially independent principles, which in this world are constantly at war with each other. This idea will be discussed more fully below.[12]

What we have looked at so far is, as it were, the Divine spilling its light downwards, but there is also an opposite movement. Just as a plant struggles up towards the source of light, so all things in this world aspire, with greater or less success, to soar upwards towards it. Matter, when illuminated by *psyche* (the blueprint) tries to be true to its entelechy. The entelechy in its turn plays its part in the order of the world or *nous*, and the *nous* is obedient to the One.

As far as human beings are concerned, it means that the fully developed *psyche* or soul seeks to understand the *nous*, and by way of mysticism it may actually come to grasp something of the One. What we call Virtue is the movement of the Soul away from matter and towards the *nous* and the One. Not every human soul manages this, any more than every acorn manages to become an oak tree. The ascent of the soul is difficult. Plato had believed that only a rigorous training of the intellect would bring some understanding of perfection, some possibility of dwelling with perfection. Plotinus thought that the intellect would help to understand the *Nous*; but the human intellect by itself could

11 see p. 45 above.

12 see p. 93 below.

never grasp the highest stage, the transcendence of the One. Only through rare moments of mystical experience were humans enabled to have a glimpse of this transcendence and to feel themselves absorbed in it. They can perhaps, up to a point, prepare themselves for such mystical experiences, but the preparation is likely to be spiritual rather than intellectual. Porphyry, in his biography of Plotinus, relates that his teacher had had such an experience four times during the four years that Porphyry was his pupil, and Porphyry himself would described the kind of spiritual preparation that may bring about some experience of the transcendental.

PORPHYRY

For Porphyry, the ascent of the Soul was even more important than it had been for Plotinus. Porphyry seems initially to have been an orthodox Christian, but after he had completed the *Enneades,* he wrote a series of fifteen books attacking Christianity, partly because he thought the Incarnation to be inconsistent with the totally transcendent nature of God. Although he had abandoned Christianity, he held on to the idea that the Soul sought Salvation, and for this, its upward ascent was necessary. Like Plato, Porphyry thought that the Soul needed to be trained for this ascent. At the lowest level we need to practise the social virtues; we cannot expect our soul to be saved if we do not treat our fellow human beings decently. Next we need to practise "apathy". This word originally meant a state in which one had freed oneself from earthly passions. Porphyry thought this could best be achieved by asceticism and especially by abstinence from meat and from sexual activity. Finally we must train ourselves to understand truth and its beauty. Then, as Plotinus had said, it was possible for the Soul to live in the *nous* and possibly to understand something of the Divine.

It is interesting how often mysticism throughout the world has been linked to asceticism. Why does an ascetic lifestyle appear to open "the doors of perception"? The phrase comes from the title of a book in which Aldous Huxley describes the mystical states induced by mescalin, and we know of many other ways – mortifications of the flesh, drugs, breathing techniques, hypnosis – which are practised by people in search of being taken "out of themselves". Two philosophical problems seem to present themselves: what truth status do we accord to altered perceptions resulting from organic changes that are sometimes deliberately induced within ourselves? And can we be at all sure that *all* mystical experiences have such a physiological basis? What about the experiences a quite unascetic person may have in contemplating a magnificent mountain landscape or when listening to some sublime music? Pythagoras and Plato believed that we can achieve insights of a mystical character by meditating on the most refined and purest reason. Jung suggested that they often spring from a very ancient "collective unconscious" and are therefore part of our psychology rather than of our physiology.

CHAPTER 11

Gnosticism

Neo-Platonism was one of several sources which influenced the amalgam known as Gnosticism. Gnosticism has many variants; but they are all basically concerned with the problem of Evil. We have seen that Plotinus had thought the created world to consist of emanations from a transcendental and perfect God (whom he had called the One) and that these emanations were like the light which became weaker as it became more distant from its source. Where the light did not reach, where there was complete darkness, that was where evil resided. Evil in Plotinus and Porphyry was simply the absence of good, just as darkness was simply the absence of light.

The Gnostics thought that Evil was not so much a negative quality - an absence - as a positive one. They believed that the world that resulted from the emanations of God (which they called *aeons*) was a purely spiritual world, which they called the *Pleroma*. The material world - which included the human body - was the creation of a *Demiurge*, a rival of God. Some of the radiance from God, sparks of the divine, had become trapped in parts of this material world; in a human being the Soul was one of these sparks. If it were to be freed from the trap or prison of the material world and to rejoin the purely spiritual world, it needed a special and esoteric knowledge or *gnosis* - hence the word given to this philosophy.

One source for this Gnostic dualism between the realm of Spirit and that of Matter, between the realm of Good and that of Evil, was Zoroastrianism. This religion had arisen in the sixth century BC and was well established in Persia. In Zoroastrianism the God of Light, Ahura Mazda, is engaged in a battle with his rival Ahriman. The God of Light will win in the end, but meanwhile his active rival will win many a battle. It was through the Persian Mani (216 to 274) that this dualism made its mark on European philosophy. For Mani, the Light and the Darkness, Spirit and Matter were originally separate worlds which had become mixed up with each other. They would one day again be separated, but until that day comes, Good and Evil were fighting on fairly equal terms.

Mani was not a Christian, but Manicheism did make an impact on a Christian version of Gnosticism. The Christian Gnostics will see Christ as part of the *Pleroma*,[1] and the *gnosis* which will free the Soul for reunion with God is the

1 There was a problem here: if Christ was the emanation "made flesh", that embodiment would fall into the realm of matter, which belongs to God's rival. This led to some ingenious solutions: "Docetism" (from the Greek *dokein* = to seem) held that the body of Jesus was not real, but a phantom. The theologian Cerinthus taught that Jesus and Christ were not the same: Jesus was purely human, and Christ was the Holy Spirit that descended on him at the time of his Baptism. It departed from him before the crucifixion, leaving the human Jesus to die on the Cross.

teaching of Christ. Some Christian Gnostics, influenced by the esotericism that is so characteristic of Gnosticism, taught that the *gnosis* was embodied not in the New Testament but in the oral teachings of Jesus which had never been committed to writing.

The adversary of God, fighting Him on almost equal terms, will become the Devil (the Prince of Darkness).

Nor was the Devil the only candidate for the role of demiurge. The theologian Marcion (100 to 165) identified the demiurge with the Yahwe of the Old Testament, who is so often jealous, angry and destructive. Christianity, for all its persecution of the Jews, accepted the Jewish Bible as part of Holy Writ, but because so much of the Jewish Bible is dominated by Yahwe, Marcion wanted to break the link which Christians accept between the Old Testament and what they considered its fulfilment in the New. Even the bulk of the Gospels was to be abandoned, as they so often claimed to be fulfilling Old Testament texts. Marcion wanted Christianity to be based exclusively on the Letters of St Paul and on some expurgated passages of Luke's writings. The Christian Gnostic, Valentius (second century) thought there were three worlds: the material world created by the Devil, the psychic world created by Yahwe and in which the Jews continue to live and the spiritual world which was created by God and is accessible through Christian gnosis.

For about two centuries Christian Gnosticism had many adherents, though all its forms were declared heretical by the Church because they all limited the absolute power of God. When the Roman Empire became Christian, the power of the state stood behind the eradication of the heresy, though variants of it kept cropping up from time to time in later centuries, especially the twelfth, with the Bogomils, the Albigensians and the Cathars. We find Gnostic ideas as late as the eighteenth century, when William Blake sets the demiurge (whom he calls variously Elohim, The Ancient of Days, or Urizen) against Christ. In a famous colour print Elohim creates Adam already in the coils of the serpent.

It is not really surprising that many people should have been tempted down the ages by the idea that Good and Evil are evenly matched. The frequent triumphs of evil seem difficult to square with the idea that God is all-powerful, all-just, and all-loving. It seems much easier to accept that God has a powerful adversary on the battlefield that is the world. As for the battlefield within ourselves, do we not often feel helplessly, with St Paul, "The good that I would, I do not do; but the evil which I would not, that I do"?[2]

The traditional orthodox answer to this problem about goodness, justice and omnipotence is that Evil is the result of the Free Will which God, in His love for mankind, has bestowed on us. Most human beings like to feel that they have Free Will and dislike the idea that they might be so tightly programmed that they have no choice at all. In other words, they value Free Will, and therefore regard Free Will as a gift from God. The corollary of having Free Will, however, is that it gives us the freedom to choose evil and not only to damage our own souls, but also so often to be the cause of unmerited suffering for others.

However, in the first place, even Christians have sometimes questioned whether we really have Free Will and whether our actions are not in fact pre-

2 Rom. 7:19

destined – an issue which will be discussed more fully below[3] – in the second place, there is an immense amount of suffering that is not caused by the exercise of Free Will, ranging from plagues and earthquakes to famines and floods.

Those who do not believe in a God who is omnipotent, just and loving (nor, for that matter, in a Devil) have no philosophical problems with all this. Those who do believe in such a God (and therefore reject the idea of an equally powerful adversary) will either believe that suffering is not an unmitigated evil but may actually make us better (but what about those whom it makes worse?), or they will accept that it is not for humans to question the ways of a loving, just and all powerful God – which is the acceptance that God demanded of Job.

3 see pp. 107 to 112 below.

PART TWO: THE MIDDLE AGES

CHAPTER 12

Christians and Authority

By the time of Origen and Porphyry, Christianity had made great strides. Eleven years after the death of Porphyry in 301, the Emperor Constantine became a Christian, and by the end of that century Christianity had become the official and exclusive religion of the Roman Empire. The Church was therefore faced with three questions which are at the heart of political philosophy: what structure of authority should there be inside the Church? What was to be the relationship between the clergy and the laity? What should be the relationship between the authorities of the Church and those of the State?

The Apostles had appointed deacons to help them – the word comes from the Greek *diakonos*, meaning helpers or servants. A Latin word for "to serve" is *ministrare*, a deacon ministered to, or served, the apostles and also the congregation. As Paul had set up new churches, he had appointed people to preside over them who were variously called presbyters (from the Greek *presbuteros*, meaning an older man or elder, and from which it seems that the word "priest" is derived) or overseers, for which the Greek word is *episcopos*. By AD 112 these arrangements had become formalized in a hierarchy of bishops and priests. The bishops claimed apostolic descent, meaning that they had been ordained by the laying on of hands in an unbroken line from the apostles, who had themselves been chosen by Jesus. The bishops in turn ordained the priests by the laying on of hands, so that each priest likewise was at the end of a continuous chain stretching right back to Jesus. This, they claimed, gave them a special authority in expounding the meaning of Christianity and insisting that their exposition was the only legitimate one. Until the time of Constantine (288 to 337) the bishops were still popularly elected, so that at the beginning there was a combination of a democratic structure with an authoritarian teaching.[1]

As the Church grew, its claims grew also. St Cyprian (200 to 258), the Bishop of Carthage, taught that not only was the clergy's interpretation of Christian teaching the only legitimate one, but that the clergy, through the administration of the Sacraments, was the irreplaceable mediator between the laity and God.

Separate though the clergy were from the laity, Cyprian also commented on the similarity between the way the Church and the State are organized. The

1 This combination will surface again in Calvinism – see Chapter 20.

Church, like the State, needed a head, and this was the Bishop of Rome. The Bishop of Rome at the time was Stephen I (254 to 257), the first to claim authority over the whole Christian Church by virtue of his office.[2] Theoretically, the basis for this claim was that the mother church in Jerusalem had been destroyed by the Romans in AD 70, that Peter had been described by Jesus as the Rock on which he would build his church and that tradition had Peter go to Rome towards the end of his life and to have become its first bishop.[3] The fact that in Stephen's time Rome was still the official capital of the Empire will have given extra weight to his claim.

Even so, Stephen's claims were not recognized at the time by rival bishops in important sees such as those of Alexandria and Antioch. Soon after the Emperor Constantine converted to Christianity (312), he in effect supported the challenge from Alexandria and Antioch by getting the Council of Nicea to give those bishops, with the new title of Patriarchs, equal status with that of the Bishop of Rome (325), and when Constantine moved his capital to Constantinople in 330 , the bishop there was also raised to the Patriarchate (as was the Bishop of Jerusalem). But a few years later, at the Council of Sardica in 343, the bishops of the western part of the Roman Empire acknowledged the claims of the Bishop of Rome.[4] The formal split between the eastern and western churches was still a very long way off,[5] but at any rate the Council of Sardica could be said to mark the moment when the western Church topped its hierarchy with a powerful ecclesiastical Head from whom authority radiated downwards and who would soon speak as an equal with the secular heads of kingdoms and empires. This is significant also from the point of view of philosophy, because these parallel institutions of Church and State developed theories of authority and obedience to match the structures of their respective organizations, and they were also to formulate philosophical arguments to define their relationship to each other.

Undoubtedly, one reason that Constantine converted to Christianity was that the church, despite all the persecution it had undergone at the hands of some of his pagan predecessors, still preached obedience to the powers that be. With such a philosophy, the church could become a potent instrument of government, and Constantine intended to make sure that it remained so by taking direct control of it, thereby putting into practice what is known as "Caesaro-Papism". It was he who had summoned the bishops of the Empire to the Council of Nicaea, over which he presided in person; it was at his insistance that the bishops of Alexandria and Antioch were made patriarchs, and it was

2 Cyprian did not accept that: he believed that, since all the bishops were descended from the Apostles, they all had equality of status. Nevertheless, he accepted that the Bishop of Rome was *primus inter pares*.

3 There is no evidence in Acts or elsewhere in the New Testament that Peter did go to Rome. Peter's original name was Simon, and he was punningly given the name Peter (*Petros* in Greek) because, Jesus goes on to say, he will be the rock (Greek *Petra*) on which he would build his church (Matth.16:18). Jesus spoke Aramaic, and in Aramaic the word for rock is *Cephas*, a name by which Peter is also sometimes known, e.g. in John 1:42 and in two of Paul's Epistles.

4 The title "Pope", meaning Father, was originally a title of respect given to many senior clergy; but from the time of Leo the Great (440 to 461) it was reserved in the Western Church exclusively for the Bishop of Rome. In the Eastern churches it continued to be much more widely applied to the present day - in the Russian church even parish priests are referred to as popes.

5 The schism began in 731 and became final in 1054.

he who put pressure on the bishops to settle the Arian controversy over the Trinity by formulating a creed that gave unity to the Church's doctrine. He did not want the Church, which was now an instrument of his power, to be weakened by fragmentation.[6]

From the time of his conversion onwards, Constantine favoured the Christian Church, but Christianity did not become the official and exclusive religion of the Empire until 380, in the reign of the Emperor Theodosius I.

Theodosius was very much under the influence of the charismatic Bishop of Milan,[7] St Ambrose. Ambrose was the first theologian to formulate the doctrine that in spiritual matters the Church has authority over the Emperor. So far, the Christians had laid stress on the first part of Jesus' saying: "Render unto Caesar the things that are Caesar's". Ambrose laid stress on the second part, "and render unto God the things that are God's". Jesus, at the time when the Roman Emperors were pagans, had meant no more than that his followers, whilst they must pay the taxes that the Emperor demanded, must not offer worship to the Emperor, for worship belonged to God alone. But now that the Emperors were themselves professed Christians, the second part of Jesus' saying assumed a new dimension. Ambrose taught that *active* resistance to the Emperor was still impermissible under all circumstances, but if the Emperor professed Christianity, the Church had the right to demand of him that he, too, should render unto God the things that are God's. So, in the name of this second part of Jesus' saying, Ambrose demanded that the Empire should end toleration of non-Christians and should destroy their temples. Theodosius complied. Then, when Theodosius ordered a massacre of the Thessalonians in 390 as a punishment for a riot, Ambrose barred the Emperor from attendance at Mass in Milan Cathedral until he had done penance. After some weeks, the Emperor complied here, too. Constantine's Caesaro- Papism had lasted no longer than about half a century. The Church had triumphantly proclaimed its independence from the Empire.

That was just as well, for the Empire in the West was shortly afterwards destroyed by the barbarian invasions and the Sack of Rome (410). But the Church of Rome did not collapse with it. The barbarians were either already Christians (albeit mostly of the Arian variety) or would shortly become so. They plundered much, but on the whole they spared the Christian churches. In due course the new rulers in Italy would even give up their Arianism and embrace orthodox Christianity. Perhaps they did this in the hope of being able to control the Catholic church as Constantine had once controlled it, but the Church put up a powerful resistance, and titanic struggles took place between Popes and Emperors in the eleventh century and again in the fourteenth cen-

6 For the Arian controversy, see note 7 on p. 81 above. It was easier to formulate a creed than actually to secure adherence to it: Arianism was declared heretical, but it continued to vex the Church for many years yet, until it was forcibly suppressed in the Empire by Theodosius I in 381. Even then, it continued to have a hold among some Germanic tribes outside the Empire until the end of the seventh century.

7 Milan, rather than Rome, had become the seat of the Imperial court in the western part of the Empire from the reign of Diocletian (284 to 305) onwards.

tury. In the course of these contests, they engaged in a debate with profound philosophical implications, which we will examine in later chapters.[8]

There is nothing particularly profound about the philosophy of authority that has been described above. Such arguments as were produced relating to the Church's position vis-à-vis the State seem little more than the byplay of power politics. St Augustine's famous *Civitas Dei*, which he began to write in 413, was likewise initially a response to a political development, namely the fall of Rome to the barbarians three years earlier, but such is the richness of reflection in everything that Augustine wrote that his chapters on the relationship between Church and State are a genuine philosophical text, and as such they have had an enduring influence on political thought.

8 See chapters 17 and 18 below. The eastern Empire withstood the barbarians, and would last until the Ottoman Turks captured Constantinople in 1453. Less than ever under those circumstances would the church in the East accept the authority of Rome, and in 451, at the Council of Chalcedon, the eastern bishops accepted the supremacy of the Patriarch of Constantinople, just as the Western bishops had accepted the supremacy of the Pope in 343. But the eastern Church remained Caesaro-Papist, and did not manage, as the western Church had done, to free itself from Imperial control. Once again, we see how, long before the formal split, the differences between the two churches grew ever wider.

CHAPTER 13

St Augustine

Augustine (354 to 430) was born at Tagaste, in present day Algeria. His mother Monica was an orthodox and devout Christian, who was often distressed by him while he was in his late teens and in his twenties. By his own account in his *Confessions,* he led a fairly riotous life as a young man during the years that he first studied and then taught grammar and rhetoric in Carthage. But he was also searching for a philosophy, and in particular, conscious as he was of the battle within himself between his conscience and his passions, he was fascinated by the problem of Evil. At first he found the answer in Manicheism[1] which the Christian Church had condemned because it challenged the idea that God was omnipotent; but his temperament needed to worship, and he soon came to question how one could worship any source of Good which seemed so evenly matched against the power of Evil.

In 383, at the age of twenty-nine, he went to teach in Rome. During his five years there he came under the influence of Plato and the non-Christian Neo-Platonism of Plotinus. Here he found not only the transcendent Deity, or the One with whom the Soul seeks to be reunited, but he also learnt to describe Evil as merely the absence of Good rather than as a power that was independent of God.

Plotinus had believed that while pure reason can help us to understand the principles of the universe (which he had called the *Nous*),[2] our highest understanding of God comes through mystical experience,and a mystical experience was vouchsafed to Augustine in 386, at the age of thirty-one. By then he had moved from Rome to Milan and there he had come under the influence of the charismatic bishop Ambrose. Ambrose advised Augustine to study St Paul. He probably saw in the young man the same psychological type that Paul had been – tempestuous, tortured by those things he did not want to do yet did, longing to escape the tyranny of the body, yearning to surrender the tortures of the logical mind to a mystically achieved haven of peace and to the certainty of salvation. The seed fell on the right ground. Augustine tells us that a voice told him to open the Bible, and his eye fell upon the passage at the end of Romans 13 in which St Paul summons his readers to "put on the Lord Jesus Christ".

Augustine now saw Christ, as St John and Origen had done, as the *Logos,* fusing, as they had done, Neo-Platonism with Christianity. This *Logos* was not only creating and ordering, but also Revealing and Redeeming. For Plato all

1 see pp. 93f above.

2 see p. 90 above.

knowledge had come either from sense experience (which is unreliable) or from innate Ideas (which can be "recovered" only through intense intellectual thought, which possibly needs the guidance of a philosopher). For Plotinus, mysticism was another source of knowledge, but that was a rare experience which happened only rarely, and then to only a very few individuals. With Augustine there is a fourth source, Revelation, which exceeds all the others, not only in importance but also in accessibility. It was available to all who chose to listen. There was no need for learning or for any special preparation, so it was as open to the humblest individual as it was for the philosopher. Revelation, which was already crucial in Christian Theology, is thus deliberately incorporated into philosophy.

This statement might be challenged as philosophy is supposed to start with human reason, not with revelation.[3] I defend the contention on the grounds that in later philosophy, in that branch of it known as epistemology (which examines the source of our "knowledge"), non-rational sources like instincts, intuition, emotions etc. will be given serious consideration. The position of reason is by no means unchallenged in the history of philosophy proper. Pascal, for example, speaking as a philosopher in the seventeenth century, said that "the heart hath its reasons which Reason doth not know".

The downgrading of reason does have its dangers, which hardly need to be spelt out. They are particularly great if they lead to a dismissal of reasoning and of secular study as not worth pursuing, being at best a distraction from what really matters and at worst positively dangerous if they challenge what is taken to be revealed truth. Ambrose had already opposed the study of astronomy, "for wherein does it assist our salvation?" Theophilus, the Patriarch of Constantinople, had no scruples in ordering the destruction, not only of the pagan Temple of Serapis there, but also of its famous library (391). St Augustine writes that there is no need for Christians to trouble themselves with "the nature of things, as was done by those whom the Greeks call *physici*"[4] and that "it is enough for the Christian to believe that the only cause of all created things ... is ... the one true God". Thereby, he defined the character of some centuries during which the Church was suspicious of scientific enquiry and held back or actually suppressed progress in this field.[5]

Even the study of medicine was distrusted. Sickness was seen as a symptom of either the fallen nature of man or of some specific individual sin, and the suffering that sickness often brought with it was regarded as an opportunity to show spiritual strength and to share the sufferings of Christ. The medical schools of Alexandria, which had preserved the Greek knowledge of medicine, faded away – a process that was accelerated when the Nestorians, whom the Church had declared heretical in 431, emigrated from that city to Mespotamia.[6]

3 see page 78 above.

4 We would call them scientists.

5 On the other hand, Augustine did value the "Liberal Arts": grammar, music, dialectic, rhetoric, geometry, arithmetic and philosophy. These, he thought, assisted the understanding of abstract and transcendental truths.

6 The charge of heresy did not relate to their continuing interest in medicine, but rather to their belief that Christ was born human and was only later imbued with divinity. (In Mesopotamia, the emigrant Nestorians set up a famous medical school at Jundi-Shapur, near Baghdad.)

> Not until the time of Aquinas in the thirteenth century[7] would a Christian philosopher try to integrate the truths found by science with the truths of religion, but even that, as Galileo would discover,[8] would not stop the Church from suppressing science when it thought that science conflicted with what was then being taught as religious dogma. Some fundamentalists (in several religions), basing themselves on what they consider to be revelations in sacred texts, would still like to do so to the present day. In some American states it is still illegal today to teach Darwinism in state schools.

Augustine returned to North Africa as a Christian in 388, was ordained a priest in 391, and eventually became Bishop of Hippo, near Carthage, in 396. But he still continued to grapple with the problem of Evil. Plotinus had located Evil in matter that the divine light had not reached and that had not yet been shaped by the *psyche*. The *psyche*, an emanation from God, having shed its light "downwards" on raw matter and infused it with entelechy, then strove to re-ascend to its original source.[9]

Original Sin

For Augustine, sin was the evil in the human *psyche* or soul. It was the result of the soul remaining attached to and contaminated with matter instead of trying to detach itself from matter in order to re-ascend to its source and thereby achieving salvation. In his early Christian writings, Augustine thought that, if the soul was contaminated by sin, it was because it *chose* to remain attached to matter instead of *willing* to detach itself. But in his later writings, he felt that the burden of sin was so overwhelming that choice or will had a very *circumscribed* part to play in salvation. Man was inherently sinful ever since Adam and Eve's "Original Sin" of disobedience to God. Not only their expulsion from Paradise, but their very mortality was the punishment for this insubordination. More than that, Chapter 3 of Genesis makes it clear that all the sufferings before death are also part of the divine punishment. The painful labour of women and the arduous labour of men merely stand for all the other pains and tribulations of humankind. Because they are inflicted by God, it is sinful to bring an end to them before God has decided to do so. The Stoics had thought that suicide was often the noble way out of disgrace or a life which had lost its meaning. St Augustine now introduced into Christianity the notion that suicide is a sin.

Moreover, not only was sin inherited from Adam and Eve, but it was also passed on and compounded in every generation by the "sins of the flesh" – the sexual act. Outside marriage the sexual act was one of the gravest of sins, and if it was permitted inside marriage, that was God's concession to human frailty. Even in marriage the sexual act remained a surrender to matter. Those who wanted to dedicate themselves most fully to the service of God would remain celibate. This had already been the position of the unmarried St Paul,[10] whom

7 See chapter 16 below.

8 see p. 208 below.

9 see p. 90 above.

10 "I would that all men were even as I myself... I say therefore to the unmarried and widows, it is good for them if they abide even as I. But if they cannot contain, let them marry: for it is better to marry than to burn". (I. Cor. 7:7-9).

Ambrose had recommended to Augustine; and indeed Ambrose was the first bishop in the Christian Church who insisted that the clergy in his diocese be celibate. Celibacy was recommended by the Catholic Church not only because families are a distraction – a priest would have to give too much attention to his family, at the expense of the attention he should be giving to his congregation and to the service of God – but also because the sexual act itself is so dangerous to the health of the soul.

Since St Augustine, so heavy has been the emphasis that the Christian Church puts on the sins of the flesh that many people have had the impression that sexual misbehaviour, rather than disobedience and the desire for knowledge, was the Original Sin for which Adam and Eve (and their descendants) were punished! Perhaps the overwhelming importance given by Augustine to sex hardly deserves to be called a part of philosophy or even of theology: one might say that it was rather a matter of psychology, if not of psychopathology. With his contemporary Jerome, the obsession with the unworthiness of sex developed into a positive loathing of sexuality in general and of women in particular. Had it not been for Eve tempting Adam into sin, the Fall might have been avoided, and her daughters continued to entice men into Sin. Hence the enormous importance attached to the idea of the Virgin Birth and, later, of the Immaculate Conception of the Virgin. Were she a woman like any other, she would, in the eyes of these Church Fathers, be too "sinful" to become the centre of veneration.

Theology? Philosophy? Psychology? Whichever it is, these views have had an immense influence on the way the West has looked upon sex, marriage and women. Sexual repression, sexual guilt, sexual shame and distrust of eroticism have been exceptionally powerful motifs in the West, and – *pace* Freud – they have possibly played a big part in channelling western creativity into other channels by way of sublimation. The monogamous and largely indissoluble marriage has, for better and for worse, been the nucleus of family life.

Wholly baleful, however, has been the influence of these ideas on the way women have been regarded in western society. This is of course not to ignore that in non-Christian societies the oppression of women has been as bad or even worse than in the West – even in societies whose religions, such as the Hindu religions, have powerful goddesses that one might have expected to become role models for the whole society. The suppression of women has much deeper anthropological causes than anything that merits the name of either philosophy or theology. It would have prevailed in any case, but it remains true that in the West the Church's view of women has been a powerful "intellectual" instrument of rationalization.

What about the doctrine of Original Sin? Perhaps we do not believe that it is an inheritance from Adam and Eve, or that it is associated so heavily with disobedience or with sex, and we may not accept that the consequences of Original Sin imperil the salvation of our souls. Even when we look at the issue in purely secular terms, did not Augustine have a point in thinking that humans are innately flawed from a moral point of view? That even the best of us, capable as we are of moral reflection, often have to struggle against the nature that we were born with, which some call our animal nature and others describe as our baser nature? That in that struggle we have often been defeated – in some areas (like lust) perhaps most powerfully when we were young, in other areas (like pride) possibly more frequently when we were older and successful?

Augustine might have given more attention to the fact that Lust is after all only one of the Seven Deadly Sins (as they would be defined in the sixth century by St Gregory the Great). Most of us still accept that there is a moral dimension involved in the proper expression of the sex instinct – though an increasing number of people will not admit even to that. But the fact that there are at least six other Deadly Sins that we can and often do commit makes the case for our flawed nature even more strongly than if there were only one. The deadliest of all the Seven Deadly Sins is actually not Lust but Pride, and if we were pleased with ourselves for not having, at the end of a day, been guilty of Anger, Avarice, Envy, Gluttony, Lust and Sloth, we would be likely to be caught by the ultimate sin of Pride!

Is it not the essence of civilization that it should control our innate baser instincts or at least canalize them into morally more acceptable channels? Kant would talk of the crooked timber of humanity out of which nothing straight could be made, and when Isaiah Berlin took the phrase "The Crooked Timber of Humanity" as the title of one of his books, it was in support of his thesis that in social and political projects we must start with human beings as they are and not with a utopian plan.

Free Will and Predestination

If, then, we are trapped in Original Sin, how can the soul achieve salvation? Augustine, again following St Paul, believed that this was possible only through the grace of God. Because Man is so sinful, nobody *deserves* this Grace; it is unmerited. But God had offered it to all mankind when He sent Jesus to take upon himself the sins of the world. It was an offer which, because men had free will, they could reject, and if they did so, they *lost* the chance of Salvation. The Latin word for loss is *damnum;* damnation originally meant simply the loss of salvation (or the absence of salvation, which was akin to Plotinus' description of evil being simply the loss or absence of good). The loss of salvation was terrible enough even if not accompanied by the eternal pains of hellfire. Salvation was impossible without the grace of God; mired as he was in sin, Man could not achieve it by his own efforts. But St Augustine went further than this: some men are predestined to exercise their will to accept the offer of grace and others are predestined to reject it. God, being omniscient, foresees[11] but does not determine who will accept His grace and who will not.[12] Those who accept

11 Augustine developed a theory about time which, strictly speaking, makes the use of the word "foresee" inappropriate. He believed that sequential time as we experience it operates in the world only after God has created it. It does not exist outside the created world, which is literally time-less (eternal), and in which there is no past,present or future - concepts which are dissolved in Eternity. (He would never have agreed with the crude suggestions of the later Catholic Church that you could *shorten* the time spent by the dead in Purgatory by praying for them or by endowing Masses for the Dead. That is a sequential idea. Time in the beyond, in the "next" world, cannot be shortened.) The whole vexed question "when did eternity begin and when will it end?" is a false question. Augustine had to address himself to this problem because people asked themselves what there was "before the beginning of time" when God created the world *ex nihilo*. But it is interesting that, on theological grounds and in theological terms, he came to a conclusion not unlike that which Kant was to reach on rational and Einstein on scientific grounds: that in "Reality" Time and Space as we experience them cannot exist. See p. 368 note 13.

12 St Paul in Romans 8:29–30 had shown the sequence. First came God's foreknowledge. This implies the course a human is destined to follow; which in turn enables the righteous to be called. That calling will be followed by justification (i.e. made just by the removal of sin), and the removal

it are helped in their struggle against sin, those who decline it reject the help of grace and are enslaved by sin.

> Why would anyone exercise his free will to reject grace? The implication of Augustine's teaching is that the capacity to use our free will to choose or to reject the offer of grace, though very small in all of us, is smaller in some people than in others. Put more simply, it seems to suggest that some people are constitutionally capable of using the little will they have to accept the grace which then strengthens that will further. The will of others is so weak that they cannot even take that step. An analogy would be of men in danger of drowning in the middle of the ocean. They can all swim a little, but none of them have the capacity to reach the far off land by swimming. They see the captain of a distant liner launch a lifeboat which can take them to salvation. The current flows strongly in the opposite direction; even so, there are some swimmers who are constitutionally capable of reaching the lifeboat whose crew will then help them to reach the liner. But there are some who, though they do try, are just too weak; the current sweeps them away.
>
> (Even the suggestion that constitutional strength or weakness are involved may sometimes be inappropriate. The strong swimmer may be strong because he has freely chosen to take a lot of exercise in the swimming pool, the weak swimmer may be weak because he has freely chosen to be a couch potato instead.)
>
> This is an intellectually subtle "squaring of the circle", allowing, as it does, validity to each of the two concepts of free will and predestination, which at first sight would appear to be incompatible with each other. The theology takes account of our experience in life and corresponds with what we feel about ourselves and indeed about others. We feel that in many situations we are free to make our own choices, but we are also conscious of the number of occasions when, "with the best will in the world", we are too weak to do what we know we ought to do. We feel there are some occasions when we are entitled to expect of a miscreant that he should "pull himself together", but there are also times when we recognize that the miscreant is not fully responsible for what he has done wrong.

Those who accept God's grace are, by that acceptance, chosen for salvation – though perhaps it would be more accurate to say that by the choice which *they* (not God) have made, they are destined for salvation. They are the Elect – the word comes from the Latin *eligere*, which means to select, though the Latin word itself comes from *legere*, meaning to choose. Once they have used their free will to accept the offer of grace, that grace helps them to strengthen their will yet further. It helps the will to make continuing choices between good and evil, so that, by making the right choice, the Elect can avoid being totally enslaved to sin in this world and can achieve salvation in the next.

> Nothing has caused more misunderstanding among the general public than the word "predestination". Many people believe the doctrine to mean that God decides in advance that only a few individuals *can* accept grace and so will be chosen for salvation, while the great majority *cannot* accept it and so will be condemned at the very outset of their lives to the opposite of salvation. Nor did

of sin makes glorification (or salvation) possible. "Whom he did foreknow, he also did predestinate to be conformed to the image of his Son... Whom he did predestinate, them he also called: and whom he called, them he also justified; and whom he justified, them he also glorified."

the medieval church generally take what would have been the line of Plotinus had Plotinus been a Christian: that the opposite of Salvation would be the absence of God – painful enough for those who had some glimmering of the joys of rejoining Him when the soul re-ascended to be in the presence of God. Instead, the medieval church taught that damnation, which, as we have seen above, originally meant the loss of salvation, meant being cast into Hell and there suffering dreadful torments for all Eternity. Understood in this way, the doctrine of predestination is seen as so harsh and so cruel that it seems difficult to reconcile with the idea of a God of Love, or of a God whom Jesus asked to forgive those who know not what they do.

The idea of eternal hellfire is as primitive as it is barbaric. It is understandable that someone whose nature is such that he *cannot* receive the Grace of God might suffer the *fate* of being without God's presence, but it is a dreadful notion that this fate should be a *punishment* when the "sin" is not the result of choice but, as it were, of a psychic constitution.

The idea that only a small minority are worthy enough to be chosen for salvation is certainly very rigorist, assuming as it does that most people are not capable of accepting the Grace of Christ's sacrifice, however, the concept of predestination as such, properly understood, is perhaps not as harsh and intolerant as it may appear.

Let us take as an example the teacher or the social worker who might look at a young man and say, "I can see what is going to happen to him. He comes from an utterly deprived background. His father is a bully who sets a terrible example of violence; his mother is totally neglectful. In addition, the boy is of subnormal intelligence and is easily led. I am afraid he is likely to end up in prison, and that will only make him still worse. I would like to save him from this fate. I try to do my best to show him a better way. I show him affection because I feel so sorry for him, but I know that this is all quite unavailing." The teacher or social worker foresees what will happen, but he does not determine it. He may of course make a mistake. He may overlook the young delinquent's capacity to respond to a really inspired individual or his inner determination to make something better of himself which needs maturity to develop. If the young man turns out in the end to be a success in life after all, the teacher may well say, "Well, I am surprised. I obviously didn't know him as well as I thought I did."

If God is omniscient, however, He would know the young man through and through, and there are no surprises. In that sense He, too, foresees, but does not determine what will happen to him. Unfortunately Luther and Calvin would be so seized of the omnipotence and inscrutability of God that they *did* teach that He not only foresees but also preordains the fate of individuals.[13]

The doctrine of predestination, both in its theological forms and in the secular form given above, is a bleak one. Most of us do not like the idea that we are so tightly programmed, either by God or by our individual make-up. Quite apart from the difficulty we may have in accepting a God who at best seems to write off so much of humanity as irredeemably lost and at worst inflicts dreadful punishments on it into the bargain. We like to think[14] that we have at least *some* choice, and at least some free will. It is true that many times in our lives we have had the experience which St Paul described as being driven to do

13 For Luther and Calvin, see chapter 20 below.

14 The extent to which that is "wishful thinking" will be examined later - see p. 134 below. The question has been raised by philosophers down the ages, not always in a theological context, but also when philosophers examine the way we actually make decisions.

that which the "I" did not want to do, but at least as often we have felt that the "I", sometimes by a personal effort of will, has managed to do the right thing rather than yield to the temptations of doing the wrong thing. When it has been the result of a struggle, we would like to take some credit for our decision. Likewise, we hesitate to accept as a general rule that anyone yielding to temptation couldn't help it and therefore does not deserve blame.

We have seen that Augustine, with some difficulty, kept free will and predestination in a theoretical balance, and the official teaching of the Catholic Church has done the same. But because Augustine gave such weight to the idea of predestination, he has generally been particularly associated with that side of the balance. In practice, the Catholic Church came to lay more stress on free will than on predestination – perhaps because it felt that the idea of predestination as commonly understood might discourage Christians from making the effort to achieve salvation by "works". Over the centuries the concept of "works" became increasingly coarse. Initially, the word had meant not only good works which one performed towards one's neighbour or towards the Church, but perhaps more importantly also the work one did on oneself – the attempt, for example, to overcome the Seven Deadly Sins within oneself. Eventually, there was too much emphasis on "works" that helped the Church in cash terms. In the end, the donation of money to the Church was counted as good work that would contribute towards salvation or towards shortening the time that the donors or their loved ones would have to spend in Purgatory. A decadent Papacy itself sold Indulgences, documents granting remission of sins in recognition of a material penance that had been paid by the purchaser.

In reaction against such abuses some Christians went back to Augustine and stressed what he had had to say about the connection between predestination and salvation by grace – namely, that "Works" by themselves, even when interpreted in the original way, were not sufficient for salvation; however freely undertaken, they could never by themselves remove the burden of Original Sin; the help of Grace was needed and God knew that most people, thinking that they could gain and indeed merit salvation by their good works alone, did not know that they lacked the necessary humility to accept the unmerited grace which alone made salvation possible. The Calvinists are the most famous, but not the only group of these Augustinian Christians, and as the Catholic Church by that time was putting excessive emphasis on salvation by works and on free will, so the Calvinists, for their part, tended to put excessive weight on salvation by grace and on predestination.

Nevertheless, the Calvinists demonstrated in practice that the idea of salvation by grace in no way discouraged them from making the most strenuous efforts to do good works and to live Christian lives. They did not use the doctrine of predestination to excuse themselves from any effort to struggle with their fallen nature.

I suggest that that is a sensible secular view also. Most of us are aware of our imperfect nature and most of us do our best to overcome it; the more understanding among us know that not only we but also our fellow human beings often struggle in vain. If we are lucky, we are strong enough to succeed in that struggle more often than not. Where, hopefully, some of us differ from the Calvinists is that we are not so judgmental and realize that our compassionate understanding should go out to those who are doomed to fail. We need not be religious to realize that many of those unfortunates live – in this world – in a hell of their own.

Augustine's emphasis on the complex of Original Sin, predestination, and salvation by Grace found a powerful critic in his contemporary Pelagius.

Pelagius (*ca.* 355 to *ca.* 425) was a Welsh-born monk who came to live in Italy in the year 400. He challenged the whole idea of an Original Sin being passed on by Adam and Eve to all future generations through the reproductive process. Instead, they had, by their disobedience to God, set a bad example to mankind, which their heirs could choose to follow or to reject. He thought that the idea that we were helpless to decide whether to be slaves to sin or to be chosen for salvation bore the traces of Augustine's former Manicheism, in which mankind was nothing more than the passive battleground on which Good and Evil strove for victory. When God created humanity, He not only gave it commandments, but also the strength to obey them. The alternative, that He should have created mankind in such a way that it was constitutionally unable to obey His commandments and then be punished on top of it, ran absolutely counter to the idea of a God who was righteous and wanted all men to be saved. So we were not sinful from birth, and death was not the punishment for Original Sin, but simply a biological necessity.

We can, therefore, achieve salvation by our own efforts. We must follow the supreme example of Jesus rather than the bad example set by Adam. God does offer grace to help the efforts we make. Pelagius compared it to the sending of a wind which helps the oarsman; it is a reward for our efforts, whereas Augustine had stressed that our Original Sin is so great that God's Grace is *unmerited.*

The battle between the Augustinians and the Pelagians was prolonged and bitter, and in the heat of the battle Augustine came to lay more and more stress on the predestination and less and less on the free will aspect of his earlier teaching. Over a period of twenty years a series of church councils debated the issue. Some decided one way, some the other, but the final victory lay with Augustine: in 431 the Council of Ephesus finally declared Pelagianism a heresy.

One does wonder why the Church eventually rejected what may seem the more seductive theory of Pelagius for that of St Augustine. Was it perhaps because by this time the idea that Jesus was the Saviour and not merely a great teacher was so deeply entrenched that it could not be challenged? Was it because Augustine's teaching rested so firmly on St Paul, whose authority stood so high? Irrespective of whether one thinks that the Council of Ephesus made the right or the wrong decision, there is no doubt that by accepting the very heavy emphasis which Augustine was by that time putting on predestination, it took a position counter to what most Christians (and not only they) would like to think. It is true, as has been mentioned above, that we acknowledge the many occasions when we seem to have been incapable of doing what we know we ought to have done and indeed may have wished to do, but to put all the emphasis on that, and to play down the element of free will, runs counter to other parts of what we think is our experience. The belief that we have some freedom of choice, that we are responsible for our failures as well as for our successes rather than that whether we fail or succeed is predestined, lies deep in human beings. For that matter, it also lies deep in the instinctive attitudes of authorities who, by and large, were unwilling, at least until the twentieth century in the liberal West, to grant their subjects the excuse that they could not help committing offences. Parents, teachers, mag-

> istrates and other authority figures tend to hold us responsible for our misdeeds and tend to praise us (and not God) for our virtues. This is, I think, one reason why the Catholic Church, after having sided with Augustine, in practice behaved increasingly as if it had sided with Pelagius and, as has been shown above, laid more stress on free will and on works than on predestination and on grace.

Once the Council of Ephesus had finally decided for Augustine, he called in the imperial authorities to root out Pelagianism wherever it existed.

Coercion and the Role of the State

This appeal to the state reflected two further elements in Augustine's thinking. The first was that excommunication of heretics was not sufficient; once excommunicated, they must also be rooted out. We have seen that Ambrose had already demanded that the state should not tolerate any religion other than Christianity. Now Augustine came, after some hesitation, to sanction the use of force to destroy heresy – nor were the Pelagians his only victims.[15] True, he deplored torture, "unnecessary" violence and capital punishment.[16] The force used against heretics was to be applied in the spirit of a loving father against an errant son. It was for the latter's own good, but also to protect the orthodox against becoming infected with heresy and thereby having their souls imperilled. He justified all this by a most extreme interpretation of the parable in Luke 14, in which the master of a house, whose feast was poorly attended by those he had invited, gave orders that his servants should "compel them to come in". Therefore, although he would have been appalled by the burning of heretics such as would become the practice of the state at the behest of the Inquisition in later centuries, Augustine is the first articulator of the persecuting church. This marked the final abandonment of the Hellenic spirit, in which questioning of received opinions was accepted as a primary intellectual virtue. Henceforth it was considered a serious spiritual failing which was to be punished and destroyed, if all else failed, by force.

The second element was that this force was to be exerted by the state at the behest of the Church. This demand, too, had already been made by Ambrose, but Augustine gave it a more detailed philosophical underpinning. He went back to Cicero: the just State must be based on justice and that meant that the

15 Another group of heretics whom he persecuted were the Donatists, named after their founder, Bishop Donatus. These had begun by challenging the validity of ordinations carried out by a group of bishops who had lapsed from Christianity during the persecutions of the Emperor Domitian (303 to 313). They then extended that challenge to ordinations carried out by any bishops whose lives they considered less than perfect. The sacraments, they argued, must not be bestowed by clergy who were defiled by sin. Augustine stressed that the sacraments were a gift of God and were independent of the worthiness or otherwise of those who dispensed them. In any case, the clergy are as burdened by Original Sin as the rest of mankind, and a sinless channel for the sacraments was therefore not available in any case.

16 The Jews, for example, should be allowed to exist, albeit in an oppressed condition, as living witnesses to the truth of Christianity. This "Doctrine of St Augustine" would be the official line taken by both western and eastern Christianity in respect of the Jews. Officially, the medieval Papacy, though it constantly urged secular governments to isolate the Jews and keep them out of any positions of influence, regularly condemned the murderous attacks which the mobs made on Jews during the Middle Ages.

state must do justice to God also and give Him what is His due. A just state is therefore a Christian state. It must be subordinate to a Christian purpose as it is explained by the Church.

Like St Paul and Ambrose, Augustine would not sanction rebellion against an unjust state. Order was too important to him, even in an unjust state the powers that be were still ordained of God, and the punishment of such a state must be left to God. Augustine interpreted the Sack of Rome by Alaric's Goths in 410 as a punishment, for the emperors' inability to root out paganism altogether. There had been riots against edicts to close down the pagan temples, and then, as Rome was being threatened by the barbarian armies, many pagans made special sacrifices to the gods under whom Rome had once become great, to induce them to protect the city from the barbarians. When Rome was sacked all the same, the pagans blamed it on the neglect of the old patron deities of Rome and claimed that if the emperors continued to support Christianity, the same fate would befall the rest of the Empire in due course.

It was to defend Christianity against this charge that Augustine embarked on one of his most famous works, *Civitas Dei* (The City of God.) In that book, his immediate answer was to point out that many of the barbarians were already Christians (albeit Arians) and had generally spared the churches and basilicas. Augustine took this as proof that God had chosen Christians to chastise the pagans.

Civitas Dei, which took thirteen years to write, developed into something much larger than a mere temporary polemic. Indeed, in the course of it he wrote that what had happened to the earthly city of Rome was not so very important in the context of his theory that Man was a citizen of both an earthly city and a heavenly one. The primary significance for each Christian lay in his membership of the City of God (which is expressed by his membership of the Church) and this would inform him of his duty as a member of the Earthly City. Clearly his duty as a member of the City of God was paramount. The Earthly City had only an ephemeral existence; secular empires had risen and fallen ever since the beginning of time and would continue to do so to the end of time, only the City of God was eternal. The Christian did have a duty to actively participate in the Earthly City. The Cynics and the Epicureans had lost so much faith in politics that they had advocated the withdrawal of the wise man into his own concerns.[17] Even Origen had advised that the Christian should not involve himself in politics, but should play an active part only in the "divine nation", which was the Church. In Origen's day (185 to 254) the state was still pagan and actually allowed no participation by an active Christian. The situation was quite different in Augustine's time. The Empire was now officially Christian, and that gave the Christian both the opportunity and also the duty to keep it up to the mark (though of course always stopping short of rebellion). Ambrose had already put this doctrine most vigorously into effect. Now Augustine drew on the philosophical inheritance from the Stoics and in particular from Seneca,[18] with their concepts of duty to the worldwide brotherhood of man, and he gave to this inheritance the theological dimension of duty

17 see pp. 59 and 62 above.

18 see pp. 70 and 73 above.

to God and, through Him, to all those who were already, or who might become, members of the Christian community.

Western society had become officially Christian in Augustine's lifetime, and during the many centuries that it remained so, his thought would be the principal yardstick against which the standards of private and public life would be measured. It would justify not only battles against heresy within Christendom, but also war against the Infidels during the Crusades. We think of the *Jihad* as a specifically Islamic concept of struggle that continues until the whole world is won for the faith, but the philosophy of Christianity during the centuries after Augustine was not so very different.

CHAPTER 14

Realism and Nominalism

The barbarian invasions of southern and western Europe during the time of St Augustine ushered in what historians have called the Dark Ages. Graeco-Roman culture disappeared in the West, and so did the spirit of philosophical enquiry which had been such an essential part of that culture. There was no serious philosophical debate in western Europe for about 600 years. True, Charlemagne (768 to 814) encouraged learning to such an extent that we speak of a Carolingian Renaissance. In 781 he invited the Yorkshireman Alcuin (732 to 804) to his capital at Aachen where he became the focus of a group of scholars, but they were largely concerned with preserving and copying ancient classical manuscripts rather than using the texts as a challenge to develop new thinking. Even that impetus faded after the break-up of the Carolingian Empire in 843. Alcuin himself had left Aachen to become an abbot in Tours, where his main interest appears to have been revising the liturgy of the Frankish church.

Church scholarship was still totally dedicated to theology, and when philosophical debate did at last resume in the eleventh century, it was closely related to theological interests. The revival of philosophy was signalled by what, on the surface, seemed to be a repetition of the argument between Plato and Aristotle about universals and particulars - which are more significant? Plato, it will be recalled, had taught that the particular things we see - horses were the example we took - are only imperfect manifestations of the universal Idea of a horse, which, like all Ideas, is stored up in Heaven, and that it behoves the philosopher to try to understand the Ideas rather than to occupy himself with the "shadowy" appearances of the senses. Aristotle, on the other hand, had described universals not so much as Ideals stored up in Heaven, but rather as useful generalizations we can deduce froma number of particular instances before us - they are classifications, rather than Ideals. The names given to the medieval versions of these two philosophies were realism and nominalism. Realism was so called because its supporters maintained that universals were real, whereas the Nominalists held that they were only the names we chose to give to groups of phenomena, and had no independent "real" existence of their own.

This may be a little confusing to the modern general public which tends to think that it is not abstractions, but those things we see concretely before us in this world that are real, but we have to remember that the philosophy of the

Christian Church had arisen out of the Neo-Platonism which had so influenced Augustine. For Plato and Christianity the world of Ideas stored up in Heaven had always been more "real" than the world here below. Now, after an interval of some 600 years, Christian thinkers were picking up Plato again and described his approach as Realism.

For the Greeks, the debate over universals and particulars had been a means to clarify their understanding of this world. Aristotle's keen interest in the particulars of this world was beyond dispute, but Plato, too, had thought that, by grasping how particulars fell short of the Ideal, we could improve this world and by acquiring wisdom, we would certainly improve ourselves. For medieval Christian thinkers, what was paramount were the implications for theological orthodoxy, and the Church was officially committed to Realism. Thus, the Church itself was seen as a universal, and more real than the members which make it up. The Trinity itself was more real than its Three Persons thought of separately.

> We might do well in the twentieth century to remember that the names we give to clusters of ideas are just that and have no independent existence. Politicians in particular tend to reify (that is, to turn into actual things) abstractions like the Nation, the State, the People, the Church etc. These reified notions are then endowed with a personality, with a will of their own, with claims and demands which, wherever they come from, cannot come from abstractions, from mere names.

ANSELM OF CANTERBURY

The most famous exponent of Realism was the Piedmontese-born Anselm (1033 to 1109) who established his philosophical reputation as abbot of Bec in Normandy before he became Archbishop of Canterbury in 1093. He took the traditional Christian Neo-Platonist view that God is the embodiment of universal Goodness, Truth and Justice. (Note that Plato's "trinity" of Goodness, Truth and Beauty have become the Christians' Goodness, Truth and Justice. Christians tended to be suspicious of Beauty as a snare and a delusion, a distraction from the pursuit of virtue.)

Anselm is credited with first formulating the Ontological Proof[1] for the existence of God. This states that the very concept of Perfection (as embodied only in God) necessitates the existence of God for the essence of perfection is that it must also exist, as nonexistence is incompatible with perfection. Therefore our very conception of Perfection implies that Perfection must exist.[2]

> Few people would accept that argument today. We might perhaps go as far as to say that *if* there is something that is supremely perfect, *then* it must exist for the reasons that Anselm gives. The argument surely depends on the prior

1 Ontology is that part of philosophy which concerns itself with the "essence" of things. The word comes from the present participle of the Greek word for "to be". (The word "essence" itself comes from the Latin *esse* = "to be"). Anselm's idea was called the Ontological Argument only in the eighteenth century.

2 Anselm does not actually use the word "perfection". He writes "We believe that Thou art a Being than which none greater can be conceived." What could he mean by "greater"? To Descartes in the seventeenth century the greatness referred to by Anselm must mean Perfection. With that substitution, the Ontological Argument can be explained as briefly as I have done here.

> assumption that Perfection does exist outside this earth – for it clearly does not exist anywhere *on* earth.
>
> Even if Perfection did exist somewhere outside this earth, Anselm made further assumptions: we have to call it God, with all the various and often conflicting ideas that we attach to the word "God"; any Perfect Essence that might exist is also somehow involved in creating or organizing the world (imperfect as this world is!) and is in some way concerned with human behaviour (by way, for example, of judging it). Furthermore, in Anselm's thought-world, "God" also implied the whole Christian apparatus of belief: Incarnation, Trinity, the meaning and requirement of the Sacraments, and much else besides.

Anselm would not have been troubled by the arguments that have just been adduced. The Ontological Argument is an example of Natural Theology,[3] but Anselm believed that Natural Theology flowed from belief rather than led to it. As he memorably put it, *"Credo ut intelligam"* ("I believe so that I may understand"). He *began* with the faith, which for him required no proof, that God did exist, that He was Perfection, that He did create the world, did judge human behaviour, and did reveal Himself in the Bible and the decisions of Church Councils. Therefore, none of the considerations raised above would have disturbed him. He merely demonstrated that, with these certainties as data, the ontological argument added a philosophical argument to support what for him was already the truth.

> That seems to be a circular argument. Taking as data what you are trying to prove is hardly a respectable procedure. Nevertheless, the proof was accepted by many future philosophers – even Descartes in the seventeenth century, whose maxim was to take nothing for granted, would have recourse to it.[4] Although all proofs in Natural Theology raise problems, none are so *circular* as the Ontological Proof.

JEAN ROSCELIN

The Nominalist view - that universals are mere mental constructs - was, in Anselm's time, propounded by Jean Roscelin (*ca.* 1050 to *ca.* 1120). He expounded this theory in a letter to his pupil Peter Abélard; but otherwise very little is known about him - perhaps it was too unorthodox a view to be broadcast widely at that time; and we do know that Roscelin was already in trouble with the church authorities for his application of Nominalism to the Trinity. He taught that only the Father, the Son and the Holy Spirit actually exist: "God" was merely the name we have attached to this group, just as "Man" is merely the name we attach to several men. Roscelin was threatened with excommunication unless he retracted this view, and he recanted (1092).

The earliest version of Nominalism can be found in Aristotle's attack on Plato's Forms,[5] but there is no reason to think that Roscelin's ideas came from Aristotle, who had only just begun to make an impact in the Islamic world

3 see p. 78 above, where Natural Theology (a branch of Philosophy) is distinguished from Dogmatic Theology (which is based in the first instance on Revelation.)

4 see p. 221 below.

5 see p. 44 above.

through Avicenna (910 to 937)[4] and would not penetrate into Europe until around 1150. It was after Aristotle had been integrated into Christianity by Aquinas that, nearly two centuries after Roscelin, we will find the next powerful advocate of Nominalism in William of Ockham (*ca.*1290 to 1349) and Ockham's Nominalism will be considered when our History reaches that period.[5]

PETER ABÉLARD

Peter Abélard (1097 to 1142) steered a middle way between Realism and Nominalism, with a doctrine called Conceptualism according to which Universals and Particulars are equally real.

> Is that not a sensible and common sense conclusion to this debate? Do we really have to choose between Realism and Nominalism? Universals surely do have an existence independent of any embodiment in particulars, and this is perhaps especially clear in Mathematics. The concept of numbers or of figures like a triangle, for example, is quite independent of embodiment in any actual collection of things or actual triangles. That had impressed Plato and would still impress as sophisticated a philosopher of mathematics as Bertrand Russell. Likewise, we may go shopping for a table without a clear idea of exactly what kind of table we will come home with, but we will have a general concept of what we are looking for which is quite independent of any particular table we may see in the shops. But then can we really deny reality to the actual table we do bring home, whose reality we may have great difficulties in manoeuvring up the stairs? Wouldn't it be ridiculous to go along with William of Champeaux (1070 to 1121), the extreme Realist under whom Abélard had at one time studied? Champeaux would have maintained that this awkward piece of furniture was actually only a mirage. The brilliant pupil would eventually rout the teacher in debate.

Abélard seemed to criticize Anselm's position that we must start with belief in order to be able to understand. Abélard stressed that all dogmas should be capable of a rational explanation. The ordinary person may not be up to using his reason, and nothing should of course be done to shake Christian faith of simple people, but anyone who claims to be a philosopher must understand doctrines rather than accept on faith formulae which he cannot understand rationally. This view ran counter to the dominant tradition in Christianity. For the Church, the most authoritative thinker was still St Augustine, who had expressed reservations about the power of reason and had taught that faith was the most important foundation for belief.

Where church authorities contradicted each other, it was particularly necessary to call in reason to arbitrate. Abélard demonstrated that they frequently contradicted each other in a book called *Sic et Non* ("Yes and No"). There he set out a number of the dogmas of the Christian faith and then printed in parallel columns mutually contradictory statements on the dogma, drawn from the Bible and the Church Fathers, and, for good measure, from pagan philosophers also. The technique is not so very different from that which Talmudic scholars

4 see p. 124 below.

5 see Chapter 17 below.

had been using for some centuries, when they pitted the opinion of one revered rabbi against that of another. The Talmudic student thus becomes aware that authorities can differ and he has to make up his own mind on the issue before him. In one of his books, Abélard staged a debate (on ethics - see below) between a pagan, a Jew and a Christian, so it is more than likely that he was familiar with this way of handling religious discussions.

Abélard thought he understood the doctrine of the Trinity. In lectures in 1170, and a subsequent book, he propounded the theory that there is only one God, but that He manifests Himself as Power in the First Person of the Father, as Wisdom in the Second Person of the Holy Spirit and as Love in the Third Person as the Son - an idea which had perhaps been foreshadowed when Philo had interpreted the three visitors to Abraham as God manifesting Himself there in his three principal emanations of Power, Mercy and Justice.[8] This view might not have caused him any trouble had it not been for the nervousness of the orthodox church after the quite different and much more radical view of the Trinity that Roscelin had been compelled to retract in 1092, less than thirty years before.

Abélard was also very interested in the rational foundations of ethics, and he explored the common ground between pagan philosophers (though he did not know of Aristotle's *Nicomachean Ethics*) and Christians on that subject. Ethics, he concluded, are based on natural laws which can be discovered by reason, and it is that same Natural Law which also forms part of the Christian Revelation.

> Here again he showed an admirable openness to the virtues of pagan ethics. But it must be noted that he assumed that pagans and Christians would agree about a Natural Law that they both shared. That was certainly not true of all pagan philosophers, nor of course of most modern writers on ethics. We have already seen, for example, that Protagoras and the Sophists[9] and then later the Sceptics[10] had taught that there were no absolute moral laws; moral precepts were merely conventions that often differed between one society and another.

Presumably, Abélard accepted the orthodox doctrine of Original Sin which is our unchosen inheritance, but he had some interesting comments to make on the nature of those sins we subsequently commit by our own choice. Sin, he taught, does not lie in the *act* that is committed but in the *intention* with which it is committed. He criticizes sentences like "killing people is sinful", as they focus on the act and ignore the intention. If you focus on the intention, then killing is not always sinful. It is not sinful if it is accidental, if it is a punishment for certain crimes, or if it takes place in self-defence or in a "just war".

> Pacifists and penal reformers today would not allow two of those categories (though there are of course even today people who believe that capital punishment is just, and that the war against Hitler was indeed a "just war", which it was necessary to fight.) But we would all agree that no sin adheres to killing in

8 see note 6 on p. 87 above.

9 see p. 13 above.

10 see p. 65 above.

genuine self-defence or in genuine accidents (as distinct from killings resulting from avoidable carelessness as, for instance, by drunken driving).

Moreover, Abélard continues, someone is sinful only if he violates *his own* moral conscience. Violation of the moral conscience of other people is not *in itself* a criterion of sinfulness. Someone who genuinely believes that he is fulfilling what he believes to be the moral law, but who is *ignorant* of God's moral law, cannot be said to be sinful. He gave the example of the executioners who, when they crucified Jesus, believed that they were morally obliged to do their duty and to obey the orders of their masters.

Jesus seems to have made the same point when he asked God to forgive his executioners, "for they know not what they do". People of liberal temperament often say that they condemn the sin, but not the sinner (which seems to be a statement along the same lines, though in fact it runs counter to Abélard's insistence that sin is not to be found in the action as such). Some modern relativists would also agree with Abélard. They are reluctant to condemn those in other societies who, sincerely believing in an entirely different code of morality (sometimes based on religious beliefs, sometimes on nationalist fervour, sometimes on age-old cultural beliefs) behave in what, by our standards, is a totally immoral and sinful way.

The Nuremberg Tribunals decided not to accept such claims as an excuse for the defendants. They particularly rejected the arguments that the defendants were only obeying orders, or that they were morally bound by oaths of allegiance. Some of the accused were executed not only on the grounds of practical expediency (that this should act as a deterrent for future war criminals) but also because the evil they had committed was absolute and could not be excused by sincerely held ideologies or by obedience to superior orders. The philosophy behind all this was not only that there is a universal moral code which should be binding on all people (with which Abélard would have agreed) but also that those who grossly break it cannot under any circumstances shelter behind alternative codes (which runs counter to Abélard's teaching).

Abélard made many enemies with his insistence that no dogmatic formulae may be accepted by a philosopher on faith alone, and even more when he suggested that the executioners of Jesus might not have been sinful. His principal opponent was the formidable St Bernard of Clairvaux (1051 to 1153), austere founder of the Cistercian Order, immensely effective preacher of the Second Crusade in 1146, and a man whom Durant calls "arguably the most powerful man in Europe" who "made and unmade popes".[11] St Bernard fought Abélard's rationalism as "a blasphemous impudence"[12] and, misconstruing Abélard's views on the Trinity as propagating the idea of there being three gods, had his teaching declared heretical at a Church Council at Sens in 1140. Pope Innocent II then imposed perpetual silence on Abélard for the rest of his life.

However, one part of Abélard's work left an immensely important imprint on medieval philosophy. He had been a brilliant and popular teacher at Paris, with an international reputation and he had taught a particular method of dia-

11 Durant – *The Story of Civilization*, The Age of Faith, p. 791.

12 ibid. p. 790.

lectical exposition, developed further by his pupil Peter Lombard, which is now known as scholasticism. This involved a technique of argumentation which was to dominate the form of debates until the Renaissance. Essentially, a proposition would be put up for debate, such as, for example, "The will is free". Students were asked to begin by producing arguments for the negative, then they were required to produce objections to the negative ideas. Then came answers to the objections. Next, they produced arguments for the positive, which in turn would be followed by objections to the positive and answers to these objections. These procedures were highly formalized, and Thomas Aquinas in particular was to use and further refine them with immense brilliance. The technique was eventually abandoned because each stage was supported not only by the use of reason but in large part by adducing texts from the Scriptures and the Fathers.

> When these texts ceased to carry the authority that they had in the Middle Ages, the method was mocked, and to this day scholasticism is associated in the popular mind with "bandying texts" and with hair-splitting debates (such as "How many angels can dance on the point of a needle?").[13] Bandying texts is indeed no longer a respectable form of debate; today we back up our arguments not by quoting texts but by appealing to experience (or sometimes to the imagination). But scholasticism deserves a better reputation than it has. The principle of being forced to state and closely examine counterarguments to the propositions one wishes to advance can be nothing but healthy. It represents an utterly different approach from that of, say, St. Augustine, who, though intensely disputatious, did not, I think, have any respect for the arguments on the other side and was very ready to denounce them as heresies to be rooted out. Carried out in the proper spirit – with the built-in assumption that in the course of inviting and then meeting refutations, we will have to refine our original conceptions – Abélard's approach might even be considered as a forerunner to Karl Popper's now widely acclaimed Principle of Falsification.[14]

13 Texts that represented angels as incorporeal beings might be set against the Bible text that has Jacob wrestling with what was obviously a very physical angel. If angels are incorporeal, clearly an infinite number of them could dance on the point of a needle. If they are corporeal, even one would have the utmost difficulty in doing so. There is also a text of St Augustine, who believed that incorporeal angels could nevertheless take on a physical presence. The Encyclopaedia Britannica comments: "The problem has not been solved to the satisfaction of later theologians". That made it an excellent subject for scholastic disputation!

14 see pp. 557f below.

CHAPTER 15

Averroism

The Arabic Origins of the Thirteenth-Century Renaissance in Europe

Soon after the death of Mohammed in 632, Islam burst out of the Arabian peninsula on its spectacular career of conquest. After Mohammed's death, Islam was ruled by Caliphs - the Arabic word actually means "successor". Under the second Caliph, Omar I (634 to 644) Islam occupied Mesopotamia, Syria, Palestine and Egypt - areas in which Hellenistic culture had been strong and in which many traces of Greek learning were still alive. For several centuries the Islamic world was ruled from Baghdad, which the Caliphs had made their capital. By 711 the Muslims had overrun the whole of the northern coast of Africa and had crossed the Straits of Gibraltar into Spain. By 721 they had crossed the Pyrenees into the South of France, where they were finally halted and then slowly driven back. In 785 the Christians re-entered Spain and began its slow reconquest. By 1035 the Christian kingdoms of Aragon, León and Castile had established themselves in the northern half of Spain.

From the point of view of philosophy, this story is important because the Arabs were fascinated by the Greek culture they encountered in the Middle East. As we have seen, the western Europeans had retained little of Greek philosophy except Platonism, whose temper was felt to be akin to that of Christianity. Such secular texts as those on medicine by the Greek Galen (129 to 199), those on Geography and Astronomy by Galen's slightly younger Egyptian contemporary Ptolemy, and those on the sciences done by Aristotle had been lost to the West, but they were still circulating in the Middle East, and the Arabs were very interested in them. In Baghdad, the Caliph Haroun al-Rashid (786 to 809) organized the systematic translation of Greek works into Arabic. This was done under the supervision of the Nestorian scholars, the successors of the refugees from Alexandria in the middle of the fifth century.[1] Around 970, a group of Arabic scholars in Basra, known as the Brethren of Sincerity, issued fifty-seven tracts which amounted to a kind of encyclopaedia of science and religion such as they existed then in the Islamic world.

They did not neglect Plato and found, as the Christians had that Platonism has much in common with their monotheistic religious outlook; assimilating Plato presented relatively few problems to the faithful. Aristotle, besides presenting metaphysical views about Universals and Particulars, also opened up a world of secular studies that captivated these intellectuals. They were greatly impressed by his work on Logic, his encyclopaedic knowledge and his applica-

1 see p. 104 above.

tion of reason in explaining the natural world. They found all this so valuable that they felt compelled to integrate it with Islamic theology. They were the first people to concern themselves with the perennial problem: what is the relationship between science and religion?

> The question would come up again and again. One such occasion, for example, revolved around Darwin's Theory of Evolution in the nineteenth century, which is so much at odds with the Biblical story of Creation. Fundamentalists totally rejected Darwinim, but those Christians who were persuaded by Darwin's arguments were somehow forced to assumilate them into their religious view of the world. This would involve looking on the biblical Creation story as conveying the truth not in a literal, but in an allegorical or poetic way. Many Christians, then and since, have found it possible to remain Christian and at the same time accept the Theory of Evolution and other scientific challenges to the literal truth of the Book of Genesis. The effort to integrate Aristotle with Islam was a prototype of this kind of assimilation.

In pursuit of that synthesis the Islamic thinkers did not initially display that nervousness which the Christian Church since Augustine had shown towards secular studies or towards excessive reliance on reason. There are many kinds of philosophy, but these Islamic scholars used the word *Falsafah* (philosophy) exclusively for this attempt to synthesize Aristotelianism with theology. They called themselves *faylasuphs,* with the same assurance with which eighteenth century French philosophers will appropriate to themselves the name of *philosophes* - as if their opponents were not worthy of the name. The greatest exponent of the new ideas, Ibn Sina, who is known in the West as Avicenna (980 to 1037) referred to Aristotle quite simply as "The Philosopher".

Avicenna was born in Bokhara and was a doctor, philosopher and courtier. He was also a prolific writer. His two most important books were the *Kitab ash-Shifa (The Book of Healing),* a vast eighteen volume philosophical and scientific encyclopaedia which has been described as "probably the largest work of its kind ever written by one man", and *The Canon of Medicine,* which the same source [1] calls "the most famous single book in the History of Medicine both East and West". Throughout he treated all questions with reason only, even those with religious implications. His theology is a prime example of "Natural Theology".[2] Throughout the history of ideas we will see repeatedly that rationalist philosophers will be met with a backlash from the orthodox, the mystics or the romantics. In St Bernard's attack on Abélard we have already seen an example - there are many more to come - in the Christian world. The backlash in the Muslim world against Avicenna is associated with Abu Hamid Al-Ghazali (1058 to 1111). He had distinguished himself as a teacher of *Falsafah* in Baghdad, but in 1095 he had what appeared to be a nervous breakdown, which, in a later autobiography, he adduced to his having lost faith in the capacity of reason to support religion. He then fell back on a strand of mysticism which had existed in Islam since the eighth century and is known as sufism. In his book *The Destruction of Philosophy (Tahafut al-Filasifa)* he "turned all the arts of reason

1 *The Encyclopaedia Britannica.*

2 see p. 78 above.

against reason",[4] brilliantly demolishing, by rational argument, the reliability of conclusions based on traditional rational procedures. David Hume would do much the same some seven centuries later[5] – though with very different intentions and results. Hume would demolish certainties based on mysticism just as effectively as he demolished the conclusions reached by traditional rational arguments.

By and large, Al-Ghazali won the battle against rationalism in the Islamic world, where he is considered the greatest Muslim after Mohammed. In 1150 the Caliph Mustanjid ordered all the works of the Brethren of Sincerity and of Avicenna to be burnt. But by then one last great Islamic champion of Aristotle and of rationalism had been born in Cordoba in Spain: he was Ibn Rushd, who is referred to in the West as Averroës (1126 to 1198). He took direct issue with Al-Ghazali's book, entitling his own work *Destruction of the Destruction (Tahafut al-Tahafut)*. In it he reaffirmed the value of rationalism, but, to ward off attacks from the orthodox, he did not take direct issue with religious doctrines that could not be based on reason and which, in any case, were of value to the unlettered. The philosopher may interpret sacred texts allegorically and in this way the texts can often yield philosophical truths. But sometimes no such interpretation is possible, and in such a case Averroës took refuge in what came to be called – mainly by Christians – the "two-fold truth" theory: some propositions are "true" in theology but "false" in philosophy. Nevertheless, propositions in philosophy can be valid in their own right, even when they may be considered "false" in the light of theology.

> This amounts to an admission that "theological truths" cannot be treated by the rules of reason. Ironically, this is exactly what theological opponents of rationalism also maintain, though they will say it assertively where Averroës perhaps put the point defensively. A pure rationalist might describe Averroës' "two-fold truth" theory as something of a cop-out. One suspects that Averroës was more interested in expounding Aristotle than he was in a serious effort to integrate him into Islam.

Averroës kept references to Islamic dogma to a minimum. Even so, in 1194 he was banished from Marrakesh (where he was then living)[6] for his opinions and most of his writings were condemned to the flames. By this time, however, many of his works had already been translated into Latin and were, as we shall see in the next section, beginning to affect Christian thought far more significantly than they ever affected the development of Islam.

Nine years after the birth of Averroës, Cordoba saw the birth of another philosopher, the great Jewish teacher Moses ben Maimon, better known as Maimonides (1135 to 1204). The two never met because, in 1148, when Maimonides was only thirteen (and Averroës only twenty-two) he and his family had to flee from Cordoba which was captured that year by the fundamentalist and fiercely anti-Jewish Almohad Berbers from North Africa. Maimonides would do for Judaism what Averroës tried to do for Islam – integrate Aristotelianism into the Jewish religion. There had been two great Jewish

4 Durant – The Story of Civilization – The Age of Faith, p. 332.

5 see Chapter 27.

6 He was allowed to return four years later, just before his death. His tomb is in Marrakesh.

philosophers before his time, the Neo-Platonist Philo of Alexandria (25 BC to AD 40) and Ibn Gabirol (ca.1021 to 1050) but these had largely been ignored by Jews and had had much more influence on Christianity;[7] philosophy had been largely neglected by the Talmudists. Indeed, Jewish religious teachers have always kept even theological speculation to a minimum. Doctrinal issues that have no bearing on human conduct were not of great interest to the Talmudists. In the Talmud, the character of God is assumed rather than argued; there is no systematic theology, there are hardly any credal debates or definitions,[8] and of course the Jews were mercifully spared such zestful controversies as wracked the Christian churches over the Trinity.

Maimonides thought that the function of the Talmud was not merely to lay down rules of conduct, but to express philosophical truths. In 1190 he published *A Guide for the Perplexed* (originally in Arabic, but it would soon be translated into both Hebrew and Latin). The foreword makes it clear that it was written for the educated perplexed – those who had some intellectual difficulties with Jewish laws or other passages in the Bible. He, too, says that anthropomorphic passages and many stories found in the Bible should be taken not literally but allegorically. He explained several Jewish ritual laws in their historical context, but stressed their continuing validity even if the historical context in which they were first formulated no longer obtained. They are divine commandments, and faith in God therefore compels obedience to them. He seems to have been a far more devout Jew than Avicenna or Averroës had been devout Muslims and he probably attached more importance to his Commentaries and Codifications of the Talmud than he attached to the *Guide for the Perplexed*, but he does stress that the religion of the Talmud cannot be at odds with the truths of reason and of philosophy, and, like his Islamic contemporaries, it was the philosophy of Aristotle which he valued most highly.

Maimonidean thought would experience the same kind of opposition from within Judaism that rational approaches had encountered from within Christianity and Islam. In Judaism, the opposition came from traditional Talmudists and also from the mystical tradition of the Kabbalah.[9] As in the Muslim world,

7 For Philo, see pp. 85ff. Ibn Gabirol lived in Saragossa and later in Granada. His original writings in Arabic no longer exist, but a book of his was translated into Latin in the twelfth century under the title *Fons Vitae* and under the name of Avicebron. This work would have a great influence on Christians and hardly any on Jews. It is so wholly lacking in Jewish content or terminology that it was not realized that Avicebron was Jewish. In 1846 a French scholar discovered a thirteenth century translation of his book from Arabic into Hebrew, and only then was it realized that Avicebron and Ibn Gabirol were one and the same person.

8 There was in fact no credal formulation until one was produced by Saadiah Gaon (882 to 942), some six hundred years after the Christians formulated the Nicene Creed in 325. Maimonides himself produced the more famous Thirteen Articles of Faith in 1168.

9 The Kabbalah (the Hebrew word means "Reception" or "Tradition") has very ancient roots, going back to the mystical visions in the Book of Ezekiel. It had two strands: a purely visionary strand which can scarcely be the subject of philosophy, and a more intellectual strand which has something in common with Neo-Platonism in that it produces an elaborate system of emanations (or "sefirot") coming from God. In the twelfth century this latter strand was greatly reinforced by an influential book published in Provence, the "Book of Brightness" or *Sefer ha-Bahir*, and in the thirteenth by the "Book of Brilliance" or *Sefer ha-Zohar*, known as the "Zohar" for short, which was published in Spain. The Sefiroth form a link between this world and God, and in an ideal world the flow from God to Man and from Man back to God would be uninterrupted. But this is not an ideal world because of the existence of evil (sitra achra), to which the Kabbalists ascribed a dynamic power in its own right. As the result of the existence of evil, one of the Sefirot, the Shekhina, is trapped in this world, and the free flow between God and Man and

the Orthodox and the Mystics won the struggle. During the century after the death of Maimonides, various Jewish religious authorities in Spain, France and Germany banned his writings. His commentaries on Jewish law were replaced by a new Codex early in the fourteenth century and the study of philosophy was prohibited at about the same time. The last edition of the *Guide for the Perplexed* for three hundred years was published in the fifteenth century, and when the Jewish authorities republished it in 1743, during the Age of Reason, they banned anyone from reading it before the age of twenty-five.

During those centuries Averroës and Maimonides made very little impact on the Muslim and Jewish world, but their influence on Christian philosophy was considerable, as we shall see.

The Impact of Averroism on Christian Europe

We saw at the beginning of the last section that the Christians had begun the slow reconquest of Spain in 785. Three hundred years later, they recaptured Toledo (1085) and for the next century and a half, before another surge (1212 to 1492) finally destroyed the Moorish kingdoms, one half of the Iberian Peninsula was under Christian rule and the other under Islamic rule.

During that period of relatively peaceful coexistence there was a good deal of cultural contact between the two parts of Spain. In the South, Cordoba, the city of Averroës, was one great centre of Islamic learning and in the North, Toledo, the capital of Castile, was to become a similar centre for Christian scholarship. Translations of Arabic texts into Latin began there in the eleventh century and gathered pace after 1150 and especially in the reign of King Alfonso X of Castile (1252 to 1284) when Archbishop Raymond of Toledo set up a College of Translators in the capital. From that centre, the translated texts were diffused all over the Christian world.

At first, most interest was aroused by the medical and scientific texts which the Arabs had translated from the Greek. Galen was translated from Arabic into Latin at the end of the eleventh century as was Aristotle's *Physics*. For the enthusiastic students and teachers of medicine in places like the medical schools of Bologna, the natural next step was to explore what else Aristotle and Averroës had written. Bologna, for example, became such a famous centre of Averroism that there was a saying that wherever you found three of its doctors, you would find that two of them were atheists (*ubi tres medici, duo athei*)

> Strictly speaking, Averroism or, for that matter, Aristotelianism, were not philosophies of atheism, if by atheism we mean, as we do today, an assertion that there is no God. We have seen that Aristotle's philosophy asserted the existence of God both as the First Cause and also as the Final Cause[10] – that the world was set going according to his plan, and that he had implanted in nature the goals towards which it should be striving; but this God was completely impersonal, did not require to be worshipped, was not interested in how peo-

between Man and God is interrupted. It is the responsibility of every individual to make every effort, by piety and meditative prayer, to restore this flow, to repair (*tikkun*) the disharmony that exists in this world, and to free the Shekhina. Within this relatively simple outline of the doctrine, however, there was a mass of esoteric symbolism and a fascination with the mystical significance of individual numbers and letters ("Gematria").

10 see p. 48 above.

ple behaved, and did not reward or punish. For believing Christians, such a God was not really a God at all so people who held this Aristotelian view were then readily described as atheists.

It was not long before Aristotelianism confronted Christianity with the same challenges with which Islamic theologians had contended. Even the Koran itself, first translated into Latin in 1156, was a challenge, presenting a religion without the complications of the Incarnation and the Trinity. (Judaism had of course done this, too, but it presented its own complications in its elaborate ritual requirements.)

When the translated works of Aristotle and the Islamic commentaries on him first reached the schools of Paris (shortly to be given university status in 1215) the first reaction of the Christian authorities was to ban them (1210). In 1215 the ban was somewhat relaxed - Aristotle's works on Ethics and on Logic were exempted.[11] In 1231 the ban on the remainder of Aristotle's thought was described as a holding operation while scholars were sifting through them. By 1255 Aristotle's *Physics* and *Metaphysics* had actually become required reading at the Sorbonne, the new college which had been founded within the University of Paris two years earlier and which would soon become the pre-eminent guardian of theological orthodoxy in France. At the Sorbonne Siger of Brabant was now the leading exponent of Averroism.

One has the feeling that by this time intellectuals may have come to feel unduly confined by the warnings that the study of subjects which we now broadly call scientific was a danger to the health of the soul – at best a diversion from thoughts that ought to concentrate on spiritual matters, and at worst a threat to religious teaching. Perhaps an awareness was growing that after all there is a world outside, a world, moreover, that had been created by God, that God had equipped us with reasoning faculties, and that perhaps He had done this to enable us to study and understand His handiwork. It is difficult to know whether this feeling created the interest in Aristotelianism or whether the discovery of the enormous richness of Aristotelianism created that feeling. At any rate, it marks a significant moment in the history of European thought after the nearly 800 years during which secular studies had been discouraged by the Church.

As in Islam, there was a powerful backlash against Averroism. It was led by the Franciscan St John of Bonaventura (1221 to 1274). Like St Augustine, St John of Bonaventura was distrustful of the study of any question which had no connection with God and no place for Christ. He condemned the use of reason in trying to understand religion. Arguments like the Ontological Argument[12] could never understand the real nature of God as the proofs of God's existence are based on His effects on the Soul rather than on rational demonstrations. The man of faith and the mystic have a better knowledge of God than the philoso-

11 There were now three philosophies of Logic: that part of Aristotle's work which had been translated by Boethius (now known as *logica vetus*) together with the four books now translated from the Arabic (*logica nova*) were now together called *logica antiqua*; and this was distinguished from the *logica moderna*, dealing with areas which had not been touched by Aristotle at all. *Logica moderna* played close attention to the different meanings which quite simple parts of language may carry – a concern with language which seems to anticipate some of the more difficult ideas of twentieth-century linguistic philosophers. See David Luscombe - *Medieval Thought*, p.78

12 see p. 116 above.

pher. Reason could not fathom the mysteries of the Christian religion – the Incarnation, the Trinity, the Virgin Birth, or the Resurrection. Was there not a danger that if Reason could not fathom these mysteries, it might actually undermine them?

Étienne Tempier, the Bishop of Paris, agreed with St John of Bonaventura. In 1269 he condemned as heresies thirteen propositions allegedly taught by certain professors at the Sorbonne, and a fresh condemnation in 1277 enlarged that number to 219. According to those pronouncements, the following ideas were widely taught in Paris (and in Italy also): natural law rules the world without interference from God; there is no Free Will; Heaven and Hell are priestly inventions to force people into good behaviour; happiness is obtained in this life, not in another; the soul of the individual dies with the body; there is no reason to believe in a bodily resurrection; God is the goal of creation, but not its cause.

Some exponents of such ideas protected themselves by adopting the "two-fold truth" theory.[13] Siger did not: he claimed only to be expounding Aristotle, without affirming that his ideas were true, and he protested his belief in all the dogmas of the Church. That did not save him from being personally accused of heresy in 1276. He fled from Paris to Italy, where he was murdered by a madman in 1282.

But the struggle was not over. If the Franciscans of this period fell back on mysticism, the Dominicans looked to reason to reconcile Christian teaching with the new learning. Their leading figure was initially Albert Magnus (1201 to 1280), though he would soon be overshadowed by his most famous pupil, Thomas Aquinas.

Albert was born in Germany, studied in Padua, and taught first in Paris and then in Cologne. He expounded the whole of Aristotle with an Averroist commentary. His reading was immense and it could be said that he did for Christian Europe what Avicenna had done for the Islamic world. He produced an encyclopaedic compilation of knowledge from all sources – from the ancient Greeks, from the Neo-Platonists, from the Islamic Averroists and from Maimonides. Indeed, he quoted Moslem thinkers so extensively that he is an important source for our knowledge of Arabic philosophy.

He did set limits to the acceptance of Aristotle. "He recognized Aristotle as the highest authority in science and philosophy, Augustine in theology, the Scriptures in everything." However, "his immense mound of discourse is poorly organized and never becomes a consistent system of thought. ... [But] he accumulated the storehouse of pagan, Arabic, Jewish and Christian thought and argument, from which his famous pupil drew for a more lucid and orderly synthesis. Perhaps without Albert, Thomas would have been impossible."[14]

13 see p. 125 above.

14 Durant – *The Story of Civilization – The Age of Faith*, p. 961.

CHAPTER 16

Thomas Aquinas

Thomas Aquinas (1225 to 1274) was born of a German family in Southern Italy, his father was the Count of Aquino. In 1239 he went to the University of Naples which, as we have seen, was then a stronghold of Averroism. In 1244 he entered the Dominican Order which had been founded in 1215 by St Dominic, and had by this time become associated (though not exclusively so) with theological scholarship. In 1245 Thomas went to Paris to continue his studies. There he was taught by Albert Magnus, and when Albert moved to Cologne in 1248, Aquinas followed him and spent four more formative years as his pupil, before returning to teach in Paris in 1252. His lectures there on the philosophy of Aristotle already attempted to reconcile it with Christianity. In 1259 he moved to Italy to teach in papal schools in and near Rome and there he met William of Moerbeke. He was one of the rare scholars at that time who knew Greek. At Aquinas' request, he made Latin translations directly from Aristotle's Greek so that it could now be studied free from the gloss that Arabic scholars like Avicenna and Averroës had put upon him.

The Papacy was alarmed at the spread of Averroism in Italy and in France. Aquinas, too, believed that the Averroist versions of Aristotle that Siger of Brabant was then expounding in Paris were a danger to the faith, but, unlike St John Bonaventura, Aquinas felt that Catholic theology must be able to accommodate what was of value in Aristotelianism, and he persuaded the Pope that "Aristotle could be sterilized". In 1268 Pope Clement IV sent him back to Paris to combat Siger and Averroism there, and for the rest of his life Aquinas was engaged in constructing a powerful synthesis between faith and reason. We will see that this synthesis will meet with criticism, notably from the three great Franciscans, St John of Bonaventura, Duns Scotus and William of Ockham. The Dominicans adopted Thomism as their official philosophy in 1278, and with the canonization of Aquinas in 1323 the Catholic Church came down on the side of Thomism. Papal pronouncements as late as 1923 make it clear that Aquinas, known in the church as *Doctor Angelicus,* has formed the basis of orthodox Roman Catholic philosophy ever since.

The Thomist Synthesis of Faith and Reason

There are thirty-four volumes of his *Opera,* but his most famous works are the two *Summae*. First came the *Summa Contra Gentiles,* which he wrote between 1258 and 1264 and was intended to help Christians in their debates with Muslims, Jews, and heretics. The arguments he used here operate largely within natural reason,: citing "rational" proofs for the existence of God.[1] The *Summa Theologiae*, written between 1265 and 1273, was intended for Christian theology students. It dealt with the "supernatural truths" of Revelation, such as the Trinity, the Incarnation, Redemption and the resurrection of the dead at the time of the Last Judgment. Aquinas' fundamental position was that, whilst Revelation is *beyond* reason, it cannot be contrary to it. Durant puts the point like this:

> Just as it would be folly for the peasant to consider the theories of the philosopher false because he cannot understand them, so it is foolish for Man to reject God's revelation on the grounds that it seems at some points to contradict Man's natural knowledge. [2]

He rejected the idea of a "Twofold Truth", that a proposition can be true in faith but false in philosophy. All truth comes from God and is a seamless whole, a continuum which we can understand through two approaches - from above, by faith in Revelation, and from below, by reason. We must not be suspicious or afraid of secular knowledge, as it helps us to understand the world that God has created. God has given us reason because He expects us to use it to understand that part of the continuum which it is capable of grasping. Science, he wrote, is "a daughter of God", God is "the Lord of the sciences."[3] But there are mysteries, parts of the truth which mere reason cannot grasp - then Revelation takes over. Theology, the expounding of Revelation, is not opposed to but is the crown of science and philosophy. Everything that can be known is of one piece.

Reason can take us so far, then Faith takes over. To use a metaphor: God dwells on the literally infinitely remote peak of a mountain which reaches from earth to Heaven. Our Reason can take us up that mountain only as far as far as the clouds that lie far below the summit. It cannot pierce the clouds, but we have the Faith that the same mountain continues above the clouds.

> The metaphor of the mountain and the clouds is, as far as I know, my own. Though it may not have been used by Aquinas, the general idea behind the metaphor will be of enormous use to the churches in later centuries. Scientific thought would make great progress and human reason found out ever more about the way the world worked. This could be interpreted as God, so to speak, raising the cloud as we used our reason to ascend the mountain. The ultimate summit would always remain veiled, but as we climb the mountain, our faith is reinforced that the same kind of climb continues above the cloud. We will have to make some adjustments to our earlier ideas. Once we may have taken it on faith (which is above the cloud) that God had created the world quite literally in seven days. Now, as the cloud moves higher and our reason can understand that that was not exactly the time span within which

1 I wonder why such a summa had to be *"contra"* gentiles. Natural theology really concentrated on grounds that all monotheistic religions would have in common. There is no reason why devout Jews, devout Muslims or devout Christians should not all accept arguments from Natural Theology, such as, for example, the Ontological Argument for the existence of God. If such an argument were rejected by anyone, it would, on logical grounds and not on theological grounds, not because they ran counter to Jewish, Muslim or Christian ideas of God, but because a member of any one of these religions might wonder about the logical steps in that argument - for which see the discussion in connection with St Anselm's exposition, p. 132 above.

2 Durant - *The Story of Civilization - The Age of Faith*, p. 967

3 "Deus scientiarum dominus". But we should remember that "scientia" included, but at the same time was much wider than what we call the sciences today. The word was applied to all knowledge, rather like the German word *Wissenschaft*.

our world came into existence, we learn to interpret the Creation story in the Bible in a poetic or symbolic rather than in a literal manner.

Though the churches have initially tended to be alarmed by developments in science and have opposed Galileo and Darwin, this metaphor has enabled them, in due course, to accommodate most scientific progress. One reason that Thomism has proved such an enduring basis for Christian philosophy is that it makes such accommodation possible. The recent recovery of Greek knowledge had led to some raising of the cloud, but Aquinas could scarcely have anticipated how much further it would be raised in future centuries that were more prolific in scientific discoveries than was his own.

There are some people who imagine that one day nothing will any longer be hidden from man's reason and that faith is therefore completely unnecessary, but many scientists, as they have climbed the mountain and seen the cloud recede, and as they came to a better understanding of the infinitely complex and wonderful mechanism of "the world that God has made", have become almost *more* religious than they were before. It is all so beautifully put by Alexander Pope writing about Newton: "Nature and Nature's laws lay hid in night./*God* said, Let Newton be; and all was light." (For "in night", read here "above the cloud". God used Newton to raise the cloud to reveal more of the way His world worked.)

One of the great books that Maimonides had written was called *The Guide for the Perplexed*, and Maimonides had explained in his introduction that it was written not for the uneducated, but for those who had perplexities and difficulties about the intellectual side of religion. The Summae of Aquinas served the same purpose. Those unaccustomed to the use of reason will believe in the existence of God as a matter of faith and Aquinas stressed that that is itself a perfectly sound basis for belief.

An interesting question that, as far as I know, is not often asked by theologians is: why is faith a sound basis for belief. Why *ought* we to have faith? Why, as it were, should we have faith in faith? Those who already have it are not troubled by that question, they do not draw a distinction, as critics might, between belief and knowledge. The knowledge they have through faith is, for them, merely a different kind of knowledge from the one they have through logical argument, but it is nonetheless knowledge and not "mere" belief. They might say that this "faith-knowledge" rests on some kind of religious experience; that they have felt the presence of God, perhaps in their prayers, perhaps in contemplating the wonders of the world. They may see such a religious experience in somewhat the same way in which they see a musical experience – that it is totally convincing, but not in a rational way nor in a way that can be adequately communicated to others who do not share such an experience. Others may have "faith-knowledge" because it has not occurred to them to question the truth of the holy books.

What of those to whom faith has not been vouchsafed in such a manner, who are nevertheless told that they *ought* to have faith, and that there is something wrong with them if they do not have it? What arguments might be adduced to persuade them to accept something that they have not so far accepted either through reason or through faith?

Let us take the musical analogy a little further. Do tone-deaf or musically uneducated people accept that Bach produced the most wonderful music? Yes, they can hear the same notes that are heard by those who affirm that the music of Bach is sublime, but the sublimity escapes them. Is the unmusical person in the same position as the peasant who would be foolish to consider the theories of the philosopher false because he cannot understand them? Perhaps he should be humble and say, "I accept that Bach is a great composer because those more sensitive, more trained, more experienced than I am can hear in the notes a sublimity that I cannot hear. Lack of sensitivity to his music is a short-coming of mine. I envy those who can respond to Bach, and it is not condescension on their part to be genuinely sorry for those who miss out, perhaps through no fault of their own." Might it not be the same with acceptance of God and of that which He tells us through the Bible and through His creation? Just as the most musically sensitive people respond to Bach, so the most spiritually sensitive respond to God. The nonmusical person hears the same notes as the musical person, but cannot get the same significance out of them. Similarly, there are people who read the same text (the Bible) or receive the same signals (from Nature) but cannot read the inner meaning in them. It might be right then for such people to admit: "My reason cannot follow the clever arguments of natural theology, and my sensitivity is too blunt to experience those sublime and nonrational emanations that come from Him. Nevertheless, I trust those people whose intellectual or spiritual equipment is finer than my own; I *ought* to trust what those people tell me about God; and so, too, I *ought* to have faith that God exists, have faith in what He has revealed in the Bible, and lead my life accordingly."

A nonreligious person might answer by suspecting that faith in God, and especially in the sublime character ascribed to Him, is not so much a matter of sensitivity as of psychological need, a kind of wish-fulfilment or self-deception. Some people *need* to have such a faith, some the certainty, firm ethical guidance that religions claim to provide. They need to make some kind of sense of the world, to strengthen their ability to cope with it, to give expression to their hope for a world beyond this one and in which they may participate after their own death. Or the sceptic might suspect that mystical experiences could be hallucinatory, possibly the result of certain physiological processes brought about by dietary deficiencies, lack of sleep, or certain breathing techniques. We know, after all, that *some* experiences that are felt to be mystical can be induced by certain drugs and therefore do have a physiological basis. Such analyses clearly would have no faith in faith.

But no one could maintain that an acceptance of the sublimity of Bach's music represents any kind of wish-fulfilment. We simply recognize musical experience as being "true" and yet inexplicable and uncommunicable in rational terms. Perhaps we should keep our minds open to the possibility that religious experience (and the resulting faith in it) may sometimes be of a similar nature.

For Aquinas, knowledge of the existence of God does not rest on faith alone. The philosopher can demonstrate the existence of God by rational arguments, and he deployed, or adapted, the range of proofs which earlier classical philosophers and Christian theologians had already produced. These included the argument from design (if there is a plan to the world – and human reason has already understood parts of this plan – then there must be a planner); the closely related teleological argument (that where things seem to aspire towards a goal, we may assume that an intelligent being is directing that process); the Ontological Argument;[4] the related argument, already used by Plato and St Augustine, that the scale by which we measure that one thing is better

4 see p. 116 above.

than another thing implies a standard of supreme goodness which is the cause of goodness in all things;[5] the arguments of God as the First Cause and as the Unmoved Mover (that at the beginning of time "something" must have set the whole causal chain into motion, and, since motion must itself be caused by something, that first "something" cannot itself have been in motion and must therefore be an unmoved Mover.)

Such arguments might convince us of the existence of some kind of Deity, but of course they stop short of proving the truth of specifically *Christian* statements about God, the Incarnation, the Trinity and the rest. This is why Aquinas had said that reason can take us only so far. Beyond a certain point, faith in Revelation must take over.

He also pointed out that these proofs merely demonstrated that a Deity must exist, but he stressed that they can tell us nothing about His nature or His attributes; even Revelation leaves these as a mystery. Strictly speaking, the philosopher can only tell us what God is *not*. For example, He is not corporeal Frederick Coplestone writes, paradoxically, "the more predicates we can deny of God in this way, the more we approximate to a knowledge of him".[6] This way of understanding God is known as the *via negativa*.

> This view has an appeal to countless numbers of people who have some feeling about the existence of a Deity that is totally unlike anything we know on earth. As a result they are impatient with what is attributed doctrinally to God in the three monotheistic religions of the West, which, as we shall see, all in some way anthropomorphize God by describing His purposes and His activities.
>
> Some of these impatient people find themselves attracted by the religions of the East (Hinduism and Buddhism) which, at their most sophisticated level, aim to achieve (by contemplation rather than by prayer or other kinds of worship) the state of *Nirvana*. This is a state in which the devotees have emptied themselves from everything connected with this world. In that state they come close to being at one with the Principle that is itself emptied in this way, and that could therefore be understood by a kind of *via negativa*.

Aquinas knew that we do attribute qualities to God, such as Goodness, Truth, Love, Intelligence, Freedom and Power. This way of understanding Him is known as the *via positiva*. Aquinas said that we can speak of God in this way only by analogy with what we praise in human beings. Such qualities are present in Creation as pale reflections of these same qualities in God – they can give us no idea of their infinity in God Himself.

> Does Aquinas find himself in a dilemma here? If the philosopher can know nothing about the nature or attributes of God, if even the *via positiva* can speak of God only by using analogies and metaphor, what, then, is the status of the language of Faith, the language that declares that God relates to us, that He commands, that He "sent" His Son, that He saves or damns? We do

5 That seems a rather odd argument. We are more likely to decide that one thing is better than another with reference to how useful or harmful, pleasurable or painful it is to us than with reference to some supreme example of perfection

6 Frederick Coplestone – *A History of Philosophy*, Vol. II, p. 348. Aquinas goes on to warn us against thinking that, because God has no body, He lacks a body. God is so perfect that He can lack nothing. He is not less than a body, but more than body, in a way that we cannot possibly grasp.

not normally take metaphors literally; when we say that someone – say, a thinker – is a child of his time, we know we do not mean that Time has literally begotten the thinker. However, at the same time as Aquinas says that all our positive statements about God are only analogies, he also expects us to take literally the statement that God sent His Son to save us, that he was crucified and rose again on the third day.

The Easter story can be treated as a beautiful analogy or metaphor. A sermon could be preached on Easter Sunday to the effect that you cannot kill the truth; you may silence it for a while, but it will rise again. This is comforting knowledge, especially during periods of persecution. Aquinas following his warning about the limitations of the *via positiva* will not have this story to be true merely as a metaphor. He believes that it must be accepted on faith as the literal truth. It therefore appears to call into question Aquinas' model of the seamless continuum between reason and faith. What we are to take as literal truth appears not to be the natural progression from reason to faith but an actual contradiction of what he has said about the *via negativa* and the *via positiva*.

How did Aquinas end up in this position? Are we not driven to the conclusion that he simply could not envisage abandoning ideas which the Christian Church had taught as truth for so many centuries and which were so deeply embedded in the thought-world of Aquinas and his contemporaries that they simply could not be questioned? It is perhaps only in the twentieth century that, in certain advanced and still rather unorthodox church circles, some of these teachings are being jettisoned, and that what Aquinas has said about the *via negativa* and the *via positiva* is held to be all that actually can be said about God.

Aquinas makes the point that we are limited by our language, which cannot express the true nature of God, but forces us into misdescriptions. When we speak of God's goodness or love, or power, we do so because we do not have the words which would express that these and all other attributes are not separate qualities in God, but are a seamless and undifferentiated whole; we use the masculine form when speaking of Him, yet He is neither male nor female.

Some feminists now refer to God as "She". That is a socially understandable reaction to God having been for centuries referred to by the male pronouns, but theologically it is of course simply substituting one misdescription for another.

We say that God foresees the future only because we cannot envisage a Being outside time, to whom therefore concepts of past, present and future do not apply.

We have seen that St Augustine had already come to the same conclusion.[7] Both men felt that time is a human construct – that human beings are made in such a way that they *have* to think in terms of sequential time, but that there exists a realm that is outside time. This is a fascinating anticipation of the position of Kant in the eighteenth century and of Schopenhauer in the nineteenth century. On grounds that have nothing to do with theology, they, too, concluded that the concept of time is an entirely human construct. We have to think in terms of time because that is the way our intellectual apparatus is made; we *impose* the categories of time on a world in which time does not

7 see note 11 on p. 107 above.

exist. It is an extremely difficult argument, running counter to "common sense" perception and experience, and it will be dealt with more fully later. In the twentieth century, Einstein, coming at the same problem from another angle, the scientific one, would also confirm that time, as we generally understand it, does not exist in the Universe.

The Problem of Evil

If one of God's attributes is omnipotence, our reason is sometimes troubled by why He did not create a better world. St Thomas says that what *we* might think a better world may not, in God's infinite wisdom, actually be so. Nevertheless, he does try to find explanations for the existence of Evil in this world.

According to Coplestone, Aquinas accounts for physical evils, like illness, death, natural disasters etc. as follows:

> The perfection of the Universe requires that there should be, besides incorruptible beings corruptible beings; and if there are corruptible beings, corruption, death will take place according to the natural order.[8]

If one were to ask *why* the perfection of the Universe should require the existence of corruptible beings, Aquinas has to fall back on God's inscrutable will. To quote Coplestone again, Aquinas argued that

> as God's power is infinite, there can always be a better universe than the one God actually produces, and why He has chosen to produce a particular order of creation is His secret.[9]

This does not seem a very satisfactory answer. It would appear to suggest that God actually willed the existence of what we consider physical evil. True, there are some physical "evils" of which we can see the point. If we did not have the capacity to feel pain, for example, then we would have no mechanism that warns us to avoid damage where we can; we might be burnt by standing too close to a fire if we were insensitive to painful heat. If no one ever died, then, *in the world as it is*, we would long ago have run out of food and living space. Humans could perhaps *imagine* a world which is quite different from the world as it is. Such might be a world which could, for instance, produce continuously more food or could even expand to make room for ever increasing numbers of people, but we have seen that for Aquinas it was a matter of faith that God had His own inscrutable reasons for not making the world other than what it is.

The belief that *all* so-called evils are of this ultimately defensible kind is known as Optimism, the idea that "everything is for the best in the best of all possible worlds".[10] But it must be fairly obvious that there are physical evils like droughts or plagues that cannot be defended in this way.

True, if one moves away from a human-centred perspective, one might argue that what is suffering for a human is probably delight for the AIDS virus, but then, from the perspective of the virus, the existence of drugs designed to kill it would be seen as much of an evil as the virus itself is from a human point of view. It is hard to see how the fact that most forms of life can sustain them-

8 Frederick Coplestone - *History of Philosophy*, Vol. II, p. 373

9 ibid., p. 370.

10 Aquinas did not hold this view, because this world cannot be the best of all *possible* worlds. As we have seen, he thought that it would be a limitation upon God if He could not produce a better world than the one He has actually created.

selves only by attacking other forms of life, sometimes with huge suffering for the animal or human victim, can possibly be reconciled with the idea a Creator who has tried to do His best for His creation.

I think it is true to say that "the world is the way it is because that is the way it has to be", and scientists can give all sorts of explanations why it has to be the way it is. A scientist who believes that a Divine Creator is, at least in some general sense, responsible for the way things are, can perhaps square his explanations with what Aquinas has said, but even he will have difficulty in countering some of the arguments in the previous paragraph.

There is of course some psychological value in accepting the inscrutability of the will of God. Many religious people find a kind of calm in resigning themselves to it, but that kind of stoicism in the face of suffering is also possible without the help of religion.

While Aquinas accepted that God must, in some sense, have willed (that is, created) the existence of what we think of as physical evils, he did not believe that God had created moral evils. In some places he followed Plotinus in seeing evil as the absence of good.[11] In others, he saw it as the inevitable consequence of free will, one of God's greatest gifts to mankind. As mankind had been given this freedom of choice, it was inevitable that some people would use it to make the wrong moral choices. We have seen how St Augustine had kept a precarious balance between free will and predestination, and how, in the course of his controversy with Pelagius, he had come increasingly to stress predestination at the expense of free will.[12] Aquinas, while also accepting the inaccurately phrased "fore-knowledge" of God,[13] tipped the balance back the other way. Once Thomism had been accepted as the cornerstone of Catholic theology, the church, though it had originally backed Augustine against Pelagius, also tended to lay more stress on free will than on predestination. Man's fallen nature was indeed accepted, as was his inability to achieve salvation by his own unaided efforts, but if he used his free will to strive for salvation, then he would be rewarded by the help of God's Grace.

Why do men ever choose to do evil? Aquinas believed that sin is really a matter of ignorance – no man sins willingly. The will of each person naturally aims for happiness, but some people have a weak intellect which gives them an inadequate understanding of how to steer their will towards fulfilment.

We might wonder whether the fulfilment of the will actually means the kind of happiness envisaged by Aquinas and which can be attained if the will is rightly directed by the intellect. Aquinas equated true happiness with virtue. The happiness a thief might feel after a successful theft is, for Aquinas, not "real" happiness at all.[14] Later philosophers (Hobbes, Schopenhauer, Nietzsche,

11 see p. 90 above.

12 see p. 111 above.

13 see note 11 on p. 107 above .

14 The distinction between the "real" and the "actual" (meaning "mistaken") runs through much of philosophy, theology and political thought. It begins with Plato's image of the Cave, where men mistake the shadows for reality. It continues with Christianity, which says that many people think they are free when they are actually slaves to sin; only in the service of Christ do we find "perfect freedom". Rousseau will translate that into a political context when he argues, so dangerously, that "real" freedom is to be found only in the service of the community. In each case the assumption is that if we listened to our "real" or "better" self, we would often reject what our "actual" self perceives as freedom or happiness.

Bergson) have much to say about the will; they see its aims as much less benign than those that Aquinas ascribes to it. For them the will is selfishly and ruthlessly dedicated to the victory of the individual or the species over competitors. Nor is Aquinas' view of the will shared by all Christians, many of whom also see the human will as inherently selfish and sinful, and teach that it must be subdued so that God's will may prevail.

A sound intellect will tell people that their true happiness lies not only in this life but in the eternal life hereafter. They must therefore not pursue a worldly happiness by evil means as this will imperil their eternal happiness in the next world. They must do in this life what God would like them to do, but in addition their intellect must discern just what it is that God would like them to do. A weak intellect may fail in this respect, and they may think that they are pleasing God when in fact they are not. Aquinas therefore stressed the importance of a sound intellect if men want to avoid evil. A sinner is a person with a weak intellect that has not grasped the knowledge of what is necessary to achieve salvation.

Aquinas here laid the same stress as Socrates had done on the intellectual basis of moral behaviour. Socrates had taught that virtue is a matter of knowledge and that wrong-doing is the result of ignorance,[15] no man does wrong willingly. This would appear to make it very difficult for someone who is not very bright to be virtuous, and it flies in the face of the fact that many simple people do good out of instinct or because they have been conditioned by a good upbringing.

Aquinas was not quite as harsh as Socrates. Socrates had denied that a man could be called truly virtuous if he had no intellectual knowledge of virtue; a purely instinctive act of goodness did not qualify as a virtuous act in his eyes. Moreover, the knowledge of virtue had to come from within; it was innate and had to be "unveiled" by intellectual effort. An educator could help by "bringing forth" this innate knowledge.[16] Knowledge of virtue which was brought to a person from outside, by a process of "indoctrination", was not regarded by Socrates as true knowledge.

Aquinas did not discriminate so sharply between knowledge from inside and knowledge from outside. Both ways of gaining knowledge of virtue were valid for him. His theology taught that salvation was possible only for the Christian, and presumably he believed that the simple soul who regularly went to church would gain sufficient training at least of that part of his intellect which made him understand that happiness lay in the service of God in this life and its reward in the next. The church would also effectively teach him what behaviour God expected of him in his daily life. Aquinas' theory has the virtue of providing one explanation (as we shall see presently, there are other and different ones) for the behaviour of someone who knows that the service of God contributes to true happiness, but whose intellect does not tell him that the *way* he is serving God is evil. Some God-fearing zealots inflict terrible ("godless") cruelties on people they consider heretics or infidels, in the belief that they are doing God's will. This belief may be the result of their inadequate intellect and/or the result of what fanatical clergy have told them is the will of God. (Aquinas himself strongly condemned the use of force against non-Chris-

15 For a discussion of this Socratic view, see p. 19 above.

16 see p. 18 above.

tians: they are protected against undue harshness by the natural law[17] that regulates relationships between Christians and non-Christians alike.)

Alternative explanations, however, seem more convincing. Such zealots suffer, not from an inadequate intellect (or at least not from an inadequate intellect alone) but from a psychological defect that cannot tolerate disagreements, or that revels in cruelty.

Universals and Particulars

When Aquinas turned to the question of Universals and Particulars, he again created a synthesis between Platonic and Christian neo-Platonic thought on the one hand and Aristotelian thought on the other. The former had deprived Particulars of any true value and made them mere shadows of the Universals or at best (as in Neo-Platonism) emanations from the Divine, which grew paler and paler as they were more distant from their source. Aristotle, on the other hand, had taught that the material things of *this* world have a valid existence entirely independent of any Ideas stored up in Heaven, but that their nature is such that they have an entelechy which strives, teleologically, for their own fulfilment and perfection. This *telos* or goal corresponded to the Divine Plan or Final Cause. Aristotle, it will be remembered, thought that the world was coeval with God and not created by Him, because His abstract nature could not be involved with making anything material.[18]

It was now, however, part of Christian dogma that God, however abstract, *had* created the world, and so Aquinas taught that the entelechy had been implanted in things by God when He created them. The Idea in God's mind is real, but so is the matter He has imbued with His Idea. Though all Matter is dependent on Him, He has endowed it with its own validity.

This approach reinforces the idea, to which we have already referred, that the Christian has no need to be afraid of studying the material world.[19] Augustine had suggested that such secular study was at best a distraction from cultivating the soul and at worst might actually lead the soul astray. Aquinas taught that when we study the world, we study God's handiwork as He means us to do.

One important consequence of the positive attitude towards the material world was that Aquinas also looked on the human body as part of God's handiwork. St Paul and St Augustine (and indeed Plato, too) had thought that the body was merely the prison of the soul, and by corrupting the soul with temptations, that it could be something even worse than a prison. Aquinas agreed that the body *could* be a trap for the soul, but he insisted that the body was also a vessel through which the Divine was expressed and should indeed be a Temple of the soul.[20]

17 for Aquinas on "natural law", see p. 143 below.

18 see p. 48 above.

19 see p. 104 above.

20 Aquinas believed that the nature of Man lies in body and soul together. True, he thought that when the body dies, the soul survives, though not as a personality until it is reunited with its body at the time of the resurrection. (That theory must have been a great disappointment to all those who hoped that, when they died, they would immediately be reunited with loved ones who had predeceased them. They would instead have to wait until Judgment Day, for only then would their souls and the souls of their loved ones reacquire their personality.) Averroës had denied the resurrection of the body, but for Aqui-

This should have been an important liberation from the disgust that Paul, Augustine and several of the early Church fathers had expressed for the physical side of human beings, but one has the impression that that idea only truly broke through into the culture of the West at the time of the Renaissance.[21]

The Thomist view now not only sanctioned, but encouraged the study of the material world. Aquinas believed that it is only after we have had sensory experience of the particulars of the material world (Aristotle) that our intellect can begin to understand *something* of the universals (*pace* Plato) of God's plan.

With this shift of attitude to the importance of the material world and the need to study it, the ground was prepared for a huge advance in western thought which might not otherwise have taken place at all. The word "Renaissance" is widely associated with the fifteenth century, and as we shall see, [22] at that time involved a new wave of Neo-Platonism. The words "Scientific Renaissance" are similarly and rightly associated with the sixteenth century, but there was also a Renaissance in the thirteenth century, which was based on what might be called the "Neo-Aristotelianism" of Siger of Brabant, Albert Magnus and Thomas Aquinas, and its implications, once they had sunk in, were arguably at least as significant and enduring as - if less seductive than - that of the fifteenth century Renaissance in Italy.

Political Thought

Aquinas was also influenced by Aristotle in his attitude to man as a member of society. It will be remembered that Aristotle had given the teleological definition of man as a political animal, meaning that any fully developed human being would be engaged in the *polis*.[23] Aquinas, too, saw the nature of man in teleological terms. He accepted Aristotle's formulation as a partial definition, agreeing that man should indeed take an active part in his community if he is to fulfil his potential, but it was for him only a partial definition. He saw man as ultimately a *religious* animal, who developed his *fullest* potential as a member of the Church, but this was not at odds with man's nature as a political animal. Man's natural need to play a social role was implanted in him by God, and society itself was ordained as an institution to deal with the quite natural secular needs of man. He did not see the state as a necessary evil, as Seneca had done,[24] and even less as a punishment for man's unruly nature.

This, too, was a departure from what was at that time the Church's official view of the state. It is true that St Augustine had seen man as the citizen of two cities, the City of God and the Earthly City, and the Christian had a *duty* to participate in the latter to make sure that it was not a godless city. Aquinas, however, did not see this participation so much as a duty as a *fulfilment* of what a

nas' belief in it was immensely important. If body and soul together constituted man, then without a resurrection of the body there could be no personal immortality of the soul in which Aquinas believed as a matter of faith.

21 The Renaissance view will be described in Chapter 19.

22 in Chapter 19

23 see p. 51 above. It will be remembered that the word *polis* had a wider meaning than polity, embracing as it did not just the political but also the social aspects of a community.

24 see p. 74 above.

properly developed man quite naturally wants to do, and he therefore had a much more positive attitude to political activity than had his predecessors. Again, Aquinas comes back to the general point that secular interests are absolutely legitimate.

One function of the secular ruler was, therefore, to enable men to fulfil both their political and their religious potential. For the latter, God had provided the guidance of the Church, which the state needs to respect. Ideally, the Church stands above the state in much the same way in which faith stands above reason, not as a contradiction, but as its ethereal crown.

As far as the form of the Church is concerned, Aquinas supported the *plenitudo potestatis*, the absolute authority of the Papacy as it had been established by his time. "It is necessary for salvation to submit to the Roman Pope", he wrote in his polemic against the Greek Orthodox Church, *Contra Errores Graecorum* (1263). But in *De Regno* (1266) he was less categorical about where authority should rest in the state. God has vested sovereignty in the people, who are then free to delegate it to one person, to a few, or to many. Provided there is good government, its actual form does not really matter.

> This teaching would not always be remembered by the Catholic Church. In practice it tended to identify itself with monarchy – strikingly so before, during and after the French Revolution. In the *Syllabus Errorum* of 1864 Pius IX gave the impression that Liberal or Socialist governments could not be approved of by the Church;[25] but in 1885 the Church sensibly came back to Thomist teaching, when Leo XIII, in the bull *Immortali Dei*, made it clear that "no form of government is condemned in itself".

Aquinas then proceeded to discuss the pros and cons of each of these three types much as Aristotle had done, and with very similar arguments. On the face of it, he says, monarchy seems the most "natural", by analogy with the rule of the father over his children, or with the soul and the heart over other members of the body. However, good monarchy is difficult to attain, and therefore constitutional safeguards should be built into the system to prevent a monarchy turning into a tyranny. Tyranny would be bad in itself and would often bring in its wake the further evil of a violent rebellion; disorder was for Aquinas, as it was for every thinker in the Middle Ages, something to be avoided at all cost. He did not go as far as St Paul did when he urged obedience to the powers that be, however cruel they might be; deposing a tyrant is legitimate, but it must be done by "the orderly action of the people".

Law

The law of the state is the lowest of four kinds of law which form a kind of "feudal" hierarchy, with a sovereign law at the top and the lower kinds dependent upon it. With only the modification required by Christianity, Aquinas here fol-

25 The Syllabus actually condemned liberals to the extent to which they defended the legitimacy of parliamentary laws which contradicted the teaching of the Church, and socialists to the extent that they were materialist. So it had no quarrel with Christian liberalism or Christian socialism and therefore was still Thomist, but the circumstances under which the Syllabus was issued made it appear a condemnation of liberalism and socialism.

lowed closely the model that had first been produced by Cicero.[26] At the apex of the pyramid is the Eternal Law, the Reason of God. From it flows the Natural Law which is reflected in Creation. This is not exactly the same as what today we call a law of nature or a scientific law, because, in Aquinas' view, it is concerned not with what a thing is now or has been at an earlier stage, but rather with what it should be if it develops as it should do according to its entelechy. Aquinas took the idea of entelechy from Aristotle;[27] and here again he marries Aristotelianism with religion by saying that this entelechy has been implanted by God. We have seen that Aristotle had said that Man is by nature a political animal and that Aquinas, while agreeing with that, had added that in addition, and more importantly, he was a religious animal. It was therefore part of the Natural Law that Man should seek the good. That does not mean that every man in fact seeks the good, but in so far as he does not, he is not developing the full potential or entelechy of his nature. That particular entelechy has been implanted in all humans, so that the Natural Law applies to Christians and non-Christians alike.

Next comes the Divine Law, God's revealed law for His Church, which is binding upon Christians.

> Although Aquinas naturally thought that the Divine Law as revealed to Christians through the Old and New Testament taken together was superior to the Divine Law enshrined in the Old Testament alone, he would recognize that the Jews were bound by that part of the Divine Law that is found in the Old Testament[28] (and he might have argued that Muslims were bound by that part of it that was revealed in the Koran). Aquinas accepted that Jews and Muslims could not be bound by the Divine Law in the New Testament unless they voluntarily accepted it. Christian teaching was against forcible conversions, though it accepted the so-called Doctrine of St Augustine which sanctioned keeping Jews "in an oppressed condition as living witnesses to the truth of Christianity"!

Finally comes Human Law, enacted by governments, which is subdivided into the *ius gentium* (international law) and the *ius civile* (national or local law). For any human law to be legitimate, it must be in harmony with the Natural Law, and, for Christian societies, with the Divine Law as well.

> Here we might comment on the confused way in which the word "law" has been used by Cicero, Aquinas, and in later centuries by many other philosophers who used the expressions "natural law" or "Law of Nature".
>
> The word "law" is used in three quite different senses, and ideally we would need different words for each.
>
> There is, first, the way the word is used in a scientific context. It is impossible to break such a law; or rather, the moment that research shows that the "law" is either wrong or not comprehensive enough, it needs to be re-formulated to take the new research into account. A single attested incident that does not conform to the scientific law as it has been perceived is sufficient to force

26 see p. 72 above.

27 see p. 45 above.

28 Jews do not accept the name "Old Testament" because of the implication that it required fulfilment by a New Testament. They refer to these books as the Tanach (a Hebrew acronym for Torah, Prophets, and Writings) or simply as the Bible.

abandonment or modification. For example, Newton's laws apply to much of nature, but once Einstein and others had shown that they do not operate when applied either on an enormously large scale (the macrocosm) or an enormously small scale (the microcosm), they no longer carried the full authority that they once did, and a reformulation became necessary. In its reformulated form it is then unbreakable unless further research shows it not to be not sufficiently comprehensive. Every scientific law purports to be descriptive.

Then there is the moral law. This is not *descriptive* but *prescriptive.* It is about what ought to be rather than about what is. It is more subject to change than a scientific law, because what is regarded as immoral by one society is not necessarily considered immoral by another. And of course, unlike a scientific law, the moral law in any given society is regularly broken. When it is broken, its guardians rarely feel compelled to abandon or modify it, but generally insist on its continuing validity for as long as possible. A single attested breach of the scientific law is sufficient to force abandonment or reformulation; but it generally requires an extremely widespread defiance of the moral law to have the same effect.

Then, thirdly, there is law made by state organs. It, too, is prescriptive; breaches of it do not necessarily invalidate it; and it will remain the law until there is sufficient pressure to enforce its repeal or amendment.

If one sees the scientific law (what Aquinas called the Natural Law) as describing things teleologically, one runs the danger of getting description mixed up with prescription, because the idea of "ought" easily becomes embedded in it; and this is particularly so if, like Aquinas, one includes moral qualities in the teleological description. By using the word "ought" in connection with human beings, we use a vocabulary that is most at home in the field of moral law. If, for example, we define man teleologically as a political animal, then a man who does not behave like a political animal – a hermit, for example – is not fulfilling his potential as he ought to do. Of course it is not *necessary* to associate the word "ought" with the moral law. We may say that an acorn ought to develop into an oak-tree without chiding it if it falls on stony ground and so does not fulfil its potential. If the tomatoes we have planted fail to thrive as they ought, we may blame our lack of green fingers, not the tomatoes. If we are liberal minded, we may not blame a human being either who, perhaps because of an unhappy family environment, is uncomfortable about involving himself in society. But even then it is hard to suppress the thought that he *ought* to be socialized, that there is something wrong with the loner. There is a tendency to see such a person, not as "unusual" or "unfulfilled" but as "unnatural". That is not only cruel (as we can see in the way in which, say, homosexuals have been regarded by Judaeo-Christian and other societies until recently); but, bearing in mind that "ought" in its moral, prescriptive meaning is so much *more* subjective than it is in its (much rarer) scientific, descriptive use, we should, I think, avoid including the concept of "ought" in teleological *definitions*, especially of human beings.

(It should go without saying, from what has been said about scientific laws above, that these, too, are subjective and liable to change over time. In theory there may be no difference between the ultimate reliability of scientific and of moral statements, and there are philosophers of science who stress this point strongly; but in practice it is generally felt that the degree of subjectivity in science is of a far lesser order, and, above all, is less tied up with emotions which make modifications so difficult.)

Thomas Aquinas and Duns Scotus

In his treatment of the Law, Aquinas has presented us with a continuum, an inevitable continuity between the lower and the higher forms, just as his metaphysics saw a continuum between reason and faith, Divine Law smoothly takes over, as it were, where Human Law stops, to become a seamless part of the Natural Law, which is the next stage upwards. That in turn soars upwards to become part of the Eternal Law, the Reason or Mind of God.

Naturally, this scheme met with criticism. This was first articulated by St Thomas' contemporary, St John of Bonaventura.[29] St John was the Minister-General of the Franciscan Order, which had been founded by St Francis of Assisi in 1209. Franciscan philosophy was generally more inclined towards mysticism than towards natural theology, and, therefore, it is sometimes seen as being in opposition to the Dominican thought of which Aquinas was the most important exponent. Whilst it is true that natural theology and mysticism represent two different approaches to religious thought, they are not necessarily in opposition to each other, but instead can be considered complementary. Tradition affirms that St Dominic and St Francis had been on friendly terms, and St Thomas and St John certainly were. Besides, out of the Dominican Order would emerge the famous mystical thinker Meister Eckhart (1260 to 1327) whilst the Franciscans produced as thoroughly unmystical a personality as Roger Bacon (1214 to 1292), on whom more in the next chapter.[30]

However, St John's criticism of Thomist natural theology would be powerfully repeated in the generation after Aquinas by John Duns of Scotland, known as Duns Scotus (1266 to 1308) and in the generation after that by William of Ockham (1290 to 1349), both, like St John of Bonaventura, members of the Franciscan Order. Aquinas had never denied the necessity of faith, but he had seen the realm of faith, as it were, as a mystical superstructure resting on top of a basis of reason - or at least it was easy to understand him that way. Scotus and the others challenged the idea that this continuity between God and His Creation, which Thomas had stressed, was inevitable or necessary; nothing that God did was either inevitable or necessary, because that would diminish both His omnipotence - He could have created a totally different world - and His radical difference from anything He had created. It was therefore presumptuous to try to understand God's work through Natural Theology, that is through the rational arguments by which Aquinas had been trying to prove, first the existence of God, and then the relationship between Him and the world. Scotus saw God primarily as will and as love rather than as reason, and he believed that the only source of insight into religious matters comes through faith in the revelations of the Bible.

There is some doubt whether Scotus actually expressed all the views which, for centuries, were attributed to him. An early work of his, the *Opus Oxoniense*, does not so much reject Thomist Natural Theology as warn that undue reliance on it might incur two dangers: it might lead to a kind of complacency in which a

29 see p. 128 above.

30 It must be added, however, that both these men were, for different reasons, accused of heresy. Eckhart's writings were condemned by the Papacy two years after his death, and Bacon spent fourteen years in prison, being released shortly before the end of his own life.

true understanding of God would be lost, and it might imperil our necessary acceptance in faith of what mere human reason might describe as God's arbitrariness. The more radical attack on Natural Theology is found in a later work, the *Theoremata,* but since 1918 some doubt has been thrown on the authorship of this work - it may have been written by one of William of Ockham's followers. However, for centuries the *Theoremata* was taken to be by Scotus, and its many supporters rallied behind it in a mighty battle for the soul and doctrine of the Roman Catholic Church. This battle was won by the Thomists in 1323, when Aquinas was canonized. Thomism was reaffirmed in papal pronouncements as recently as 1879 and 1923.

Scotus was never declared a heretic, he was too powerful a theologian for that. Indeed, he is known in Catholic teaching by the title of *Doctor Subtilis.* Even so, his followers were ridiculed for a long time by the victors; and in popular parlance his name, in the form of "dunce", remains a synonym for an ignoramus. His reputation has risen again in recent years, and in 1993 he was actually beatified.

> It seems strange that it took quite so long to honour Scotus in this way. One might have thought that the process should really have begun much earlier, certainly not later than the eighteenth-century Age of Reason. At that time many leading supporters of reason turned against faith and mocked religion. At the climax of the French Revolution religions were outlawed, churches closed down and priests guillotined, all in the name of the Goddess of Reason. Aquinas had invited reason to take an honoured place within religion, but it may have seemed to the victims of the French Revolution that what he had done was to invite a cuckoo to lay its eggs in the religious nest. Now the cuckoos had grown to throw religion out of the nest. At that moment, surely, one might have expected the church to give the critics of Aquinas more prominence, and even having regard to the slowness of the procedures for beatification or canonization, one might have envisioned Duns Scotus to have been honoured rather sooner.

The fact is that, since the eighteenth century if not before, Aquinas' magnificent attempt to marry reason and faith had come under enormous stress. Even the Jesuit writer Coplestone, writing with the seal of the *nihil obstat* and the license of the *imprimatur,*[31] describes the bringing together of philosophy and theology as a honeymoon which could not endure. The tension between the two, which was built into the system, was too great. Quite soon "the charter granted to philosophy tended to become a declaration of independence." [32] The point is so brilliantly expressed in an extended metaphor by Knut Tranøy that I quote it here in full:

> The Thomist synthesis in which all truth, theological or philosophical, is in principle of one and the same kind could be described metaphorically as a ship with only one room. The advantages of such an arrangement are considerable. Everybody in it is a member of one and the same community, although at different stations. There may be quite some distance from one end of the ship to the other, but nevertheless it is in principle possible to communicate all the way. However, a ship of this kind suffers from the serious disad-

31 The *nihil obstat* (nothing stands in the way) and the *imprimatur* (let it be printed) are, respectively, declarations by a high Roman Catholic authority that a book presents no danger to the faith and that it may be published.

32 Coplestone - *A History of Philosophy*, Vol.II, p.430

vantage that if it starts leaking, no matter where, then the whole ship and everybody aboard it are imperilled. If, for some reason or other, the philosophical end of it (which was also that of the sciences) does not hold water, there is imminent danger that the theological and religious end may become uninhabitable too. To exploit the metaphor, the critics of Aquinas wanted to protect the ship against such dangers. For them, there was still one ship only, but they introduced a water-tight compartment by which the ship was divided into two sections. A ship of this kind will not so readily sink even if its philosophical section - frailer because more human - should take to leaking. But the vessel now suffers from another weakness. In rough seas, it may break in two, each section taking its own course. The separate sections may even begin to behave as separate ships, and their masters may quarrel and fight each other, each claiming to sail the better ship on the safer course.

It seems to me that this metaphor can be used to illustrate, in the first place, the ideal relationship between faith and reason which Thomas Aquinas tried to institute in his system - and, secondly, some of the reasons why his critics found the system unacceptable, its attractions notwithstanding.[33]

33 Knut Tranøy in *A Critical History of Western Philosophy*, ed. D.J.O'Connor, Macmillan 1964, p. 123.

CHAPTER 17

The Franciscans

ROGER BACON

Roger Bacon (1214 to 1292) was a Franciscan, but there was little of Franciscan mysticism, such as had been advocated by his contemporary, St John of Bonaventura, in Bacon's philosophy. He was born in Somerset and studied in Oxford, Paris, Italy and the near East before returning to teach, first in Paris in the 1240s and then, around 1250, in Oxford. In Paris his studies and teaching were influenced by the Aristotelianism that was then recovering from its initial ban at that university. He was drawn most strongly to those aspects of Aristotle that investigated this world and much less so to the metaphysical aspects of his philosophy. By the time he took up his post in Oxford, he had become fascinated by science and mathematics, and had become positively disgusted with metaphysical speculations and with self-contained logical structures. As a Franciscan he was of course religious, and he accepted that there was a world beyond the physical world, so he acknowledged the metaphysical *truths* (not subject to speculation) taught by the Church. It was part of Franciscan thinking that those truths have to be taken purely on faith and cannot otherwise be philosophized about. That left him free to devote his philosophical thought largely to the physical world; and true statements about that world must in the last resort be tested by experience. Logical deductions made from the results of experiments must then be put to the test of further experience.

That experience is the basis of all knowledge was of course not a new idea: Aristotle had already said that all knowledge begins with the senses which provide us with experience.[1] Although Aristotle had built up a large body of knowledge on empirical observations, that statement was, for him, primarily an epistemological one; he was describing *how* we can know anything. For Bacon, it was a statement about how we can *know the truth* of anything. Moreover, for Aristotle empirical observation was the basis of a great metaphysical structure, embracing theories about entelechies, causes, and the nature of God. Roger Bacon eschewed such speculations, and would draw no conclusions other than those which experimental evidence would support. Theology had been the central concern for Aquinas, and it had been important for him to show that the study of this world was compatible with it. One feels that for Bacon the central concern was a study of this world. He was at pains to assert his approach to this world was perfectly compatible with a theology that rested, not on reason or experiment, but on genuine faith in the Church's authority.

1 see p. 45 above.

Errors result not only from drawing conclusions that are not tested by experience, but also from relying on received opinion. Bacon listed four sources of error: the first was the acceptance of "frail and unworthy authority". No one can manage entirely without relying on earlier authorities, and indeed some of them are reliable. But the only sure way to decide which source is reliable and which is frail and unworthy must ultimately be to test each against experience. Even Aristotle was not exempt from this test. Bacon railed against the way in which Aristotle had come to be regarded second in authority only to Holy Writ, first by the Arab philosophers, and then by Christian theologians after Aquinas had incorporated so much Aristotelianism into his doctrines. Far from standing in awe of Aristotle, "he declares", says Durant, "that if he had the power, he would burn all the books of the Philosopher as the fountain of error and a stream of ignorance – after which he quotes Aristotle on every second page."[2] There was only one source of authority whose pronouncements must be accepted even though they are not capable of being tested, and that was "the solid and sure authority which has been bestowed on the Church". That was not merely a prudential safeguard. Bacon was, after all, a Franciscan, and as such accepted, as we have seen, that religious truths were subject neither to rational nor to experimental proof.

The second source of error is "long established custom". The third is "the sense of the ignorant crowd" and the fourth is "the hiding of one's own ignorance under the shadow of wisdom." By this last, Bacon meant not so much a kind of conscious bluffing, pretending to knowledge which one does not have, but a lack of humility. Not conscious pretence, but an unconscious self-deception that one understands a situation perfectly when in truth one does not, or knows the truth only in part.

> These seem obvious sources of error once they have been identified; their listing seems scarcely worthy of being elevated to the status of philosophy. However, when Bacon sees a careful reliance on evidence as the only protection against them, he is actually striking a cutting blow against any proposition that cannot be tested by evidence – and by implication against much that the revered Thomas Aquinas represented. For many propositions in metaphysics cannot be so tested; nor can statements which begin with definitions from which other statements are then deduced and accepted without being tested by experience.
>
> I think Bacon should have included a fifth source of error: the love of tidy intellectual systems. An intellectual system arises in the first place from inductions – a series of observations suggests a systematic explanation. In *Das Kapital*, for example, Karl Marx adduced a collection of social facts and statistics which suggested to him a theory about the nature of capitalism. Once that theory had been formulated, there was an enormous temptation for some thinkers to force other social facts into this same system without genuinely testing whether they fitted. In other words, the system led to deductions which were then insufficiently tested against experience, and gross errors resulted. It is a point that will be treated extensively by Karl Popper.[3]

2 Durant – *The Story of Civilization – The Age of Faith*, p. 1008. Perhaps Bacon was not quite as inconsistent as Durant's passage suggests. He might have wanted to burn the works of Aristotle because they contained so many metaphysical arguments; but he would have quoted him on every other page for the validity of the empirical part of his work.

3 see Chapter 45.

Bacon carried out experiments from which he made many discoveries of what can be done with lenses by way of refraction, magnification etc. One result was the manufacture of spectacles in his own time, and telescopes would follow three hundred years later. He produced a formula for making gunpowder, which would be used in guns in the following century, and, although he was not able to provide experimental proof, he believed that machines could be invented for flying and for locomotion on land and in water. He had the vivid imagination of a good writer of science fiction. Passages in his writings in which he forecasts such things are as powerful and poetic as they are uncannily prophetic.

These ideas have struck posterity because they would one day be put into practice. Less attention has been paid to those of his ideas that most intellectuals would today reject. Like many of his generation he made experiments in alchemy and he believed in astrology.[4] This last belief got him into trouble.Iif our fate is governed by the stars, then there can be no free will. For this reason the Church had condemned astrology, most recently in a work by Étienne Tempier, the Bishop of Paris. Bacon had said he respected the solid and sure authority of the Church, but for him that did not mean that he had to accept the authority of the Bishop of Paris. In 1277 he criticized Tempier in a book called *Speculum Astromiae*, and this probably contributed to his imprisonment in the following year.

He had already incurred the displeasure of the Church authorities. His views were so unorthodox and his attacks on theologians with whom he disagreed so intemperate that in 1257 he had been banned from teaching in Oxford and from publishing any further works. Bacon took hope when, in 1265, Clement IV was elected to the Papacy. The new Pope was a Frenchman whom Bacon may have known when both men were living in Paris. Bacon now appealed to him against the ban, and in 1266 Clement invited him to send him his writings in secrecy, notwithstanding any prohibitions from the Franciscan Order. It was in response to this invitation that Bacon wrote the massive encyclopaedic work, 800 pages long, for which he is most famous: the *Opus Maius*. Fearing that this might be too much for the Pope to read, he sent along two summaries of the work, the *Opus Minus* and the *Opus Tertium*. These books were a plea that the papacy should encourage in the universities scientific study of the world that God had created. Bacon, of course, took great care, as we have seen, to protest that he accepted the authority of the Church's teaching. He also stressed that scientific work must always respect moral considerations as they are, "of no account except as they help forward right action... The science of morality is the mistress of every department of philosophy."

We have seen that Bacon thought of astrology as a science. In the *Opus Maius* he defended his work on astrology against the condemnation of the Church. He argued that the influence of the stars no more destroyed free will than did the influence of the weather. When we know that a snowy season is

4 It may be an example of western cultural arrogance to dismiss alchemy and astrology out of hand. Jung found much subtlety in alchemy. It might be chemical nonsense, but he thought that if we approach alchemy as a mystery religion, it has many valuable insights. And a belief in astrology is so widespread among otherwise apparently sensible people in the Far East that we might perhaps keep an open mind about it.

> an inauspicious time to sow crops, we exercise our free will to sow in the spring instead. Likewise, if we learn that, being born under the sign of certain stars, we are predisposed to be choleric, we know that we have to make more of an effort to control our anger than if we were born under another sign. If the stars tell us that certain constellations are inauspicious for a particular enterprise, we can use our free will to choose a different date for the undertaking. the more we know about the influence of the stars, the more effectively we can use our free will to make the best use of these influences and to avoid possible bad effects.
>
> It is to be noted that the nature of this defence accepts that if astrology did actually imply that everything was predetermined, then, given that the assertion of free will was such an essential part of the moral teaching of the Church that it would indeed be immoral to study or to propagate astrology. Bacon, in other words, probably would not have agreed with the arguments of many scientists today that their researches are "value-free". Scientists must push forward pure research as far as it can go. Its results can be applied either for good or for ill (nuclear power for example). It must be up to society, acting through its political leaders, to decide how it wishes to use the results, and to legislate on what limits it wishes to set on the application of the research findings. Of course, the techniques of even pure research must respect certain ethical limits. Research into the characteristics of twins, for example, is perfectly valid, but if it is carried out by the brutal methods of a Dr Mengele, it is obviously unacceptable.[5]
>
> As for applied science, there are scientists who will refuse to work on *unethical applications* of research on moral grounds , such as the development of germ warfare or of certain genetic techniques like cloning for human beings, but even they would not normally wish to bar research on germs because this could be beneficial for medicine or on cloning techniques which could increase crop yield.[6]

It is not known whether Clement IV read these works; it is most unlikely, as he died in November 1268. Bacon continued to defy his superiors and continued to publish works in which, as usual, he made scathing onslaughts on his contemporaries. At last they lost patience with him. Perhaps his attack on the Bishop of Paris was the last straw. In 1277 he was summoned to Paris by the head of the Franciscan Order, condemned "for teaching novelties" and imprisoned in 1278. There is no record of when he was released; one record suggests that it might not have been until shortly before his death fourteen years later. If so, he made good use of the last few months of his life. Combative to the last, he wrote one more aggressively worded book which was published in 1292, the year he died.

5 It is on these grounds that some people oppose experiments on animals also, even if the resulting research were beneficial to humans.

6 The medical profession has set up ethical committees to decide which experiments are ethically acceptable and which are not. These committees sometimes take into account not so much the ethical nature of the experiments themselves as the unethical use that might be made of the results. Much unease has already been felt about the cloning of sheep, and at the moment of writing, there is a prohibition on experiments involving human cloning, even though the results of such experiments might be used for beneficial ends, such as the multiplication of humans who are free from certain diseases. But the fear that the results would almost certainly be used sooner or later for unacceptable ends – say, aggressive individuals being cloned to staff armies – at present imposes an absolute bar on human cloning. We have to stress the words "at present". In the Middle Ages it was considered unethical to dissect human corpses, but the benefits for science were so great that society came to accept it. Society may, in the future, yield to pressure to accept human cloning also.

WILLIAM OF OCKHAM

William of Ockham (*ca.* 1290 to 1349) was another Franciscan who was born in England and had both studied and later taught at Oxford. We will see him developing some of the ideas we have already encountered in the work of Duns Scotus and Roger Bacon.

He combined Bacon's suspicion of logical arguments based on concepts rather than on experience with a renewed engagement with the two-hundred years old debate between Realism and Nominalism.[7] Officially, the Church had favoured Realism, the philosophy that everything we see in this world is imperfect and therefore less real than the Ideas or Universals stored up in Heaven or in the mind of God. Nominalism, the philosophy which held that these Ideas are only names which we give to groups of particular things, but which have no real or independent existence apart from the particulars, had been taught by Roscelin, but he had been threatened with excommunication and had recanted.

Ockham's Nominalism

Ockham was a thorough-going Nominalist. Our sensations, he held, are the only source of certain knowledge: we can have reliable knowledge only of *things*. Because the concepts we create by grouping certain particulars together have philosophical validity only to the extent to which they refer to actual particulars, further concepts which we derive from them cannot have the same reliability unless they are in turn tested for reference to particulars of which we have experience. Logical arguments and hypotheses, based merely on concepts, are suspect if not so tested. All reliable conclusions, in other words, are reached by *induction* from the experienced particular to the general, and not by *deduction* from the general to the yet inexperienced particular.

> The difference between deduction and induction may be explained like this: we observe a number of phenomena and we make *inductions* about them. For example, we may infer from observation that hay-fever is prevalent in the summer. From this we might go on to make accurate or inaccurate *deductions*: it is related to the amount of sunshine and therefore we should spend as much time as possible in north-facing rooms. This would be an inaccurate deduction (which tests would soon demonstrate). It would be a correct deduction (which can also be tested) that it is related to the amount of pollen in the atmosphere and that therefore an air-conditioning system that traps the pollen might alleviate the condition.
>
> As we move from fairly straightforward physical questions like this to more abstract questions, concerning, for example, psychology, ethics, or social questions, the inductions that can be made from observed phenomena (how humans behave) and the deductions (how we ought to treat them to achieve certain goals that we might consider desirable) vary hugely. The inductions may be right or wrong – sooner or later, further experience may confirm or challenge the induction. The damage of inaccurate induction is likely to be more limited than that of elaborate deductive structures based upon them and which demand, but are not always subjected to, the test of experience; the more elaborate they are, the more wildly they may diverge from reality.

7 see p. 115 above.

> Deduction is a valuable and suggestive tool of thought and is indeed an essential requirement for discovering truths that were hitherto unknown, but its "logical" nature is not in itself a guarantee of truth.

Ockham knew, of course, that we cannot do without deduction: logic is not possible without it, and without logic we cannot extend our knowledge. Before we can use either induction or deduction, we first have to organize the phenomena we experience in groups (or Universals) – hay-fever sufferers, in the example we looked at above. As a Nominalist, he insists that we create these universals; they are fabricated within our own minds and have no independent reality outside our minds; we give names to these groups, and names is all that they are. We must never forget that if these names do not refer back to statements about *specific* things, they are merely empty talk, of no use as tools of *rational* [8] thought. Coplestone puts it like this:

> [The Universal] owes its existence simply to the intellect: there is no universal reality corresponding to the concept. It is not, however, a fiction in the sense that it does not stand for anything real: it stands for *individual real* things, though it does not stand for any *universal* thing.[9]

So, where a concept does not refer back to a real thing, it is unnecessary and should be eliminated. It is this principle that has become famous as Ockham's Razor, generally (though inaccurately) quoted as stating that "Entities are not to be multiplied beyond necessity."[10] There is a necessity for us to use the name "horses" for a particular group of quadrupeds, but there is no necessity *in philosophy* for us to use any names which do not correspond to anything we have actually experienced.

Faith and Reason

If Ockham insisted that we should not use Universals that are not based on experience, what then would be the status of statements about angels, for example? Or about God as the author of all things, when we cannot learn *by experience* that God is the cause of anything?

Ockham accepted the distinction which had been made by Aquinas between philosophy and theology,[11] but he did not agree that the two dovetailed in the way in which Aquinas thought they did. Philosophically, we cannot say anything about angels. The name "angels" does not correspond with any experience we have of particular angels. Philosophically speaking, therefore, angels should fall victim to Ockham's razor. But theologically speaking, we have the warrant of the Bible that angels exist, and on those grounds Ockham accepted, as a matter of faith, that they existed, even in the absence of any experience we might have of them. *Theological statements are not subject to philosophical tests.*

Here Ockham, as a good Franciscan, picked up the theme first put forward by St John of Bonaventura. He maintained that his teaching on the importance of

8 The significance of putting the word "rational" into italics will emerge presently.

9 Coplestone – *A History of Philosophy*, Vol.III, p. 57. (My italics.)

10 *Non sunt multiplicanda entia praeter necessitatem*. That particular formulation was actually not his own, which was slightly different; and he also expressed the idea in the words *frustra fit per plura quod potest fieri per pauciora*: "it is vain to do with more what can be done with fewer."

11 see p. 78 above.

experience referred only to the processes of rational (that is, philosophical) thought. Like St John, he insisted that rational thought will never lead to a profound understanding of religion.[12] He did not accept the Thomist philosophy that the truths about the rational world and the truths of theology are all of a piece; that there is a continuum from rational to theological truths; that there are sound rational arguments which can be deployed to reinforce our faith in the existence of God; that once the existence of God had been confirmed by reason, we can accept His revelations in the faith that, if we could penetrate the metaphorical veil of clouds that screens Him from us, we would find that the same ladder of reason which had taken us as far as the clouds also continued above them.

Ockham, however, held that we have no cause to think that God is constrained by what we call the laws of reason. In His omnipotence He could have created a world along lines which are totally different from those grasped by human rationality, indeed, it is likely that parts of Creation do not conform to anything that human reason can possibly grasp.

Apart from this general position, Ockham also took direct issue with some of the rational arguments that Aquinas and others had adduced to prove the existence of God. These arguments could not be logically conclusive because they could not be verified by experience. To the argument that there must have been a First Mover to set the world going, for instance, Ockham replied that, in the first place, there can be no experience of that event, and secondly, that even if there were a First Mover, we cannot verify by experience (i.e. philosophically) that it was God and not some being lesser than God, like an angel. Ockham believed that God created the world in the beginning, but he believed it because the Bible said so, not because he saw any logical need for this belief.

To the argument that the existence of God as the Final Cause explains why all things strive towards goals, he objected that though we can find by experience that there is an entelechy which makes all things strive to develop in a certain way, we cannot demonstrate that they are striving towards a set goal or that any such goal has been set by God. The belief that God has set such goals rests entirely on religious faith.

Ockham accepted the existence of God, of the Trinity, of the Real Presence of Christ in the Eucharist and of the immortal soul,[13] but he maintained that this acceptance rests only on faith. So, like some Averroists – Siger of Brabant, for example – Ockham believed in the Twofold Truth. Siger and the Averroists had probably propounded this theory at least in part as a matter of prudence, to carve out a safe place for reason and at the same time to protect themselves from the charge of heresy. Ockham, on the other hand, passionately believed in God's absolute freedom from humanly conceived rational restrictions, at the same time as he was genuinely a complete rationalist as far as earthbound experiences were concerned.

12 see p. 145 above.

13 He did, however, question at least one article of faith, most strongly held in the Eastern churches but also having supporters in Roman Catholicism, that Mary was the Mother of God (*theotokos*), on the grounds that that would mean that, because God the Father, God the Son and God the Holy Ghost are One, she was the mother of her father.

Ockham also challenged Aquinas' concept that human law and moral law were part of the structure of one immutable and rational natural law,[14] and that moral evil was the result of a faulty intellect.[15] Ockham thought it was not provable by experience that there is such a thing as Natural Law; still less that it was natural and rational for man to comply with it. It follows that we cannot affirm that certain acts are evil because they run counter to a Natural Law which is rational. Instead, Ockham declared that some acts are evil because our faith tells us that God has forbidden them. In matters of morality we should indeed do what our "right reason" tells us to do, but a man of faith will build God's demands into the very structure of this right reasoning. If he does not do that, his "right reason" may lead him to conclusions which may be rational, but which are at odds with what God has commanded and on that score alone are wrong.

> To take an example, Aquinas knew that homosexuality had been condemned by the Bible. That being so, he would also have taken it for granted that homosexual behaviour was contrary to the Natural Law, and that therefore its prohibition had a natural and rational basis even if he were not able to demonstrate it. But in fact, he would have thought that he was perfectly able to prove to his own satisfaction, with arguments he considered rational, that homosexual behaviour was "unnatural" and therefore wrong.
>
> Yet those arguments, rational though he would have thought they were, were not universally compelling. The ancient Greeks, for example, had seen nothing wrong with homosexuality. The Natural Law to which apparently all moral laws must conform, does not seem to have implanted in the Greeks a natural revulsion against homosexual behaviour, and when they engaged in it, they did not think they were *breaking* a natural law and so behaving in an *un*natural way – they found it natural and acceptable.[16]
>
> Ockham would have taken this debate right out of the sphere of what was rational or natural. We need only trust in the word of God as revealed in the Bible that such behaviour was condemned by Him, and use that faith as an integral building block of our "right reasoning" when confronted with such an issue.
>
> Aquinas was certainly not a relativist; his faith precluded that. However, when morality is said to be rational, the door is opened to an element of relativism, because reason may lead different people to different conclusions. There are, for example, some clergy today who maintain that they have faith in God but that their reason tells them that the condemning of homosexuality is irrational. Therefore, they are prepared to assert that, because God is reason, He cannot actually have condemned homosexuality as drastically as traditional church teaching maintained. Thus they are willing to ordain homosexuals and to preside over homosexual marriages. Ockham's position on the moral law had a more fundamentalist basis. There are biblical texts condemning homosexuality, and faith in the Bible is a sufficient ground to oppose it, irrespective of whether human reason accepts or rejects it.

14 see p. 143 above.

15 p. 139 above.

16 True, according to Aquinas' scheme, the Greeks, living before Christianity, knew nothing of the Divine Law which was binding only on Christians (and, to an extent, on Jews and Muslims). But in that scheme the Divine Law must be *supplementary* to the Natural Law – must add new obligations, like, for example, keeping the Sabbath Day holy – but cannot be *contrary* to the Natural Law. The idea was that each form of Law must conform to the principles of the law that was higher up in the pyramid. See p. 143 above.

Ockham and Politics

Aquinas' political thought had been entirely theoretical, as he played no active part in public affairs himself. Ockham, however, found himself deeply engaged in a political battle with the Papacy, and this would shape his ideas on the relationship between Church and state and also on that between the Papacy and the Church.

Soon after the death of St John of Bonaventura in 1274 there had arisen a tension within the Franciscan Order between the Spirituals and the Conventuals. The Spirituals preached absolute poverty, because that had been the way, not only of St Francis, but also, they said, of Christ and the Apostles. By 1274 the Franciscan Order had acquired buildings and a certain amount of communal wealth. The Conventuals saw nothing wrong with this, but the Spirituals thought that even communal wealth was wrong. They criticized not only the Conventuals, but also, with good reason, the enormous wealth of the Church at large and of the Papacy in particular. The Pope, John XXII (1316 to 1334) naturally sided with the Conventuals, and in 1317 published a bull declaring the Spirituals' contention that Christ and his Apostles had possessed nothing either individually or communally as heretical. This went too far even for the Conventuals. In 1322, at a meeting of its General Chapter in Perugia, the entire Franciscan Order declared that Christ and his Apostles had indeed owned nothing of their own. John XXII now denounced the Perugia declaration as heretical (1323). The majority of the Order submitted to the Pope in 1325, but a large minority did not. This group was led by Michael of Cesena (the General of the Franciscans), Marsilio of Padua and William of Ockham himself. William, already in trouble for his stance on apostolic poverty, was now (1326) additionally censured by the Pope for his nominalism, and so came under the same pressure that had led his nominalist predecessor, Roscelin, to recant.[17] Ockham, however, did not recant. Instead, together with Michael of Cesena and Marsilio of Padua, he fled from the papal court to that of the Holy Roman Emperor, Ludwig IV of Bavaria (1328).

At this time a struggle was raging between the Popes and the Emperors for the control of Italy. In 1309, as the Emperor Henry VII was gaining the upper hand, the Papacy had fled from Rome to Avignon. After the death of Henry VII in 1313, Ludwig had been elected emperor, but in 1323 Pope John XXII had declared Ludwig's election invalid, and in the following year had excommunicated him. Ludwig, for his part, supported the Franciscans in their rebellion against the Pope, called John a heretic for his condemnation of the Perugia declaration and appealed to a General Council of the Church.

When William of Ockham and Marsilio of Padua fled to the Emperor's court, they formulated theories that suited their new patron. They attacked the very basis on which the Papacy had rested its ever increasing claims for supremacy in Church and state alike. It is to the development of these claims, and then to the challenges to them, that we turn in the next chapter. In its third section, we shall encounter William of Ockham and Marsilio of Padua again.

17 see p. 117 above.

CHAPTER 18

State and Church

The theories describing the proper relationship between Church and state passed through four phases between the proclamation by the Emperor Theodosius I of Christianity as the official religion of the state (380) and the end of the Council of Constance in 1418.

The First Phase: Cooperation

The establishment of Christianity as the religion of the state happened just before the time that the *Pax Romana* was breaking down and western Europe was succumbing to the barbarian invasions. There followed a period of about five centuries which historians have called the Dark Ages. During that time the top priority for both the secular and the spiritual authorities was to cooperate against the threat of disorder, and not to engage in a struggle for supremacy. The somewhat combative way in which Ambrose had stressed that, though active rebellion against a ruler was still impermissible, a Christian Emperor must do the Church's bidding in spiritual matters, was toned down. It will be remembered that St Augustine, writing the *Civitas Dei* soon after the barbarians had sacked Rome, reiterated the teaching of St Paul that active rebellion, even against an unjust State, was illegitimate.[1] The spirit of cooperation was further stressed in the doctrine of the Two Swords which was promulgated by Pope Gelasius I round about 480 AD. According to this theory, God had entrusted the secular sword to the state and the spiritual sword to the Church, and had commanded that the two were to be wielded in harmony (*concordia*) with each other. The autonomy of each institution within its own sphere was recognized. The concept of sovereignty – that in the last resort one institution was sovereign over the other – was still alien to the Middle Ages, though Gelasius spelt out that where the policy of the state touches on spiritual matters, it must accept the authority of the Church. The Emperors accepted this, just as Theodosius had done, and for several centuries both clerical and lay authorities concentrated on, as it were, honing their respective swords and wielding them within their own realms.

The emperors found this more difficult than did the Papacy. In those centuries feudal princes and barons ruled their fiefdoms as well-nigh independent rulers, and they regarded emperors and kings as no more than first among equals (*primi inter pares*). They were often in open rebellion, and it was not until the sixteenth century, at the beginning of what we call the Early Modern

1 see p. 113 above.

Period, that the monarchs in some countries – by no means in all – managed to truly become masters in their realms.

The Papacy, however, was much more successful. Its control over the Church, which had always been strong, became even stronger. The barbarian invasions had done terrible damage to agriculture on the land and to the fabric and the commerce of the cities, but the Church had suffered a good deal less, as many of the barbarians were already Christians and had generally spared churches and monasteries. So the Roman Catholic Church survived when the western Roman Empire did not.

The monasteries did sterling work in further strengthening the Papacy, both institutionally and theoretically. In 529 St Benedict founded the Benedictine Order at Monte Cassino. Its rule imposed such order, discipline and obedience that the monks became an élite within the Church, all totally at the service of the Papacy. Indeed, the Order would eventually produce no fewer than fifty Popes. Benedictine monasteries were founded all over Europe, and they helped to keep the Church strong and coherent during the Dark Ages, while the secular authorities had a much more difficult time.

The Second Phase: The Papal Bid for Supremacy

So, when the last of the barbarian invasions exhausted itself during the first half of the tenth century, the Church was stronger than the state. It had become more ambitious, and as cooperation against disorder was no longer quite so necessary, the Papacy became more provocative in asserting its supremacy. The Cluniacs, named after the Benedictine monastery that had been founded at Cluny in 910, were responsible for propagating doctrines that claimed ever wider powers for the Papacy. They based themselves on a set of forgeries that are known as the False Decretals and which had gained currency around 850. They purported to be documents that greatly strengthened the authority of the Popes over both Church and state. Some claimed to be papal decrees that had reduced the powers of archbishops and had encouraged bishops to go over their heads in appeals to Rome. The most famous of the forged documents is known as the Donations of Constantine, according to which the Emperor Constantine was supposed to have granted Pope Sylvester I (314 to 335) temporal rule over the western part of the Roman Empire.

This claim was tantamount to a papal claim of sovereignty – indeed, the words *plenitudo potestatis* express that concept quite dramatically. In secular affairs, the concept of sovereignty was still quite unknown in medieval Europe. Rulers were far too weak to think of making any such claim. They knew that they would have to share power with their nobles, and that they were at most *primi inter pares*. The prevailing idea in secular affairs was that of *concordia*: the stability of a state rested on the harmonious cooperation between the King and his estates. Indeed, the Gelasian theory mentioned above rested on the same concept: state and Church need to cooperate in harmony.

Now Pope Gregory VII (1073 to 1085) who himself came from Cluny, used the False Decretals and the Donations of Constantine to assert his sovereign control over Church and state alike, and soon he was engaged in a titanic battle with the Holy Roman Emperor Henry IV, a struggle known as the Investiture Controversy. Gregory asserted that the Pope could impose bishops on the Emperor against the latter's will, that he could tax the Emperor's clerical subjects and that the clergy should be immune from secular taxation and from punishments by the secular courts. The angry Henry IV was unwise enough to convene a synod of German bishops who declared Gregory deposed, whereupon Gregory excommunicated him and claimed the right to depose the Emperor and absolve his subjects from their allegiance. Henry IV was then engaged in a desperate struggle against his barons, whose rebellion was now legitimized by the Pope, and Henry was forced to go to Canossa to do penance and seek absolution (1077).

The Third Phase: Resistance to Papal Claims

The scene at Canossa has captured the imagination of posterity, but Henry's submission was a temporary one. The struggle between Popes and Emperors continued. In the thirteenth and fourteenth centuries, at stake in the struggle between the Imperial party (the Guelphs) and the Papal party (the Ghibellines) was not only the matter of authority, but control over Italy. At one stage, the Imperialists gained such a hold over Italy that the Papacy had to flee Rome and take up residence in Avignon (1309), from where, as we have seen,[2] Pope John XXII had declared the election of the Emperor Ludwig IV invalid in 1323. At the same time, William of Ockham and Marsilio of Padua were locked in dispute with Pope John over the Perugia declaration. In 1328 they fled to Ludwig's court, and now supported the efforts that had already been made in Imperial circles to undermine the papal theories and to erect rival theories in their place.

The most important text on the imperial side had already been published. It was the *De Monarchia* (1310) by Dante Alighieri (1265 to 1321).

Dante hated war and violence, and he looked for a universal empire which could establish universal peace, the Commonwealth of God on this earth. God had directly charged the secular power to establish this Commonwealth, and Dante blamed the disorders in Europe on the Papacy, which had exceeded its God-given spiritual role by playing at politics, by raising armies, fighting wars, and making alliances, by abusing the weapon of excommunication in matters which had nothing to do with the faith and by generally meddling in temporal affairs. In other words, Dante was harking back to the Gelasian theory of the Two Swords and wanted to rein back the intrusion of the Papacy into secular matters.

> His criticism of the Papacy was fair enough, but the hopes he placed in a universal secular empire establishing universal peace was utopian indeed – not least because he never discussed what force might be needed to sustain such an empire. Instead, he claimed that a universal empire would be based on justice and freedom because its rulers would be so well endowed that they would not be tempted to rule badly!
>
> Some historians have seen Dante's vision of a universal and peaceful secular empire as the earliest formulation of an idea which eventually found its embodiment in the League of Nations. President Woodrow Wilson, the beget-

2 see p. 157 above

> ter of the League, was, like Dante, an idealist. The hard-headed politicians who created the League to humour Wilson saw to it that, like Dante's universal empire, it would lack the force to make its decisions prevail.

Marsilio of Padua and William of Ockham now added to this literature, Marsilio with his *Defensor Pacis* (Defender of the Peace, 1324) and William with a whole series of works of which the most important one was the *Dialogus inter magistrum et discipulum de imperatorum et pontificum potestate* (Dialogue between a teacher and his pupil about imperial and papal power). In essence they follow a very similar line. They flatly deny that the Church can make any binding laws beyond those that are found in Scriptures. Violation of the laws in the Scriptures will be punished by God; the Church has no authority to punish. Its decretals and other pronouncements are merely human and have no divine authority whatever. As human laws, they may be enacted, supported and enforced by the state. A community has the right to decide what is an offence and how it should be punished. It may very well follow the advice of the Church about what is heresy and may punish it as such, but in that case the punishment is for an offence against what the *community* has decided.

Marsilio and William define the source of authority in both state and Church. Secular power, they say, derives from God through the people, who delegate it to their representatives. How exactly the representatives are chosen can vary from place to place. In the Middle Ages noone envisaged that choice being made by universal suffrage, of course, but both Marsilio and William insisted that the authority of the rulers, however they are chosen, is ultimately derived from the corporate body of the people as a whole.

When they turn to authority in the Church, they follow similar principles. Here, too, God has vested power in the whole Christian community (William specifically includes its female members) who also delegate it to representatives who in turn choose the ultimate authority: the General Council of the Church, to whom the Pope himself is subject.

This idea was still a little ahead of its time. For one thing, at the time it found no significant support within the church itself. The cardinals who had been appointed by the Papacy continued to support the Popes' claims to the *plenitudo potestatis*. But when the Imperialists organized the election of a rival Pope in Rome in 1378 (some three decades after the deaths of Marsilio and William of Ockham) and the Church underwent the Great Schism, the scandal was so great and the Papacy was so weakened that the idea of calling a General Council to settle the dispute grew apace.

The Fourth Phase: The Conciliar Movement

The Conciliar Theory was adopted by the University of Paris in 1381. A General Council could settle the dispute between the rival popes only on the assumption that it had the authority to do that, and that assumption in its turn implied that the ultimate authority in the Church could not be the Pope. So the theory initially held that it was vested in the Pope-in-Council instead, expressing much the same idea as was expressed in England, for example, by the concept of the supreme secular authority resting in the King-in-Parliament.

The rival popes proved recalcitrant to this idea. When a General Council met at Pisa in 1408 to bring the schism to an end, neither Pope would cooperate. This forced the Council to go further, implicitly claiming not just partnership but superiority. It deposed both the rival Popes and elected a third, but the other two would not step down, so now there were three Popes! As a result, the next Council in Constance (1414) made explicit the claim to superiority which at Pisa had still been implicit. It also managed to persuade the governments of Europe to withdraw their support from whichever Pope they had supported. Of the three Popes, one then resigned, the second one fled and the third died shortly afterwards. The Schism was over, and the Council elected Martin V (1417).

Some members of the Council had wanted to devise a new and more representative constitution of the Church before they proceeded to the election of a new Pope. These were the lower and more radical clergy, who wanted to restrict the power of the cardinals as well as that of the Pope. The threatened cardinals and the conservative upper clergy, fearing this, managed to proceed to the election of the new Pope before any institutional reforms could be enacted. Martin V had no intention of surrendering any part of the papal authority, and indeed, many people accepted that a strong Pope was now needed to restore the shattered Church. He simply ignored the Council's decree that it was superior to the Pope. Indeed, he met it with one of his own, just after the Council had dispersed in 1418, that any future appeals from the Papacy to a General Council would be illegal.

The whole episode is highly significant. The Papacy strengthened itself shortly before most Western monarchies were able to do the same later that century and it managed to resist demands for the reform of abuses and corruption. As a result, when change did come with the Reformation in the following century, it was only achieved by a schism far more fateful than the schism between Rome and Avignon.

The dispute had also produced arguments for a more representative form of government in the Church. In reply to this, the victorious Papacy reiterated the most thoroughgoing exposition of absolutism. The doctrine of papal infallibility, though not formally pronounced until 1870, was, by the end of the fifteenth century, well established in practice.

Both arguments – for representative government and for absolutism – would before very long be shorn of their ecclesiastical context and would transfer into the secular field, where they would dominate political thought for several centuries.

Forerunners of the Reformation

The four phases described above all concerned themselves with the material power and the secular authority of the Papacy. Perhaps in reaction to this concentration on essentially structural issues, there sprang up Christian movements that wanted to renew the mystical, spiritual and inner life of the Church. Prominent among these Pietists were Meister Eckhardt (1260 to 1328) Geert Groote (1340 to 1384) who founded the Brethren of the Common Life, and his successor Thomas à Kempis (1384 to 1472). They practised what was called the *devotio moderna,* in distinction from the *devotio antiqua* of Thomist scholasticism. They did not challenge the authority of the Church, but worked within it to renew its spiritual life.

There were, however, others - John Wycliffe (1328 to 1384) and Jan Hus (1369 to 1414) were the most famous - who thought that the existing Church had become so corrupt and worldly that it had forfeited its authority and in the course of their rebellions they also developed doctrinal positions which were at odds with the teaching of the Catholic Church.

Historically speaking, Wycliffe and Hus were "before their time" Wycliffe's Lollards were crushed in England, Hus was burned as heretic at the Council of Constance (1414) and the Hussite armies in Bohemia were defeated twenty years later.

But the ideas of the Lollards and Hussites, like those of the Pietists, did not die out. They were to be the seed from which sprang the ideas of the Reformation in the sixteenth century.

PART THREE: RENAISSANCE AND REFORMATION

CHAPTER 19

The Humanist Renaissance

The word "Renaissance" was coined by Giorgio Vasari in 1550 to describe what had been happening in the artistic world between the lifetimes of Giotto and Michelangelo. He showed how during that period artists were increasingly and very consciously influenced by the arts of Ancient Greece and Rome, whose ideas were thus "reborn". Since then, the word "Renaissance" has been extended from the visual arts to all areas of thought which were shaped by the rediscovery of the classical world. The general public probably still associates the word mainly with fifteenth-century Italy, with artists like Masaccio, Piero della Francesca and Botticelli, and with the Medici, the Sforzas and the other princely families of Italy who patronized the arts so generously during this time.

In truth a renaissance of the ideas of Antiquity goes back a good deal further than this. In 1927 the American scholar C.H. Haskins coined the phrase "the twelfth-century Renaissance". He stressed how in that century, which most people still place firmly in the Middle Ages, there was already a revived interest in Latin Antiquity. Even so, there was as yet hardly any knowledge of classical Latin literature. Medieval Latin was effective for its purpose, but it was stylistically crude by comparison with its elegant predecessor. Cicero's writings had disappeared; his letters would not be rediscovered until the end of the fourteenth century, nor his books until the nineteenth century.

Greek antiquity, too, made its reappearance in Europe during the twelfth century Renaissance. Western Europe had totally lost contact with the Greek world. In the fifth century, the western Roman Empire had been overrun from the north by barbarians who knew nothing of the Greeks, while the eastern Roman Empire continued in existence for another thousand years. In the eighth century there had been the final schism between the Roman Catholic Church in the West and the Greek Orthodox Church in the East. Since then, a virtual intellectual iron curtain had separated the Latin from the Greek world, on which even two centuries of Latin crusading in the East in the twelfth and thirteenth centuries had no effect. When Greek ideas were reintroduced into the West, it was not by direct contact between them, but by a very circuitous route.

In Chapter 15, we saw how, in the eleventh, twelfth and thirteenth centuries, the writings of some of the ancient Greeks had been translated into Arabic after the Arabs had overrun parts of the Byzantine Empire; how Greek ideas, especially those of Aristotle, had been integrated into Muslim thought, notably by the Arabic scholar Averroës (1126 to 1198); how Averroism came to Spain, the southern half of which was at that time still ruled by the Arabs, while the northern half had by then been reconquered by the Christians. There had followed about a century and a half during which there had been relatively peaceful coexistence between the Christian North and the Arabic South, and indeed, a good deal of cultural contact between the two. Christian and Jewish scholars in Spain translated the Averroist texts from the Arabic into Latin.

Chapters 15 and 16 have described the momentous results, which I would like for the sake of convenience to call the "Averroist" Renaissance, to distinguish it from the "Humanist" Renaissance of the fifteenth century. The works of Aristotle in particular had represented a challenge to early medieval Christian thought. The Christian church had initially opposed Averroism, but had then been compelled to work out a synthesis between secular and religious study. The major figure to undertake this task had been Thomas Aquinas (1225 to 1274). His canonization in 1323 meant that this proto-Renaissance had become firmly bedded down in Christian thought.

The impact of Aristotle had therefore been profound and significant. But it must be recognized that the reception of Greek ideas suffered from certain limitations. To begin with, it was entirely dependent on Arabic texts: the Greek language was almost entirely unknown in the West in the late Middle Ages. Furthermore, the Arabs had translated only those texts which had interested them. They had not been interested in Greek poetry, drama or history. Almost all of Aristotle had been translated, but Plato hardly at all.

Before the advent of Averroism in Europe, the West did have some knowledge of Plato, but he was known to Christians largely through Neo-Platonism. The Neo-Platonists had concentrated on those of Plato's works that concerned themselves with the soul and with emanations from the Divine. Those Neo-Platonists who were Christians had done for Plato what Aquinas would do for Aristotle - they had integrated particular aspects of Plato into Christian theology. This had actually been less of a challenge than Aristotelianism would be. Aristotelianism represented a different temper and a different way of looking at the world; only relatively minor adaptations had had to be made for Neo-Platonism to fit into the otherworldly outlook of early Christianity. St Augustine had loved Plato and the Neo-Platonist Plotinus ("through whom Plato lived again") and it was through St Augustine that the Middle Ages had remained aware of Plato. But this awareness was very selective - it had passed through the sieve of those aspects which had been most congenial to St Augustine. Plato and Neo-Platonism were only known through the expositions made by Latin writers. No one knew Greek, and Plato's original writings - the range and beauty of his dialogues - were not known at all at the end of the Middle Ages.

The Italian Renaissance - the one with which the general public is probably most familiar - began in Florence with the recovery of classical Latin, and then of classical Greek. This recovery was instigated by Petrarch.

PETRARCH

The scholars of The Averroist Renaissance had learnt to admire the writers of Antiquity for their knowledge of logic, of the sciences, of medicine and of metaphysics: the Ancients were revered as paragons of learning. Petrarch (1304 to 1374) however, was not interested in these subjects. He found this adapted Aristotelianism and the whole apparatus of Scholasticism dry and boring. The letters of Cicero were not rediscovered until after Petrarch's death, but their influence on the last years of the Roman Republic could be traced in the surviving writings of Cicero's contemporaries. They made Petrarch think of these Romans as paragons of style, elegance and *façon de vivre.* They had seen the art of living as an end in itself rather than as a preparation for the next life. They had written in praise of friendship and of dignified leisure. Instead of relying on what Petrarch considered arid scholastic disputations, they had used eloquence in writing and in rhetoric to win assent.

> We all delight in a case made with eloquence, it is satisfying, enjoyable and easier to follow than a scholastic argument. But it is easy to understand how some historians have thought that, by and large, the thinkers of the Renaissance were shallower than those of the Middle Ages.

The various philosophies current in the last days of the Republic, whether Stoicism, Epicureanism or Scepticism, had all claimed to develop the teaching of Socrates (who was known only through the works of Plato). None of them claimed descent from Aristotle, who had fallen out of fashion after the city-states, to which his political philosophy was so closely bound, succumbed to the Hellenistic and Roman Empires. Petrarch, bored with Aristotelianism, set Plato up against him, though he knew little of Plato's work and misinterpreted much of what he did know. No matter. The discovery that there had been a Plato who was not merely a proto-Christian would be very influential.

The Romans of Cicero's time had freely acknowledged their debt to Greek culture, and their leading thinkers had been familiar with the Greek language. Petrarch himself knew no Greek. He tried to learn it, but he had a bad teacher and could find no other because they were so scarce. This drove him to launch a campaign for the study of Greek, which bore fruit a generation after his death, when a Chair of Greek was established in Florence (1397).

When Cicero's letters, with their brilliant style, were rediscovered in 1392, they gave a further impetus to what Petrarch had been preaching. Cicero had valued grammar, rhetoric, poetry, history and moral philosophy. These he had defined as *litterae humaniores*, and their study as *studia humanitatis*. Hence these particular areas of thought became known as the Humanities, and the study of them Humanism.

> It will be noted that the "Humanities" excluded, on the one hand, doctrinal theology and, on the other, natural philosophy, which was what Science was called at that time.
>
> The exclusion of theology did not mean that the Italian humanists were necessarily irreligious. The meaning of Humanism in the Renaissance should not be confused with the use of that word today, when it is really another word for Atheism. Many atheists dislike describing themselves negatively by a name

which only stresses what they do not believe – it comes from the Greek *a* (without) + *theos* (god). They prefer a name which expresses positively that their beliefs rest on human or humane values which, in their view, owe nothing to divine commandments.

All the humanists of the fourteenth and fifteenth centuries professed – usually with total sincerity – a belief in God, but another overtone of the word Humanism as used at that time was the insistence that, because humanity was God's finest handiwork, there was nothing wrong with the pursuit of human excellence in all fields. It therefore set itself against the medieval theological view that all is vanity that does not prepare the soul, by piety, prayer and contemplation, for the life in the next world.

The Humanities are often erroneously identified with the "Liberal Arts", or even "the Arts" (as opposed to "the Sciences") for short. That phrase goes back to the Middle Ages, which had identified seven Liberal Arts. These were divided into a higher group of four, called the *Quadrivium*, consisting of Arithmetic, Geometry, Astronomy and Music, and a lower group of three, the *Trivium* of Grammar, Rhetoric and Logic.[1] Why were these seven subjects called "liberal"? The word comes from the Latin *liber*, meaning "free". It was the study that was appropriate for free men (or gentlemen), as opposed to the pursuit of subjects that had a practical application, like science or mechanics. In this respect the Middle Ages picked up from Plato and Aristotle the idea that studies which are not an end in themselves but are pursued for practical ends were suitable only to "mechanics" or slaves.[2] That, by our standards, was snobbish enough, and it held back the development and status of the sciences for centuries.

It can be seen that Cicero's "Humanities" are not the same as the "Liberal Arts". The subjects of the *Quadrivium* are not represented among them at all. As we shall see, Renaissance scholars did not stick so closely to Cicero's prescriptions that they neglected the *Quadrivium*, to which they also attached the greatest importance.[3]

THE REVIVAL OF CLASSICAL LEARNING

Florence identified itself particularly with the Roman Republic, as it was itself a Republic and would continue to be so nominally even after the Medici dynasty established itself in 1428. Their interest now extended beyond the letters of Cicero. The rediscovery of Vitruvius led to a scholarly revival of architecture based on classical models, Quintilian as well as Cicero became a model of rhetoric, and the comedies of Terence and Plautus were revived, as were the satires of Juvenal. Those earnest medieval scholars had not on the whole been interested in rhetoric, comedy or satire, so these were revelations of a sort.

When the study of Greek began, Italian scholars began to scour the eastern world for Greek manuscripts, and they brought back a huge haul in the years

1 Oddly enough, the word "trivial" is related to *Trivium*: not because it was the lesser division of the seven liberal arts, but because the earliest meaning of *trivium* as of *quadrivium*, was "the place where three (or four) roads (*viae*) met", where the public tended to congregate, so that *trivialis* came to mean "belonging to the public streets", and hence "common".

2 See pp. 35 and 51 above.

3 When Holbein painted *The Ambassadors* in 1533, he indicated the educated and gentlemanly status of the two men by arranging on the table and shelves behind him the instruments that were associated with the *Quadrivium*.

that followed. In 1423, just one such scholar, Giovanni Aurispa, returned from his journeys with 238 important manuscripts. The western world now rediscovered the original texts of Plato and of Aristotle. These included some that had never been translated into either Arabic or Latin, for example, Plato's *Symposium,* that great hymn to love and friendship, and Aristotle's *Poetics*, whose theories about the dramatic unities[4] would, from time to time, have such a strong influence on theories of literature until the early nineteenth century. Other works that now reached the West in the original included the epics of Homer and the dramas of Aeschylus, Sophocles and Euripides and the historical writings of Herodotus, Thucydides, Xenophon and Plutarch.

What a feast all this was for scholars! The most important of these was Francisco Filelfo, who in 1429 started a great series of lectures expounding these works in Florence. He revived for the Liberal Arts (Grammar, Rhetoric, History, Poetry and Moral Philosophy) the name that Cicero had given to them: the *studia humanitatis*.

The intellectual iron curtain between East and West had become permeable, and soon it broke down altogether. The Byzantine Eastern Empire had been under the pressure of the Turks for three hundred years. Back in the eleventh century, the Greek Christians of the East had called for help from the Latins of the West. The Latin armies had arrived on Crusades to drive the Turks out of the Holy Land, but instead of restoring it to the Byzantine Empire they had turned it into a Latin kingdom. The Fourth Crusade was actually diverted to sack Constantinople in 1204. This was hardly an inducement for Greeks and Latins to come closer together. By the end of the thirteenth century, the Turks had driven the Crusaders out of the Middle East, and the Byzantine Empire continued to lose territories to the Turks. By the beginning of the fifteenth century its situation was desperate. It had shrunk to a small area on either side of the Straits, surrounded on all sides by the Turks. The fall of Constantinople seemed only a matter of time. The Greek Christians were desperate. They felt that only if there were a reunification of the eastern and western churches in the face of Islam could the East expect help from the West. In 1439 they sent a delegation to the western Church Council which met that year in Florence, to negotiate reunification. It was led by the Emperor John VIII Paleologus in person and the theologians in his train were headed by the Archbishop of Nicaea, John Bessarion. The two churches were temporarily reunited, but then the treaty was repudiated by the clergy in the East and by the turbulent mob in Constantinople. Bessarion, who had been created a Cardinal of the Latin Church for his services, remained in Italy.

Bessarion was a distinguished advocate of Plato, and he had brought with him a large library of Greek manuscripts, which he later donated to the Senate of Venice. He gathered around him other Greek scholars. Their number was reinforced when, in 1453, the Turks finally captured Constantinople and many other Greek Christian scholars fled to Italy. This group greatly contributed to the interest in Plato, which had already been stimulated by the enthusiasm of

4 He had said that a noble work of drama should concentrate on only one plot (that is, have no sub-plots) and that it should ideally take place on one day. He had not actually stipulated that it should also be set in only one place, though the theory of the Dramatic Unities came to be thought of as demanding unity of plot, time and place.

Marsilio Ficino, who, in 1445, is said to have founded the Platonic Academy in Florence.[5] Ficino translated all the twenty-seven dialogues then attributed to Plato[6] into Latin. Ficino was a Christian, and his aim was to fuse Plato with Christianity. This had also been the aim of the Neo-Platonists of Antiquity,[7] and Ficino also translated into Latin the most important Neo-Platonic text, the *Enneades* of Plotinus.[8] In addition, he wrote commentaries on seven of the Platonic dialogues he had translated. Between 1469 and 1474 he published no less than eighteen volumes of a work called *Platonic Theology on the Immortality of the Soul.*

The inclusion of the word "Theology" in the title is significant - Plato and the Bible were to be synthesized. Neither was to be taken literally, but both, he thought, enshrined sacred mysteries that had to be deciphered.

This attempt to synthesize everything that was valuable in Christian and pagan thought is typical of the Renaissance. Another member of the Platonic circle, Pico della Mirandola, went even further. Like Bessarion he sought to integrate Aristotelianism with Platonism and both with Christianity. He also found much of value in the so far exclusively Jewish mystical tradition of the Cabbalah.[9] He saw truths of Christianity embedded within it and was responsible for creating a Christian Cabbalah. This attempt to create a synthesis of all the great intellectual creations of the past became known as "The Perennial Philosophy", after the title of a book published in 1540 by Augustino Steuco.

Alas, by 1540 the Reformation was already in full swing. The syncretism of the Renaissance strikes me as one of the most attractive aspects of the Italian Renaissance, and on that score alone the period is a high water mark in the history of civilization. I am drawn to it because it was based on respect of what non-Christians had achieved intellectually, and it concentrated on those things which Christians and non-Christians had in common instead of focussing on what made them different. It was an all too brief period of intellectual tolerance and breadth of mind. The Protestant Reformation, when it came, and the Catholic Counter-Reformation which was a response to it, was totally sectarian and intolerant. Not only did both reject Renaissance syncretism, making it clear that trying to find any common ground between Christianity and paganism was subversive of Christianity, but they focussed on the differences between Protestantism and Catholicism, and on the differences between various kinds of Protestantism (Lutheranism, Calvinism, Zwinglianism, Anabaptism etc.). For over a hundred years international and civil wars about religion would be the result.

The philosopher Michel de Montaigne (1533 to 1592) was a witness to the long religious civil wars in France (1562 to 1598). He loved classical antiquity and did not believe in the absolute truth of any religion. He therefore urged an attitude of tolerance, but was forced by the Inquisition to amend some passages to this effect in his *Essais* (1580) for later editions. Not until the eighteenth century do we find another attempt made, this time by Theists and

5 There is some question whether such a formal body ever existed, or whether it was merely an informal gathering of friends such as Pico della Mirandola, Politian and Alberti.

6 see p. 21 above.

7 see p. 58 above.

8 see p. 89 above.

9 See p. 126 above.

Deists,[10] to concentrate once more on what all religions have in common. At that time these were campaigners against persecution by the propagators of what they considered obscurantism and superstition, so they treated the doctrinal differences in the name of which there was so much intolerance with scorn and ridicule rather than with respect. Perhaps it is only since the Second World War that the hold of fanatical sectarianism has weakened in Europe (alas, not everywhere – we have only to think of Northern Ireland) and that some serious efforts have been made by religious leaders to recreate respect for the beliefs of other religions.

Renaissance thinkers like Ficino and Pico della Mirandola had gone further than respect; they had not stopped at a courteous agreement to differ from the pagans (who were of course no longer available to engage in dialogue with them). The Perennial Philosophy had aimed to *integrate* pagan with Christian thought. That attempt has been abandoned by most churchmen today. There was, for a time, some hope in certain quarters that the Christian churches might actually somehow fuse their doctrines and reunite, but this has led nowhere. Respect for differences between Christians, between Christians, Jews and the Muslims, or indeed between those who believe in God and those who do not, is the most that we *can* hope for, and is, I believe, the most that we *ought* to hope for. Only among small sections of the laity have there been attempts to integrate the wisdoms of other systems of belief (mostly those of the East: like Hinduism and Buddhism, but also some very ancient pagan concepts, like those about the Earth Mother) into our philosophies of life.

The universities, who had played such a leading part in shaping the Averroist Renaissance, had little use for the ideas of the Humanist Renaissance. They remained almost unaffected and persevered with Thomist orthodoxy and scholastic Aristotelianism for at least another century. It could be said that, whereas the attempt to integrate the learning of Antiquity with the teaching of Christianity was a huge intellectual endeavour, the attempt to recapture the lifestyle of Antiquity was, by comparison, a shallower intellectual enterprise. It required not so much a challenging struggle with ideas, rather it was the creation of a fashion, to copy a way of life and of expression that struck Petrarch and his contemporaries as immensely attractive. Of course, the intellect was involved to a certain extent, but the *seriousness*, the concern with theology and the earnestness of the Averroist Renaissance was often missing. The scholastic arguments may have been dry, pedantic and boring, but they attempted to be rigorously logical. To present a theological argument in an elegant rhetorical manner would have struck medieval, and did strike some of their contemporary theologians, as quite inappropriate. Their priority was to create a convincing intellectual structure. They would have seen the shift of focus to a preoccupation with lifestyle as essentially frivolous, especially when it involved such *jeux d'esprit* as seeing in the Roman Venus a prototype of the Virgin Mary.

10 Theists believe that there is a God who cares about how humans behave and that there is therefore a relationship between Him and His creation. Beyond that, at least in the eighteenth century, they mocked the stories in both the Old and the New Testament as fables not worthy of belief, and considered the rituals and ceremonies of the different religions to be basically absurd. Deists believe that there must be a Deity which has created the universe, but that this God no longer shows any interest in it, and that there is no further relationship between Him and human beings.

If Humanism found little acceptance in the universities, it did find warm support from the princely courts. That worldly setting in itself helps to explain the interest in the secular aspects of the lifestyle of Antiquity and the occasionally merely perfunctory obeisance to theological doctrine. The most famous of the princely patrons of Humanism were the cultured Medici dynasty of Florence. Cosimo Medici (1428 to 1464) and his son Lorenzo the Magnificent (1469 to 1492) were enthusiastic supporters of the Platonic Academy, and Ficino read ten of his translated Platonic dialogues to Cosimo as the latter lay dying in 1464. Humanism penetrated even the Papacy. Several Popes were patrons of the new ideas: Nicholas V (1447 to 1455), Pius II (1458 to 1464), Julius II (1510 to 1513) and Leo X (1513 to 1521), who was the son of Lorenzo the Magnificent. Only a Humanist Pope could have supported the scheme that Michelangelo created for the Sistine Chapel, the very heart of western Christendom, between 1509 and 1511. There we see, in the frieze on either side of the chapel, Biblical prophets and the Sybils of Pagan Antiquity alternating as they prophesy what is to come. In the following year, Rafael placed the two magnificent *fresci* known as the *School of Athens* and the *Disputà* within the papal library. The former shows the great figures of pagan Antiquity, grouped round Plato and Aristotle. The Fathers of the Church face them on the opposite wall.[11]

Painting often gives visible expression to Ficino's interpretation of Platonic ideas as allegories of Christian ones. For example, the spiritualized Goddess of Love and Beauty is the central figure in Botticelli's *Birth of Venus* (1485; Uffizi). The pagan goddess of Love arrives on a shell or scallop (the symbol of Christian pilgrimage). She illustrates Ficino's teaching that Plato's love of Beauty was an allegory of St Paul's love of God. Plato had equated Beauty with Truth, so the goddess of Beauty is also the goddess of Truth. Venus, the daughter of Zeus, is an allegory of Truth, the daughter of God. Truth dwells in purity in the realm of Ideas, but is veiled when she appear to us here below. So, in the painting a figure on the shore of the land where humans dwell holds out a robe that will veil "the naked truth" when she comes to dwell among us.[12]

Plato had had an almost mystical reverence for mathematics and geometry, which he had regarded as a particularly pure form of truth, beauty, and harmony. This, too, was revived by the Florentine Platonists. The serene classical proportions of Renaissance architecture – so different from the Gothic – testify to this, as do the compositions of Rafael. In at least two of Botticelli's paintings, art historians have seen hidden references to numbers whose allegorical significance only trained Neo-Platonists could understand. This is not the place to

11 Though Rafael respects both the pagan philosophers and the Christian theologians, the scheme of the two paintings shows that he thought the latter were superior. In the *School of Athens*, Plato and Aristotle debate whether Ideals stored up in Heaven (universals) have more reality than their manifestations on earth (particulars):. The central axis of the painting – what Anthony Bertram has called "the axis of certainty" – falls between them: no pagan thinker has access to the central truth. In the *Disputà* there is also a debate, this time between the Church Fathers; about the exact significance of the Eucharist. Whatever their disagreements, there is no doubt about the central truth of Christianity, for on the central "axis of certainty" of the composition are aligned the Father, the Son and the Holy Spirit represented in the monstrance on the altar.

12 Titian makes the same point in *Sacred and Profane Love* (1515; Borghese Gallery). Contrary to a civilization which still thinks there is something naughty about nudity, it is the unclothed woman who represents Sacred Love and the clothed woman who stands for "profane" (i.e. non-religious; the Latin word originally meant "outside the Temple") love.

describe in detail the symbolism that some scholars have detected in the *Primavera* (1478; Uffizi), but among the many layers of meaning they have seen in that painting is one that relates to an elaborate Ficinian programme of numbers.

Plato's *Symposium* was a great hymn to Love. It contains the myth that the gods had split the original human beings into two, and that ever since each half tries to find the other with which to reunite. Ficino took such myths to be the equivalent of parables in the New Testament: allegories, not to be taken literally. He believed that God who is Love manifests Himself in the love that humans have towards each other; the Love that God has for mankind is immanent, not transcendental. Therefore, love between humans – not just an awareness that we are all brothers in the sight of God and ought therefore to treat each other well as a matter of Christian *duty* – is to be cherished as a gift of God. Ficino rejects the medieval notion, expressed in clerical celibacy, that strong attachment to an individual – what we call friendship – diverts from God the love that is owed to Him. Through love between humans, the soul ascends to love for God; it graduates from the communion of bodies in physical love, through the communion of souls between humans,[13] to the love for God. This theme, too, has been seen as underlying the *Primavera*. Presided over by Venus (whom we now know to represent spiritual love in Ficinian philosophy) the soul passes through the physicality of the three Graces to the contemplation of heavenly love as Hermes (the god of hidden, "hermetic", knowledge) points the way through the clouds.

Plato had seen the object of education as training the soul to attain wisdom so that after death it could rejoin the realm of Ideas from which it had descended to dwell within its human shell. Ficino, too, wanted to prepare the soul for its ascent to Heaven. The good active life on this earth is the first stage; the contemplative life is the next, preparing it for its reunion with God after death.

In all this we see that for Ficino it was important to reconcile pagan with Christian thought. This was why he singled out Plato for special attention, just as the Neo-Platonist Christians had done. But Greek philosophy had had other strands, such as Epicureanism and Scepticism (and to some extent Stoicism), which had debunked religion. No original texts of these schools were available during the Renaissance, but Latin commentaries on them by Cicero, Diogenes Laertius and Sextus Empiricus were rediscovered during the revival of interest in Roman Antiquity. These ideas now found their Renaissance exponents in writers like Lorenzo Valla (1407 to 1457) for Epicureanism, and Michel de Montaigne (1533 to 1592) for Scepticism. Such thinkers did not openly attack Christianity – that would have been too dangerous for them personally. Besides, many of them did not want to undermine the faith of the uneducated. They recognized religious belief as an important support of social and moral discipline. Many of the educated, however, looked upon traditional Christian teaching with what R.G. Collingwood has called "the discreet smile of the Renaissance". William Durant puts it beautifully when he writes that, for many Renaissance thinkers:

13 Since Plato too had valued this above physical attachment, Ficino coined the phrase "Platonic love".

> the revelation of a Greek culture lasting a thousand years and reaching the heights of literature, philosophy and art in complete independence of Judaism and Christianity, was a mortal blow to their belief in Pauline theology, or in the doctrine of *nulla salus extra ecclesiam* – 'no salvation outside the Church'. Socrates and Plato became for them uncanonized saints; the dynasty of the Greek philosophers seemed to them superior to the Greek and Latin Fathers; the prose of Plato and Cicero made even a cardinal ashamed of the Greek of the New Testament and the Latin of Jerome's translation; the grandeur of imperial Rome seemed nobler than the timid retreat of convinced Christians into monastic cells; the free thought and conduct of Periclean Greeks or Augustan Romans filled many humanists with an envy that shattered in their hearts the Christian code of humility, otherwordliness, continence; and they wondered why they should subject body, mind and soul to the rule of ecclesiastics who themselves were now joyously converted to the world.[14]

It is certain that the Renaissance picture of the Ideal Complete Man was very different from that of the medieval Christian Man. He was now seen largely in secular terms; he had a noble place in the scheme of things, whereas the Middle Ages had stressed his essential corruption by Original Sin. He may glory in his body and train it to excellence, rather than be ashamed of it[15] and called upon to mortify the flesh. Had not God created man in His own image as His finest handiwork? Man is therefore not a miserable worm who has to pass through this earthly life as best he can to prepare himself for the life hereafter, he is endowed by God with Dignity. One of Pico della Mirandola's books has the significant title *De Hominis Dignitate*. In it he has God say to Adam: "I created thee as a being neither heavenly nor earthly ... that thou mightest be *free* to shape and overcome thyself." (My italics). "Free", not predestined to either Salvation or Damnation. Not only Salvation but secular success also comes to Man through his own efforts and strength of will. Human love is one of Man's noblest achievements, whereas the Middle Ages had extolled celibacy for those noble spirits who were capable of it. The Renaissance found a place for respecting real women of character and scholarship, where the Middle Ages had ignored the real woman behind chivalric idealizations of her, if indeed they did not treat her as mere chattel. Now her individuality was noted, as indeed was that of each man. This emerges strikingly in Renaissance portraiture. The often stylized or idealized representation in medieval portraiture gives way to recognizable human beings which differ from one another, whether it be by a broken nose as in Piero della Francesca's portrait of Federico Montefeltro, the Duke of Urbino, or by the bulging eyes of his obviously rather plain wife Battista Sforza (both 1465; Uffizi).[16]

Where the Middle Ages advocated austerity, Renaissance Man was entitled to pursue pleasure. He should strive for honour by fulfilling all his innate capacities for growth – an ideal which contrasted with the medieval one of humility. He should pursue personal fame and claim recognition for his individual achievements, rather than do his work anonymously in the service of

14 W. Durant – The Story of Civilization – The Renaissance, p. 84

15 Compare the hunched deformed body of Adam in Masaccio's *Expulsion of Adam and Eve from Paradise* (1428; Carmine, Florence) with the still handsome and sinewy body he is given in Piero della Francesca's *The Death of Adam* (1452; Duomo, Arezzo).

16 although it must be admitted that striking individual likenesses are found more often in portraits of men than in those of women.

God.[17] He should aim for honour in the public service and engage in civic affairs rather than follow the monastic life.[18] Renaissance Man was interested in real History, in what people really did, and he used myths and legends for allegorical purposes only, rather than believing them to have actually happened. He admired versatility[19] and delighted in wit. The state, which had been seen as an instrument of God in the Middle Ages, was now seen as a secular institution. This comes across most strongly in the writings of Machiavelli, who saw statesmanship in purely pragmatic terms, free from all theological imperatives.

MACHIAVELLI

The self-confidence of the Italian Renaissance states was badly shaken by the French invasion of 1494. They had been indulging in continual quarrels and petty wars. Many of them had come to rely on mercenary armies rather than on their own troops. The Popes, who had secular interests as rulers over territories in Central Italy, played their own part in intrigues, shifting alliances and wars. In 1494, the ruler of Milan was engaged in a dispute with the King of Naples, and invited Charles VIII of France to assert dynastic claims on Naples. To his astonishment, the French armies poured into Italy. He had to let them through Milan. They next expelled the Medici rulers of Florence, who had sided with Naples. Within five months they had occupied Naples itself. This badly upset the balance of power, and the Spaniards now took a hand: they invaded Naples to drive out the French. Soon afterwards, the Habsburgs were drawn into the struggle with claims of their own on Milan. For the next three centuries Italy was one of the principal battlegrounds on which France, Spain and the Holy Roman Empire fought out their battles for supremacy. The hitherto independent Italian states became, at best, satellites of the surrounding great powers. The Papacy threw its weight now on one side, now on the other, in a desperate attempt to maintain some balance of power in the peninsula.

It was a terrible humiliation for the Italians, who, during the glory days of the Renaissance, had regarded the French, the Spaniards and the Germans as little better than barbarians, and there was much heart-searching about the causes of this disaster.

One explanation was offered by the Florentine Dominican Girolamo Savonarola. For him, the barbarian invasions were the punishment of God on a society that had turned away from true religion to worship pagan antiquity. The Papacy itself was at fault: instead of resisting this flirtation with paganism, it had itself patronized it. Savonarola revived the demand for a General Coun-

17 We know the names of the sculptors and painters who produced the Renaissance masterpieces. The creators of many medieval works of art, by contrast, are unknown to us because they worked for the greater glory of God, not for themselves. In the course of the Renaissance the status of the artist grew immeasurably – the Emperor Charles V felt proud to pick up the brushes that had been dropped by Titian. Medieval artists, on the other hand, saw themselves as humble artisans and were treated as such.

18 Here, the worldly Aristotle still had something to contribute. Leonardo Bruni (1370 to 1444), the scholar-Chancellor of Florence, made a new translation, into a Latin that was more elegant than the medieval versions, of Aristotle's *Politics* and *Ethics*. See p. 51, for Aristotle's conception of honour.

19 The Florentine Leon Battista Alberti (1404–1472) was honoured for this quality. He was a linguist, a musician, a philosopher, a poet, a craftsman, an architect, a criminologist, a sportsman and an animal breeder. Leonardo da Vinci was, of course, also renowned for his versatility.

cil to reform the Papacy. He called for repentance and organized the burning of "vanities", of those paintings of naked pagan goddesses and of worldly depictions of the Christian story. Temporarily, he had a powerful impact,[20] but he was excommunicated for his attacks on the Papacy and was hanged and burnt in 1498. The synthesis between Antiquity and Christianity was not abandoned by the Papacy – the paintings by Rafael and Michelangelo in the Vatican were still to come. It would only be after the Catholic Church had lost half of Europe to the Reformation that its religious art would turn its back on pagan "precursors" of Christianity.[21]

A very different explanation for the disasters that had struck was offered by Niccolo Machiavelli (1469 to 1527). His most famous book, *The Prince*, written in 1513, offers a cure for the sickness of Italy. The cynical view of human nature expressed in it, and the equally cynical advice about how a prince should manipulate it, have given Machiavelli a terrible reputation. The adjective derived from his surname has become a word of abuse and when the Index of forbidden works was introduced by the Catholic Church in 1559, *The Prince* figures on the list. Indeed, he has so outraged Christian moralists that his first name has become an addition to the list of names (Satan, Lucifer, Beelzebub etc.) by which the Devil is known: "Old Nick".

We ought to remember that Machiavelli had this cynical view not so much of mankind in general as of his Italian contemporaries in particular. In a longer and much less well known work of his, *Discourses on the First Ten Books of Titus Livy*, begun in the same year as he wrote *The Prince*, he shared the Renaissance admiration of Antiquity. The subject of Livy's books was the early history of the Roman Republic, and Machiavelli praised the virtues that the people of Italy had had during that time.[22] He believed that the Italians of those days had been full of republican virtues, they had been public-spirited, and wise in exercising their suffrage to elect worthy magistrates. Their qualities had set them on the path to creating a united Italy, and they had been ready to defend their state with their own bodies.

Machiavelli believed that, by contrast, the Italians of his own time were incapable of such virtues. They had split into warring princedoms which relied largely on mercenaries or *condottiere*. The mercenaries had no patriotic allegiance, and they were actually a source of lawlessness and disorder. They often turned against their employers and occasionally overthrew them, as the

20 Botticelli is said to have brought armfuls of his own paintings to throw upon the bonfire of vanities that Savonarola organized in 1497 in Florence's Piazza della Signoria. We have only to compare his two treatments of the *Nativity* to see the effect which the friar's preaching had on him. That of 1476 (Washington National Gallery) shows the Infant Jesus being worshipped by recognizable members of the Medici family and their courtiers. These make up the foreground, and some of them were so keen to be recognized that they face out towards us and away from the crib. In the Nativity of 1500 (in the London National Gallery) there are no recognizable individual portraits, and, in a clear return to the language of medieval religious painting, perspective is ignored and the human beings, though in the foreground, are tiny in relation to the Holy Family and to the angels dancing above the stylized stable.

21 Whereas Michelangelo's Sybils join the Prophets in looking towards the east wall of the Sistine Chapel, there would be no room for any pagan figures when that wall was covered with his terrifying Last Judgment thirty years later (1541).

22 Livy's work consisted of 142 books. Book 10 took him only to the end of the Samnite wars in 290 BC, long before the Republic reached its apogee in the days of Cicero (1st century BC) but Machiavelli detected republican virtues even in those early days.

Sforzas had overthrown the Visconti of Milan. The ancient city of Rome was now the home of the Papacy which, instead of being a force for Italian unity, was deviously playing off one part of the country against another, and that at a time when France and Spain were becoming united national states. The Italian body politic was diseased, and in the absence of republican virtue, autocracy was the only medicine. *The Prince* was written as a manual for autocrats.[23]

Machiavelli shows a prince how he can secure and maintain his power. He believed that that power should be exercised for the benefit of the state, to make it strong and secure at home and abroad. It was not his intention to help a prince pursue his personal self-interest at the expense of his subjects, which is how so many dictators have abused their absolute power. The lessons of *The Prince* are, however, of benefit both to public-spirited and to corrupt autocrats, and they have been applied as least as often by the latter as by the former.

> Machiavelli was neither the first nor the last to see autocracy as the necessary medicine for a diseased political system. It is the argument used by every dictator and by every military leader who has staged a coup. Some are openly contemptuous of democracy, others claim that the restoration of a healthy democracy is their ultimate objective. Machiavelli never made that point in *The Prince*. There is plenty of advice on how an autocrat should keep power, none on how he should prepare to relinquish it when order has been restored. Yet, the *Discorsi* suggest that Machiavelli did not see autocracy as the best model of government.

A prince needs to remember that human beings are in general selfish: "One can make this generalization about men: They are ungrateful, fickle, liars and deceivers, they shun danger and are greedy for profit; while you treat them well, they are yours. They would shed their blood for you, risk their property, their lives, their children, so long ...as danger is remote; but when you are in danger they turn against you." To rule over such people, a prince must be as strong as a lion and as cunning as a fox, and the book is full of advice on how to be both strong and cunning. He must be ruthless, "it is better to be feared than loved if you cannot be both". He cannot be fettered by rules of morality, and indeed Machiavelli anticipated Nietzsche in thinking that the Christian morality has made men feeble. Of course, if the subjects are good Christians, they will be easier to govern so the prince should claim to rule over them by divine authority - but he himself must be amoral. "Let the prince ... take the surest course he can to maintain his life and state; the means shall always be thought honourable." Of course, Machiavelli expected that the prince would not be interested in self-aggrandisement as an end in itself; he is to remember that his function is to make the *state* strong, healthy and orderly. In a diseased state he has to be its master, but at the same time he also has to be its servant. A healthy

23 It has often been pointed out that it was also written for a much more mundane purpose: to restore Machiavelli to the good graces of the Medici. When the Medici had been expelled from Florence in 1494, Machiavelli had joyfully served the Republic in diplomatic and military affairs. He had persuaded the republican government to do without mercenaries, and had been put in charge of setting up a citizen militia. Doubtlessly his work at the centre of government taught him that even a republic does not live on fine ideals alone and that all governments attract their fair share of ruthless and self-seeking individuals. In 1512 the Medici had been restored to power; Machiavelli was imprisoned and tortured, but was shortly afterwards released and sent to live on his farm in the country. There he wrote *The Prince* and dedicated it to Giulano de Medici, but it did not secure for Machiavelli a return to office.

republican state likewise sees, as the Romans did, that the welfare of the people is the supreme law *(salus populi suprema lex)* and that this interest must override, as he writes in the *Discorsi,* every consideration of "just or unjust, pitiful or cruel, honourable or dishonourable".

> Machiavelli works on the assumption that politics is a rough and dirty game; to be successful a ruler must not hamper himself with moral scruples. In democracies politicians often feel that that is only partially true of domestic affairs: there are limits to the amount of deviousness that is acceptable. If it is permissible, for example, to be "economical with the truth", an outright lie to the House of Commons is regarded by all British statesmen as morally reprehensible. In a democracy, the game is played according to certain rules which have a moral basis and which all parties respect.
>
> But even democracies engage in cynical and immoral operations in the international field. The assumption is that there is no common moral basis accepted by all states in international affairs. Any foreign minister who truly aims to follow a moral foreign policy, when other states are not so constrained, will serve his country's interests badly as a result. Yet democratic statesmen are reluctant to be openly as amoral and ruthless as such a view of the world might demand. A cynic might say that the reason for this is the need to clothe the nakedness of national self-interest in the garments of morality. But there is also the realization that, though a completely moral foreign policy is unachievable, the abandonment of the *aim* to be as moral as possible under the circumstances would in fact lead to a world which is more immoral than it has any "need" to be. Here lies, I think, the main mischief of Machiavelli's point of view. One may not always be able to observe morality in politics; one may have to accept that politics is often a dirty game; but if one abandons morality as an ideal and settles for pure self-interest, the game will become dirtier and dirtier. The too-ready acceptance that politics has nothing to do with morality is as dangerous as the too-ready acceptance that politics must be conducted with an absolute respect for moral principles. How to strike the balance between these two in practice is of course enormously difficult.
>
> It is not always easy, especially in foreign policy, to be clear what the moral imperatives would be. To take only one example: it is perhaps immoral to stand by and see a savage dictator commit unspeakable atrocities inside his own country, but it is nowadays also considered immoral to interfere directly in the internal affairs of other countries and to violate their sovereignty, so long as there is no threat to international peace.

The princes of Renaissance Italy were notorious for their guile, treachery and ruthlessness, but in truth the same could be said of most medieval rulers, whatever lip service they paid to religion. The most striking feature of Machiavelli is that he did not pay such lip service. He regarded politics as a science based on the lessons learnt from observation; his books are full of examples from recent and classical history to illustrate his maxims.

He did not build up a wider framework within which to set his teaching. There is no reference in his work to metaphysics, such as we find in the writings of medieval political thinkers, nor does he underpin his conclusions with a comprehensive theory of psychology such as we will find in Hobbes. For this reason, some authorities do consider him not really to have been a philosopher at all. Nevertheless, he was a thinker whose influence was soon acknowledged by clear-sighted, cynical and effective statesmen. There is a story that, in the days when they were still colleagues, the deeply religious Sir Thomas More wrote to Thomas Cromwell that his bedside reading was Plato. Indeed, More's own book, *Utopia* (1516), which is a description of an ideal state, is obviously influenced by Plato's *Republic;* both books describe the model of an ideal state laid up in Heaven, and of which any real state that actually exists on this earth is of necessity an imperfect copy. The worldly Cromwell, who would help to make Henry VIII the unfettered ruler of England, advised More to read *The Prince* instead: there More would find an account of how the world *really* works, and that is of much more use to a statesman than a description of an unrealistic ideal state. In his idealistic youth, Frederick the Great had written a book attacking Machiavelli, but as soon as he had assumed the responsibilities of kingship, he openly made *Raison d'État* the principle that allowed him to set aside all moral inhibitions in his foreign policy. Neither Cromwell nor Frederick allowed himself to be influenced by religious considerations, and in this, each man was a true disciple of Machiavelli.

Yet there is an irony here. Machiavelli had looked upon religion as no more than a useful method of social control. He had no conception of the explosive force which religion demonstrated only four years after *The Prince* was written, when Martin Luther nailed the Ninety-Five Theses upon the church door of Wittenberg.

CHAPTER 20

The Reformation

Northern Humanism

The rediscovery of ancient Greek was not confined to Italy, it soon spread north of the Alps to Germany and the Netherlands. In Italy it had led scholars to study the pagan authors in the original. The Italians were surrounded by vestiges of Antiquity; of the Roman Republic that was such a self-declared admirer of the heritage of Greece. In northern Europe such vestiges were absent, and the climate among the scholars in the North was altogether more religious. The mystical and pietist movements in the fourteenth and fifteenth centuries, like the Brethren of the Common Life,[1] created quite a different atmosphere from the more worldly one that characterizes the Italian Renaissance. As a result, in the North the rediscovery of Greek led to studying the New Testament in the original, and it was a short step from there for scholars to wish to be able to study the Old Testament also in its original Hebrew. The scholar most associated with promoting these studies was Johannes Reuchlin (1455 to 1522).

One result of this newly concentrated study of the Bible was that it privileged the texts of the Scriptures over those of the Church Fathers and of Church Councils. As a result, many people began to think that the writings of the Fathers, the decrees of the Councils and the very apparatus of the Church did not rest on biblical authority at all. There was nothing in the Bible about Popes. The word *episcopos*, from which the word "bishop" is derived, is mentioned a few times in Paul's letters, and it did mean "an overseer", but more commonly Paul and the Acts of the Apostles had spoken of the churches being managed by elders (*presbuteros*). These were senior members of the congregation; their title did not carry the sacral overtones either of the word *hiereus* used in the New Testament for the Jewish temple priests or of the word *sacerdos* which was its Latin translation. When the Catholic Church came to use the word *sacerdos* to describe the leaders of the churches, it transferred to them this sacral aura. It was then also carried by the translation into other languages (*Priest, Priester, prêtre* etc.) and all these titles implied that their holders were set apart by their calling from the general laity.

None of this meant initially that the scholars rejected the authority of Popes, Councils and priests. They did not want to challenge the authority of the Church, but wanted to work within it. One call was for the renewal of its spiritual life by meditation and a concentration on the inner life. Another was for the raising of the calibre of the priesthood. Many individual priests were seen to be

1 See p. 163 above.

worldly, ignorant and superstitious. Again, there was no attack on the priesthood as such, even if there was, to an extent, a challenge to its pretensions to be a group of men set apart from others. Post-Biblical stories about saints and the miracles connected with them were beginning to be treated with scant respect, and the material interest in pilgrimages to their shrines were touched upon. Even the learned clergy, so the Humanists thought, were often too concerned with hair-splitting scholastic debate and with inventing theological refinements and definitions which Christ and the Apostles had never considered for a moment. Such defects in the clergy were famously exposed to mockery by Erasmus of Rotterdam (1469 to 1536) in his satirical work, *The Praise of Folly* (1509).[2] This book achieved an immense circulation. In Erasmus' lifetime there were no fewer than forty-two editions of the Latin text, as well as translations into French and German. It has been said that "Erasmus laid the egg of the Reformation; Luther hatched it". But Erasmus thought of himself as a faithful son of the Catholic Church; he would oppose Luther's break with Rome and was even offered a cardinal's hat towards the end of his life by Pope Paul III.

JOHN WYCLIFFE AND JAN HUS

Better candidates as forerunners of Luther had been John Wycliffe (1328 to 1384) and Jan Hus (1369 to 1415). Wycliffe (whose followers were known as the Lollards) has in fact been called "The Morning Star of the Reformation". Like Marsilio of Padua in the generation before him,[3] he had preached apostolic poverty for the clergy, this being the way in which Christ and His apostles had lived. Worldly possessions corrupted. This applied to the laity also. Jesus had addressed his remark that it is easier for a camel to pass through the eye of a needle than for a rich man to get into Heaven to a layman. This line of argument won Wycliffe much support from the poor, as we shall see shortly.

But clergy had a quite particular obligation to lead a life uncorrupted by property, and Wycliffe launched a powerful attack on the wealth of the Church. Huge sums flowed from the church in England to fill the coffers of Italian Popes in Rome. The Popes used much of this wealth to promote their secular interests as rulers of the papal states. They were elected by a College of Cardinals consisting predominantly of Italians and quite often appointed Italians to vacant sees in England and elsewhere. Another source of the Pope's income was the sale of papal indulgences.[4] Like Luther after him, Wycliffe

2 Its Latin title was *Morae Encomium*. It was in fact written for Erasmus' friend Sir Thomas More and the title is a pun on More's name.

3 For Marsilio of Padua see chapters 17 and 18.

4 Indulgences were a by-product of the Catholic teaching about Hell, Purgatory and Salvation. Those with a huge burden of sin were condemned to eternal hell fire. Most Christians are sinful to some extent, and their sins need to be purged in Purgatory – for a greater or lesser time, depending on how sinful they were, before they are fit to go to Heaven. Some preachers depicted the process of purgation as involving fire. Acts of contrition or repentance were rewarded by absolution from sins, and so could shorten the time that souls have to spend in purgatory for sins that have not been absolved. Contrition could be shown by good deeds undertaken to make up for bad deeds that had been committed. The emphasis was on "Salvation by Works". High on the list of good deeds were such acts as the endowment of masses for oneself or for one's dead relatives, charitable donations to the church or to other good causes. Eventually, the Church hit on the idea of indulgences: people could buy a papal document granting a shortening of the time in purgatory for sins that had been committed by oneself or by one's dead relatives, and – in the crudest versions – even for sins that might be committed in the future. The medieval and

poured scorn on the idea that people could be absolved from their sins by buying indulgences: they were only another device foisted on the ignorant in order to increase the wealth of the papacy.

All these abuses were already resented by many people in England, and Wycliffe's attack on payments to Rome won him the support of a proto-nationalist party in England. Its patron was John of Gaunt, the uncle of Richard II and, during that king's childhood, the virtual ruler of England.

Wycliffe went on to question papal authority over the Church in general and over the English Church in particular. The papal schism which occurred in 1378 merely reinforced his argument. Finally, he came to challenge the necessity of priests as intermediaries between the congregation and God. Essentially, each man was his own priest.

Congregations should not have to depend on priests to tell them what was in the Bible, whose Latin text had been carefully left untranslated into the vernacular. If each man was to be his own priest, he would need to have access to the Scriptures in English. In 1381 Wycliffe issued the first English translation of the Bible (from the Latin, of course, not from the original Greek or Hebrew). Such an enterprise was soon to be declared heretical, and a later translator, William Tyndale, would be martyred in 1536 for it.

In addition, Wycliffe challenged two aspects of Catholic theology. Where the Church had increasingly tipped the balance between free will and predestination towards the former,[5] Wycliffe took a strongly predestinarian view, and he propounded the idea of Consubstantiation against the Catholic doctrine of Transubstantiation which had been officially adopted by the Fourth Lateran Council in 1215.[6]

In almost all these disagreements with the papacy, Wycliffe anticipated Luther. Luther would savagely repudiate the Peasants' Revolt in Germany of 1525 that had inscribed Lutheran slogans upon its banners. Similarly, Wycliffe, though less violently, also dissociated himself from the English Peasants' Revolt of 1381 that was likewise strongly tinged with Lollard ideas. Under the challenge of social uprisings, both men, for all their attack on wealth, turned out to be socially conservative and feared that their creeds might be equated with social disorder. This enabled Luther to keep the support of his princely patrons. Wycliffe, too, was protected by John of Gaunt from his enemies in the English Church, and he died peacefully in his bed. However, after his death the

Renaissance Papacy resorted to this way of raising money whenever it was involved in a war or needed funds for great architectural enterprises.

5 see Chapter 13.

6 The doctrine of Transubstantiation is that at the moment of Communion the substance of the wafer and the wine cease to be bread and wine and are miraculously transformed into the actual body and blood of Christ. It is based on a literal interpretation of the words of Christ at the Last Supper, when, giving the bread to his disciples, he said, "Take, eat, this is my body", and when he gave them the wine, he said "this is my blood of the New Testament" (Matthew 26:26–28). The doctrine of Consubstantiation also takes Christ's words at the Last Supper literally, but holds that at the moment of communion the substance of the body and blood of Christ coexists with the substance of the bread and the wine. Wycliffe and Luther both held this view. Calvin did not think that the words at the Last Supper should be taken any more literally than other expressions of Christ, such as "I am the vine, ye are the branches" (John 15:5) or "I am the door" (John 10:9). The bread and wine remain bread and wine, but if communion is taken in reverence, the spirit of Christ miraculously enters into the communicant. Zwingli did not believe in any miracle at all: communion is taken as an act of remembrance, rather as we often stand in silence to remember the dead.

Lollards were ruthlessly suppressed by Henry IV and Henry V. The Lollard movement was, as the saying goes, "before its time". This was not so much because the ideas were premature as because at the time the bishops were, as often as not, close relatives of the nobles in the government. The nobles saw an attack on the church as an attack on members of their families. When the Tudors began to promote men of humbler birth to bishoprics, not only was the link between nobles and bishops broken, but an attack on the property of the Church might even result in the nobles acquiring a share of the Church's wealth.

At any rate, Wycliffe was more fortunate than Jan Hus, the Bohemian reformer who was much influenced by him.[7] When Hus, like Wycliffe before him and Luther after him, led a campaign against the sale of papal indulgences, he was excommunicated (1411). By that time he had gained so much support in Bohemia that the Emperor Sigismund hoped he could arrange a reconciliation between Hus and his enemies. He promised Hus safe conduct to explain himself to the Church Council at Constance, but when the Council condemned him as a heretic, Sigismund declared that promises made to heretics were not binding, and Hus was burnt at the stake (1415).

MARTIN LUTHER
1483 to 1546

Luther was an Augustinian monk who, in 1508 ,began to teach at the university of Wittenberg in Saxony. Brought up by a ferocious and punitive father, he was obsessed by a sense of guilt and of his own sinfulness and by the fear of damnation. He tried to live as holy a life as he could, and he knew that he was doing his best to avoid the Seven Deadly Sins. That was fairly easy for the three sins which involved wrong action – Avarice, Gluttony and Sloth; but the others are sins of the mind. In the case of Lust, for instance, it is not enough to abstain from sinful carnal action. Had not Jesus said "whosoever looketh on a woman to lust after her hath committed adultery with her already in his mind" (Matth. 6.28)? A strongly sexed man, Luther could not keep "impure thoughts" at bay. It was the same case with Anger. It did not have to be expressed in action; it was already sinful to feel it (and Luther was a hot-tempered man). The same was true with Envy. If, at the end of the day, he could claim to have committed none of these sins in thought or deed, then Pride, the deadliest of all the Deadly Sins, lay in wait to ensnare his soul. Luther did endless penance without feeling that by Works [8] he had significantly reduced the huge burden of sin that would damn his soul. St Augustine, after whom Luther's order was named, had come to preach the grim doctrine that, while there were those who were predestined to be saved, there were others who were predestined to damnation.[9] Luther, conscious that he had no power over his sinful feelings, and that he seemed to be programmed to have them, was terrified that he might belong to this latter

7 Richard II of England had married Anne of Bohemia. While she was queen, a number of students from Bohemia came to attend English universities. There they learnt of Wycliffe's ideas, and took them back to their own country when they returned.

8 see note 4 in this chapter.

9 For a full discussion of what St Augustine meant by Predestination, see Chapter 13.

group. Then, in 1509, he was suddenly struck by passages like those in which Jesus said, "He that believeth on me hath everlasting life" (John, 6:47). Luther, sure that he did believe in Jesus, now felt an enormous burden lifted from him. Jesus, knowing that we could never rid ourselves of our sins by our own efforts, had taken them upon his shoulders his blood had washed away the sins of those who believed in him. Luther was now convinced that, whereas Works could never by themselves bring us salvation, we could be justified (i.e. saved) by Faith alone.

It is obvious that if genuine penance and good works by themselves could not ensure salvation, the purchase of indulgences certainly could not do so. Nevertheless, in 1517 Pope Leo X, who had lavished huge sums on the building of the new St Peter's, launched a sales drive for plenary indulgences. In an area just outside Saxony, a salesman called Johann Tetzel advertised these in a particularly crude manner. His practices came to the ears of Luther. Strengthened by his new convictions that Works were not in themselves sufficient to achieve salvation, Luther felt moved to proclaim, in a notice pinned upon the church doors at Wittenberg, the famous Ninety-Five Theses which he was prepared to defend in debate. These allowed that the Pope, by his prayerful intercession, could possibly lift the burden of sin from repentant sinners, but they denied that the purchase of indulgences could have any such effect. Leo X had actually accepted much criticism from within the church. He had shown benevolence towards Erasmus despite the latter's satirical treatment of clerical abuses and he repudiated the excesses of Tetzel's campaign, but he could not permit an all-out attack on indulgences in general, as that struck at his revenues; and he summoned Luther to Rome.

Luther refused to go, and now successively widened his attack. In 1519 he espoused the Conciliar Theory which had been routed by the Curia a hundred years earlier.[10] He asserted that the decisions of Church Councils were superior to those of the Pope. He went further still, saying that even Councils might err, as had been shown by the condemnation of Jan Hus for heresy. His alignment with Hus made it inevitable that Luther, too, would be condemned as a heretic, and in 1520 he was excommunicated. Defiantly, he publicly committed the Papal Bull of excommunication to the flames, and developed his doctrines in an ever more radical direction. Like Wycliffe and Hus, he proclaimed that the Scriptures were the only binding authority on Christians; that each Christian was his own priest and had the right to interpret the Scriptures for himself (giving, as it were, a theological twist to the secular individualism which we have seen was a feature of Renaissance philosophy);[11] that there was nothing in the Scriptures which set the clergy apart from the laity, and that therefore the clergy, like the laity, should be allowed to marry. He rejected the doctrine of Transubstantiation as a superstition: the bread and wine remained bread and wine, though respect for the words of Christ in the Gospels led him to espouse Consubstantiation[12] instead.

10 See p. 162 above.

11 see p. 176 above.

12 see note 6 in this chapter.

Just as Wycliffe and Hus had struck the national note, so now did Luther. It was wrong that Germans should be bound by an Italian Pope with Italian interests, and that German money should be syphoned off (not only in the form of indulgences, but in a host of other contributions also) to support him.[13]

These positions won him enormous support in Germany, not least from the Elector of Saxony and some other German princes who also resented the drain of money to Rome. When, in 1521, the exasperated Leo demanded that the young German Emperor Charles V should act against Luther, Charles - faithful Catholic though he was - knew that the Imperial Diet (or parliament) would not allow this if Luther had not first been given a hearing before it. Luther was summoned to appear before the Diet at Worms, and the Emperor promised him safe conduct. Luther's friends urged him not to go, reminding him that an earlier Emperor had revoked the safe conduct he had given to Hus. Luther famously answered that if every tile on the roofs of Worms were the devil himself, yet he would go. In fact, although Luther was found guilty of heresy at the Diet, the safe conduct was honoured. Luther, however, found it prudent on his return to Saxony to shelter for some ten months in one of the Elector's castles, the Wartburg. There, true to the idea that every Christian ought to be able to read the Bible for himself in the vernacular, he made a German translation from the Greek of the New Testament (to be followed twelve years later by a translation of the Old Testament from the Hebrew.)

After his emergence from the Wartburg, Luther developed his theology and practice further. He preached against the idea that the most perfect dedication to God was shown by those who withdrew from the world into the monastic life. On the contrary, the religious life required not withdrawal from the world - he came to condemn monasticism as mere parasitic idleness - but engagement with it and regarded even the humblest secular work as a *calling* (vocation, *Beruf*) to which one had been summoned by God.

Luther wanted the congregation to be far more involved in church services than they were in the Catholic practice of the time, when celebration of the Latin Mass, carried out by priests on behalf of the congregation, was the centrepiece of the service.For Lutherans the sermon in the vernacular became much more central. Instead of intricate church music being sung for the most part by choristers, the laity was invited to join in with the splendidly simple and four-square hymns that Luther composed. He condemned the worship of the Virgin Mary and of the Saints, because this led to much superstition so readily exploited materially by the guardians of shrines, besides which it was based on the idea that they could intercede with God for sinners, when only faith in Christ was an effective means of Salvation.

Luther considered some books in the Bible as inauthentic, but those he accepted he believed to be *literally* true, and he rejected any attempt to treat them as allegories. Such an attempt was, he thought, a misguided attempt to

13 Luther, unlike Calvin, showed very little interest in spreading his idea outside Germany. Calvin always answered letters from people living outside Switzerland who wanted to know more about his ideas or asked for his advice. Luther hardly ever bothered. Outside Germany only the Scandinavian countries and small communities in the Netherlands became Lutheran. Calvinism had a much wider international distribution: Switzerland, the Netherlands, France (the Huguenots), Scotland (the Presbyterians), England and the New England colonies; it also had a presence in Hungary and, briefly, in Poland.

reconcile Faith with "that Whore, Reason". That was one way in which he differed sharply from Christian Neo-Platonism and from the Renaissance Humanist enterprise that had developed from it. At the same time, however, it might be argued that going back to the original texts of the Bible was a theological version of the importance that the Renaissance had attached to going back to the original texts of the ancient Greeks.

He crossed swords also with the Humanist Christian, Erasmus of Rotterdam. The humanist concept of the dignity of man would be impaired if man could not freely exercise his will but was instead helplessly predestined to either salvation or damnation. In 1524 Erasmus wrote a book to this effect, *De Libero Arbitrio*, but Luther did not break away from his Augustinian training, and he attacked Erasmus' book in his own *De Servo Arbitrio* in the following year. True, we will be saved if we have faith in Christ, but we cannot command ourselves to have that faith. The capacity for faith is not within our control, and the all-knowing God knows whether we have this capacity or not. If we lack faith, we incur the wrath of God, of which Luther was as convinced as he was of the love of God; his belief in the Devil and in the terrors of Hell was as vivid as that of any preacher of indulgences.

> In several respects Luther went well beyond the teachings of St Augustine. Chapter 13 has a long discussion of St Augustine's teaching on free will and predestination. That discussion suggested, firstly, that at the time the idea of damnation (from the Latin word *damnum* meaning loss) implied the loss of salvation rather than the pains of hellfire and secondly, that St Augustine avoided the idea that God *ordained* whether a person used his free will to accept or reject the Grace of God through Jesus Christ – He merely *foresaw* how strong a will a person had and how he would exercise it. The discussion explained that "foresaw" is not really the appropriate word, as Augustine believed that past, present and future are all dissolved in the timeless eternity in which God dwells. It would therefore be more accurate to say that God "knew", rather than "foresaw", the strength and capacity of any individual's will. In any case, foreseeing does not imply ordaining. A teacher may foresee that one of his pupils will fail because the pupil will not use the abilities he has, but that certainly does not mean that the teacher ordains the pupil to fail. Luther, however, possibly influenced by his own earlier feelings of helplessness and terror, specifically says that God not only foresees, but also ordains. His text says that God "foresees, *foreordains* and accomplishes all things by an unchanging, eternal and efficacious *Will*" (my italics). This clearly means that God ordains whether or not an individual is capable of having the faith in Jesus which would save him. Luther admits that "common sense and natural reason are highly offended that God by His mere Will deserts, hardens and damns ... If it is difficult to believe in God's mercy and goodness when He damns those who do not deserve it, we must recall that if God's justice could be recognized as just by human comprehension, it would not be divine."

The ferocity of the language Luther unleashed against the Papacy during his revolt suggests that his temperament was that of a violent rebel against authority, and his early book on the subject of secular authority (*On Secular Authority: to what Extent it should be Obeyed*, 1522) seemed to bear that out. In it he paid lip-service to St Paul's commandment that one should obey the powers that be, because they are ordained of God, but this was followed by a scorching passage on the rarity of pious princes, and a warning that "men ought not, men cannot, men will not suffer your tyranny and presumption much longer", and in his private letters at that time he expressed himself more forcibly still. When, in 1524, the German peasants rose in revolt against the economic exploitation to which they were subject, Luther published a pamphlet that blamed the princes and bishops for their oppression and urged them to meet the grievances of their subjects. At the same time, though, he reminded the peasants of the Pauline doctrine of obedience. The peasants had expressed their cause in religious terms by referring to the communism they saw in the Gospels – a good example of what might be the result if each man is his own interpreter of Scripture – and they had naturally looked upon Luther as their champion. They were bitterly disappointed that Luther now quoted Scripture against them. They refused to heed his call; the revolt continued and grew in strength. Characteristically, Luther now raged against those who would not accept his authority [14] – and indeed by now he also feared that if he continued to support the peasants, he would alienate those princes who had given Luther essential support and protection in his battle against the Papacy and the Emperor. In another pamphlet of 1525 he exhorted the princes (not that they needed such exhortation) to "smite, slay, and stab, secretly or openly, remembering that nothing can be more poisonous, hurtful or devilish than a rebel".

These neurotic outpourings would have little to do with the history of philosophy if they did not mark the point at which Luther accepted not only the authority of the princes over the peasants, but also over the new church. In matters of church structure, he simply replaced the Pope by the Prince as head of the Church. The Prince could appoint bishops who in turn would appoint the lower clergy; he should insist that all his subjects follow his religion (as long as it is Lutheran) and should punish heresy (against Lutheranism). The policy that the Church should be controlled by the state has been known since the seventeenth century as Erastianism, after a fairly obscure Swiss theologian Thomas Erastus (1524 to 1583) who had expounded it.

Like the Roman Catholic Church, therefore, the Lutheran churches were organized hierarchically. No room was left for any democratic governance; as

14 He would show the same characteristics in his relationship with the Anabaptists and with the Jews.

The Anabaptists are so called because the believed that people should be baptized again (Greek *ana* = again) when a person makes a commitment to Christ as an adult. They may also be considered proto-anarchists, in the sense that they were suspicious of all government, would not swear oaths of allegiance, take public office, or have recourse to the law courts. They believed in religious toleration, not only for themselves but for all religions. Some of them were pacifists, and many of them believed in communal living and property. They attracted many followers among the poor and naturally excited the hostility of governments and of the propertied classes. It is said that by 1530 some 2,000 Anabaptists had been put to death. In 1534, one group, under John of Leyden, seized control of the city of Münster and held it for sixteen months. All were slaughtered when the city was recaptured. Initially, in 1524, Luther urged that the Anabaptists be tolerated, arguing that they, like all men, had the right to interpret the Scriptures for themselves, but by 1530, in his usual violent language, he was urging the princes to be ruthless in exterminating the sect.

As far as the Jews were concerned, Luther had hoped that, once he had condemned their persecution by the Catholic Church and had acknowledged that Jesus himself was a Jew, the Jews would be ready to convert to his version of Christianity. When the Jews would not convert, his early benevolence turned to vicious hatred and abuse, expressed in his pamphlet *Against the Jews and their Lies* (1542). So we find Lutheran Saxony and Brandenburg expelling their Jews in the mid-16th century just as Catholic Bohemia did.

in Catholicism, authority flowed from the top downwards. This was only one respect in which Luther differed from that other great protestant reformer, John Calvin.

JOHN CALVIN
1509 to 1564

Calvin was born in France, and was trained as a lawyer. In his early thirties he joined a circle of friends who, like him, had come under the influence first of Erasmus and then of Luther. King Francis I and the Sorbonne were determined to stamp out the reforming movement, and in 1534 Calvin fled, originally to Protestant Basel. By that time he had developed ideas which differed considerably from Luther's. They found expression in his most influential book, *The Institutes of the Christian Religion*, which he published in 1536. It made him instantly famous in Protestant circles. The leader of Protestantism in Geneva, William Farel, who had just won over the city council to the new religion, urged Calvin to take up a ministry in that city. In 1538 both men were banished because of the harshness of the puritanical regime that they inspired, but events developed in such a way that in 1541 Calvin was invited back. From that time onwards he effectively became the ruler of Geneva, and the doctrines of the *Institutes* dominated the city.

Luther, as we have seen, had by then developed an Erastian position, accepting that the secular rulers should be at the head of the Lutheran churches. That prescription worked in northern Germany, where so many princes were already committed to Lutheranism, but it would make the establishment of Lutheran Erastianism impossible in a country like France, whose king already had as much control as he wanted over the apparatus of the French church and had no wish to place himself formally at the head of it.[15] Calvin already had the loftiest view of the role that religion should play in dictating to conduct of the state, and the situation in France can only have reinforced this belief in Theocracy: the church must supervise the state, rather than the state supervising the church. This concept was now put into practice in Geneva.

Unlike the Lutheran church, that of Calvin had a democratic structure. To begin with, the word priest was replaced by that of pastor (original meaning "shepherd") or minister. The original meaning of the word "minister", still captured by the expression "to minister to someone's needs", was "servant". A minister of religion was to serve rather than to master his congregation – though in practice it was of course his task to exercise ecclesiastical discipline over his flock. The congregation chose its elders or presbyters. In Geneva, the city council chose a mixture of pastors and elders to form the Consistory or

15 The secular policy of the Papacy had led it to create the Holy League in 1512 with the intention of driving French influence out of Italy, but in 1515 Francis I had won a great victory in Italy, and Pope Leo X had had to come to terms. By the Concordat of Bologna (1516) he permitted the kings of France henceforth to nominate the bishops in his kingdom – the subsequent investiture by the Papacy would be a pure formality. The King of France thereby acquired control over the entire apparatus of the Church in France. The abuses in that apparatus, which had previously been exploited for the benefit of the Papacy, were now exploited for that of the King. The French Crown, therefore, was not interested in the reform of abuses, which was such an important part of the Protestant programme. As for the doctrinal part of the reformers' programme: with their material interests safeguarded by the Concordat, the kings of France were perfectly happy to recognize the Papacy's supremacy in doctrine in exchange.

Presbytery which governed the church, but in those communities where the government was not Calvinist, the system would be more democratic. When a new minister was needed by a congregation on the promotion, resignation or death of an incumbent, the presbyters would invite suitably qualified candidates to apply, to be interviewed by them on their religious beliefs, perhaps to be invited to preach a specimen sermon or two; after which the elders who would make an appointment. The ministers in an area would choose some of their number who might represent them in synods; synods in turn would elect, usually for a fixed term, the head of the church. In Scotland the title would, significantly, be the Moderator, which means little more than chairman. Eventually this system will become known as Presbyterianism.

> This structure, in which authority flowed from the bottom up, was democratic only within the Calvinist church. We have something like what Leninists would call "Democratic Centralism". The Leninist theory (though not the practice) was that the Communist Party was democratically organized for its members, but that its decisions should then be imposed, not only on party members, but on society at large. No other parties were tolerated. The same was true in Calvin's Geneva, and during the English Civil War, the English Presbyterians put forward the same demand. It meant, both in Geneva and in England, that, for example, Unitarianism (the belief that Jesus was a great religious teacher but was not divine or part of a Holy Trinity) should be suppressed. Sects like the Unitarians or the Baptists said that they wanted a system of Independence. The Independents claimed that each congregation should have the right to decide for itself what to believe and how to worship, and they rejected any compulsory national religion. They are therefore the first people to preach religious toleration and to hold that the state should not dictate the religious *beliefs* of its citizens. (They did, however, often give the state the right to dictate the *behaviour* to the society at large. It was during the rule of the Independents in England, for instance, that the theatres were closed down.)

Out of the Calvinist democratic organization of the church grew the demand that the state should be similarly organized. This was, therefore, one obvious reason why Calvinism would be opposed by governments which were Catholic or which had adopted an Erastian form of Protestantism. Both wanted church and state to be ruled from the top downwards, and both saw in Calvinism a training for subversion of state and church alike.

In addition to this disagreement about structures, there were also theological differences between Luther and Calvin. We have already seen that Calvin did not believe in Consubstantiation; he taught that the miracle that happened during the reverent partaking of Communion was that the spirit of Christ entered into the communicant.[16] Then Calvin's version of Predestination was even more uncompromising than Luther's. Luther had realized that it was not given to everyone to have Faith in Christ – some are destined to have it and some are not – but if they do have Faith (and Luther knew there were large numbers who did) then Salvation is their reward. Once Luther had convinced himself that Faith alone would secure Salvation, he had shaken off all his old crippling guilt feelings and had become quite indulgent towards certain sins which were simply unavoidable aspects of human nature. He was no puritan. A verse is attri-

16 see note 6 on p. 185 above.

buted to him: "Who loves not woman, wine, or song / Remains a fool his whole life long." His recorded table talk showed that he allowed himself to be coarse and obscene in expression, and in a letter he enjoined upon his reader that if he must commit certain sins, he should "be a sinner and sin strongly (*pecca fortiter*), but more strongly have faith and rejoice in Christ".

We find none of this in the austere Calvin. A Calvinist not only demands what he considers the highest standards for himself, but will also wish to impose them on the society around him. Calvinist regimes showed no tolerance for human weakness: they insisted on the strictest morality in conduct; they were puritanical in sexual matters; they reproved feasting, sumptuous clothes, and any kind of extravagance. In Calvinist churches, everything that might distract the congregation from prayer or the sermon was abolished: statues, stained glass, incense, the splendid raiments of the priests. Calvinism introduced the puritan Sunday, which permitted of no entertainment on that day. It also suppressed much entertainment on the other days of the week; there was to be no theatre, no dancing. Profanities in speech were severely punished.

Even the most godly way of life, though, was no guarantee of Salvation. Calvin stressed that Salvation is in no way a reward for anything, certainly not for Good Works, but not for Faith either – it is totally unmerited.

> One may have some sympathy with Calvin's contention that the mere possession of faith did not merit salvation. Throughout history the most terrible cruelties and injustices have been wrought upon dissenters by people who are undoubtedly possessed of an unshakeable faith in their religion. Luther himself was a case in point: his faith in Jesus did not stop him from encouraging barbaric violence against Anabaptists and Jews. Luther might have replied that, even if these incitements were a sin (and he did not believe that they were) Jesus would take that sin, too, upon his shoulders.
>
> Calvin obviously had faith in Jesus also, and that faith led him, too, to commit what we now consider the barbarity of having an opponent burnt alive for heresy.[17] He, too, thought this was the right thing to do, but even if it were a sin, Calvin would not have availed himself of Luther's comfortable argument that he would be forgiven because he had faith.

Even more harshly than Luther, Calvin insisted that God not only foresees, but ordains everything. For him, the doctrine of Predestination meant that God "ordains some to eternal life and others to eternal damnation" because, "He has determined what He wants to do with each individual". He saw God not as a sorrowful observer of how some of his creatures misuse the free will He has given them, but as a deity who, by any merely human criteria, decides in a totally arbitrary manner, unrelated to the merit of either good deeds or of faith, to whom He will grant Salvation and whom He will condemn to eternal damnation. (These were the stark alternatives: there was no place in Calvin's theology for Purgatory.)

17 This was the case of Michael Servetus. Servetus had denied the doctrine of the Trinity, had seen Jesus as a human being who was a divinely inspired prophet. He also accepted the Anabaptist view that baptism in adulthood was necessary, and indeed that infants should not be baptized at all. He also rejected the doctrine of Predestination. Servetus was burnt in 1553.

The picture becomes even grimmer. Luther believed that all the millions of people who have faith in Jesus can look forward to Salvation, but Calvin believed (one wonders on what grounds) that those chosen by God for Salvation – the Elect – were only very few, and that the great majority of mankind was destined to be damned.

> If Salvation is not a reward, either for good works or for faith, but depends entirely on the will of God; if, as Calvin said, the will of God is totally inscrutable; if the Elect are only a small number, then no Christian, however well he behaves or however solid is his faith, is given any grounds for believing that he will be saved. What is even worse, he must fear that the odds that he might escape eternal hellfire are heavily against him.
>
> Given that well-nigh everybody in sixteenth-century Christian Europe believed in Heaven and Hell and had the most acute fear of eternal hellfire, one may well ask how such a terrible doctrine managed to secure the large following that it undoubtedly did. How can you have faith in the Saviour if you are not sure whether he will save you? What is the point of leading a virtuous life if, despite that, you may still be destined for damnation? Catholicism held out much more promise of reward for good works, Lutheranism for belief in Christ. If you were conscious of being a sinner, Catholicism offered the possibility of absolution; Lutheranism told you that if you believed, Christ would take your sins upon his shoulders. Why should either saint or sinner follow the doctrines of Calvin?
>
> If you live soberly, thriftily and honestly, the likelihood is that your affairs will prosper. If you prosper – and if you know that you have prospered for that reason and not because you have cheated or stolen – it might seem that God has smiled upon you on this earth, and you then have a reasonable hope, though of course you cannot be certain, that you may also be among those who have been chosen for salvation. Where a Catholic might lead a good life in order to get to Heaven, a Calvinist might see leading a good life as an indication that he had already been chosen for Heaven. That may be one reason why Calvinism has appealed to such people. Calvin approved of prosperity honestly gotten. He was not even categorically opposed, as Luther was, to charging a reasonable rate of interest in commercial transactions. There is a somewhat disputed theory that a moderate version of Calvinism appealed to the sober and hard working mercantile classes which were growing fast in some parts of Europe (Switzerland, the Rhineland, the Netherlands, England) in the sixteenth and seventeenth centuries, though this does not explain why so many poor people in those countries responded to Calvinism also. It is probably a mistake to look too much to material causes: the missionary zeal, the centrality of the sermon, the involvement of the congregation through the lay elders will all have played an important part.

Some By-Products of the Reformation in Protestant Europe

The Protestant reformers had an instant effect on their followers' religious life and on the structure of their churches. They also had long-term effects on thought and attitudes, not all of which had been intended.

When the Reformers asserted the individual conscience against the authority of the Catholic Church, they further strengthened the individualism which we have already seen to have been a feature of the Renaissance. Once people are asked to use their own judgment and not to take traditional authority for granted, no authority can claim the infallibility that the Catholic Church had claimed. The infallibility of Scriptures alone was, in theory, intended to replace that of the Popes and Councils; but in due course the spirit of enquiry would for some people call the Scriptures themselves into question and open the way to Biblical Criticism, to Theism, Deism, and even to Agnosticism and Atheism. Reason is bound to play a part once people are asked to use their judgment. It has been said that Erasmus had laid the egg of the Reformation and that Luther hatched it. In the same way one could argue that Luther, notwithstanding his hatred of "that Whore, Reason" had laid the egg of the Age of Reason which would be hatched by the *philosophes* of the eighteenth century.

That is looking a long way ahead, but even while the Scriptures were still regarded as Holy Writ, that text was now subject to rival individual interpretations, and there was no longer any authority to adjudicate between them. No wonder that once the unity of the western Church was broken in two, the Protestant half would rapidly fragment into a whole series of sects.

In most Protestant countries, that would leave the state as the only defining unit of authority. This was just one feature among others that contributed to the process of nation building and the centralizing of state power that was taking place in the sixteenth century. Nation building in turn creates a stronger feeling of national identity, and in protestant countries this was reinforced by the use of the vernacular in religion. The universal use of Latin had been one manifestation of a universal church. It now lost its role as the *lingua franca*.[18] In Catholic countries, Latin remained the language of the Bible, but even there monarchs were wresting control of the churches in their countries from the Papacy.[19]

Whether Protestant or Catholic, governments still claimed that their legitimacy rested upon religious foundations. They continued to quote St Paul on the injunction to obey the powers that be, and they invoked the Divine Right of Kings and of hereditary succession. But that was an increasingly shaky basis – if resistance to the Papacy was justified on the grounds of conscience, resistance to the state would be seen as legitimate on the same grounds. The right of men to have their individual consciences respected in matters of religion may be asserted against states that aim to control church doctrine and organization, and this can easily broaden out into demands for wider political rights. We have already seen how easily the Presbyterian model of church government could be translated into a demand for a similarly democratic organization of the state. It is not surprising therefore, that those who were Puritan in religion were also the driving force behind the demand for parliamentary as opposed to autocratic government in Elizabethan and early Stuart England. The first parliamentary governments in the early modern period are found in those countries – England, Scotland, Switzerland, the United Provinces (the name of what we now call the Netherlands) and the New England colonies – in which Calvinist Puritanism was most influential. Autocracies lasted longest in Catholic,

18 The Treaty of Westphalia, which ended the Thirty Years' War in 1648, was the first international treaty to have been drawn up in French and not in Latin.

19 see note 16 on p. 191 above on how the French monarchy achieved this. The Spanish monarchy also managed to have the Inquisition under royal rather than under papal control.

Lutheran and Orthodox countries, because their religious structures were also based on the autocratic principle.

For a time, opposition movements aimed to replace the prescribed religion of the state with their own, equally prescribed: intolerance was met by intolerance. Eventually, after decades of passionate religious strife both between and within states, people began to see the case for religious toleration: that no one's conscience ought to be coerced, that religious convictions of citizens are a private matter and not a proper subject for state interference, and that the state might actually be stronger as a result.[20]

Luther and Calvin rejected the teaching of St Thomas Aquinas that Reason and Faith are part of a seamless continuum, and that the knowledge of God and of our moral obligations is vouchsafed to us not only by revelation, but also by reason. St John of Bonaventura, Duns Scotus and William of Ockham had disputed this approach: our knowledge of God and the demands of morality cannot be reliably based on human reason, only faith in His revelation and in His commandments provides a sure foundation.[21] We have already seen Luther refer to Reason as a whore, and both he and Calvin agreed with the Ockhamist view.

However, they did not go back to the Augustinian and medieval view that a concern with understanding the physical world was at best a distraction from spiritual concerns.[22] Aquinas had taught that God had given us the faculty of reason so that we could use it firstly to understand Him and His moral laws (an idea that Luther and Calvin rejected, as we have just seen) and secondly, to understand the way in which the world He had created actually worked. This second argument Luther and Calvin did not reject. Along with their insistence that the Christian should involve himself with this world (rather than retreat from it into monasteries) was an acceptance that the attempt to understand and investigate the material world was legitimate. Here the use of reason is recognized, justified, and even encouraged. That created a benign climate for the Scientific Revolution, which in turn would bring about momentous changes in European thought and attitudes.

REFORMATION POLITICAL THOUGHT

The Renaissance rulers in Western Europe – Henry VIII in England, Francis I and Henri II in France, the Spanish monarchs from Ferdinand and Isabella to Philip II – had all strengthened absolutism. They had done this with only the lightest theoretical clothing, as this seemed hardly necessary. It was usually sufficient to fall back, if need be, on St Paul's injunction to the Christians of

20 This is a rather sweeping generalization. It is true of Britain, of the United Provinces and of some German states like Prussia from the sevetneenth century onwards. There was less of it in countries where the government was Catholic. During the exhausting religious civil wars in France between the Catholics and the Huguenots, a middle party, the Politiques, began to advocate religious toleration. Its philosopher was Montaigne (see above, p. 175), though he died in 1592, six years before the Edict of Nantes established toleration as the official government policy. That lasted less than a century; state repression of the Huguenots began again with the Revocation of the Edict of Nantes by Louis XIV in 1684 and lasted officially until the French Revolution.

21 For a full discussion of this debate see Chapter 16 on Aquinas and Chapter 17 on William of Ockham.

22 For St Augustine on this point see p. 104 above.

Rome to obey the powers that be (Rom. 13:1). In the early seventeenth century this was embodied in the theory of the Divine Right of Kings, but it had not been much invoked by the Machiavellian rulers of the sixteenth century. They might almost have agreed with a slight paraphrase of Edmund Burke, who would write that "one sure symptom of an ill-conducted state is the propensity ... to resort to theories". Confident rulers probably thought that a strong government should not theorize too much, since that might be giving a hostage to fortune by inviting counter-theories. It has often been remarked that this was the reason why Queen Elizabeth, who certainly believed in her Divine Right to rule, never specifically invoked it, even when her policies were challenged by groups in Parliament. She retained just enough power and enjoyed just enough respect from her subjects not to have to fall back on the defence of Divine Right. James I, on the other hand, invoked it frequently as the monarchy began to weaken under the challenges of Parliament, of the Common Lawyers and of the formulation of theories of resistance that had developed in the previous century to counter absolutist claims.

Theories of Resistance: Historical Arguments

These theories based themselves on historical grounds and, once the Reformation had started, on religious grounds also.

The historical arguments were that the absolutism of the Renaissance monarchs was an innovation. In medieval times the apparatus of government and communications was so bad that every ruler depended on his nobles to maintain order in the remoter areas of his kingdom. This practical fact lay behind the theory of *concordia* – that good government depended on the Crown and the nobles acting in harmony to prevent chaos. The monarch was only *primus inter pares*. He did not have, and should not claim, absolute power in the state. Power was shared, and the aristocracy, the estates or parliaments and local bodies all had rights and privileges which the monarch could not take away. So when the monarchy in France aimed at absolutism, nobles, local assemblies and law courts asserted their ancient privileges and "liberties" against it.

> The original meaning of the word "privilege" was law that protected the rights of private persons. Its present sense derives from the fact that the poor had next to no rights, so that privilege was in practice only invoked by the rich and powerful. Similarly, the word "liberty" meant the freedom of individuals or institutions granted to them by custom or charter. It, too, was at the time claimed on behalf of the upper classes, but in the eighteenth century it was to be demanded by democrats against the "privileged", so that "liberty" and "privilege", which once meant much the same, came to be seen almost as opposites.

If the monarch ignored the rights of his subjects, he was chipping away at the foundations on which his own authority rested. Shakespeare enshrined the theory in *Richard II*: if the king takes away from Bolingbroke

> his charters and his customary rights,
> Let not tomorrow, then, ensue today;
> Be not thyself – for how art thou a king
> But by fair sequence and succession? [23]

23 Act II, Sc.1.

When James I in England claimed to be the source of all law and that the judges were merely "lions under the throne", his own Lord Chief Justice, Edward Coke, objected. The king is subject to the law just as his people are; the English Common Law rests on custom and precedent, not, like the Roman Law, on princely *fiat*.[24]

Religious Arguments

The Reformation had split not only Europe, but many countries within Europe. Protestant subjects were in revolt against Catholic rulers and Catholic subjects were in revolt against Protestant rulers. Each looked for theories that would justify rebellion against a monarch whom they considered heretical. We find these first in the *Vindiciae Contra Tyrannos,* an anonymous Huguenot work published in 1579, during the protracted civil wars in France between the Catholics and the Huguenots. The author defends rebellion against a heretical (here Catholic) ruler on the grounds that the king has broken a contract or covenant which he has made with his people.

From Plato onwards, there have been occasional references to a theory of contract: rulers and subjects enter into a contract by which the former promise to rule well and the latter promise their obedience in return. In the twelfth century, John of Salisbury had spelt out that if the ruler breaks this contract and governs as a tyrant, his subjects are absolved from their side of the agreement and are entitled to depose or even to slay their king. It is obvious that such an argument was flatly opposed to the teaching of St Paul that even pagan governments have been ordained by God and that resistance to them is not lawful. In the Middle Ages there was too much fear of disorder, and too much respect for the Pauline injunction to obey the powers that be, for the Contract Theory of Government to become a widely accepted justification for rebellion, but now the Pauline teaching was breaking down, and from the *Vindiciae* in the sixteenth century to Rousseau in the eighteenth century, the Contract Theory plays an increasingly important part in political thought. The *Vindiciae* postulates a Double Contract. The first is made jointly by the King and his people with God - they promise to give the community a religious character. The king and his subjects are, as it were, surety for each other. The king makes certain that his people follow God's commandments, and the people undertake to guarantee that the king does likewise. In return, God sanctified the *office* of kingship. There is then also a contract between the king and his people: he promises to rule them well in return for their obedience. The promise involves not only that he abstain from tyranny, but, more importantly, he has to be true to his covenant with God, for which the people stood surety. The people are therefore entitled to rebel against their ruler, in the first instance if he becomes a heretic and, in the second, if he becomes a tyrant.

Some Catholic thinkers accepted these arguments – except, of course, that for them it was the Huguenots who were the heretics. Popes had often called for the deposition of rulers who had offended against the Catholic Church. Now the Spanish Jesuits Luis Molina (1535 to 1600) and Juan De Mariana (1536 to

24 see the discussion on p. 72 above.

1624) defended rebellion against an unjust ruler – a ruler who did not give to God His just dues – and even endorsed tyrannicide in such a case. Juan de Mariana vindicated the assassination of Dutch Protestant leader William of Orange in 1584, and that of Henri III of France five years later, for having come to terms with the Huguenot Henri of Navarre.

> William of Orange had been a rebel against King Philip II of Spain, and the Spaniards never recognized him as a lawful ruler, but Henri III of France was king by what had been considered the Divine Right of Hereditary Succession. Juan de Mariana was therefore sanctioning not merely tyrannicide, but regicide. In this he was unusual, for regicide was still regarded by most people with some trepidation and even horror. Psychologically it was almost identified with parricide, and was normally subject to quite powerful taboos. Kings rarely approved of the murder of fellow-monarchs. Such approval could easily rebound on themselves, and there was a general understanding that they would refrain from ordering each other's assassinations.
>
> Remnants of such misgivings remain to the present day, for instance, the CIA had to deny that it had sought to murder Fidel Castro. States vow vengeance against terrorists, but they rarely try to murder the heads of "terrorist states" (though perhaps bombing raids on Libya and Iraq had the true aim of killing their rulers). It may seem odd that, when there are few scruples in killing "enemy" civilians or the soldiers whom the heads of enemy countries have sent to fight for their "evil" causes, there still appears to be a deep-seated taboo against killing their leader.

For Cardinal Robert Bellarmine (1542 to 1621) deposing a monarch was all the less problematical becausehe did not believe that the institution of monarchy had any divine sanction. For him, it was a purely secular arrangement, and the authority of the king was based only on a contract between the rulers and the ruled. Those who had preached the Divine Right of Kings had held that the kings' authority over the people depended not on a contract but on the fact that they were the Lord's Anointed. For Bellarmine, however, it was the people who appointed a ruler, even if the Church might subsequently anoint him and give its blessing to such a secular arrangement. It was in such a secular form that the contract theory would develop.

JOHANNES ALTHUSIUS
1557 to 1638

The Dutch Calvinist Johannes Althusius saw the contract as an element in the formation of societies. His book, *Politica methodice digesta,* was published in 1603, and later thinkers adopted his concept of a Social Contract. Of course, they knew that historically there can never have been an explicit agreement of this kind when communities first developed, but when they asked themselves how societies had come into existence, how it was that, in general, authority appeared to be accepted, they assumed that there must originally have been some tacit understanding between the rulers and the ruled. When rebellions break out, the theory continued, it will often be because the subjects feel that the rulers had broken this unspoken agreement and that they are therefore absolved from their duty of obedience.

Today it seems ridiculous to postulate even a tacit agreement underlying the *creation* of societies. To begin with, there has never been a presocial "state of nature" – every person is already a member of some kind of society – the extended family and the tribe – at birth. Then, when tribes have amalgamated, it is more likely to have been as the result of conquest, of the exercise of power by one tribe over another, than by any acceptance, tacit or otherwise, of mutual obligation. It is best to see the theories of seventeenth- and eighteenth- century philosophers not as primitive and unhistorical versions of anthropology, but rather as rationalizations of the kind of political attitudes they favoured. The refusal to see the lack of historicity in the theory and the insistence on the contract idea was an attempt to delegitimize governments whose authority rested on mere force – until Hobbes cleverly subverted the whole idea of the contract to legitimize absolutism![25]

The political stance that influenced Althusius' version of the social contract was a democratic one, as befitted a citizen of the United Provinces who had successfully revolted against autocratic and aristocratic government by the Spaniards: the legitimization of power flows from the bottom upwards. He maintained that the earliest social contracts were those that created families; in every family there is a recognized system of rights and obligations.

Say that to a rebellious teenager! The idea would be challenged by theorists like Sir Robert Filmer (1588 to 1653). Like Althusius, Filmer extrapolated from the smaller units to the larger ones, but in the smaller unit, the family, he saw the authority of the *paterfamilias* as absolute. Such authority is therefore natural throughout the larger arrangements of society, and it culminates in the absolute authority of the monarch.

The families then make agreements among themselves to form local corporations, again creating both rights and obligations. The corporations in turn get together to form local communities; those will come together in provinces and the provinces will agree to form states. In each case, the larger unit derives its legitimacy from the smaller units which have contracted to form them and the right to resist if the contract is broken lies with these smaller units.

Althusius insisted that the smaller units must act through their representatives or through magistrates. The magistrates might have been elected, might have been appointed by the king or might have inherited their posts: it did not really matter all that much - the point was that only people who had some weight and standing in a society could call upon the people to rebel against a king who had broken his contract. Althusius, and most other contract theorists who followed him, did not give the right of rebellion to individuals. If every individual were to decide for himself that a contract had been broken and that therefore he was entitled to rebel, that would really be an invitation to anarchy. It is for the representative bodies or magistrates to decide that the breaches of the contract were sufficiently serious and persistent to justify rebellion, and then to call upon the people to rise.

It could be argued that the French civil wars in the late sixteenth century and the English Civil War in the mid-seventeenth century were started by calls from such "senior" members of society, and yet to many who experienced

25 See Chapter 26 below.

these conflicts it appeared that anarchy was not thereby avoided. A rebellion against the monarch, even when called for by senior people, created chaos. It seemed to some political thinkers, therefore, that order could be reestablished only by restoring the authority of the monarch, but this would require new theories of absolutism that did not rely on the now discredited theory of the Divine Right of Kings.

JEAN BODIN
1530 to 1590

Arguably the worst turmoil of the period afflicted France in the forty years that followed the death of Henri II in 1559. He was succeeded by three weak sons, one after the other, and the French nobles used the opportunity to undo the growing absolutism of the previous two reigns. Many of them espoused the Huguenot cause, which then provided them with a religious excuse for defying the Catholic monarchy. Even the Catholic nobles exploited the dependency of the monarchy upon them to reassert their former powers. The Crown sank into pitiable impotence and the country fell into chaos as Huguenots and Catholics battled it out in eight civil wars between 1562 and 1598.

Jean Bodin concluded from all this that the medieval doctrine of *concordia* had broken down, and in his main work, *La République* (1576) he set against it the concept of the ruler as *souverain*, sovereign or supreme. Monarchs had been called "sovereign lords" before, even if the theory at the time called for them to share their powers with nobles or other bodies. Bodin insisted that shared power was not sovereign power. In the last resort, sovereignty must be undivided, and all individuals and institutions of the state must be subordinate to the sovereign and owe whatever rights they have to his permission for the time being.

Like Althusius, Bodin extrapolated the principles that govern the state from those that he thought governed the basic building block of society, namely the family. Althusius saw the family as naturally based on mutual consent and a kind of proto-contract; Bodin turned that notion upside down.[26] He saw the undisputed authority of the father, the *paterfamilias,* as the natural principle within the family, and the undisputed authority of the sovereign as the equally natural extension of this.

> I suppose it is possible that fathers in Althusius' relatively democratic Holland may actually have been a little less authoritarian at home than their counterparts in France – French fathers could apply to magistrates for a *lettre de cachet* to have disobedient sons imprisoned. All the same, it looks fairly clear that both Althusius and Bodin read back into the family the political ideas that they wanted to foster anyway.
>
> We will find this same phenomenon of accepting a basic building block (here it is the family, but in Hobbes and Locke it will be the nature of individuals or the notion of a contract) and reading back into it the character that would support preconceived political structures. If the desired structures are diamet-

26 Strictly speaking, it was Althusius, Bodin's junior by twenty-seven years, who turned Bodin's notion upside down.

rically opposed to each other, so will be the perception of the nature of the building blocks.

In theory, Bodin conceded, the sovereign might be an assembly, in which case it may delegate its power to a head of state who would, in the last resort, be its servant. In practice, however, Bodin said, it is best for a state if sovereignty resides in a hereditary monarchy: it is the best guarantee of order; its hereditary character normally avoids the risks of wars of succession; its decision-making is more likely to be crisp and consistent.

This last seems to be a rather sweeping generalization. Historically, there have certainly been weak and/or dithering monarchs under whom policy making was neither crisp nor consistent. French history was particularly bedevilled, in Bodin's own life time and for parts of the succeeding two centuries, by the chaos that ensued when a child succeeded to the throne by way of hereditary succession; in later societies, which were infused by a genuine democratic spirit expressed through parliaments, presidents, prime ministers or political parties, power would usually alternate without bloodshed.

Nevertheless, Bodin recognized some limitations on sovereignty. Most importantly, the ruler had to obey the laws of God. By this Bodin did not mean any theological dogma such as had set Catholics and Huguenots at each others' throats. Bodin himself belonged to the small party known as the *Politiques*. This party, more out of weariness and the recognition that credal conflict was tearing the states of Europe apart than out of any kind of idealism, had, for the first time in Christian history openly abandoned the idea that the state had the right and duty to foster "true" religion and suppress dissent. Instead, it should tolerate religious differences. The laws of God that Bodin thought were binding on the sovereign were the more general moral laws of nature, including, for example, that a ruler should keep agreements.

Bodin did not explain what, if anything, subjects were entitled to do if the sovereign did not obey God's laws. If he thought that subjects should leave the punishment of such a ruler to God rather than rebel against him if the king had not kept his agreements, then perhaps in this respect there were no legitimate checks on the ruler's sovereignty in this world.

Bodin thought that the sovereign had no absolute right over the property of his subjects – the right of an individual to his own property was inalienable. From this it followed that the sovereign could not take away property by taxation except, through estates, by the consent of those who were taxed.[27] This seemed to contradict his main idea that individuals and the subordinate institutions of a state owe their rights to the consent, for the time being, of the sovereign.

So Bodin's ideas are not very consistent, nor very well worked out. He did not examine closely why a subject should obey an absolute ruler, or under what circumstances and on what grounds (in the absence of a contract between him and the ruler) a subject is entitled to rebel. He did not explain at all clearly the steps that lead from the absolute authority of the *paterfamilias* to that of the sov-

27 We will postpone until we come to Locke – p. 268 below – another problem about the inalienability of property without your own consent. If it is truly inalienable in that way, can you then be bound by the decision of representatives who do not in fact represent you in this respect?

ereign, and whereas the *paterfamilias* has absolute rights over the property of his dependants, the sovereign, as we have seen, has no such rights over the property of his subjects.

Bodin's conception of sovereignty, then, rests on some unexamined theoretical foundations. It would be left to Thomas Hobbes to remedy these defects and produce one of the most closely argued analyses of sovereign power that has ever been produced.[28]

28 See Chapter 26 below.

CHAPTER 21

The Scientific Revolution

The Renaissance had made relatively little progress in what we now call the sciences, because it had such reverence of the Ancients in these as in other matters. Some people have called Aristotle the father of science; he was, after all, the first person to have carried out systematic studies in the various branches of science, giving to many of them the names that they still bear today. The Ancients had taken only the *first* steps in science. However, when their work was rediscovered, first by the Arabs and then by the Christian world,[1] such was the reverence then given to Antiquity, and to Aristotle in particular, that what they had said about how the material world works was regarded as almost the *last* word. It was incorporated into theology by Thomas Aquinas. For the Renaissance, Plato was more attractive than Aristotle, and Petrarch and Ficino more congenial than Aquinas, but the Humanists accepted, as had Aquinas, that what the Ancients had said about science was authoritative. If this was true of the intellectuals who had moved in courtly circles, it was even more so of the universities, where Thomist Aristotelianism had established itself as orthodoxy, and, as we have seen,[2] the universities had on the whole remained impervious to the Renaissance.

The impulse towards the Scientific Revolution, then, did not come from the universities, nor did it come from the courts. It really arose out of practical needs. With the increasing refinements of artillery, military engineers wanted to make it more effective and began to work on the science of ballistics. Sailors who were venturing further and further into uncharted waters called for compasses which in turn required an understanding of the earth's magnetic fields. Miners needed to understand hydrostatics if their pumps were to work properly.

Such needs and others led to great technological advances in the manufacture of precision instruments: telescopes and microscopes; micrometers, barometers and thermometers; accurate pendulum clocks and balances. All these instruments made precise quantifications possible, so that theories could be expressed in mathematical formulae and experiments could be carefully measured - something that was vital, for example, in investigations involving motion.

1 see Chapter 15.

2 see p. 173 above.

This in turn led to immense refinements in mathematical techniques. In the seventeenth and early eighteenth centuries we see the invention of decimals, of algebra and equations, of coordinate geometry, of logarithms, the calculus, and slide rules.

From Pythagoras and Plato onwards[3] there had been an intuitive feeling that mathematics was the purest form of intellectual training and that it was a mystical key to *philosophical* understanding. The new developments in mathematics took it out of the area of the arcane – it was now a key to *practical* knowledge of how the material world actually worked.

Not that this change was devoid of philosophical implications, quite the contrary. Socrates had associated knowledge with virtue, and ever since his time it could be said, with only slight exaggeration, that the most important task of philosophy had been seen as bringing about spiritual improvement. That had been the main purpose of the Socratic injunction to "know thyself".[4] Now, knowledge was equated with a grasp of the material world outside oneself.

The success of mathematics, and of the sciences dependent on it, in explaining the material world meant that, even before Newton, these disciplines gained an immense prestige. By the mid-seventeenth century they were beginning to be applied to areas that had not so far been considered parts of the material world at all: perhaps concepts like attraction and repulsion could explain the ways our minds worked.[5] But this attempt to "know oneself" was spiritually neutral, concerned simply with understanding mental mechanisms and not with moral judgements. Then, once the psychology of individuals had become subject to what were believed to be scientific explanations, the next step would be to look at how large collections of individuals, how societies could be understood and managed.

ASTRONOMY

Astronomy was an area of scientific progress that had an exceptional bearing on philosophical thought. Unlike discoveries in ballistics or hydraulics, astronomical theories have immense implications concerning man's place in the universe and, it was feared, even for traditional religious belief.

The astronomer Ptolemy (second century AD) had given his imprimatur to the belief of the ancient Greeks that the stars were points of light fixed in a series of transparent crystalline spheres which revolved around the earth. This theory by itself did not account for the movements of the planets, whose courses were more irregular,[6] and various elaborate explanations were given for this from Ptolemy onwards. As the circle was regarded as the symbol of perfection, the heavenly bodies were assumed to have circular motions, and the irregular movement of the planets was explained by the postulation of epicycles: each planet revolves in a circle around a centre which rests on the circumference of

3 for Pythagoras see p. 9 above; for Plato, p. 34f above.

4 see p. 19 aboe.

5 Democritus had already had a similar idea in the fifth century BC.

6 The stars never seem to change their relationship to each other, but the planets do. The word planets comes from the Greek *planetes* which meant "wanderers". The Ancients had believed that there were seven of them: the Sun, the Moon, Mercury, Venus, Mars, Jupiter and Saturn.

the sphere in which it is fixed. None of these explanations were totally satisfactory because they all assumed that the basic course of planets is circular, when in fact it is elliptical.

Among the ideas of Antiquity which Thomas Aquinas had incorporated into Christian thinking in the thirteenth century were those of Ptolemaic astronomy, which fitted well enough into the Christian view of the world. Dante's *Divine Comedy* (1310 to 1314) had God, the Prime and Unmoved Mover, dwelling beyond the ninth sphere, in the Empyrean, and an archangel or an angel governing each of the lower spheres. As one moved below the surface of the earth, one entered the successive circles of Hell. The Christians assumed that, naturally, God had sent Christ to the centre of the universe, and this idea further reinforced Ptolemy's geocentric view. Indeed, as long as it was thought that the earth was a flat circular disc surrounded by the River Oceanus, the maps of Christian Europe placed Bethlehem at the exact centre of that disc and arranged the rest of the known world around it.

The Greek geographer Eratosthenes had worked out, as long ago as *ca.* 200 BC, that the earth was round and not flat, but that knowledge was lost long before either the Arabs or Aquinas had incorporated Greek learning into their world picture. It surfaced again in the fifteenth century, and Columbus had enough confidence in it to sail westwards in 1492 in the expectation of reaching the East Indian Spice Islands. True, he hit the West Indies instead, and it was found that there was a whole continent between the Atlantic and the Pacific, but there could no longer be any doubt that the earth was a globe, and that therefore Bethlehem could hardly be the central point of it – at least the belief could persist that God had sent Jesus to this earth because it was the centre of the universe.

That belief was soon to be shaken. In 1514, Copernicus (1473 to 1543) suggested that some of the complexities of epicycles would disappear if the sun, and not the earth were seen as the centre of the planetary system. He continued, however, to believe in epicycles, and it would take another century before Johannes Kepler (1571 to 1630) would at last interpret the data of planetary movements correctly by showing that their paths must be elliptical.[7] Copernicus was, however, utterly radical in his momentous postulation of a heliocentric universe.[8]

When Copernicus lectured on his theory in the presence of Pope Clement VII in 1533, the Pope was willing to entertain the notion that the sun might be the centre of the universe. Clement was still a son of the Ficinian Renaissance, and the Florentines had been much taken with the symbolism of the third-century Neo-Platonists like Plotinus. Plotinus had seen the world as an emanation from God, and he had compared emanations to the light which streams forth from

7 Kepler could demonstrate *that* the paths were elliptical, but could offer only suggestions *why* they should be so. He guessed that gravitation might have something to do with it, for by that time Galileo's telescopes had shown that the planets were solid bodies, not just points of light. It was Newton, a century and a half later, who would finally work out the mathematical laws of gravitation that explain the shape of the ellipses.

8 Today we should of course use the word "galaxy". The sun is the centre of the solar galaxy, and there are many galaxies that make up the universe. But in the sixteenth and seventeenth centuries that was not known: what we call the solar galaxy, the astronomers of that time believed to be the entire universe.

the sun – a light that at its source is so bright that no human being can look upon it, but which becomes dimmer the further one is from its source, until it is lost in darkness – the absence of God.[9] So Ficino had seen the sun as symbolizing God, the centre of everything. A Ficinian Pope would therefore not be so appalled when an astronomer presented a universe that was heliocentric not only in symbolism, but also in actual fact.

The first attack on Copernicus came from the Protestants, from Luther and Calvin. For them, they only source of authority were the words of the Bible, and Copernicus' theory contradicted several biblical passages.[10] That the Papacy was willing to flirt with attempts to reconcile Christianity with the pagan Plotinus was merely another example of the theological slackness it had promoted.

As the Catholic Church lost half of Europe to Protestantism, it began to be sensitive to such criticism. The Counter-Reformation turned its back on the pagan world. The Council of Trent, which first met in 1545, two years after the death of Copernicus, insisted on complete Catholic orthodoxy, and the heliocentric theory was henceforth under a cloud, though not yet actually banned.

In 1613, Galileo Galilei (1564 to 1642) published the discoveries he had made with his telescope – notably that the planets were made of solid matter and were not merely points of light. That there were other material bodies just like the earth out there in the universe was in itself a mind- boggling idea for many people. In the course of his book, Galileo also adduced further evidence that the sun was the centre of the universe, as Copernicus had said. The work was a sensation, partly because of the discoveries Galileo had made, partly because it had been written in Italian to reach a wide audience, and possibly because it reasserted the heliocentric theory, which was in disfavour in orthodox church circles. Pope Paul V was stung into declaring that the teaching of Copernicus was "false and erroneous" (1616). The next Pope but one, Pope Urban VIII, was a personal friend of Galileo's. In 1624 he allowed him to write another book describing both the Ptolemaic geocentric and the refined Copernican heliocentric system, as long as he did not formally commit himself to the latter and supplied the caveat that we could not understand the works of God. Nevertheless, when the book was actually published in 1632, Galileo's enemies accused him of heresy, and Urban could not prevent him from being tried by the Inquisition. Galileo saved his life by recanting the heliocentric theory (1633). After his recantation, he is said to have muttered to a friend, "*E pur si muove*" – "for all that, the earth does move (around the sun)".

Despite the censures of the Church, that is what most intellectuals continued to believed. The philosophical implications were immense. If the earth is not the centre of the universe, then the central place of Man in nature was less certain, and his significance in the cosmos seemed reduced. It was also thought-provoking that something that was so counter-intuitive could be true. We *feel* that the sun revolves around us and we continue to use phrases like "the sun is rising" as if the earth was fixed, but now we see that the world cannot be as it appears. The knowledge that we look at it from a constantly shifting view-

9 See p. 90 above.

10 e.g. Psalm 96:10: "the world also shall be established that it shall not be moved."

point casts further doubt on what our senses tell us. Philosophy will have to turn from scrutinizing the world that is observed to examining the role of the observer. That in turn will, in due course, open up a new area of philosophy, that of Epistemology, the branch that examines the nature of our knowledge and how we come by it.

Today we use the phrase "Copernican revolution" for ideas that totally transform the way we look at the world, such as would result, for example, from the work of Kant or Darwin or Freud. The original Copernican revolution was one such. Originally a revolution in our understanding of astronomy, it turned out to have repercussions well beyond astronomy, in areas that profoundly affect the way in which we think of ourselves. The first philosopher who spelt out some of the implications of Copernicus was Giordano Bruno.

GIORDANO BRUNO
1548 to 1600

Whereas the theories of Copernicus, Brahe, Kepler and Galileo were based on finding mathematical explanations for the observations they had made, those of Bruno were entirely speculative and philosophical. Unlike Spinoza, some of whose ideas he anticipated, Bruno was not a systematic philosophical thinker. His language was often wild and visionary, and he wrote much mystical nonsense which has no real place in the history of philosophy at all. However, some of his speculations were extraordinarily prophetic. He was the first to conclude that, as the movement of stars would look different when observed from the earth than from some other point in the universe, measures of motion must depend on the observer's position in the universe. As we measure motion by time, time, too, must be variable in this way. Even before Galileo had devised the first telescope, Bruno postulated that Copernicus had not gone far enough. Not only was the earth not the centre of the universe, but neither was the sun: there are an infinite number of worlds outside the solar system.

The idea of infinity was familiar in relation to God (who has no beginning and no end), to time (eternity) and to mathematics, but Bruno was the first thinker to be impressed by the spatial infinity of the material universe.

> It may be difficult for us today to appreciate the enormity of this idea. Galileo's telescope had yet to demonstrate that the planets and the stars were material bodies and not points of light. Most people still thought that these points of light were fixed in concentric crystal spheres, and the outermost of these was believed to circumscribe and therefore to limit the entire universe. God dwelt outside the universe, beyond this last sphere. Now Bruno was suggesting that the solar system and an infinity of other systems existed in boundless, infinite space. For many people, Copernicus had already reduced the significance of man by placing him on a planet that was not the centre of the universe. Against the traditional background, the implication of the idea that man dwelt within a system that was itself not unique and probably not central either must have been even more startling than it is today. As Bruno could offer no proof of his idea, most of his contemporaries dismissed it as simply a crazy figment of his imagination.

Now we have a new problem: can there be two infinities? Can there be any room outside something that is infinite, let alone for another infinity? If there cannot, does it not follow from this that the infinity of the universe and the infinity of God are the same, and that therefore God and the Universe are one and the same? If that is so, must it not mean that God cannot be transcendent, totally outside the universe, but must be wholly immanent, present in every particle of matter?[11] That is what Bruno sometimes seems to think, as when he writes in one of his dialogues, "God is not an *external* intelligence ... It is more worthy of Him to be the *internal* principle of motion." Elsewhere, in another dialogue, he seems to have drawn back from this position. Here, whether out of prudence or out of genuine belief, he drew a distinction between the two infinities. The infinity of the universe, he says, is divisible into finite components (from stars down to the minutest particle of matter) but God in His infinity is indivisible, and here he also asserted the orthodox Christian view that God is transcendent.

People who believe that God is wholly immanent are pantheists: they think that God is present in all creation, in every tree and in every stone. Orthodox Christianity was very suspicious of that idea, thinking that it could easily degenerate into pagan worship of trees, stones etc. Bruno was no pagan, but he could not possibly be an orthodox Christian either. If God and the universe are one, God will be immanent in all human beings, and it is difficult to find a place for Him being uniquely so in Jesus Christ. Bruno could not believe in such a special incarnation, and he was not afraid of making intemperate attacks on Christian theology. From 1576 onwards he was constantly on the move in Europe as he successively fell out with the authorities in Italy, France, Switzerland, England and Germany. It is amazing that he remained free for as long as he did. He was finally arrested by the Inquisition in 1592. He was interrogated in a leisurely manner for eight years before being burnt as a heretic in 1600. He was condemned not for his beliefs about astronomy and the universe - the ideas of Copernicus would not be declared as "false and erroneous" until 1616 - but for refusing to recant his rejection of the Incarnation and the Trinity.

FRANCIS BACON
1561 to 1626

Francis Bacon was not the first philosopher of science. That title should be bestowed on his namesake, Roger Bacon who had lived over three centuries earlier, from 1214 to 1292.[12] Roger Bacon had first laid down the central idea of scientific enquiry that induction rather than deduction must be the beginning

11 The word "immanent" comes from the Latin *manere*, meaning "to stay" or "to dwell". Some theologians, like William of Ockham (see Chapter 17) had stressed that God is totally transcendent, that is, outside the world. Others, like the Neo-Platonists (see Chapter 10) had allowed that, although He is transcendent, there is a degree of immanence also, by way of the emanations that stream forth from Him and mingle with the world. The metaphor used was that of light: the pure source of light is transcendent and so intense that we cannot look at it, but as that light floods the world, it infuses the world in something less than its original intensity. If God were wholly immanent, dwelling *entirely* within the world, then He would be dwelling also in everything in this world which is perishable, corruptible, impure and evil. That idea is deemed to be incompatible with the idea that God is pure perfection, and was therefore regarded with abhorrence by all orthodox Christians.

12 see pp. 149 ff above.

of material knowledge, and that any deductions which seemed to follow logically from experiments must be tested and confirmed pragmatically.[13] Roger Bacon had lived when the intellectual life was still dominated by theology and long before the Scientific Revolution. Although he had taken care to exempt the teachings of the Church from the tests to which he would subject knowledge of the material world, he had been imprisoned by his Order for unorthodoxy; and the scholastic climate of the time was not very favourable to his ideas. Francis Bacon was more fortunate in the time in which he lived. Scholasticism was in decline; scientific work was taken more seriously, so his work fell upon much more fruitful ground.

In 1620 Francis Bacon wrote an outline, about twenty pages long, of his plan to bring about a great renewal of knowledge. It was called the *Instauratio Magna*.[14] Before this he had already published a number of books which were to be part of this renewal. The most important of these was *The Advancement of Learning* (1603 to 1605). His other major work, the *Novum Organum*, was published five years after the *Instauratio*. In the *Advancement*, he classified knowledge into three broad areas: Poesy, which he said primarily involves the faculty of the imagination; History, which particularly engages the faculty of memory; Philosophy, for which the faculty of reason was crucial.

Only about one-fiftieth of the *Advancement* is devoted to Poesy. A little less than one-tenth dealt with History, in which Bacon, who was intimately involved with politics, was rather more interested. In 1622 he published a *History of the Reign of Henry VII*, in which he admired the king's statesmanship for its Machiavellian qualities. Bacon, who himself indulged in much subtle intrigue at the court of James I, possessed these qualities himself in good measure, and he admired Machiavelli for studying human behaviour "scientifically"; for being concerned with how human beings actually behave rather than with how they ought to behave ideally.

It was the third area, Philosophy, which interested him most – it takes up nearly nine-tenths of the *Advancement*. He first divided philosophy into two branches. The first was the knowledge of the Divine. Here he accepted the authority of the Church, which absolved him from having to say much about it. He made no attempt to reconcile any contradictions that might appear between theological truths that relate to the world beyond this one, and the truths of science which operate in the study of this world, so he avoided ecclesiastical censure.

The second branch of philosophy was natural knowledge, and this is what interested him most. He subdivided this into two further fields. The first is physics, the knowledge of which we acquire with our senses; the second is metaphysics, the laws which account for what our senses have observed. It is metaphysical knowledge, thus defined, which is the main object of the sciences.

As Roger Bacon and William of Ockham had said earlier, we discover these laws by induction.[15] For Francis Bacon induction was a much more valuable

13 In deductive reasoning we begin with a very few propositions and then draw conclusions from them. Inductive reasoning is the opposite: we begin by collecting a number of phenomena and work out by experiments what conclusions they suggest.

14 The Latin word *instaurare* means "to renew"; and Bacon's title is sometimes translated into English as "The Great Instauration" and sometimes as "The Great Renewal".

15 See chapter 17.

intellectual tool than deduction. Formal logic and mathematics work entirely by the deductive method. The first proceeds from premises, the second from axioms. In formal logic, many errors can creep into the formulation of premises and thus into the conclusions derived from them. Mathematics is more watertight in this respect. Even so, Bacon thought that neither formal logic nor mathematics can ever produce anything really new; they can only tease out what is already contained within the premises or axioms.

Bacon, therefore, downgraded the importance of formal logic and of mathematics. Philosophers down the ages, from Pythagoras to Ficino, had regarded mathematics with mystical reverence; they saw it as such a pure form of truth that it was a symbol of divine truth.

Bacon refused to endow mathematics with this kind of sovereignty and mystique. Far from it being the queen of philosophy, he regarded it as merely an auxiliary to science. It is of course an auxiliary without which much of science cannot go very far, and Bacon, by his extreme privileging of induction over deduction, has been accused of not giving sufficient importance to it when he described the techniques a scientist should use. He devoted a large section of the *Novum Organum* to it.

There are particular procedures that should be followed for inductive work. If we want to find out what might be the cause of heat, for instance, we should not start with a hypothesis about what the cause might be and then look for facts that would fit in or confirm the hypothesis. Instead, we would collect as many examples as we can of where heat is present (the rays of the sun, the interior of animals etc.), follow this with a list of situations where heat is not present (the rays of the moon, for instance - which appeared to show that heat is not likely to be a function of light) then list cases where it is present in varying degrees (how the heat of animals increases when they exercise or are ill). We can then begin to induce something about the nature of heat. The induction that Bacon made was that heat is a form of motion - and there is indeed a modern theory that heat is molecular motion.

Bacon regarded that conclusion as only a "first vintage". It holds good only as long as no cases of heat crop up that could not be explained in that way. The "first vintage" would then have to be either abandoned or modified so as to incorporate the new-found phenomenon. A large number of cases may be found that appear to verify a conclusion, but it takes the discovery of only one case that does not fit in for the conclusion to be falsified; we should always be *systematically* on the lookout for such cases. Any scientist who has formulated a new theory tends to become so proud of it that he forgets to look out for, or is actually tempted to reject, anything that might falsify it. It is therefore important that he publish his work, so that other scientists can repeat the experiments or can challenge them with material that does not fit the theory. In these respects Bacon was a forerunner of ideas that are especially associated in the twentieth century with Karl Popper.[16]

> Bacon was unduly condemnatory of beginning with a hypothesis. The very act of collecting examples is already based on selection: one would not collect randomly but systematically, and what informs the system is usually already

16 See p. 557 below.

some preliminary theory. The way scientists generally make progress is not by collecting a large number of examples from which to make an induction, but by having a hypothesis to start with and then seeing whether experiments would support it or not. Scientists working, for example, on cancer research may ask themselves, "I wonder what would happen if we did so-and-so." Progress is also made when a scientist happens to notice a chance phenomenon which puzzles him and for which he then tries to find an explanation. Louis Pasteur once said that progress in science was often made by the accidental discovery of the prepared mind. In that way, Alexander Fleming made the discovery that led to the development of penicillin. Here, too, the first stage would be an informed guess – that is the formulation of a hypothesis based on the phenomenon that has been observed. The next stage is testing whether that hypothesis would work when applied to similar phenomena.

Nonetheless, Bacon was right to stress how essential this testing is and to warn against accepting logical deductions from a hypothesis. There are two types of situations where we could go wrong. The worst mistake is to begin with an assumption that is not based on deductions, has not been tested by experiment, but is regarded on some other ground as a certainty. This had been the case with the astronomers who had begun with the conviction that the planets were fixed in crystalline spheres. When they found that the movement of the planets did not appear to conform to this assumption, they did not abandon it, but tried to force their observations into formulae that became ever more complicated. The trouble was that they had begun with an untested assumption and then tried to make their observations fit this assumption.

But we can also go wrong if a hypothesis is the result of induction but from which inaccurate deductions, untested by experiments, may then be made. To repeat an example given on page 153: we may induce from observation that hay fever is prevalent in the summer. From this we might go on to make accurate or inaccurate deductions. One deduction, which tests would soon show to be inaccurate, might be that hay fever is related to the amount of sunshine and that therefore we should spend as much time as possible in north-facing rooms. It would be a correct deduction (which can also be tested) that it is related to the amount of pollen in the atmosphere and that therefore an air-conditioning system that traps the pollen might alleviate the condition.

In Bacon's view, then, one of the great dangers to accurate thought was to begin with a hypothesis. But he listed many other ways - he called them "Idols" - which lead our thinking astray. Here again there is an echo from Roger Bacon, who had identified four sources of error: the acceptance of "frail and unworthy authority"; "long-established custom"; "the sense of the ignorant crowd"; "the hiding of one's own ignorance under the shadow of wisdom".[17] Francis Bacon also presents us with a foursome, which is a little more sophisticated.

The first he called *Idols of the Tribe*. Under this heading he listed

> Reliance on the senses alone. We know how our senses can lead us astray (for example, how the sense of sight can tell us that a straight stick in a glass of water is bent). There are also things that our senses cannot observe directly and fail to pick up. An example would be the properties of air: when the air is still, we can neither see, smell, hear, taste nor feel it.

17 See p. 150 above.

Creating abstractions or generalizations from our sensory experiences which are then thought of as constant instead of as subject to change in the light of new experiences or the discovery of faulty reasoning.

Ignoring ideas which do not fit in with existing ones, or else distorting them so that they do fit.

Assuming the existence of final causes which are not subject to experimental demonstration. Final Causes were initially defined by Aristotle as the purpose for which anything is organized. The concept had come to play an important role in Theology, where God was seen as the Final Cause. Bacon did not challenge it in religion, where it was defined by the Church and was, therefore, not subject to question or experiment, but if the concept was to be used in science, it would need to be subject to experimental proof. When we ascribe purpose to natural processes, we too easily drift into thinking of Nature in anthropomorphic terms. We can learn much about the nature of clouds from observation: how they are made up, or under what circumstances they precipitate water, but we cannot establish that they exist for the purpose of watering the earth.

Bacon called *Idols of the Den* the errors an individual will make as the result of his temperament, education, or other special influences to which he has been subjected.

Then there were the *Idols of the Market Place*. These were errors due to the way we use language. Sometimes we give names to things that do not actually exist, in which case conclusions drawn from those non-existent entities are at best not provable in science and at worst plain nonsense.

An example might be the theory that "universals" are not just names that we give to groups of things but that they have an independent reality.[18]

Also, we sometimes use the same word to describe things which are not the same, or which may mean one thing in one context and another thing in another, without us being aware of the difference. The confusion that arises from that is obvious.

In the days of the Soviet Union, communist regimes used to call themselves People's Democracies. They clearly had a very different conception of democracy from the one that prevailed in the West. Before any sensible discussion could take place between a communist and a liberal, one would have to begin by clarifying what each side meant by the word "democracy". The phrase which in those days Professor C.E.M. Joad used on the original Brains Trust became quite a catchphrase. When asked a question whose terms were ambiguous, he would respond: "It all depends on what you mean by ...". This simple phrase introduced millions of people to one of the essential tasks of philosophy: to be very precise in the way we use words.

Idols of the Theatre was the name given by Francis Bacon to the fourth source of careless thinking, and it corresponded exactly to what Roger Bacon had called "the acceptance of frail and unworthy authority". Francis Bacon meant by this the uncritical acceptance of philosophical systems of the past, which often represent unreal worlds of the philosopher's own creation. Francis, like Roger,

18 see the discussion in Chapter 14 on Realism and Nominalism.

believed that far too much reverence had been given to the theories of Plato and of Aristotle. Some of their ideas were not testable, but in any case, Francis Bacon criticized the implication that the task of philosophy was the essentially backward looking one of integrating the wisdom of the Ancients into Christian or Renaissance thought. He thought that the task of philosophy was to look forward, to open up new fields of knowledge through the inductive method, and to contribute to the practical "relief of man's estate".

> At the French Academy in the early eighteenth century there was a famous controversy known as the Battle between the Ancients and the Moderns. The Ancients saw the imitation of the models of Antiquity as the only guarantee of excellence in thought, in literature and in the arts; the Moderns thought the time had come to emancipate themselves from these models and that when they did so, their best work was superior to what Antiquity had produced. Bacon, who had no great reverence for tradition, would have sided with the latter. It is not a coincidence that he had called his prospectus "The Great Renewal"; he had the ambition to replace Aristotle and Aquinas with what he considered a more modern approach to philosophy. Faint echoes of Bacon's temper perhaps reverberate in Blair's Britain: we must not dwell too much on our heritage and ancient traditions, but must embrace the future with zeal. Some people shiver at this, regarding it as a betrayal of the roots of our past and our culture. At the very least, they say, we need to keep a balance between our treasured past and the beckoning future. Bacon would probably be rather impatient with this nostalgia, but we have seen that in the zeal for his new approach he had perhaps rather excessively downgraded the importance of formal logic, of mathematics, and now of tradition.

Just as Bacon had no particular veneration for the philosophy of the past, he had none for the so-called accumulated wisdom of the law. As Solicitor-General (1607), Attorney-General (1612), and Lord Chancellor (1618 to 1621) successively, he was the great opponent of Edward Coke, the Lord Chief Justice from 1612 to 1616. Coke was the great defender of the Common Law, which is firmly bound by precedents from the past, however outdated or inefficient they might be. Bacon, on the other hand, was an advocate of the principles of Equity, which originally[19] meant that, where they conflicted, natural justice (as interpreted by the Court of Chancery over which he presided as Lord Chancellor) rather than precedent (as followed by Common Law courts under the Lord Chief Justice) should prevail.

Constitutional and political philosophy played a part in this conflict also. In its medieval origins the Court of Chancery had enabled the King's chief minister, then called the Chancellor, to deliver the justice (which is what "equity" means) which the slow and precedent-laden procedures of the Common Law had denied. It was therefore in some sense a tool of the King, which the Common Law was not, the more so since Chancery was presided over by the King's chief minister, the Chancellor, whereas the Lord Chief Justice was the head of the legal profession. Bacon had been appointed Lord Chancellor by James I, who was then engaged in the struggle with Parliament that would erupt into Civil War during the next reign. James claimed the Divine Right of Kings,

19 The system of Equity Law, as it developed from the fourteenth century onwards, would in due course develop its own set of precedents, so that in practice it became just as cumbersome as the Common Law.

demanded that judges do his bidding and act like "lions under the throne". Coke, who was also a member of the parliamentary opposition to James, held that the Common Law of England was above the King and that it enshrined certain principles of English liberty that the King had to respect. In the struggle between Bacon and Coke, therefore, Bacon represented not only a different legal philosophy, but he was also a supporter of the King. In 1621, Parliament impeached Bacon for corruption and James had to let him go, but the King owed much to Bacon and was able to save him from the terrible consequences that generally followed a successful impeachment. He merely had to retire, and it was during his retirement that he wrote the *Novum Organum*.

Many later philosophers were to acclaim Bacon as the initiator of the Age of Reason. This is not so much due to the originality of his ideas, almost all of which we find in his predecessors, but that he wrote at the right time. Great progress was being made in science, and philosophy was slowly beginning to emancipate itself from theological constraints. Theologians increasingly tolerated this state of affairs, providing that there was a profession of belief in the world beyond this one. This profession was not always merely a matter of form; there have always been philosophers who restrict the area on which philosophy can usefully speak. Not all of them do so for prudential reasons; some of them are happy to remain in the religious faith in which they have been brought up. Not until the eighteenth century will we find philosophers who make frontal attacks on the teaching of the Church. When they do, they will include religion among Francis Bacon's "Idols of the Tribe and of the Theatre".

PART FOUR:
THE SEVENTEENTH CENTURY

CHAPTER 22

René Descartes

1596 to 1650

The great exponents of the inductive methods in philosophy – Roger Bacon, William of Ockham and Francis Bacon – were all Englishmen, and perhaps there was something in the English turn of mind which puts a wide practical experience in the forefront of philosophy, both as a starting point for reasoning and as a method of checking conclusions.

The opposite, deductive approach, of beginning with a proposition of which we can be certain and then seeing what conclusions logically flow from this, is particularly associated with the great French philosopher René Descartes, and the Cartesian method which is named after him is said to be as characteristic of the French turn of mind as the pragmatic approach is held to be of English thought.

Descartes was an excellent and creative mathematician. He established analytical geometry, did important work that would culminate in the invention of the infinitesimal calculus, solved several mathematical problems and developed much of the algebraic notation that is in use today. We have seen that Francis Bacon had given a subordinate role to mathematics, the deductive activity *par excellence*. Descartes, however, believed that it underlay all sciences. He did not neglect scientific experiments himself and made important discoveries in mechanics and optics. These of course have a strong mathematical character. He also studied physiology. He believed that physiological processes, like all processes in the sciences, are mechanical and are therefore also ultimately explicable in mathematical terms. More than that, he thought that, because mathematics gives answers that cannot be clearer or more definite, its deductive *method* should be a model for "all the things which come within the scope of human knowledge".

In mathematics, one begins with indubitable axioms, and Descartes looked for an axiomatic truth from which one could deduce the rest of one's knowledge. He said he would begin by doubting everything (*"de omnibus dubitandum"*). That is of course what a Sceptic does also, but a Sceptic is content to stay within his scepticism, whereas Descartes was looking for a way of escaping it. Such an escape was possible if he could find an axiomatic proposition which was clearly recognized as true *by his intellect*. He would not start with sense experience, because our senses so often play us false. To give just one example: our sense of touch may suggest to us that we hold a straight stick in our hands, but when we put it into a glass of water, our sense of sight suggests that it is bent. In the end, he concluded that the very act of doubting must prove that there is a doubter (*dubito ergo sum*) or, more famously, that if I am thinking, I must exist: *cogito ergo sum*. Even if my thoughts are deluded by my senses, even if a malign spirit makes me think erroneously, it is still indisputable that, if I am thinking erroneously, I exist (*Si fallor sum.)*[1] Similarly, I exist when I am perceiving, imagining, feeling, desiring or willing.

Does that mean that there is no certainty of my existence when I am unconscious or dreamlessly asleep? Descartes held that we think continuously from the moment of conception onwards, but that we do not remember certain kinds of thinking.

> That is true in so far as our brain is continuously active even when we are unconscious or dreamlessly asleep, but as Descartes will distinguish sharply between what he considered the mechanical function of the body on the one hand and thought processes on the other (see below), it is hard to see in what way he could have arrived *deductively* at the conclusion that he was thinking when he was not aware of thinking and therefore to the further conclusion that he must exist when he was not aware of thinking.

Our existence and identity are guaranteed by these mental processes alone – not by the fact that we have a material body. The mind and its workings, he thought, were completely immaterial. When we exercise them, we find that the object, particularly of perception, appears to be the outside world of material things, but the only thing we can initially be aware of is that there is a particular activity – thought and perception – which takes place in our minds. The next thing Descartes has to show is that this activity of thought and perception actually correlates with something that actually exists outside our minds. He had already said that *perceptions* can be faulty, as in the example of the way we see a stick in a glass of water. If we doubt everything, we may also doubt whether the laws of logic we employ when we *think* correspond with anything outside ourselves.

Taken to extremes (as it would be by philosophers in the following century) that course of thinking leads to solipsism: the idea that the only thing of which we can be absolutely certain is the content of our mind, and that we can have no idea whether there is anything outside our mind at all; everything we call the outside world may simply be a figment of our imaginations. When, for example, I see a table, I can have no certainty that there actually is a table; when I

1 These phrases come from the first edition of Descartes' *Meditations on First Philosophy*, which was published in Latin in 1641. Four years earlier he had published, in the *Discours de la Méthode*, the first outline of his philosophy, and this had been written in French because he wanted to reach out beyond the academic world to the general public. There, the famous phrase is *je pense, donc je suis*. The *Meditations* was a more detailed working out of the ideas of the *Discours* and wasaddressed to the academic world. He had circulated the *Meditations* in manuscript to several famous contemporary philosophers and invited them to respond to it. Their criticisms and Descartes' replies to them are included in the published work. A French translation of the *Meditations* followed in 1647. Descartes wrote these books attractively in the first person singular, conveying his own train of thought. His French was elegant and clear, and it contributed to making his ideas widely accessible. His avoidance of any cloudiness of expression established an admirable tradition of lucidity in philosophical writing in France of which Frenchmen are very proud – and which,in due course, will contrast powerfully with the obscurity of much German philosophical writings.

bump into it, I can be aware only of the sensation of being bruised. If I have no certainty that there actually is a table when I see it, I obviously cannot have certainty that it exists when I no longer have the sensation of seeing it because I have left the room. If a friend tells me that the table still exists because he remained in the room and saw it, I am not certain that the friend exists, only that I have the visual and auditory sensation that he is giving me that information. My mathematical or logical thought processes may similarly strike me as convincing, but I can have no certainty that phenomena that seem to obey mathematical or logical rules exist outside my mind. I can be certain of the existence of only (*solo*) my self (*ipse*) – hence the name given to the extreme consequence of Descartes' *cogito ergo sum*.

Descartes was not a solipsist. He had said he could not trust our *perceptions* to be reliable, as in the case of the stick that appears bent in a glass of water, but he was sure that there *was* a stick and a glass of water, and that if we applied careful and logical *thought* to our various perceptions, we could correct our unreliable perceptions and understand why the stick appeared bent when it fact it was not.

The reason he had this confidence was that he was certain that God would not deceive us if we used our minds correctly. God would not allow the mind to think that one could make sound logical deductions from axioms if He had not created a world in which sound axioms were sound axioms and sound logic was sound logic.

But if we must doubt everything that cannot be clearly apprehended to be true, how can we be sure that God exists, and that, if He does exist, He would not deceive us?

Here Descartes used the arguments of medieval natural theology as advanced by Anselm, Thomas Aquinas and others who had based their belief in the existence of God on two grounds: faith in Revelation and Reason. The most famous of the rational arguments is known as the Ontological Argument for the existence of God. It runs, it will be remembered, something like this: the very concept of perfection (as embodied only in God) necessitates the existence of God, for the essence of perfection is that it must also exist, as nonexistence is incompatible with perfection. Therefore, our very conception of perfection implies that perfection must exist.

It would of course be incompatible with God's perfection that He should try to deceive us.

> Few people would accept that argument today. We might perhaps go as far as to say that *if* there is something that is supremely perfect, *then* it must exist for the reasons that Anselm gives. The argument surely depends on the prior assumption that perfection exists outside this earth – for it clearly does not exist anywhere *on* earth.
>
> In view of this, we can understand Durant's comment: "As we follow Descartes, we see the infant Age of Reason recoiling in fear from the hazards of thought and seeking to reenter the womb of faith." That is not completely fair. Descartes did indeed tell us early in the *Discours* that he had faith in the Bible, but the Ontological Argument itself takes no account of faith and claims to establish the reality of perfection (which we call God) on the basis of reason alone. However, as one of his critics, Antoine Arnauld II (1612 to 1694),

pointed out, even when reasoning, Descartes had put the cart before the horse. On Descartes' own principles: "We can be sure that God exists only because we can clearly and evidently perceive it. Therefore, *prior to being certain that God exists*, we should be certain that whatever we clearly and evidently perceive is true."

When, therefore, we come to a generation which finds Descartes' *reasoning* for the existence of God fallible and which does not think in terms of mysticism or Revelation either, then we quickly get to the solipsism, scepticism and idealism which has been described above.

Now that he was sure of the existence of God and of the fact that He would not deceive us when we employ our reason properly, Descartes thought he was safe in making a number of logical deductions, relating to what he thought were three *separate* substances: God, the Mind, and Matter:

1. God: By employing our reason, he thought he had safely deduced that God exists.

2. The Mind: We could also deduce that the self existed, which Descartes identified with the thinking or rational mind or soul. (Descartes did not distinguish between them and used those terms – *l'esprit* and *l'âme* – interchangeably.) Because thoughts have no length or breadth or any other qualities that belong to matter, the soul must be immaterial, a substance separate from and independent of the body. It will therefore not perish when the material body perishes. Because he made no distinction between the mind and the soul, his belief in the immortality of the Soul made it possible for him to think that the brain, a bodily organ, is not essential for the existence of the mind or the soul.

3. Matter: We can safely accept the mathematical qualities of the outside material world, namely the reality of length, breadth and depth, of time and of motion. Descartes saw further proof of their reality in that they operate even in our dreams, in which everything else is fantasy. We do not come to accept their reality through experience; the mind, when it engages in thought, rightly perceives them as axiomatic. Later philosophers will describe the potential recognition of such qualities as *innate*, meaning that this recognition is there at birth, though it may remain unconscious until experience brings it up into consciousness. A baby has no grasp of mathematics at birth, but as our thinking powers develop, we realize its necessary and ineluctable truth. Because mathematical characteristics were so objective and reliable, they would be called *primary* qualities. On the other hand, our perception of nonmathematical characteristics in the outside world – of colour or smell, for example – came to be called *secondary* qualities. Descartes believed that these were actual minute particles given off by objects which then stimulate not our rational minds, but our senses, and they may affect these differently in different persons and are therefore more subjective and less reliable.

Since the days of Pythagoras and Plato, mathematics had been given this very special place in philosophy, as the purest and least corruptible kind of knowledge there is. While avoiding the almost mystical reverence given to it in Antiquity and the Middle Ages, Descartes powerfully reinforced that tradition.

It would be further enhanced by the work of Newton, and even after later philosophers had whittled away and finally abolished the distinction between primary and secondary qualities, the special veneration for mathematics would affect much more than philosophy and science. It would, for example, influence the criteria by which works of art were often judged in the seventeenth and eighteenth centuries, during what is called the Classical Period.[2] Some artists (Poussin, Descartes' contemporary, is a striking example) and philosophers of aesthetics (like Kant in the following century) would proclaim that mathematical relationships should underlie the composition of a truly great work of art. There is a strong mathematical quality in the regular rhythms of poets like Racine, Dryden or Pope; in the façades of great public buildings and the layout of avenues and flower beds; in the music of Bach.

Just as Descartes believed that the mind could exist separately from material bodies, so he also held that there can be material bodies without minds. This is obvious in the case of inanimate matter, but Descartes believed that it was also true of plants and of animals. Because he thought that animals cannot reason, they cannot have minds either. When he had said "I am thinking, therefore I exist", he assumed that the mind which did the thinking was *conscious* that it was thinking. For him, thinking without the consciousness that one was thinking was not a mental activity and so was not thinking at all: processes in the brain of which one was not conscious were merely mechanical. Animals, he assumed, were not conscious of thinking and were therefore simply rather complex machines, moved by stimuli to their physiological mechanisms.

Although modern behaviourists maintain that we cannot deduce from the behaviour of an animal that it is capable of thought or feeling, such conclusions must seem very odd to anyone who has much to do with animals. For even if one agreed that they might not have reasoning faculties, any dog owner, farmer or hunter could have told Descartes that relationships with animals are radically different from relationships with machines.[3]

In human beings also the processes of the body were mechanical, as are *to an extent* those movements in the brain which respond to stimuli, like our instincts and emotions. Only the mind, because it is nonmaterial, does not work like a machine. Our reasoning and our will are free, and we ought to use our will to think as rationally as we can. The more rationally we think, the better we are able to understand the mathematical and physical laws that govern the behaviour of matter.

If minds and bodies are such different essences, how do they interact with each other? How does the mind set the body to move, and how do bodily events like physical pain make themselves felt in the mind? In the latter case,

2 The word "classical" first appears early in the seventeenth century. It comes from the Latin *classicus* which meant "of the highest class or excellence". In a world which venerated Antiquity, the word was applied generally to that period in history; but in aesthetics is applies particularly to that aspect of Antiquity which had extolled mathematics as the "highest class" of intellectual endeavour.

3 There are modern philosophers who, while not thinking of animals as machines, still deny them the capacity of thought: R.G. Frey because thought requires language and animals cannot speak; Stuart Hampshire because in the absence of language, they cannot have concepts. Yet the simplest observations of how animals communicate with each other and even with humans would seem to suggest that thought, concepts and reasoning do not depend totally on human language. There is an excellent discussion of this issue in Mary Midgley's *Animals and Why They Matter* (University Press of Georgia, 1984)

the mind clearly does more than observe the pain: it actually experiences it. Descartes recognized that mind and body, though different, are closely "united and intermingled", and that appetites like hunger and thirst, passions like anger and love, sensations such as those communicated by the five senses, are neither purely mental nor purely physical phenomena. He also had to explain in what way the wish of the mind, say to greet a friend, is translated into the gesture of extending a hand; how the mind can make the body resist certain stimuli (like deciding not to have another alcoholic drink when the bodily stimuli are setting up a craving for more) or how it reinforces certain physical stimuli, like sexual urges, with mental reinforcements (like deciding that the person who triggers the sexual urges also has other admirable qualities).

Descartes conjectured that mind and body were linked through the pineal gland which is situated at the base of the brain. The nerves, he thought, transmit pain from (say) the foot to the pineal gland. The gland then transmits it to the mind, so that the mind *experiences* the pain, but not as a pain in the mind but as a pain in the foot.

In fact, we now know that the pineal gland has quite a different function. It responds to the light falling on the eye's retina. The light causes it to release melatonin into the bloodstream, which in turn controls our body clock, telling the body how to regulate its sleep patterns. If we suffer from jet lag, it is because the gland takes time to adjust its secretions if the normal rhythm of light and darkness is disrupted.

A later Cartesian, Arnold Geulinckx (1624 to 1559), rejected the idea of the pineal gland being responsible for the connection between mind and body, and instead invoked the activity of God. When a physical event happens, God puts into our mind the idea of the physical event. It is as if body and mind are two synchronized but separately working clocks. This theory is called Occasionalism.

This seems an even more desperate attempt to explain the interaction of mind and body. Some philosophers would therefore try to escape the problem by denying the need to establish a connection at all, and they do this in two opposite ways. Hobbes claimed that all "mental" processes are entirely physical, whereas Hume said that we can be certain *only* of mental events and can have no certainty that body or matter actually exist outside our minds.

The Importance of Descartes

The advances of Science make many of the ideas of Descartes appear quite ludicrous. Although he introduced the important Mind-Body problem (as distinct from the theological concern with body and soul) the distinction he made between mind and matter is particularly vulnerable. Although we still do not fully understand mental processes and have not reduced them entirely to physiological ones, we do now know that they are accompanied by electrical and chemical activity, and we find it increasingly difficult to define the difference between the mental and the physical. Likewise, most of us are no longer prepared to make Descartes' sharp distinction between humans and animals. Most people would also think that the Ontological Argument for the existence of God is logically flawed, and that its introduction by Descartes as a defence against solipsism was something of a sleight of hand. The Ontological Argument is a prime example of reliance on faulty deductions from possibly faulty premises, and we are suspicious of Descartes' excessive reliance on the deductive principle. Later philosophers, like Berkeley and Hume,[4] have demolished the distinction Descartes drew between primary and secondary qualities.

Yet Descartes is recognized as a seminal and immensely influential figure in the history of philosophy. Many people consider that modern philosophy began with him.

The first reason for this is that he made epistemology the prime concern of philosophy for generations, dominantly so until the time of Kant a century and a half later. Hitherto, the main question of philosophy had been: "What is the world like?" Now it was "What is the nature of our knowledge? How do we come by it? How sure can we be that the knowledge we think we have of the physical world corresponds accurately to what the physical world is like?"

Descartes believed that whatever knowledge we have must be acquired by reason and logic. He claimed that even his belief in God was rational and logical, though he proclaimed his faith in revelation also. As Richard Tarnas has strikingly put it:

> Human reason establishes first its own existence, out of experiential necessity; then God's existence, out of logical necessity; and thence the God-guaranteed reality of the objective world and its rational order. Descartes enthroned human reason as the supreme authority in matters of knowledge, capable of distinguishing certain metaphysical truth and of achieving certain scientific understanding of the material world. Infallibility, once ascribed only to Holy Scripture or the supreme pontiff, was now transferred to human reason itself. In effect, Descartes unintentionally began a theological Copernican revolution, for his mode of reasoning suggested that God's existence was established by human reason and not vice versa.[5]

So Descartes is considered to have been the originator of the Age of Reason, which came to its full flowering in the eighteenth-century. As far as the deity is concerned, Descartes' followers among eighteenth century Deists had less faith than he had, and dismissed revelation altogether. They would accept that reason tells us that there must be a God, however, they would base this conclusion not on the shaky Ontological Argument, but mainly on the fact that the universe seemed to follow a plan and that, if there is a plan, someone must have created the plan. They saw no rational evidence for believing that the creator of the plan still cared about his creation, was concerned about the behaviour of human beings, demanded to be worshipped, or distributed rewards and punishments. In fact, they would train their reason on debunking these so-called "revealed" aspects of the deity.

The Deists thought that philosophers can properly concern themselves with debates about God. Thomas Hobbes, however, thought not only that theology was separate from philosophy - a distinction that had been made before - but that philosophy must regard the vocabulary in which theological debate was carried on as absurd nonsense.

4 see Chapter 27 below.

5 Richard Tarnas - *The Passions of the Western Mind*, p. 279.

THOMAS HOBBES (Epistemology) 1588 to 1679

Hobbes was one of the people to whom Descartes had sent the original manuscript of his *Meditations* and whose comments, with Descartes' own replies, the latter had incorporated in the first printed edition of 1641.[6] Like Descartes, Hobbes had been fascinated by mathematics before he had turned to philosophy, though he turned to both subjects quite late in life: he was already forty-one when he "discovered" Euclid, and fifty-two when, in 1640, he wrote his first work on philosophy. By then he had met Galileo in Florence and, soon afterwards, he met Descartes and his circle in Paris.

It was probably after meeting Galileo that he came to the idea that not only the course of the stars, but everything else could be explained in terms of the movements of material things.

> The Universe, that is the whole mass of things there are, is corporeal, that is to say body.... Also every part of body is likewise body, and that which is not body is not part of the Universe. And because the Universe is all, that which is no part of it is nothing, and consequently nowhere.

Such a view made him reject Descartes' dualism between mind and matter. He explained mental processes entirely in mechanistic terms. Sensations enter the physical organism as motions, and they trigger other movements in the nervous system. Like any other movements, those in the nervous system persist unless something slows them down or stops them. This, in Hobbes' view, accounted for memories and dreams – they are, as it were, like ripples in water, set off by the impact of the sensations on the nervous system and becoming fainter as they spread. Accurate memories tend to be those which are reinforced by a repetition of the original stimulus. Ideas, too, arise from the original impact of the sensation, and each idea in its reverberations produces other ideas. The ideas might have an immediate connection with the original input or the connection may be remote. The more immediate the connection is, the closer the ideas are to reality; the more remote, the more they lose touch with the original material and become fantasy. "Imagination", Hobbes wrote, "is nothing but decaying sense".

> We describe a philosophy that aims to account for everything in terms of one basic concept (here that everything can ultimately be explained in terms of motion) as "reductionist". However much neurophysiology has seen mental processes accompanied by electrical or chemical manifestations, most scientists are reluctant to go quite as far as Hobbes, namely that mental processes are *nothing but* physiological ones.

As with reliable memories, Hobbes said that the most reliable ideas were those that are continually reinforced by a repetition of the sensations that produced them originally, in other words by experience. In this sense he agreed with Francis Bacon's emphasis that we must constantly test the validity of our ideas by making inductions from our experiences and by repeating experiments; but he had more respect than Bacon had for the value of the kind of deductive

6 See note 1 on p. 220 above.

thinking that finds its purest expression in mathematics.[7] Mathematics was at the heart of the laws of motion; the laws of motion were at the heart of physics; and physics, not metaphysics, was at the heart of what, for Hobbes, was philosophy. Philosophy had to concern itself entirely with those causal explanations that we can study scientifically. That is why it could not concern itself with God. The vocabulary in which theologians discussed religion was "absurd, insignificant,[8] nonsense". Describing God as an "incorporeal substance", for example, was a contradiction in terms. Although Hobbes could understand what "infinite" meant in mathematics, the application of that word to describe the nature of God made no kind of sense to him. The concept of transubstantiation, as it was used by religious people, ran absolutely counter to any experimental evidence. "Spirit" had to be for Hobbes, who saw everything in terms of material motion, a meaningless idea.

Not only were our ideas created by motion, but so was our behaviour. This was governed entirely by our appetites and aversions. The root of the word "appetite" comes from the Latin word *petere*, meaning to seek; "aversion" means "turning away from". So appetites or desires are motions towards something that gives us pleasure, aversion or fear is a motion away from what gives us pain or discomfort. Our will is merely the motion that results from the tension between pain and pleasure. If a course of action leads to more pleasure than pain, we will embark upon it; if it leads to more pain than pleasure, we will avoid it. Our reason merely has the function of working out, sometimes by the trial and error of experience, how to maximize our pleasure and minimize our pain. As we shall see in later chapters,[9] some analyse the foundations and institutions of our society as determined by reason working out how to minimize the pain caused by the fear of rampant lawlessness and to maximize the pleasures of security. All these elements - desires, aversions, and the use of reason to achieve the one and avoid the other - are in essence mechanical and are therefore also subject to the laws of motion.

It also means that the will is governed by this balance between pain and pleasure, and as it is governed it cannot be free. Ever since the Middle Ages the debate between free will and determinism had been a theological one (though Empedocles in the fifth century BC had already postulated that particles of the Four Elements came together by attraction, which he also called Love, or moved apart by repulsion, which he called Hate.) In Hobbes we have the first nontheological theory of determinism, and also the first statement that our individual and social behaviour is completely governed by the Pleasure-Pain Principle.

> The idea that all our conduct is aimed at maximizing our pleasure and minimizing our pain implies that we are all egoistic. If that is true, how do we explain altruism in which we sacrifice something of our own pleasure for the sake of others? Do not martyrs deliberately forego pleasure and accept pain?
>
> It can be argued that we never perform any actions purely for the sake of others and without any regard to our own pleasure. If we make sacrifices for

7 for Francis Bacon, see p. 212 above.

8 meaning that it was incapable of signifying anything

9 on Enlightenment thinkers (Chapter 28) and on Utilitarians (Chapter 36).

> the sake of others, we do so because we would feel uncomfortable within ourselves not to do so – it would be more painful to us avoid the sacrifice than it would be to make it. When we say, as we sometimes do, "I couldn't live with myself if I had acted other than the way I did", we express very clearly that we have acted ultimately to avoid the pain of guilt. All this suggests we are all selfish and that there is no such thing as genuine altruism.
>
> Yet the word expresses something real if properly understood. Perhaps altruism should be defined as a higher egoism, and selfishness as a lower egoism. When we say somebody is selfish, we ought to mean that he is a person whose conscience is so absent, weak or blunted that he *can* live with himself without discomfort when he betrays an ideal or does nothing to alleviate the pain of others. The fact that "altruism" is only another word for higher egoism is no reason not to admire it when we see it.

Hobbes thought that we define as "good" those things which give us pleasure and as "evil" those which give us pain. As what gives pleasure and pain is not the same for every individual and every society, good and evil must be relative notions. Again, Hobbes broke away from what theologians had been saying for centuries, though, here too, he was saying something that Protagoras had been saying in the fifth century BC – at the time when the Greeks had emancipated themselves from the idea that the gods had laid down what was right and wrong. Hobbes is the first thinker of modern times who constructed his philosophy without any recourse to theology at all. From that point of view he is perhaps the most revolutionary philosopher of the modern period. Others would follow him down that path in later generations, but in his own time he stood alone. Of his contemporaries, we have seen Descartes feeling the need to call theology in aid of his system, and for Pascal and Spinoza religious concerns were absolutely central.

CHAPTER 23

Blaise Pascal

1623 to 1662

Like Descartes, Pascal was a great mathematician and physicist. At the age of fifteen he produced a new theorem in geometry which still bears his name; at the request of a gambler he invented a calculus of probabilities which is still used by insurance companies today; he invented the use of mercury to measure barometric pressure; he devised a mechanical adding machine. He sent one of these to Christina, the scholarly Queen of Sweden, who promptly invited him to her court. Pascal suffered from poor health and declined (*c.* 1643), which was perhaps just as well; Descartes, who would some six years later accept an invitation from her to come to Stockholm and teach her philosophy, died there after three months because she insisted that the frail and habitual late riser should arrive for her lessons at five o'clock every morning in the midst of the Swedish winter (February 1650).

When Pascal's father died in 1651 leaving him a sizeable inheritance, his health suddenly improved for a while. For the next three years he lived a life of pleasure and some extravagance. Many of his friends during this period were *libertins*, the disparaging name given at that time to freethinkers and men of unconventional customs and morals. This phase of his life came to a sudden end when, in 1654, his coach crashed into the parapet of a bridge and nearly plunged into the river below. The closeness of death shook Pascal to his core and brought him a vision of God. Henceforth, he abjured the pursuit of pleasure and devoted himself to the religious life. His sister Jacqueline had already become a nun at Port-Royal-des-Champs. Blaise joined this community, and it was there that he began the philosophical work for which he became famous.

Port-Royal was then the centre of a form of Roman Catholicism called Jansenism, after the name of a Dutch theologian Cornelius Jansen (1585 to 1638). Jansenism could be described as Catholic Puritanism. Jansenist churches were plain and austere, in contrast to the theatrical paintings and sculptures favoured by the Counter-Reformation in general and the Jesuit churches in particular. More important was its theological stance. Like Luther and Calvin before him, Jansen had espoused the most rigorous doctrine of Predestination, claiming in his work, the *Augustinus*, that this derived from St Augustine.

We have seen in the previous volume that originally St Augustine had struck a delicate balance between free will and Predestination. He had taught that

Divine Grace is essential for salvation. Man has free will to accept or reject the unmerited Grace offered by God, but God, in His omniscience, knows the extent to which each person will exercise that free will and therefore whether that person is destined to salvation or to damnation. This view had been challenged by Pelagius, who thought that, while the Grace offered by God was indeed a help, salvation was essentially the reward for our own efforts. In the course of his bitter struggle with Pelagius, St Augustine had come to lay ever more stress on Predestination and less and less on the free will aspect of his earlier teaching. It was these later writings which had inspired Luther and Calvin, and which subsequently inspired Jansen also.[1]

The official teaching of the Catholic Church was that of the earlier Augustine: that there is a balance between free will and Predestination. But whereas Augustine had come to lay the emphasis on Predestination, the Church tended to stress that whether we were saved or not depended to a large extent upon our own efforts, by way of good works, upon confessing when we fell short and atoning for our failings by penance. The priest can then lift the burden of the sin committed by granting absolution.

The Jesuits were particularly notable in tipping the balance away from Predestination. Indeed, some of them seem to have gone as far as to maintain that "no action can be imputed as a sin if God does not give us, before we commit it, the knowledge that it is sinful and an inspiration from Himself which strengthens our will to avoid it".[2] If that were so, it would indeed make absolution rather easy.

The Jesuits were founded by St Ignatius Loyola in 1534. Within a century they had become the elite of the Catholic Church. Highly educated and sophisticated, their contact was more with the educated ruling classes than with the general public. They tended to be employed by kings and aristocrats as tutors for their children and also as their own father confessors. If one were a cynical historian, one might say that the reason they played down Predestination was because the kings and aristocrats of Catholic Europe expected easy absolution from their confessors in return for confessing the many sinful deeds that Machiavellian politics involved, not to mention all the sins of the flesh which they had committed. France was then engaged in a lengthy struggle with the Habsburgs. Although French kings carried the title of "the Most Catholic King", Machiavellian politics required that they ally with German Protestants and Muslim Turks against the Catholic Habsburgs. For this they needed absolution from the Catholic Church. In such a case the Jesuits were willing to grant absolution for attrition, without insisting on contrition. Attrition in practice meant sorrow for an offence without a promise not to commit the offence again: contrition implied a serious effort not to re-offend.[3] It is not perhaps unduly cynical to suppose that in the matter of the kings' amatory affairs also, their

1 see p. 189 above for Luther; p. 193 above for Calvin; and Chapter 13 above for St Augustine.

2 This, at any rate, is the proposition which Pascal, in Provincial Letter No. 4, had a Jesuit defend in a debate with Jansenism.

3 That was the difference in practice. In theory, attrition expresses sorrow for fear of damnation, whilst contrition arises purely from the love of God.

Jesuit confessors might not insist on contrition before they granted absolution, and that here, too, the penances they imposed were not too arduous.

The Jansenists were good Catholics who believed in confession and absolution, but they accused the Jesuits of laxity in granting absolution. The Jesuits retaliated by securing papal condemnations of the *Augustinus* in 1653,[4] the year before Pascal joined the community at Port Royal.

At that time the head of Port Royal was Antoine Arnauld II, who was also a member of the Sorbonne. Under the joint pressure from Louis XIV, the Jesuits and the Papacy, the Sorbonne was about to expel Arnauld just at the time when Pascal came to Port Royal, and Pascal's first philosophical work, the *Lettres Provinciales*, was written in defence of Arnauld. It was published anonymously in 1656. In it he attacked easy absolution as harmful to piety and the spiritual life, and he chastised the Jesuits for what he thought were the over subtle arguments and fine distinctions for which they were famous. It is Pascal who coined the word "casuistry" (*casuistique*) to describe the use of such techniques.

The book was very popular, both because it was brilliantly written and also because the Jesuits had many enemies. However, it was condemned by the Congregation of the Index in 1657, and Pascal did not publish his next and most important work, the *Pensées* in his lifetime. Indeed, it was not finished at the time of his death. It is not a systematic work of theology or of philosophy. The thoughts range from aphorisms of a line or two to more extended passages, some jotted down in haste, others already carefully worked up. They were written down on loose sheets that he had only begun to arrange in bundles by the time he died. In 1670 they were printed for the first time, and there have been many different arrangements of the material since then.

The most interesting of his thoughts examine the proper relationship between reason and faith. This is an old question, as we have seen: Natural Theology gives reason an important, though of course not an exclusive, role in religious understanding, while its opponents assert that religious truths are of a radically different order from any that are within the grasp of mere human reason.[5] Pascal placed himself with this latter group. We have seen that Descartes had used the Ontological Argument from Natural Theology as the keystone of

4 This put the Jansenists into a dilemma, because, unlike the Protestants, they regarded themselves as faithful sons of the Catholic Church and had no wish to break with it. When, in 1653, Pope Innocent X declared that five propositions in the *Augustinus* were heretical, they maintained that those propositions could not be found in the book. The following year the Pope declared that they *were* in the book, whereupon the Jansenists said that, if they were, they did not bear the meaning that the Pope read into them. In 1656 Pope Alexander VI declared that he did not accept that defence, and the Jansenists said that, whereas the Pope was infallible when he pronounced on doctrine, he could be mistaken when he pronounced on matters of fact. Louis XIV would have some secular and organizational disputes with the Papacy himself, but he was unwavering in his support for any papal pronouncements on doctrine: he was consistently hostile to the Jansenists. Although he closed down Port Royal in 1709 and had the buildings razed to the ground in 1711, neither the Crown nor the Papacy were ever able either to crush the Jansenists or to drive them out of the Church. This was partly because, for prudential reasons, the Papacy's continual and severe harassment stopped short of actual excommunication. The excommunication of Luther had lost half of Europe to Catholicism, and the Papacy perhaps feared that excommunication of the Jansenists would merely swell the ranks of the Huguenots. So the Jansenist would trouble both Pope and King until the French Revolution.

5 For the difference between Natural Theology and Dogmatic Theology see p. 78 above. See also pp. 145 and 154 above for the differences between Aquinas as an important exponent of Natural Theology, and St John of Bonaventura, Duns Scotus and William of Ockham as critics of it.

his whole intellectual structure,[6] though one has the feeling that he was not of a particularly religious temper. Pascal wrote, "I cannot forgive Descartes. He would have liked to be able to bypass God in the whole of his philosophy. But he could not help making God give a shove to set the world in motion; and after that he had no more to do with God."

> Medieval critics of Natural Theology, like St John of Bonaventura, were not exactly *afraid* of reason: they had thought it merely presumptuous to think that reason might fathom anything about God. By Pascal's time, however, it was beginning to look as if reason might actually *undermine* religion – it was already doing so in the hands of Hobbes. Was that perhaps why Pascal found it impossible to forgive Descartes?

Pascal agreed with Descartes that there are some things we can reason about and that deductive mathematical reasoning is the most reliable form of reasoning there is. He recognized the value of the inductive and experimental methods in the physical sciences, provided we remember that in this field our conclusions must be merely provisional.

In religion, as we shall see, Pascal believed that the most precious and certain truths were understood by our intuition, and he regretted that it was not given to us to understand all the aspects of this world by intuition alone, "Would to God ... that we never needed Reason and that we knew everything by instinct and feeling! But Nature has denied us this advantage, and has on the contrary given us but little knowledge of this [intuitive] kind; all the rest can be acquired by Reason only."

The kind of conclusions we can reach in mathematics and the physical sciences, and the reasoning we employ in them, leave us ignorant about everything that really matters: the mysteries and significance of life, morality, and the Christian Revelation. Disowning the value of the brilliant work he had himself done as a mathematician and scientist, he now wrote that, in comparison with the things that really matter, "we do not think that the whole of philosophy is worth an hour's labour... To mock at philosophy is to philosophize truly."

Unlike philosophers like Socrates, Plato, or Descartes, Pascal did not believe that reason properly pursued must lead to undisputed truth. He agreed with what Hume would say in the next century, that as often as not "Reason is ... the Slave of the Passions". In the matter of morals it so easily turns into mere rationalization of what suits us. It produces not absolute verities but merely relative criteria which suit particular communities, so that the most atrocious acts have been justified as dictated by reason in various societies: "Theft, incest, infanticide, parricide have all in their time been regarded as virtuous acts ... Three degrees of latitude reverse the whole of jurisprudence; a meridian decides about truth... A pleasing justice which is bounded by a river! Truth this side of the Pyrenees, error beyond."

> That is true enough, but unfortunately the same can be said when we take faith rather than reason as our guide to morals. "Truth in Teheran, error in New York" (or vice versa.) Pascal believed that there was only one true faith to

6 p. 221 above.

guide us – yet even then he might have realized that what was truth in Port-Royal was error at the Sorbonne.

Pascal was filled with what, in the twentieth century, would be called existential *angst*, which reason cannot allay. Science had demonstrated the terrifying immensity of the universe. *"Le silence éternel de ces spaces infinis m'effraie."*[7] What rational meaning could the life of man have within that context?

Why does man, that most feeble of reeds, have the capacity to think, to feel, and to agonize? What rational meaning could explain the apparent senselessness of human suffering? "Picture a number of men in chains, all condemned to death. Each day some are strangled in the sight of the rest. Those who remain see their own condition in that of these their fellows, looking at one another with sorrow and without hope, each awaiting his turn. This is the picture of the condition of man." What is the point of it all; the meaning of life? As Durant puts it, "How shall we redeem this obscene slaughter called history, except by believing, *with or against the evidence,* that God will right all wrongs in the end?"[8]

Only faith, therefore, can give us that relief. Our reason may question that faith; but the heart believes it, and we should listen to it. It is in this context that Pascal wrote the most famous of his poetic sentences: "The heart hath its reasons which reason doth not know."

That sentence is often quoted out of the religious context in which it appeared, and with good reason. We have had so much experience of things we know intuitively but which cannot be proved. It also describes the many occasions when, rightly or wrongly, we follow the dictates of our emotions and intuitions while the intellect would prompt us to take a different course.

Pascal did not reject the proofs of Natural Theology, but that was because he already believed. "It is upon the knowledge gained by the heart and the instinct that reason relies." He had come across atheists who, because they did not believe to begin with, found the arguments of Natural Theology unconvincing. In any case, Natural Theology can lead only to Deism. Deism argues that, as the world follows a plan, it is reasonable that there must be a planner, but that we have no reason to think that the planner is still interested in what He had created. Natural Theology had never been used, and indeed *could* never be used, to support the most important tenet of Christianity, that Christ fulfilled the prophecies of the Old Testament and that only through him could mankind be redeemed.

Many people would think that Pascal was right here. The belief in the divinity and role of Christ, the willingness to accept that what the Gospels and the Epistles say about him is true, must surely be based on the emotional and nonrational side of the believers.

Pascal produced a famous argument to persuade sceptics to have faith in the existence of God. He had once, at the request of a gambler, developed a calculus of probabilities and now he told the doubter that a belief in God was a good bet. If He existed, the chance was that His grace would be granted to the believer

7 The eternal silence of these infinite spaces [*sic*] terrifies me.

8 Durant – *The Story of Civilization – The Age of Louis XIV*, p.65. My italics.

who tried as a result to lead a godly life and might thereby be saved. Indeed, Pascal believed that the doubter who managed to give up worldly pleasures would soon acquire real faith.

> Really? What evidence is there that people who develop and practise an autonomous value system that thinks little of worldly pleasures must necessarily end up by having faith in God, let alone in Christ? Does that assumption not ignore sober members of other religions or indeed of none?

If God did not exist, Pascal continues, at least the belief that He did would have done no harm and might actually have led the believer to behave better than he would otherwise have done.

> The argument has itself amused the sceptics. Can one will oneself into true faith in this nonspiritual and carefully prudential way? Faith surely has to be based on a conviction, not on a hedging calculation. Besides, given that Pascal was committed to the more extreme form of Predestination, he could not assure the doubter that Grace was given as a reward to all who believed and acted accordingly. Like Calvin, Pascal thought that it was foreordained that only a small minority of people would be saved; the odds must therefore be strongly against any one individual, let alone any one hedging believer, achieving salvation.

Was Pascal addressing the wager argument to himself? During his pleasure-loving years he had been much influenced by the scepticism of Montaigne, which he cannot have discarded without a struggle. Certainly after he had entered the community of Port Royal, there was nothing tepid or half-hearted about his faith. Yet when we see how troubled he was about the apparently arbitrary cruelty and suffering in the world, one feels he could hardly have borne it without his faith in God and in Christ. He said so himself:

> I look on all sides, and everywhere I see nothing but obscurity. Nature offers me nothing that is not a matter of doubt and disquiet. If I saw no signs of divinity, I would fix myself in denial. If I saw everywhere the marks of a Creator, I would repose *peacefully* in faith. But seeing too much to deny [Him] and too little to assure me, I am in a pitiful state, and I would wish a hundred times that *if a God sustains nature*, it would reveal Him without ambiguity.[9]

Pascal, then, saw a torturing dichotomy between Nature and God, and even his faith in God seems to have something desperate about it. Not for him, then, the serenity of Spinoza, for whom no such dichotomy existed.

9 My italics.

CHAPTER 24

Baruch (Benedict) Spinoza

1632 to 1677

The philosophy of Spinoza is a good example of Hegelian synthesis.[1] Hegel believed that every idea (or thesis) eventually produces it opposite (or antithesis), and that out of the clash between the two arises a synthesis which embraces the best of the thesis together with the best of the antithesis. So Descartes' thesis that the truth is to be found by relying entirely on reason produced Pascal's antithesis which exalts faith and intuition over reason. The philosophy of Spinoza, a contemporary of both Descartes and Pascal, is the synthesis: it provided a tightly structured rational argument which resulted in a mystical acceptance of God and Nature.

Baruch Spinoza was born in Amsterdam into a family of Jewish Portuguese/ Spanish ancestry. He was fortunate that he lived in seventeenth-century Holland, which was then the most liberal country in Europe. It was also the only one in which the Jews enjoyed full religious toleration and more civic rights than they enjoyed anywhere else. True, there were limits even to Dutch toleration, and Spinoza did not dare to publish all his views in his lifetime, but what he did publish, and the opinions for which he was known, would have landed him in severe trouble in any other country in Europe.

His education had been in synagogue schools, but quite early on he was influenced by the rationalist doubts that some Jewish scholars had about the literal truth of the Old Testament and about the Talmud. The great Jewish philosopher Maimonides (1134 to 1204) had accepted that some statements in the Bible must be interpreted allegorically rather that literally; his teaching had been banned by orthodox rabbis in the fourteenth century. Now, in the seventeenth century, the dawn of what we call the Age of Reason, the fundamentalist teaching in all religions was, again, called into question by some daring spirits; Spinoza was one of these. It became known that he had lost his faith in the dogma of the Jewish religion (although he remained of a deeply religious temperament and had, as we shall see, his own understanding of God.) The Jewish

1 Georg Wilhelm Friederich Hegel, German philosopher, 1770 to 1831. For a full treatment of the idea of Hegelian synthesis see Chapter 33.

authorities were alarmed. This was partly because he questioned what they taught, but they were also nervous about harbouring in their midst someone whom Christians might also consider to be undermining the literal truth of the Old Testament, to which orthodox Christians were as committed as were the Jews. In 1656 the Jewish authorities excommunicated Spinoza.

In 1670 he published, anonymously, the *Tractatus Theologico-Politicus*. This is an important early work of Higher Criticism. This is the name given to the study of the Bible not as revealed truth, but as a series of texts produced by human beings at various times. It may lay bare the agenda of its different authors, will try to establish dates, will examine contradictions and apparent impossibilities, etc. Fundamentalists regard this as a profoundly subversive activity, and Spinoza's book created such a storm among orthodox Jews and Christians alike that he left instructions that his remaining works were to be published only after his death. He died in February 1677, and by the end of that year they appeared under the title *Opera posthuma*. These included his two most important works, the *Tractatus Politicus*[2] and the work best known by its short tile, the *Ethics*.

In the *Ethics*, Spinoza writes that his aim was to search for "anything that might be truly good and able to communicate its goodness, and by which the mind might be affected to the exclusion of all other things". Wealth, fame and the pleasures of sex cannot do any of this, as they are too often accompanied by turmoil and grief.

> Only love towards a thing eternal and infinite feeds the mind with pleasure ... free from all pain... The greatest good is the knowledge of the union which the mind has with the whole of nature ... The more the mind knows, the better it understands its forces and the order of nature; the more it understands its forces or strength, the better it will be able to direct itself and lay down the rules for itself; and the more it understands the order of nature, the more easily it will be able to liberate itself from useless things. This is the whole method.

We can see from this that Spinoza was aiming for something spiritual, just as Pascal was. But he prided himself so much on having reached his spiritual conclusions by rational methods that he set out the whole book in the form of geometrical proofs, beginning with definitions and ending with "Q.E.D." (with interspersed *scholia* or explanations). The full title of the book was actually *Ethica Ordine Geometrica Demonstrata* (Ethics demonstrated by the rules of Geometry). All this makes the book very difficult to read. The method, like that of Descartes, is purely deductive. Induction plays next to no part in it.

The *Ethics* consists of five parts. In the first four parts Spinoza builds up a picture of the world which, as we shall see, is largely deterministic. By using our reason we understand that things are the way they are because that is the way they have to be, and that includes our own nature over which we have very little control. The fifth part of the book aims to show how humans can achieve a degree of ethical freedom in a deterministic world by using their reason. Reason, which has given us a full understanding of how little freedom we have, enables us at the same time to become better people. It gives us a better understanding of how we relate to other people and to the world at large, and thereby it enables us to enter into the mystical joy of accepting the world as it is. This

2 This work will be discussed in Chapter 26, pp. 261ff.

area of understanding is what Spinoza calls "Ethics", though it seems to me that the mystical and spiritual quality which was its essence gave to his use of the word a much wider meaning than we normally ascribe to the word "ethics". It was because he believed that the proper understanding of the world will lead up to what he considered the most important aim in life – namely the understanding of this "ethical" dimension – that he gave the name of *Ethics* to the entire work.

God or Nature

Spinoza began with the concept of "substance". Today we generally use that word to mean something material, but that was not its original meaning. The word comes from the Latin *substare*, meaning "to stand underneath" or "to support". For Spinoza, in the last resort, God and the laws which governed the whole universe underlay everything.[3]

He took the same line that Giordano Bruno had taken: God is infinite, so is the universe. There cannot be two infinites and therefore God and the universe (Spinoza called it Nature) must be one. Whenever we speak of God, we speak of Nature, and whenever we speak of Nature, we speak of God. Like Bruno, Spinoza believed God to be wholly immanent, and the phrase he uses – *Deus sive Natura* (God or Nature) was profoundly shocking to all those who believed that God was wholly or at least predominantly transcendent.[4] Indeed, many of his critics thought it was tantamount to atheism, and that view was so prevalent that right into the early eighteenth century a philosopher like Leibniz thought it prudent to disavow his considerable indebtedness to Spinoza's thought.[5]

In fact, it would be truer to describe Spinoza as a pantheist. He spoke of "God or Nature" with religious reverence, and although he did not think that God loved us, there was every reason for us to love Him. Loving is an action. God could not love us (or, for that matter, be angry with us) because He does not act; He simply is. He does not design the universe; He simply *is* Design. Being immanent in everything, He is not the external cause of anything. He is a Principle, not a Person.

He is not Goodness as opposed to Evil, because everything that we *call* evil (suffering, violent death etc.) is also part of Nature. Sometimes we understand the place of suffering and violent death in the grand design, but very often we do not understand it. We simply cannot get our minds around how certain things we call evil *can* be part of the design. Even in such cases, Spinoza thinks, we would be wise to accept it as such. For him, "good" and "evil" are the words with which we describe our reaction to certain things. It is absolutely natural for us to abhor certain things and to value others and it is legitimate for us to

3 For Spinoza, the concept of substance is the starting point of his structure in the same way in which Descartes' *cogito* was the foundation upon which he built his entire edifice. Spinoza's definition of substance is highly technical. So is the way in which he argues from that definition to the conclusion that only one substance can exist and that this substance must be infinite. I am asking the reader to accept these conclusions of Spinoza's as the basis of the rest of his philosophy.

4 For a discussion of transcendence and immanence, refer back to pp. 85f. above and to note 12 on p. 210 above.

5 On Leibniz see p. 247 below.

describe such things as evil or good – but the words describe *our reaction* to these things; they cannot rightly be applied to describe a quality of the world, of Nature, or of God.

> For example, we can understand that there is an aspect of Nature which is "red in tooth and claw", which involves animals preying on each other, and involves suffering by the victims. That is obviously part of the scheme of things – some animals have to kill other animals if they are themselves to live. Few of us would think of this aspect of nature (and remember that Spinoza equates Nature with God) as "evil". Unless we are vegetarians, we don't usually think that it is evil for us to kill animals for our food: it is what Nature/God seems to have ordained for us, and that is all there is to it.
>
> It is much harder for us to see how we can avoid describing the Nazi extermination camps as evil. Spinoza would say that we quite legitimately express *our abhorrence* of the camps by using the word "evil"; he also believes that it is natural to feel abhorrence (and this will be explained in a little more detail later in the chapter). In the last resort "good" and "evil" are, for him, the words with which we describe *our reaction* to certain things, not the things themselves. They cannot rightly be applied to describe a quality of the world, of Nature, or of God. Extermination camps happen in Nature; and therefore, in a way that is totally beyond our capacity to understand, they must therefore be part of the Design that is God or Nature.
>
> Again the acceptance that cruelty and violence are part of God or Nature does not mean that the philosopher should make no effort to combat them. It is as natural for some men to be cruel as it is natural for others to combat cruelty. What, according to Spinoza, makes some men cruel and others crusaders against cruelty will be discussed a little later in this chapter. Fighting against certain aspects of Nature is itself part of Nature, will itself have an effect on Nature, and may possibly succeed. However, where it does not succeed – and certainly where it *cannot* succeed – the philosopher will accept that stoically: "what can't be cured must be endured".

We have seen that for Spinoza there was ultimately only one infinite substance which underlies everything that there is, and that this was Nature (or God). Therefore, Nature must be all of a piece. All mind is part of Nature, as is all matter. Moreover, as everything is part of Nature, everything is also part of everything else. Nothing exists in isolation; everything is affected by the environment and has its own effect upon it, however minute or apparently imperceptible.

> The twentieth-century Chaos Theory gives some scientific support to this. World systems, according to this theory, can be affected by events whose repercussions, though they are part of a chain of cause and effect, are so complex as to be unpredictable. An often quoted example is the so-called Butterfly Effect, according to which the beating of a butterfly's wings in China may ultimately have an effect on the weather in Argentina. One can go on to say that the butterfly effect does not stop there: the climate of Argentina influences everything that grows or is produced there. This in turn affects Argentina's economic activities, which in turn have a relationship with the economy of the rest of the world. Butterfly wings, climate, production are all matter, but they also interact with mind – they cause or are the result of thought processes. Mind and matter, part of Nature, are, therefore, also part of one another.

Mind and Matter

Mind and matter are two modes or aspects of "God or Nature". The totality of all the mental aspects in Nature make up the mind of "God or Nature" - and every individual mental phenomenon is therefore a part of God's mind. In the mental mode, Nature shows its creat*ive* aspect (*Natura naturans*). The totality of all matter makes up the body of "God or Nature", and this mode is the creat*ed* aspect of Nature (*Natura naturata*).

To most transcendentalists, who believed that God was wholly spirit, the idea that God might have a body was totally repugnant. But there is a totality of matter in Nature, and if Nature and God are the same, then it is logical that every part of material nature must be a part of the body of God.

Descartes had believed that mind and matter were totally different. He had had quite a struggle to explain how, if that were so, the one could influence the other. It will be remembered that he had to have recourse to the idea that they act on each other through the pineal gland.[6] There had also been the even more extraordinary idea of Geulinckx, known as *Occasionalism*, that God had created mind and body like two synchronized but separately working clocks.[7]

Spinoza rejected this Cartesian Dualism. For him, mind and matter are simply different modes of experiencing the same thing, or in which the same thing appears; there is no need to find as problematic a link as the pineal gland between them. Descartes had seen the pain I feel when I cut my finger as two events: a physical event in the nervous system which is transmitted through the pineal gland to create a mental consciousness of pain. For Spinoza it was a single event, of which the damaged finger was the material aspect and the consciousness of pain the mental one. He writes that "the mind is the body felt from within; the body is the mind seen from without".

When you see me crossing a room to pick up a book, you see a physical action, but you quite rightly deduce that this is the physical mode in which a mental event – my willing to move across to pick up the book – manifests itself. My own awareness of crossing the room is the mental mode that is an integral part of my physical movement.

Another way of putting it is that we can observe any phenomenon in the world from two different perspectives – it is the same phenomenon, but we can see it from either the mental or the physical perspective, rather as a mountain is the same mountain whether we look at it from the north side or the south side. (Strictly speaking, that analogy may be questioned on the grounds that, in this case, both perspectives are actually physical. Perhaps a better analogy might be a piece of music, which we can consider either from the perspective of seeing the arrangement of notes on a piece of paper or from that of the feelings that the harmonies set up in our minds.)

There seems to be some support for Spinoza's refusal to make a distinction between mental and physical events in the findings by neurologists that mental events are directly physical. Every thought process is an electrical discharge from the brain. Even if I appear to make no physical movement at all, the mere act of thinking *involves* (N.B. "involves" rather than "causes") such a

6 see p. 224 above.

7 see p. 224 above.

physical event. Sometimes we actually experience thought processes in a physical way, such as when our stomach churns with apprehension or when certain thoughts lead to physical sexual arousal, but when our emotions are not involved, for example in mentally adding up a row of figures, we usually do not experience thought processes as something physical.

Even so, although thoughts involve electrical impulses, we cannot be sure that they are *nothing but* electrical impulses. For example, if I add up two rows of figures of similar length and complexity, one accurately and the other inaccurately, the electrical discharges would be different if I realized while doing it that I had made a mistake in the second row and experienced annoyance as a result. But if I was not aware of the mistake in the second row, then the measurable electrical impulses are presumably much the same; and yet the one thought has a quality which the other one does not, and that difference cannot be expressed in physical terms.

So while Spinoza's refusal to make a separation between mental and physical events receives much support from neurology, we ought not to give this a totally reductionist interpretation. There is still a mystery there.

It might be thought to follow from Spinoza's theory that when the body perishes, the mind must perish with it. In one sense, of course, the body does not perish – its matter breaks up and is absorbed into other matter. It therefore remains part of the body of Nature or body of God. Spinoza believed that, in so far as the mind trained in philosophy can understand the relationship of things, it becomes, as it were, an integral part of the mind of God or Nature; as the Mind of God or Nature is eternal, the philosophic mind has a share of this eternity.

Spinoza here shares with Plato the idea that the philosophical mind has a better chance of being reunited with the Divine than the unphilosophical mind. But is there not some sleight of hand here? When the body crumbles and is absorbed back into the body of Nature, there is no distinction in this respect between the trained body of the athlete and the crippled or exhausted body of the sick or aged. Why then should the unphilosophical mind be less capable of being absorbed into the mind of God-or-Nature than the philosophical mind? It seems to me that we have here an arrogant élitism which we tend to find in many intellectuals. They like to believe that people like them are not only blessed in this life by their innate intellectual gifts supplemented by their efforts, but are in addition entitled to further rewards in the next life which are denied to those who are not so clever nor as wise!

The training of the mind in philosophical understanding. was for Spinoza, (as it had been for Plato)[8] of the greatest importance – not only for some kind of survival after death, but also in this life, so that we can understand, and to that extent serenely accept, the workings of "God or Nature".

A trained mind will also help us to understand the springs of human action – to know where we have choice about what we do and where we do not, and, in general terms, to know ourselves better, and to that extent to have a little more control over our actions than we would otherwise have.

8 See Chapter 5 above.

The Springs of Human Action

We have seen above that Spinoza did not identify "God or Nature" with Goodness as opposed to Evil, because everything that we call evil is also part of Nature. As human beings are a part of that nature, their actions, too, cannot properly be praised for being good or condemned for being evil, any more than we can condemn a spider's actions as evil because of the way it traps, poisons and eats flies. When humans trap and kill their victims (whether of other species or even of their own) that is as much a part of their nature as it is part of the spider's nature to behave as it does.

We might argue that humans are different from spiders because they have a moral sense which enables them to distinguish between good and evil. Spinoza thought, as Hobbes had done, that we merely define as good those things which correspond to our desires, and as evil those for which we have an aversion. We do not desire something because it is good; we call it good because we desire it. Very often our definition of good and evil is not even a personal definition, but is taken over from what *society* calls good and evil. Society, for its part, will describe as good those things which it considers as desirable and as evil those parts which it considers undesirable (more on this below). As not every person or every society desires the same things, the meaning carried by "good" or "evil" will be subjective and relativistic.

Spinoza thought that desire and aversion arise from the fact that it is of the nature of mind and matter to strive to preserve themselves (*conatus sese preservandi*). In what we call animate beings this striving is closely linked to the desire to achieve pleasure and to avoid pain. Again, like Hobbes, Spinoza believed that our actions result from one desire being stronger than another. This view sees our decision making as determined by the relative strengths of our desires, and from that it followed that any free will we have is extremely limited. Spinoza wrote, "Men think themselves free because they are conscious of their volitions and desires; but they are ignorant of the causes by which they are led to wish or to desire."

> I may feel, "I had to choose between being a doctor or a lawyer. Both careers had their attraction for me. I thought the matter over carefully, and freely chose to study medicine rather than law." But in fact this was not a free choice: my nature (temperament, talent or upbringing) is such that the balance between the pleasures and difficulties of medicine was more attractive to me than that between the pleasures and difficulties of law. The career of being an actor seemed to me very desirable, but this desire was counteracted by my knowledge that I lacked the necessary talent. Of course, there are many careers that I did not consider at all: my nature is such that, for instance, I would derive no pleasure from training to be a bricklayer, so if anyone had suggested that career to me, my nature would have rejected that out of hand.
>
> Fortunately, the money was there to enable me to study medicine, so I was free to follow my nature. The only freedom there is, is freedom from external hindrances (like poverty in this instance), but that is not the same as freedom of the will.
>
> In this example, I have been kept away from a career as an actor because I was aware of my lack of talent in this direction. Had I known, before I

embarked on it, that I lacked the stamina to pursue a medical career, that awareness would have counteracted my desire to become a doctor and would have prevented my starting a course which I had to abandon half-way through. Perhaps I even had an unconscious knowledge of this weakness, but I now know that that was more than counteracted by the desire to please my ambitious parents."

All these considerations apply of course over a much wider area than our "choice" of a career. It applies, for example, to what we call moral choices. In someone who runs away from a conflict, for instance, the aversion from danger is stronger than the desire to stand up for a cause. In a "brave" person the opposite is the case. In someone who loses his temper, the desire to lash out is stronger than the desire to act reasonably; of someone who can curb his temper the opposite is true. Whether we are "brave" or "reasonable" is not a matter of our choice, although we may think it is. Martin Luther was literally right when, risking martyrdom at the Diet of Worms for maintaining his ideas, he said, "Here I stand; *I can do no other.*" He was undoubtedly afraid of what might happen to him, but a combination of his nature and his nurture, of his possibly genetic drives and of the way society had shaped him, had made the "coward's" way out literally impossible for him.

(Is there a philosophical problem here? Spinoza had postulated that the most powerful drive in every living thing is the *conatus sese preservandi* – and clearly for anyone who espouses the possibility of death for a higher cause, the urge of self-preservation cann*ot* be the universally dominant drive.)

The same goes for people we call "altruistic". Such a person "can – in the end – do no other" than do what he considers to be his moral duty. In a selfish person, the pull of idealism is, by definition, weaker than the pull of his egoism. One might therefore describe altruism as itself being a kind of selfishness, but we give it a different name because we recognize it to be a "higher" kind of selfishness than the baser kind in which idealism plays no part.

There are, of course, more than just two drives to consider in many situations. If we are tempted to tell a lie, there is not only the conflict between avoiding a painful situation or telling the truth because "we can do no other": there may also be the fear of what happens if we are found to have been lying. In such a case our course of action will be the result of the relative strengths of three or four "pulls": the pull to avoid the unpleasant consequence of telling the truth; the pull of our "moral" conditioning (by upbringing, the pressures of society etc.) to tell the truth; the pull of the unpleasant consequence of possibly being found out; and the pull of the possibility of getting away with it through our skill or cleverness.

To the extent that the ultimate outcome of these rival pulls are part of a person's *nature*, he obviously cannot escape it; to the extent that *nurture* has shaped the outcome, Spinoza believed that nurture is *almost* as inescapable as nature. We accept as a general rule that children who have been nurtured by parents who have a strong moral sense have their own moral impulses strengthened thereby, whereas the children of feckless parents find fewer forces within themselves to check their own feckless impulses. But parents are only one aspect of nurture.

Society as a whole plays a big part in moulding us into the sort of people we become. It does that because society, like everything else in Nature, strives to preserve itself, and in its efforts to do so it creates a number of counterweights to impulses which its members think is necessary to control. These include such things as "the exhortations of the moralist, the ideals of the philosophers, the stigma of public condemnation, and the penalties of the courts." [9] The purpose of punishment, Spinoza urged, is purely to control behaviour that would damage the society's aim to preserve itself. It should not have the character of retribution, nor should it be seen as something that is merited by guilt. In the absence of free will, there can be no such thing as *real* guilt (though, paradoxically, guilt *feeling* is what the above counterweights to anti-social impulses are intended to create.) The fear of retribution in the afterlife, in the form of Hell or Eternal Damnation, is for many people also a counterweight, but Spinoza believed that this is based on mere superstition which no *rational* person of knowledge and understanding ought to entertain.

The proper use of knowledge, reason and understanding, can free our actions to a certain, though limited, extent from being *entirely* the outcome of the battle between our desires and our aversions. It enables us to have some *control* over what we do and therefore to have *some* freedom.

There are three grades of knowledge, according to Spinoza. The lowest is the knowledge that we derive from our senses or experiences. The next is our knowledge of the causes of things. The highest is intuitive: it gives us the understanding that God and Nature are one, that Nature is all of a piece, and that, therefore, everything in Nature is part of everything else.

The first kind of knowledge - derived from our experience - tells us that the immediate pleasures which we naturally desire sometimes hinder a greater or longer-lasting pleasure. We may have to accept pain to give ourselves a better chance of pleasure at a later stage.

> For example, most of us are willing to undergo painful operations if that will make us better and enable us to live a more pleasurable life in the long run. Those who will not make that "choice" are mostly those who do not expect to have a more pleasurable life after the operation.

Like Epicurus,[10] Spinoza stressed that we need a rational understanding not only of the nature of our desires, but also of the consequences of indulging them.

The second kind - which tells us of the causes of things - includes the understanding of why we act as we do. If we are aware that our temperament is irascible - even better, *why* our temperament is irascible - then that insight can act as a counterweight to the desire to lash out. "Know thyself" was the prescription of Socrates that Plato has presented to us[11] - it was Spinoza's also.

> It is also the fundamental principle of the psychotherapy of Freud and others. A person may constantly find himself in trouble because he is always rebelling against the authority of his employers or other superiors. There may, of course, be objective reasons for being at odds with his superiors, but the reason may also lie, say, in a childhood in which he resented his father, and he is now transferring the rebellious feelings he had about his father to whatever person is currently in authority over him. In that case, the psychotherapist's

9 Durant - *The Story of Civilization - The Age of Louis XIV* - p. 643.

10 See p. 61 above.

11 see p. 19 above.

task is to bring the patient to an understanding of the real reason for his rebellion – not by simply *telling* the patient what the problem is, but by bringing him to discover that fact for himself deep within his unconscious. The theory then is that this discovery frees the patient from emotional and unconscious identification between his employer and his father. This should give him a wider range of choices about how he should now behave towards the employer. He may still find himself at odds with his employer, but now it may be for the right objective reasons and not simply as a transference of emotions from the father to the employer. The patient is no longer *driven* to flare up in a bull-headed, unproductive or dangerous way and is now free to think of other strategies to remedy the situation. He might now state his own position in a way that will not antagonize the employer and might actually persuade him. Or he might now seek redress through a trade union or an industrial tribunal. He might even shrug his shoulders and accept that, unsatisfactory as the employer-employee situation is, it is a fact of life which he cannot change, but which should not be allowed to upset him so much. (That would be a truly Spinozan reaction.) He might even come to the conclusion that the employer had actually behaved quite reasonably and that his own irritability with him has been unreasonable. The psychotherapist has not prescribed to the patient how he should act once the neurosis about the father has been dealt with, but as the result of his new insight into himself, the patient has now available to him a much wider choice of action and attitude than he had previously. To that extent he is more free. He is, of course, not completely free, because, given that he has a wife and large family to support, he needs to be in employment.

The third and highest form of knowledge understands that, as everything is part of Nature, everything is also part of everything else. From this follows the awareness that if we forget this interconnection between ourselves and the environment, or between ourselves and other human beings, we may actually damage our own capacity to preserve ourselves. It will, therefore, counteract the desire to follow our own narrow self-interest at the expense of other people. Properly understood, Spinoza insisted, self-preservation should lead us to treat the environment and other human beings with respect. We are all members one of another, and "no man is an island", as John Donne had said.

There is scarcely anyone who does not today understand the applicability of this insight to our relationships with the environment and our fellow human beings. We are aware of global warming being produced by our own actions, of the damage we can do to the food chain, even of how the attempt to preserve ourselves by excessive use of antibiotics can produce the opposite effect as viruses mutate and become more deadly. We have begun to understand it in economic affairs also – it is in the interests of rich countries not to exploit their strength to impoverish rivals, but that their prosperity can contribute to our own. We are uneasily aware that an underclass alienated by social deprivation is a danger to the stability of our society. We draw back from major wars because we have reason to believe that no one can emerge victorious in any meaningful sense from a major war.

All of this we *know* with one part of ourselves. We all know, for example, that the benefits we get by the lavish use of pollutants or the felling of the rain forests are short-term benefits. Clearly it is better to have the knowledge than not to have it. If we were ignorant, we would not be aware of the need for any

> restraint at all, whereas knowledge may lead to *some* restraint being exercised here and there. However, all too often greed and other selfish motives are such powerful drives that they stop us from doing everything that our knowledge tells us we should do.

Spinoza, however, never claimed that all our actions can be controlled by knowledge. It will certainly act as a counterweight to our drives, but it may not be able to cancel them out if they are too strong in our make-up. In that case, we just have to accept them. For, just as we need to understand that there are some things that we can control, so equally we need to know what we cannot control, either in ourselves or in the Nature of which we are a part. This includes not only physical impediments - we can obviously not become good tennis players if we totally lack the ability to coordinate eye and hand movement, or good musicians if we are tone deaf - but it may also include temperamental aspects.

> In other words, even the knowledge that one is of a generally timid and fearful temperament because of a series of incidents in one's childhood may not be of itself sufficient to control one's fears, however hard one tries.

Spinoza believed that, once we understand what we cannot control, both in Nature and in ourselves, we are less likely to rage against the world as it is, and more likely to accept it in a spirit of stoic acquiescence.

The word stoicism suggests a certain grimness, but Spinoza's stoicism had something serene and even joyous about it. Perhaps it was because he identified Nature with God. For Pascal, they had never been the same. He had experienced Nature as pointless and terrifying. His reason could never make sense of it, and he had clung to faith in God and Jesus Christ as a refuge from, and an antidote, to Nature.[12] For Spinoza, reason will help the wise man to understand and to accept Nature as it is and to see God in it. The wise man recognizes that he himself and everything that happens to him is part of "divine nature". That recognition should be a source of joy because it liberates him from the passions of fear, anger and despair.

We have seen, however, that the recognition by itself is not sufficient to liberate men from the passions which enslave us. In most men, reason is not strong enough to conquer the other desires, either because the reasoning faculties are inherently defective or because their passions are stronger than their love of reason. Such men tend to use their reason merely to serve the passions, to justify ("rationalize") them, and to work out ways in which they can be satisfied. The philosopher is fortunate; in his case, his nature, his nurture, his inborn intelligence, and the influence of his environment (parents, school etc.) have combined to make the desire for reason and for understanding so strong that it overcomes and masters all the other passions.

> We can now see what Spinoza's determinism had in common with the Christian doctrine of Predestination and in what respects he differed from it.[13] The most important difference was that the Christian predestinarians believed in sin, and we have seen that Spinoza had no use for that concept. Like the predestinarians, he allowed us very little free will. The predestinarians believe that the little free will that we have can be strengthened by accepting the

12 see p. 233 above.

13 See especially the treatment of the question of Predestination on pp. 107 ff.

> Grace of God, which will enable us to make more choices than if we reject it. For Spinoza it was reason, not Grace, that slightly widens our choices. For the predestinarians, it was God who "knew" (the concept was, of necessity, anthropomorphic) whether we were capable of accepting His Grace or not. In some versions of predestinarianism He not only knew, but (arbitrarily, as our limited human understanding saw it) ordained it. For Spinoza, it was also a matter of chance whether our reason was strong enough in quality and in drive to give us that extra bit of choice. The predestinarians saw salvation as the unmerited reward of the acceptance of Grace; Spinoza believed that only in so far as the mind of an individual had acquired a philosophical quality could it hope, after the dissolution of the body, to survive by merging with the mind of God or Nature.

Here, then, at the climax of Spinoza's intellectual structure we have arrived at what Spinoza meant by ethics. Ethics did not mean for him what the word is generally taken to mean - a set of moral rules or principles laid down by God or Nature and which can be obeyed by any person whether he is intelligent or not. Spinoza did not believe that we are "commanded" by God or Nature to "do good". He thought that if (and, really, only if) we have a true understanding of Nature, we cannot help comporting ourselves in a particular manner. Because we are filled with reverence for God or Nature, we will love everything in Nature and treat it with respect. Because we understand that we are all part one of another, we will behave accordingly. Because our understanding and acceptance of Nature for what it is has liberated us from fear, hatred, resentments and despair, we are able to live lives that are not corroded by these qualities. All this is not really for Spinoza the result of a *moral* effort, striving to live up to a set of rules. It is rather the result of an *intellectual* effort, which enables us to live an ethical and a noble life.

The Influence of Spinoza

During the century following his death, Spinoza's teaching fell between two stools. Religious people mostly reviled him as an atheist, and the *philosophes*, the eighteenth-century rationalists, who agreed with his biblical criticism, his philosophical method, his psychology and his determinism, were put off by his mysticism. However, the German romantics, from the end of the eighteenth century onwards, loved his pantheistic identification of Nature with God. Spinoza's concept that everything in nature tries to preserve itself will be developed by Schopenhauer into the Will to Live and by Nietzsche into the Will to Power. Hegel would say, "to be a philosopher, one must first be a Spinozist". That he should say this is not surprising; as mentioned at the beginning of this chapter, it was Hegel who would develop the concept of the synthesis, and before Hegel there had been no more striking an example of synthesis - between reason and mysticism - than the philosophy of Benedict Spinoza.

CHAPTER 25

Gottfried Wilhelm Leibniz

1646 to 1716

Like so many other seventeenth-century philosophers, Leibniz was a considerable mathematician, and his first published works were on mathematics. In 1675 he discovered the differential calculus, and in 1676 the infinitesimal calculus. He published his findings in 1684, unaware that Newton had already made them ten years earlier - but Newton did not publish his work until 1687. Leibniz's notation was considered superior to Newton's and has been in use ever since.

Employed as a courtier and diplomat, first at Mainz and then at Hanover, he was sent on frequent diplomatic missions all over Europe, and he became a well-known figure at the courts of Berlin and Vienna. Wherever he travelled, he sought out philosophers and scientists. He had met Spinoza at The Hague, and absorbed some of his ideas as he did the ideas of all the other philosophers he met. Some critics have accused him of having "used" them all in the prolific writings he published in his lifetime. Bertrand Russell describes those publications as "optimistic, orthodox, fantastic, and shallow", though Durant pays tribute to the quality of many of his occasional writings.[1] It was only in his major works, the *Nouveaux Essais sur l'Entendement Humain* and especially the *Monadologie*, that Leibniz's true stature as a philosopher was revealed. The former was written between 1694 and 1704, and the latter in 1714. Neither was published in his lifetime. The *Nouveaux Essais* were left unfinished and only saw the light of day in 1765. The *Monadologie* may have been held back because Leibniz possibly feared that, for all the pains he had taken to distance himself from the "atheist" Spinoza, his enemies might nevertheless point to certain Spinozist influences - the book was not published until 1720. It was those works that made Bertrand Russell say that, after all, Leibniz was "one of the supreme intellects of all times".[2]

Leibniz was indeed anxious not to be controversial or provocative - partly for prudential reasons (it has been said that he wanted to be all things to all

1 W. & A. Durant - *The Story of Civilization - The Age of Louis XIV*, Vol. III, p.676.

2 Both quotations from Bertrand Russell from *A History of Western Philosophy*, p. 604

men) and partly because of a temperament that wanted to find harmony, unity, compromise and conciliation wherever possible. We shall presently find this temperamental inclination very prominent in his metaphysical view of the world. As a diplomat he took some initiatives in trying to reunite the various Christian creeds, and he received some hearing for a time in those political quarters which were interested in Christian unity against the Turks. But that interest was spasmodic; he quickly ran up against the entrenched positions of theologians, and, besides, Louis XIV actually allied himself with the Turks against the Habsburgs.

La Théodicée

The one major work that Leibniz allowed to be published in his lifetime, the *Théodicée*[3] (1710), does not appear to have been at all revolutionary. On the contrary, it was a conservative defence against the dawn of the so-called Age of Reason. In 1697, Pierre Bayle, a precursor of the *philosophes*,[4] had published in Amsterdam his *Dictionnaire Historique et Critique.* Bayle had suggested that it was impossible to reconcile faith with reason, Man's freedom with God's omnipotence, and the existence of earthly evil with divine goodness and power.

Leibniz, who had made a closer study of medieval scholasticism than had most of his contemporaries, fell back on arguments drawn from Aquinas. God has given us divine revelations in the Bible and He has also equipped us with reason, therefore, faith and the right use of reason cannot contradict each other.[5] Although Leibniz was a Lutheran, on the matter of free will he aligned himself with Aquinas against Augustinian Lutheranism.[6] Although science may suggest the existence of invariable laws that govern us, and although theology stresses God's foreknowledge, yet we know within ourselves, even if we cannot prove it, that we have free will.[7]

> We are mistaken about so much of what we feel or perceive that this seems a singularly weak argument.

On the problem of evil, Leibniz took a view which differs somewhat from that of Aquinas. Aquinas had argued that, in the words of Frederick Coplestone, "as God's power is infinite, there can always be a better universe than the one God actually produces, and why He has chosen to produce a particular order of creation is His secret".[8] Leibniz argued differently: God, he said, could not have created perfect beings, for then He would have created Himself. Therefore, he necessarily created limited and imperfect beings, and their imperfect existence is better than nonexistence, and God's creation is therefore the best possible

3 Leibniz coined the word "Theodicy", and since then it has been used of that branch of theology that concerns itself with reconciling God's Justice (Greek *dike*) with the existence of physical and moral evil.

4 Bayle will be treated more fully in Chapter 28, p. 301 below, on the Enlightenment.

5 See p. 132 above.

6 On Aquinas, see p. 138 above; on Augustinian Lutheranism, see p. 189 above.

7 God knows how we will use our freedom, but that does not mean that He determines how we will use it. For a full discussion of this argument, see pp. 107f above on St Augustine.

8 Frederick Coplestone – *History of Philosophy*, Vol. II, p. 373. For a discussion of this argument, see p. 137 above.

creation. "Imperfection", he wrote, "is the part that may be required for the greater perfection of the whole". Leibniz believed that the perfection of the world required that God's finest creation, humankind, should not be mere machines, but should have the dignity of free will. If that leads to the imperfections of sin, that is a lesser imperfection than if we had no free will. "This world," Leibniz writes, "must be the best that God could have created so long as He left man human and free. If a better world had been possible, we may be sure that God would have created it".[9]

We shall see later how this view fitted in with what Leibniz wrote in the *Monadologie*. It became known as Optimism, and it would be famously mocked by Voltaire in his novel *Candide* (1758), where the egregious Dr Pangloss insists that everything that appears to us evil and deplorable is really part of "the best of all possible worlds".

> One may detect a trace of Spinoza in this aspect of Leibniz's philosophy. Spinoza had argued that everything that happens, however difficult it is to accept, has to be what it is because it is part of God or Nature. But of course Leibniz's God is the traditional and transcendental God of the theologians rather than the immanent and pantheistic God of Spinoza. Besides, Spinoza had refused to describe human motivations as either "good" or "evil". Leibniz recognized evil deeds, but thought they were a lesser evil than the absence of free will would be.

Nouveaux Essais sur l'Entendement Humain

There was nothing dangerous or unorthodox about the *Nouveaux Essais sur l'Entendement Humain.* As their title suggests, they were written as a series of reviews and commentaries on Locke's *Essay Concerning Human Understanding,* which had been published in 1689. When Leibniz heard of Locke's death in 1704, he stopped work on them, and they were not published until 1765. Locke's book will be treated in more detail in Chapter 27 below. Here it suffices to say that Locke had set himself against the then prevailing orthodoxy, which had been reinforced by Descartes, that we are born into the world with innate concepts or ideas. Instead, Leibniz maintained that all our ideas are derived from the experience of our senses after we have been born. In his answer to Locke, Leibniz once again showed himself as a conservative, aligning himself with the Cartesian view and adding to it certain refinements of his own. His answers to Locke are also best considered in Chapter 27.

La Monadologie

This was Leibniz's most original work. Ideas as highly technical as are the ideas in *La Monadologie* would not generally be discussed in this book, which is written for nonspecialists. If the technical arguments are difficult to follow, the conclusions that Leibniz reached as a result did, in the end, have a sufficient impact on cultural attitudes in western Europe to justify their inclusion here. The word "monad" was of early seventeenth-century coinage, and was originally applied to mathematics, where it meant "one" or "a unit". Leibniz used it to

9 There is a detailed discussion of this argument on p. 137 above.

mean the simplest, smallest separate and therefore independent units of which everything is made up. It was to be distinguished from the word "atom", because all those who had written about atoms had described them as the smallest *physical* units of which matter is composed. Leibniz believed that the basic stuff of the universe was not material, but nonmaterial units of energy. Each of these had its own inner purpose or will. Leibniz's concept was possibly inspired by Spinoza's *conatus sese preservandi*,[10] but we have already seen that Leibniz was nervous about any of his ideas being identified with those of Spinoza, and so he preferred to use the word "entelechy". This came from Aristotle [11] and had entered the vocabulary of the medieval schoolmen with whose ideas Leibniz was anyway thoroughly familiar. Aristotle had used the concept, for example, to explain why an acorn turned into an oak tree. For Leibniz even an acorn was made up of a cluster of monads, each one of which had its own individual purpose (here, to form an acorn).

In the twentieth century, the material atom has been split, and we now know that the atom itself consists of protons and electrons and that these in turn are subject to energy which makes them orbit the nucleus of the atom. Leibniz's idea that the basic stuff of the universe consists of units of energy therefore seems to us an astonishing piece of intuition. Durant suggests that he might have been influenced by what he had seen through microscopes, which had revealed throbbing life in the smallest cells.[12] In fact, Leibniz had arrived at his conclusion neither by intuition nor by observation, but by an independent use of logic, the steps of which are set out as follows by Ruth Saw:

> An atom of matter is presumably reached by a process of division. It is either the end of the process or not. If it is the end, it is the smallest particle of matter and it can be no further divided; but then it is not extended, and so *not* a particle of matter. If it is not the end, then it can be further divided, and so it is not the smallest particle of matter. The simple elements, then, cannot be described in spatial terms, and we must seek some other way of speaking of them.[13]

One of the aspects of energy, for Leibniz, is that it does not involve extension.

So here we have a new approach to the Mind-Matter debate. Dualists like Descartes had said that mind is one thing and matter another. Materialists like Hobbes had seen all the processes of the mind as material ones. Spinoza had taught that mental and physical appearances are different ways of looking at the same thing. Now Leibniz advanced the proposition that everything we call material is in the last resort mental. Because it does not appear to us as such, it follows that the material world of appearances is not the world of reality, which we cannot see at all. All our science is therefore only an account for appearances.

> We are reminded here of Plato, who had believed that only with the utmost effort of philosophy can we have any grasp of reality, which is only apparent to us in a defective form, but Plato had not thought that material bodies were not material. Leibniz was perhaps closer to certain Eastern philosophies (which

10 See p. 241 above.

11 See p. 45 above.

12 Durant, *op. cit*, p. 669.

13 *A Critical History of Western Philosophy*, ed. D.J. O'Connor, p. 222.

> were unknown in the Europe of his time) which describe our world as a world of appearances only. His most important link is with Kant, who would, following a different line of argument, say that we are not capable of any certainty about the nature of reality, *das Ding an sich*.[14]

Leibniz's explanation of how nonphysical monads come together to make up what we perceive as physical bodies is very complicated and technical. Frederick Copplestone calls it "extremely obscure".[15] I will not go into it here, but in any such aggregation Leibniz believed that there was a hierarchy of monads. Athough each monad has its own separate entelechy or purpose, the entelechy of the lesser monads generally makes them respond to that of the dominant monad, which organizes them in a particular way so that they become the thing that we observe. For example, the dominant monad of a sheep organizes the other monads to behave in such a way that we can recognize the sheep.

Leibniz defined each monad as totally self-contained. That meant that it must be independent of all other things. It is therefore independent of all the other monads which make up the world, and this must mean that no monad can be affected by any other monad, nor, therefore, can any monad affect any other monad. So if the lesser monads respond to the dominant monad, it is not a question of the dominant monad directly affecting the lesser ones or of the lesser ones being directly dependent on - i.e. affected by - the dominant monad.

> Before we move on to look at Leibniz's explanation of the hierarchy by which the dominant monad of a sheep organizes the other monads in such a way that we recognize the aggregation as a sheep, we may perhaps wonder why anything that is independent and self-contained should be incapable of affecting or being affected by anything else. It seems a difficult chain of argument if we relate it to anything in our experience that we consider self-contained or independent. We might take as an example a magnet that is lying on the table. It is self-contained – it does not depend on anything else, but it undoubtedly has the power to attract any iron filings in the vicinity. These filings were likewise independent when they were a good distance away, but they lose their independence and are affected by the magnet when they are brought close enough to it. Similarly, the magnet itself will lose its independence and be affected by a more powerful magnet nearby. Philosophically speaking, this independence is an illusion. Even an "independent" magnet is not truly independent, as even by merely resting on the table it has to respond to the forces of gravity that keep it there. Leibniz's monads, by definition, are so self-contained and independent that nothing can affect them – except God.

Here, then, is Leibniz's explanation of why monads come together in certain aggregations without affecting each other. The entelechy that God has implanted in each monad is programmed to make it behave in a way that brings each of them, independently of being affected by the others, to make the world what it is. God has created them "in perfect mutual agreement ... in virtue of which each, ... following its own laws, agrees with what the others demand." Elsewhere, he writes more famously of "the pre-established har-

14 See pp. 365 ff. below. For another way in which Leibniz links with Kant, see p. 277 below, which deals with Leibniz's challenge to Locke's epistemology.

15 Coplestone - *A History of Philosophy*, Vol. IV, p. 300

mony" which regulates the world. The whole Universe is a beautifully ordered and harmonious Nature which Leibniz compared to "the clock of God (*horologium Dei*), and God wills what is most harmonious."

Here, too, we may detect a Spinozan note. Spinoza had argued that what we consider unharmonious in the world is actually part of the plan that is God or Nature, though we may not understand it.

Of course, there have been theological systems like that of Aquinas which had come to similar conclusions without the unorthodox equation between God and Nature, and Leibniz aligned himself with the orthodox argument about a transcendent God *arranging* rather than *being* the way the world works.

So, for Leibniz, a fatal illness, for example, would not be a case of the entelechy of a lesser monad being at variance (and therefore out of harmony) with that of the dominant monad. God would have arranged for the entelechy of a virus to destroy the rest of the aggregate for some reason of His own that is compatible with His vision, perhaps incomprehensible to us, of what a harmonious universe required.

The clock image reminds us of the Occasionalism of Geulinckx, who had believed that God merely synchronized the workings of mind and body as if they were two separately working clocks.[16] Leibniz's *horologium Dei* was far more elaborate, in that it synchronized each of the innumerable monads that made up the world. When Antoine Arnauld commented that this idea meant that God was continuously enacting miracles, Leibniz answered that we define as a miracle something that is an exceptional event – something that happened regularly all the time was not a miracle.

We might also notice how Leibniz's insistence that God's purpose was a pre-established harmony fitted in with his own longing for harmony in the political world.

For Leibniz, the hierarchy of the monads was determined by their degree of consciousness. The lesser monads were driven by an entelechy of which they were not consciously aware – they merely had, in Leibniz's vocabulary, "perceptions" of their purpose. The dominating monads, in humans or, to a lesser degree, in animals, had "apperceptions": a conscious awareness of their striving. In human beings, the dominating monad was the soul which presided over the aggregation of the lesser monads.

Even the higher human monads have some mere "perceptions"; they respond to things that are below the threshold of consciousness. Obvious examples were what Leibniz called *les petites sensations* which make us register without being aware of, for example, background noises. We may not have a focused apperception of these *petites sensations*, and in a rare poetic phrase Leibniz writes that "our clear concepts are like islands which rise above the ocean of obscure ones".

This metaphor about the relationship between the conscious and the unconscious will be much used in the romantic period, which was so interested in the unconscious. Even more interested was the twentieth century, in which a further distinction was made between the subconscious and the unconscious. The subconscious is something that lies just below our consciousness. We

16 see p. 224 above.

> notice background noises subconsciously, meaning that, if someone says to us, "what is that noise?", we can focus on it, and what was subconscious becomes conscious. In other words, it is not too difficult to recover the subconscious, all we have to do is to pay attention to it. The contents of the unconscious, on the other hand, are in the unconscious because we find the conscious thought about then embarrassing or painful, relating, as it may do, to traumatic experiences in our childhood or to unacknowledged guilt feelings. They are in the unconscious because we have deliberately repressed them and put them there, and it may need the skill of a psychotherapist to bring them back, painfully, into our consciousness. I am not suggesting that the unconscious is a discovery of the twentieth century. Poets like Shakespeare knew about it long before then. When Shakespeare has King Lear point out, in his "madness", that the man who whips the whore in an orgy of self-righteousness is actually fighting his own temptation to use her services, he showed an awareness of that psychological complex long before Freud. But it was perhaps Leibniz who first accounted for the difference between the conscious and the sub- or unconscious in philosophical terms.

Leibniz said that the *petites sensations* also include our unanalyzed aesthetic responses. He thought that our appreciation of music, painting or architecture depends on our unconscious response to "the secret arithmetic" of intervals and other relationships.

> In this, he was child of his time, the time when aesthetic theory was basically classical. A work was then thought beautiful if it conveyed a strong sense of "mathematical" organization. It is the age of formal gardens; of classical architecture; of Boileau's teaching that great painting should conform to the principles underlying Poussin's mathematical organization of a picture; of the basically regular metres of a Racine or a Pope; of the compositions of a Bach or a Mozart. The creators of these gardens, paintings, buildings, poems and compositions etc. consciously gave their works these mathematical qualities, but Leibniz thought that conscious awareness of them was not necessary for their appreciation. We may know nothing about the theory underlying classical works of art, but we instinctively appreciate them because our *petites perceptions* respond to this "secret arithmetic". As we shall see,[17] even Kant, writing seventy years after the publication of the *Monadologie*, when the aesthetics of Romanticism were already in full swing, still adhered to these aesthetic criteria. Today we are aware that aesthetic criteria can be time-bound – those of Leibniz are no exception.

The Significance of Leibniz

More than in other chapters of this book, the reader may ask himself in what way Leibniz's very technical philosophy has affected any of the issues with which we are still concerned today, and indeed, the way he argued and came to his conclusions seems very abstruse. Only his most straightforward text, the *Théodicée*, deals with traditional issues in theology that still exercise the minds of religious people trying to grapple with the relationship between faith and reason, with the problems of free will and with the existence of Evil in a world that God has created. On those issues, he did not really have anything to say

17 see pp. 377f below.

that had not already been said by theologians in the past, and he resonates down later ages mostly through phrases like "the best of all possible worlds" because of Voltaire's devastating mockery of it.

His views on Epistemology, which are discussed more fully in Chapter 27, were not in themselves so very original either, but his formulations of them would be a jumping-off ground for Kant, whose own theories on the intellectual equipment we have were not dissimilar from those of Leibniz. After Kant had elaborated them and worked out their implications, the thought world of Europeans, especially those of continental Europe, would be radically transformed. The reader is therefore advised to return to what has been said in this chapter and in Chapter 27 about Leibniz after he has read the chapter on Kant, when Leibniz's influence on the future will stand out more clearly.

For the rest, developments in twentieth-century science and psychology have made people return to Leibniz with renewed interest. The way he argued his positions may be regarded as obscure or unconvincing, but who could fail to be interested in his conclusions: that non-material phenomena like energy, once hidden, are now revealed as lying within the atom that used to be thought of as the ultimate building block of the material world; that what Aristotle and Leibniz had called entelechy has been found embedded in genetic material; that depth psychology has given to unconscious perceptions an even greater role in our thoughts than Leibniz's formulation had suggested. It is for reasons such as these that Leibniz is still of great interest today.

CHAPTER 26

Seventeenth Century Political Thought

THE POLITICAL THOUGHT OF THOMAS HOBBES 1588 to 1679

Like Bodin,[1] Hobbes lived in turbulent times. Just as Bodin's La République of 1576 had come out of the French religious civil wars, so Hobbes' Leviathan of 1651 was a response to the English Civil War (1642 to 1651). Hobbes had approved of the attempt of Charles I and his ministers to rule without Parliament from 1629 to 1640. When the King was forced to call the Long Parliament in 1640, Hobbes was already nervous enough to leave England, even before the Civil War had broken out. He moved to France, where, in due course, he would act as mathematics tutor to the future Charles II at the exiled Stuart court. In France he witnessed more disorders in the shape of the Frondes (1648 to 1652). He tells us that he was of a timorous disposition, and that this was probably due to the fact that he had been born prematurely because his mother had been so frightened by the approach of the Spanish Armada. The Frondes merely reinforced his temperamental fear of insecurity and his longing for strong government.

If his book grew out of his own psychology, he claimed that it was firmly based on human psychology in general. Before one could understand the character of the state, one would need a proper understanding of what human beings were like in the state of nature, before societies had developed. Only then could one understand the nature of the state which men had created.

We have seen above[2] that, even before he wrote *The Leviathan*, Hobbes had already developed a wholly mechanistic view of psychological and mental processes. He thought that our behaviour is governed entirely by the competing pulls of pleasure and pain. We have no innate moral sense; the main function of our intellect is to work out rationally how to minimize pain and maximize pleasure, and such moral codes as we obey are purely the result of this calculation.

Hobbes considered that one of the most important sources of pleasure is Ownership. In a state of nature, ownership of property is insecure because other people are prepared to go to great lengths, singly or in groups, to seize it –

1 see p. 201 above.

2 See Chapter 22, pp. 226f above.

they may even kill for it. Hobbes described death as the *summum malum*, the evil we fear above all others, and obviously such fear is as painful as ownership is pleasurable.

To protect one's possessions one needs power; to seize the belongings of others also requires power. Everyone is, therefore, after power, and one can never have enough of it. Hobbes writes, "I put for a general inclination of all mankind a perpetual and restless desire of power after power, that ceaseth only in death."

> One of Freud's early followers, Alfred Adler, broke from his master when he proclaimed that the Urge for Power, not the imperatives of sex, is the mainspring of human psychology. Freud thought that Adler did not probe deeply enough, had Adler done so he would have acknowledged that we want power not for its own sake;, but to deal with something more fundamental, which Freud thought were the imperatives of sex. The way in which Hobbes has built up his argument shows that he, too, recognized that men wanted power not for its own sake, but for something more fundamental, which for him was to satisfy the pleasure of ownership.

So life becomes a race, "which we must suppose to have no other goal, no other garland than being foremost". Under those circumstances, life in the State of Nature, where every man is against every other man, must be, in Hobbes' famous phrase, "solitary, nasty, poor, brutish and short". The fear of death, the *summum malum*, is ever present.

This fear afflicts all men in the State of Nature. Their reason tells them all that even the strongest individual may be defeated by guile or by a combination of weaker individuals.

> ... and not just in a State of Nature, we might add. The most powerful and despotic men in the world never really feel secure. They surround themselves with bodyguards whom they hope they can trust, and some of them sleep in a different bed each night for fear of assassination.

Reason also tells them that there is only one way in which to make life tolerable, and that is by a Social Contract. However, the Social Contract that Hobbes devises is not one between the governed and a government, such as we have seen in the *Vindiciae*, in Bellarmine and in Althusius. Instead it is a contract or Covenant which individuals in a state of nature make *with each other* to set up and obey a Sovereign. Hobbes envisages the terms of the Covenant as follows: "I authorize and give up my right of governing myself to this Man or to this Assembly of men on this condition, that thou give up thy right to him and authorize all his actions in like manner."

> In a State of Nature, all men are armed up to the teeth. What Hobbes proposes is a sort of "decommissioning of weapons" – all men simultaneously throw their weapons onto a pile which they then hand over to the Sovereign.

He goes on: "This is the generation of that Great Leviathan, ... of that mortal God to which we owe under the Immortal God[3] our peace and defence."

3 The phrase "under the Immortal God" is inserted prudentially. Hobbes was actually a Deist - that is, someone who believes that a God must have created the intricate mechanism that is this world, but that there is no evidence that this God has any interest in whether we behave morally or not. Although it would be reasonably safe (never entirely so) to hold this view in the eighteenth century, it was still a dangerous one to hold in Hobbes' lifetime.

In the Bible,[4] the Leviathan is referred to as an unconquerable sea monster, whom only God can subdue. The etching which was the frontispiece of Hobbes' book shows a gigantic crowned monster whose scales consist of innumerable tiny human beings. It is a potent image – countless individually weak and insignificant men have merged their feeble powers to produce and become part of an irresistible might. Some men do in fact feel strong by identifying with the power of the state or its charismatic leader.

So we see that, unlike some other authoritarian philosophers, Hobbes has not treated the idea of a contract, as such, as subversive. What he has done instead is to subvert the idea at the heart of the contract theory, so that, instead of justifying resistance against an autocrat, it becomes the actual justification of autocracy. As has been pointed out in the section on Bodin,[5] the basic building block – the contract idea – is accepted, but reinterpreted so that it can serve Hobbes' preconceived political theory.

The wording of the Covenant makes it clear that in theory, Hobbes, like Bodin, thought it possible that the sovereign might be an assembly rather than an individual, but, like Bodin, he believed that in practice a single individual is better capable to provide steady and orderly government than an assembly, and he said that hereditary rule is more conducive than any other to a peaceful transfer of sovereignty. He made this judgement strictly on practical, rather than on theoretical, grounds.

Whether sovereignty is vested in an individual or in an assembly, Hobbes, like Bodin, insists that it cannot be divided; there must be just *one* source of *ultimate* authority. If that source is an assembly, then any king exercises his powers on the assembly's sufferance; if it is a king, then the same is true of the assembly.

Thus, the early Stuarts asserted their sovereignty by claiming that they could dissolve parliaments at will and indeed rule without them. The Revolution of 1688, by declaring James II deposed and inviting William and Mary to assume the crown on terms, would eventually lead to the establishment of parliamentary sovereignty in practice.

Where would Hobbes have located sovereignty in the United States, where the Separation of Powers between the Legislative, the Executive and the Judiciary was built into the Constitution because its authors were determined that power *should* be divided and diffused? Hobbes would have seen that idea as a prescription for a return to chaos, and he would have been amazed to see the success of that arrangement in the United States.

We note that no condition, no covenant is put upon the sovereign power thus created. Like Bodin, Hobbes believed that if the sovereign were bound by a covenant, he would not be sovereign. Hobbes maintained that reason tells us so. It is reason also that tells us that, "we ought not to resist the sovereign" thus created, for resistance would destroy the very security for which we have set him up.

It is to be noted that for Hobbes, obedience to the sovereign is not the result of a contractual obligation towards the sovereign, nor is it in any way a moral obligation, it is dictated purely by reason. Reason can discover what Hobbes calls the Laws of Nature. We may *call* some of these laws moral laws, but that

4 Job Ch. 41, Isaiah Ch. 27, Psalms 74 and 104.

5 see p. 201 above.

is not because they have an intrinsically moral quality, but only because we refer to their subject matter in this way, rather as we might talk about the laws of biology or chemistry – in other words, they describe the way the world *does* work rather than to the way it *ought to* work – they are *descriptive* rather than *prescriptive*.[6] Hobbes sets out sixteen laws of nature which include that, "men should seek peace and follow it", that they should make the covenant in the way he has stated, that, "men perform their covenants made" and that "every man strive to accommodate himself to the rest". In Hobbes' view, laws depend not on the will of God, but describe the way things naturally are. They are not really different from the laws which say that we should have regular periods of sleep or that we should not step into a fire. Nature is such that sleep is necessary if we are to remain healthy. Similarly, these Laws of Nature are necessary if we are to avoid the "disease" of the intolerable condition in which people find themselves in a State of Nature. A number of important questions arise:

1. Do men in fact use their reason to work out how to maximize pleasure and minimize pain?
2. If they do, does reason tell all men that, if they want to lead a tolerable life, they ought to form a covenant with each other in the terms Hobbes has set out?
3. Does reason really tell them that they must neither fetter nor resist the sovereign? Could such unquestioned obedience not strike at least some men as *unreasonable*?
4. Do all men regard death as the *summum malum*? It is true that many people submit to dictatorships out of fear – "rather red than dead" – as millions might have said who submitted resentfully to communist dictatorship, but others would say, like the American patriot Patrick Henry, "Give me Liberty or give me Death." Such people are prepared to risk death in pursuit of a cause or an ideal. There are always *some* such people, and if there are enough of them (and this may of course depend on the feeling that for some reason or another dictatorships are already weakening), powerful rulers are overthrown.
5. Should we accept Hobbes' picture of the state of nature? We have already discussed[7] that there has never been a time when humans have not lived in social groupings and that there has obviously never been in history a moment when men came together to create a political society by Covenant. We may assume that our philosophers knew that perfectly well. For them, the state of nature and the Covenant was a myth that embodied a truth about basic human psychology and therefore about the nature of obedience. Hobbes saw man's basic nature as extremely greedy, violent, and yet fearful. Is that an accurate picture of human

6 For a fuller discussion on the three different senses - moral, scientific and legal - in which the word "law" can be used, see p. 144. There it is pointed out that one essential difference between moral and scientific laws is that moral and legal laws may remain valid even if they are frequently broken, whereas once a descriptive law is shown to have been "broken", it ceases to be a law. Hobbes is one in a long line of philosophers who seems to me to go wrong because he thinks of law as being descriptive even when it is in fact prescriptive. Having consistently described the dictates of reason as laws of nature, he does admit in the last paragraph of Chapter 15 that, strictly speaking, the dictates of reason are *improperly* called laws: they become laws only after they have been decreed by the sovereign. Yet, he also says, they may properly be called laws if we remember that they are "delivered by the word of God". This sudden reference to God is wholly out of tune with Hobbes' Deistic temper, but in any case, in the passage referred to he merely recognizes the category of legal law; nowhere does he seem aware of the distinction between moral and scientific laws.

7 See p. 200 above.

nature or is it unduly pessimistic? We will discuss this further when we come to see how John Locke will interpret the myth of the state of nature and the social contract.[8]

Hobbes insisted that any limitations on the powers of a sovereign was tantamount to denying sovereignty, so that limited sovereignty was a contradiction in terms. He did stress, rather as Machiavelli had done, that a prudent ruler will be careful how he uses his theoretically absolute power. If he provokes a serious rebellion, he deprives his subjects of the security for the sake of which, along with others, they have surrendered all their power to him. If he cannot keep order, he is, *by definition*, no longer a sovereign; his power has disintegrated, and disintegrated power, again by definition, cannot be sovereign power.

It is not a question of the sovereign having broken a covenant which he had never entered into, it is simply that the covenant which his subjects have made *with each other* has broken down. They had promised to surrender all *their* powers, to give absolute obedience in the knowledge that others were giving absolute obedience also. It follows from the fact that a serious rebellion has destroyed the character of the sovereign. For whatever reason, a sizeable number of subjects have resumed the weapons that they had promised to hand over to the sovereign, and so the contract they had made with their fellow subjects is broken. Everyone is therefore free from the contract he has made with his fellows, and as a result they are all back in the dangers that existed in the State of Nature. The justification of sovereignty is not any kind of divine right, it is simply the ability to maintain order.

Like Machiavelli,[9] Hobbes gives some advice on how a ruler should avoid provoking his subjects to the point of serious rebellion and what is helpful for the maintenance of his authority. He has no contractual or even moral obligation to rule his subjects fairly, but it is in his own pragmatic interests not to inflame them beyond endurance.

He did not add that he might be deeply hated by his subjects, yet cow them for a lifetime by a totally ruthless reign of terror, such as we have seen in our own time. Even then, however, such tyrants know how to brainwash large numbers of their subjects by propaganda. Cowed though Stalin's subjects were by the KGB, many of them actually wept when he died.

In Hobbes' time, religion was perhaps the most powerful propaganda machine, not just in the religious, but also in the secular field. Machiavelli had said that a prince should see to it that his subjects believed sufficiently in religion to make them obedient to him, but not to the extent that they renounce warlike qualities when the prince requires them to fight for him or for the state. Since Machiavelli's time the Reformation had shown religion to be a cause for destructive civil wars. This made it even more important for Hobbes than it had been for Machiavelli that the ruler should control and use religion in the interests of the stability of the state. Needless to say, Hobbes believed that the church had to be totally subject to the sovereign and could not have any power independent of him.

8 See p. 265 below.

9 see p. 179 above.

A ruler who cannot protect his subjects against disorder has destroyed his own sovereignty. Any successful usurper who can keep order has thereby acquired the sovereignty which the previous ruler has lost – legitimacy depends entirely upon this ability.

> Hobbes is, I think, a good analyst of sovereignty. His definition of it seems to me incontrovertible. Sovereigns may accept ethical or legal restraints on their power – and fortunately many do, and behave in a reasonably moral manner – but if they choose to ignore them *and get away with it*, their sovereignty remains unimpaired thereby. We do, for example, have parliamentary sovereignty in England. It was once said, before the days of sex-change operations, that Parliament can do everything except turn a man into a woman. It can. in theory, pass laws that abolish all civil rights (and there have, for instance, been periods when it has made trade unions illegal). It can ignore the times set for general elections (and did so during the Second World War). Of course, if it did exercise its powers in too tyrannical a way, it would risk provoking an uprising – just as any individual sovereign would do if he tried his people beyond endurance – and its sovereignty would be destroyed.
>
> Where Hobbes went wrong, I think, was not in his analysis of sovereignty, but in his view of human nature. Whether or not there is a contract between them and their sovereign, people feel they have natural rights which their ruler must respect.[10] They expect more from him than merely security for their lives. Aristotle had said that political societies are founded so that people may live, but they are continued so that they may live well. Spinoza would also assert this view. In many countries, sovereigns are aware of, and even share, the wider value systems of their subjects. In countries where they do not, the people sometimes manage to impose their wishes on their rulers. Maybe that is a limitation of sovereignty (which Hobbes thought was a contradiction in terms) but it does not necessarily lead to intolerable chaos, and may make life better. That gives the moral dimension a much more important role in politics than Hobbes had been prepared to consider.

Hobbes' cold analysis made everyone feel uncomfortable. People felt the need to clothe the gaunt Hobbesian skeleton with moral garments. Parliamentarians thought they were morally right to fight against absolute sovereignty. Royalists wanted to rest their claims on the religious ground of the Divine Right and not merely on the *de facto* possession of power. For them, the ineffectual exiled Charles II was the rightful sovereign of England by Divine Right of Hereditary Succession, and Oliver Cromwell, though he was in full control of England after 1651, was an illegitimate usurper. As Hobbes had no respect for theories of divine right, he was ordered not to attend the exiled Court any longer. So he made his peace with the actual *de facto* government and returned to England in 1652 from his voluntary exile in France.[11] When Charles II was successfully restored in 1660, he in turn headed a *de facto* government which Hobbes readily supported. If Charles II's courtiers had had their way, Hobbes would have suf-

10 We will leave aside for the moment whether there are in fact such things as natural rights: Locke made their existence a major part of his criticism of Hobbes, whereas Bentham would call the notion of natural rights "simple nonsense".

11 This is not to suggest that Oliver Cromwell was enamoured of Hobbes' idea. Cromwell had no respect for the Divine Right of Kings, but he did believe that he was ruler not simply because he had won the Civil War, but because the Lord had blessed his godly Puritan cause.

fered for trimming in this way. Fortunately for him, Charles II did not see it as trimming but as the logical outcome of his philosophy. Charles was a charming cynic who almost certainly did not believe in the Divine Right of Kings which he and his supporters asserted. More generous than his courtiers and more tolerant, he allowed his former tutor to live out his life peacefully and in receipt of a royal pension.

THE POLITICAL THOUGHT OF BENEDICT SPINOZA

Spinoza's political thought is found mainly in his unfinished *Tractatus Politicus*, which was published just after his death in 1677. He had read the *Leviathan* and saw the origins of the state rather as Hobbes had seen it. Spinoza also saw man in the state of nature as characterized by selfish and aggressive lawlessness. We remember that, for him, it is in the nature of all things to strive to preserve themselves (*conatus sese preservandi*)[12] but this instinct of self-preservation is not the only one. In Hobbes, each individual man was basically interested only in himself, and it was purely fear that led him to form societies. However, Spinoza thought that, even in a state of nature, man also has a social instinct. For Hobbes, society was the result of reason, not of instinct, and it is only after fear has driven men to hand over all their powers to the Leviathan that they learn to act as social beings. For Spinoza, however, the same social instinct which led men to found families then led them to establish social relationships with other families – fear had nothing to do with this. Fear only arose afterwards because, in the state of nature, such natural groupings are still at the mercy of the aggression of other groups.

Like Hobbes, Spinoza believed that men's reason showed them how they could escape from the state of nature by making a social contract, in which they hand over their powers to a ruler who, "whether he be one or many or the whole body politic, has the sovereign right of imposing any commands he pleases". Again, like Hobbes, he points out that this *right*, though unlimited in theory, is in practice limited by what the subjects expect from the ruler. Hobbes' men had surrendered their authority on the sole condition that the ruler could maintain order and protect their lives. Spinoza's expected more of the sovereign; they expected him to make possible not just security of life, but also quality of life.

> This is what Aristotle had said long ago: "A *polis* is not ... founded for the purpose of men's living together, but for their living as men ought."

A life without freedom is a life without quality and men expect the state to give them as much liberty as is consonant with order, "The last end of the state is not to dominate men, nor to restrain them by fear; rather it is to set free each man from fear ... The end of the state is really liberty."

Hobbes, while granting that sovereignty could be vested either in an individual or in an assembly, had argued that, in practice, government by an individual was more desirable, as being more likely to create an orderly society. Spinoza did not agree. With his Dutch background he believed that for all the fickleness of a democracy, it is preferable to the arbitrary whims of a single

12 see p. 241 above.

ruler or the vested interests of an aristocracy. Not only do these latter deprive men of their right to exercise their reason, they are more likely by their excesses to create disorder than the outcome of rational debate: "... for it is almost impossible that a majority of a people, especially if it is a large one, should agree in an irrational design. And moreover the basis and aim of a democracy is to avoid the desires as irrational and to bring men as far as possible under the control of reason, so that they may live in peace and harmony."

> Spinoza shared the optimism of John Stuart Mill in the nineteenth century that, given freedom of discussion, the most rational view would prevail in the end. He seemed to have little fear that demagogues might play effectively upon the emotions – often on the baser, warlike and intolerant emotions – of an audience. Most democrats today are aware of this weakness; even so they still prefer democracy to any alternative. E.M. Forster would famously give two cheers for democracy: one could hardly give it three; and Winston Churchill described democracy as "the worst form of government – except all those other forms that have been tried from time to time."

There should therefore, according to Spinoza, be freedom of expression for all opinions that do not aim at sedition. This included religious doctrines, which Hobbes had wanted the state to control because religion was dynamite and could so easily be a cause for disorder. Hobbes had drawn this conclusion from the contribution that the development of Puritanism had made to the outbreak of the Civil War. He thought that if the governments had ruthlessly nipped Puritanism in the bud, the Civil War might never have happened. Spinoza, however, drawing on his experience of Holland, realized that religious toleration made disorder less, rather than more likely, than it was in a state whose prescriptions of religious dissent forced such believers into violent resistance in defence of their faith. So religious toleration is not only morally right - denying people religious freedom is damaging their quality of life - but also helps the society to remain united.

THE POLITICAL THOUGHT OF JOHN LOCKE 1632 to 1704

Background

John Locke had studied medicine, and in 1667 he became the personal physician and then a good friend of the first Earl of Shaftesbury. In the 1660s, Shaftesbury had been a member of Charles II's government. While he was President of the Council of Trade and Plantations, he had his friend Locke appointed Secretary to the Council, and therefore, Locke had more experience of government than philosophers usually have. Shaftesbury enjoyed discussing philosophy with him and urged him take that subject up seriously. In particular, he wanted him to produce a philosophical justification for Shaftesbury's own political programme when, in the 1670s, he moved from government into opposition to the king.

The Restoration Settlement of 1660, which had allowed Charles to return to the throne, tried to keep the power of the king and that of Parliament in balance, and this produced great instability. It was almost a proof of the contentions of

Bodin and Hobbes that divided "sovereignty" was a contradiction in terms and was bound to produce disorder. During the 1670s, all sides in England seemed to realize that the Restoration Settlement would not work – the balance would need to be tipped decisively towards either king or parliament. Those who wanted it tipped towards the king became known as Tories, while the Whig opposition, of which Shaftesbury was by then the leader, wanted the king's powers effectively subordinated to those of parliament.

Other issues were also involved. The Whigs supported equal political rights for all varieties of Protestantism, while the Tories wanted to make local and national government an Anglican monopoly. Both Whigs and Tories wanted to exclude Roman Catholics from local and national government. Because James, the heir to the throne, was a convert to Catholicism, the Whigs wanted to exclude him from the succession. The Tories supported his right to succeed, because they believed that interference with the Divine Right of Hereditary Succession would weaken a monarchy they were committed to strengthen. They could only hope that James would accept the Anglican monopoly of local government. (The determination of James II, after he became king in 1685, to break this monopoly would turn almost all the Tories against him and would make the bloodless revolution of 1688 possible.)

The struggle between the two parties aroused tremendous passions. Plots and rumours of plots abounded, and the country came close to another civil war. In 1681, Charles tried, but failed, to have Shaftesbury convicted of high treason. Even so, the Earl's life was in danger, and in 1682 he fled to Holland, where he died early in the following year. Some of his followers who remained behind in England were accused of a plot to assassinate the king. The leading conspirators were executed and a witch-hunt was launched against other prominent Whigs. In the autumn of 1683 John Locke thought it prudent to flee to Holland also. From there he saw Charles II, and then his brother James II (who had converted to Catholicism) apparently totally victorious in reestablishing royal absolutism.

James II's Catholic policy so infuriated the majority of his subjects that they wanted to get rid of him. The nearest Protestant member of the dynasty was James' daughter Mary, who had married William of Orange. The rebellious subjects asked William of Orange to bring an army to overthrow James II and Locke was one of the intermediaries between the English rebels and William. The invasion succeeded in 1688, and James fled. The Crown was then offered to William and Mary.

The way this was done in 1689, in the Declaration of Rights, was interesting from the point of view of political philosophy. James II was declared to have abdicated by his fleeing and the throne was declared vacant. (This set aside the Divine Right of Hereditary Succession, by which James' Catholic baby son should have succeeded his father).[13] There were then thirteen clauses declaring certain autocratic practices of James II illegal, and listing the rights which Englishmen enjoyed; the fourteenth clause then offered the Crown to William and

13 However, in deference to the sensitivities of the Tories and of some Whigs also, the official theory was that James II's flight amounted to an abdication and that his wife had not given birth to the baby who grew up as the Old Pretender. That baby had been smuggled into the Palace in a warming pan, and therefore Mary was the next heir to the throne by hereditary succession. That story fooled nobody.

Mary. The Declaration was quickly interpreted by the Whigs as a contract between the Crown and the People – it was an offer of the Crown which was conditional on William and Mary having accepted these rights. The implicit corollary was that if they violated these rights, they had broken the contract and the people were absolved from their allegiance. The Social Contract which established government was no longer something mythical that had occurred in the State of Nature, but was felt now to have been a concrete event in seventeenth century England.

Locke's Ideas

John Locke now returned to England, and in 1690 he published his most famous book on political philosophy, the *Two Treatises on Government*, which soon came to be regarded as the Bible of the Whig Revolution.[14] Because of the date of publication, it is often taken to have been a retrospective blessing on the Settlement that had been made the year before, but it is important to realize that the book had actually been written in 1681, when the struggle between Charles II and Shaftesbury had been at its height. At the time it was written, therefore, the text was not a calm exposition of the *status quo*, but rather a challenge to the absolutist claims of Charles II and a call to revolution. Locke was so unsure of the durability of the new regime and so nervous about the danger to himself if the exiled James II or later his son, the Old Pretender, were to make a comeback that he had the *Treatises* published as written "by an Englishman" and denied his authorship throughout his lifetime.

The Two Treatises on Government

The First Treatise has rightly received very little attention from philosophers. Entitled *False Principles*, it is an attack on Sir Robert Filmer's *Patriarcha*, a royalist tract that was first written in 1642 at the beginning of the Civil War, but was not published until 1680, when the royalists were again advancing extravagant claims for absolutism. Filmer had based such claims on the Bible, and had seen absolute royal power as the natural development of the absolute patriarchal power. He had described Adam as the first king and Charles I and Charles II as his rightful heirs. Locke found it easy to demolish such interpretations of, and deductions from, the Bible as "glib nonsense".

Some commentators have suggested that the real target of Locke was not the easy target of Filmer, but the more formidable one of Hobbes. Locke did not agree with Hobbes, but in 1680 it was Filmer who was quoted by the royalists, and not Hobbes who, as we have seen, had little respect for the Divine Right of Kings which, for the royalists, was central in the Exclusion Crisis. Certainly in the Second Treatise, entitled *The True End of Government*, Locke takes direct issue with Hobbes, even though he never mentions him by name.

14 Leading Tories, devoted members of the Church of England, had joined in issuing the invitation to William and Mary, so strictly speaking it inaccurate the refer to 1688 as the "Whig Revolution". However, the Settlement accorded more closely with what Shaftesbury and the Whigs had been fighting for since the 1670s than with the support that the Tories had given to Charles II and, initially, to James II also.

Perhaps the reason he does not mention him is that he built up his theory on three fundamental ideas that he actually shared with Hobbes: there was once a state of nature which was unsatisfactory; a social contract was then made to create a state; to understand why the contract and the resulting state take the form they do, it is necessary to understand what human beings are like in their natural state. Filmer's theory had been built on quite different foundations; he had relied on biblical arguments, and he had found no place for any contract at all. Although Locke agreed with Hobbes on the buildings blocks which had to be the basis of political structures, we have another example of the men perceiving these building blocks in radically different ways. They both begin with basic human nature, but see this differently, consequently, the next building block - the social contract which these individuals make - will be a different kind of contract, and the political institutions that arise out of the contract will be very dissimilar, too.

Locke, then, like Hobbes, begins with his understanding of basic human nature. Hobbes had envisaged that, in the State of Nature, each person regards his neighbour as at least a potential enemy out to rob or destroy him, whereas Locke thought that, even in a State of Nature, men were generally in a state of "good will, mutual assistance and preservation". In other words, the human species finds cooperation quite natural. Locke agrees with Hobbes that reason gives man an understanding of the law of nature, but whereas for Hobbes the "law of nature" was merely *descriptive*, for Locke it was a *prescriptive* moral law. It laid down the basis of how we ought to behave towards one another because God has made us all equal and independent and has laid upon each man an obligation to do "as much as he can to preserve the rest of mankind". So, for Locke, humans are not fundamentally predators of one another, but are more like a peaceful flock of sheep or perhaps like a swarm of ants who instinctively cooperate with each other.

> Which of them has a better grasp of what most human beings are naturally like? Is it arguable that Hobbes saw humankind from a mechanistic and Locke from a teleological point of view?[15] It will be remembered that the mechanistic view tends to see the essence of something in what that something is in the beginning: an acorn is just an acorn, and the essential nature of the oak tree lies in the acorn. A teleological view sees the essence of something in what it is meant to become if nothing obstructs the process: so the essence of the acorn is the oak tree into which it should develop. If one sees the essence of a human being to lie in its beginnings, one might agree with Hobbes: we know that babies have a lot of violent, aggressive and possessive emotions which have to be tamed in the process of growing up and becoming socialized. For Locke, maybe the essence of a human being lies in the socialized form which is as much the normal development of a human as the oak tree is the normal development of the acorn. Perhaps in a civilized society people do behave quite "naturally" in a cooperative manner; but, alas, we know how easily in stressful situations many people may revert to the violent, aggressive state in which they were born. So it is not so easy to determine whether Hobbes or Locke were right in their analysis of what human beings are "naturally" like.

15 For a discussion of teleology and mechanism, see p. 33.

There would be no need of any government if the cooperative qualities which Locke considers natural in human beings were shared by every single member of the human species in the state of nature. But there are always a few freak individuals who are not like the rest of the species, who are "degenerate" (the word comes from *genus*, the Latin word for "species") and men realize that they need to protect themselves again these relatively few corrupt and vicious individuals.

In a state of nature, the majority of cooperative individuals could deal with the small degenerate minority by taking the law arbitrarily into their own hands, but they realize that this is not very satisfactory. It would be much better to set up a society in which it was made clear to everybody exactly what constitutes a transgression of the rules and how such transgressions would be judged and punished. What is needed therefore is "an established, settled and known law", "a known and indifferent [meaning impartial] judge" and, "a power to back and support the sentence ... and to give it due execution".

The purpose of the Social Contract, then, is to set up such an organization, which will be endowed with the three functions just described: a legislative, judicial, and executive power.

> This formulation of the three functions of government became a classic. Some later philosophers, like Montesquieu, will urge that to prevent a government from becoming too strong and endangering the liberties of the individuals requires that these three branches should not be combined in the same hands, but should be entrusted to separate bodies of men. This idea is not found in Locke, even though the whole thrust of his philosophy is against giving too much power to the government. Nor, despite much talk about the need to respect the difference between the three functions, is it found in British constitutional arrangements. Members of the executive (i.e. ministers) sit in the legislative body; and in judicial matters the supreme court of appeal is made up of the law lords who sit in the Upper House. The authors of the American constitution followed Montesquieu[16] and provided for such a formal separation of powers – the President and his ministers (the executive) do not sit in Congress, and neither do the members of the Supreme Court.

Because the great majority of men are peaceful and cooperative, the state, in order to deal with the relatively few degenerate men, does not need to be equipped with the unlimited and overwhelming powers of the Leviathan. It is not necessary for an individual to give up all his rights to it. So, in Locke's Social Contract, all the individual surrenders, in common with his fellows, is his right to take the law into his own hands to deal with miscreants. Moreover, everyone agrees to *delegate* these powers to the government, and what they delegate, they may resume if it exceeds the limited role for which it is set up. Hopefully they can do this by electing a different government. If, however, they are prevented from doing so, if the government behaves in too oppressive, arbitrary or unconstitutional a manner, then the citizens are entitled to rebel. Locke was as nervous about disorder as any other conservative thinker, and he was at pains to stress that his teaching was not, and could not, be taken to be an invitation to rebellion whenever citizens had a minor grievance against the government.

16 see p. 272 below.

Human nature, he believed, was such that it would put up with quite a lot of misrule – it was only if this became too gross that the people would turn to rebellion as a last resort.

For Hobbes, the state had been created by men as a piece of machinery to serve their purpose, but in the end the machinery had turned into a sort of Frankenstein monster with a life of its own. The imagery of Hobbes' famous frontispiece is that the Leviathan is not so much a piece of machinery as a living organism that had turned the individuals who had created it into mere parts of itself.[17] This idea was totally alien to Locke. The state never becomes more than a piece of machinery at the service of its creators. If it fails them, they can dismantle it and create a new structure which serves them better. Locke left the judgement of whether what the government does is acceptable or not firmly to "the majority".

> Presumably he meant the majority of qualified voters, who, in Locke's time, were of course only a small propertied section of the male population. There is no suggestion that he was considering universal suffrage, however, it is easy to see how later generations could use Locke's language to claim universal suffrage.

Locke never used the word "sovereign" in describing the government. The functions of the government are very limited. If all men are potentially as violent as Hobbes thought they were, then the state needs enormous powers to maintain law and order; it has to be what we now call a repressive police state, with all the paranoid characteristics that involves. If, on the other hand, it needs to control only a few "degenerate" men, then it does not need such powers; it needs to be little more than a glorified village policeman, whose job it is to keep an eye on a few local rogues.

In Locke's state, individuals retain all their natural rights, which he described as the right to Life, to Liberty, and to Property. Hobbes' frightened man was prepared to give up his rights to liberty and property to secure his right to life. If Hobbes' sovereign respects liberty and property, he does it for prudential, not for contractual reasons. He may be aware that if he deprives too many people of their liberty and property, enough of them may rebel to prevent him from protecting the lives of his other subjects, who accepted his sovereignty only if he could provide law and order. If he could no longer do so, he would, by definition, no longer be sovereign. Locke's man, on the other hand, contracted with the state that it should protect *all* his natural rights – his liberty and his property as well as his life.

Of course, these rights cannot be totally absolute. A person may forfeit life, liberty or property as a prescribed punishment for specified transgressions. We find that the loss of liberty or property is accepted as a penalty for crime in even the most liberal of societies, and Locke took this so much for granted that he never even discussed it. (At least he did not make the mistake of calling these natural rights "inalienable", as the authors of the American Declaration of Independence were to do.) Presumably, Locke took the view that, so long as it

17 The notion of the state being an organism rather than being a piece of machinery is first found in Aristotle (see p. 52 above) and will be discussed again in the chapter on Rousseau, p. 335 below.

is the majority that decides that a particular offence merits a deprivation of life, liberty or property, no violation of an offender's natural rights has taken place.

It will not be until the nineteenth century, with De Tocqueville and John Stuart Mill, that political philosophers will go back to the insights of Plato and Aristotle:[18] that majority rule can degenerate into a tyranny of the majority which is as damaging to individual rights as was the tyranny of an individual or of an oligarchy. A majority can be very oppressive, either in what it defines as a crime or in the punishments it ordains. In such cases, the natural rights of an "offender" are certainly violated, but it is also very difficult, if not impossible, to lay down any absolute rules about what a majority can legitimately define as a crime and punish as such. What seemed obvious crimes to eighteenth-century people may not seem not to be crimes at all to their twentieth-century successors.

Western Europe today is sympathetic to the idea that Life is sacred (except when we are involved in war!). Certain states in the USA do not go so far and, despite their apparent belief in the "inalienable" right to Life, have retained capital punishment; at least they would say that Life is so important that it can be forfeited only as the result of such grave offences as murder.

What about Liberty? Again, in general terms democracies give Liberty a very high valuation, but we accept deprivation of liberty not only as a punishment, in addition, we accept the most enormous restrictions on our liberties when we have committed no offence at all, so that the restrictions do not therefore have the character of punishment. To take just one example, we accept regulations which deprive us of the freedom to build a house wherever we like. In Locke's time, too, there were such restrictions, if not quite so many. We have agreed to them, at least in theory and implicitly, by the majority decision of our representatives.

Just as in the case of Life and Liberty, Locke knew that the right to Property cannot be absolute. Not only can it be taken from you as a punishment for transgression, it may be taken from you when you have committed no crime at all, by taxation:

> Government cannot be supported without great charge, and it is fit everyone who enjoys his share of the protection should pay out of his estate his proportion for the maintenance of it. But still it must be by his own consent – i.e. the consent of the majority, giving it either by themselves or by their representatives chosen by them.

Notice the slide from "his own consent" to "i.e. the consent of the majority". I may disapprove of paying taxes which go to finance weapons of mass destruction. Even my representative in parliament may vote against money being spent on such armaments, but both he and I may be overruled by the majority inside and outside parliament. If that happens, I cannot withhold my taxes on the grounds that my property is being taken away from me without my consent and that therefore my natural right is being violated. When Locke makes the slide, just quoted, he seems uneasily aware that whereas any man is free to surrender his own natural rights – whether to life, liberty, or property – they can hardly be natural if an individual in a minority can be forced to surrender them by the majority.

Nor does Locke examine what he means by "the majority". In his day, the majority of the population of England did not have the vote, therefore did not have any representatives. He never considered by what right the representa-

18 For John Stuart Mill, p. 429 below. For Plato and Aristotle, see p. 39 and p. 53 respectively.

tives elected by only a minority could make any decisions that were binding on the unenfranchised. Did the question never occur to him? The traditional answer to that question is that, like the people for whom he wrote, he simply took it for granted that the unenfranchised were thus bound. Yet, in his youth during the Civil War, the idea of a very wide suffrage had been vigorously canvassed by the Levellers and the Diggers. Locke should therefore have been well aware that one could not really take a narrow suffrage so much for granted that it was quite unnecessary to state the case for it. Here, as elsewhere in his political theory, he left loose ends.

Locke assumed that the minority accepts, as part of the Social Contract, that it will be bound by majority decisions even where such decisions made inroads into its natural rights. The fact that the functions of government agreed under the Social Contract were so very limited seemed to him to reduce the possibility that there could be many major objections to the way they were exercised.[19] The minority confirms its acceptance of what the majority decides by remaining in the country instead of emigrating or joining another society. In due course this idea was expressed in the formula that "residence implies consent".

It is a somewhat harsh dictum, it is, after all, a major step to uproot oneself from the land of one's birth. Not everyone is willing, or able, to do that, even if the disagreement or oppression is very severe. Of course, some Englishmen had done just that. The Pilgrim Fathers, for instance, had been prepared to emigrate because they could not consent to being forced to follow the religion of the majority of their fellow citizens.

Locke thought that the Pilgrim Fathers should never have been put into the position where they could not practice their religion peaceably in England. The very limited functions given to the state in Locke's Social Contract did not include the right to dictate the religion of its citizens. Louis XIV was arguing that suppression of the Huguenots was necessary to prevent them from causing trouble to the state. Locke took the opposite view. Quite apart from the fact that men have a right to freedom of worship, religious oppression actually *provokes* disorder in the state. These were the arguments he used in a series of *Letters Concerning Toleration* which he published from 1689 onwards, though some of these, too, had been written in Shaftesbury's lifetime, and in support of the Whig policy of toleration for the Dissenters. There were some exceptions. Clearly, there should be no toleration for religions that demand human sacrifices, neither should there be any for the preaching of Atheism, because Locke thought that no one who does not fear God could be trusted, nor could any country tolerate a religion which demanded allegiance to a foreign power. These were the grounds on which Roman Catholics should be excluded and on which the Whigs resisted the succession of James II.

What made Locke think that Property was such a natural right in the first place? Today we would not endow it with anything like the same importance as

19 Actually, the functions of the "Lockeian" English state in the eighteenth century went far beyond merely keeping the few "degenerate" men under control. We have only to remember that the economic theory of the time was Mercantilism (roughly what would later be called Protectionism), which meant that the control of trade was one of the State's most important functions; and this of course deprived its citizens from trading freely with other countries or from buying in the cheapest markets. Laissez-faire theorists in the nineteenth century would consider this a function which the State should not have.

the right to Life or Liberty. Yet to Locke it was just as fundamental. In the State of Nature a man acquires the right to land and its products by "mixing his labour with it" so that it becomes, as it were, an extension of himself. He enjoys this right under two conditions. The first of these is that there is enough land for everyone.

> Locke, with typical looseness, does not define "enough". In the England in which he lived, one might argue that almost all the land (except "common land") was in ownership and that there was "not enough" to satisfy the needs of the landless peasants who therefore had to labour for the landowners. One could therefore take Locke literally and argue for land reform – the redistribution of land so that everyone has "enough".
>
> It was different in America, where there were at that time, and for long afterwards, vast stretches of land which (conveniently ignoring the American Indians) were owned by nobody. The American pioneers could therefore take Locke literally. The advice was "Go West, young man"; there was no need for anyone on the east coast to labour for an employer as anyone could stake out his claim out in the west where there was enough for everyone, and could mix his labour with the wilderness by clearing it with his own strong arm. The land he had cleared and cultivated thereby became his own.

The second condition that limited the right to own land was the requirement that the owner could make use of its product "before it spoils", for "nothing was made by God for man to spoil or destroy". Money, of course, does not spoil, so it is all right for the owner to exchange his produce before it is spoilt for money that keeps its value.

If these two conditions are fulfilled, then, "the grass that my horse has bit, the turf my servant has cut, and the ore that I have digged in any place where I have a right to them in common with others, become my property without the assignation or consent of anybody."

> One might argue that this entitles a man to the ownership of the grass, the turf and the ore rather than to the ownership of the land. And anyway, it seems rather obvious that in the second case it is the servant and not the employer who has cut the turf. For all that slavery and serfdom had disappeared from England, it seems that for Locke the servant is rather how Aristotle had described a slave: merely an animated instrument, a living tool, the property of its owner like his horse or like the spade with which he dug the ore. He owns the servant who cuts the turf (or at least he owns his labour in return for the wage the servant receives). Essentially, this is how the capitalist thinks. The socialist, however, says that it is the servant who is entitled to the results of his labour.
>
> Locke never even considered such points – one might say they seem never to have occurred to him, or, if they did, he made no intellectual effort to tidy up loose ends. In this he was very different from Hobbes before him or from Hume after him: whether one agrees with Hobbes and Hume or not, there is no doubt that they were much more rigorous in following through all the implications of their arguments, so that they left few, if any, loose ends. Locke lacked this rigour in his political writings. We have already seen how he equated a man's own consent with that of the majority and how he assumed that representatives of a limited electorate represented "the majority" etc. Some might think that this lack of rigour makes Locke a rather lightweight political thinker, but the influence of a thinker may have little relationship to the

precision of his thought, and that is certainly true of Locke.

Ultimately, he relied on what men of his class considered only common sense and this characteristic actually endeared him to his English readers. It has been said that Locke is the most English of political thinkers, describing a polity with which the English like to identify themselves, one that was based on what is "only common sense"; that was moderate, pragmatic and not too rigidly theoretical (here the contrast will be made by Burke and others with the disasters that befell the French when the revolutionaries and especially the Jacobins based themselves rigidly upon theory); that set limits to the powers of government; that shrank from the Hobbesian idea that power, not morality, lay at the bottom of government; that was basically tolerant; that assumed that people were not easily roused (after 1688) to rebellion or revolution; that was in favour of liberty and property (note the boast that an Englishman's home is his castle).

The Influence of Locke

Locke's political theory became immensely influential. In England it was cited to give philosophical underpinning to the Revolution Settlement. We have seen above how the Declaration of Rights, for example, which in effect offered the Crown to William and Mary as the last clause in a document whose preceding clauses recited a series of constitutional rights, was quickly interpreted by most Whigs as a Lockeian Contract of Government. The Whigs, who dominated England for half a century after 1714, stood for limited government, for the consent of the governed, for the inviolability of property, and for all Protestants having equal civil rights – all Lockeian ideas. Locke had the great merit of making his thought palatable to his countrymen for many years to come. Few Englishmen could recognize themselves in Hobbes' portrayal of man: tense, aggressive and timid at the same time, ready to surrender their liberties to an all-powerful ruler. It is in Locke's pages that we meet the Englishman as we like to see him today: easy-going, temperate, friendly but individualistic, tolerant, proud of his liberty but not bombastic about it, pragmatic and full of common sense, capable of holding beliefs which seem inconsistent or poorly worked out, but which somehow work in conjunction. Whether this was the picture of Englishmen in Locke's lifetime it is difficult to say, certainly it was their character as it developed under the easy rule of the Whigs in the eighteenth century.

Locke's influence was not confined to England. Voltaire believed that England was governed in a Lockeian manner. It was not governed autocratically, there was religious toleration and much else that he admired and thought greatly superior to the way in which France was ruled. He did much to popularize Locke's ideas in France. However, whereas in England Locke was interpreted in a conservative way, in France his ideas were more subversive. In the eighteenth century, Locke's ideas were held to justify the *status quo* in England, whereas they were obviously a condemnation of the *status quo* prevailing in France.

Looking back into the past, Lockeans equated the natural rights of man with the traditional rights of Englishmen. Like Sir Edward Coke at the beginning of the seventeenth century, Locke believed that it was the Stuart attempts to introduce absolutism into Britain that were revolutionary and that resistance to them was conservative, drawing on established traditions which were, with romantic exaggeration, traced back to the Magna Carta of 1215 and indeed further back, to an equally glamourized picture of the consensual way in which Anglo-Saxon communities were said to have governed themselves. The Glorious Revolution was not believed to have done anything radical or innovative, it had simply put England back on the historic track from which the Stuarts had tried to divert it. Had Locke's book been published when it was written, before the Glorious Revolution, it would have been more subversive of the *status quo* than it was after 1688, but Locke would still have maintained that it was essentially a conservative, not a revolutionary work.

In France, however, the myths and traditions to which Lockeans appealed were very weak. France had been at her greatest under autocratic rulers like Henri II, Cardinal Richelieu and Louis XIV. The most important opponents of the centralizing monarchy in France were the aristocracy, who called in aid not the natural rights of man, but their ancient privileges and powers; for these, Voltaire had no love whatever. The French could not equate the natural rights of man with rights that Frenchmen actually enjoyed. They became, of necessity, a more abstract conception, and they were made still more abstract by the *philosophes* who, unlike Locke himself, had always been outside government. Their demand for natural rights had a much more revolutionary and explosive flavour.

We have seen how struck Montesquieu would be when he read in Locke the description of the three functions of government being the legislative, the judicial and the executive. In his dislike of absolutism, Montesquieu would advocate that those functions should never be combined in the same hands, and so introduced the idea of the Separation of Powers. That never made much headway in France, but in America it would be built into the Constitution of the United States. The Americans did not endow property with quite the same importance that Locke had done - their Constitution proclaims that among men's inalienable rights are Life, Liberty *and the Pursuit of Happiness.* Nevertheless, we have already seen how attractive Locke's concept that a man makes land his own by mixing his labour with it was to the American pioneers in the west.

We have looked here only at the influence of Locke's political ideas. Even more far-reaching was the impetus that his philosophy gave to epistemology - that branch of philosophy which examines the nature of our knowledge. It is this area that the next chapter will examine.

PART FIVE:
THE EIGHTEENTH CENTURY

CHAPTER 27

The British Pragmatists

JOHN LOCKE
1632 To 1704

The branch of philosophy which concerns itself with the nature of knowledge, which investigates how we acquire it and how reliable it is, is called epistemology (from the Greek *episteme*, meaning knowledge). John Locke made it the central concern of his pure philosophy and started off a new wave of epistemological thought, especially in British philosophy. It had admirers on the continent during the eighteenth-century Age of Reason, but when continental thinkers turned to Romanticism, epistemology did not remain their prime concern, and most of them returned to a preoccupation with metaphysics and with the question of how we ought to live. Their approach did not appeal to the British temperament, which tended to dismiss continental metaphysics as too full of cloudy mysticism. English thinkers were not so dismissive when it came to questions of how we ought to live, but few of them were pure philosophers. They were mostly political theorists, like Burke, Bentham and John Stuart Mill; and even then, as Locke had done in his *Treatises on Government*, they addressed social and political policy rather than "the human condition". English pure philosophy was rather barren during the Age of Romanticism, but it revived in the twentieth century with the analytical philosophies of Moore, Russell and Ayer, which once again dealt with logical and epistemological questions; with what we can truly know.

Locke was of course not the first of the philosophers with epistemological interests, or even the first for whom they were central to their enquiries. We have seen, for example, that Plato and Descartes had believed that some of our knowledge is *innate*, meaning that we are born with it, even if for a time we remain unconscious of it until experience brings it into consciousness.[1] Aristotle, on the other hand, had believed that all our knowledge is acquired *by experience in the first place* – a view known as empiricism (from the Greek *empeirikos*, meaning practised).[2] William of Ockham, Roger and Francis Bacon also held this view. Empiricism seems to have had a special appeal to the English, even before Locke became one of its most famous exponents.

1 For Plato, see p. 36 above. For Descartes, see p. 222 above.

2 For Aristotle, see p. 45 above.

Locke's empiricism was far more influential in shaping the outlook of future philosophy than that of his predecessors had been. This was because the latter had confined their empiricism only to this world, which they accepted as, in the last resort, less important than the transcendental world; they had lived at a time when theology was sovereign. Descartes, Pascal, Spinoza and Leibniz still wrote under its sway, but by the time that Locke wrote his *Essays Concerning Human Understanding* (1689/90) that was no longer the case – still less so in the following century. Locke was not interested in theology at all, nor in any other kind of metaphysics about which he thought we could know next to nothing.[3]

He thought that what human beings were born with, what was innate in them, were reflexes and instincts, but these he described as physiological habits which are the same in all normal babies. Also the *faculties* by which we acquire knowledge are innate, but the *knowledge itself* or the ideas we have (which constitute our knowledge) are not innate. A child's mind is, he thought, a *tabula rasa.* Some philosophers had said that moral concepts or ideas about God were innate. How could that be, Locke asked, since these differ so widely in different parts of the world?

Leibniz's Response

As mentioned in Chapter 25, Leibniz had written the *Nouveaux Essais sur l'Entendement Humain* between 1694 and 1704 in response to Locke's *Essay Concerning Human Understanding.* When he heard of Locke's death in 1704, he stopped work on his own refutation, and the *Nouveaux Essais* were not published until 1765, half a century after the death of Leibniz in 1716. Leibniz elaborated the idea that we are born with some innate ideas, and as Descartes had asserted this more than half a century earlier, the *Nouveaux Essais* could already be seen as a rearguard action when they were written. By the time they were published, they seemed positively outdated, because by then the philosophy of Locke (and that of Berkeley and of Hume who had extended it) had carried all before it.

We have seen that Locke had allowed that the faculties are innate by which we acquire those ideas which later constitute our *factual* knowledge. Leibniz went further: he believed that each normal person also has the innate capacity to acquire logical, moral or religious ideas. He did not suggest that new born babies have even rudimentary *ideas* about logic, morality or religion – merely that each normal individual is born with an innate *capacity* or *receptor* for them, just as Locke's "faculties" were the receptors for factual ideas.

> We might perhaps also add a receptor for aesthetic responses. In the twentieth century Noam Chomsky[4] would add, as it were, a language receptor, with the capacity to master, and to manipulate, with amazing speed, the complex grammar and syntax of whatever language experience will fill it. Science has meanwhile discovered that, for example, aesthetic, linguistic and factual activity are carried out by different areas of the brain; so the idea that there are

3 But, as we shall see, Bishop Berkeley, who carried forward Locke's epistemology, not only gave God a place in his philosophy, but actually needed God to help him to resolve a problem in his epistemological theory.

4 See p. 602 below.

different "receptors" does not look so odd.

Some experiments have even shown that there is an area of the brain which is particularly active in conjunction with religious experience. This might account for the fact that religious experiences can be found in societies all over the world. This would raise a number of speculations: How has such a "receptor" evolved in humans? Does that area of the brain *create* religious feelings or does it *receive* some kind of a signal from outside itself?

What goes into these "receptors" is handled within them in different ways. We handle factual belief in one way, religious belief in another, aesthetic belief in a third. We come to know how we should handle factual belief; to what tests we should subject it to discover whether the facts are really facts or not. But many philosophers have stressed that religious belief cannot and should not be handled in this way, but rather through faith. Likewise we know that when we make a factual statement, that this table is made of wood, we are saying something essentially different from asserting that this table is beautiful: an aesthetic statement cannot be handled in the same way in which a factual statement is handled.

Of course it often happens that the contents of one receptor overflow into another one. Things that ought to be treated in the way in which factual information should be treated may instead flow into the religious receptor and are there treated with an unquestioning reverence that they do not deserve. Conversely, religious people might complain that sceptics treat religious ideas with the methods that are appropriate in the "factual" receptor but that they miss the point when they are applied to ideas that belong into the religious one.

What specific morality, religion, factual or logical material eventually fills these receptor depends on later reasoning, education and other kinds of social conditioning. The receptor or capacity itself can develop as it is filled with moral ideas; it can grow just as a muscle can grow and the capacity of a very small child to absorb moral ideas is less than the capacity of a normal mature person.

On similar lines, Leibniz believed that most humans are also born with a receptor for what we call religious ideas. Here again, what specific religious ideas will fill this receptor depends on the environment. Locke had said that religious *ideas* could not be innate because they differ so widely. For Leibniz the religious *instinct* was innate. That is why throughout history most human beings have apparently thirsted for, or at any rate been ready to accept, a "religious" dimension to their thought. What fills the religious receptor will vary greatly. A great variety of theologies may fill it, but so may nontheological intimations of the numinous (in Nature or in music, for instance), and so may quasi-religious attachments to secular ideologies (as, for example, when some communists treated their creed with all the reverence and ritual that are characteristic of a religion.)

There are other explanations for religious attitudes – for example, that they reflect our feeling of insecurity. Another theory is that we transpose to a deity or to a system characteristics which we have found in our childhood experiences. For example, we may transfer to God the Father some of the features we associated with our own father (that he might be loving or angry) or which we discovered our father did not actually have (such as omnipotence). Such explanations would treat religious concepts merely as the result of associations of ideas and would not involve looking for a separate religious receptor in human beings.

Even where we are talking only of factual knowledge, Locke had said that we only had the innate *capacity* for this knowledge, but that this "receptor" was, as it were, empty of ideas or concepts at birth and could be filled only by experience. Leibniz, however, thought there were some "tools of understanding" which were already present in each individual at birth. These include a grasp of the concepts of being, of substance (in its everyday meaning), of unity, of identity, of contradiction and of cause. It is with these tools that the mind handles the sensations it receives.[5] They help us to make sense of our knowledge. Without them, the mind would indeed receive sensations, but it could never sort or order them or make sense of them. At birth these tools and our use of them are still very rudimentary. They develop in much the way in which our muscles develop, and to use them properly requires much practice and training.

Even babies know, in a rudimentary, confused and unrefined way, that things exist (being),[6] that there is a difference between air and solid matter (substance), that there is one thing that "is" their hand (unity), that that hand is the same thing in successive moments of time (identity), and that its hand is not at the same time its foot (contradiction). Leibniz believed that these, the most elementary and rudimentary ingredients of logic, are innate.

On the other hand, can it really be said that babies have any innate concept of *causes*? Does not the awareness that B often follows A come only with experience? And is it not only after one has seen many As "causing" Bs that one assumes that there are As that "cause" the Bs that one will notice in future? (I put "cause" into inverted commas because, as we shall see later in this chapter, Hume will deny that we are entitled to assert causal connections between A and B.)

Locke had conceded that reflexes and instincts are innate. Yet some of these, like the sexual instincts, are latent at birth and show themselves only at a later stage of life. Could not the same be true of the principles of logic? Locke did not think so, as some adults never grasp the principles of logic – but then some adults remain impotent. If we take the Leibnizian view, could it not be said that in each case there are innate capacities – physiological as well as intellectual (and, I would add, moral) – which, though latent at birth, develop in so many humans that we call that developing "normal", while we call "abnormal" the failure to do so?

Locke on "Simple" and "Complex" Ideas

Like his predecessors in pragmatic philosophy, Locke believed that all ideas and all knowledge are derived from the experience of our senses, and then from our *reflections* upon that experience. He divided the ideas we derive from our sensations into *simple* and *complex* ideas. Simple ideas are derived directly

5 Note in Chapter 31, p. 364 below, what happens when Kant substitutes "*has* to handle" for "handles" in this sentence. Leibniz may have been considered old-fashioned and backward-looking when the *Nouveaux Essais* were published in 1765, at the time when pragmatic epistemology was at its height, but his prestige revived after what Kant would have to say in the 1780s about our "tools of understanding".

6 That may not actually be true. It is suggested by some psychoanalysts who belong to the school of Melanie Klein that at the *very* beginning of life, a baby does not realize that its mother exists independently of itself, but sees the mother as an extension of itself.

from the five senses of sight, hearing, touch, smell and taste. The colour, perfume, and texture of a rose are simple ideas. Our reflections tell us that when a bundle of sensations constantly coexists - for instance, the colour, smell, feel, and behaviour of a plant - there is something that holds all these sensations together and supports them. That something is the substance, in the philosophical sense that has been described in chapter 24 on Spinoza.[7] We *infer* the existence of a substance, though we can have no direct perception of it, and therefore no knowledge of what it *is*. We do have an idea of what it *does*: it is what holds simple ideas together to give us a complex idea - in the above context, the complex idea of a rose, in which colour, perfume, and texture are combined.

We need to be reminded that, whereas what in everyday language we call "substance" is material and can be experienced through the senses, the philosophical meaning of the word is nonmaterial and therefore something of which our senses can have no direct perception. In the philosophical sense nonmaterial substances hold together not only material things like roses, but also things that are in themselves immaterial. In a rare excursion into theology, Locke believed that we could infer that God is the substance that holds together all the different aspects of perfection: perfect goodness, perfect truth, perfect beauty, perfect knowledge, perfect justice, perfect love, omnipotence etc. He thought that the soul was the substance that held together our thinking, doubting, fearing, loving etc.

> If we are sceptical about the existence of the soul, we might like to substitute here the concept of the individual personality.

Reflections can lead to further complex ideas. To some extent these result from *memory*; ideas in the memory are not simple ideas because they do not result *immediately* from sensation.

The material stored in our memory is grouped in certain *associations*. These may be reasonably reliable, or they may be faulty, giving rise to erroneous thinking. Sometimes they may be so faulty as to give rise to hallucinations.

> This idea became the foundation of a new approach to mental illness and madness, which would soon be explained in terms of such "misassociations" rather than of diabolical possession, and it contributed to deranged women, for example, no longer being regarded and treated as witches.[8]

Reflections may also be the result of *interpretation*. A swan hisses: the sound we hear is a simple idea; the interpretation of the sound - that the swan is angry - is a complex one. Like associations, interpretations may of course be either faulty or reasonably reliable.

Interpretation itself often depends on the *generalizations* we make; we group together certain things we have perceived. Sometimes we group spaniels and terriers together under the generalization to which we give the name "dogs", at other times we may group together spaniels, terriers and cats and give the

7 See p. 237 above.

8 See Roy Porter - *Enlightenment*, pp. 216 to 223.

name "pets" to that generalization. Here Locke, like a good nominalist,[9] was at pains to point out that generalizations have no independent existence; they are merely the names we give to sensations that we have chosen to group together.[10]

Other complexities derive from learning vocabularies. For example, we will almost certainly have some experience of seeing animals killed, either by other animals or by ourselves. We also have experience, through all our senses, of other human beings. We learn that there is a word, "murder", which describes the killing of human beings, so now we know the idea of murder even if we have personally never experienced the killing of a human being.

Finally, our reflections may lead us to create new ideas by combining known ideas in a previously unexperienced manner. In this way, for example, we make inventions.

"Primary" and "Secondary" Qualities

To what extent do the ideas we derive from our senses actually correspond with the objects outside ourselves that give rise to those sensations and produce those ideas? Locke had no doubt that there were real objects outside ourselves: he was no solipsist.[11] But he knew that our sensations are often unreliable. Like Descartes, he thought that they would be at their most reliable and objective if they could be checked or corrected by mathematics, by measurement, and by reason. Therefore, he thought that the qualities of an object that we can be most certain about were those of shape, solidity, extension, number, motion and rest. He called these *primary* qualities. He was sure that they were really "out there" in the world. *Secondary* qualities were more subjective and less reliable. They are known by our senses only and, he thought, cannot be objectively tested. For example, objects appear to change colour in different lights, and in darkness they cannot be detected at all. The same bowl of water will feel warm to a cold hand and cool to a warm hand. Locke therefore thought that we cannot know that objects out there in the world "really" possess these secondary qualities, nor that these qualities do not in fact depend on us.

9 A reminder: Nominalism was the name given during the Middle Ages given to those philosophies which generalizations or universals are man-made. Realism, deriving ultimately from Plato, held that universals are the ultimate reality of which the individual particulars we perceive are merely imperfect manifestations. See Chapter 14.

Locke also reminded us not only that all names are man-made, but also that some of them – those that do not refer to ideas ultimately resting on sense experiences – are "but empty sounds".

10 That names have no independent existence could also be demonstrated by the fact that the same name is so often used in quite different ways. What western Liberals mean by "democracy" is quite different from what the communists meant by that word. This perception will lead to the main concerns of twentieth century analytic philosophy, which eventually grew out of the nominalist inheritance, and which tried to pin down the precise meanings of the words we use (the names we give to things). Professor C.E.M. Joad, who brilliantly simplified philosophical concepts on the radio, would coin the phrase "it all depends on what *you* mean by" democracy or by whatever concept was under discussion. The italics here are mine, to emphasize that what one person means by the concept may not be the same as what another person means by it.

11 A solipsist is someone who feels he can be sure only (*solo*) of the thoughts one has oneself (*ipse*). One cannot be sure anything exists other than our thoughts, or that there is any object "out there" that correlates with the ideas we have.

Today we know that this distinction is an invalid one. Science can explain in mathematical terms, through measurable light waves and sound waves, what a colour or a sound "really" is, what the measurable chemical components of a smell are etc. In Locke's day, one could demonstrate by measurement to someone whose angle of vision suggested to him that a coin was oval or a stick in a glass of water was bent that these were optical illusions. Today one can demonstrate by measurement to a person who is colour blind or tone deaf that there are "real" differences between different colours and different notes. In this way the distinction between primary and secondary qualities disappears; and a "common sense" view would be that the so-called secondary qualities are really "out there" just as much as the so-called "primary" ones are.

As we shall presently see, even before these scientific discoveries were made, the difference between primary and secondary qualities would be whittled away and ultimately destroyed by Leibniz, Berkeley and Hume. But, as we shall also see, in philosophy, as distinct from "common sense", that whittling away led, not to both being considered really "out there", but to the opposite: that we could no longer assume that either primary or secondary qualities were really "out there". In his *Nouveaux Essais*, Leibniz had already said that we are wrong to trust our perceptions when they tell us that space, time and motion (all included among Locke's primary qualities) are absolute: they are instead relative perceptual relations. By the time we come to Hume, it appeared that we cannot know that there is anything "out there" at all; and even when Kant will teach *that* there is something "out there", he will say that we cannot know *what* that something, that *Ding an sich*, is really like.

What is interesting in Locke's distinction between primary and secondary qualities was that he lived in a classical culture. Classicism always attached great importance to mathematical qualities which emphasize regularity, symmetry, order, and an underlying permanence. It dominated theories of aesthetics right up to the time of Kant, and we see it applied in the painting, music, poetry, architecture, and garden and park design of the time. Romanticism, on the other hand, paid more attention to the temporary, to the fleeting, to "natural" qualities, which escape mathematical regimentation. Locke's distinction may well have been influenced by the classical canons of his time.

GEORGE BERKELEY
1685 to 1753

Long before the Irish-born George Berkeley became Bishop of Cloyne in 1734, he had become a major figure in British philosophy. As a young man he had been enormously stimulated and challenged by John Locke's proposition that all our ideas and knowledge originate in our sensations and in subsequent reflections upon them. At the astonishing age of 25, he had published his *Treatise Concerning the Principles of Human Knowledge* (1710). In this and the later *Three Dialogues between Hylas and Philonous* (1713), he took Locke's work very much further.

If Locke, for example, was a nominalist, Berkeley could be described as an ultranominalist. Locke had contented himself with saying that generalizations (universals, abstract ideas), though ideas that we have in our mind, can have no independent existence, but are merely the *names* we give to groups of particular sensations that we have.[12] Berkeley thought that it was actually impossible to conceive of anything that was properly a universal. We think we can have a general idea of a triangle, but when we concentrate on the idea of a triangle as such, we are always forced to picture a particular triangle: *either* right-angled *or* equilateral *or* isosceles *or* scalene. The moment we try to form an idea of "pets", the images we form for ourselves are *either* of dogs *or* of cats – or rather, of a *particular* dog or a *particular* cat. So a *general* idea of a triangle or a pet cannot actually exist even in our minds, and the notion of a general idea must therefore, strictly speaking, be a contradiction in terms!

> This is convincing enough, but we all use abstractions, however imperfect they may be, to useful effect. One can hardly think or make any argument without them, and that includes any arguments that Berkeley himself will put forward. Hume, who will come to even more radical conclusions than Berkeley, will readily admit that the conclusions of philosophy do not always correspond with how we *have to* carry on our lives.[13]

We recall that Locke had been sure that there was a substance (of which, however, we could have no direct perception) which supported both primary and secondary qualities; that the primary qualities of objects existed independently of our perception of them, and that we could not be sure that the objects "really" possessed the secondary qualities we perceived, as our perception of these was subjective.

Berkeley believed that when we asserted the existence (the *esse*) of anything, we could not mean anything other than that it was being perceived or that it was itself the mind which was doing the perceiving: *"Esse est percipi aut percipere."* Everything was in the mind;[14] nothing – whether objects we consider real (like tables) or objects most of us consider to be phantasmagorical (like unicorns) – could be imagined that was not in the mind. He challenged his readers to think of anything that might exist independently of the mind: the moment they tried to think of such a thing, an image formed in the mind, and without a mental image it was impossible to think of it at all and therefore to be sure that it could exist independently of the mind. If Locke said – and Berkeley agreed – that we could have no perception of Substance (in the philosophical sense), then it followed that we had no reason to say that it existed. Similarly, there could not be any difference between the existence of primary and secondary qualities. In each case the existence could be asserted only and exclusively because it could be perceived: primary qualities – like shape, solidity and the rest – were not privileged over secondary qualities in any way. They, too, existed only in the mind. If we try to think of a material object separately of the perceptions we have of it – of its colour, its shape, its texture, its smell, etc – we are left with nothing: no substance, either in its philosophical meaning or its everyday meaning (of "matter") remains. The ground vanishes for a materialist view of the world; everything is all in the mind.

12 See p. 280 above.

13 See p. 288 below.

14 Like Descartes, Berkeley thought he could perceive, by introspection, that we have a mind that does the perceiving. Where Descartes said, "I think, therefore I exist", Berkeley would have said, "I perceive, therefore I exist." Hume will deny that we can have any perception of the mind as such: we can have perceptions of perceptions, but not of a mind which is supposed to do the perceiving. See p. 289 below.

When Boswell said to Dr Johnson that he found Berkeley's arguments difficult to refute, "Johnson answered, striking his foot with mighty force against a large stone till he rebounded from it, 'I refute it thus!'" Many people might agree with this "common sense" way of dealing with philosophical subtleties; but it was not really a refutation at all. Berkeley would have answered that the sound of Boswell's comment, the appearance and solidity of the stone and the pain in Johnson's foot were all perceptions of Johnson's senses which were experienced in the Doctor's mind.

Was Berkeley then a solipsist? Were all our perceptions and thoughts purely subjective? Did they correspond to nothing outside ourselves? Was there no way of determining whether our perceptions had any degree of objectivity? Berkeley shied away from that conclusion. To begin with, when I meet another person, what I perceive is only his behaviour, but from this I can often infer that a mind similar to my own directs his behaviour. On a great many matters I can see that his perceptions are the same as mine, and my perceptions may thus be rescued from total subjectivity (though not, of course, if we were both drunk and both saw pink elephants).

Would a full-blooded solipsist argue this way? Would he not say that the other person has no existence outside of my perception not just of his behaviour, but of his autonomy?

Berkeley believed that, just as we infer what another person perceives from what we perceive him doing, so we can infer some of the perceptions which are in the mind of God from perceiving what He is doing, namely the effects He is producing.

Hume would point out that this is rather an odd argument for Berkeley to have used. Berkeley had demonstrated that we can be certain only of our perceptions and that these do not warrant the inference that anything exists outside of them. As we have no direct perception of God, our inferences about His existence would be unwarranted as, for the same reason, are inferences about the existence of substance.

Of course, even a solipsist constantly makes inferences from perceptions: he could not live otherwise. A solipsist thinks in terms of probabilities. From the perception he has of a car speeding along a road he is about to cross he will infer a high probability that he will have the perception of being knocked down if he were to cross the road before the car has passed. He merely maintains that perceptions cannot make inferences 100% reliable: the driver of the car may suddenly brake, for example. But for Bishop Berkeley of course the existence of God was not merely a probability: it was a certainty.

So Berkeley, like Descartes,[15] claimed that the existence of God rescues many of our perceptions from being wholly subjective. But there is a difference between Descartes and Berkeley: Descartes had believed that in God's world there were real material objects with primary and secondary qualities "out there" which caused our perceptions.[16] Berkeley believed that neither we nor God derive perceptions from a material world. Just as the world which *we* perceive cannot

15 see p. 220 above.

16 see p. 222 above.

be material[17] and is all in our mind, so, for the same reasons, God's world must be immaterial and all in His mind.

> Is not the idea that God's world *must* be immaterial rather an extraordinary one to be held by an orthodox believer in God? Is it not rather an anthropomorphic idea of God? Does it not assume that God is limited in the same way as we are? *We* may not be able to make any reliable statements for what exists "out there", outside our perceptions, but why should this limitation apply to an omnipotent God? Why should we assume that God cannot go beyond perceptions to the very source of those perceptions? True, as mere humans we cannot know whether what is "out there" is material or not: all *we* can be sure of is that we have perceptions and Berkeley has defined existence accordingly. But for all we know what is "out there" *could* be material; and, if it were, could not an omnipotent God be sure of it? If God *had* created physical objects in the universe, He would have direct knowledge of their material nature, even though this would be denied to us: we could be sure only of the perceptions we would receive from such material objects. That Berkeley does not take this position is all the stranger since elsewhere he asserts, as we have seen, that he "did not take away existence", and continued, "I only declare the meaning of the word so far as *I* can comprehend it."
>
> The explanation for Berkeley's position was that he believed that *any* concession to materialism was the thin end of a wedge which would eventually leave no room for the spiritual. He said himself that he saw it as his mission to demolish materialism, which he saw unmitigated in "*Epicureans, Hobbists and the like*" and to which he thought that Locke had made too many concessions.

In so far as the perceptions in our mind have objectivity, they correspond to the perceptions that are in God's mind. Berkeley believed that those of our perceptions which are objective are given to us by God directly.

The idea that the world exists in God's eternal mind had another advantage. Without such an idea, we could have no certainty that anything could exist while it was not being perceived by us. The existence of a table consists of our perception of it, so could the table continue to exist when the room is empty and there is no one there to perceive it? The fact that the perception of the table is always in God's mind guarantees the continuity of the perception and therefore the continuity of the table's existence.[18]

(Berkeley also used this argument in reverse, as an additional proof for the existence of God: convinced as he was that tables continued to exist in a room without observers, he concluded that, as they cannot exist in the mind of a human observer, they must exist in an eternal mind. There must therefore be an eternal mind, and there is only one eternal mind, the mind of God.)

Also in God's mind are the *so-called* Natural Laws which govern the way the world works and according to which the world normally behaves in a regular way. So, when we perceive things that do not obey these "laws" we are either

17 that is because, after something has been stripped from all the aspects we can perceive, no residual "matter" remains.

18 Berkeley's theory gave rise to the famous limerick by the Oxford theologian, Monsignor Ronald Knox: "There was a young man who said 'God/Must think it exceedingly odd/If he finds that this tree/Continues to be/When there's no one around in the Quad.' Reply: 'Dear Sir: Your astonishment's odd:/*I* am always about in the Quad./And that's why the tree/Continues to be,/Since observed by, yours faithfully, God.'"

perceiving chimeras (like the pink elephants of the inebriate) or we are perceiving miracles. (The latter is quite possible, since we cannot *know* that in God's mind Nature always behaves "normally".)

I have italicized the word "so-called" in the above paragraph because Berkeley did not ascribe to Natural Laws the *necessity* which earlier philosophers had done. Instead, he believed that the sequences we perceive in nature are *contingent.*[19] If we say that A is the cause of B, we imply a necessary connection, but Berkeley anticipated Hume in saying that all we could say with certainty is that the perception of A is customarily close to the perception of B; we cannot perceive such a thing as "cause" any more than we can perceive such a thing as "substance". The same goes for concepts that we use for causal explanations, like attraction, gravity, force etc. We can have no direct perceptions of these, so none of them have any existence in themselves, they are merely words we apply descriptively to groups of perceptions, such as observing things moving closer to each other etc.

Nevertheless, the perceptions we do have, in so far as they correspond with the perceptions in God's mind, can be trusted. Berkeley stresses that by his philosophy "we are not deprived of any one thing in Nature. Whatever we see, feel, hear or in any way conceive and understand remains as secure as ever and is as real as ever... and the distinction between realities and chimeras retains its full force".

The idea that the perceptions in God's mind can validate the objectivity of some of our own perceptions has saved Berkeley from solipsism. It was, even by Berkeley's own philosophy, a frail protection. No doubt he had a perfectly sincere faith in the existence of God, but we have already seen above that Hume would turn Berkeley's own arguments against him: we cannot actually perceive God, and therefore we cannot assert His existence. But if God is removed from Berkeley's argument, we then have a dramatic and unsettling breakthrough into pure subjective solipsism. Hume had the courage to take that step, to reveal and develop the full implications of Berkeley's philosophy.

DAVID HUME
1711 to 1776

Hume, too, was still very young - only twenty-seven - when his seminal book, *A Treatise of Human Nature,* was published in 1739. In a posthumously published autobiographical essay he claimed that it fell "dead-born from the press" - perhaps because he had pushed the ideas of Locke and Berkeley to such an extreme conclusion that those people who had already accused Berkeley of intellectual sleight of hand were not prepared to take Hume seriously. He had confessed in the book that sometimes his speculations, "appeared so cold, and strained and ridiculous that I cannot find in my heart to enter into them any further". Hume seemed to say that Philosophy can lead us to conclusions which are totally at variance with the "common sense" that guides our everyday life. Yet, as we shall see, his philosophy did have some practical consequences on atti-

19 Events are described as contingent (literally "touching each other") if they happen in close proximity (one event being simultaneous with, just preceding or just following the other) without *having* to happen in proximity. If they *have* to happen close together, their connection is described as necessary.

tudes to life, and his formulations would become increasingly relevant to the ways in which scientists think of their work.

Certainties in Mathematics

Most of us are happy in our everyday life with "knowledge" that has proved to be *useful*, but, like most epistemologists at that time, Hume was concerned to establish what we can and what we cannot know *with certainty*.

> Philosophically speaking, "certainty" must mean 100% certainty. In ordinary parlance we may say that we are "98% certain of something", and we are much more comfortable acting on that than on a mere "25% certainty". But actually the expression "98% certainty" is a contradiction in terms – if there is 2% uncertainty, then, by definition, certainty cannot exist. Hume will insist repeatedly that a very high degree of "certainty" is a perfectly adequate guide for living, but as a philosopher he must constantly remind us (and himself) that what is adequate for living may not satisfy the rigorous demands that the pursuit of philosophical truth makes on us, and that notions which are useful may not be logically tenable.

Certainty, he thought, was to be found only in what he called Truths of Reason. Mathematics provided such truths. If we define a square as a rectangular figure with four equal sides at right-angles to each other, and if we divide a right-angle into ninety degrees, then various theorems involving squares can be proved to be necessarily true and certain. If we use the decimal system , and if we call the number of xs in "xx" two, the number of xs in "xxx" three, and the number of xs in "xxxxx" five, then there is no possibility that two plus three could ever equal anything other than five. Enormously elaborate and accurate calculations involving the manipulation of numbers are therefore possible.

Thinkers in the past had often treated mathematics as the most valuable yardstick for philosophical thinking precisely because it provided such certainty. Often they had enthroned it (perhaps next to Theology) as the philosophy *par excellence* – Hume, although he agreed that it dealt in certainties, did not attach any special importance to it. (It also so happened that, unusually for a philosopher of the seventeenth and eighteenth centuries, he was not very interested in or knowledgeable about mathematics, though this fact has no bearing on his argument.) He thought it was totally self-contained, of interest to mathematicians and those who used applied mathematics like architects or engineers, but that it had no bearing on most of the matters that concern us as human beings. The truths of mathematics were in a sense self-evident, merely the unpacking of definitions.[20] Its Truths of Reason could not be a model for what he called Truths of Fact. The truth of the statement that "This table has a square top" is not implicit in the words used, as the truth of " 2 + 3 = 5" is implicit. Whether the table has a square top or not can be checked only by observation.

20 Berkeley had thought much the same, although, unlike Hume, Berkeley was a very knowledgeable mathematician and had published two early works on mathematics three years before his *Treatise Concerning the Principles of Human Knowledge*.

Impressions and Ideas

What are observations? In the first place they are *impressions of sensations*. Unlike Locke and Berkeley, Hume did not speculate on what the source of these impressions might be. Locke had believed that they come from objects outside ourselves, and Berkeley had said they are implanted in our minds by God. Hume said that we don't know where they come from - there may very well be objects "out there", but we have no way of knowing whether there are such things or not; all we can be aware of is that we have impressions of sensations. If we do not know whether there is a world out there, we cannot even be certain that mathematical truths, though certain in themselves, correspond with anything in the outside world - another reason why he would not privilege them.

There are also what he rather oddly called *impressions of reflection*. By "reflection" he did not mean what Locke had meant when he had said that reflections create "complex ideas" out of a collection of "simple ideas".[21] For Hume, "impressions of reflections" give rise only to our feelings, or "passions" as he called them: desires, aversions, fears etc - about which more below.

Impressions make fainter copies of themselves in our memories; these copies we call *ideas*. Impressions, and consequently ideas that are copies of them, form certain clusters. If a group of impressions or ideas cluster together sufficiently often, we attach a word to signify such a cluster. For example, the impressions of a particular colour, shape, texture, taste and perfume cluster together to form a thing to which we attach the name "orange". When we use the word "orange", we refer to such a cluster of impressions or ideas, which it is different from the cluster of the same shape, but of different colours and texture to which we might give the name "cricket ball". Hume, like Locke and Berkeley before him, was a nominalist:[22] "orange" and "cricket balls" are merely the *names* which we have created for ourselves to classify clusters of impressions.

The clusters do not require a substance to hold them together, as Locke had postulated. Like Berkeley, Hume said that we can have no impression of substance. The clusters of ideas come together by being frequently associated with each other. Hume greatly admired Newton, and he described the association in Newtonian terms: there is, *"a kind of ATTRACTION*[23] *which in the mental world will be found to have as extraordinary effects as in the natural and to show itself in as many and as various forms"*. But the attraction between ideas is in *us*; we have no reason to think that it is in substances or in anything else in the world outside us.

> Psychologists recognize such "associations of ideas". Every association is a personal construct. Some of them may be social constructs, but a social construct is merely many individuals making the same associations. For social constructs to work for us, we have to make them part of our own – they will not work for everyone in the social group. For some of us the idea of "pork" may be associated with pleasurable ideas like "delicious crackling", for others with distasteful ideas like "forbidden food". (That it is "forbidden food" is a Jewish social construct that works for orthodox Jews but not for secular Jews.)

21 see p. 279 above.

22 For Nominalism, see p. 115 above.

23 Hume's capital letters.

Sometimes ideas cluster together from impressions that our senses have not received together. We may have had an impression of a horse, and we may have had an impression of wings. If we have never had a visual impression of a winged horse before (i.e. by looking at a picture), nor an aural impression of one (i.e. by having heard somebody tell us about it) – in short, if we have never had an impression of a winged horse through any of our senses, but *have* had separate impressions of a horse and of wings – then we are capable of having the idea of a winged horse.

As impressions and ideas are the only source of our knowledge, we cannot be sure that words and concepts that are not derived from them refer to anything that really exists. Therefore, Hume, like Berkeley, said that we could have impressions only of one event being followed or preceded by another, but could have none of "causes" that connected them. Therefore, there could be no certainty that causes existed.

"Laws of Nature"

We must have strong reservations about what we call the Laws of Nature. These may have a high degree of probability, but if we can have no certainty of causes, we can have none of laws that assume causes. Our experience may have found a particular cluster of impressions or sequences of events to be totally regular, but our experiences are finite and we cannot be certain that the sequences will be the same at some future date. That is true even of our perceptions of space and time, which Newton had thought to be independent. Hume said that when we talk about space and time, we are merely expressing our repeated but finite experiences of physical or temporal distance.

> These are of course ideas which all scientists hold today and which were explained most compellingly by Karl Popper.[24] Europeans observed for years that all swans were white – until they discovered that in Australia there were swans that were black. We may have observed that when we heat water to 100°C, it begins to boil, and we may therefore conclude that this is one of the properties of water or that raising the heat to 100°C always causes it to boil, but if we were to heat it at high altitudes, where the air is very thin, it boils at temperatures lower than 100°C.

None of this means that the concept of a cause is useless: we cannot do without it in life. We find by experience that a refined notion of cause and effect is more useful than a crude one, and we are so constituted that the notion of cause is a part of the cluster formed by impressions and ideas. Hume confesses quite cheerfully and engagingly,

> Should it be asked me whether I sincerely assent to this argument which I have been to such pains to inculcate, and whether I be really one of the sceptics who hold that all is uncertain ... I should reply ... that neither I nor any other person was ever sincerely and constantly of that opinion.... I dine, I play backgammon, I converse and am merry with my friends, and when, after three or four hours' amusement, I would return to these speculations, they appear so cold and strained and ridiculous that I cannot find in my heart to enter into them any further. Here then I find myself absolutely and necessarily determined to live and talk and act like other people in the common affairs of life... Thus the sceptic still continues to reason and believe, though he asserts that he cannot defend

24 See p. 557 below.

> his reason by reason; and by the same rule he must assent to the principle concerning the existence of the body, though he cannot pretend, by any arguments of philosophy, to maintain its veracity.

He therefore advocates what he calls *"mitigated scepticism"* as a rule of life.[25]

It was not only in ordinary life that Hume needed to use the concept of causes. As we shall see, even in his philosophical arguments he had to use it often enough. But we can have only a *belief* in causes, not a knowledge of them. The necessity of a cause, he says *"is something that exists in the mind, not in objects"*.

Continuity

This quotation, referring as it does to "the mind", is a good example of how Hume has to use a word which, he says elsewhere, does not stand for anything that can be perceived by sensation, and that therefore we cannot be sure that the mind exists![26] We cannot experience the mind,[27] we can only experience the thought of thinking. Here is what he says:

> That which we call mind is nothing but a heap or collection of different perceptions... [28]. For my part, when I enter most intimately into what I call myself, I always stumble on some particular perception or another, of heat or cold, light or shade, love or hatred, pain or pleasure. I never catch myself at any time without a perception and can never observe anything but the perception... And were all my perceptions removed by death, and could I neither think nor feel nor love nor hate after the dissolution of my body, I should be entirely annihilated; nor do I conceive what is further requisite to make me a perfect nonentity.[29]

25 As much as anything in this book, this passage of Hume's touches upon a relationship between Philosophy and Living. And on this matter I would like to quote here the comment made by Frederick Coplestone in his *History of Philosophy* (Image Press) Vol.5, p.317. Coplestone was a Jesuit theologian, and as such set limits to the encroachments that philosophy was entitled to make on areas in which philosophy was not competent; but one does not have to share his theological views to be struck by the wisdom of what he writes here: "Hume's remarks about scepticism ... should not be understood in a purely ironical sense or as indicating that the philosopher had his tongue in his cheek. Scepticism was a matter of importance in his eyes, partly because it was a living issue at the time, though more in France than in England, and partly because he was well aware of the sceptical conclusions which followed from the application of his own principles. For one thing, it was, he thought, a healthy antidote to dogmatism and fanaticism. Indeed, 'a true sceptic will be diffident of his philosophical doubts, as well as of his philosophical conviction'. [Hume - *Treatise*] He will refrain from showing dogmatism and fanaticism in his scepticism. At the same time, a thorough-going scepticism is untenable in practice. This fact does not prove its falsity; but it shows that in ordinary life we have inevitably to act according to natural belief or the propensities of our human nature. And this is how things should be. Reason is a dissolvent; at least, there is very little that it leaves unshaken and unquestionable. And the philosophical spirit is the spirit of free enquiry. But human nature is far from being governed and directed by reason alone. Morality, for example, is grounded on feeling rather than on analytical understanding. And though the philosopher in his study may arrive at sceptical conclusions, in the sense that he sees how little reason can prove, he is at the same time a man; and in his ordinary life he is governed, and ought to allow himself to be governed if he wishes to live at all, by the natural beliefs which common human nature imposes on him as on others. In other words, Hume had little sympathy for any attempt to turn philosophy into a creed, a dogmatically propounded standard for belief and conduct. It is, if you like, a game; a game of which Hume was fond, and one which has its uses. But in the long run 'Nature is always too strong for principle' [Hume - *Essays*] 'Be a philosopher; but, amidst all you philosophy, be still a man.' [*ibid.*]"

26 For that matter, he should not really have used the word "objects" in the quotation either. He has told us that we could not be sure our impressions come from - let alone are "caused" by - objects.

27 It will be remembered that Berkeley had thought that he could perceive by introspection that we have a mind that does the perceiving. See note 14 above.

28 In other words, we cannot know that there is a mind holding ideas together any more than we can be sure that there are substances holding clusters of impressions together.

29 Durant comments: "Berkeley had demolished materialism by reducing matter to mind; Hume compounded the destruction by reducing the mind to ideas. Neither 'matter' nor 'mind' exists. Forgivably,

There is a problem here: who or what is the "I" that enters, stumbles, and fails to catch or to observe? The word would imply that it refers to the author's self; yet so radical is Hume that he says there can be no knowledge that the self exists – he out-solipsizes most solipsists. Berkeley had said that we can be sure of the continued existence of objects when we do not perceive them because they continue to be perceived by God, but Hume said that we cannot be sure of that because we cannot have a direct perception of God. Continuing existence can therefore not be guaranteed by impressions – and this is true not only of objects, but of our self, because we are not continuously aware of our self. What gives us the *belief* in continuities of existence is memory: we remember that we perceived a table in the room yesterday and we perceive it when we are in the room today: so we *believe* that it has always been there. Similarly, we remember what we thought and did yesterday (though that, after all, only partially – and what we thought or did when we were babies we remember hardly at all) and that makes us believe that there is a self that has continued from babyhood to our present "I".

> Strictly speaking, here as elsewhere, on Humean grounds we cannot even be certain that *memory* exists. Just as we cannot observe the mind but only perceptions that are "in the mind", so we cannot observe the memory, but only ideas which are "in the memory". It seems to me a good example of Hume's philosophical arguments requiring the use of concepts that, by his own principles, cannot support them with philosophical certainty!

It follows, incidentally, that if we can have no sure knowledge of our personal continuity, we can have even less of immortality.

Religion

Hume also concluded that, if we can have no certain knowledge of this or any other religious assertion, clearly we have no justification for persecuting people simply for not sharing our religious beliefs. In this he was in tune both with the Whigs of his day and with his *philosophe* colleagues in France.

> One might comment that a good deal of persecution actually takes place precisely *because* the persecutors, for all the certainty they profess in their own beliefs, are not at bottom as confident about them as they appear. At some deep psychological level they feel threatened by criticism when others do not agree with them, and this makes them lash out.
>
> Of course this is not the motivation of *all* persecution. Some persecutors feel certain enough about their own beliefs, but fear that critics may lead others astray. That could lead to those others losing the chance of salvation, in which case the persecutors feel that they owe it to those others to protect them from beliefs that they are certain will imperil their souls. Or, the persecutors might fear that their vested interests would be undermined by the critics and their followers.
>
> In any event, the case against persecuting other people must rest on other grounds than merely that we cannot be *certain* of the truth of our beliefs, for that would imply that if we *could* be certain of them, we would be justified in persecuting others. The case against persecution must rest on the rights of

the wits of the time dismissed both philosophers with 'No matter; never mind.'" (Durant – *The Story of Civilization – The Age of Voltaire* – Book I, p. 143).

> people to have and express beliefs as long as such beliefs do no damage to society. Unfortunately, there is no universal agreement on what does and what does not damage society.

In his own writings on religion, Hume demolished the deistic views which were fashionable among some of his philosophical contemporaries. Deists believed that there was no evidence of the existence of God who cared about how we behaved, but they accepted the Argument from Design. Because the world seemed to them to follow a design, they thought they could infer that there must be a divine Designer. Even if that were granted, argues Hume, we cannot infer from whatever design we might perceive that the designer has the attributes of Infinity, Perfection, or Unity. What reason, he asked, would we have for believing that there was an overall design, when we could observe only so small a part of the universe that we could not reliably extrapolate on the huge parts of it which we cannot observe? If there were a design, what justifies the belief that there was only one Designer and not several? Why could not one Designer have designed everything that is good and another Designer everything that is bad, as the Manichaeans believed?[30] Human designers do not live forever, so what would make us think that a Divine Designer, if there is one, is infinite? What reason, also, to think that He is perfect? The design of this world would appear to be less than perfect and to leave much to be desired. Hume had no patience with theological arguments that purport to explain that, despite the existence of physical suffering and moral evil, the world has to be the way it is, and that what we think to be evil is nevertheless part of God's design. If there is such a design, perhaps it is a botched one. Moreover, it could be one of several, neither the first nor the last.

Again we need to remind ourselves that Hume did not state that there was no God, merely that, if He did exist, we could have no certain knowledge of Him. He was an agnostic, not an atheist, but he denied that, in any meaningful sense, certainty could be provided by faith.

Beliefs, Reason, Desires

Religious beliefs, Hume thought, were obviously among those which cannot be based on experience. Beliefs which *are* based on experiences we call "true" in as much, and for as long as, they are not contradicted by other experiences. The comparison between experiences is made by our reason: the person who believed that water *always* boiled at 100°C was using his reason to compare various experiences when it did so; the person who experienced that at altitudes it boils at less than 100°C (or who worked out that it must do so and consequently carried out an experiment to verify it) used his reason to declare the earlier conclusion wrong.

We never use our reason unless we *desire* to do something with it. All desires are feelings, or what Hume calls passions. Feelings are shaped by real or anticipated pleasures and pains – we desire to do those things which make us feel pleasure, and we desire to avoid those things which make us feel pain.

30 See p. 94 above.

I think this is tantamount to saying that pleasurable feelings cause desires and painful feelings cause aversions. If that is so, we would have here another example of Hume being unable to avoid using the notion of cause, even though he had said that we cannot be sure that there actually are such things as causes, and that we accept beliefs in such things as cause and effect not because we can be sure of them, but because we *feel* them to be useful.

Hume says the passions may be calm (what we call unemotional) or violent (what we might call passionate today). They may be what he called direct (meaning instinctive) or indirect (meaning acquired by being associated with experienced pains or pleasures). Even if we use our reason for something entirely neutral like making a mathematical calculation, the driving force behind making the calculation is our desire (a "calm" or "unemotional" one if we think of the task as a "neutral" one) to work out the answer. Without a desire to do anything, we never perform any conscious actions at all, reasoning included. It is therefore desire alone, and never just reason, that is our primary motivation. Reason serves the function of satisfying desire, of finding ways of making action possible. We are first and foremost creatures of passion, and only secondarily rational beings. Hume expresses it famously as follows: "Reason is and ought only to be the slave of the passions and can never pretend to any other office than to serve and obey them."

We have already seen that Hume has taken the last step that the Age of Reason can take: he has used reason to undermine our belief that reasoning can ever give us certainties about anything – about logical necessity, about cause and effect, or about the authority of scientific "laws". Now he has made reason the *slave* of the passions instead of urging us, as so many philosophers and moralists have done in the past (and do still), to make it their *master.*

Hume's language here is deliberately provocative. Had he, for example, used the word "servant" instead of "slave", the impact of the sentence would not have been so strong. One may also wonder why he inserted the phrase "and ought only to be": if reason *is* (meaning "has to be") the slave of the passions, then the assertion that it *ought* to be so is hardly meaningful. The extra phrase *seems* to be a clarion call with which Hume – himself the ultimate product of the Age of Reason – has, as early as 1739, ushered in the Age of Romanticism, one of whose characteristics would be precisely to elevate the emotions above reason.

But this can hardly have been Hume's intention. Hume was a rationalist, not a romantic. His reasoning was, as it were, the ladder by which he had painstakingly climbed up to show that the passions are our ultimate guide. He had his reservations about reasoning, as we have seen, but he did think that the ladder was ultimately as serviceable a piece of equipment as any we *could* have. The Romantics, on the other hand, leapt to the primacy of the emotions without using the ladder of reason at all, and they were rather proud of doing so. They did not believe that reasoning, as the Age of Reason understood it, was by its very nature the *servant* of the passions: it was more often their *enemy.* They accused the rationalists of denigrating the passions (*"surtout, messieurs, pas trop de zèle"*),[31] of being rational when they ought to be emotional, and of preaching that reason ought to *master* the emotions. The Romantics did not think that reason *was* the slave of the passions, but they did

31 ("above all gentlemen, let us not have too much zeal"), Voltaire.

> believe that it *ought* to be so. For them, if not for Hume, the word "ought" in this context had a real meaning.
>
> At first sight, the proposition that reason is the slave of the passions may seem absurd. For example, when we feel a desire to have that extra alcoholic drink at a dinner party, is it not our reason which tells us that we may have an accident in the car on the way home and which masters our desire for that other glass of brandy? Or is it the feeling (or passion) of fear: fear of an accident or of a breathalyser test and the loss of our driving license which masters the desire (another passion) for another drink? And if the desire for another drink overrules the fear of the consequences, do we not often "rationalize" rather than reason, thus: "I know I can hold my drink", or "I've never seen the police out and about on my way home at this time of night" (which would be a good example of the invalid assumption that what has never happened in the past will never happen in the future!). Strong passions so often lead to rationalizations to justify them, in private life, in political or religious beliefs, in value judgements. Only if our passions are what Hume calls "calm", or if the passion for objectivity is the overriding one, will we allow reason to serve us as reasoning and not as rationalization.
>
> Hume's position certainly threatens those people who are afraid of their feelings, or at least frightened by the possibility that they are not in control of them.
>
> All the same, it seems that there are still some situations that do not look as if they could be analyzed in this way. Let us assume that A holds a belief with what Hume would call "violent" (and we would call "passionate") feelings and that he has used his reason to construct an argument that serves these feelings. He engages in an argument with a friend, B, who holds a different belief (either with violent or with calm feelings) and who has constructed an argument to serve these. B argues his case so convincingly that A not only abandons his own initial belief as wrong, but *as a result* has different feelings on the subject under discussion. Do we not here have a case where reason has shaped the new feelings rather than the new feelings constructing new reasoning?

Hume also asserts that it is not our reason but our feelings, based as they are on sensations of pleasure and pain, that are the source of our ethics and our aesthetics.

Ethics

The rules of morality rest, so Hume thought, on two aspects of feelings; on two elements which cause us pleasure or pain. The first of these is when our feelings instruct our reason what best serves our enlightened self-interest. We then make rules of justice accordingly. A law which prohibits theft or murder is one which gives us a pleasurable feeling of safety and reduces the painful feeling of fear. For most of us, the feeling of the consequent long term advantages of obeying the law (as well as the feeling of fear that we might be caught and punished) overcomes the desire we may have to break the law for our own short term advantage.

It follows that when we describe any act as wicked, we are describing not a characteristic inherent in the act itself, but are expressing the revulsion in our feelings about it. It is the offence against our feelings rather than offence against reason that then often drives us to entertain feelings of revenge and to demand punishment – not simply as a deterrent (for which we could make a rational case), but to assuage our feelings of outrage.

This would mean that killing people is wicked because it offends our feelings, not that our feelings are offended because killing people is wicked in itself. We need only note how many people see nothing wrong with capital punishment or with killing in wartime. A soldier may have conflicting feelings about, say, bayonetting an opponent. On the one hand, there may be the revulsion against killing him (based on compassion, which will be discussed below), on the other there may be the fear that if he does not kill the opponent, the opponent may kill him. In addition, he may fear the consequences if he disobeys the orders of his officer. Military training does it best to strengthen the latter two feelings and to weaken the first so that in the end the stronger feeling prevails, and subsequently gives rise to reasoning or to a rationalizing justification.

Some moralists might object to this conclusion. They would say that a deed can be wicked even if it does not offend the feelings. Vegetarians, for example, know that the feelings of most people are not offended by killing animals for food, yet, irrespective of that, they think it is morally wrong to kill animals.

Hume would answer that any moralist who takes that kind of position is, by doing so, merely expressing what his own feelings are. The fact that they are often not shared by his fellow humans means that there can be no absolute morality. That has been the argument of sceptics throughout history, and throughout history it has caused much alarm among theologians and "upholders of standards". Kant, for example, will try rather desperately to reinstate some absolute rules of morality.[32]

Political Thought

Hume is aware that it is in the interest of the rich and powerful to create a system of justice that enables them to remain so and which is actually unjust to the poor and the weak. No wonder, then, that they support unfair laws. However, even those who suffer from such a system often feel that they would suffer even more if it broke down, and *for as long as they feel this* (but no longer), they, too, will be inclined to support, it or at least accept it without active revolt.

Hume certainly does not recognize any duty of obedience arising out of "Natural Laws" or "Natural Rights", neither of which were demonstrably true. He derided the "State of Nature" and any contract to form a government as invoked by Hobbes and Locke as "a mere fiction". Government is not founded on consent – far more often it is based on force and violence. The authority of governments is purely *de facto*, and obedience to them is enjoined not by contracts, the implied consent of residence, or divine right, but only by one's perception of the advantages that stable government brings with it.

Hobbes had argued, firstly, that the sovereign, not being party to any contract, has no obligations towards his subjects at all, and secondly, that if a government cannot maintain the order for the sake of which it has been set up, then *ipso facto*, it is no longer a government. Hume came to the same conclusion, but he reached it without employing Hobbes' infrastructure of a contract (made between the sovereign's subjects and *not* between the sovereign and his subjects).[33]

32 see pp. 374ff below.

33 See p. 256 above.

We set the pain we may feel – about what governments may be doing and the painful consequences that might follow from rebellion – against the pleasures we may feel from whatever advantages the existence of even a disliked government may confer. If the perceived pain is greater than the perceived pleasure, we may want to revolt, and if enough people feel that, then there may be a revolt; that revolt may be successful, and if it is, the government loses the force that sustains it and thereby ceases to be a government. It cannot fall back on claims of "legitimacy" – legitimacy (including the legitimacy of hereditary succession) and moral or legal contractual obligations (whether between subjects alone, as in Hobbes, or between subjects and their government, as in Locke) simply don't come into it.

Governments find it convenient to indoctrinate their subjects with the idea that they have a moral obligation to obey. The subjects may come to believe it, just as a nurse can make a child believe that a witch will come and punish them if it doesn't behave. However, the fact that the subjects may come to believe this no more proves that there is a moral obligation than the child's indoctrination proves that there are witches. The subjects are not bound by moral or contractual obligation to the government any more than the government is bound by such obligations to the subjects.

In fact, there are many governments that acknowledge no contractual relationships and exercise power without any legitimacy; their power rests entirely on the balance that their subjects perceive between the pain of their oppression and the pleasure that might result from a successful (or even an unsuccessful) rebellion.

That balance will not be the same in all societies. Some societies find intolerable things that other societies might accept. For example, enough Englishmen have historically felt that nonparliamentary taxation is such an intolerable evil that they are prepared to rebel. Rulers also have to strike a balance between the pleasures of exercising power and the feeling of fear about having to face a rebellion. English governments know the temper of their people and have, since the Civil War, refrained from trying to levy taxation without the consent of Parliament.[34] Other societies may resent their kleptocratic governments, but that resentment is not sufficient to rouse the masses to rebellion. Their rulers are either able to intimidate their subjects (so that their *feeling* of fear is much more powerful than other feelings) or they may live in a culture of hopelessness (the *feeling* that nothing can ever change) and therefore one that has inculcated acceptance of suffering. In some societies this feeling is reinforced by the prevailing religious teaching, God's will be done, *inshallah*.

Compassion

This bleak picture of human motivation is modified by an aspect not so far considered. Hume says that crude self-interest is not the only feeling that shapes our views of morality. We also have the capacity for empathy with the suffer-

34 One must also add that there are some rulers who try to make their subjects happy because they derive pleasure from doing so, and not because they want to stay in power. To give one example: I believe that the reason for Gladstone's mission to pacify Ireland was that he wanted to right historic wrongs, even at the cost of facing defeat at the hands of the House of Lords or of a split in his party. I believe that for him the feeling of compassion (which is dealt with in the next section) was stronger than the feeling for power. There are some politicians (a Vaclav Havel or a Nelson Mandela) whose moral stature is almost universally recognized, but even they do what they do because they would feel the pain of guilt if they behaved otherwise.

ings of other sentient beings because, by the process of association, we perceive them as being like us. This perception results from what he rather loosely calls "the laws of humanity"[35] which make it "impossible for such a creature as man to be totally indifferent to the well- or ill-being of his fellow creatures". And he specifically includes animals: "We are bound by the laws of humanity to give gentle usage to these creatures."

Again, when we observe cruel behaviour, it gives us pain because it offends our own feelings of compassion, and we blame the perpetrator not so much for any defective reasoning in him, but for supressing his innate feeling of compassion. It is not our reason which calls for revenge, but our outraged feelings.

Compassion, too, is of course a feeling, but if we act in accordance with it, we are, as it were, yielding to "finer" feelings, and people are capable of feeling to a greater or lesser extent. For example, many who have empathy with the sufferings of human beings lack it when it comes to the suffering of animals, or, if we do understand that they suffer, we allow other feelings (the desire for cheap food which is the basis of battery farming, for example) to override any feeling of compassion we may have. Hume believed that an ethical education requires that we should not only teach people to reason correctly about where their self-interest (cheap food, for example) lies, but also that we should try to deepen and strengthen the *capacity* to feel compassion that is innate in all people.

> Of course, if Hume were asked why it was *better* to have that capacity strengthened than not to have it strengthened, he would, by his own theory, have to answer that his conclusion ultimately rested not on reason, but on his own well-developed feelings of compassion.

Aesthetics

Hume deals with Aesthetics in two places: *The Treatise on Human Nature* (1739) and again in *Four Dissertations* (1757). In the earlier work, his treatment of the subject is what we might expect from the rest of that book – aesthetics has nothing to do with reason, but rather with our feelings, which are shaped by "the primary constitution of our nature", by custom, and by caprice.

By "custom" he means the conditioning by the tastes of our society; and by "caprice" he means our personal idiosyncrasies in taste. An individual may find something beautiful not because he has been conditioned into this by society, but because it is, for him, personally associated with some pleasurable feeling which he has experienced in the past. Hume does not concern himself with any aesthetic "credo" – he does not say that one kind of aesthetic appreciation is better than another – one's standards must be subjective, because, like all other feelings, they are related to individual pleasures and displeasures.

> If our society influences and educates us to consider classical forms as the hallmark of a great work of art, then a classical work of art will give us a feeling of pleasure, and one lacking in such qualities will give us one of displeasure.

35 See p. 144 above for the several uses of the word "law", which can easily be confused. I think that the sense in which Hume uses the expression "laws of humanity" must be in the prescriptive sense of the "moral laws" – which means that they can be broken and still remain moral laws – rather than in the descriptive sense of scientific laws – purporting to describe the characteristics that are a necessary part of all human beings, which they clearly would not be if one found human beings "breaking" them.

(Hume urges us to learn the aesthetic norms of any given society if we want to understand its art.) Likewise, one person's individual idiosyncrasy may appreciate order and discipline so that he responds more pleasurably to classical art, when another person's idiosyncrasy may respond more pleasurably to what is wild and untamed, so what we call romantic art may be the source of aesthetic pleasure for him. Yet another person may be interested solely in sweetly sentimental content and have no interest at all in formal qualities, and so may take pleasure in the most mawkish of Christmas cards.

Hume writes that "Beauty is nothing but a form which produces pleasure, as deformity is a structure of parts which conveys pain."

This would rule out, for instance, Grünewald's pain-wracked Crucifixion in the Isenheim Altarpiece as a work of beauty. The purpose of that painting was not to produce pleasure, but empathy with the pain of the Crucifixion – though it is just arguable that one might admire the skill of the artist in evoking such a feeling, and that this admiration is itself a form of pleasure. I doubt whether Hume would have availed himself of that argument: he had classical tastes and would almost certainly have preferred the elegant figure of the crucified Christ in Rafael's Mond Crucifixion and have found Grünewald's painting ugly. But even a classical and formally beautiful painting like a Deposition by Poussin can, by depicting grief, produce grief rather than pleasure in the spectator.

Hume ventures that the "primary constitution of our nature" is such that in many cases it takes pleasure if the appearance of an object or an animal expresses its function well; if a castle conveys a picture of strength or a horse one of swiftness. Displeasure is caused when the appearance *seems* to belie function. Hume specifically mentions pillars which taper downwards even if they are strong enough to do their job.

There is a school of thought which is enamoured of functional beauty – the streamlined shape of Concorde has often been cited as an example; there are other people who admire the beauty of those houses by Frank Lloyd Wright which look a little like inverted pyramids and therefore appear to be precariously poised, even though they are technically stable.

So, with the consideration of "the primary constitution of our nature", Hume begins to abandon the idea that aesthetic tastes are wholly subjective - and he does so with a vengeance in the *Four Dissertations*. There, he includes among the aspects of beauty on which "*all agree*" the very eighteenth-century and time-bound classical requirements for "*elegance, propriety and simplicity*". That would of course rule out complex and flamboyant art (say, the Baroque) or anything that is "discordant", "inelegant" (such as pictures that portray violence, that convey the reality of the "ugly" side of life, or that portray "improper" subjects).

He still admits that beauty cannot be an absolute quality, and depends on the eye of the beholder, but he also says that we need to use reason alongside of feeling to establish canons of judgment, and so they cannot be wholly subjective or arbitrary. He writes: "Whoever would assert the equality of genius and elegance between Ogilby[36] and Milton, or Bunyan and Addison, would be

36 John Ogilby (1600 to 1676) was a very minor poet whom Charles II had entrusted with "the poetical part" of his coronation, and who was ridiculed by Dryden and also by Pope in his *Dunciad*.

thought to defend no less an extravagance than if he had maintained a molehill to be as high as Teneriffe or a pond as extensive as an ocean."

> The fact that most people today would think more highly of Bunyan's artistry than of Addison's merely goes to show the subjectivity of Hume's judgement – and of ours, too.

Hume goes on to say that anyone who prefers Ogilby to Milton lacks the training that would validate a correct appreciation of beauty, "especially in the fine arts". The training would involve extensive experience and comparisons, close attention and comprehension of the skills and techniques required. We should, therefore, pay attention to the views of someone who has had this training. Hume calls him the "qualified observer". Today we call him an art critic.

> The history of the arts is studded with examples of art critics who look silly to later generations because they derided the work of men whose greatness is today regarded as unquestionable. So today, we no longer accept so readily the criteria laid down by some high priest of aesthetics like Hume's contemporary, Sir Joshua Reynolds. In the twentieth-century revolt against élitism, some people go as far as to assert that the pronouncements of the so-called expert have no more validity than those of an ordinary person. Are there any grounds on which to give weight to the opinions of the expert?
>
> There can surely be no argument about the statement that someone who has given much time to *any* activity knows a great deal more about it than someone who has not. I might assess the performance of a batsman simply by the number of runs he scores, but a cricket enthusiast might say of him that, although he was an effective scorer of runs, his strokes lacked style, grace, fluency – all qualities of which the enthusiast is conscious because he has become knowledgeable through much watching, comparing, discussing, and perhaps playing himself. If I were to say that I cannot detect these qualities, he would rightly pity me for what I am missing. Moreover, as I know that I have devoted no time to any serious study of cricket, I am ready to accept both my deficiency and his expertise and discrimination.
>
> Perhaps an element of native sensitivity comes into it as well. A violinist might play a note that is an eighth too high or too low, and I might not notice it because my ear is not sensitive enough to hear such minute intervals, but I accept that for someone with absolute pitch the beauty of the passage would be spoilt by the slightest sharpness or flatness. To some extent, most people can train themselves to hear more exactly, but this cannot be expected of someone who may be slightly tone-deaf. In the same way, the relationships between the figures of a painting by Raphael may possess a subtle rightness that only a trained sensitivity can appreciate.
>
> Of course, there is no definable criterion of relationships that is common to all trained critics; the subjective element must come into it. Asymmetry, for example, may create an exciting tension, but it can easily topple over into ugliness, and critics may disagree on exactly where the dividing line between the two might be.
>
> Take the representational content in a painting like Botticelli's *The Birth of Venus.* An untrained mind may respond to it simply for the beauty of its subject matter: a lovely wistful nude borne on a large shell towards the shore where an attendant is holding out a cloak ready to receive her. However, that same person might derive exactly the same pleasure from a pin-up that may not be a

work of art at all. The *aesthetic* response to this painting is of a different level. It will delight in the *formal* qualities of the work – the relationship between the shell and the shore, or between the shell and the architecture created by the figures, or the contrast between the flowing lines of much of the pictures and the rigid tree trunks on the right. Then there is the appreciation of the deliberate blend of Christian and pagan symbolism, representative of a period that tried to find a synthesis between the classical and the Christian world. Next, there is a response to the ambivalent meaning of nudity in the picture, playing on the quite unerotic symbolism contained in the phrase "the naked truth" which is veiled when it dwells on the land among men. The wistful expression of Venus then conveys something more than titillation experienced at the sight of a vulnerable and bashful nude; it now speaks of the sadness that mankind cannot comprehend the naked truth. The picture becomes as rich in allusions as a great poem whose quality is revealed as layer upon layer of meaning is discovered by a mind in appreciation.

So, a certain respect for the aesthetic judgements of the "qualified observer" is defensible. The critic may indeed be fallible, bound by the conventions of his time or social group, too ready to condemn the new and the unfamiliar. He may also be too snobbish in rejecting what he has not tried to understand: the enthusiast of jazz and perhaps even of rock music can often discriminate more subtly between good and bad jazz, good and bad rock, than can a music critic who deems a study of these art forms as beneath him. When all this has been said, however, the worst offence, in art as in morals, is the stance that one man's judgement is as good as anothers' – that because there can be *no absolute* standards, there can be *absolutely no* standards. Ignorance is no sin, but there are things to be known, however imperfectly. There are sensitivities to be trained, though these may occasionally have blind spots, and there are things to be learnt, which enrich our response to what great art has to tell us. There is something to be said for Hume's later retreat from total subjectivism in aesthetics.

British and French Thought in the Eighteenth Century

Hume is the greatest British ornament of the Age of Reason. Frederick Coplestone, in his *History of Philosophy*, gives four chapters to Locke, three to Berkeley, and four to Hume. By contrast he devotes only two chapters to the whole *philosophe* movement in France, from Bayle's Dictionary of 1697 to the death of Holbach in 1789. Bertrand Russell, in his own *History of Western Philosophy*, gives five chapters to the three British pragmatists between them and does not deal with the French at all. It appears that Coplestone and Russell consider the thought of the French Enlightenment to be rather superficial, little more than a footnote to British thought, and it is true that the French *philosophes* generously acknowledged their debt to the inspiration they had from British philosophers and from Isaac Newton. Nevertheless, a book entitled *Philosophy and Living* cannot deal so cavalierly with the French. The social, political, religious and economic impact that the writings of the *philosophes* had on France was immense. Moreover, ever since the days of Louis XIV, the cultural prestige of France on the continent had been enormous: continental élites still looked to France for their tutors and for their culture, so that the direct influence of the *philosophes* was not confined to France alone. They may not have been as profound or original as the British (though I suspect some unconscious chauvinism in Coplestone and Russell here), but they formed a self-conscious group of philosophical propagandists. They aimed – with great success – to be read by a much wider public. It could be said that in England the radicalism of its philosophers affected few people who were not primarily interested in philosophy, but *ancien régime* France had such a creaking social and political structure that the radicalism of the *philosophes* became a weapon in the struggle to reform them. This book, interested as it is in the relevance of philosophy to life outside the philosopher's study, will therefore give these French thinkers proportionately rather more attention than they received from Coplestone and Russell.

CHAPTER 28

The Enlightenment

The term "Enlightenment" is generally applied to the eighteenth century, and its most famous exponents are a group of Frenchmen who are known as the *Philosophes.*[1] Like the word "Enlightenment" itself, the name *philosophe* was adopted by the leading thinkers of that school, with the same sublime confidence that the Arab Aristotelians had displayed in taking the name *Faylasuphs* in the ninth and tenth centuries. The implication was that there was no philosophical approach worthy of respect other than their own. They claimed that too much of what had previously gone under the name of philosophy had been debased by superstition, and by religious superstition in particular; even the boldest spirits of the past had been inhibited by the fear of trespassing against orthodox theology. Therefore, they claimed, it was only the eighteenth-century generation of *philosophes* that was truly enlightened and that had at last enthroned reason as the one true guide to Philosophy. Historians have tended to take them at their own valuation - even if some professional philosophers have not - and have often named the period in which they flourished as "The Age of Reason".

Before we come to consider their work, we will have a brief look at their precursors. These were seventeenth-century Frenchmen and early eighteenth century Englishmen. They were the first who dared to undermine revealed religion.

The French Precursors

PIERRE BAYLE
1647 to 1706

Bayle's subversion of revealed religion was found primarily in his two-volume *Dictionnaire Historique et Critique* (1697). He was a Huguenot who had fled from Louis XIV's persecution to Rotterdam in 1681, and it was there that his Dictionary was published. It anticipated the great eighteenth-century *Encyclopédie.* Its entries poke fun at Bible miracles, which Bayle claims to be no different from the pagan miracles which Christians rejected. He asked how one could revere biblical characters who behaved as badly as King David had done, and cast

1 In his brilliant book, *Enlightenment: Britain and the Creation of the Modern World* (Penguin, 2001), Roy Porter protests agains the Enlightenment being associated primarily with France. As we shall see later in this chapter, many of the French *philosophes* paid generous tribute to England as the country in which their ideas were not only first propagated, but first put into practice, and a later section of this chapter will say something about these English precursors.

doubt on a God who would have created Adam and Eve in the foreknowledge that they would succumb to the Original Sin. He showed incomprehension at the idea of the Trinity, could not believe in Transubstantiation and condemned the imposition of such ideas by religious persecution. Even the Dutch might have balked at these views had they not generally been followed by perfunctory rebuttals from Scripture. Bayle was in fact summoned to answer for his work by the consistory of his church in Rotterdam, and he promised to tone down some of the entries for the second edition of 1702; even in that form it remained an enormously influential work.

BERNARD DE FONTENELLE
1657 to 1757

It is amazing that Fontenelle escaped the Bastille, though he was twice threatened with it, and even more remarkable that, while Louis XIV was still alive, he was elected to the French Academy in 1691. Three years earlier he had published *L'Histoire des Oracles*, in which his exposure of prophesies and priestly trickery could easily be applied to Christianity, were it not for the prudential exception that he made of the prophesies in the Bible and of the Christian clergy. As a young man of twenty-three, he had written another subversive tract, *L'Origine des Fables* (1680), in which he showed how the imagination of primitive men led them to invent gods because they could not understand natural phenomena. Again he protected himself by saying that no such process was at work in the understanding that Christians had of God, but he did not publish this little work until 1724, in the more relaxed atmosphere that followed on the death of Louis XIV in 1715; the early days of the Enlightenment proper.

In 1685, he published the *Relation de l'île de Bornéo*. This was an imaginary account of a voyage to Borneo, where the traveller finds two tribes, the Mréo and the Eénegu, involved in a squabble over a trivial and meaningless issue. Those who could read an anagram saw it as a skit on the disputes between the churches of Rome and Geneva about what actually happens during the Communion service. This story was the precursor of several later books by other authors, which use the device of mocking in a foreign land some custom which could easily be seen as an allusion to customs nearer home. Thus, Montesquieu's *Persian Letters* of 1721 would describe abuses in Persia that obviously refer to those in France, and Jonathan Swift would use the same conceit in 1726 when Gulliver describes the passionate struggle in Lilliput between the Big Endians – who believe that one should break open an egg at the big end – and the Little Endians who believed the converse.

The English Precursors

In England, it was a little safer than it was in France to be sceptical about revealed religion, and to express theistic or even deistic opinions.

> Theists believe that there is a God who cares about humanity and wishes it to behave in a moral manner. He is a personal God, and prayer and worship are ways of communicating with Him. Theists reject the idea that He has revealed

> Himself in the sacred books of Judaism, Christianity, Islam or of any other religion. Naturally, therefore, they think that the quarrels between different religions and sects about the meaning of the texts or about ritual are pointless, and that persecution to enforce creeds or rituals are indefensible.
>
> Deists believe that there is a God who has created the universe and established the scientific laws according to which it operates. They see Him as an impersonal Creator and can see no evidence that He is still interested in His creation. The analogy was later drawn by William Paley (1802) that when we see an elaborate watch which has been abandoned on the sea-shore, we know that some Watchmaker must have made it and set it going, but we may conclude that that was the end of his involvement with it.

A number of English thinkers felt it safe enough to question revelation. The third Earl of Shaftesbury, for example, denied that revelation by itself could be the source of our morality. We could not assert that God and His laws were good if we did not have standards of goodness which were independent of God. Shaftesbury believed that we do have such a standard because we have, irrespective of God, an innate faculty to perceive moral beauty and an innate sense of right and wrong, though these could be deformed by a bad environment (upbringing or the customs of a society). In this he was really closer to Leibniz than to John Locke, who had been asked by the earl's grandfather, the first Earl of Shaftesbury, to supervise the education of his grandson. It will be remembered that Locke had rejected innate ideas, whereas Leibniz had argued that we have an innate capacity for moral ideas.

More swashbuckling attacks on what they considered the preposterous stories in the Bible were penned by Thomas Woolston in the late 1720s and Matthew Tindal in 1730. Henry St. John, Viscount Bolingbroke spent several years in exile in France, from 1714 to 1723, and again from 1735 to 1744, where his Deistic views were well known and influential, although it was only in 1754 that they posthumously appeared in print.

However, the Englishman who, unintentionally, did most to provide the Enlightenment in England and France with a theistic or deistic interpretation of God, was Isaac Newton.

ISAAC NEWTON
1642 to 1727

There was a massive irony in the fact that Newton's ideas should have played such an important part in underpinning a cavalier attitude to the Bible, because Newton himself accepted every word in scriptures as the word of God, and considered texts like the Book of Daniel and the Book of Revelations to be the literal truth. He had written a commentary on the Apocalypse, and had identified the Antichrist in that text as the Pope. Only when it came to post-Biblical teachings did he feel free to question doctrine. He believed that the doctrine of the Trinity, and even of God's incarnation in Christ, were superstitions which had been foisted onto Christianity by Athanasius and the various Church Councils. On all these matters he left writings which were far bulkier than his writings on science. He also left extensive manuscripts on Alchemy, and in his laboratory in Cambridge he hoped to find the elixir of life and the Philosopher's Stone which could transmute base metals into gold.

That side of his work is scarcely known today, and seems strangely at odds with his enduring achievements in science. He was one of the inventors of the Calculus,[2] and his work on optics (the composition of light) was path-breaking, but it was his discovery of the mathematical laws of gravitation that seemed to his contemporaries to have a significance that went far beyond the discovery itself.

That gravitation was involved in the movement of the stars had been guessed from about 1600 onwards, but no astronomer before Newton had been able to work out the mathematics of it. In his *Philosophiae Naturales Principia Mathematica,* published in 1687, Newton had accounted mathematically for the movements of the planets, the trajectory of comets and the movements of the tides.

In the Preface to that book he states that "all the difficulty of philosophy seems to consist in this – from the phenomena of motions to investigate the forces of nature, and then from these forces to demonstrate the other phenomena".

> On the face of it, this statement about "*all* the difficulties of philosophy" seems strange from someone who believed not in the God of Deism but in the God of Christianity; Newton seems to have made the distinction that had often been made between Theology and Philosophy. Statements about the *nature of God* are ultimately a matter of faith in revelation, but He invites us to use our reason to study of the *nature of the world* He has created, and holds out the assurance that that world is subject to laws which reason (here called philosophy) can discover.
>
> So, in the Preface he speaks as a philosopher and not as a theologian, but not all philosophers would have agreed with his conviction that all the difficulties of philosophy rest on an understanding of the phenomena of motions. Such a statement implies a wholly materialist view of *this* world. Philosophers like Descartes had seen immaterial minds as separate from material bodies. Therefore, they would certainly not agree that *all* the difficulties of philosophy relate to understanding the laws of motion. An understanding of motion may elucidate physical problems, but it will not help us to understand the mind or the soul, or how these interact with the body. Hobbes, on the other hand, had been an out and out materialist. He had described all mental activity in terms of motions triggering off other motions, in terms of appetites and aversions which are themselves movements towards or away from what gives us pleasure or pain, and this notion of mental activity was also shared by Locke, and after him by Berkeley and Hume.[3] It is their understanding of *this* world (as opposed to Descartes') that Newton also seems to accept.

He said that his work was only descriptive and that he knew nothing about the essential *nature* of gravitation. In the second edition of the Principia (1713) he added that "Gravity must be caused by an agent acting constantly according to certain laws; but whether this agent be material or immaterial I have left to the

2 See p. 247 above.

3 The earliest examples of that idea are with Democritus and the "atomists" of Ancient Greece – see p. 5 above. Newton recognized this: the passage I have quoted from his Preface actually begins with a recognition that the Ancients had used mechanics in the investigation of natural things. He points out that the medieval schoolmen had forgotten this, and that the moderns have once again become interested in the laws of mathematics which govern movement.

consideration of my readers." He would not advance a hypothesis on this matter: *"non fingo hypotheses"*. We should note that this famous phrase applied to his refusal to make an assumption in this particular case. He did not mean that he never made any hypotheses - no scientist could possibly do any research without constantly making and then testing hypotheses. He simply was not prepared to venture whether God was the immediate Creator of gravitation or whether later research might not discover an intermediate material explanation. If such an intermediate explanation were ever found, his religious faith told him that it would still be one for which God was ultimately responsible. Indeed, in that second edition he made clear his opinion that God had created the design of the world and the laws according to which the whole planetary machinery worked; He had spaced the celestial bodies sufficiently far apart so that gravity did not make them all coalesce in one gigantic mass; He had given the system its initial impetus although He must periodically correct certain irregularities which Newton had noticed in the solar system and He sustained the machine and thus prevented it from running down.

Alexander Pope wrote the famous couplet: "Nature and Nature's Laws lay hid in night. God said, 'Let Newton be!' and *all* was Light." The italics are mine, not those of Pope, who was a believing Catholic. Obviously, it was possible to be hugely excited by what Newton had demonstrated in the *Principia* and, at the same time, reject Newton's other work, notably his unquestioning acceptance of scriptures. This is what many theists and deists - in England, in France and indeed further afield - would do.

The Enlightenment was a European phenomenon; and if the sections that follow concentrate on its French exponents, it is because the French Enlightenment was so particularly eloquent and influential. Also, because French had become the *lingua franca* of the ruling classes on the continent [4], it was mainly through the French *philosophes* that Enlightenment ideas were diffused through continental Europe.

THE FRENCH PHILOSOPHES - GENERAL

England had acquired enormous prestige in France after the victory of England and Holland in the War of the Spanish Succession. It suggested to many Frenchmen that there was a great weakness behind the glitter of the ideas and institutions brought to their apogee by the *Roi Soleil*, and that they could learn from those of his enemies. English ideas, therefore, powerfully supported the reaction against the system of Louis XIV and reinforced the spirit that had begun to make itself felt in France itself by Bayle and Fontenelle. Locke and Newton had already made an impact in France: *"les Anglais pensent profondément"* wrote Fénelon, the future Archbishop of Cambrai, in 1693. In 1734, Voltaire, who had spent three years in England in exile, published his first important book, *Lettres sur les Anglais*, in which he acclaimed Locke and New-

4 When the Protestant countries rejected the authority of the Roman Catholic Church, Latin gradually ceased to be the international *lingua franca*, and because the France of Richelieu and Louis XIV had such great prestige, French gradually took the place of Latin. A landmark was the Treaty of Westphalia, which, in 1648, ended the Thirty Years' War. It was the first international treaty whose text was French and not Latin.

ton,[5] and praised English political and religious liberties. Montesquieu, too, had in 1731 returned from an eighteen months stay in England full of admiration for Locke and the British constitution.

We have already seen how Locke's political theory was interpreted in France,[6] we now have to see what Frenchmen (and, as mentioned above, many other Europeans) extrapolated from Newton's scientific theories.

Intuition had told the ancient Greeks that the world must be an orderly place. They had never been able to prove it, but they backed their intuition by using the same word, *cosmos*, for order and the universe. Later, theologians taught that God's actions must be rational, although, as human reason was too weak to understand the ways of God, this belief, had to be a matter of faith rather than something that could be proved. As science developed in the seventeenth century, human reason had come to understand more and more of the laws that governed the physical universe, and now Newton had *demonstrated* that even the movements of the stars can be explained by human reason.

Modern man, therefore, had done much better than the ancient Greeks and the Medievals, for these had had to rely on intuition and faith; what science they had was often pure guesswork, like their understanding of the humours, for example. Medieval thought had paid antiquity the compliment of incorporating much of Plato and Aristotle into its philosophy, and the Renaissance was so called because it claimed to be a rebirth of classical culture, and to draw more directly than the Middle Ages had done on the well of antiquity – its artists, architects and philosophers regarded themselves as humble pupils who aspired to match the perfection of classical achievements. The men of the French Enlightenment, however, thought that they had excelled their teachers and no longer needed to stand in such awe of the Ancients. The science of Antiquity did not deserve the name, and its philosophy was outdated. Aristotle was too closely identified with medieval scholasticism, and Plato's Idealism was overthrown by the fashionable Lockeian Empiricism, with its rejection of innate ideas and suspicion of metaphysics. Only in the field of aesthetics did the classical model still command allegiance. French dramatists still obeyed the unities of time, place and action which were supposed to have been laid down by Aristotle,[7] and in art and architecture there was still a respect for the varied vocabulary of Antiquity as opposed to what was considered to be the barbaric style of the Middle Ages.[8]

Even in literature, some late seventeenth- and early eighteenth-century authors wanted to emancipate themselves from classical models. The defenders of Antiquity fought back; much more than literature was felt to be at stake. From 1687 onwards, the Battle between the Ancients and the Moderns raged in

5 He even gave grudging praise to Shakespeare, even though Shakespeare's plays ignored all the classical canons of drama, which had been sanctified by Corneille and Racine, and which Voltaire held dear.

6 See p. 272 above.

7 The idea was that a great drama should ideally have only one plot (i.e. no subplots). Its actions should be confined to one day and to one location. Aristotle had indeed laid down that great drama must have unity of plot, and he had recommended unity of time (there were, in fact, classical dramas whose plot – perforce – extended over more than one day) but he had actually said nothing of unity of place.

8 It was Voltaire who coined the word "Gothic" for that style, because the Goths were the barbarians who had overthrown the Roman Empire.

France , with Claude Perrault and Bernard de Fontenelle championing the Moderns and Nicolas Boileau defending the Ancients. In England the dispute was known as the Battle of the Books, with Sir William Temple on the side of the Ancients and William Wotton championing the Moderns (1690 onwards). These arguments continued throughout the early part of the eighteenth century.

The Moderns, then, thought that what made them modern was that they had substituted reason for intuition, faith or guesswork. It had been found that reason could discover the natural laws underlying the physical world. What made the Enlightenment such an all-embracing intellectual movement was the assumption of the *philosophes* that natural laws were not confined to the physical world, but also underlie social phenomena. Reason could discover these laws, and once they were discovered, reason could shape human laws and institutions along rational lines. The *philosophes* asked whether the forces that had shaped laws and institutions in the past were rational, or whether they were merely based on what at best could be described as rationalizations of irrational traditions or superstitions. One often has the impression that their primary interests were political and social rather than philosophical. For them, philosophy was not an activity carried on as an end in itself in a metaphorical ivory tower; it was at least in part a weapon in their political struggle against aspects of the *Ancien Régime*. The *philosophes* were, in a word coined by their twentieth-century successors, *engagés* - committed to a political agenda - and their ideas made a powerful contribution to the crumbling of the old order and the inspiration of the French Revolution.

They were certainly not detached. They wrote with open partisanship, and they addressed themselves not to fellow philosophers so much as to educated laymen. In order to reach that public, they used wit (*esprit*) and a simple yet graceful and polished style. Their favourite media were not learned and lengthy treatises, but short essays, fables known as *contes*, imagined exchanges of letters, or subversive ideas slipped into the dictionaries they compiled.[9] We find little *gravitas* in their work. Instead, they frequently employed a tone of mockery or satire, and often spiced their writings with elegantly described indecencies. They were not much concerned with their own consistency. In one of his *contes*, Diderot has a character say, "I pursue ideas as young men pursue

9 The prototype had been Bayle's *Dictionnaire Historique et Critique* of 1687. Voltaire published a *Dictionnaire* philosophique in 1764. The most famous example was that great collaborative enterprise of the philosophes, the *Encyclopédie ou Dictionnaire Raisonné des Arts, des Sciences et des Métiers*, of which Diderot was the main editor. It was published between 1751 and 1780 and consisted of twenty-one volumes of text and twelve volumes of engraved plates. Inbetween a host of extremely useful, practical and politically quite innocuous entries, the editors slyly slipped in some very controversial ones; subversive asides would be inserted into straightforward explanations of a particular word's meaning. For example, in the article on the wafer (*pain béni*) written by Diderot, there was the calculation that about four millions livres a year was being spent on the wafers, and that this money could really be better spent; for good measure, the same article also calculated that all the candles lit in French churches probably cost something in the region of eight million livres. The article on Fanaticism opines that it had done much more harm to the world than impiety had ever done. Diderot's article on Refugees calculates the loss to the French economy caused by the emigration of many Huguenot refugees as the result of their persecution by Louis XIV, and de Jaucourt's article on Jews deplored the persecution to which they had been, and were still being, subjected. The article on the Press demands that it should be free. The article on *Egalité* begins by discussing the word in its mathematical and scientific meaning, then describes what it signifies when used in connection with voice production, and then goes on to a discussion of natural equality in political thought, which clearly expresses a democratic position.

loose women". The author could have said it of himself. He was quite capable of extolling the idea of the Noble Savage in one book (*Supplément au voyage de Bougainville*, 1772), yet, in the very next year (in *Jacques le Fataliste*, 1773) saying that only reason prevents man from giving way to his natural wickedness.

All this is anathema to the academic philosopher, and it accounts for the scanty treatment, or even total exclusion, of the *philosophes* from some histories of philosophy, like that of Bertrand Russell, for example. If they were not very original thinkers, nevertheless, they popularized certain philosophical positions. They rejected supernatural and metaphysical explanations. Most of them were Deists, some were Theists and a very few, like Holbach, were actually Atheists. In epistemology they followed Locke's Empiricism: all ideas are derived from sensations. They adopted Hobbes' materialism - one of La Mettrie's books was actually called *L'Homme Machine* (1748). They believed that our behaviour is wholly determined by the mechanical seeking of pleasure and avoidance of pain; and they saw no discontinuities between the physical and the mental aspects of man, nor, for that matter, between animal and human nature.

Natural laws governed not only the physical world, but the moral world also, and they could be discovered by Reason: our morality should be based not on arbitrary religious commands, or on fear of hellfire, but on Reason.

> Some people claim, even today, that religion is a sounder foundation for morality than reason, and that a decline in religious belief increases amoral or immoral behaviour in society. Reason, after all, comes up with different answers according to whoever is doing the reasoning, and some people are not so much reasoning as rationalizing. Where their rationalisation seems to justify (to them) indulging in sinful conduct, it would actually be desirable that they should be held in check by a wholesome fear of God's wrath. In his old age, even Voltaire came to the conclusion that religion was necessary as a social discipline,[10] at least for the uneducated people who could not, he thought, use their reason properly. The "enlightened" Emperor Joseph II would tolerate all religions in his empire except Deism, for this taught that, though God had created the world, He was no longer interested in how His creation behaved. Joseph knew that his police could not keep an eye on all his subjects and he wanted them to think that God could see what they were doing and would punish the evil doers. But the argument could be extended: the reason of all humans, of the educated and the uneducated alike, was, according the rationalist David Hume, always the slave of the passions, so a morality which purported to be based on reason was ultimately only serving our passions.[11]
>
> The *philosophes* might have replied that that was equally true of religious commands. Most of them maintained that it was not Man who was created in God's image, but God who is always being created in Man's image, and God's commandments, which are actually devised by human beings, serve what are, whether by way of reasoning or rationalisation, human passions.

It was reason, the *philosophes* believed, that worked out what the consequences of a particular action would be in terms of pleasure and pain. Where religious preachers stressed the duty of man in this world so that felicity should accrue to

10 See more on this on p. 320 below.

11 See p. 292 above.

them in the next, the *philosophes* believed that all humans naturally, necessarily *and rightfully* sought pleasure and happiness in this world. The doctrine that w *should* maximize pleasure would later be called Hedonism.[12] The pursuit of happiness was, as the Founding Fathers of the United States would proclaim in the Declaration of Independence (1776), one of the inalienable Rights of Man. The state, therefore, has an obligation to maximize the happiness of its people. Reason will also tell us that people are happiest when they enjoy Liberty. Governments should therefore impose the minimum of restraint.

This applied to economics also. Most of the *philosophes* espoused the ideas of the Physiocrats. These were the followers of François Quesnay (1694 to 1774). His *Tableau Economique* anticipated the criticism of mercantilist restrictions on trade and advocated the *laissez-faire* free-trade economics later proposed so famously in Adam Smith's *Wealth of Nations* (1776).[13] The *philosophes* accepted the arguments of the Physiocrats, partly because they agreed that these restrictions were inefficient deformations of the economy (efficiency being one of the pragmatic tests they applied to any social arrangement), but also on the basis that anything that limited freedom (here the freedom of traders) was regrettable on ideological grounds.

The *philosophes* thought that reason would also make us understand that it was in our own enlightened self-interest to treat each other with humanity and to cooperate peacefully with one another.

> Peaceful cooperation is clearly of great benefit to society in general, but an individual may not always agree that he should behave in a cooperative manner. How, for instance, would one appeal to the reasoning of a successful criminal that it was not in his own interests to prey on his fellow citizens? One could show him that society would break down if everyone behaved as he did and that therefore he would suffer along with the rest, but he might answer that his reason showed him both that everyone did *not* behave like him, and also how he could best enrich himself. He would say that *he* would not suffer from any breakdown in society. Even if society were to break down completely, he would continue to flourish – he is skilled, ruthless and better equipped than his fellow citizens, because he can use his reason unfettered by moral inhibitions. Only the certainty of inescapable punishment could have any effect on the reasoning of such a man.

The *philosophes* had a theory of punishment also. Reason would instruct us that, while its purpose should be to protect society by deterrence and reform, nothing rational was gained by a vindictive or cruel penal policy. They were all disciples of Cesare Beccaria (1738 to 1794) whose book *Of Crimes and Punishments* (1764) immediately established itself as a classic of penal reform.

The *philosophes* believed that it is only because so many societies are not rational that in practice moral codes are not the same throughout the world but are relative. (This at least is how they rather uneasily married their belief in relativ-

12 Judging by their portraits, they were generally happy individuals. Whereas seventeenth-century philosophers had themselves painted looking stern, the portraits we have of Voltaire, Diderot and d'Alembert mostly show them smiling.

13 A crucial difference between the Physiocrats and Adam Smith was that the former believed that agriculture was the most valuable of economic activities and, while they supported free trade in manufactured goods, they expected governments to protect agricultural interests.

ism with their confidence that reason could discover the presumably invariable laws of nature that governed morality.) A rational approach to politics will judge institutions and legislation by the degree to which they maximize the happiness of the people – the idea that would later be called Utilitarianism.

All these were proper philosophical ideas. The *philosophes* saw their promotion as a crusade. They wanted the Light of the Enlightenment (*Éclaircissement, Aufklärung*) to dispel the Darkness of Obscurantism. Every belief was to be tested by reason; no belief that could not stand up to that test commanded respect. Foremost among their targets were the fables and miracles taught by the clergy - these were sheer superstition. Worse was the dogmatism which brooked no rational debate, the imposition of these superstitions by brainwashing or by force, the fanaticism, censorship and persecution to which they gave rise. The *philosophes* were intensely anticlerical.

The clergy not only exercised a stultifying power, it also enjoyed great privileges, and privilege, whether of the clergy or the nobility, could not be justified by reason and was therefore another target of the *philosophes*. In France, the nobles and clergy enjoyed extensive tax-exemptions; if a commoner wanted to take an aristocrat to court, there was no equality before the law. There could be no rational defence for such arrangements. They were resented by the growing middle class, which did not enjoy exemption, and it was manifestly unjust that the wealthiest in the land escaped a burden which, therefore, fell with crushing weight on the poor. If the privileged orders called tradition in aid, that cut no ice with the *philosophes*. They had no respect for traditions as such, only for those which were rational, corresponded to natural justice, could be justified by their overall results, or contributed to overall efficiency.

Certainly mere birthright gave no title to power. This applied not only to the nobility, but to the monarchy also. The *philosophes* did not accept that kings had absolute power by divine right or hereditary succession. Governments, too, had to justify themselves by producing enlightened policies. Beyond that, the *philosophes* had no common stance about the best form of government. Some believed in contract theories of one kind or another as the source of authority; others were more interested in the fruits than in the origins of government. We shall see that Voltaire, for instance, seemed prepared to back any autocracy, however it had arisen, as long as it was an enlightened one. Montesquieu thought that an enlightened aristocracy would be the best system of government. Others argued that the English system, in which it was believed that there was a balance of power between monarchy, aristocracy and commoners, would produce the most enlightened results. Rousseau, who at least set out as a *philosophe*, came to put his trust in the absolute sovereignty of the people.

One reason that made Rousseau part company with the *philosophes* was that he revelled in emotions, whereas they were suspicious of the passions which so easily overwhelmed reason. *"Surtout, messieurs, pas trop de zèle"* ("above all, gentlemen, let us not have too much zeal") advised Voltaire. He knew how religious zeal in particular had led to intolerance and civil wars. Critic though he was of the *Ancien Régime*, he would have been appalled by the ferocious political zeal that would lead to such violence in the French Revolution.

Like all the *philosophes*, Voltaire believed that change could, and should, be brought about by education. Education would eliminate prejudice (the word after all, means judging before reasoning) and superstition. They were essentially optimists, not in the sense (which was mocked by Voltaire in *Candide*) that all *was* for the best in the best of all possible worlds, but in the sense that everything *could* be made better, that education and wise government could and should improve human life. They thought they knew how this should be done, and they had great confidence in their own ideology, so much so that their opponents referred to them in a derogatory way as *idéologues* (as if their opponents - and indeed all governments - did not have an ideology of their own which they, too, want to inculcate in the schools!)

In the French educational system, there is an interesting spin-off of the *philosophes'* desire to teach enlightenment philosophy in the schools. In France, philosophy is today a compulsory subject in the examination for the *Baccalauréat*, which is taken at the end of secondary schooling. In English secondary schools, philosophy was not taught at all until fairly recently, and even now is studied by only a tiny handful of students. The reason is probably more an English distrust for theorizing than a commitment to Plato's view that philosophy should not be taught to anyone under the age of thirty – below that age, he thought, students would be too immature, and would probably give passionate and radical interpretations of the philosophy they studied. As the French *philosophes* were rather radical themselves, they did not have this distrust of the young.

One can criticize the *philosophes* for seeming to have no conception of a pessimism that was based not on the religious ideas of Original Sin, but on a dark secular view of man such as we will find in Schopenhauer, Nietzsche, or Freud. Their warning that emotions could so easily overwhelm reason was sound enough, but they seem not to have understood that humans have emotional needs and that Man cannot live by reason alone.

Reason can destroy so much of what humans cherish. Many people do not feel that every tradition must justify itself by reason; they like ritual and ceremonial, and they fear that if there is a wholesale demolition of traditions on the grounds that they are not rational, an essential part of the fabric of society may be destroyed. The ideological blueprint which takes its place (and is often forcibly imposed, as it was by the Jacobin heirs of the Enlightenment during the French Revolution) may itself be flawed and could easily become a strait-jacket which constrains human nature.

The cult of efficiency is also often defended on the grounds of reason, yet efficiency can be bought at too great a price if it tramples over too many human needs and interests. Free trade, for example, may be more efficient than protectionism; it may lower prices and increase trade and prosperity. However, it often destroys the livelihood of entire communities.

As Pascal had said (and not regretfully): "The Heart hath its Reason which Reason doth not know".

CLAUDE ADRIEN HELVÉTIUS
1715 to 1771

Helvétius' *De l'Esprit* (1758) was one of the most characteristic products of the French Enlightenment. His father had come from Switzerland and had settled in France where he had become physician to the Queen. This helped his son (one of twenty siblings) to land the profitable job of Farmer-General. He met all the leading *philosophes* and was soon a member of their circle. In due course ,he and his attractive wife presided generously over their own *salon,* which became a focus for the stars of the French Enlightenment. By the age of thirty-six he had accumulated an immense fortune and was able to retire from his post to devote himself entirely to philosophy.

He incorporated both Hobbes and Locke into his thinking. From Hobbes he took the idea that our actions are *wholly* dictated by what we *perceive* to bring pleasure and avoid pain. Therefore, all human actions are totally egoistic. If we engage in what we call virtuous or altruistic activities, it is because the sacrifices they would entail are less painful to us than the guilt we would have if we acted otherwise. Whether we have guilt feelings or not in turn depends entirely on the way we have been conditioned by our personal and individual environment: real choice does not come into it, and Helvétius denied that we have any free will.

From Locke, he took the notion that all ideas begin from sensation and experience. All men, he believed, were endowed by nature with equal *mental* capacities.

If, as Locke had argued, minds are *tabulae rasae* at birth, like blank sheets of paper, then these blank sheets would all be the same, ready to receive whatever the sensations and experiences might inscribe upon them. Helvétius did not seem to consider that even blank pieces of paper are not necessarily the same. Some are so smooth that they hardly absorb ink; others quickly soak up whatever is written upon them. Leaving analogies aside, he thought that, genetically (a concept, of course, which he did not know) our mental equipment is identical. It is now quite clear that it is not: some individuals are genetically quicker and abler than others to learn and to handle ideas – in other words, some are genetically more intelligent than others.

In some quarters this is not regarded as a politically correct idea, and it is particularly unacceptable to those quarters if applied to make statistically significant statements about groups of people (Asians, West Indians, Whites etc.) Because some people draw dangerous political or social conclusions from scientific statements about genetic differences between individuals or (on a statistical basis) between groups, the statements themselves are deemed incorrect. However, science itself is value-free. What is not value-free are the uses we make of scientific information in our social attitudes or arrangements. Just as the knowledge of nuclear energy can be used for good or for ill, so can knowledge about genetic differences. We use it ill if we claim that it justifies racist attitudes and behaviour; we use it well if we think about ways in which we can help genetically "disadvantaged" people to overcome either the disadvantages or the consequences to which it might lead. If it is illegitimate to draw racist conclusions from genetic data, it is equally illegitimate to draw conclusions about the science from whatever political ideology we may hold.

The political ideology of the *philosophes* was the admirable one that all men should have equal rights, and I think that made Helvétius in his time (and other ideologues since then) look for, or at least accept, a "scientific" (but actually pseudo-scientific) basis for his ideology.

Helvétius goes on to argue that, if we are all born with equal mental capacities, then the differences between individuals and between nations are the result, not of natural inequalities, but of the different environmental influences to which they have been subjected. Human progress therefore depends entirely on the social, legislative and, above all, educational environment.

> The educational environment begins in the home, of course, but many homes, for one reason or another, do not provide a good educational environment. It may be because the parents are actually bad parents, or because they are ignorant and superstitious. This is not uncommon in twentieth-century society, but in the eighteenth century, the problem was very much worse: only a very small proportion of society had any significant degree of education at all and this was, in the opinion of the *philosophes*, under the influence of the clergy. The *philosophes* did not believe that the clergy helped to educate people, on the contrary, in Helvétius' opinion, it was in the interest of the clergy to keep the people ignorant.
>
> One sometimes hears the point being made that pupils' shortcomings cannot be blamed entirely on inadequate schools, and that the home has to bear the main responsibility. It is, of course, true that the home has such a responsibility, however, there are only a very few measures that the state can take to help parents to be good parents, such as giving financial help to enable one parent to stay at home instead of having to go out to work. That may help parents to provide a good educational background for their child, but it is not a guarantee that they will do so. Wherever for whatever reason the home is deficient, it is the schools and only the schools that can help the children, not only to become good citizens themselves, but in due course to become parents who *can* provide a good basic educational environment for the next generation. This is why the *philosophes* were constantly stressing the need for good education in the schools: get that right, and the whole society can be put on the way to progress. No other reforms can compare with educational reform for long-term effectiveness.

The task of education was therefore to condition us to value those actions we call virtuous or altruistic and to inculcate guilt about actions we call selfish. To bring this conditioning about, we do not have to resort to what we today call "brainwashing". Indeed, as an anticlerical, Helvétius condemned the clergy for brainwashing their flock from childhood onwards with superstitious fears of Hell and hopes of Heaven.

The Church condemned his book, and the *parlement* had it burnt in 1759. It would have gone worse with Helvétius himself had he not, in a second edition, printed an abject retraction, professed his full adherence to Christian teaching and deplored the perverse and pernicious influence of the *philosophes*. He published no more in his lifetime, but reiterated the condemned ideas in a book – *De l'Homme, de ses Facultés et de son Éducation* – which appeared a year after his death.

Instead of playing on people's superstitions to condition them, Helvétius thought that we should encourage them to think for themselves and to use their reason. No one today would argue with this, but we may have some doubts about the next stage in his argument. The use of reason, he believed, would show individuals that their own happiness depended on that of the society at large more specifically – picking up a phrase which had first been coined by the Irish philosopher Francis Hutcheson in 1725 – he announced that we should aim for "the greatest happiness of the greatest number". All laws should aim for this "single principle – the utility of the public", which "contains all morality and legislation". These phrases would become famous when Jeremy Bentham adopted and explicated them thirty years later.[14]

> We have seen in the last section that the use of reason alone will not convince a clever criminal that his happiness depends on the happiness of the society he victimizes. To make men behave morally, we need to do more than train their reasoning, we need to train their moral sense. The *philosophes* tended to assume that the latter is based on the former, whereas in fact they are two distinct forms of education.
>
> In its best form, moral education is a training and heightening of the empathy for the suffering of other people ("how would you feel if someone stole from you?", for example). This was the view of David Hume.[15] There is a less perfect form which has in it an element of conditioning by precept and by example so that, without being able to reason it out for ourselves, we feel guilty if we offend against it. Because we approve of the end result, we may not apply to this the pejorative name of "brainwashing" – and yet the technique of this less perfect form is not so very different from it.

Helvétius believed that the principle of the greatest happiness of the greatest number required a fairly equal diffusion of wealth. This would never be possible in a society whose primary aims were mercantile or commercial, for such economies were bound to produce great concentrations of wealth. Instead, he wanted an economy based on widespread land ownership, with a penal taxation system that would prevent the extension of estates beyond a certain point.

The Durants say that, although he is little known today, "educated Frenchmen, in the third quarter of the eighteenth century, ranked Helvétius as almost the equal of Voltaire, Rousseau and Diderot, and gave his first book such popularity and acclaim as was hardly accorded to any other volume of the age".[16] Unlike his contemporaries, he had written only two books. These were all of a piece, systematic, and he did not contradict himself. The same could not be said of the more prolific and diffuse writers, who did not seem to worry unduly over the inconsistencies that can easily be found over the long series of their works. Yet, it is they whose fame has endured – none more so than the greatest icon of the Age of Enlightenment – Voltaire.

VOLTAIRE
1694 to 1778

The *engagement* of the *philosophes* with the political and social issues of their time is strikingly illustrated in the life of François-Marie Arouet Jr who, at the age of twenty-four, assumed the name of De Voltaire, an anagram of AROVET L(e) J(eune). He first used that name as the author of his earliest and immedi-

14 See p. 421 below.

15 See p. 296 above.

16 W. & A. Durant – *The Story of Civilization – The Age of Voltaire* – Vol. III, p. 689.

ately successful play, *Oedipe* (1718). He was lionized for it in aristocratic circles, where he was already appreciated by some as a disrespectful wit, a mocker of political and religious conventions and a composer of lampoons. The appreciation was not universal; the Chevalier de Rohan, effete scion of a famous aristocratic family, made disparaging remarks about the presumptuous "de" in Voltaire's new name. Voltaire then circulated a lampoon about his detractor; and the Chevalier retaliated by looking on while six of his footmen beat up the young upstart to teach him a lesson. Voltaire challenged the nobleman to a duel, and for this effrontery the De Rohan family had the commoner committed to the Bastille. After a fortnight he was released on condition that he left France for a while. He went to England (1726) and stayed there for three years.

We can imagine how this episode helped to shape Voltaire's attitude towards the privileges of the aristocracy. In England, he found a society which was far less snobbish and far more tolerant than that of France. There was equality before the law, irrespective of status. The English nobles did not claim tax exemptions, nor did they profess, as so many French aristocrats did, to look down on money-making as a sordid activity. Commerce flourished as a result, and its creators were well represented in Parliament, and although the English were "a foolish people which believes in God and trusts in ministers", at least every kind of belief in God was tolerated. Voltaire came across Locke's epistemological theories and found them superior to those of Descartes, and when he discovered Newton's physics, he was immediately aware of their philosophical implications. After his return to France, he published his favourable impressions of England in a book which first appeared in English in 1733 under the name of *Letters Concerning the English Nation*, and later in French as *Lettres Philosophiques*. When it appeared in France, it was burnt by the public executioner as "the greatest danger for religion and public order", and, to escape arrest, Voltaire went abroad, to Germany and then to the dukedom of Lorraine, until he was given permission to return to France in 1736.

The *Philosophes* and the "Enlightened" Despots

Voltaire then began a correspondence with the Crown Prince of Prussia, the future Frederick the Great. Frederick espoused the progressive ideas of the *philosophes*, both because he was an intelligent young man who was fascinated by the *avant garde* ideas of his time, and because he was in rebellion against everything that his boorish father, Frederick William I, stood for. In his youthful idealism, the Crown Prince composed a political tract, the *Anti-Machiavel*. It criticized Machiavelli's *The Prince* for having been concerned merely with building up, as an end in itself, the personal power, mastery and security of the ruler.[17] After he became king, Frederick would define himself as the first *servant*[18] of the state. If a ruler is interested only in his own power ,but does not put the interests of the state before anything else, then he is merely a selfish tyrant.[19]

17 This is rather unfair to Machiavelli – see p. 178 above.

18 *domestique* – Frederick wrote in French.

19 See p. 180 above. Those pages suggest that this was not a fully justified criticism of Machiavelli. Machiavelli was a patriot who attributed the weakness of Italy to the lack of civic virtue among his Italian contemporaries. In the absence of such virtue, he thought that the interests of the state required the

There were also conventional passages in the *Anti-Machiavel* praising the blessings of peace.

Frederick had been in correspondence with Voltaire since 1736, and in 1739 he invited Voltaire's opinions on his manuscript. Voltaire was not only flattered, but thrilled that, with such views, the future King of Prussia looked like becoming a philosopher king, an enlightened ruler who would put the ideas of the *philosophes* into practice. He saw the book through the press, and it was published in September 1740, four months after Frederick II's accession.

The King promptly suppressed the publication in Prussia. Once in power, he showed himself to be a disciple, rather than a critic, of Machiavelli. True, he would always claim that he was acting in the interests of the state rather than in his own personal interest,[20] and he scorned the idea that he was king by Divine Right. As the first servant of the state, he would never have claimed, as Louis XIV had so famously done, that *"l'état, c'est moi"*. No, Frederick the Great believed in *La Raison* – but in politics that meant *Raison d'État*. Where the interests of the state were concerned, there could be no moral constraints, neither for him nor for his fellow "enlightened" despots, Catherine the Great and Joseph II.

These rulers did not even trouble to conceal the nakedness of their aggression with any moral fig-leaves. In December 1740, Frederick launched a war against Maria Theresa, who had succeeded to the Habsburg throne two months earlier. He had inherited a powerful army and a strong state and he believed that Maria Theresa had neither. It was a good opportunity to seize the rich province of Silesia. When his ministers asked him what lawful claim he was asserting to this territory, he replied, "That is for you to work out: I have already given the order to march." This is a striking contrast to the behaviour of Louis XIV. Louis had been just as aggressive as Frederick when he had invaded the Spanish Netherlands in 1667, but before embarking on this campaign, he first set his lawyers to producing an elaborate and not totally hollow justification for his claim to that territory. As one of his nobles, the Duc de la Rochefoucauld had sardonically observed, "Hypocrisy is the tribute that Vice pays to Virtue". The "enlightened" rulers did not bother with such a tribute; they quite openly espoused the idea that might is right. The example that Frederick the Great had set in Silesia would be followed within a generation when Prussia, Russia and Austria carved up Poland between them without the slightest legal justification, and simply because they were strong and Poland was weak. Again, Frederick made no bones about it, "Catherine and I are simply brigands", he admitted, and he jeered at the fact that the more morally sensitive Maria Theresa had been forced to join in the plunder.[21]

That, then, was how Frederick the Great interpreted the *philosophes'* prescription of "enlightened self-interest". It showed up on an international scale the problem with the *philosophes'* bland assumption that it was in an individual's

rule of a strong and ruthless prince as distinctly a second best. But as the book was also written to restore Machiavelli to the favour of the Medici ruler of Florence, it deals more fully with the technique than with the purpose of effective government.

20 He genuinely despised royal pomp and ceremony. As often as he could, he wore simple clothes, and once described a crown as "merely a hat that lets in the rain".

21 *"Elle pleurait quand elle prenait"*, he said caustically. (She was weeping whist she was helping herself.)

enlightened self-interest to behave virtuously and peacefully.[22] What attitude were the *philosophes* to take when the philosopher princes behaved in such a ruthless manner? Neither Voltaire nor Diderot showed up very well under the challenge – they were too flattered by the attentions the princes paid to them. So Voltaire wrote a poem to Frederick in which he deplored the carnage with which Frederick had defiled the German lands, but ended weakly, "I pardon all, if only you will sigh."[23] After the Partitions of Poland, Diderot dealt in a similar way with his benefactress Catherine the Great. He assumed, he told her, that she had no choice but to take part in the Partition as, if she did not join in, the other powers would go ahead without her.[24]

At least Diderot told her without mincing words that the draft which she had circulated of her intended domestic reforms left her despotism untouched (though, he added, she was not a tyrant), that he disapproved of despotism, and that there "can be no true legislator other than the people". Voltaire never made such an unqualified rejection of despotism.

Voltaire and Montesquieu had found that, in England, a mixed government worked very well. The Baron de Montesquieu thought that it amounted to government largely by the nobility. The King needed to work through Parliament, which consisted of two houses; the House of Lords was made up of nobles and the House of Commons was practically controlled by them because their unchallenged local influence or the ownership of rotten and pocket boroughs enabled them to place their own relatives or other nominees into parliamentary seats. There was, therefore, a balance of power between, on the one hand, the nobles who controlled the legislature, and, on the other, the royal executive. The result was a healthy, free and prosperous society that Montesquieu admired so much that wanted to apply the same formula to France. His thesis became known as the *thèse nobiliaire*, and was vigorously propounded by his fellow aristocrats in France. The trouble was that most French aristocrats, though they might be *salon philosophes*, were actually quite unenlightened when it came to political reforms. They clung to their tax exemptions, tended to

22 see p. 309 above.

23 "*Je vous pardonne tout, si vous en gémissez.*"

24 Actually, it was Catherine who had started the trouble by sending her troops into Poland, which was rebelling against being a Russian satellite. Prussia and Austria then threatened to ally against Russia, and Catherine could only buy them off by suggesting the First Partition (1772). In 1765 she had given considerable and tactful help to Diderot. When she heard that he was in financial difficulties, she bought up his beloved library for 15,000 *livres*, and appointed him as its librarian with a generous annual salary during his lifetime, after which the books would go to St Petersburg. Charming though the gesture was, it was cheap at the price. The enlightened despots knew how influential the philosophes were, and how their own praises would be sung by them throughout Europe. Diderot at least continued to criticize her domestic measures as not being sufficiently enlightened. In 1767 she drew up draft instructions (*Nakaz*) for domestic reforms. These cited Montesquieu 250 times and Beccaria 100 times. She sent the draft to Frederick the Great, to Voltaire, and to Diderot. Frederick and Voltaire approved of them, but Diderot thought the reforms did not go far enough: why, for example, did she not introduce an elective legislature, and above all, why did she not abolish serfdom? Catherine could never venture to antagonize her serf-owning nobles to that extent, and she later reported having told Diderot, with her usual charm: "In all your plans of reform, you forget the difference between our positions. All your work is done upon paper, which does not mind what you do to it: it is all of a piece, pliable, and presenting no obstacles either to your person or to your imagination. But I, poor Empress, must work upon the human skin, which is terribly ticklish and irritable." It is a gentle hint that, in her opinion, even philosophers who were "engagés" and concerned themselves with practical political and social matters really dwelt in ivory towers.

look down on commercial wealth and obstructed all attempts by the King's ministers to introduce reforms.

This is why Voltaire thought that the English formula would never work in France. France did best under a strong monarch. If there were to be any reforms in France, they would have to be introduced by an enlightened despot who would first have to break the power of the privileged orders (the nobility and the clergy). This view became known as the *thèse royale*, and it was espoused by some of Louis XV's ministers, notably by the Marquis d'Argenson (Minister of Foreign Affairs from 1745 to 1748), Jean-Baptiste Machault (Comptroller-General of Finances from 1749 to 1757) and René Nicolas Maupeou (Chancellor of France, 1768 to 1774). Unfortunately, Louis XV was a weak man, easily influenced by the nobles at court and quite unsuited either to be an enlightened despot himself or to give consistent support to ministers who wanted to strengthen the power of the executive against the privileged orders. This made Voltaire particularly admire those rulers like Frederick the Great who he thought showed determination to make domestic reforms and showed an active interest in the ideas of the *philosophes*. Even an unenlightened despot like Louis XIV had much to be said for him. While staying at Potsdam from 1750 to 1753 as the guest of Frederick the Great, Voltaire completed and published his book *Le Siècle de Louis XIV* (1751). In it, he praised the Sun King for reducing the political power of the aristocracy (though at the cost of leaving them their tax privileges) and for his munificent support of the arts and letters. Under Louis, he wrote, "the State became a perfect whole with all lines leading to the centre".

Of course, Voltaire's praise of Louis XIV's despotism could not be unqualified: the blackest mark against that king was his religious intolerance and the persecution of the Huguenots. Not that Voltaire sympathized with the Huguenot religion – all sects were ridiculous in their superstitions and credulities. Both Huguenots and Catholics believed in the divinity of Jesus; Voltaire did not. Neither, of course, did the Jews, but he scorned them too, for their belief in the absurdities he detected in the Old Testament and for religious observances which he thought even more bizarre than those of the Christians. Having devoted some pages in the *Dictionnaire philosophique* to a diatribe against the Jews (laced with the crude stereotyping that were then the common coin in Christian Europe) he concluded, "Still, we ought not to burn them." That expressed, in a condescending form, the opinion which he expressed more famously when writing to an opponent, "I detest what you say, but I will defend with my life your right to say it." A religion may be absurd, but it must be tolerated – not least because persecution is itself carried out in the name of equally absurd traditions.

Voltaire was a passionate crusader against religious fanaticism. This man, who urged that a wise man should never become too emotional, claimed to run a fever every year on the anniversary of the St Bartholomew's Massacre of the Huguenots (1572) and his rage against injustices committed in the name of religion was unquenchable. More than on any other issue, he showed his *engagement* in his crusades to right such wrongs. In 1730, the Church refused a Christian burial to the great actress Adrienne Lecouvreur, because it held that her profession had rendered her unworthy of it. The body, which had delighted Voltaire and not a few of the theatre-going clergy, was buried under quicklime in unhallowed ground – a monstrous contrast with the burial in Westminster Abbey that year of the actress Anne Oldfield, as Voltaire pointed out in a scathing poem. In 1768, after having mobilized an international campaign of indignation, he secured posthumous acquittal of the Huguenot Jean Calas, who had been broken on the wheel in 1765 after a wrongful conviction for murdering his son, who had converted to Catholicism. In the following year, Voltaire took up the case of the Chevalier de la Barre, who had been convicted of blasphemy in 1766 and had his tongue torn out before he was executed and his corpse burnt together with his copy of Voltaire's *Dictionnaire philosophique*. Voltaire had briefly fled abroad for a few days, but soon returned and launched a campaign against this latest example of infamy. "*Écrasez l'infâme!*" is the battle cry he had coined some years before, and which he constantly repeated for the rest of his life.

Sometimes, it looked as if he felt worn out with *engagement*. In *Candide*, written in 1758 when he was sixty-four, we have a hint of this. After having wittily excoriated the follies and wickedness of mankind, it seems as if he felt that it was vain to keep on struggling against it. His *alter ego* Martin is made to say, "Let us work without arguing: it is the only way to make life bearable",[25] and the book ends with Candide's agreement, "We must cultivate our (own) garden."[26] Voltaire himself, however, did nothing of the sort: he fought the campaigns about the cases of Calas and de la Barre several years after *Candide*.

In 1766, at the age of seventy-two, he wrote a work significantly called *The Ignorant Philosopher*. He felt that for all his pursuit of philosophy, he was not sure of any of the answers, "If you tell me that I have taught you nothing, remember that I set out by informing you that I am ignorant." Here he harks back to Socrates, but he also affirms, with the Greek sage, that the unexamined life is not worth living – "My baffled curiosity is ever insatiable." He might have been happier if he had not thought so much, but, "I concluded that although we may set a great value upon happiness, we set a still greater value upon reason. But ... I still thought that there was great madness in preferring reason to happiness."[27]

Voltaire hovered between Theism and Deism. In *The Ignorant Philosopher* his assertion that there is a Supreme Intelligence which governs the universe does not go beyond Deism. If he ever believed in Theism – that there is a God who cares for his creation and to whom it makes sense to pray – that belief was badly shaken by the Lisbon Earthquake on All Saints Day 1755, when thousands died in the midst of their worship as the roofs of the churches crashed down upon them. How could one continue to believe in a caring God when He allowed His faithful worshippers to die in the very act of worshipping him? Surely this cannot be, as Leibniz had argued, the best of all possible worlds, and Voltaire would famously satirize this "optimism" in *Candide* (1758). In his famous *Poème sur le désastre de Lisbon* (1755) Voltaire's Theism only just survived as he embraced a kind of stoic acceptance of God's will: "What then is needful to us

25 "*Travaillons sans raisonner, dit Martin, c'est le seul moyen de rendre la vie supportable.*"

26 "*Il faut cultiver notre jardin.*"

27 This sentence comes from a fable he had written in 1761: *L'Histoire d'un bon Brahmin.*

mortal men?/O mortals, we must suffer, must submit,/Must worship, must have hope - and die."[28]

"Powerful God, I believe!" he once exclaimed, prostrating himself on the top of a hill from which he had watched the sun rise over a glorious panorama, but then, for the benefit of his companion, he added, "As for monsieur the Son and madame his Mother, that's a different story." (1774). On his deathbed, when asked to acknowledge the divinity of Christ, he is said to have exclaimed, "in the name of *God*, monsieur, do not speak to me of that *man*!" but in 1760 he erected a church on his property at Ferney, although his own name figured in larger letters than that of the Deity in the inscription over its entrance:

DEO EREXIT
VOLTAIRE

By that time, the landlord of Ferney had come to see religion as a necessary social discipline, even "if God did not exist, we would have to invent Him" he wrote famously in 1769. In 1764 he resorted once more to one of the favourite means which the *philosophes* used to spread their ideas; he published another *Dictionnaire philosophique*. Here, in an entry on the subject of Hell, he suggested that, though philosophers could not believe in it, it was no bad thing that ordinary people should fear it so as to restrain them from evildoing. As Durant comments, "After preaching a religion free from fables, the great sceptic ended preaching the worst fable of all."[29]

The fact is that, towards the end of his life, Voltaire seemed to see almost more danger in atheism than in Christianity. He began to see some good in a clergy which would teach morality; he referred to Jesus as "my brother" and even as "my master". From 1760 onwards he attended Mass every Sunday in his church. In 1769 he signed a document that he wished to die in the Catholic religion, and, strangest of all, he became a lay Capuchin friar in 1770. It is not surprising that the more radical *philosophes* thought that he had betrayed them. Many of them were now disciples of Holbach, who had gone beyond Theism and Deism and was an uncompromising Atheist.

BARON D'HOLBACH
1723 to 1789

Holbach was born in Germany to a very rich family. He settled in France in 1748 and spent some of his immense inherited wealth on buying a French aristocratic title and organizing, on two days every week, the most important anticlerical *salon* in Paris and in his country villa. Like his close and equally wealthy friend Helvétius, he was a charming host, and this attracted many *philosophes* to his table, like Voltaire and Diderot, in whose own work the Baron's ruthless consistency was often conspicuously absent and who would shrink from the radicalism and atheism which Holbach expounded so delightfully.

28 *"Que faut-il, O mortels? Mortels, il faut souffrir, se soumettre, adorer, espérer, et mourir."* The fact that we have to adore the Intelligence that governs the universe does not necessarily imply that the Intelligence cares whether we do adore it, or not.

29 Durant - *The Story of Civilization - The Age of Voltaire* - Vol. III, p. 748.

Holbach's best known book, prudently published under another name, was *Le Système de la Nature* (1770). Helvétius had concentrated his attack on the clergy, but had (perhaps only out of fear) professed his full adherence to the Christian faith. Holbach scoffed at all religious beliefs. At worst, he thought, they were based on fear, superstition and the inability to face Nature's indifference to suffering. At best, it was the making of hypotheses for who might be the architect of what we call Creation. Like his disciple, the scientist De Laplace, Holbach would have said that he had no need of such a hypothesis. Nor would Holbach have any truck with Spinoza's equation between God and Nature (*Deus sive Natura*). For Holbach, this was merely an attempt to anthropomorphize or pantheize Nature. Nature consists entirely of matter and motion; the causes that operate in it come wholly from within itself and not from anything outside of it. It is entirely indifferent to what we call good or evil; everything within Nature is governed by egoism (what Spinoza had called the *conatus sese preservandi).*

Of course, that applies to Man himself, as part of nature. We are reminded that twenty-two years earlier, La Mettrie had already entitled one of his books *L'Homme Machine,* in which he had dismissed, as Holbach now did again, that this machine housed an immaterial soul which could survive it. According to Holbach, our behaviour is entirely dependent on our hereditary constitution from within and on the impact of the environment from without. Our constitution from within does not include any inborn moral sense; it makes us respond only to pleasure and pain. What we call good or evil is what contributes to pleasure or will cause pain. We realize as clearly as our Reason allows us to do that behaviour which is injurious to society is ultimately injurious to ourselves; and so we devise social structures, educational systems, laws and punishments and "moral" codes that will contribute to pleasure and minimize pain.

> The problems that arise from this idea have been discussed in the introductory section of this chapter.

It is, therefore, incumbent on us to train our reason properly, so that we can understand what social structures can best deliver that result.

> The problem here is that reason does not deliver the same understanding even to those who aim to follow its dictates. Holbach, for example, unlike Voltaire, absolutely rejected even enlightened despotism, which annoyed Frederick the Great so much that he took up his own pen to write a *Réfutation du Système de la Nature.* Reason led Holbach to espouse Atheism, whereas it told Voltaire to support Theism.

In *Le Système de la Nature,* the French Enlightenment's total dedication to reason probably reached its climax. Yet, twenty years earlier, when the worship of reason was already a commonplace among the *philosophes,* its sovereignty had been challenged in Rousseau's *Discours sur les Arts et les Sciences* (1750). Rousseau had initially been in the circle of the *philosophes,* was a friend and protégé of Diderot's, had contributed articles to the *Encyclopédie* and had attended Holbach's *salon,* but he was so shocked by the atheism that was under discussion around Holbach's dinner table that he ceased attending. His departure, and the publication of the *Discours,* ushered in the Age of Romanticism.

CHAPTER 29

The Early Romantics

Introductory Remarks on Romanticism

Before turning to Rousseau, who is arguably the founder of unalloyed Romanticism in philosophy, it would be helpful to consider what we mean by the term Romanticism. The best way to do this is to contrast the values it held with those held by the Classicism which preceded it. Of course the following profile of Romanticism will not apply in its totality to every Romantic, let alone to every Romantic philosopher, but each of them would subscribe to some of the aspects that will now be described. Conversely, even the most classical philosophers occasionally exhibited some of the features that will be listed as characteristic of Romanticism.

Classical values are so called because they are supposed to have come from Classical Greece. Classical Greece's canons of taste and beauty had a powerful influence on Europe for about four hundred years, from the Renaissance to the Enlightenment. In this section, I am concentrating on their manifestations in the eighteenth century, the period when they were challenged by the Romantic movement.

One reason why we talk about Classicism in the Enlightenment is that, like the Classical Greeks, the philosphe put a very high value on the intellect and the search for rational explanations. By contrast, the Romantics believed that the rationalism of the Enlightenment was arid because it had not only neglected the emotions but had actually prmoted suspicion of them. The Romantics extolled the emotions over reason, the heart and the soul over the head. The word "sentiment" was originally another word for "feeling", and the Romantics were indeed often what we now call "sentimental". They were thrilled by the passions of love and hate, even by their excesses; lack of moderation was not an intellectual or a character defect for them. Even violence exercised a spell over many of them. The more extreme of them despised the placidity, the flaccidity, even the degeneracy of peace, and they would make a cult of war. War was not only the result of passions like patriotism; some believed that it brought out the best in you, and that it was a phenomenon ordained by Nature herself, which was everywhere, they thought, a picture of strife, and not of the harmony that so many classical thinkers saw in it. It is not surprising that many Romantics would in due course embrace the distortion of the Darwinian concept that life is a struggle in which only the fittest will survive.

I am not suggesting that classical rationalists rejected war. We have already seen[1] how readily Frederick the Great, a classicist *par excellence*, would

1 see p. 316 above.

> resort to war, but he did not glorify war as such. It was simply an instrument of what was, significantly, called *Raison d'État*; the result of the use of reason to show the advantage that a strong power would have over a weaker one. The attitudes towards war of a calculating rationalist on the one hand and a passionate romantic on the other have a totally different *feel* to them. For the former, war, under certain circumstances, was a rational activity, for the latter, it was an instinctual one for the healthy individual.

Classical thinkers believed in the values of maturity. A mature person, they thought, has put the impetuous passions of youth behind him. For them, the function of education was to educate the young to leave their instinctual and "primitive" tendencies behind them, or at least to control them, and to become sober and mature adults. Maturity aims for harmony, balance, moderation and restraint. Newton appeared to have demonstrated that there was a natural balance in the universe which kept all the stars and planets in their allotted place. Adam Smith extended this notion to the field of economics - if the state does not interfere, then economic forces will work in much the same way as gravitational forces do and create a natural balance of economic relations.

Many Romantics despised these ideas. Instead of maturity they made a cult of youth which they set against the "stuffiness" of their elders. They were not interested in controlling intense and extreme feelings, which they preferred to moderation. Instead of desiring to find a state of harmony and balance, which they considered static, they valued striving, restlessness, aspirations and longing. Nothing for them was ever perfect, so perfection would always elude them - hence "divine discontent", an alienation from so many human arrangements which made them outsiders, and the need to always strive for something better. There was the romantic cult of the Wanderer, the alienated individual who was at home and at rest nowhere (whereas the cosmopolitan classicist claimed to be at home everywhere). They showed special interest in what was nonrational, like intuition and the imagination.

For the Romantic, it was the artist who was the high priest, whereas for the classical philosophers the scientific thinker was the role model. The scientific thinker discovers laws and rules in the physical world, and tries to find them also in psychology and society. He also looks for rules of conduct (based on reason, of course) whereas the Romantics admired the rebels or heroes who were alienated wanderers and defied rules or conventions.

This applied also in the arts. The Romantic artist prided himself on not being bound by rules, but on following his imagination. Even the greatest classical artist saw his role primarily as a craftsman who satisfied the existing taste of cultivated patrons. What imagination he had, he put at the service of educated society. The Romantic artist felt little obligation to contribute to society; he owed his first responsibility to himself, to express *himself*. This could mean having to ignore the conventions and upsetting his clients, so that he would not receive as many commissions. In case a such his integrity demanded that he must be prepared to starve in a garret - an image that became popular in the nineteenth century, but was never found in the eighteenth.

Classical culture showed a liking for mathematical qualities in the arts and in literature. We see it in the geometry underlying their pictorial compositions and their architecture, the regularity of their scansions and rhyme-schemes, and the rather tight formal structure of their musical compositions. The Romantics liked freer forms in all those areas. Classical culture had imposed formalism even upon their gardens; it was rather afraid of the wilder aspects of nature, which must be tamed and controlled, rather as our own natural emotions must be tamed and controlled by our reason. The Romantics, on the other hand, admired nature uncontrolled, wild and rugged. The classical Grand Tour took in the cultivated cities and country houses of Europe; the 19th century tourist enthused over untamed mountains, turbulent streams, and all the awe-inspiring manifestations of nature against which the individual was small and insignificant.

While the Classicists were seeking out objective and rational explanations of how the world worked, many Romantics were fascinated by what was apparently irrational and subjective, like the unconscious, dreams, nightmares and hallucinations. We can see this reflected in many paintings, for instance, of Goya, Blake or Fuseli.

If the classicists preached prudence and moderation, the romantics rather admired recklessness. Heroic and reckless men were driven above all by their will, and the notion of the personal will (and of a general will or a cosmic will, too) will play a big part in nineteenth-century Romanticism, as we shall see.[2]

Classical thinkers sought out the universal, concentrating on what they believed all men or societies had in common. They believed that by the laws of nature, men were in some sense created equal. The Romantics had no use for this idea. They were interested in men who naturally rose above the common ruck – the élites, the geniuses, the heroes, the supermen and master races.

> I am not suggesting that the classical rationalist did not admire heroes – no one nurtured on Greek and Roman legends could fail to sing the praise of heroes, but again, I think that the classical and romantic heroes have a different *feel* to them. The classical élites had reached their eminence as much through education as through innate superiority. The classical tradition believes that people have a more or less equal potential, and it therefore thinks that people should be helped to realize their potential. This is why it attached so much importance to education. Good education and training would enable everyone to raise his or her capacity towards the level of the élites. If genius of all kinds consists of one percent inspiration and ninety-nine percent perspiration, as Thomas Edison would put it, then education and training could provide the ninety-nine percent and could significantly diminish the gap between the élites and the ordinary man. For the Romantic, on the other hand, that one percent represented an unbridgeable gulf between the hero and the common man. The typical romantic hero has no belief in the innate equality of man and, therefore, far from trying to lift the common man up to his level, he will simply walk all over him.

Romantics valued the particular; classical philosophers were interested in the universal. The latter thought in terms of what people (humankind) have in common – they spoke of the Rights of Man. A Romantic is interested in what makes individuals or nations different one from another. So he would underline that the Rights of Frenchmen and the Rights of Englishmen were rooted in

2 See chapters 32, 34 and 39 on Fichte, Schopenhauer and Nietzsche respectively.

a different past and that it was therefore wrong to expect them to be the same. The classical thinker was cosmopolitan, where the Romantic easily became a nationalist. (When he did, he would often identify his brand of nationalism with the cult of youth, and would call his movements by such names as "Young Germany", "Young Italy", "Young Ireland" etc.)

Cosmopolitan culture was shaped by sophisticated and educated elites. The Romantics found the root of national character not in those classes, but in folk traditions. German Romantics would coin the word *völkisch* for the traditional culture that they admired, and the Brothers Grimm collected folk tales, which romantics now found more interesting and valuable than the legends of classical antiquity. In this way, nationalism and populism formed an alliance which remains to the present day.

The folk-traditions were, of course, expressed in the local language - not in the cosmopolitan French which members of the educated classes on the continent sometimes spoke more fluently than they did their own (in the conviction, so brilliantly fostered by Louis XIV, that the culture of Versailles was the acme of civilization). The Romantics in Germany and in Russia rebelled against the domination of French culture and the French language. The *Sturm und Drang* movement[3] in Germany, founded in 1772, was dedicated to promoting pride in the native literary traditions of Germany. It was outraged when, in 1780, Frederick the Great delivered a lecture to the Academy of Berlin entitled *De la littérature allemande*. Speaking in French, the king told his audience that German literature would never be of much value unless it copied the literary models of France. The Slavophil movement in Russia also rejected western, and specifically French, influence on the upper classes in their country.[4]

Where Eurocentric classical thinkers tended to despise cultures that did not meet western criteria, the Romantics often made a cult of the primitive, of the "noble savage" who was uncorrupted by sophistication, and they were fascinated by the "exoticism" of cultures of the East, which were untouched by Western "civilized" influences.[5] (Another strand of Romanticism, however - the one that believed in master races - was utterly ruthless in the way it regarded and treated races it regarded as inferior.)

3 It would acquire that name from the title of a play written in 1776 by Friederich Maximilian von Klinger.

4 An interesting example of this is Tolstoy's *War and Peace*, published in 1868/9. The novel opens in 1805 and ends with Napoleon's retreat from Moscow in 1812. In the opening pages, the dialogue of the upper class characters is in French while the rest of the text is in Russian - in Russian editions this makes an even more striking typographical picture than it does in English ones. When Napoleon invades Russia, the Russians at first have to retreat. The implication is that a society which has become Frenchified and alienated from its true character cannot stand up to the French invader. The desperate Tsar puts General Kutusov in charge. Kutusov comes from Russian peasant stock. His military thinking is not based on French military manual,s but on a deep understanding of the Russian character, the Russian spaces and the Russian winter. By making these his allies, the enemy is at last defeated.

5 The Classical thinkers also professed great admiration for China. For them "China appeared the land of tolerance, of virtue without Christianity, of philosophical rulers with charming manners, of Deism, of Reason triumphant: the very ideal to which Europe must strive to conform." (Vincent Cronin - *The Wise Man from the West*.) The absolutism of the Son of Heaven was taken as an example of true Enlightened Despotism. Leibniz started a fashion for Chinese philosophy, Voltaire praised Confucianism, and the German Enlightenment philosopher Wolff embraced Confucianism so fervently that he was expelled from the University of Halle. (Hugh Honor - *Chinoiserie*.) The fashion for Chinoiserie in the arts therefore owed much to both classical and romantic thought.

The classical thinker thought of societies as being aggregations of individuals, and of the institutions of society as something that these individuals had created to serve their purpose, rather as a machine is constructed to serve the purpose of its manufacturer. If the machine does not work as it should, you replace the malfunctioning part with one that works better, and if necessary, the machine can be taken apart or totally dismantled and rebuilt - this is what the revolutionaries did in France during the French Revolution. For the Romantics, society was an organism which had an existence over and above the individuals who made it up, in the way in which the body is something more than the sum of its parts.

> A Romantic, being less concerned with consistency than a classical thinker, was not troubled by the fact that the organic theory of society subordinated the individual, while at the same time the Romantic admired the individual who defied society.

The individuals do not stand outside, but are an integral part of the organism. Where the classical philosophers believed that individuals had created the state to serve them, the Romantic was inclined to teach that it was the duty of the individual to serve the state. Whereas a machine is something that can be built from scratch, an organism is something that grows and develops over time, and has a history which one needs to understand.

Classical thinkers had always been sceptical of traditions, because so many traditions seemed to be unreasonable. They had to be questioned because they were likely to be an impediment to progress. The *philosophes* had no reverence for the past as such, and very little for history. The only past periods of history that they admired were Antiquity and the Renaissance which drew upon it - even then there was a dispute among the *philosophes* about just how much reverence should be accorded to these periods: the famous Battle between the Ancients and the Moderns.[6] Both Ancients and Moderns were at one in despising the Middle Ages, for which they coined the word "Gothic", because the Goths had been the barbarians who had destroyed the last embodiment of Antiquity - the Roman Empire. They had no concept of *growth* or *development* in history. The Romantics would not be so high-handed. The traditions of the past embodied wisdom that should not be lightly cast aside, and they are an organic part of present society. Classical artists had been interested in the ruins of classical architecture, but for the Romantics, remnants of the medieval past also evoked a nostalgic reverence, not mere contempt. This was particularly so in Germany. After the Middle Ages, Germany had so often been the battleground of foreign armies that the Holy Roman Empire of the German Nation had become a pale shadow of what it had been in the Middle Ages. The Germans thought that in those Middle Ages their culture had reached a peak, and they now proudly described the architecture of that time as "Gothic", a word which Voltaire had coined as one of contempt.

Classical thinkers in the Age of Reason had often mocked Christian doctrine and observances as based on superstitions which no rational person should entertain. That was another reason why they had despised the Middle Ages, when, in their view, religious superstitions had reigned unchallenged. The

6 See p. 306 above.

Romantics admired the medieval centuries as an age of unquestioning faith and of deep religious feelings. In many art forms, therefore, we find a new interest in the Middle Ages. In England, for example, we have the novels of Sir Walter Scott, the pre-Raphaelite painters (note the significance of the name), and above all the Gothic revival in architecture which, especially for churches, was to recreate the settings in which medieval religious faith had found its expression. Where the classical philosophers would accept only those religious precepts that could be supported by reason, the Romantics valued the mystical side of religion, which appealed to the feelings.

Such, then, was the spirit of Romanticism which grew during the eighteenth century in opposition to Classicism. The man who most self-consciously made the break from the Age of Reason was Jean-Jacques Rousseau.

JEAN-JACQUES ROUSSEAU
1712 to 1788

Rousseau's *Confessions*, a posthumously published work which he started in 1762, is one of the most self-revealing autobiographies that have ever been written. Where another author might have concentrated on the narrative of his life or on his intellectual development, Rousseau, like a true Romantic, constantly tells us about his feelings. He emerges from his self-portrait as a nervy, wimpish, weepy, masochistic, neurotic, manic-depressive personality. He was capable of plunging from the heights of elation to the depths of despair, and even joyous emotions would often manifest themselves in him in a flood of tears. When he was in love, he was sick with love, when he contemplated nature, he almost swooned with religious adoration. In general, he was a profoundly unhappy man, ill at ease with the etiquette of polite society, and paranoid to a degree. At the same time he must have had great charm, for he never lacked patrons. He often fell out with them (rather than they with him) and his restless nature meant that he could never settle down anywhere for long, but he always found other people who were willing to help him or to give him a home in his perpetual peregrinations.

He was born in Geneva of Calvinist parents. His mother died of puerperal fever after giving birth to him; his father remarried and more or less abandoned Jean-Jacques and his brother. At the age of thirteen he was apprenticed to an engraver, but fled from him after a thrashing when he was fifteen. He was taken in by a Catholic priest and presently converted to Roman Catholicism. The priest introduced him to Mme de Warens, an aristocratic lady with whom he fell passionately in love and who would secure for him various posts with other aristocratic families. Eventuall,y a series of such introductions brought him to Paris, in 1742.

Four years earlier he had become interested in philosophy and had begun to educate himself in the subject, initially by reading the works of Voltaire. These readings destroyed his belief in the Catholic faith, but did nothing to cool down his fervent religious temperament.

The first philosopher with whom he became friendly when he came to Paris was Denis Diderot. Rousseau was then earning his living by copying music, and he was a good enough musician himself to compose operettas and ballets which were successfully and profitably performed in aristocratic homes and, eventually, even at court. Diderot commissioned him to write the article on music in his forthcoming *Encyclopédie.*[7] Rousseau had other patrons, too, one of whom secured him a lucrative post in the civil service. As an official, he was now required to wear gold braid, white stockings, a powdered wig and a sword – all of which made him feel profoundly uncomfortable.

In 1749, Diderot was imprisoned in the fortress at Vincennes for some remarks he had made in his *Letter on the Blind*, which challenged the idea of a benevolent creator. The imprisonment was not very harsh: Diderot could receive his friends there, and Rousseau walked the five miles from Paris to Vincennes to visit him several times . On one of these trips, he had taken a newspaper with him in which he saw an advertisement inserted by the Academy of Dijon. It offered a prize for the best essay submitted to the Academy on the subject, *Has the restoration of the arts and the sciences contributed to corrupt or to purify morals?* The title suggests that a controversy on this subject was already going on, but most of the submissions at the height of the Age of Reason could be expected to take the line of the *philosophes* – that, after the Renaissance and the Scientific Revolution had swept away many medieval prejudices, the application of the principles that governed the taste in the arts and progress in the sciences could only contribute to improve the morals of society.

Rousseau described in a letter, many years later, the revelation that came to him as he read the title. He seems suddenly to have seen in a flash of inspiration that, so far from being a benefit, civilization as the *philosophes* conceived it had led mankind astray and had corrupted its nature. This is what he wrote:

> All at once I felt myself dazzled by a thousand sparkling lights. Crowds of vivid ideas thronged into my mind with a force and confusion that threw me into unspeakable agitation; I felt my head whirling in a giddiness like that of intoxication. A violent palpitation oppressed me. Unable to walk for difficulty in breathing, I sank down under one of the trees by the road, and passed half an hour there in such a condition of excitement that when I rose I saw that the front of my waistcoat was all wet with tears.... Ah, if ever I could have written a quarter of what I saw and felt under that tree, with what clarity I should have brought out all the contradictions of our social system! With what simplicity I should have demonstrated that man is by nature good, and that only our institutions have made him bad.

In this state of mind he made his way to Vincennes and there told Diderot of his illumination and his intention to enter the competition. Would this mean a breach with Diderot, whose projected *Encyclopédie* was so committed to everything the Age of Reason stood for? I have mentioned in the first paragraph of this chapter that several *philosophes* were not wholly immune to Romanticism, and Diderot was one of these. Anyway, he was broad-minded enough to encourage Rousseau to submit this challenge to the Age of Reason and to assure him of his continuing friendship. Rousseau feverishly composed his *Discours sur les Arts et les Sciences*, and so fresh and original was his approach that the Academy, probably weary of reading countless conventional expositions of *philosophe* ideas, awarded him the first prize. Diderot arranged the publication of the *Discours* in 1750.

7 The first volume would appear in 1751.

Le Discours sur les Arts et les Sciences

Rousseau's argument begins with the historical dimension. In every ancient civilization, and in many modern ones, cultural refinements were accompanied by moral laxity, corruption and enfeeblement. These sapped their strength and contributed to their overthrow by more primitive and vigorous invaders. Their philosophers were always much to blame, for in these latter stages they would "sap the foundations of our faith and destroy virtue. They smile contemptuously at such old words as patriotism and religion, and consecrate their talents ... to the destruction and defamation of all that men hold most sacred." Rousseau set against such decadent civilizations:

> those happy nations, which did not know even the name of many vices that we find hard to suppress – the savages of America, whose simple and natural mode of government Montaigne preferred, without hesitation ... to the most perfect visions of government that philosophy can suggest.

The concept of the Noble Savage had arrived upon the scene. He was a creature who possessed virtue uncorrupted by learning. He lived close to nature, and it is to nature that we should all return. In an orgy of exaggeration and anti-intellectualism he extols, "that happy state of ignorance in which the wisdom of Providence has placed us... Let men learn for once that Nature would have preserved them from science as a mother snatches a dangerous weapon from the hands of her child."

The *philosophes*, except for Diderot, despised the essay, but it struck a powerful chord elsewhere and made Rousseau famous overnight. It liberated him, too; he now discarded the ceremonial clothes in which he had felt so uncomfortable, and henceforth his favourite garment was a simple kaftan.

Significantly, he also abandoned France for a while, returning to Geneva for a few months in 1754 and renewed his citizenship there. He now extolled the virtues of the small and intimate city-state. This, he believed, gave all its inhabitants the possibility and the responsibility for practising civic virtues for which there was so much less scope in a large state like France. (We will see him developing this idea in the *Social Contract* a few years later.) In Switzerland, he saw a nation that still preserved the rustic virtues, and he returned to the more austere Calvinist religion. The puritan city fathers of Geneva did not permit the establishment of a theatre in their city. When, in an otherwise laudatory article on Geneva in the *Encyclopédie*, D'Alembert suggested that the city might benefit from allowing plays of quality to be performed there, Rousseau leapt to Geneva's defence in the *Lettre à M. D'Alembert sur les spectacles* (1758). The theatre and the acting profession were essentially frivolous and undermined morality; even classical tragedies were full of crime, sex and violence, and comedies often held the virtues up to ridicule. We seem to hear Plato speak again.[8]

8 See p. 29 above. Although Rousseau had written plays himself, his *Letter* was generally seen as an attack on Voltaire, who enjoyed a rather greater reputation as a playwright and who had possibly encouraged D'Alembert to insert the passage on the theatre into his article. Since 1755, Voltaire had been living on Genevan territory, at *Les Délices*, a house just outside the city, into which he had fitted a private theatre. The Genevans had immediately forbidden their citizens to attend it, and over the next few years showed increasing irritation at Voltaire's anti-clericalism. In 1758, Voltaire had abandoned *Les Délices* and moved back to France. Rousseau's *Letter*, appearing at that very time, simply rubbed salt into the wound. Voltaire condemned Rousseau as a deserter from the Enlightenment when it was in trouble (the *Encyclopédie* was banned in France that year) and so the *Letter* marked the final breach between Rous-

Le Discours sur l'Inégalité, 1755

Meanwhile, he had entered another essay competition, again instituted by the Academy of Dijon. The new title was *What is the origin of inequality among men, and is it authorized by natural law?* He did not win the prize this time - for one thing the examiners may have found quite an overlap between this submission and his previous one - but the essay was published all the same (with a dedication "to the Republic of Geneva"). It marked another step in his philosophical development. He began by describing the State of Nature, though he admitted that it was a concept rather than a historical reality.[9] As it had done for Hobbes and for Locke, it gave Rousseau the opportunity to describe what he thought men were "naturally" like. He rejected Hobbes' view that in a State of Nature every man is against every other man and strives for dominance. For Rousseau, men were naturally equal (meaning that none have natural rights over others) and naturally good. All they need in the State of Nature is food, sex and sleep, and if they have enough of these, they are content and peaceful. It was a vision closer to Locke's picture of what most men are naturally like.

When he wrote *Émile* in 1762 he would go further and say, as Hume had done,[10] that, because we aim at the well-being of both our bodies and our souls, the well-being of our soul requires that our natural feelings of compassion for our fellow human beings also need to be satisfied. This makes men naturally unwilling to inflict suffering on their fellows! As Coplestone comments:

> Morality is thus the unthwarted and unprevented development of man's natural passions and feelings. Vice is not natural to man: it constitutes a distortion of his nature, created by the rise of civilization, multiplying men's wants and needs, and giving rise to selfishness and to the hateful and angry passions.[11]

In the State of Nature, Rousseau believed, the only natural society is that of the family; larger units are not "natural", but artificial. In an echo of his earlier essay, he says that in this blessed primitive stage, there is no intellectualizing. In his love of dramatic sentences, Rousseau proclaims that *"a thinking man is a depraved animal"*.

In Locke's State of Nature, any man could lawfully acquire property by mixing his labour with the soil,[12] but in Rousseau's there is no private property, because everything was owned in common. This state of affairs ends with a "fatal accident": the claim to individual property. "The first man who, having enclosed a piece of ground, bethought himself of saying, This is mine, and found people simple enough to believe him, was the real founder of civil society." From that moment onwards the decline into "civilization" was both inevi-

seau and the *philosophes*. The break was all the more complete as, for good measure, Rousseau included in his preface a repudiation of his friendship with Diderot, although the break between them had nothing to do with philosophy but was occasioned by Diderot's well-meant, but indiscreet, intervention in one of Rousseau's affairs with a married woman.

9 He is the last major philosopher who will allow himself the luxury of inventing a hypothetical and unhistorical state of nature. In the nineteenth and twentieth centuries, the speculations of philosophers on this subject will be replaced by the fieldwork of anthropologists.

10 See p. 296 above.

11 Coplestone - *A History of Philosophy*, Vol. VI, p. 77.

12 See p. 270 above.

table and irreversible. How much better would it have been if someone had protested at the time:

> From how many crimes, wars, and murders, from how many horrors and misfortunes, might not anyone have saved mankind if he had pulled up the stakes, filled up the ditch, and cried out to his fellows: 'Beware of listening to this impostor! You are undone if you once forget that the fruits of the earth belong to us all, and the earth itself to nobody.'

This is the forerunner of Proudhon's argument in 1840 that *Property is Theft*.

Now force had to be organized to protect property, and this eventually took the form of the apparatus of states, which then perpetuated unnatural inequalities, protecting those who have property and oppressing those who have little or none. The whole process is riddled with corruption of the natural virtues.

Proudhon was an anarchist; that is, he believed that the state is an evil, and that men would live more happy lives without a central government (Greek *an-* meaning "without", and *archos* meaning "government" or "rule".) Proudhon and Bakunin combined socialism (the belief that property should be held in common) and communism (the belief that the small commune rather than the large state is the *ideal* unit of government). Both ideas derive from Rousseau, and it would be Marx who did his best to drive the anarchists out of the communist movement, though anarchocommunists would still play a part in, for example, the Spanish Civil War.

For Rousseau once the state has come into existence, there is no remedy in dismantling it so as to go back to the State of Nature which, we must remember, was for him a kind of paradise, a time of innocence and equality. If we were now to dismantle the state, we would not recover that paradise. Instead, we would descend into what Hobbes had seen as the State of Nature, which is worse than the present. So all we can now do is to look to the Gospels to remedy the ills of the present and to recover some of the virtues we had before our fallen state.

Note his difference with the *philosophes* here. They believed that we could look to reason to make us virtuous, because reason tells us that it is in our enlightened self-interest to be virtuous. Rousseau, who has no belief in reason, believes that only religious faith can restore our virtue.

The essay drew down upon itself more scorn from the *philosophes*. It was expressed most sardonically by Voltaire, to whom Rousseau had sent a copy:

> I have received, Monsieur, your new book against the human race. I thank you for it... You paint in very true colours the horrors of human society ... no one has ever employed so much intellect to persuade men to be beasts. In reading your work, one is seized with a desire to walk on four paws. However, as it is more than sixty years since I lost that habit, I feel, unfortunately, that it is impossible for me to resume it.

Voltaire then went on more seriously,

> The great crimes [in History] were committed by celebrated but ignorant men. What has made and will always make this world a vale of tears is the insatiable cupidity and indomitable pride of men (he means their "natural" bad qualities) ... [whereas] literature (he means the product of the intellect, the arts and the sciences which Rousseau had so much despised) nourishes the soul, corrects it, and consoles it.

The Article on Political Economy, 1755

In 1755, when the *Discours* was written, Rousseau had not yet fallen out with Diderot, who continued to support him and commissioned further articles from him for the *Encyclopédie*. That year, the fifth volume of that work was published, and in it was Rousseau's article on Political Economy.

In his *Discours sur l'Inégalité* only a few months earlier, Rousseau had declared that in a state of nature there was no property, and that its subsequent acquisition and then its confirmation by civil society had been the result of oppression and corruption. Now he proclaimed that property was *"the most sacred right of all the rights of citizenship, and even more important in some respects than liberty itself."*

> There may be less of a contradiction here than appears at first sight. Rousseau seems to have regarded the transformation from the idyllic propertyless state of nature to a civil society which enforces the rights of property as being a development rooted in the very nature of Man. He has already said that the change was both inevitable and irreversible. We simply have to make the best of this civil society, otherwise, once the unregulated acquisition of property has started, life in the state of nature would be as "solitary, nasty, poor, brutish and short" as Hobbes had portrayed it. The difference between Hobbes and Rousseau then seems rather academic: for Hobbes, Man was naturally aggressive and acquisitive from the very beginning, whereas for Rousseau, he naturally became such very soon after the beginning, when a hypothetical first man enclosed a piece of ground and proclaimed it as his own.
>
> All the same, the emotional resonance of Rousseau's two passages is totally different – the first protesting against the oppression and corruption implicit in both the process and the outcome, the second hallowing the outcome as "sacred".

Rousseau next involves himself in the same contradiction as Locke had done – yes, property is sacred, but not so sacred that society cannot and should not interfere with it. Locke had confined that interference to taxation in order to provide for the "great charge without which governments cannot be supported".[13] The charges that Locke had in mind were the necessary expenses of administration and defence; but Rousseau expanded the grounds on which "sacred" property could be taken away by taxation, namely to level out some of the unequal distribution of wealth within a society: there was to be a progressive system of taxation, and part of the proceeds should be devoted to a national system of education in which children should be brought up, "in the bosom of equality" and should be "imbued with the laws of the state and the precepts of the General Will."

What is this "General Will"? Rousseau had already explained, a few pages further back, that

> The body politic is also a moral being, possessed of a will; and this general will, which tends always to the preservation and welfare of the whole and of every part, is the source

13 See p. 268 above. A reminder here that the contradiction lies in the fact that, as long as a majority has consented to it, an individual will have to make a contribution even if he himself or his representative have not consented. Under those circumstances, his right to his own property can hardly be said to be a "natural", let alone a "sacred" right.

> of the laws, and constitutes for all the members of the state, in their relations to one another, the rule of what is just or unjust.

Here, in the notion of the body politic being an organism with a life and a will of its own, we have the germ of the notion which would dominate Rousseau's next and most famous work, *The Social Contract*.

Le Contrat Social, 1762

The opening sentence of the first chapter is a famous clarion call: *"Man is born free; and everywhere he is in chains."*

In connection with his previous writings, one would expect this sentence to introduce a condemnation of society which has enslaved free individuals, but the paragraph continues,"How did this change come about? I do not know. What can make it *legitimate*?[14] That question I think I can answer."

Although he claimed that he did not know how the change came about, in fact he posited a state of nature which was ended by a Social Contract, just as Hobbes and Locke had done. All three of them really knew that from the *historical* point of view, the Social Contract is a fiction, but for each of them that fiction underpinned a philosophical legitimation of a just society, and will sanction whatever just restraints there are on the individuals. Restraints imposed by a tyrant who does not acknowledge any tacit contract have no legitimacy. If lawful restraints in accordance with a social contract deserve the emotively charged description of "chains", they are, in Rousseau's view, as we shall see, at any rate freely chosen. Rousseau loved paradoxical formulations; they are dramatic and arresting, but they scarcely make for clarity of thought!

Like Hobbes, Rousseau now believed that the state of nature is intolerable.

> His earlier theory had shown man in the state of nature in a pre-lapsarian state of goodness and innocence. I don't think Rousseau would have been very troubled by the contradiction. Romantics accepted contradictions more readily than classicists. Life *is* full of contradictions, and eighteenth-century rationalists were wrong in trying to neaten up the phenomena of nature.

In Hobbes, men had escaped from that condition by a contract in which they had surrendered all their powers to an absolute ruler who had authority for as long as he could enforce it.[15] Rousseau rejected this as a legitimate basis of authority as he could not see that force could rest on any kind of morality. Locke had provided a moral basis of government – it needed to rest on consent, without which there could be no legitimate encroachments on the natural rights to life, liberty and property. However, we have already seen that Locke fudged the problem when a majority agrees to such encroachments but a minority withholds its consent.[16] Rousseau tried to square this circle:

> the problem is to find a form of association which will defend and protect with the whole common force the person and goods of each associate, and in which each, while uniting himself with all, *may still obey himself alone and remain as free as before.*

14 my italics.

15 See p. 259 above.

16 See p. 268 above.

The Social Contract, as Rousseau has it, is formulated as follows:

> Each of us puts his person and all his power under the supreme direction of the General Will; and in our corporate capacity we receive each member as an *indivisible part of the whole.*[17]

He goes on, "This act of association creates a moral and collective body, composed of as many members as the assembly contains voters, and receiving from this act its unity, its common identity, its life and its will." In other words, once the community has been created by the Social Contract, it is something more than the sum of its individuals. It is not some administrative mechanism that they have put together and that stands outside of them as a separate structure. What the Social Contract has brought into being is a living organism endowed with a personality, and the members are as much part of it as the limbs are of a human body. The real interests of each and every individual cannot be distinct from that of the society as a whole, indeed, the individual's life has no meaning unless seen as an integral part of the organism, any more than a limb could have if separated from its body.

The idea that a community has a corporate personality is often expressed in such phrases as "national character" or "*esprit de corps*". The latter especially seems to be a common experience; we do and feel things as a group which we might not be doing or feeling as individuals. This happens even in amorphous groups like football crowds. Though we may only be spectators and may do little more than cheer on our team from the sidelines, our will to win appears to be the same as that of the team, and we take pride in its achievements as if they were our own. And in the grip of communal emotions, our normal inhibitions often vanish or we abandon natural fears.

It is, however, arguable whether this is best described as a transformation of a mere sum of individual wills into a collective will. What may happen is that when activities are shared, some feelings are intensified (this happens a lot in a theatre audience and at sports events) whilst others (like guilt feelings) are reduced. If we do have any reservations, group pressures against maintaining them are often effective. Besides, individual perceptions can be influenced and deliberately manipulated by symbols. This is especially the case when individual behaviour patterns reflect a rather thin veneer of reason or civilization over basic irrational or uncivilized instincts, which are often looking for an excuse to break out. Then there is an instinctual, but individual recognition that, for good or ill, aims are more easily achieved if action is collective than if it is individual. We should remember that in all situations there will always be members of the community, few though they may often be, who resist all those pressures. They could hardly do this if the General Will of the community really had the capacity to subsume all the individual wills.

From Hobbes to the *philosophes* the theory had been that societies were constructed to serve the enlightened self-interest of individuals. What they had constructed they could dismantle and reconstruct if it did not serve them well. The Organic Theory of society, on the other hand, is profoundly hostile to the idea that the individual is more important than the community, that the community exists to serve the individual and not *vice versa*. It is only through the Social Contract creating an organic society that one is turned, in Rous-

17 my italics.

seau's words, from "*a stupid and unimaginative animal into an intelligent being and a man*".

Incidentally, that means that Rousseau has abandoned his earlier idea of the "noble savage" and of civil society being a necessary evil. Civil society has now become the means of our redemption – without it, we are not fully human at all.

The community which the Social Contract has created then sets up a government to deal with the practical way of translating its will into action. Whilst the *community* is an organism, the *government* is merely a piece of machinery. Sovereignty, which Hobbes had ascribed to the government, for Rousseau resides in the community. The government's function is merely to carry out what the will of the community has decided. Nevertheless, Rousseau frequently forgets the distinction - sometimes the book appears to endow the state with the same organic character that he sees in the community, and some of Rousseau's political disciples (like the Jacobins) or philosophical descendants (like Hegel) will consistently identify state and community.

This confusion is important. There can be a kind of intimacy in small communities which makes it possible to speak of a general will – though I have suggested above that even in that context it is more properly described as a collection of conditioned individual wills. In very large political units like the so-called nation states, there are so many and such varied smaller communities that there are bound to be many different primary loyalties, and "national consensus", except in situations of national danger, is much less likely to exist; where it does, it is most probably created by propaganda. Rousseau himself wrote that, for this and other reasons, small states (like his native city state of Geneva) were preferable to large states like France, where the exercise of direct popular sovereignty was impossible. Even in smaller states, he thought it required superhuman citizens to make the General Will work.

We shall see below that Rousseau endowed the General Will with infallibility – itself an extraordinary and sinister idea – and that he claimed that it could impose itself on dissidents on the grounds that that was what they "really" wanted. Therefore, when the concept of the General Will, dubious as it is when applied to small communities, is transferred to the state, it paves the way for the worship of the state and of the leaders who personify it.

True to the idea that government is "only" the machinery through which the General Will translates itself into action, Rousseau was, on the whole, indifferent to the forms it takes. He pointed out, quite rightly, that different communities may require different forms of this machinery. He also showed that every government developed its own vested interest and "unavoidably" tended to forget that it was merely the servant of the sovereign. There is little detailed discussion of what a government can and cannot legitimately do, although it is obvious that it acts legitimately when it acts in accordance with the general will and illegitimately when it does not, so the principal question is: how is the General Will discovered?

The General Will is found by counting votes, but Rousseau makes an important distinction between what he calls the General Will and the Will of All. Let us take as an example the *principles* of a taxation system. (Once these have been decided, it is up to the government to work out the practical details). A society is asked, shall we say, whether taxation should in principle be progressive or not. If the members of the community, when voting on this, consider where their own personal interests lie, then what emerges would not be the general will, but merely an aggregation of self-centred individual wills; the will of all. Only if all the members of community ask themselves what is in the interests of the community as a whole does the General Will emerge.

> Can we ever expect to find a society in which most voters will disregard their individual interests when they vote? A few wealthy men may vote out of idealism for a socialist programme. Most will either vote unashamedly for their own material interests or they will produce some rationalizing argument, like invoking the "trickle down" effect that society as a whole will benefit from capitalism. Conversely, of course, most poor men will vote for a redistribution of wealth, either unashamedly for their own materialist interests or by producing some rationalizing argument such as that a redistributive society is a more efficient one. There may be something to be said for each of these rationalizations, but generally, each group adopts those that most seem to support their personal interest.
>
> Rousseau must have realized that, just as he realized that even in small states, superhuman qualities are required to make them work properly. That is not *in itself* necessarily a condemnation of his theories – an ideal may be philosophically right in the sense that, if everyone lived up to it, a better society would result. Many political theories advance ideals in the full knowledge that they cannot be fully achieved but in the hope that, if they are accepted as ideals, a society may come closer to fulfilling them than if they have never been put before them.

Rousseau was deeply opposed to what we call "pressure groups" and he called "factions" and "partial associations", as these, though they have a general will with regard to their members, represent self-centred particular wills with regard to the community as a whole. "It is therefore essential, if the General Will is to be able to express itself, that there should be no partial society within the State."

> In this condemnation of political parties and interest groups, we have the first hint of the dictatorial tendencies that will increasingly surface as the work develops.

Rousseau maintained that where the general will does emerge, it is infallible: "The General Will is always right and tends to the public advantage."

This is an extraordinary assertion, though, as we shall see, it is again a necessary one for the authoritarian structure he will base upon it. He assumes that the people, if genuinely trying to discern what is best for their society, will always have the wisdom to come to the right conclusion. He does admit that, even if people do so vote, they will not all come to the same conclusion, but he has the confidence that "the pluses and minuses cancel one another, and the General Will remains as the sum of the differences". Then follows (twenty-nine chapters later on!) the following passage:

> When in the popular assembly a law is proposed, what the people is asked is not exactly whether it approves or rejects the proposal, but whether it is in conformity with the General Will, which is their will. Each man, in giving his vote, states his opinion on that point; and the General Will is found by counting votes. When therefore the opinion that is contrary to my own prevails, this proves neither more nor less than that I was mistaken, and that what I thought to be the General Will was not so. If my particular opinion had carried the day, I should have achieved the opposite of what was my will; and in that case I should not have been free.

For the final line of this argument we have to go back again, this time by thirty-four chapters. The Social Contract:

> tacitly includes the undertaking, which alone gives force to all the rest, that whoever refuses to obey the General Will shall be compelled to do so by the whole body. This means nothing less than that he will be forced to be free.

This last phrase again shows Rousseau's love of paradoxical formulations, and it both draws on earlier ones and inspires later ones. For an earlier one, we may take the phrase in one of the Collects in the Book of Common Prayer, in which Jesus is described as "the author of peace and lover of concord, in knowledge of whom standeth our eternal life, *whose service is perfect freedom.*" In normal parlance that would be a contradiction in terms, but what is meant is that freedom exercised for ill is imperfect freedom, indeed is not freedom at all, but enslavement (service) to our baser instincts. What we *really* want is salvation ("eternal life") and therefore it is no contradiction to say that serving this aim is perfect freedom.

Kant will make the same distinction as Rousseau had done between our Real Will and our Actual Will: the Real Will is what our better natures want; the Actual Will often significantly diverges from that.

To distinguish between these two is not an invalid notion, and indeed we have all experienced the struggle between the two. St Paul had given expression to it when he said "The good that I would I do not: but the evil which I would not, that I do." (Rom.7.19). However, it is one thing to be aware of that struggle within myself; it is quite another for others to determine for me what I *really* want and therefore in what my real freedom consists. Even less is it justifiable – paradox or not – for them to "force me to be free". Under certain circumstances we may indeed legitimately be forced to obey the wishes of the community, but the claim that this is in my own interests is usually doubtful, and the claim that it gives me "real freedom" is a self-deluding and pernicious play on words – though there are cases when people can be so thoroughly indoctrinated by a totalitarian system that they actually accept that their real will is what the system tells them it is, and that their real freedom consists in serving the system.

It should by now be clear how much the theories of totalitarianism owe to Rousseau: the reliance on plebiscites to give expression to the "General Will"; the claim that the leader, acting as the representative of that general will, is infallible; the cult of the national community, only through serving which can the individual fully realize himself; the dislike of "faction" or "partial association" (i.e. independent parties, autonomous trade unions, churches, or other organizations); the intolerance of minority dissent and the cant with which its suppression by the apparatus of the state is justified.

Of course Rousseau saw himself quite differently. His theory, like that of many of the *philosophes*, was directed against the *Ancien Régime* in France, which represented the interests only of the ruling classes and in which the people had no say at all. The move from the sovereignty of monarchs to the sovereignty of the people had to be an improvement. That is perhaps *some* excuse for Rousseau, but it cannot be an acquittal even in terms of the eighteenth century. The intellectuals of the eighteenth century were well acquainted with the main ideas of Classical Greece, and Rousseau must surely have come across Aristotle's six-fold classification of governments[18] in

18 See p. 53 above.

which he indicates that there is a form of democracy in which the majority exercises an oppressive dictatorship over the minority.

Even so, in the French eighteenth-century context, the fact that he developed an organic theory, rather than a more individualistic theory like Locke's, seemed less important than that both wanted to promote democracy.

For France in Rousseau's lifetime, it was still all theory. It is only when the French Revolution broke out that the practical differences between the two approaches became clear. In the early stages of the French Revolution the Lockeian idea seemed to prevail. The first constitutions thought in terms of checks and balances, freedom of association and expression, legal protection of the rights of individuals, and a Lockeian respect for property. When the Revolution moved into its Jacobin phase, it became Rousseauist. Indeed, the Jacobin leader St Just once claimed of his party that, "we are the General Will" and we know how in its name all the worst excesses of totalitarian states have been justified from that time to our own.

That self-justification would be used by many future regimes in the history of Europe. By the end of the nineteenth century, only the Tsars of Russia still relied exclusively on the Divine Right of Kings to justify their autocracy. All other autocrats based their legitimacy on Rousseauist popular sovereignty. Their form of government is known as "Caesarism", because, like Caesar Augustus, they claimed that they exercised dictatorship by public demand. Their plebiscites – not always totally rigged – had demonstrated this. The French Revolution had let the genie of democracy out of the bottle and it could not be put back in; it could only be hypocritically perverted. It is another example of De la Rochefoucauld's dictum that, "hypocrisy is the tribute that vice pays to virtue".

To what extent can Rousseau be held responsible for the way in which his ideas were interpreted by later generations? He had written *The Social Contract* as a critique of the *Ancien Régime* and might well have been appalled at the use that was made of his ideas by the Jacobin Terror or the Caesarist regimes of the nineteenth and twentieth centuries. A philosopher cannot always know into what fruits the seeds he has sown will develop, though he should listen to contemporaries who are sometimes more far-sighted than he is. Edmund Burke, for example, detested Rousseau's ideas and forecast what they might lead to. As for posterity, while we should make an effort to judge a philosopher's ideas without bringing into play the hindsight we possess, it is hard for us to avoid the saying in the Sermon on the Mount: "By their fruits ye shall know them" (Matth.7.20).

Émile (1762)

What is certainly illegitimate, in my opinion, is to mock a philosopher's (or, for that matter, anybody's) *ideas* simply on the grounds that there is some serious defect in his private or public life, or because his personal conduct falls short of the standards he lays down. One may denigrate the *person*, but unworthy persons have often produced ideas (or works of art) of some power, profundity, or originality, and these ought to be considered for themselves alone.

This is particularly apposite when we consider Rousseau's next work, *Émile*, which was a tract on the education of an imagined pupil of that name.[19]

19 Rousseau envisaged it as a sequel to *Julie, ou La Nouvelle Héloïse*, the hugely successful romantic novel he had published in the previous year. In this novel, the religious Julie lives in faithful monogamy with the

Many people have questioned Rousseau's right to propound any ideas on education because, immediately after their birth, he had deposited each of the five children born to him by his common-law wife at the door of a foundlings hospital; Rousseau wondered about this himself. It is certainly odd that he should have had the nerve to write on the subject, but I think that ought to be irrelevant when we come to consider the ideas in the book. We should judge them on their own merit. We may take into account what use has been made of them in later years, but we should treat them as if we did not know anything about the author's private or public life.

Émile has had as far-reaching an influence as *Le Contrat Social*, which was published in the same year. Rousseau proposed that children should be given as much freedom as possible. That included not wrapping babies up in swaddling clothes. He disapproved of wet nurses; mothers should breastfeed their own children, for this would strengthen the bond of affection between mother and child. A study of animal life showed that such bonding is natural and important, farming children out to wet-nurses is therefore unnatural and artificial.

Once education begins, there should be no rote learning, which is stultifying and so often a torture. Indeed, there should be no intellectual training at all before a child is twelve years old.

He does not seem to have considered that there are ways of training the intellect other than by rote learning (quite apart from the fact that *some* rote learning is valuable as a useful tool and can actually be enjoyed by children), and that it is never too early to invite a child (within its capacities) to think for itself and lay the groundwork for later intellectual development.

Until the age of twelve, concentration should be on moral education (not by precept, but by example), on encouraging it to love nature in the countryside, and on the healthy development of the body, for which a vegetarian diet was best. A child's sexual consciousness should be retarded for as long as possible.

Serious intellectual education should begin at the age of twelve.[20] At this stage it is to be technical and scientific, and it should be based on getting the child to discover how things work by doing experiments rather than by having information imparted to him.

The influence which some of these ideas have had on the theory of education even to this day can hardly be exaggerated, though it took a long time before they made any headway. The first advocate of Rousseau's methods, Pestalozzi (1746 to 1827) in Switzerland, was disappointed by how little attention he attracted. Froebel (1782 to 1852) in Germany was a little more fortunate, though nineteenth-century education is still a byword for stultifying learning by rote. In the twentieth century, Maria Montessori (1870 to 1952) in Italy and the Netherlands and A.S.Neill (1883 to 1973) in England made much more of an impact, and researches by Piaget (1896 to 1980) into the various stages of children's learning confirmed much of what Rousseau had advocated. Since the Second World War, "child-centred" education has dominated

agnostic philosopher Wolmar, though her true love is her Abelardian tutor Saint-Preux, who is as religious as she is, but to whom she had lost her chastity before her marriage. In fear of her father's revenge Saint-Preux has fled abroad, but Wolmar shows his nobility by not only forgiving their lapse, but inviting Saint-Preux back to tutor their children, and the three live happily and virtuously together. Rousseau wanted to show that love can transcend any quarrel between religion and rationalism. The ideas of the tutor in *Émile* are a more elaborate version of those of Saint-Preux.

theory, at least in Britain, and only at the very end of the century has there been a reaction against some of its excesses.

Rousseau's advocacy that children should be allowed to remain "natural" for as long as possible and should be taught early on to love nature was, of course, part of the Romantic cult of untamed nature, which we can see in the literature, the paintings, and the goals of much of the tourism of the time.

The study of history should not begin before the age of fifteen, and formal religious education should not begin before the age of eighteen, when a young man can think for himself and is beyond the impressionable age at which he can be conditioned (often by the inculcation of guilt feelings) into religious orthodoxy.

Not only does religious teaching often begin in very early childhood (note the expression "cradle Catholics"), but most religions expect children to make their commitments (through Confirmation, Bar-Mitzvah etc.) at an age when many of them are still rather uncritical of the ideas they have been taught.

It will be remembered that Rousseau wanted *moral* education to begin very early, but that he had stressed that it should be by example rather than by precept. For him, the example set by parents and teachers had a religious basis, so in effect did rest on religious precepts, though these should not be conveyed as such until much later.

Today, many people also see that religion could be taught, long before the age of eighteen, in much the same way as poetry or history are taught, as descriptions of how people have thought about religions (note the plural) without the teacher trying to inculcate one particular religion as orthodoxy.

Émile's religious tutor is a parish priest in Savoy, and Rousseau later published this section of the book separately, under the title *Le Vicaire Savoyard* (1765). The vicar showed himself sceptical about much Christian dogma and doubted the authenticity of the Gospels. As he held the Rousseauist belief that Man may be corrupted by civilization, but is naturally good, he rejected the notion of Original Sin. Nevertheless, though he could proffer no intellectual arguments, he trusted his intuition, which convinced him of the existence of God, of free will and of Heaven, Purgatory and Hell. There could otherwise be no meaning to Man's life, no consolation at times of grief and suffering, nor an explanation of the glories of nature. On many points of religion the vicar, like Rousseau him-

20 Rousseau makes it clear that he is talking only about boys. His view on the education of women was an extreme example of male chauvinism, and is totally incompatible with his general theory of the Social Contract giving people "real" freedom. Women, he says, "have, or ought to have, little freedom". The education of a girl should prepare her for a life of "the strictest and most enduring restraints, those of propriety". The duty of a woman was to submit to her husband and make his life as pleasant as possible, and of course to be utterly faithful to him and be on her guard that her reputation should never be called into question. "She should learn early to submit to injustice and to suffer the wrongs inflicted on her by her husband without complaint." She should have only just enough education for her company not to be too boring for her husband, but not enough to enable her to entertain independent thought about society or religion. (Altogether, it is a picture of his uncomplaining housekeeper and common-law wife, Thérèse Levasseur, who had even tolerated having her children by him left at the door of a foundling hospital.) There are many other quite pathologically misogynist comments about the nature of women, so ridiculous that they ought not really to feature in a book on philosophy at all – indeed one wonders how someone considering himself a philosopher could allow such totally unphilosophical ideas to appear in print. Moreover, this was written in a period when educated women had a considerable role in French society, and Rousseau must have been to some of the salons over which they presided. He implied that it was their freedom that contributed to the infidelities that were accepted by many men and women in eighteenth-century aristocratic society. He was more in tune with some of the ideas of the nineteenth-century bourgeois paterfamilias than he was with his own century.

self, had *intellectual* doubts even about what his *intuition* told him, but he was sure that religious beliefs produce good results – we live better lives if we act "as if" they are true – a position that will later be argued by Kant.

> Intellectual humanists can perhaps work out an ethical system which they can take as a guide in life; they can perhaps see a meaning in life even without religion, and can have the resources without religion to cope with grief and suffering. However, for many people who are not given to working things out from first principles, the acceptance of what the religions teach do help them to lead a better life.

Many of the *philosophes* mocked what they considered to be an abdication of reason, and it was easy for them to show that religious beliefs had often produced practical results which were far from good: superstitions, persecutions, and the like. On the other side, the Catholic Church was outraged by the vicar's dismissal of much Christian orthodoxy, and it was of course dedicated to teach religion to the youngest children when they were at their most impressionable. "Give me a child until he is seven years old and I shall have him for life" was a Jesuit saying.

The publication of *Émile* led to much harassment of Rousseau in Catholic France. The *Parlement* of Paris ordered it to be burnt. By that time he had fled to Switzerland, but the Calvinists were no more enamoured than were the Catholics of his attitude to the Gospels. The rulers of Geneva also had the book burnt, and when Rousseau fled to Bern, he was asked to leave again. Frederick the Great then gave him shelter in Neuchâtel, a part of Switzerland that was under his jurisdiction, but even there the Calvinist clergy arraigned him for heresy. Then he accepted an invitation from David Hume to come to England, but by this time he had become so paranoid that he suspected Hume to be behind unfriendly articles which appeared about him in the press. In 1767 he returned to France. There he was now left more or less in peace, though he wandered restlessly from one residence to another. He died in Paris five weeks after the death there of his great rival Voltaire. The French revolutionaries of the Constituent Assembly, direct heirs of the Age of Reason, moved Voltaire's body to the Panthéon in 1791; in 1794 the Jacobins, who had claimed to represent the General Will, did the same for Rousseau's remains. From there, as the Durants say, "their spirits rose to renew their war for the soul of the Revolution, of France, and of Western man."[21]

EDMUND BURKE
1729 to 1797

Edmund Burke was another exponent of the Organic Theory of the State, but where Rousseau was seen at the end of the eighteenth century as a thinker of the radical Left and as having contributed to bring about the French Revolution, Burke, who detested the Revolution and the thinkers who prepared the way for it (whether *philosophes* or Rousseauists) came to be seen as the defender of the conservative Right.[22]

21 W.& A. Durant – *The Story of Civilization – Rousseau and Revolution*, Vol. IV, p. 887.

22 The terms "Left" and "Right" are used anachronistically when discussing eighteenth-century politics as they derive from the seating arrangements in the French Assemblies of the nineteenth century.

Rousseau had envisaged popular sovereignty. In his ideal state (which was a small one) the people would meet frequently to decide on policy, and those to whom it delegated the functions of government would be constantly under its immediate control. He admitted that in a modern, large state, this would be difficult, indeed well-nigh impossible, but Burke had an objection that rested on something more fundamental than the difficulty of such an arrangement. He famously asserted that those whom the people had chosen to carry out the functions of government were not *delegates*, but *representatives*. He was a member of parliament for Bristol, whose merchants disapproved of Burke's advocacy of removing trade restrictions from the Irish. When his constituents protested that, as their MP, he should support their interests, he responded (1778) that it was not for that purpose that they had elected him - they had chosen him because they trusted his character, his integrity, his general principles and his judgement. He should indeed consider the interests of his constituency, but he was and should be more than just their messenger boy as his responsibility as a member of parliament was towards the interests of the country as a whole. At the next election, he would give an account of what he had done as their representative and if they did not like how he had exercised his judgment, they would be free to choose a different representative.[23] Rousseau had specifically rejected that argument, when he had written, "The people of England regards itself as free; but it is grossly mistaken: it is free only during the election of members of parliament. As soon as they are elected, slavery overtakes it, and it is nothing."

Burke was also opposed to the whole notion of a Social Contract. The Social Contract, as Rousseau saw it, had brought an organic society into being. This society then set up the machinery of the state, and Rousseau had specifically denied that a contract existed between the society (which was the sovereign) and the government. A sovereign, he had said, cannot be bound by any contract. But Rousseau was never very consistent: six chapters earlier he had envisaged a government "breaking the social treaty" by which it had been created.

Burke was suspicious of the very word "contract", with its legalistic connotations and the implication that one side is released from it when the other side breaks it. In a famous and sonorous passage he denies that the state has come into being through some legalistic contract which ends when one side breaks its terms. First, he blurred the distinction between "Society" and "State", then, he preferred the word "partnership" to "contract":

> Society is indeed a contract. Subordinate contracts for objects of mere occasional interest may be dissolved at pleasure - but the State ought not to be considered as nothing better than a partnership agreement in a trade of pepper and coffee, calico or tobacco, or some other such low concern, to be taken up for a little temporary interest and to be dissolved by the fancy of the parties. It is to be looked on with other reverence; because it is not a partnership in things subservient only to the gross animal existence of a temporary and perishable nature. It is a partnership in all science; a partnership in all art; a partnership in every virtue and in all perfection. As the ends of such a partnership cannot be obtained in many generations, it becomes a partnership not only between those who are living, but between those who are living, those who are dead and those who are to be born. Each contract of each particular state is but a clause in the great primeval contract of eternal

23 He did indeed lose his Bristol seat in 1780, though his patron, Lord Rockingham, swiftly found him another one in the following year.

society, linking the lower with the higher natures, connecting the visible with the invisible world, according to a fixed compact sanctioned by the inviolable oath which holds all physical and all moral natures, each in their appointed place.

It is to be noted that nowhere does Burke describe, as Hobbes, Locke and Rousseau had done, how such a contract or compact came into being. This might seem very sensible of him, as the contracts of these earlier thinkers, couched as they were as a legal and binding agreement, were after all mere fiction. Burke will not speculate how governments came into being, "A sacred veil is to be drawn over the beginnings of all governments."

(A view which anthropologists might consider a little defeatist).

The state is not merely a political organism; because it is a partnership in all science and all art, it is also a social organism, and because it is a partnership between the living and the dead, it is deeply rooted in the history of each society. It shares its organic nature with other states, much as an oak tree shares an organic nature with a poplar.

Moreoever, the roots of an English oak tree are different from those of a French poplar; their organization is different, and these differences need to be respected if the trees are to be healthy. Just as it would be unnatural to graft the branch of a poplar onto an oak tree, so the attempt to impose on any state or society a character that is alien to its nature is bound to fail. This, Burke thought, was something the ideologues did not understand. The ideologues of the Age of Reason constantly thought in abstractions which were formed by what they liked to think was pure reason. They talked of the nature of Man as if this were everywhere the same; they took no account of the fact that Frenchmen had been shaped by their history to flourish in one kind of political, social and cultural soil, and that this was different from those which had shaped Englishmen.

As we shall see in the next chapter, this charge can certainly not be laid at the door of all the French *philosophes*. Montesquieu, in a cool and rational tone very different from Burke's mystical language, had shown in some detail how the history and character of nations are shaped by their different environment.

During the War of American Independence, Burke had spoken up for the Americans. They were of British stock and had taken British characteristics with them to the colonies. It was part of a British tradition going back to Magna Carta that there should be no taxation without representation. When the Americans rebelled, they defended a way of life which was rooted in the British past and had therefore contributed to the strength and success of Britain as a nation. It was not the Americans, but the government of Lord North which was the true revolutionary, trying to impose on British people something that was alien to British traditions – just as it had been Charles I and James II who had tried to impose an alien system of government on their subjects at home. It was these monarchs who were the would-be revolutionaries, rather than the men who executed the former king in 1649, or who drove out the latter in 1688.

There is indeed a significant difference between English and French revolutionaries at that time. The English always sought justification in the history of the past. The Glorious Revolution of 1688 was called glorious not because it had brought about a new dawn, but in part because it had reasserted what the revolutionaries took to be the ancient traditions of British liberty. The French, on the other hand, claimed that the French Revolution had indeed produced a new dawn – so much so that the Jacobins renamed the year when the Republic was established in 1792 as Year I.

France, Burke maintained, had never had traditions of liberty. France had been at her strongest and most successful under absolute governments, and had been at her weakest when that absolutism had been undermined - never by genuine parliamentarians (such as had resisted Stuart attempts at absolutism) but usually by selfish nobles. It was being undermined again now in the name of theories which ignored the lessons of French history. In 1790, when Burke wrote his *Reflections*, the French Revolution was still in its moderate phase. Burke believed that even at that stage its philosophy (when it was still owing more to the *philosophes* than to the Rousseauists) was alien to the French genius. The result was sure to be chaos which, before long, would become so intolerable that Frenchmen would once again demand and get strong and authoritarian government. In this way, after much bloodshed and possibly in a twisted form, the native traditions of France would reassert themselves. Burke prophesied the authoritarianism which Napoleon would establish after 1799 - two years after Burke's death.

What Burke did not realize was that if wisdom manifests itself in history in the centuries that lie behind us, it will also manifest itself in those that lie ahead. So he did not foresee that what Frenchmen did during the French Revolution would itself become a significant part of tradition in France. In the revolutions of 1830, 1848 and 1871, sections of the population would invoke the traditions of 1789, 1792 or 1794 (dates which represent moderate, radical and extreme programmes respectively). Moreover, the attempt by Charles X to go back to the traditions of the *Ancien Régime* had no resonance in the country and led to his overthrow.

On the other hand, there is some truth in his insight that if constitutions are to endure, they cannot make too radical a break with the traditions of the existing society. This is especially the case when the constitutions are imposed from outside, as they were, for instance, by the imperial powers when they bestowed constitutions on their African colonies prior to their departure. The Westminster model broke down very quickly in many of Britain's former colonies, while ancient tribal traditions, both in terms of allegiance and in terms of power structures, reasserted themselves.

The long passage quoted on pp. 343–4 comes from Burke's *Reflections on the French Revolution*, published in 1790, when the Revolution was still in its moderate phase. Some of the early revolutionaries had long admired the English constitution and wanted to give France something similar. Burke felt that even then they were imposing on France a form of government that, though deeply rooted in the history of England, was alien to the traditions of France. The *philosophes*, it will be remembered, had no respect for traditions as such. They claimed to measure the worth of a tradition against reason, but there is a wisdom embodied in traditions which goes beyond the weak and fallible reason of individuals:

> The individual is foolish; the multitude is foolish for the moment, when they act without deliberation; but the species is wise and, when time is given to it, as a species it always acts right.

> Politics ought to be adjusted, not to human reasoning, but to human nature, of which the reason is but a part, and by no means the greatest part.

In particular, the reasoning of the revolutionaries rested on abstract theories, and, "one sure symptom of an ill-conducted state is the propensity of the people to resort to theories".

> Here, Burke gives expression to how the British generally see themselves. They pride themselves on their pragmatic and common sense approach, and tend to be suspicious of the theoretical structures erected by many continental thinkers. What they really mean is that their theories (here, that wisdom is enshrined in tradition) are sounder than those of the continentals (in this case the application of "abstract" principles to politics).

Of course, there has to be change, but change should always be evolutionary, going with the grain of a nation's history, never revolutionary, informed by hatred or contempt for the past. To go back to the metaphor of the tree, every organism grows and develops, and rotten branches need to be pruned, but radical reform lays an axe to the very roots (Latin: *radices*) of the organism and that is sure to inflict irreparable harm. Using another metaphor, he wrote, "Even when I changed, it would be to preserve ... I would make the reparations as nearly as possible in the style of the building."

> This passage is echoed by the language of Peel's Tamworth Manifesto of 1834. In it, Peel explained the principles that were to guide the Tory Party, which he renamed the Conservative Party to show that the resistance to any change which characterized it, in the period immediately following the Napoleonic wars, had been abandoned. Peel said he was willing to reform, but only in order to be better able to conserve the valuable character of British institutions. This principle of Burke's has been at the heart of British conservatism ever since, and has saved it from becoming rigid or excessively doctrinaire. Rarely since that time has conservatism fought in the last ditch. When pressure for reform became too great, it generally made concessions in good time,[24] and Britain has therefore been spared the revolutions which have violently overthrown so many inflexible governments on the continent. If that means that reform in England has always been rather slow and piecemeal, it has also reduced the pressure for *root*-and-branch reform and has therefore drawn the sting of genuine radicalism in Britain.

The concern that Burke had that change should go with the grain of a nation's history is not unconnected with the attempt of the *philosophes* to look for laws that would illuminate the understanding of the social sciences (of which history was one) as they were bringing better understanding of the physical sciences. During this quest, philosophies of history emerged to which we will turn in the next chapter.

24 I have deliberately spelt conservatism with a small c here because some of the concessions have been made by conservatives in the Whig and Liberal parties.

CHAPTER 30

Eighteenth Century Philosophies of History

Before the Eighteenth Century

Before the eighteenth century, few historians had concerned themselves with philosophical aspects of history, and most general books on the philosophy of history begin with the eighteenth century. (R.G. Collingwood's *The Idea of History* is an exception, and I owe the following paragraphs to it). It is only then that historians began specifically to ask themselves questions about the nature of history and to produce systematic theories about how history works. Are there laws that govern historical processes? Are there patterns in history? If so, are they patterns of general progress or do we see cycles of growth and decline? Is there some sense in which history repeats itself? Are there impersonal forces which throw up leaders of a particular type, or are the processes of history shaped by the personalities, the strengths and weaknesses of particular individuals?

Of course such questions must, from time to time, occur to anyone who thinks about history. Historians before the eighteenth century made the odd comment about them, but it did not generally occur to them to formalize a theory. They sometimes saw their subject as an encouragement of patriotic or religious virtues, which provided a framework for their narrative. This was only sometimes conscious; all historians, even those who are not given to conscious reflections, nevertheless *have* a philosophy of history, of which they may be quite unaware. They will have certain unconscious assumptions about who or what is important and who or what is unimportant. These assumptions shape what they write, even if they think that all they are doing is writing down a narrative.

The first glimmering of reflections on what they are doing comes with the awareness of some writers that they ought to sift fact from fiction, history from myth or legend. That separation had never occurred to the rhapsodes, those early writers and reciters of epics like Homer's *Iliad*. The first great writer to undertake this task was Herodotus (*ca.* 484 to 425 BC) who, therefore, is rightly called the Father of History. Indeed, he was the first man to use the word "history" in the title of his work on the twenty-year war between the Greeks and the Persians. The word then meant "inquiry", and itself came from the word *histor*, meaning "a judge". Herodotus therefore announces that he is doing more than merely write down stories or legends passed down to him. He did not need to fall back on myths (other than perhaps those that are born in any war) because he has carried out his own research, enquired into the past, cross-examined witnesses, weighed up or judged what he was told. (There was not much documentary or archival material in those days.) He does not even do all the judging himself, but leaves it to his readers. When given conflicting accounts of what has happened, he often confined himself to telling the reader that "some says this" and "others say that". Examining witnesses involves confining the subject under investigation to a short timespan and one close to the period in which the writer lives; the Persian War had ended in 479, shortly after Herodotus had been born.

A generation later, Thucydides (*ca.* 460 to 404 BC) wrote of the Second and Third Peloponnesian Wars between Athens and Sparta (431 to 404 BC) in which he had actually taken part. He could therefore tell an even more reliable story than Herodotus (though he did not scruple to invent speeches which his characters were *likely* to have made). He made it clear that his aim went beyond that of his predecessor - he was not only providing a narrative, but hoped that the way he explained it would help in "the study of similar events which are likely in human nature to occur in after ages". This is a hint - nothing more - that there might be recurring features in history and that its course might depend, not on the arbitrary will of the gods, but on earthly causes which we could understand. These include, for example, the different "national characters" of Athens and Sparta, described with great impartiality by someone who fought for the one against the other.

> The notion is not completely useless in trying to understand certain periods. Some countries are, for long periods, imbued by a military ethos like that of Sparta – this has been held to explain some recent German history. Other countries seem to pay more attention to civilian values, as Athens was said to have done, and when such societies find themselves at war with a "Spartan" country, they may initially be unprepared for it and suffer setbacks as a result. The danger is that such notions can lead to unjustifiable generalizations about an entire country – ignoring the more pacific elements in German society, for example, or the strident chauvinism that often characterizes the popular press in a country whose statesmen are not themselves aggressive.

Then there are geographical factors and the respective advantages of sea-power and land-power.

> The American Admiral Mahan's famous book, *The Influence of Sea-Power upon History*, published in 1890, would elaborate on this, showing how a country with a long coastline is encouraged to develop a navy and how this in turn stimulates overseas commerce and may result in creating a commercial empire. He also describes how possession of a powerful navy makes aggressive blockades possible without having to use the same numbers of men that a landlocked country would need for similar aggressive intent, but that, to bring about a conclusive victory, there is generally a need to defeat the enemy's forces on land.

Next there are social tensions, always present, but exacerbated during a war, between oligarchs and democrats.

Athens was hampered by the already existing tension between these two classes. The expenses of war tend to fall most heavily on the poor (through taxation and price rises as the result of shortages, especially of food.) The resentments may then often boil over. In this way, war would radicalize the French Revolution and would trigger the two Russian Revolutions of 1917.

Then there is the influence on the course of a war of the characters and ambitions of individual leaders.

The personal ambitions and corruption of Alcibiades played a major role in the war between Athens and Sparta. Likewise, the particular character of Hitler would stamp its mark on the course of German history. In the next section we will look at the argument that Hitler was brought to power by certain "impersonal" forces in Germany at that time, which he represented and exploited cleverly, and that, had Hitler died before 1933, these impersonal forces would have thrown up another leader very like Hitler.

It is to be noted that we are still a long way away from the notions that one can "learn lessons from history" or that there is a pattern to history, let alone that "History repeats itself". Thucydides is merely inviting historians of a future epoch to pay attention, just as he has done, to such factors as national character, geography, social tensions etc. This will enable them to write a fuller history of the period in question and to gain a deeper understanding of the events that are being narrated.

During this period, there was a rapid rise and fall of many states and empires: of Athens and other city-states, of Macedon, of the short-lived empire of Alexander the Great, of Carthage – all sooner or later to fall to Rome. So the notion of history being cyclical naturally surfaced from time to time, but it was not explored in any detail.

In general, for all the popularity of Herodotus, Thucydides and Xenophon, history as a subject of study did not enjoy great prestige among philosophers. A generation after Thucydides, Aristotle (384 to 322 BC) clearly did not take the hint of that great historian that we might find some recurring features in history. One could say of Aristotle that, although he had developed a philosophy of science, a philosophy of literature, a philosophy of ethics, he did not think there was such a thing as philosophy of history. He famously wrote that poetry was "truer" than history, because history dealt with everchanging and particular circumstances whilst the subject matter of poetry was eternal and universal, and as such the proper subject of philosophy. History, therefore, had nothing to do with philosophy for Aristotle, and I believe that Thucydides would have agreed with him. I doubt whether he would have thought that there was such a subject as philosophy of history, or have claimed that the remarks he had dropped – that future historians might benefit from taking geography etc into account – qualified him to be considered as a philosopher.

Being a historian and being a philosopher of history are obviously two different things. Anyone who does serious detailed research in history must surely realize that every situation, every individual, is unique. He may find it difficult to avoid making generalizations – he, too, is likely to have what I have earlier called an unconscious philosophy of history which tells him what is significant and what is less significant – but the more scholarly he is, the more suspicious

> he will be of them because he knows – or should know – where generalizations break down.

Rome produced great narrative historians, influential, not least because of their care for literary style. Where Herodotus and Thucydides had confined themselves to a short and recent period of history, Livy took the whole of Roman history as his canvas. His early books therefore relied heavily on legend, and he could certainly not rely on eye-witnesses. In addition, for him there were moral lessons to be drawn from history. He was a patriotic Roman republican, and he traced the decay of republican virtues in Rome and hoped that his readers might revive the ancient virtues. However, the decay continued, and Tacitus would illustrate its continuation. Both believed that the purpose of history was not only instruction, but also moral edification and a call to patriotism. So, the task of the historian was, among other things, to make moral judgments.

Collingwood says that the Romans had a poor conception of causality - many of them still ascribed disasters to the whims of the gods, and taught that they should be borne stoically. With such a superficial attitude, it followed that there was little one could learn from history.

Christian historiography also saw history as divinely influenced, but where the pagans had seen the influence of the gods as arbitrary, depending sometimes on the rivalry between quarrelling gods, the Christians regarded history as the working out of the one and only God's long-range providence or purpose, which is to establish Heaven on Earth. We may not always understand His purpose, but history reflects divine wisdom not a divine whim and is a carefully worked out plan in God's mind. We find this idea as late as the writings of the French Bishop Bossuet (1621 to 1704) who, in 1681 published a history of the world up to the reign of Charlemagne (*Discours sur l'Histoire universelle*). This showed history as God's relationship with His chosen people; originally the Jews. When they were defeated by the Assyrians and the Babylonians, it was because God wanted to chastise them for having gone astray; he then used the Persians to reestablish them in their land, and then the Romans to protect them from the Syrians. When they rejected Jesus, God used the Romans to punish them. Since then, the Christians have been His chosen people, who, under His Providence, converted Rome. When the people of Rome had been tempted to worship once again at pagan temples, God had brought the barbarians upon them to sack the city. Providentially, many of the barbarians had previously been converted to Christianity. Charlemagne's coronation by the Pope set the seal on the Christianization of much of Europe, since which time, the faith had gone from strength to strength.

Some sixty years later, Montesquieu would provide a very different explanation for the rise and fall of the Roman Empire.

MONTESQUIEU
1689 to 1755

Montesquieu did not believe that the key to the understanding of the course of history was the idea that God sporadically intervened in human affairs to bring about Heaven on earth. As a child of the Age of Reason, he believed that everything in the universe is governed by regular laws which, even if God were their providential author, can be discovered by reason. More and more of the laws that governed physical nature had been discovered during the Scientific Revolution, which had culminated so dramatically in Newton. This gave confidence to some *philosophes,* Montesquieu included, that the application of reason would also reveal the laws that governed social affairs, which included history. In his *Considerations on the Causes of Greatness and Decadence of the Romans* (1734), he wrote:

> there are general causes, moral or physical, which operate in every monarchy, raise it, maintain it, or overthrow it. All that occurs is subject to these causes; and if a particular cause, like the accidental result of a battle, has ruined a state, there was a general cause which made the downfall of this state ensue from a single battle.

Montesquieu was surely right here. True, we may jib at the word "accidental" when considering some victories on the battlefield – brilliant or incompetent generals have obviously had a decisive influence on some battles and even campaigns. However, a battle lost does not invariably cause the downfall of a state. Some countries have recovered from even the most catastrophic defeats (like Pearl Harbour) to win wars in the end, whilst for others, a single battle like Königgrätz (Sadowa) or Sedan are fatal. Consider, for example, that Russia acknowledged defeat in the Crimean War when she had lost Sebastopol, which really was no more than a pimple on the vast body of Russia, but she could lose Moscow to Napoleon and vast stretches of land to Hitler, without losing the war. At the time of the Crimean War, the structure of the Russian Empire was so ossified that the loss of Sebastopol was crucial, whereas Stalin had for years prepared a military and industrial back-up system east of the Urals that could produce the counter-attacks that won the war for him.

Montesquieu's view is today called the "structuralist view" of history. One aspect of this is usually the contention that, for example, the character of individual leaders in itself has a very limited influence on the course of history. It assumes that such a leader gets to where he is not so much because of his own talents, but because society is looking for just such a man. Montesquieu spells this out specifically. Cato had wanted to preserve republican institutions through the powers of the Senate, but this policy was doomed, and would have failed even if Caesar and Pompey had been on Cato's side rather than against him. "If Caesar and Pompey had thought like Cato, others would have come to the same ideas as those of Caesar and Pompey; and the Republic, destined to perish, would have been led to ruin by some other hand." I believe that in a democracy, the structuralist view is almost wholly true, especially in the longer run, a leader cannot become or remain a leader unless he reflects the balance of forces in his society. He may for a while retard certain developments of that society or, more rarely, perhaps speed them up, but he cannot, over a period, go against the stream and impose his views or policies on a society that does not like them.

It is, I think, also true in modern history that society, in a period of crisis or chaos, sometimes "calls for" a strong man. The dictators who then arise may be said to answer that call. Once a dictator comes to power by going with the stream of history, the personality he then displays can be a crucial moulding form of the future. If he is utterly ruthless, has paranoia, megalomania, or an obsession with, for example, antisemitism, then once he has absolute power, he can use terror and his control of the media to impose his view of the world

> on his country's policies. He could eliminate all potential rivals as Stalin did, or plunge the world into an epoch-moulding war and embark on the elimination of the Jews as Hitler did. The Weimar Republic may have been ripe for overthrow, but the strong man who replaced it might have had the personal moderation of a Bismarck, the friendly attitude towards the Jews that Mussolini originally had, or the basic respect for political decencies that De Gaulle had.

Montesquieu detected a process in the history of Rome, which he believed could be found in the rise and fall of other states as well. He thought that initially the small Roman Republic had a balanced constitution and a strong sense of civic virtue. These qualities enabled it to grow, and as it grew, it needed a strong central authority to rule its dependencies. This in turn was bound to weaken the civic spirit of the citizens and would, in due course, lead to despotism, corruption and decadence. There would come the time when the Empire was too bloated and too self-indulgent to be able to resist the assault of vigorous barbarians and so it declined.

In his more famous book *L'Esprit des Lois* (1748), Montesquieu made a more thorough attempt to create a philosophy of history. Here he propounded the idea that what primarily influences history is the physical environment within which societies develop. That means, in the first place, climate, coastlines, mountains and the nature of the soil. These determine the temperament of the people, their customs and the economy of their society. These in turn underlie the laws, the forms of government and other social arrangements.

Montesquieu illustrates these general statements with a wealth of examples. Some of these are shrewd and suggestive, whilst others can only be described as dotty. He claimed that the colder climates of the north make people more vigorous, more independent-minded and therefore more in love with liberty, more temperate in their enthusiasms, and he even believed that they were more virtuous than the people in warmer southern climates. Southern people succumb more easily to despotism, whilst the northern spirit of independence and liberty caused the people there to embrace Protestantism. (This was only one reason why the book was initially banned in France.) It is because in hot climates people are more passionate that women have to be secluded and it is the early fading of women's beauty in hot climates that explains polygamy in Muslim countries.

> Montesquieu anticipates Marx in providing a materialist explanation of history, but he is far wilder in his supportive material, and Voltaire and others had no difficulty in demolishing the examples and thereby undermining the generalizations. Climate and geography are fairly constant, but the character of a nation is not. The Turkish and Persian governments may have been effete in Montesquieu's time, but governments and soldiers from that region had been formidable enough in the past. The Italians of Montesquieu's time, treated more or less like colonial subjects by the Great Powers, were very different from the Romans of old who had set out from the same geographical and climatic setting to subdue much of the rest of Europe.

The Catholic Church attacked Montesquieu for the relativism it perceived in his work. Relativism did indeed seem to be a logical implcation of his theory, but that did not stop him from making moral judgments in his book. His political theory, which has been mentioned in Chapter 28,[1] is part of *L'Esprit des Lois*, and we have seen that it was opposed to absolute monarchy. If material factors predispose people to unattractive customs, a good legislator should try to control and correct these, just as a doctor will understand the factors that predispose someone towards illness and can control and cure it by a judicious medical regime. The legislator will find it difficult if he goes too much against the grain of the society; so he has to work prudently, conservatively and with sensitivity. The task is not impossible, however, and Montesquieu was not an out-and-out determinist in his view of history. However, he did believe that there were natural laws at work in history. His understanding of these laws was crude, and his illustrations of them often even cruder. It was a contemporary of his, Giambattista Vico, who produced a subtler version of what these laws might be and how they worked.

GIAMBATTISTA VICO
1688 to 1744

Montesquieu's work had achieved instant fame among his contemporaries; Vico had to wait much longer for recognition, even though his *Scienza Nuova* of 1725 preceded Montesquieu's *Considerations* by nine years and *L'Esprit des Lois* by twenty-three years.

Montesquieu knew Vico's book and privately acknowledged that it had influenced his own book on the rise and fall of the Roman Empire. In it was the notion, central to Vico's *Scienza Nuova*, that Rome's civilization had gone through a cycle of youth, maturity and decay and the suggestion that similar cycles might be found in other civilizations. The language of the youth, maturity and decay of a society suggests that society is seen as an organism. The organic view of society was, as we saw in the last chapter,[2] characteristic of Romanticism. Romanticism did not sit so easily with Montesquieu, nor was it yet the dominant cultural influence of his day. His classical contemporaries had a more mechanistic view of society. It was seen more like a machine which is formed by various bits being put together than as an organism and that was the temper of Montesquieu's second and more influential book, *L'Esprit des Lois*, written fourteen years after his book on the Roman Empire. Here, in classical style, he focussed more closely on the *external* forces (like climate, geography, size and the economic possibilities stemming from them) which affect the way a society functions. Change the parts (substitute rich farming land for desert) and you create a different kind of society.

Vico was, therefore, even more out of touch with the classical temper that prevailed in 1725. For him, the organic phases of society had psychological characteristics very similar to those of a human being. Of course, external factors (climate etc.) have an effect on it, just as they have an effect on individual humans. The essence of a society is to be found in its internal development rather than how it is shaped by external factors. That notion has to wait for general acceptance until the Romantic movement has become really significant. It

1 See p. 317 above.

2 See p. 327 above.

is difficult to give a precise date to that moment, but it must correspond roughly with the impact of Rousseau's *Social Contract* of 1762. After that, it gradually gathered in strength until one could say that it had become dominant by the end of the Napoleonic period, by which time, long after Vico's death, his ideas had begun to receive wider acclaim.

Let us look more closely at the organic cycles which Vico had detected in the life of societies. In its earliest stage, the primitive or heroic one, a society is strong on the imagination, on the passions, and on the hold that religion has upon it. In this stage, a society, like an individual, is vigorous, enthusiastic and impetuous. In the next stage, the classical or reflective, its feelings and emotions are more controlled by reason. In the third, the decadent, the emotions and enthusiasm are actually looked down upon, and reasoning, which in the reflective phase has been employed creatively, is used destructively in an all-embracing scepticism which will eventually undermine all the values and institutions that are needed to keep a society healthy. As a result, it will eventually collapse, and a new cycle will begin.

> As an example, let us see how this applies to morals. In the primitive phase moral teaching is accepted from the priests without too much reflection. Because it is not questioned, the moral code is intensely felt, but it may also have elements in it that are superstitious and unreasonable. The reflective phase will try to trim the superstitions and will aim to base morality not so much on received religious opinion, but on reason.Once it is based on reason, however, we cannot be sure whether it can withstand some of the attacks that are made on it in the name of reason. In a decadent and sceptical phase there may be no confidence in the rational basis of any (or at least of an agreed) morality, and the cohesion of society, which depends on a commonly agreed moral position, is fatally undermined.
>
> To take another example, a primitive society may vigorously and confidently propound and enforce a family structure in which women are unreasonably oppressed. In the reflective phase, the women are treated in a more rational and liberal manner and the family structure is the better for it. In the decadent phase, reason is deployed, if not against the family, then at any rate to liberate women – and men, too – from family obligations if these are seen to be "unreasonable". This strikes a damaging blow at a structure that is seen by many people as an essential part of a healthy society.

The cycles are not mere repetitions; they allow for progress. History is, as it were, an upward moving spiral. Vico believed that the religious phase of Christian civilization represents an advance over the religious phase of pagan culture, and such progress he saw as part of the Divine Providence which shapes the course of history.

Unlike the *philosophes*, Vico valued the early, primitive phase of the cycle. Primitive societies may not have so much wisdom resulting from rational reflection, but their religion, in particular, reflected the "poetic wisdom" of a people, and was not, as so many *philosophes* believed, the result of ignorance and imposture, "Civilization", he writes, "in every case began with religion, and was completed by sciences, discipline, and arts."

Like Montesquieu, Vico believed that law sprang out of custom, but where Montesquieu had seen custom shaped by the material factors of geography and climate, Vico said that it sprang out of imagination and feeling. He was also a pioneer in the importance he attached to language, myths and folklore as helping us, if we will use our imagination and capacity for empathy, to enter into the minds of earlier periods and to understand a society's roots. The notion of the "noble savage" was yet to be invented by Rousseau; but Vico had already seen nobility and a (nonrational) wisdom in the civilization of our distant forefathers.

This is another reason why Vico was ignored during the Age of Reason and would come into his own only when Romanticism had established itself. The *philosophes* had dismissed most earlier periods of history as benighted, "Gothic"; they had paid little attention to the imagination and could see no value in "primitive" religion or the "wisdom" of the uneducated. Vico shared the romantic feeling that the past was valuable and formative, and that religion played an important part in this. Vico's time would come. He was first "rediscovered" by Goethe in 1787 during that thinker's own romantic period; he was praised by Coleridge in 1816, translated into French by Michelet in 1827, treated as a major figure by Croce in 1920 and then introduced to the British public in the 1960s and 1970s by that great historian of Romanticism, Isaiah Berlin, and some of Vico's ideas would be developed by Johann Gottfried Herder at a time when they would fall on much more receptive ground, but between Vico and Herder we need to consider another "classical" philosopher of history, the Marquis de Condorcet.

THE MARQUIS DE CONDORCET
1743 to 1794

Condorcet was a *philosophe*. He had been a friend of d'Alembert, the editor of the *Encyclopédie*, and had played a part in preparing that great work. Like so many *philosophes* he was strongly anticlerical and a great believer in the power of education to eliminate ignorance and to pave the way to progress in society. When the French Revolution broke out, he became associated with the Girondins, and in 1792 he was the architect of the secular educational system enacted by the Convention. Shortly afterwards, in the summer of 1793, the Girondins were overthrown and then proscribed by the Jacobins. Condorcet went into hiding, but was discovered in March 1794 and taken to prison, where, two days later, he was found dead.

While in hiding he had written his *Esquisse d'un Tableau Historique des Progrès de l'Esprit Humain*, published the year after his death. Whereas Vico's picture of history had been of a cycle of birth, maturity and decline (albeit that each cycle was at a higher level than the preceding one) Condorcet's was one of continuing progress from the barbarism at the beginning of human history to the present civilization and indeed to the civilizations of the future. This vision of continuing progress throughout the whole of history was a slight refinement of the view held by many *philosophes*, who did not trouble to look for any sign of progress during the Middle Ages; they had simply seen those centuries as a gaping hole between Antiquity and the Renaissance.

The motor of this progress was education. Condorcet had seen the extension of education becoming a feature of many European states during his lifetime, not only in France, but also in the lands ruled by the so-called Enlightened Despots, with Joseph II having set the pace. Those countries which had not yet expanded their educational system were bound to follow soon: they would see how it strengthened the states who had made the reform, and would need to follow suit if only to match the strength of their rivals. As education was the key to all progress, progress would be infinitely extensible into the future.

This optimistic picture of history is a forerunner of the influential philosophy of Auguste Comte (1796 to 1857) which is known as Positivism. In the second half of the nineteenth century it dominated the outlook of western countries, where the Industrial Revolution was delivering power, prosperity and progress, and where there was every reason for believing that this was only the beginning of improvements for all mankind. Until the slaughter of the First World War, many tended to ignore the darker side of the picture, the imperfectablity of human nature. This aspect will be discussed more fully in the section on Comte.[3]

In the meantime, the ideas of Comte form an interlude between Vico's more sophisticated view of human development and the elaboration of parts of his philosophy by Johann Gottfried Herder.

JOHANN GOTTFRIED HERDER
1744 to 1803

Herder published a four-volume work between 1784 and 1791, called *Ideas for the Philosophy of the History of Mankind*. He took up Vico's point that we should never use one stage of a society's development as a yardstick by which to assess earlier ones. Each culture has its own merit. As Vico had said, the earlier "primitive" phases of a people's history have an intrinsic value of their own. Herder added that above all they are important for an understanding of the present. These early phases account for the *differences* between nations today. The *philosophes* had laid stress on what all men have in common, but, like all romantics, Herder was more interested in the differences between nations than in their similarities. These differences stemmed from a people's innermost nature, and this nature is expressed, above all, in the *language* spoken by the common people, the *Volk*. Since 1772, the *Sturm und Drang* movement had urged the Germans to resist the influence of the French language in Germany;[4] it was alien and could never express the native spirit of the German people. Herder now widened this idea by stressing that *every* nation finds its true spirit incorporated in the language of its common people. A nation is *defined* by its language.

The *Sturm und Drang* movement was initially cultural rather than political. It was not part of its agenda in 1772 (nor was it part of Herder's) to call for the political unity of all those who spoke the German language, but as the cultural hegemony of France was transformed into direct political domination of much of Germany during the Revolutionary and Napoleonic period, so cultural

3 See p. 437 below.

4 See p. 326 above.

nationalism was transformed into the political nationalism which has been one of the most potent forces in European history ever since. This nationalism almost invariably defined a nation as a community using the same language.[5]

As the struggle for independence moved from the cultural to the political field, it assumed characteristics which were alien to Herder's ideas. When, during the Napoleonic period, Johann Fichte published his lectures under the heading *Addresses to the German Nation* (1808/09), he was already asserting not merely the independence, but the superiority of German over other languages. He claimed that the German language was pure, unlike French or Italian which he thought were bastard derivatives from Latin, or English, which he described as an entirely composite language. People who spoke corrupted and impure languages, he thought, could not possibly be in true touch with their innermost nature. The claim that German was therefore culturally superior to those other languages would very quickly become the claim that the German *race* was likewise superior to other races, and therefore had a right to lord it over them. In reaction against this, other nationalists would assert the superiority of their own language and race, and these rival claims provoked the nationalist arrogance and hatred which have bedevilled the history of the nineteenth and twentieth centuries.

All this was far from the teaching of Herder. The culture of one country should not be used to assess the value of other cultures, any more than one period should be used as a yardstick against which to assess other periods. Herder saw all the different cultures of Europe coexisting peacefully and with respect and tolerance for each other. Political nationalism would soon develop into the worship of the national state, but Herder prophetically warned that the modern state, which is so often based on the conquest of other peoples, was no improvement on the sometimes homogeneous ethnic groupings which preceded it. He disliked authoritarian governments, militarism and imperialism. He was even more liberal than those so-called liberal nationalist parties in Germany, who were willing to extend citizenship and equal rights to all those who identified themselves with the German language and culture. Herder believed that within every state people should be respected for their *own* national identity. For example, he respected the Jews as a people with its own language and culture, and challenged the prevailing assumption of many Germans, and a section of the Jews themselves, that the Jews should drop their culture and assimilate with the peoples among whom they lived. He would have been very unhappy had he lived long into the nineteenth century, which so perverted his ideas.

5 There are some exceptions, of course. The Swiss were proud of their national unity despite their linguistic diversity, and so, by and large, were the Belgians after their state came into existence in 1830.

PART SIX:
THE NINETEENTH CENTURY

CHAPTER 31

Immanuel Kant

1724 to 1804

Towards the end of the eighteenth century, around 1780, there were several strands in European philosophy which appeared to be pulling in different directions. It was Kant who made a titanic effort to pull them all together and in the process launched continental philosophy in particular in a new direction. His influence on the continent is not exhausted yet.

His original interests and writings related to science, which in the eighteenth century was thoroughly deterministic. It held that every event was determined by the causes which had preceded it; that these causes could be discovered by a combination of experiments and reasoning and could be formulated as laws; that the same reasoning which had discovered the laws operating in the physical sciences should in due course discover the laws operating in the social sciences as well; and that the knowledge gained by the proper application of scientific reasoning was real and certain. This was the earliest formative influence on Kant's thinking.

Then, in 1755, he came across the work of David Hume, who, Kant famously said, awoke him from his dogmatic slumbers. Hume had demonstrated that we can have no *certain* knowledge of anything beyond our direct experience and observation. Radically, he showed that we can have no *philosophical* certainty that causes, laws, space, time, or even identity exist: they are the names we give to clusters of impressions which are generally associated with each other. If we cannot be *certain* that anything lies behind the perceptions of our five senses, then we can hardly make reliable statements about anything of which we can have no direct perception, and that strips all metaphysical and all religious ideas of any reliability.[1] Kant had had a very religious upbringing, so now he had to reconcile three strands of thought – the certainty of his religious outlook, the confidence he had that science gave reliable answers, and now the *philosophical* uncertainty which Hume had cast on our ability to be sure of anything other than our direct perceptions.

> I keep putting the word "philosophical" into italics to remind us that Hume was well aware that for practical purposes the assumptions we make about cause and effect are useful enough, and that we are so constituted that we cannot

1 For a full discussion of these ideas, see the section on Hume in chapter 27.

> live without them. Much of philosophy is "counter-intuitive" – meaning that it often undermines what we would like to call "common sense". At first sight, therefore, it seems that such philosophy is so abstract and theoretical that it has little to do with actual living. If one's business is philosophical thinking, then clearly one can be troubled by counter-intuitive ideas, and very few philosophers have so much reliance on common sense that they do not take counter-intuitive theories seriously enough to grapple with them on a philosophical level.

The next influence on Kant came in 1765, when he read Leibniz for the first time. Leibniz had posited that in the mind there are certain inborn principles according to which our later experiences are organized. He called these "the tools of understanding", and they included the concepts of being, substance, unity, identity and contradiction. Without these tools, the mind might *receive* sensations, but it could never order them or make sense of them. He also thought that, just as our minds are equipped to receive and order the impressions of the senses to give us *factual* knowledge, so they are also equipped from birth to receive and work on another kind of input which will give us *moral* knowledge. Admittedly, Leibniz had said, the factual knowledge which our senses convey to us gives us a fundamentally inaccurate picture of the world. They seem to tell us that the world is material, consisting of a mass of physical atoms; but that is an illusion: all "matter" is, in the last resort, not matter at all but is made up of units of energy.[2] Kant will absorb both the notion of the tools of understanding and the idea that the world may be totally different from the way in which we perceive it.

Finally, we need to consider the impact made on Kant by Rousseau's *Émile,* which he read soon after it appeared in 1762. Kant was, famously, a creature of habit. It was said that the inhabitants of Königsberg could set their clocks by his daily constitutional walk. He is reported to have been so absorbed by *Émile* that for once he forgot to follow this routine. What gripped him so much was the Romantic challenge in that book to the preeminence of reason and the instruction that we should listen to our feelings. This would reinforce Kant's conviction, derived from his religious upbringing, that, where rational *proof* of the existence of God is missing, we (he really means "*he*") can confidently accept what our religious feelings tell us.

His interests now shifted from the sciences to philosophy, and we can see in his theories the four formative influences on him. Two of these were aspects of the Age of Reason – the existence of Natural Laws as shown by Newton, and subjectivism as shown by Hume. The other two belonged to Romanticism: a respect for what the feelings, the inner self tells us – the so-called "categorical imperative" – and a transcendentalism[3] that came from Leibniz and makes possible a return to metaphysics.

We see the germ of his later ideas in the inaugural lecture on Epistemology which he delivered, when, at the age of forty-six, he was appointed Professor of Logic and Metaphysics at the University of Königsberg in 1770. In it, he distin-

2 For a fuller discussion, see the section on Leibniz in on p. 278 above for his notion of our innate ideas, and p. 250 above for the idea that matter is in the last resort immaterial.

3 Transcendental: beyond our *experience* of phenomena.

guished between the world that can be perceived by the senses and that which can be perceived by the intellect. By that distinction he showed that he rejected the claim of philosophers like Locke, Berkeley and Hume that all knowledge derives from sensation, but all those philosophers in the past who believed in a metaphysical dimension would have agreed with Kant. Even Aristotle and Berkeley thought that the metaphysical dimension could be inferred from the knowledge we derive from the senses.[4]

Kant would develop the distinction between these two worlds in a way which had never occurred to his predecessors. It took him another eleven years before he was ready to publish, and then he wrote in a tremendous hurry. The 800 pages of *The Critique of Pure Reason* (1781) were written down within four or five months. He admitted in a letter to Moses Mendelssohn that he had not taken the time to polish his method of exposition so as to make his ideas easier to understand - and the work is difficult. It is made even harder because it is one of the earliest philosophical treatises to be written in German rather than Latin. Where Latin is crisp and compact, German tends to be ponderous. Kant made his own translations of the Latin philosophical vocabulary, but in addition had to invent a new vocabulary to express new concepts. Even the German reader might be confused. The word "Critique" for example, could mean "criticism", or "assessment" (as, for example, of a work of literature) but Kant used it in the sense of "investigation" or "analysis". As for the word "Pure", we shall presently see the significance of that adjective.[5] The programme that the title of the book was intended to convey was an investigation into Epistemology, a description of how our rational faculties operate, of what they can and cannot do, and of what we can and cannot know. When Kant had established that, he turned, in *The Critique of Practical Reason* (1788) to the more "practical" question of how what he had discovered about reason in the first book might help to establish a foundation for ethical behaviour. The third of the great trilogy was *The Critique of Judgment* (1790) which investigated the foundations of a theory of Aesthetics. The second and third Critiques are therefore obvious subjects for a book on the relationship between Philosophy and Living, the first initially appears to be very abstract and to have little relevance to the way we actually live. Yet today, very few people would agree with the arguments and conclusions of the two latter books as they seem rather time-bound. I think we will see, however, that the first book created a perspective of Man's relationship to the World which still has enormous relevance today. Its implications affect the mindset of modern man - and therefore the way he lives - more than might at first sight appear.

The Critique of Pure Reason, 1781

Hitherto, philosophers had divided propositions into two kinds, under the technical names of "analytic" and "synthetic" propositions, and they must be either the one or the other. *Analytic* propositions followed up the implications of definitions. If we designate the number of asterisks in *** as "3", the number in ** as "2", the number in ***** as "5" and the symbol for addition as "+", then it

4 For Aristotle, see pp. 48f above; for Berkeley, see pp. 283f above.

5 p. 364 below.

must be true that 3 + 2 = 5. If we use the word "man" for the male of the human species and the word "father" for the male progenitor of a child, then it must be true that "fathers are men". The truth of these propositions is self-evident, and experience will confirm them, but they could never be falsified by, and are therefore independent of, experience. They are prior to experience, and such propositions are accordingly called *a priori*.

Whether a *synthetic* proposition is valid or invalid is known only after it has been experienced, and its truth is therefore said to be *a posteriori*. Philosophers describe knowledge based on experience as *empirical*. The truth of empirical propositions is inferred from the world of appearances which we perceive through our senses. Kant will call these appearances *phenomena*. Examples of synthetic propositions would be, "Napoleon was a great general" or "men are by nature aggressive".

Kant now significantly extended the range of *a priori* truths. He held that we bring to bear on the phenomenal world not only our senses, nor only those *a priori* truths which unfold from definitions. The way in which our minds operate on the phenomenal world is dictated by the way our minds are constituted, and this constitution is also *a priori*, that is, it does not *derive from* experience, though, like the unfolding of definitions, it will subsequently be *applied to* experience.

Hume had demonstrated that we have no evidence to be certain that there is such a thing as a cause. All we can *know* is that very often, or even always within our finite experience, A is followed by B. Similarly, he showed that when we talk about space and time, we are merely expressing our repeated experiences of physical and temporal distance. He had then added that we cannot in real life, of course, do without the notions of cause, space or time. We constantly show that we have a *belief* in causes etc. but he insisted that they were only beliefs, and that we had no *philosophical* reason for *knowing* that they really existed.[6]

Kant now asked himself why "we cannot do without" these notions. Hume had suggested that it was because they were useful and that without them we just couldn't live, but he was clear that entertaining such notions lacked philosophical rigour and was therefore a kind of intellectual laziness. Kant was sure that there was a great deal more to it than that. He held that thinking in terms of causes was not a philosophical aberration, but arises out of the very essence of the way the human mind is constituted, the essence of the way it is compelled to reason, even in reason's purest form. (We can now understand why he included the word "Pure" in the title of the work.) When the mind looks at the phenomenal world, it has no choice but to view it with ideas (or tools of understanding) that are built into the mind. This looking Kant called *Anschauungen*. This German noun means quite literally "viewings", and the technical translation into English – "intuitions" – does not, in its everyday sense, capture that meaning at all (although it, too, comes from the Latin *intueri*, meaning to "look upon"). These ideas (or tools of understanding, as Leibniz had called them, or concepts and categories as Kant will call them) are *a priori*; they come *before* any experience and shape the experiences we subsequently have.

6 See p. 288 above.

Both Leibniz and Kant knew that these tools of understanding are not present in a baby, but in their view they are genetically programmed to develop without having to rely on experience. A baby cannot play football because its leg muscles are not developed, but they are programmed to develop naturally (if the baby is not afflicted by a disease) as it matures. In the same way, a baby is not aware of tools of understanding, but they, too, in the absence of disease, naturally develop as the baby matures. Locke had said that the mind at birth is a *tabula rasa* and that there are no innate ideas. Leibniz and Kant differed from him in positing that such developments *are* innate and not the result of experience, though experience and training may speed up and above all refine the development of these tools so that we can use them more effectively.

So, the world reaches us already mediated through these tools of understanding. What follows from *that* is that we can have no direct knowledge of the world as it is before this mediation has happened. Kant calls the world as it is before mediation the *noumenal* world,[7] or, in a memorable phrase, *Das Ding an sich.* This phrase literally means "The Thing in itself", but its sense would be more accurately caught by translating it as "the Thing (or World) as it *really* is" (as distinct from how it appears to us). In so far as we have an awareness that there is such a noumenal world which we understand either not at all or only very imperfectly (as we shall see below, Kant was sure that there was a God, even if we can grasp His nature only very imperfectly), we are making use of a form of reason which Kant calls *Vernunft.* We have already seen that he calls the world as it appears to our senses (after mediation through our tools of understanding) the *phenomenal* world,[8] and that world we grasp with a form of reason which Kant called *Verstand.*[9]

Twentieth-century philosophy makes a point about language that is similar to the point that Kant makes about our tools of understanding. Language is a tool we have to use; we have to understand things through our language, and we find it hard or impossible to conceptualize anything for which our language does not equip us.

But is this true of musical and other aesthetic or spiritual experiences?

These tools of understanding (as we have seen, Kant calls them "concepts" and "categories" – they will be described in detail below) also have what is called a *transcendental* character. This confusing word does *not* refer to the world that is beyond the world of appearances (for which Kant uses the word *transcendent*) but to ideas which go beyond any one person's ideas and are shared by all human beings, not by any one self but by the *transcendental self,* and are therefore not merely individual constructs. The subjectivism necessarily involved in

7 From the Greek *noein,* meaning "to think" – in other words, it is a world that we can grasp, not through our senses, but by using our intellect.

8 From the Greek *phaenestai,* meaning "to appear"; *phainein* meaning "to show".

9 Kant's vocabulary is not only difficult when translated into English – even a non-philosophical German would be confused by it. Just as such a German may not understand that Kant uses the word *Kritik* in a sense which it no longer has today, so he will be puzzled by the meaning Kant gives to the words *Vernunft* and *Verstand.* In modern German those words have exactly the opposite meaning to Kant's. If you ask a modern German to use his *Vernunft* you ask him to apply common sense, and the notion that the world as it appears to us is the real world seems only common sense. The modern meaning of the word *Verstand* is understanding, and might be applied to the notion that, if we think about it rationally, we would understand that the world of appearances is not the real world at all and that reality is "super-sensible".

a situation where the objective nature of the noumenal world must be hidden from us is therefore a *collective* subjectivism. As such, it presents a *kind* of objectivity against which the subjectivity of an *individual* can be assessed. For example, in their developed state these collective *Anschauungen* present a system of reasoning in the context of which we can say whether an individual is using reason properly or not. At least this means that we are not condemned to solipsism, let alone to what I called Hume's "out-solipsizing the solipsists".[10] That part of Kant's teaching which deals with the nature of the ideas that all human beings share is therefore called *Transcendental Idealism.*

Bertrand Russell explains Kant's theory with an analogy, which I am extending a little here.[11] If all people were born with blue-tinted spectacles that they could never take off, the non-philosophical person would assume that all the colours of the world have a bluish tinge. But philosophers, once they have realized that these tinted spectacles (since we *all* wear them, we might call them "transcendental spectacles") are an irremovable part of our visual equipment, will know that we cannot know what the colours of the world are *really* like because they can only reach us as mediated by our "transcendental spectacles". The philosopher will know that he is receiving signals from outside, and he will also know that there is something "out there" which is sending the signals, but he will know that the signals he is capable of receiving depend on the nature of our receiving apparatus. That apparatus may, by its very nature, distort the signals and indeed miss out a whole range of them. To those signals we cannot receive we are (in this example) blind, and we can have no conception of them. We might also add that the apparatus which we all have is often not even used by individuals as it should be: by not paying enough attention to his spectacle lenses a person could have allowed them to become smudged, so that for him they would produce an unreliable picture even of the phenomenal world.

> But will the philosopher really *know* that there is something that is sending the signals? Should Kant not rather have said that he will *assume* the existence of an external source of the signals? Indeed, later critics will go further. If the "Ding an sich" is unknowable, we can have no reason for assuming that it exists at all. Some of them, therefore, reverted to pure Idealism – our ideas are the only things of which we can be certain. Such critics would be unimpressed by the analogy, for example, that astrophysicists receive signals from outer space without knowing their source, or, if they do know the source, without knowing what that source is like. If the critics are pure idealists, they would say with Berkeley and Hume[12] that, philosophically speaking, all we can be sure of is that we have ideas about these sources, irrespective of whether they are "known" or "unknown", but that we can have no grounds for thinking that there really are sources "out there" which cause these ideas.

Again, to extend Russell's analogy further, we know that the eye of a fly is so constituted that the single images we see appear to the fly as multiple images. We think that the fly's vision of the world is inaccurate because it does not correspond to our vision, but how do we know that our vision accurately picks up

10 See p. 290 above.

11 Russell – *A History of Western Philosophy*, p. 734 in the 1946 edition.

12 See pp. 282 above for Berkeley, p. 287 above for Hume.

the signals the world sends out? In fact, we know that it doesn't. The human eye is incapable of registering ultra-violet or infra-red colours, just as the human ear is incapable of receiving high-pitched sounds that a bat can receive.

These examples are all crude and misleading because science can come to our rescue and tell us that there *are* signals which we cannot perceive directly through our senses alone or which we perceive inaccurately (though a full-blown Kantian would have to say that science comes to our rescue only as far as the phenomenal world is concerned – we cannot know whether or not science gives us a reliable picture of the noumenal world). To understand the full significance of what Kant was saying requires us to extend the above examples of the limitations of our *sensory* equipment (of sight or hearing) to the limitations imposed on us by our *reasoning* equipment. Our reason does not read off or deduce from the signals of the noumenal world what that world is like. The way our rational equipment interprets those signals constitutes the phenomenal world. This interpretation *forms* our "knowledge", and because knowledge is interpretation, it is not so much something we *have* as something we *do*. We shape the phenomenal world with our tools of understanding. For example, because we cannot perceive the noumenal world directly, we cannot know whether it has an order or not. Therefore, such sense as we have of the universe being orderly is not imposed by the universe on us, but is imposed by us on the universe.

Kant believed that by this insight he had brought about a "Copernican Revolution". Copernicus had replaced the old idea that the earth was the centre of the universe with the idea that the sun was at its centre. This radically shifted the perspective with which men looked at the world and their place in it. Kant created a similar shift of perspective, from the idea that the world is something that is *given to* our mind to the notion that it is a *product* of our mind. The Germans particularly took to this revolution. The conception that the world is a product of the mind (and, later, of the will) ran riot there in the course of the nineteenth century. More soberly, twentieth-century scientists and philosophers will reinforce the notion that we can only understand the world through the conceptual apparatus, the tools of understanding, that we have.

It is important to realize that, although the tools of understanding are not adequate to reveal to us the real nature of the *Ding an sich*, they are, within that limitation, extremely "high precision" tools and give us an understanding of the phenomenal world. There are the most rigorous rules for using our reasoning faculties properly. The phenomenal world on which we use them therefore of necessity conforms to these rigorous rules – it is a rational world. If we impose an "erroneous" view on the world of appearances – for example, the idea that the earth is flat or that blood is made in the liver – it is because our tools of understanding have not been deployed properly. However, as long as we do impose faulty reasoning on the world of appearances, we will believe that that world conforms to our faulty reasoning; in other words we will still see the world as conforming to the rules of reason as we understand them at any given time. When subsequently our reasoning is used more precisely, our view of the world of appearances changes accordingly.

> This accounts for the fact, for instance, that every European in the Middle Ages believed that the earth was the centre of the universe or that Man was created in the way the Bible describes. In later ages, Copernicus and Darwin deployed their reasoning apparatus in such a way that they eventually persuaded most people to look at the world with tools of understanding that were more sophisticated and gave us a better understanding of the *phenomenal* world of appearances (though we should still remember, firstly, that even the more refined tools of understanding used by Copernicus and Darwin may not have delivered the last word on astronomy or evolution in the phenomenal world, and, secondly, that we still have no certainty about what the *noumenal* world is like.)

What, then, are these "tools of understanding"? Kant calls some of them *concepts* and others *categories*, though he sometimes refers to concepts as categories. Both have the characteristic of imposing order on our perceptions.

There are first the *concepts* of space and time. Our minds are so constituted that we *have* to order our perceptions in a spatial and temporal way, and we cannot imagine a world which has more than three dimensions or does not obey a temporal sequence. If, therefore, more than three dimensions or some kind of nonsequential time did exist in the noumenal world, we would be incapable of grasping that.[13]

When he comes to *categories*, these are an elaboration of Leibniz's "tools of understanding".[14] For Leibniz, these had been the innate notions of being, substance, unity, identity, contradiction and cause.[15] Kant divided categories into four groups, each of which he then subdivided into three further groups.

> These neat threesomes might arouse some suspicion. Threesomes seem to have a powerful psychological appeal, from the Trinity in Christian thought to the neat triads we shall see in Hegel.[16] Could it have anything to do with a child's earliest experience of the threesome made up of itself, its father and its mother?

Here is Kant's elaboration:

First we have "categories of quantity": the notions of unity, plurality and totality.

13 In fact, Kant deployed arguments to show that time and space as we conceive them are *merely* concepts of the human mind and *cannot* exist in the noumenal world. This seems contradictory to me. If we can know nothing about the noumenal world, we surely cannot know whether our notions of time and space do or do not exist in it. I suspect that he believed in a timeless and spaceless noumenal world because of his religious beliefs. Christian thinkers held that God and souls exist outside of time and space. St Augustine had believed that sequential time as we experience it operates in the world only after God has created it. It does not exist outside the created world, which is literally time-less (eternal), and in which there is no past, present or future - concepts which are dissolved in eternity. This was Augustine's answer when people asked themselves what there was "before the beginning of time" when God created the world *ex nihilo.* It is interesting that, on theological grounds and in theological terms, he came to a conclusion which was not unlike that which Kant was to reach on rational grounds and Einstein on scientific grounds that in "reality" time and space, *at least as we experience them* cannot exist.

14 I prefer Leibniz's terminology, as the words "category" and "concept" have non-technical meanings which are quite different from the sense in which Kant uses them. In modern parlance, the word "category" carries no implication of anything *a priori* - we consciously create categories or groups into which we classify things, and when we talk about a concept like democracy, that is something that we have defined, but is not *a priori* either.

15 For a discussion of these, see p. 278 above.

16 p. 390, note 2 below.

So we have, prior to experience, notions which we subsequently apply to experience, of "one thing", of "several things", and (more arguably?) of "universality" or "completeness".

Then there are "categories of quality": reality, negation and limitation.

We apply to experience the *a priori* notions of what we consider "real". We have a tool of understanding which discriminates between "is" and "is not" and also applies an alternative to "is" and "is not", namely, "is only in part".

The "categories of relation" are: substance and accident; cause and effect; activity and passivity.

We expect, prior to experience, to see a relationship between a basic object or substance (say, what makes a rose different from an orchid) and variable "accidents" (like the rose's colour.) One wonders, however, whether the distinction between substance and accident is really innate. Surely it is not intuitive, but learnt from experience? [17] As far as cause and effect are concerned, we have already seen above that this notion, which Hume had considered to be the result of philosophical laziness, was thought by Kant an essential part of our make-up. We may, of course, think that A is the cause of B when in fact it is not, but that merely means that we use the *a priori* tool, "cause", inaccurately. Kant also thought that the notion of the difference between "acting" and "being acted upon" was also part of our *a priori* equipment.

The "categories of modality" are, possibility and impossibility, existence and non-existence, and necessity and contingency.

When we consider a proposition about the world and decide that that proposition is impossible, our decision may be wrong; but we do not need to have learnt from experience what "impossibility" is. The same goes for existence and non-existence. The belief in the existence of fairies may be wrong, but our *notion* of existence is inborn.

Again we may be wrong in deciding that B *must* always follow from A (necessity) rather than it merely happens to accompany A in this case (contingency) but in that case we have merely applied our innate notion of the difference between necessity and contingency inaccurately.

Here again, one may wonder whether this particular "category" is really innate and *a priori* or whether it is the result of experience.

What distinguishes the concepts of time and space from the categories, is that the latter are all essential ingredients of logic. Every logical argument aims to use these tools of understanding correctly. *Formal* logic, as it had been developed since the time of Aristotle, consists of rules that should help to ensure the correct handling of these tools. As we have noted above, a tool can be used accurately as well as inaccurately. The fact that, for example, we have an *a priori* concept of cause and effect does not mean that we always argue rationally from cause to effect. The more effectively we use our reason, the more fully comprehensible the phenomenal world will be for us. Kant, as a child of the Age of Rea-

17 The notions of substance and accident (or predicates) go back to Aristotle – see p. 44, n. 4. But Aristotle had believed that substances and accidents *really* existed. Berkeley had then shown that, because we could have no perception of substance, therefore it could not exist – see p. 282. Now Kant reintroduced the idea, but not as something that really exists in the noumenal world, but as an innate tool of understanding which is part of our mental make-up, not part of the world "outside" on which we are compelled to impose this distinction.

son, trusted implicitly and explicitly that reason, properly handled, will give us a wholly reliable and coherent account of the *phenomenal* world, and an increasingly perfect understanding of the Laws of Nature which govern that phenomenal world.

> If reason is properly used, therefore, it should ultimately reveal enduring truths about the phenomenal world. If truths are enduring, then they are essentially static. Kant's contemporaries had thought that, for example, as far as a particular branch of the natural sciences was concerned, Newton had discovered the truth for all time, and it gave them the confidence to believe that if the same methods of reasoning were applied to social problems, they too would ultimately produce an enduring truth. As we shall see, Kant believed that reason could produce an enduring moral code. Those who thought in that way did not allow for the notion of truths dynamically changing over time. Hegel will introduce the notion of dynamic change, and in that way will fit in with the idea of perpetual striving and restlessness that was such a characteristic of the Romantic mindset. Kant's vision of permanent truths was more in tune with the classical attitudes of the eighteenth century.

As we have seen, Kant assumed that all human beings have pretty much the same conceptual apparatus with which they handle the signals that reach them from the one and only noumenal world. This explains why human beings have much the same perceptions of the phenomenal world – pre-eminently, but not exclusively, in matters relating to mathematics and the sciences. The world of appearances is the result of an ordering which we all do in much the same way. Different human beings therefore have common experiences, as does the same human being at different times. We do not see the world as purely arbitrary; we think it is subject to laws (though they are laws through which we order appearances).

> How then do we account for the fact that the experiences of human beings at different times or in different cultures are *not* the same? Presumably by realizing that, though they have the same tools of understanding, they apply them differently – sometimes erroneously, sometimes in a way that is crude and can be refined. For example, the knowledge of the world we receive through our five senses alone tells us that the earth is flat, but, around 200 BC, Eratosthenes became aware that this did not fit in with other visual information he received. The shadows cast by the sun suggested to him (using his conceptual apparatus, in particular the category of "possibility and impossibility") that the surface of the earth cannot be flat and must in fact be curved. That rational approach was forgotten for many centuries after Eratosthenes; the world of appearances to the Middle Ages was one in which the earth was flat, so here again we have the problem of how Kant could be sure that the world of appearances is a rational one.

Kant was very conscious of the fact that our conceptual apparatus often delivered ideas which cannot be reconciled with each other, though each is supported by perfectly sound arguments. For example, our human understanding tells us that everything must have a beginning, therefore time must have a beginning, but other considerations tell us that time cannot have had a beginning. The notion of space usually implies bounds to space, but we can also understand the notion that space is literally boundless. Kant referred to such contradictions as *antinomies*. These antinomies are only apparent - that is, they belong to the world of appearances. They cannot exist, he believed, in the noumenal world, and their existence in the phenomenal world is merely another illustration that our rational conceptual apparatus is inadequate for a comprehension of the *Ding an sich*.

Religion

Antinomies are also found in the field of religion. Here Kant introduces another part of our *a priori* mental equipment, which does not seem to fall into the concepts or categories that he has listed and seems to be almost at odds with some of them. Our mind, he maintains, affirms certain religious concepts so strongly that they transcend all the conflicting metaphysical arguments about them and indeed exist alongside of logical arguments such as Hume had advanced and which would appear to render them philosophically untenable. Kant agreed with Hume that we cannot be said to *know* religious truths, but where Hume had again put down belief in religious truths as a philosophical aberration, for Kant our inability to know them rested on our inability to *know* anything that was in the noumenal world, as metaphysical truths obviously were.

That argument might lead some people to conclude that, in the absence of *knowledge* of metaphysical truths we should be agnostics, meaning that we don't know whether the metaphysical truths exist or not. (An atheist, who claims to know that there is no God, cannot be a Kantian, because he does not admit that we cannot know whether the grounds for such a claim exist in the noumenal world or not.) But Kant's conclusion was not an agnostic one. To begin with, he identified the *Ding an sich* with God.

> Later philosophers argued that if we cannot know the *Ding an sich*, we cannot know that it exists. Even if we did believe that there is such a thing, its identification with God is an assertion rather than an argument. After all, it is perfectly possible to imagine an unknowable noumenal world without identifying that world with a deity.

He thought that the signals that our conceptual apparatus picked up and through which we were then compelled to impose upon the world a view that is religious (in the traditional sense of that word, namely of being connected with a deity) had the same unavoidability as any of the other concepts or categories through which we were compelled to view the world. He admitted - though he is not consistent about this throughout his work - that what we have is not religious knowledge, but religious faith which we are entitled to trust.

That trust, he thought, was supported by its intellectual usefulness. Faith offers us guidance in interpreting the world; it gives us a reassurance without which our sanity and our peace of mind would be imperilled. We are, therefore, better off if we act *as if* our faith told us the truth about the world:

> In the domain of theology, we must view everything as if the sum of all appearances (the sensible world itself) had a single, highest, and all-sufficient ground beyond itself - namely a self-subsistent, original, creative reason. For it is in the light of this idea of a creative reason that we so guide the empirical employment of our reason as to secure its greatest possible extension.

The phrase "as if" smacks to some of intellectual dishonesty – it seems that the pretence that we have the truth is so useful that it doesn't really matter whether we actually have it or not. But that is doing Kant an injustice. After all, he said we could not know the ultimate truth, the *Ding an sich*, anyway, not just in matters of religion, but also in our perceptions of the phenomenal world. In the latter case we use concepts and categories to make sense of the world, and we are better off by doing so and by acting "as if" they told us the truth of the world. It is perhaps revealing that he used the "as if" phrase only when discussing religion.

Perhaps the most important reason for trusting faith is that it is the indispensable underpinning of morality,

> If there is no primordial being distinct from the world, if the world is ... without an Author, if our will is not free, if the soul is ... perishable like matter, then moral ideas and principles lose all their validity.

It is an argument one still often hears today, when people attribute what they consider the collapse of moral standards to the decline of religion. They argue that without faith in a divinely ordained moral order, each individual shapes his own moral rules according to his inclination, and moral chaos is the result.

Our minds are so constituted, argues Kant, that we *must* have a belief in God. (He writes a little later in the passage that the *necessary* belief does not go beyond a deistic view of God - i.e. we are not compelled by our very nature to believe in all those attributes which the Bible attributes to Him.) We can see from the passage just quoted that we *must* believe in more than God; we are so constituted that we must also have faith in free will and in the imperishability of the soul.[18]

Here Kant goes further than Leibniz. Leibniz had said that most humans are born with an innate *capacity* (I likened them to receptors) to acquire and process religious ideas, but the exact religious ideas which fill the religious receptor depend on later reasoning, education and other kinds of social conditioning. In the case of some people, that receptor is filled with ideas which have no strictly theological content at all, but are an overflow of secular information from the factual receptor into the religious one.[19] As a result, we may have a person who has quasi-religious feelings of reverence for, say, Marxist ideas, but he is likely to be totally devoid of ideas about God, free will, or the immortality of the soul. When Kant described religious concepts as *a priori*, the word "religious" meant what it normally means, and ruled out the idea of a "secular religion" such as the ideology and worship of, say, liberty, equality and fraternity. In any case, there are some people in whom the receptor is either missing or is never filled. They totally lack *any* type of religious sensibility, and do not even have an *a priori* "secular religion".

Kant's view of these ideas being the inescapable tools of understanding with which we have to interpret the world is truly astonishing. For a start, he must have known that there were countless Christians who believed in pre-

18 He bases his idea that belief in the immortality of the soul is *a priori* on a surprisingly feeble argument. Prior to the so-called *a priori* nature of that belief is another, which is also *a priori*: virtue creates happiness. As virtue and happiness manifestly do not always coexist in this world, God must make sure that they coexist in the next world. This argument would turn belief in the immortality of the soul into an *a posteriori* one, but in fact, neither that belief nor a belief in God has a *rational* foundation.

19 For a fuller explanation, see p. 276f above.

destination or determinism and denied free will.[20] Nor can he have been unaware that some people were atheists – Holbach's *Système de la Nature* had been published eleven years before the *Critique of Pure Reason*. All this should have shown him that he was plainly wrong when he extended to religion the innate, *a priori*, inescapable characteristics of the concepts with which we reason. Our minds are clearly *not* so constituted that they *must* have these concepts of God, free will and immortality of the soul or *must* view the world through them.

The only way in which one could possibly defend Kant's view is if there were something seriously defective in a person who did not believe in God, free will or the immortality of the soul – that the absence of a receptor for such concepts was akin to a disease like psychopathy (the constitutional inability to tell right from wrong) or like the absence of a limb as the result of exposure to Thalidomide. The argument would be analogous to one that could be made in respect of concepts and categories. We have likened these to an apparatus that receives signals, or to spectacles through which we have to view the world. The apparatus may be incorrectly tuned; the spectacles may be smudged or distorted. These would be defects which would prevent a person from having a correct view of the phenomenal world. In the same way, Kant may have felt that a person who cannot see that there must be a God is like a person who cannot see that the earth is round – there is something defective in the tools of understanding that he is using. But there is a great difference: one can compellingly demonstrate that someone who thinks the earth is flat is using defective tools of understanding, whereas no such *compelling* demonstration can be deployed against an atheist.

There is surely a difference between the concepts and categories with which we see the "truths" in the phenomenal world and those with which we see "truths" in religion. (I put the word into inverted commas because, according to Kant, they are truths as far as we can establish through our concepts and categories. We cannot know whether they tell us the truth about the *Ding an sich*.) In the former case, it is possible to reach at least a temporary consensus about what those "truths" are. For example, once it had been demonstrated by refining our tools of understanding that the earth was round and not flat, it became impossible to refute that idea. The arguments for it being round were logically so compelling that no one who used the tools of understanding properly could refute the idea. No such logically compelling arguments can be advanced for religious "truths"; believers in God and free will have never been able to convince Atheists or Determinists. It is surely sheer arrogance to assume that the latter can be dismissed on the grounds that their tools of understanding are defective, and that a belief in Determinism is therefore on a par with a belief that the earth is flat.

As we have seen, Kant had so far, rather like Rousseau, justified his faith in these religious ideas by the strength of the affirmations that we *feel* about them. He based himself on reason as far as his ideas of concepts and categories were

20 Those who believe in Determinism, like Hobbes, were materialists who thought that human beings, like the rest of Nature, work on mechanical principles. Kant's scientific training had led him to accept determinism in the phenomenal world. Man, as a physical being, was part of the phenomenal world, but Kant maintained that Man's soul and his moral nature were not physical. They were part of the noumenal world, and not subject to determinism. It seems an odd assertion to make, as he had said that the noumenal world is something of which we can have no direct knowledge, so we cannot know whether our souls or moral sense are or are not part of that world. However, the idea that Man straddles the noumenal and the phenomenal world in this way will be taken up by Schopenhauer.

concerned, but when he came to religious ideas, he initially aligned himself with the Romantics. He had also claimed that, without such feelings, "moral ideas and principles lose all their validity". However, he felt uneasy about vacating the base of reason, and he came to think that moral truths are based on more than mere feelings (however inescapable these are) and that they also have an equally inescapable logical and rational basis. He concluded that he needed to work out the nature of moral precepts in a separate book. The result was *The Critique of Practical Reason*. Influential though this book was, in its absolutism it merely compounded his disregard for the variety of views that people actually have about morality.

The Critique of Practical Reason, 1788

Kant tells us that moral precepts are *a priori*, absolute and invariant, and based on pure reason.

They are *a priori*, not *a posteriori* – that is, they are not inferred from experience. Like mathematical statements, moral precepts would be true even if we found by experience that men everywhere ignored them. We need no other kind of knowledge to learn what they are. They are not dependent on a sociological setting and they do not flow from people's psychology.

Like the laws of mathematics, moral precepts are invariant and absolute – they are applicable to all people in all societies at all times.

> It is an idea which many people in western societies today totally reject – and there were people in Kant's own lifetime who rejected it also, but in his time, most people probably believed that there was only one belief that was right and that all the others were wrong. For example, Catholics were convinced that only they were right and that Protestants were wrong, and vice versa. Also, many of Kant's contemporaries were disturbed by the relativism taught by some of the *philosophes*. Was it not a dangerous and subversive idea and an invitation to the moral breakdown of society? (That is an idea which is not unknown today). In such a climate, Kant's view was not so unusual.

Moral precepts are not prudential, meaning that their validity relates to the good effects they produce or are intended to produce. Their imperative is *categorical*, not hypothetical.[21] A hypothetical imperative would tell us that we must do A if we want to achieve B. The categorical imperative tells us that we must do A without regard to any end. A moral action must be judged irrespective of any consequences it might have.

> Historically there has been some danger here. Some people have felt it their moral duty to obey society or the state irrespective of the consequences. That was hardly what Kant had in mind.
>
> We admire it when people stand up for what they think is right irrespective of the consequences to themselves; if they die in a noble moral cause rather than compromise, we respect them as martyrs. We are less inclined to admire people when the consequence of their high moral principles may be the suf-

21 Kant had used the word "category" for *a priori* ways of looking at the world, and he believed that the genuine moral imperatives are also *a priori*, so we can understand why he called them "categorical". Since his time the word "categorical" has entered our language, but today it no longer carries quite the same meaning. We use it to mean "unqualified"; a categorical statement is one which admits of no qualifications.

fering of others – as, for example, in the case of the Christian Scientist whose moral convictions will not allow him to call in a doctor to save his sick child.

Kant says that the categorical imperative takes two forms, from which all other moral precepts flow. The first is: "Act so that the maxim of your will can always hold good as a principle of universal legislation." The reasoning behind this is that, if moral maxims are invariable, what is moral for one must be moral for all - they must therefore form a universal moral law.

Taken by itself, there is a problem here. If we look at sexual morality, for example, we find that different societies have different views of this. Kant would have to believe that all except one of those views are "wrong" (not *a priori*, not absolute, not based on pure reason.) Yet the adherents of the "wrong" views would be perfectly prepared to see them observed not only just in their society, but universally.

An important corollary of Kant's maxim is that if we claim freedom for ourselves, we must also allow it to others. Kant had absolutist views on morality, but he opposed the idea of any political or clerical absolutism to enforce them.

The second form of the categorical imperative runs like this: "So act as to treat humanity, in your own person or in that of any other, in every case as an end, never only as a means." The reasoning behind this admirable dictum is that using another person as a means ignores or overrides his position as a rational judge of his own actions. It is claiming for oneself a position (of superiority) which one denies to the other, and one is thereby refusing to extend one's own position into a universal one. That in turn violates the first injunction, that one's own actions should conform to a principle one would be willing to see applied universally, i.e. towards oneself as well as to other people. No one ever wants to be treated only as a means to an end.

Like the laws of mathematics, moral precepts are based on pure reason. In the *Critique of Pure Reason* Kant had based religion and morality on the strength with which our feelings assert them. Now he says that essentially they rest on a rational basis, though it is feelings that give them their exceptional strength.

So, if he had been asked how he would explain that many people hold "wrong" moral precepts, he would have replied in much the same way as he would have explained that some people continue to believe that the earth is flat: they are simply not using their reason, their tools of understanding (here the tools of moral understanding) properly. This may be either because the tools are in some way defective because not properly maintained, or because, in the field of morality as elsewhere, reason is often overwhelmed by Passion.

The corollary must be that in any given situation there is only one correct moral position, and that all the others are false. It is not that Kant laid down a rigid code of morals; he was well aware that moral imperatives may collide (if, for example, one is torn between two conflicting loyalties) but it is pure reason that should work out what the moral precept in such a situation requires – it should not be left to the pull of conflicting emotions. To help us in this task, Kant had identified the two basic principles of the categorical imperative, from which all other moral precepts flow.

Every moral decision we make, then, is the result of a choice between reason which may pull one way and feelings, habits, or conventions which may pull in the opposite direction. Kant does not believe, as Hobbes and his successors had believed, that the self responds mechanically to the relative strength within us of our appetites and aversions, of our pleasure and pain, so that choice (except for the fact that our reason is used to weigh up the one against the other) hardly comes into it.[22] Kant says that we are free to make moral choices and indeed have a *duty* to make them. Somewhat paradoxically, he also holds that, if we use that freedom to give in to our passions rather than to our reason, we are not truly free but are enslaved by our passions.

> Kant here differs from Hume, who had famously said that "Reason is, and ought to be, the slave of the Passions".[23] He also differs from those Christians who believe that we should not presume to try to understand God by reason. They stress that true freedom lies in serving God and Christ in faith rather than in serving reason, which in human beings is fallible and sometimes leads them to challenge faith. Conversely, there is also the Thomist position in Christianity that reason, properly understood, is complementary to faith and not a threat to it. In this respect, Kant was a Thomist, for he, too, saw no contradiction between serving God and serving reason.

For anyone who believes in free will, as Kant did, it is not very novel or revolutionary to say that the making of moral choices involves an act of will, and this was indeed what Kant said. The German philosophers who would build on Kant's philosophy, however, will take this fairly obvious reference to the will and inflate it into the mainspring of our entire view and handling of the world. For them, Man is governed primarily neither by reason nor by feeling, but by the will.

For Kant, the greater our struggle against our feelings in order to do our duty, the greater is the moral value of the dutiful action. So someone who does the right thing effortlessly, out of natural goodness, performs an action which, though clearly good and desirable, is of less moral worth than if an effort were involved.

Our duty, Kant says, is recognized by us in our capacity as autonomous, independent and *rational* agents. It is not imposed on us by any external secular authority. Nor is it imposed by God, as God belongs to the unknown noumenal world, so we could not perceive it as such. Indeed, Kant says, the moral law leads to religion, not *vice versa*.

For Kant, God, the soul and freedom of the will are not part of the phenomenal world of appearances, they belong to the noumenal world. It follows that, though our *intellectual* tools of understanding cannot pierce through the phenomenal world to the noumenal world that lies behind it, through our *moral and religious* sense we do have an entrée into the noumenal world that we do not have through our intellect. Human beings, therefore, straddle the noumenal and the phenomenal world; through their soul and moral nature, they are part of the noumenal world, at the same time as through their physical nature they are part of the phenomenal world. Moreover, whereas our physical nature is not free (being subject, like the rest of the phenomenal world, to determinist and mechanical principles) our religious and moral *nature* is free (even if religious

22 See p. 227 above.

23 See p. 292 above.

and moral *principles* rest, as Kant asserted, on the same "high precision" tools of reason as those that govern our understanding of the phenomenal world).

We have already seen above that the religion towards which the moral sense leads us is a deistic religion, so that the only obligation it puts upon us (and which our innate reason has already accepted as an obligation we have *towards ourselves*) is that we should do our moral duty. God does not require any more of us, and makes no doctrinal demand on us, such as a belief in miracles or in the divinity of Christ, acceptance of particular forms of worship or church structures, baptism etc. Religious doctrines are *taught and learnt*: they may be true (Kant was an observant Christian) or they may be erroneous, but because they are *taught and learnt*, they cannot be *a priori*. Thus, the Church should never be an institution compelling belief in such things and exercising censorship to that end. Theocracy is indefensible, and any claim the Church puts forward to monopolize the interpretation of Scripture or the way to salvation is illegitimate. In a later essay called *Religion within the Limits of Reason Alone* (1793), Kant wrote: "Everything which, apart from a moral way of life, man believes himself capable of doing to please God is merely religious delusion and spurious worship of God."

> Karen Armstrong comments that, "in this perspective God was simply tacked on to the ethical system as an afterthought. The centre of religion was no longer the mystery of God but man himself... It would not be long before some would take his ideal of autonomy one step further and dispense with this somewhat tenuous God altogether." [24]

The Critique of Judgment, 1790

In the third of the Critiques, Kant addressed himself to the question of Aesthetics. Were the principles of Aesthetics also *a priori* – in other words, did we have, prior to any experience of the world, aesthetic concepts through which we were compelled to view the world? Kant veers uneasily between the admission that *"the judgment of taste cannot be anything but subjective"* and his own temperamental hankering after absolute and really rather restrictive standards, such as he had advanced in his discussion of morality. His treatment of aesthetics in fact runs against the admission that taste must be subjective. He did believe that, properly understood, standards of taste must be absolute and, like all absolute standards, must be based on reason. If they seem in fact to be subjective, therefore, that is because people had not based them on reason. So Kant set about defining what (his) reason told him were the criteria of aesthetic qualities.

24 Karen Armstrong – *A History of God*, p. 362. It is not surprising that Kant's essay of 1793 called down upon him the wrath of the church in Prussia and consequently that of King Frederick William II. In 1788 the Prussian government had issued an edict demanding that all preachers and teachers adhere to orthodox religious teaching. The *Critique of Practical Reason*, published in that same year, had already overstepped that mark, and the even more outspoken language of the essay of 1793 exhausted the government's patience. The King demanded an explanation of Kant's subversive ideas and ordered him, on pain of "unpleasant consequences to yourself", to desist from expressing such views in future. In his reply, Kant explained that the essay had been intended only for scholars and not for the general public, but he promised in future to make no more public statements on religious matters. Under the more tolerant reign of the Frederick William III, however, he restated his ideas in a booklet tracing the history of the dispute (1798).

As anyone who has ever discussed aesthetics is likely to have discovered, criteria of beauty are assertions and have little to do with demonstrable rational arguments, and today it is deeply unfashionable to lay down any absolute rules for what has and what does not have aesthetic qualities. We are very aware that the aesthetic standards laid down by one century have often been rejected by the next. Even more so does this apply to different societies. Since the days of museums, art galleries and the worldwide availability of images from different ages and different societies, we are far more aware than were Kant and his contemporaries of the illimitable variety of aesthetic criteria. One might almost say that today nobody, at least in the artistic establishment, *dares* to describe anything at all as totally devoid of aesthetic merit.

Kant's general assertion – it is really a definition – is that aesthetic qualities are those that are capable of giving us *disinterested* pleasure.

We might agree that a work of art or something beautiful in nature that we happen to come across gives us disinterested pleasure, but when we actually *seek out* or create something beautiful, the phrase "disinterested pleasure" might be thought of as a contradiction in terms, as we do it to gain at least the benefit of the pleasure of contemplating it.

That said, there are different kinds of interest that may be involved. What Kant meant by "disinterested pleasure" was that it had no ingredient beyond the pleasure of contemplation, that beyond that it served no other purpose – "self-contained pleasure" might have been a better phrase. Certainly, many aesthetic experiences are of that kind. When we rejoice in the beauty of the countryside, thrill to the sounds of an orchestra, or stand in front of a painting in an art gallery, we generally do have exactly that kind of pleasure.

Of course, there are also occasions when we seek out something of beauty because we get something more out of it than self-contained pleasure: we may, for example, want a beautiful piece of music to relax us when we are tense, or we may ask for a particular piece of music because it gives expression to our sense of mourning. We may acquire a piece which is genuinely beautiful because its possession confirms to ourselves and our acquaintances an image we like to have of ourselves. Such works of art do not lose their aesthetic qualities simply because what we bring to bear on them is not unalloyed disinterestedness. So aesthetic qualities that are *capable* of giving us self-contained pleasure often give secondary pleasures beyond that.

It is also possible to *create* something with aesthetic qualities even though the act of creation is motivated by impulses which are far from disinterested. Works of political propaganda, such as many of Jacques-Louis David's paintings, aim to produce not only aesthetic but political responses and many religious paintings are intended to teach people what is in the Bible, or to produce a pious and sometimes even a sectarian response in the viewer. Nevertheless, to a nonpolitical nonreligious person, who appreciates them simply as beautiful images, they can give a "self-contained" pleasure.

What qualities, Kant goes on, can give self-contained pleasure to the person *whose aesthetic responses are sufficiently rational*?

We must remember this qualification. Kant knows that people may not properly apply the aesthetic tools of understanding with which they are equipped, just as they may incorrectly use logical or moral concepts.

One quality is in harmony of *form*, which Kant believed to be more important than "accidents" like colour. In this assertion of course he displays the classical taste of his time, which had been given a philosophical underpinning by, for example, Locke's distinction between "primary" and "secondary" qualities.[25]

Then we take "disinterested pleasure" in the "sublime". Whereas the emphasis on form has roots in Classicism, "the sublime" was a notion much cultivated by Romanticism. Sublime qualities are those of grandeur or power. They do not inhere in the objects themselves (the starry heavens, the majesty of mountains, the forces of nature unleashed in a thunderstorm) so much as in our response to these phenomena. That response has a moral quality - it makes us aware of our physical insignificance (but at the same time, Kant argues, *"raises the energies of the soul above their accustomed height"*.)

We also see aesthetic qualities when we see phenomena as striving to be or as actually being part of a design:that implies a harmony which is in itself an aesthetic quality. Our nature as religious human beings requires us to see a divine mind that has organized and sustains the design. This fits in with Kant's view in *The Critique of Pure Reason* that, without the notion of a divine plan, the world would seem totally incoherent and would have neither any rational nor any moral meaning to keep us sane.[26] So Kant integrates his views of religion with his views of aesthetics.

The pay-off that we are kept sane by the aesthetic pleasure in seeing an order in the world hardly makes that pleasure "disinterested".

The Influence of Kant

Kant was seen by many as saving religion and morality from the rationalist assaults of Hume and Holbach, and the fact that he had done so by calling on both reason and feelings in aid made him acceptable both to rationalists and to romantics. German nationalists in particular saw him as representing German profundity and moral virtue against French frivolity and spiritual corruption.

He had also rescued metaphysics, and many philosophical minds, especially in Germany, have an urge to look beyond the physical world to find significance for our lives. True, Kant said that we could not know what the noumenal world was really like, which made it rather difficult to talk about it in clear words, but that did not trouble German thinkers. On the contrary, one might unkindly say of German philosophy after Kant that obscurity of expression was considered a hallmark of profundity of thought.[27] Kant's immediate followers, Fichte and Schelling, were impressed by Kant's notion that our minds shape the world as we know it, but they thought that they could jettison Kant's notion of the noumenal world as being necessary. This did not help German philosophy to gain in clarity, and, as we will see, they merely substituted one metaphysic for another.

25 See pp. 280f above.

26 See p. 374 above.

27 Durant gives us a quotation from a letter of Goethe's in 1824: "On the whole, philosophical speculation is an injury to the Germans, as it tends to make their style vague, difficult, and obscure. The stronger their attachment to certain philosophical schools, the worse they write."

In the short run, then, Kant's influence seemed to be strongest with the romantics, but in the longer run it goes far beyond that. The notion that the world we perceive is shaped by the nature of the mind that does the perceiving will be greatly extended in later years. Though philosophically the notion of rational and *a priori* tools of understanding is important, it may not make much difference in the practical world. If we all have the same tools of understanding, as Kant believed, then by deploying them properly, we will all interpret the world in much the same way. However, it came to be realized that the mind is also stocked with certain concepts and categories which, though not *a priori*, are unconscious and often unquestioned. Because they are not *a priori* and, therefore, by their nature not universal among humans, interpretations of the world through them are far more varied and, once we become aware of them, more mutable than Kant conceived. These concepts and categories are *culturally* conditioned, and are generally - until challenged - those of the dominant culture. They may be determined, for example, by class, by gender, by race, by the way we use language, or by a combination of all these. We can make an effort to identify the often unspoken assumptions that lie behind them, and then, if need be, change them, but we cannot rid ourselves of *all* assumptions - at any given moment many of them will be unconscious. So, our perception or observation of the world is never uninfluenced by our cultural tools of understanding; we interpret in the very act of "observing" or "perceiving". This is a concept which has been influential even in science. Scientists have shown that there are certain scientific events which we can never observe as they really are, because the very presence of the observer influences the behaviour of what is being observed. All this supports Kant's contention that we can never know *das Ding an sich*, Reality as it really is. The teaching in Ancient Greece of Protagoras and the Sophists - that truth is relative - has proceeded from the field of observation (that different societies in fact have different values) - to a philosophical assertion that, by the innermost nature of the world, the truth must always escape us.

These notions have had an enormous impact in the late twentieth century where they have culminated in Post-Modernism and in the philosophy of Deconstruction in particular.[28] The fuse that Kant had set would detonate long after his lifetime.

28 See chapter 48.

CHAPTER 32

Kant's Successors

JOHANN FICHTE
1762 to 1814

Kant's notion that the world we perceive is a world shaped by our own tools of understanding resonated down German philosophy throughout the nineteenth century. It is a crucial aspect of the thought of Fichte, Schelling, Hegel, Schopenhauer and Nietzsche. Kant had clung to the idea that, behind the phenomenal world we perceive, there is a noumenal world, *das Ding an sich*, whose nature we can never really know because the signals which it sends out can be handled only by such tools of understanding as we have - Russell's "blue spectacles" analogy, to put it crudely.[1] Fichte, Schelling and Hegel argued that we do not really need the concept of the *Ding an sich* as something that exists independently of the mind and if we cannot know it, we cannot know that it exists. We cannot know that the perceptions we have of the world are our interpretations of signals we receive from an outside source. Instead, they believed that our perceptions are simply the product of our minds - they come from within us and their source is not outside of us. It is not the world that shapes our thinking; it is our thinking which shapes the world. Kant's successors agreed with him that the world that we know is shaped by our minds, but that world, shaped by our minds (Fichte uses the word consciousness or Ego), they thought was sufficient. Our consciousness must, of course, be conscious of *something* - it must have an object. That object is the non-ego. the non-ego is the world outside of our consciousness, but it is created by our consciousness.

This philosophical position, left like that, would amount to solipsism, the idea that I cannot be sure that anything exists other than my individual thoughts. For all I know, having done away even with Kant's *Ding an sich,* the whole world is merely a figment of my thoughts. Fichte avoided solipsism by retaining Kant's concept of the transcendental self that had provided an objective criterion against which the individual's perception of the phenomenal world could be measured.[2] Just as the individual ego creates an individual non-ego as the object of its consciousness, so the transcendental ego creates a transcendental non-ego for itself. That transcendental non-ego is what we call nature. The transcendental ego or consciousness manifests itself in the mind of every individual, and so it often guarantees to us that the reality created by our individual consciousness is also a reality in transcendental consciousness.

1 See p. 366 above.

2 See p. 366 above.

Berkeley had been rescued from solipsism by the conviction that many of the perceptions in our minds are also in the mind of God,[3] and in Fichte, Schelling and Hegel that rescue role is played by the transcendental ego (also called the Absolute) to which a quasi-religious significance is assigned.

One might conclude from this that the reality in the transcendental consciousness is objective, but that does not seem to be Fichte's position. On the one hand he wants to save reality from being merely an arbitrary, and therefore possibly a fantastical creation of the mind. On the other hand, as we shall see, Fichte insisted that we each have the freedom in every respect to create our own reality. That is true even of a madman, and some charismatic madmen can create a world not only for themselves but for many of their contemporaries also. Heine commented ironically on the notion that Fichte, for one, created his own world, "Himself as everything! How does Mrs Fichte put up with it?"

Kant had believed that, while we did have freedom in the moral sphere, we have none in our understanding of the phenomenal world. We order the world of appearances by ascribing to it objective laws of nature which themselves are derived from our tools of understanding. We have already seen in the previous chapter[4] that there is a problem here: our tools of understanding, rigorous though their demands were said by Kant to be, do not deliver immutable laws of nature, otherwise, there would be no room for the many occasions when scientists have modified or even contradicted the laws of nature of which their predecessors had felt certain. It had admittedly been a Copernican revolution to argue that we shape the phenomenal world rather than that the world shapes us, but Kant had stopped short of pushing this revolution through to its logical conclusion. For all the careful use which we may make of our tools of understanding, the laws of nature which we see in the phenomenal world are not objective, but are in the last resort subjective – "in the last resort" because there is often so much agreement about the laws of nature at any given time in any given society that, if we do not look at other times or other societies, we assume them to be objective.

Fichte pushed Kant's revolution through to the conclusion that we do not always have the same tools of understanding. Everyone fashions the tools he uses in his own way, often by accepting the tools used by his own society, but occasionally shaping quite new ones for himself. In both cases, therefore, they give us a subjective rather than an objective knowledge of the world – they give us the "take" we have on the world.

> In this he was even closer than Kant had been to twentieth-century philosophy of science and to the Deconstructionist philosophy of Roland Barthes, Jacques Derrida and others.[5]
>
> In many fields this is perfectly obvious. A person who is, consciously or unconsciously, steeped in the classical mode of perception will see the world differently from one who is steeped in the romantic mode. A religious person will have a "take" on the world which is different from that of someone who is not religious. A feminist does not see society in the same way as a non-feminist

3 For Berkeley's arguments, see p. 284 above.

4 See p. 370, above.

5 See Chapter 48, below.

> does or even as women saw it before feminism had come along, and so on.
>
> This also applies, though perhaps to a lesser degree, to science. After Newton and Darwin, many people looked in quite new ways not only at strictly scientific aspects of the world, but also at social issues. Where Kant had believed, in Bertrand Russell's analogy, that *everyone* wears the same type of spectacles and all we need to do is to make sure that they are properly polished, in Fichte we find many different kinds of spectacles, all of them potentially changeable, and each of which produces a different way of looking at the world. There can be no permanent truth.
>
> There are, of course, some potential dangers in this. Not only may some ways of looking at the world be wrong in the sense that they run counter to all considerations of logic, but other ways may actually be vicious, such as a racist "take" which is sometimes espoused by an entire society. All Fichte is saying is that all these people – those who fly in the face of logic, or those whose view is vicious – are creating their own world and can sometimes convince other people to see it in the same way as they do.

It seemed to Fichte to follow that, in theory, the mind has freedom in the way it shapes the world of appearances,[6] just as it has in the moral sphere, even if in practice most of us, at any given time and in any given society, do not make active use of that freedom. We generally accept certain ways of proceeding, and there is therefore widespread agreement (again, at any given time and in any given society) on what the laws of nature are like. But in theory, we have the freedom to choose our own reality.

Kant had said that in the moral sphere we have the freedom to make choices, and that these choices are made by exercising our will. Now Fichte applied that same idea to our knowledge of the world of appearances – we create the world (reality) by an act of will.

> Although twentieth-century deconstructionists believe that our subjectivism is the result of ideological or other assumptions which are, *for the most part*, unconscious and therefore unarticulated, they do agree that quite often a conscious act of will is involved. For example, the Soviet scientist Trofim Lysenko asserted in 1927 that by modifying the environment in which wheat grew, one could transform its genetic nature, so that the characteristics acquired by the modification would be inherited by future generations of the crop. This theory was rejected by qualified scientists, but it was approved by Stalin and imposed as "Soviet Science" on overtly ideological grounds: it fitted the Marxist theory that man is shaped by his environment, so that if you modify the environment, you can permanently (!) alter the nature of man. Similarly, the rejection of Darwinism in favour of "Creationism" is willed by religious fundamentalists in the United States.

So does that mean that each individual can shape his own reality by an act of will alone? We have just seen that in the area of science the will, at any given time and in any given society, accepts certain ways of proceeding so that there is likely to be (again at a given time and in a given society) widespread agreement. Fichte called that agreement the "dogmatic" view of the world. (The Greek word "dogma" means "teaching" – a dogmatic view is a view we accept

6 More strictly speaking, in the way it shapes reality. As Fichte did away with the noumenal *Ding an sich*, the world of appearances was to him the only world there is, or, in short, the world of appearances is reality itself.

because we have been taught it.) This view can be conscious - when we are aware of the reasoning that lies behind it - or it can be unconscious - where we simply accept the consensus as "given" and where it does not occur to us to question it. For Fichte, however, scientific activity was not particularly significant. Those who pursue it tend to be seized of the determinist nature of what they are studying. Even the original scientist who breaks from the views of his colleagues and creates a new reality will merely substitute one manifestation of determinism for another.

Fichte attached much more significance to moral, religious, artistic or political activity. Firstly, those who pursue this are conscious of their own consciousness (or ego) in a way in which the scientist, who focuses on the *object* of consciousness, is not, and secondly, they are conscious of their freedom in the way a scientist cannot be. Here the will can create a reality that it totally new. Where, for the *philosophes*, the scientist was the guide to true knowledge, for Fichte, the arch-Romantic, it was the artist who was the High Priest, and artistic creation was the model of all creativity. The artist does not, as Plato had argued, copy some pre-existing *ideal* pattern, nor is art "a mirror held up to nature", slavishly copying the world of *particulars*; the creative artist does not follow rules. By a heroic act of will the artist creates his own, original reality: he shapes his own existence into a work of art; he does not allow the "dogmatic" view to dictate his life; he, above all others, creates his own truth and the vision of it he must follow.

> How true this is of the great artists of the twentieth century. If we look at Picasso, for instance, who is the archetypical twentieth century artist, we can see at once how Fichte's views apply to him. Art, for Picasso, was neither about creating an ideal pattern nor about holding a mirror up to nature, and he certainly broke every artistic rule in the book. Instead, he powerfully created his own world – so powerfully that he has won a large following, and has transformed the way in which many people look at art today and the expectations they have of it.

What is true of the demands of art is also true of morals and religion, and of science, too. The heroic thinker will be prepared to suffer whatever penalties the "dogmatic" world may impose on him: the artist will be prepared to starve in his proverbial garret; the "Byronic" individual will fly in the face of convention and be prepared to endure exile; a Darwin or a Freud will persist in the face of vitriolic abuse. In all this Fichte anticipates the stress the Existentialists will put on "authenticity".[7] They begin by reshaping only their own world, but in due course many of them, by gaining acceptance, reshape the transcendental or consensual world. These are the really great individuals.

He applied this notion of the heroic individual to politics also. He admired historical figures like Napoleon, who impose their will upon an age, and who shape both themselves and the society into a work of art.

> This admiration of the Great Man who stamps his mark on history will have some sinister consequences in Fichte's Germany, and of course the theory is the very opposite of the Marxist notion that the Great Man is he who gives expression to the dominant forces that are already at work in history. This is a

7 See p. 486 below.

> theory that has history shaped by impersonal forces, not by great individuals. According to this theory, all that a Great Man can do is to speed up the work of those forces. Such a man is, in the last resort, an instrument and not a shaper of history.

Although individual freedom and the individual will were of great importance to Fichte, in his political thought he took the Rousseauist view that when individuals merge their will with the will of the state they achieve true freedom. He bestowed this mixture of democracy and authoritarianism on his beloved German nation, for among his other influences was a strongly nationalistic one. Philosophers were probably the only readers of his *Wissenschaftslehre*. Far more popular were his *Addresses to the German Nation* of 1807, a foundation document of German nationalism (and, incidentally, of virulent nineteenth-century antisemitism.)

FRIEDERICH SCHELLING
1775 to 1854

Schelling was a pupil of Fichte's, and he, too, believed that, in the end, the world was pure mind, but he differed from his teacher in maintaining that it had not always been so. For Schelling, it had evolved to that state, had striven teleologically to attain it. (Here, Schelling followed Kant's *Critique of Judgment*, which had derived aesthetic satisfaction from the awareness that nature was part of a design or was evolving according to a design that was set before it.) Originally, he thought, nature had been inorganic, then organic life developed and organic life then evolved into mental and intellectual life, and from there into spiritual life.

Schelling calls the ultimate stage of this evolutionary process, from the inorganic stage to nature being aware of itself, "the Absolute" or "the World Soul". He also identifies it with God. Kant had asserted that we must believe in God because, if there were no God, the world would be a meaningless chaos – we lead saner lives if we acted "as if" God existed. He had gone on to say that there was no need to believe in the paraphernalia of Church teaching about, for example, the divinity of Christ. Schelling, son of a Lutheran pastor, had been a student of theology before he became a philosopher, and he was a believing Christian – indeed he converted to Roman Catholicism. For him, God was not an abstract organizing principle, as He had been for Spinoza, nor was He an intellectual construct or a way of making sense of the world, as He had been for Kant. Schelling was sure that there was an independent *personal* God who was continually creating and revealing Himself to Man over time; initially through myths and the most primitive of religions, and then culminating in the redeeming God of the Christian revelation.

If God is independent and equated with the Absolute, it would seem to follow that the Absolute, too, is independent, and so not unlike Kant's *Ding an sich*. Yet the notion that there is a difference between the *Ding an sich* and the world as we perceive it is rejected by Schelling. Somehow, Schelling marries the idea of an independent God with the Fichtean notion that the world in all its aspects (physical, moral, aesthetic, spiritual etc.) is a product of the mind. Our mind evolves *pari passu* with God evolving from myth to Christianity, "we are not only part of that process; we are its consciousness and means of expression".[8] That in turn would imply that even the Absolute (or God) was not independent of our consciousness of it, but depended for its self-awareness on being articulated by the human mind at its highest level.

The highest level of the mental life, we have seen, is the spiritual one. At the level before that, the intellectual one, the mind studies nature as something outside itself and is often unable to grasp that it is itself an integral part of nature. Only at the spiritual and artistic level does the mind see itself in that way, so that it grasps nature *from within nature itself.* Conversely put, when nature has evolved to this point, nature, too, understands itself from within itself. At that point the inorganic matter of the earliest stage and the mind and spirit of the later stages are interfused: they have become alternative manifestations of the same thing; different aspects of a single world order. This was an idea very close to the conception of Spinoza,[9] who was at this time widely read by the Transcendental Idealists.

Such awareness from within itself is of course an act of consciousness. Now Schelling believed that the highest kind of consciousness seeks, creates and finds harmony and aesthetic qualities, which is why it manifests itself most fully in the artist and the philosopher. So Schelling, like Fichte, thought that ultimate reality was a product of the transcendental ego as it manifests itself in the individual ego of the profound thinker; Heine's mocking comment on Fichte and his wife might equally have been made about Mr and Mrs Schelling.

The philosophies of Fichte and Schelling are exceedingly difficult to understand. Even sympathetic accounts complain about the obscurity and vagueness of the language in which they are expressed, and it is quite impossible to summarize their key concepts with any degree of clarity. They are,, anyway, intensely speculative, and quite incapable of being tested. Pragmatic philosophers have dismissed them as so much mumbo-jumbo. Romantic thought poeticized the infinite and the boundless, and it exalted the mystical merging of Man in the Universe. For a generation or so the reputation of transcendental idealism stood very high in Germany and, to a much lesser extent, in England, too. Even from the point of view of this book, which is concerned with how philosophy affects the way people live, some of the notions of these thinkers have trickled down in a generalized form to shape attitudes. These include the idea that it is the human mind which imposes some kind of order on the physical and moral universe rather than that the universe has an order which the mind detects.[10]

Then there is the allied idea that we can, to some extent, shape the world by our will. This has had particular repercussions - sometimes very baneful ones - in the social and political field.

8 Robert C. Solomon - *Continental Philosophy since 1750*, p. 44. (Oxford University Press).

9 For Spinoza, see chapter 24, and in particular p. 239f.

10 Not that this idea was completely novel: over 2,000 years earlier Protagoras has said - a great deal more simply than the transcendental idealists - that "Man is the Measure of all things." And Montesquieu had shown how differently the world appears to a Persian from the way a Frenchman sees it.

The way we view the role of the artist also owes something to Fichte and to Schelling. As late as the eighteenth century, even the most princely of artists, for the most part, still saw it as their role to serve their patrons. Now the artist will claim much more independence. His creative genius must be respected, but even where it is not, the artist must follow his own course – his integrity demands that he be authentic at whatever cost to himself. For this reason alone, Fichte and Schelling, obscure though they are, deserve a place in a book on Philosophy and Living.

CHAPTER 33

Georg Wilhelm Friederich Hegel

1770 to 1831

When Schelling was a student at the University of Tübingen, he shared a room with his friend Hegel, where both studied Theology and Philosophy. Later ,they were again together at the University of Jena, where Schelling was Professor of Philosophy and Hegel a lecturer in the same subject. The university suffered terribly during and after the Battle of Jena (1806) and student numbers fell drastically. Hegel was penniless and left the university, first for Bamberg, where he had been offered the editorship of a journal, and then for Nuremberg, where he was headmaster of a school from 1808 to 1816. It was at Bamberg that he published his first work, the *Phenomenology of Mind* (1807).

From Descartes to Hume and even to Kant, the preoccupation of epistemological[1] philosophy had been how the mind processes the sense impressions it receives from the outside world. Kant had said that there is such a world (*Das Ding an sich*), but that the tools of understanding we have compel us to understand it in terms of those tools, without any assurance that they enable us to understand what *das Ding an sich* is really like. In that case, Fichte had said, if we can have no knowledge of the *Ding an sich* or of the *noumenon,* then such a concept is unnecessary. All we have is the knowledge of *phenomena* and these are shaped, as Kant has said, by our consciousness or Ego, that is, by our mental activity. To this, Schelling had added the idea that this mental activity has historically evolved over time, from primitive organisms, in which mental activity as we understand it is absent, to thought, which in humans can rise from unreflective mental activity to the artistic and spiritual level.

The Dialectic

Hegel now examined more closely how this evolutionary process happens in human consciousness. He coined the word "Phenomenology of Mind" to describe the way the mind works, not on external objects, but on the ideas it already has. In other words, it describes how the mind examines one of its

1 Epistemology is that part of philosophy which deals with how we know things.

ideas, intellectually reflects on it, finds where it clashes with an opposing idea, reflects on this clash, and works out a way of resolving it. The original idea was the Thesis; the opposing idea (or ideas, for there may of course be several of them) the Antithesis, the resolution the Synthesis.[2] The Synthesis, however, is not enduring: in due course it will be seen as a new Thesis which generates its own Antithesis, and a new Synthesis will emerge from that clash. The process continues *ad infinitum*, or, more accurately, continues until all contradictions are resolved in the Absolute.

The world, as we have seen, is consciousness, so Absolute Consciousness, the end of the Phenomenology of Mind, must be consciousness of the whole world and of that world being conscious of itself. This implies that *in the end* the Absolute must be knowable, not the unknowable *Ding an sich* that Kant had posited. Hegel, like Kant, was a religious person, and indeed a Christian, so just as Kant had found it natural to equate the *Ding an sich* with God, so for Hegel, God and the Absolute were really the same: in both God and the Absolute all contradictions and differences would be dissolved.[3] Using Kant's distinction between *Vernunft* and *Verstand*,[4] Hegel calls *Verstand* the understanding of concepts as being separate from one another, and *Vernunft* an understanding that the Absolute is what we would today call "holistic" – in the Absolute all divisions disappear and everything is part of everything else.[5] This notion satisfied the mystical feeling he had had as a young man that all separateness is ultimately unreal, and he was satisfied that he had reached this conclusion by a rational process.

Hegel was convinced that the development of ideas from Thesis through Antithesis to Synthesis embodies the highest form of reason. Hegel described the process as a *dialectic*. The word has the same root as *dialogue*. Both come from the Greek *dialegesthai*, meaning to converse and *dialektike* meaning the art or skill (*techne*) of argument. A dialectical argument is designed, not to prove that one side is right and the other wrong, but to find a resolution of the differences.

In that respect, it reflected Hegel's psychology. In his youth he had been attracted to mysticism, and he had felt the "unreality" of separateness especially strongly, and had the intuition that only the whole is real. In an early essay of 1801 he had written that *"Division is the source of the need of philosophy"*. The task of philosophy was to overcome opposition and division, the "splintered harmony" between subject and object, body and soul, religion and the sec-

2 Those three terms (together they are sometimes referred to as Triads) have been much identified with Hegel's philosophy ever since they had been identified as central to it by Heinrich Moritz Chalybäus in the middle of the nineteenth century and were then perpetuated by Karl Marx. They had been used extensively by Fichte. Hegel actually used them very sparingly, but the triadical arrangement of ideas pervades everything he wrote. Like Kant, he seems to have been attracted by the archetypal notion of trinities. However, perhaps the word "triad" conveys the wrong idea anyway. He knew quite well that the opposite of a thesis need not be just one but could be several antitheses, out of whose clash a new synthesis would arise.

3 Because Hegel did not agree with Kant that there was some permanent *Ding an sich* outside our capacity to understand it, his notion of God was not of a deity that was always there, but rather of a Deity that was always developing itself by the dialectical process in which human minds participated.

4 see p. 365, note 9 above.

5 This notion, that to the philosopher everything is part of everything else, reminds one of Spinoza. See p. 238 above.

ular life, private and public interest, reason and feeling, reflection and intuition.

The dialectic, then, describes the process by which ideas in the mind evolve, and because, as Fichte and Schelling had said, the mind creates the world, it also describes the way in which the world evolves. This is especially true when mental processes are translated and shaped into social institutions, for these reflect the thoughts that gave rise to them - they are Mind or Spirit (Hegel uses the word *Geist*) "solidified in the world". The idea comes first, then the world reflects them. This philosophy is therefore called *Dialectical Idealism.*[6]

> The whole scheme suggests that, *over the long term*, the development of ideas and their solidification in the world represent progress – especially when we consider that in the end it all culminates in the Absolute (which Hegel identified with God). Any relapse into regress, reaction or barbarism, which the world has experienced often enough, is, in this scheme, part of the necessary motor of the Dialectic, an antithesis to be overcome in an eventual synthesis which is seen as an improvement over both the thesis and the antithesis. Moreover, the clash between ideas that represent thesis and antithesis, when solidified in the world, is often a violent and bloody one. That, too, must be accepted as the necessary price of progress, which Hegel specifically accepted when he dismissed as unphilosophical Kant's vision of a supranational authority to prevent war.[7]

Kant had had the confidence that reason, properly used, can give us an understanding of what the phenomenal world is like. Hegel, for his part, was confident that the dialectical *process* moved in a rational way.

True, any given thesis or antithesis cannot be wholly rational or it would not have to give way to a synthesis (and even a synthesis, in so far as it forms a new thesis, cannot be wholly rational) but Hegel believed that the process by which ideas refine themselves is a rational one.

> One might have some reservations about this. Hegel certainly uses the word "rational" in a rather special sense. The antithesis of a rational thesis might be itself rational, but it might also be irrational. If the thesis, for example, were the rational democratic ideas which solidified in the constitution of the Weimar Republic, the antithesis of the Nazis in many ways took what we would consider a passionately and often consciously irrational form. Is it not playing with words to say that, because there were reasons (i.e. thought processes) that induced the Nazis to think antithetically, it was a rational process that was at work? Altogether, the notion that lies behind the dialectic is that it is not only a rational but also, as we have seen above, a progressive process in the course of which, things should get better and better, as each synthesis embodies the best of the thesis and the antithesis that preceded it. But that seems to be an unduly optimistic interpretation of history (though Positivism held just that view). In fact, history often regresses rather than progresses. We have the Dark Ages, for example. Even if modern revisionism suggests that the name

6 The opposite view was later held by Marx. He also believed in a dialectical process, but he fell back to the earlier position that the material world "out there" is the cause of our ideas. He maintained that a dialectic is involved in the natural evolution of that material world, and that, therefore, the ideas which respond to this evolution are also dialectical. That view will be known as Dialectical Materialism, and will be more fully discussed on p. 444 below.

7 See below, p. 396.

> is a misnomer and that they were not as dark as all that, one could hardly in any normal sense suggest that they represented a more progressive, let alone a more rational phase of thought than did the age that preceded them.

Hegel believed that the dialectical process of ideas was rational, and therefore, he argued, the development of the solidified manifestations of these thought processes – in history, in institutions, in art and in science – is likewise a rational development. Things in the world are what they are because they have to be that way, so what is, is properly so, or, as Hegel put it aphoristically – "The Real is the Rational and the Rational is the Real".

This dictum can be interpreted either in a conservative or in a radical way. A conservative would emphasize that any given status quo is rational and should therefore be accepted. That idea in turn easily slips into the notion that Might (which has established the prevailing state of affairs) is Right. Hegel's critics have accused him of justifying such a state of affairs.

A radical, on the other hand, might stress that, because what is rational is always evolving, the status quo must evolve also; that, in so far as it is rational, it is so only for a limited time; that the dialectic, proceeding along rational lines, will demand change; and that one should therefore strive to bring that rational adjustment about. In many ways, as we shall see below,[8] Hegel did not envisage the idea of social organization, and the idea of the state in particular, evolving beyond the state they had reached in his own lifetime, but he was well aware of the radical possibilities inherent in his dictum, and he once told Heine to pay as much attention to its second as to its first half. The followers of Hegel will in fact divide between the Right Hegelians and the Left or Young Hegelians, who would give Marx his left-wing starting point.

The notion of the dialectical process, first sketched out by Hegel in *The Phenomenology of Mind,* will later be applied by him to a vast range of subjects.[9] (Sometimes one wonders whether the application is particularly illuminating, as when he posits Being as the thesis, Not-Being as the antithesis, and Becoming as the synthesis.) Even that triad conveys the idea that nothing in this world is static; the dynamism of the dialectic is always at work. This notion, of course, fits in well with the Romantic view of striving and restlessness, as opposed to the Classical search for what is permanent.

There is an application to human nature, where the *philosophes* had believed it essentially to be always the same, for Hegel, human nature changes and develops from one epoch to another.

For Kant, Ethics were embodied in an eternal moral law, but Hegel naturally saw ethics, too, in a continual process of dialectical change.

> We can certainly observe in history how the strict ethics of one society (the thesis) eventually creates its antithesis of what we call "permissive" ethical attitudes. The opposite can also be observed. A society that is felt to be too permissive will create an antithesis of a very authoritarian ethic. A synthesis is

8 p. 396 below.

9 Hegel published some of these applications in his lifetime: to Logic (in *The Science of Logic,* 1816) and to private and public ethics (in *The Philosophy of Right,* 1820). Others were the subject of lecture series, and these were published after his death by students from Hegel's notes and from their own notes of what they had heard him say. They include *Lectures on Aesthetics, The Philosophy of Religion, The Philosophy of History,* and *The History of Philosophy.*

certainly possible in theory – a society which replaces external controls and an uncontrolled permissiveness with sound internal controls. Have we seen such a synthesis?

Truth, likewise, evolves in a dialectical manner – it is relative to the stage which the dialectic has reached. However, because we are here dealing with Dialectical Idealism and not Dialectical Materialism, the relativism of truth is not (as Montesquieu, for example, had said) *created* by environmental circumstances, rather the dialectical process of truth-producing ideas *produces* an environment which, as a result, displays the same dialectical development.

The history of ideas does quite often show a dialectical pattern. Hegel himself saw it in the history of religion. This starts, with the ancients, believing in many gods in solid human form and in a relationship to particular functions and peoples (thesis). It proceeds, with the Jews, to the idea of one God in disembodied form who is both particular to the Jews and at the same time is the author of universal ethical and natural laws (antithesis). Then Christianity has a universal God who is no longer the God of a particular people and who is both disembodied and embodied in Jesus Christ (synthesis).

He also saw it in the history of philosophy. This begins with the idea, found in the Ionian cosmologists, that everything is basically one thing, like Air, or Fire, or Change (thesis).[10] Then come dualistic philosophies, seeing a division between Body and Soul or between Mind and Matter or between Good and Evil (antithesis). The synthesis is then the thought of such philosophers as Spinoza[11] and Hegel himself, in whom everything is ultimately part of everything else.

One could apply the same notion to certain ideologies in cultural and political history. In culture we may see classical canons of restraint (say, in Poussin) generating the antithesis of a freer expression of form (say, in the Rococo) and emotions (say, in Greuze) and then finding a synthesis in what some people call classical romanticism (say, in David) where classical forms are married to the expressions of stormy emotions.

In history, there are many examples of an old-fashioned theory of government (the *ancien régime*) generating the antithesis of a radicalism, which, though bringing reforms, becomes excessively violent, extreme and disorderly (the Jacobins, followed by the chaos of the Directory). Napoleon, representing the restoration of order whilst retaining some of the reforms of the revolutionary period, could be seen as the synthesis. Napoleon will then produce his own antithesis leading to the Bourbon "Restoration", but it is not a complete Restoration: the restored Bourbons had to accept some kind of parliamentary government, which had not existed in any significant way either under the Ancien Régime or under Napoleon. With an effort, one might be able to fit (force?) the later developments into the same pattern.

Many other revolutions in history have followed the same pattern, but is it only theory that generates other theories? Are not historical events in particular best explained by combining Hegel's Dialectical Idealism with Marx's Dialectical Materialism?[12] It was, after all, material facts of the ancien régime –

10 See p. 5 above.

11 See p. 238 above.

12 See p. 391 above.

the injustices, the inability to accommodate the interests of new economic forces or to relieve the material pressures on the poor – that created the ideas of revolution. The ideas were then in turn translated into changes in the material world. After that, it was then again the experience of material distress – of terror and of chaos – which gave rise to the ideas that Napoleon translated into the transformation that he brought about.

The "truth" of ethical, cultural and political systems is indeed not fixed and is continuously evolving, possibly in the dialectical manner proposed by Hegel and Marx. Hegel accepted that nature does not exhibit the dialectical process at work, but he did not calculate the implications of this admission. For example, the Black Death in the fourteenth century was an event in the material world, not the solidification of any ideas at all. That event subsequently *shaped* ideas, as the shortage of labour affected the economy and social structure in all sorts of ways. This would appear to be a clear case of the dialectic being drive by material events rather than by ideas.

Even if we take the Kantian position of saying that our understanding of the phenomenal world is conditioned by our tools of understanding, these tools give us some ideas of the world that are unchanging through the ages. To take a simple example, no dialectical process of thought could possibly alter the truth that in the phenomenal world the sun rises in the East. Our *ideas* about nature occasionally clash in an antithetical way, as, for example in the opposition of the heliocentric to the geocentric view of our part of the universe, but this is the result of closer observations of the material phenomenal world and not of the geocentric view *generating* the heliocentric one. Scientific progress is not the result of one idea *by itself* producing an antithetical idea, and scientific progress is very often not a matter of antitheses at all, but rather of some refinement which (if you like) synthesizes some new discovery in the material world with existing ideas about it. Biology and Chemistry have never been thought to be antithetical, but they can be synthesized into biochemistry. (Conversely, those who believe that mind and matter are antithetical, rather than complementary, could point to psychosomatic medicine as resolving this clash into a synthesis.)

Freedom

In Hegel we find a development of a notion going back to the Christian idea that there is within us a better self which is often at war with a worse self. If we follow the worse self, we may think that we are doing this freely, but in fact we are not free at all, rather we are enslaved to our baser nature. Only if we are not thus enslaved and follow our better self are we "really" free. Rousseau had then given this notion a crude institutional form, by identifying real freedom with the General Will of society. The General Will, he said, was never wrong and always superior to any individual will which aims to promote a person's narrow self-interest - the freedom to do so is only "actual" freedom, but not real freedom.[13] He then produced a series of paradoxes, such as that if one is compelled to accept the General Will against one's own actual will, one is in fact being "forced to be free". Kant reverted to the less crude analysis, that actions based on mere desire are not free, even if they seem to be so. Real freedom is to be found only in actions based on the proper use of reason (and we need to

13 See p. 338 above.

remember that for him, the categorical imperatives of morality are based on reason).

Hegel drew another distinction between real and actual freedom. He agreed with Kant that real freedom is to be found in actions based on the paths of reason, but because Hegel believed, unlike Kant, that the path of reason is a dialectical one, he believed that we enjoy real freedom only in so far as we go along with the dialectic's progress towards the Absolute. Reality conforms to the dialectical progress of reason, hence, it will be remembered, the equation between what is real and what is rational. Therefore, "Freedom consists in the knowledge of reality" (which Marx will re-phrase, more famously, "Freedom is the recognition of necessity.") Most dramatically, "The history of the world is none other than the progress of the consciousness of freedom."

Where Christianity and Kant had seen "actual" freedom as often not freedom at all, but slavery to one's baser self, Hegel pointed out that when we think we are free, we are often unwitting slaves of environmental influences. Some of these are social pressures, ideas inculcated by the educational system, by propaganda, or by advertising (what we would now call "brainwashing"). These all make it hard to think rationally for oneself. A person who is really free has to be able to liberate himself from this kind of conditioning. More subtle still are the social and historical forces of any given time, which many people take for granted without realizing that they are not permanent, but subject to the dialectical process.

At this point it seems clear that Hegel is not saying that, to be really free, one has to go along with things as they are; the dialectic involves an oppositional stance, when the antithesis is in necessary, though temporary, conflict with the thesis. The freest person would perhaps be the one who, even while engaging in the clash between thesis and antithesis, can look beyond this to realize what shape the synthesis would take.

The State

Freedom of course can take many forms – the freedom to make moral decisions, the freedom to make decisions about everyday life, etc. One of its most important forms is political freedom, freedom in the state, but in Hegel, the dynamic process of the dialectic comes to a halt with the state. Here again, we notice Hegel's tendency to assume that, contrary to his theory, the dialectical process comes to an end with ideas of which Hegel approved. It seems that he could not envisage a rational antithesis beyond the state, and so he believed that real freedom consists in accepting the state, rather as Rousseau had thought that real freedom means accepting the will of the community as represented by the General Will.[14]

The state has come into being through a dialectical process. The thesis was the family or tribe, in which individuals were seen only as members of such groups. The antithesis was the assertion of the rights of individuals against the group; the clash between the idea of groups denying independent right of individuals and the idea of individuals having no particular allegiance to the

14 See p. 337 above.

groups is resolved in the modern synthesis of a state, which claims to subsume (without destroying) the rights of individuals or lesser groups, because these all find individual fulfilment in the state. This last idea, expressed by Rousseau and put into practice in the course of the French Revolution, finds conscious expression in the so-called Organic Theory of the State,[15] and it is supposed to differ from the original thesis because in that earlier phase the organic nature of the society was taken for granted without being consciously articulated.

> One might question this: Aristotle, for example, had expressed the idea quite consciously,[16] and we find a very full statement of the theory in the speech which Shakespeare gives to Menenius Agrippa in the first scene of *Coriolanus*. It is one of several examples of where what Hegel considers a synthesis – i.e. the last stage of the triad – could be found in a much earlier phase of the history of ideas.

A twentieth-century person might accept that the state was such a synthesis, but he would remember that a synthesis becomes a new thesis, creating its own antithesis and then a further synthesis. There is after all not one state, but several. These assert the rights of individual states against each other, and the resulting clash might then produce the synthesis of the supranational state, such as is currently developing in the European Community. The supranational states may clash, and one could imagine the synthesis of a world state emerging from this.

Why did Hegel not envisage this? He did say that philosophers are not in the forecasting business - they are too bound to their own times and cannot transcend the contemporary world. The philosopher can only understand how the past has dialectically moved to the present, and he can realize that, only at the moment when the present phase is about to give way to the new one. In a poetic phrase, he writes "The owl of Minerva flies only at dusk."

> That would certainly be an excuse for the several occasions on which he assumed that the synthesis that happened in his own time (the state, Christianity, or, for that matter, his own philosophy) was the last word in that particular field. Of course, he could not be expected to specify exactly what form the next phase – the new antithesis to the current (syn)thesis – would take, but in accordance with his own theory he should have anticipated some such challenge.

There were contemporaries of Hegel who did envisage that the clash of states should be superseded by some organization that should keep the peace. For one thing, there was the claim of the Catholic Church that allegiance to it transcended any allegiance to the state - a claim that the Protestant Hegel would not accept.[17] Then Kant had, in one of his works (*On Perpetual Peace*, 1795), sketched out a League for Peace, and after the Napoleonic Wars the continental powers joined in a Holy Alliance to maintain peace and stability in Europe. The

15 See p. 338 above.

16 See p. 52 above.

17 We might note in passing that the word "Catholic", from the Greek *katolicos*, means universal; and that this concept historically *preceded* the concept of the modern state. Again, that would be a case of a synthesis preceding a thesis!

Concert of Europe, set up at the same time, was the earliest forerunner of the League of Nations and of the United Nations.

Admittedly, the theory of a supranational authority was quickly contradicted by the practice. All these bodies have been ineffective when the threatened the interests of the individual states. Hegel thought that this was only natural and he poured scorn on such arrangements: they were impossible, and indeed, undesirable, because conflict between states has a positive value as part of the dialectic. In every age one nation is charged with the mission of expressing the *Zeitgeist* (or Spirit of the Times). If the world is to move along to the next stage of the dialectic, then wars, the solidification of the idea of struggle, is inevitable. History is the World's Court of Judgment on this process. This view seems at odds with the notion that the state is the highest *possible* manifestation of the dialectic, for in the Absolute, the ultimate synthesis, all theses and antitheses must be dissolved.

Over and over again, Hegel uses rapturous and mystical language about the idea of the state: it is "the Divine Idea as it exists on earth"; "we must therefore worship the state as the manifestation as the Divine on earth"; "the State exists for its own sake"; "the State is the march of God through the world".

No wonder that many critics, like Karl Popper,[18] have accused Hegel of exalting existing states, and his native Prussia especially, as the incorporation of the Absolute. Peter Singer mounts a defence of Hegel. The last of the phrases, he says, is a mistranslation: it should read *"It is the way of God with the world that the State exists"*.[19] That would make possible the notion that it must exist as part, but not necessarily as the end, of the dialectical process. Moreover, Singer frequently uses the word "community" when he is discussing Hegels' theory of the State, as if Hegel meant the whole of political and social life.

> Rousseau had realized that community and state were two different things. He had been sceptical and hostile towards all the institutions of his time, and had been very clear that it was not the state which was sovereign, but the General Will of the community, of which the existing states – and certainly those which were bigger than city-states – were only imperfect instruments. Neo-Hegelian liberals like T.H. Green[20] would also see the General Will as a valuable concept in small social groupings, but a dangerous one when applied to the machinery of the state.

Finally, Singer denies that Hegel saw the actual Prussian State of his time as an embodiment of the Absolute, as it was clear to him that it fell far short of granting individuals or subsidiary institutions their rightful self-fulfilment within the state. It was only the *idea* of the state that embodied the Absolute - the actual states of Hegel's time still had much evolving to do before they could correspond to the ideas.[21] Yet one can see how Hegel's theories, like Rousseau's, have been enthusiastically embraced by authoritarian states that claim to be the embodiment of the national General Will.

18 In *The Open Society and its Enemies*, Vol. II, p. 31.

19 Peter Singer - *Hegel* (Oxford University Press, Past Masters series), p. 42.

20 See p. 432 below.

21 Singer, *op. cit.*, p. 43/4.

The *Zeitgeist* is expressed not only by certain nations, but by certain individuals also. "He who tells the time what it wills and means, and then brings it to a conclusion, is the great man of his times." A great man's actions have a significance of which he may or may not be aware. Was Julius Caesar aware that when he crossed the Rubicon he set in motion the inevitable process by which the Roman Republic would be transformed into the Roman Empire? Others are very conscious of their world role. Napoleon was such a one, and Hegel admired him even when the French Emperor defeated Prussia at the Battle of Jena. The admiration lasted right up to his downfall, when Hegel commented that Napoleon was "an immense genius destroyed by mediocrity".

> As we have seen before, Napoleon could be seen as representing the synthesis that arose out of the clash between the *ancien régime* and the French Revolution. But a synthesis then forms the new thesis that engenders its own antithesis. The man or men who represent that antithesis would be those who express the evolving *Zeitgeist*. The antithesis of government by colourful individuals and the excitement they generate is often the government of mediocre, grey and prosaic men. In the Hegelian sense perhaps even such mediocre men are, paradoxically, "the great men of their times".

The Influence of Hegel

We can see how many of Hegel's ideas have had an influence on modern thought. Perhaps his most important influence was on Karl Marx, who brought the idea of the dialectic down to earth, from the realm of abstract ideas generating each other to the interplay in the first instance of material developments, to which ideas then respond. Marx's view was the vision officially propagated by Communism and as such would have a worldwide influence.

Both in its Idealistic and in its Materialistic form, the Dialectic is shown as an ultimately progressive force in history and society. The clashes between thesis and antithesis, painful as they often are to live through, are healthy and are the necessary birth-pangs of progress. The inevitable synthesis, resulting from these clashes, could also be be taken as representing the triumph of the best idea, or, stretching it a little further, as the survival of the fittest. Those notions fitted in well with nineteenth-century Positivism[22] and with Social Darwinism[23] which had the optimistic view that, despite the occasional slipping backwards, the story of mankind is one of progress. The twentieth century is more aware of the possibility of regress, which has been prevalent in so many societies for many decades at a time.

In ethics, the Hegelian system is a synthesis between values being fixed and eternal on the one hand (which many people find hard to accept) and being purely relativistic on the other (which, disturbingly, gives no firm foothold to any system of values). An ethical system has, in relation to a particular time and society, a validity of its own.

22 See p. 437 below.

23 see p. 442 below.

> In practice, however, that may not be of much help, as anyone who questions the ethics of his time or society may be preparing the ethical outlook of the next stage in the dialectic.

The notion that certain historical figures express the stages of the dialectic has also been enormously influential. Some statesmen in the past have had faith in their destiny, believing that there was something *in them* that singled them out for greatness. Others have believed that God had chosen them for a particular mission. Since Hegel's time, there have been statesmen who have been less subjective and more philosophical: they have believed that they must study the objective forces of history so that they can work along with them. A striking example is the future Napoleon III, who wrote in 1841, "March at the head of the ideas of your century and these ideas follow and support you. March behind them, and they drag you after them. March against them and they overthrow you."

> Napoleon III was certainly the midwife of many forces of nineteenth-century history, though their very dynamic overwhelmed him in the end.

Finally, Singer's defence of him notwithstanding, Hegel, like Rousseau before him, was interpreted as glorifying the community as it manifests itself in the state. Hegel professed a belief in freedom and would very likely have been appalled at the way "actual" and "real" freedoms have been crushed in some modern states. In the course of the nineteenth and twentieth century the state has become ever more ambitious, and in some countries the distinction between state and the community became increasingly blurred and even obliterated. Hegel had said that the Absolute manifests itself in the state. No wonder, then, that some states have espoused Absolutism. Another revealing word for modern absolutism is Totalitarianism, in which the state, whether fascist or Marxist, claims the right to control the totality of human activity. In this respect, Hegel's legacy has been a sinister one.

CHAPTER 34

Arthur Schopenhauer

1788 to 1860

We have seen in the preceding chapters how Fichte, Schelling, and Hegel had rejected Kant's distinction between the unknowable noumenal world and the phenomenal world which we perceive through our tools of understanding. Schopenhauer restored that distinction.[1] In particular, he accepted Kant's idea that the concepts of space and time are *mere* tools of understanding and *cannot* exist in the noumenal world.[2] It is only in the phenomenal world, therefore, that we differentiate things from each other *because* they do not occupy the same space and do not happen at the same instant. We cannot conceive of two *different* phenomena occupying the same space at the same time, so that, if they do, they must be identical, but if space and time do not exist in the noumenal world, then there can be no differentiation there - in the noumenal world everything merges into the One.

> I have the same problem here as I have with the notion that time and space cannot exist in the noumenal world. If we cannot know the noumenal world, not only can we not know that time and space do *not* exist there, but neither can we know that in that world our logical tools apply as they do in the phenomenal world. *Our* logical tools of understanding the phenomenal world tell us that if time and space did not exist *there*, everything would merge into one. But can we assume that the logic we use would apply to the noumenal world when we can actually have no knowledge of the noumenal world? It seems to me that Schopenhauer had no justification for applying to the noumenal world the logic that applied to the phenomenal world. He would therefore not be entitled to assume that in the noumenal world everything *must* be One – quite different logical rules might very well apply there.

Schopenhauer had already formed this conclusion and written about it, when a friend who was an orientalist introduced him to Hinduism and Buddhism. In Hinduism he found the same idea, the notion of Maya, the veil of appearances which separates us from the ultimate reality, which was One. A Latin transla-

1 For much of this chapter I am heavily indebted to Bryan Magee's brilliant exposition in his *Philosophy of Schopenhauer*, Oxford University Press, revised edition of 1997. There is also an excellent chapter on Schopenhauer by Richard Taylor in *A Critical History of Western Philosophy*, edited by D.J. O'Connor and published in 1964 by Macmillans.

2 I have already expressed some puzzlement about this idea in note 13 on p. 368 above.

tion of the *Upanishads* now became his nightly bedtime reading, and he found similar insights in Buddhist thought. In his later writings, Schopenhauer would frequently refer to eastern thought, and he became the first western philosopher to be a serious student of eastern philosophies. He was particularly impressed by the fact that the Hindu and Buddhist thinkers had taken quite different routes from those taken by Kant and himself to come to these conclusions.

In the *Critique of Pure Reason*, Kant had stressed that the noumenal world, *das Ding an sich*, must be unknown to us, but he had also opened up the possibility that we might have some glimmerings of the noumenal world. Whilst as a physical being Man is part of the phenomenal world, as a moral being, with *a priori* moral and religious intuitions, he is part of the noumenal world.[3] Schopenhauer developed this idea further. We can have *intimations* of the noumenon, as it were, from the inside; we can feel the noumenon working within us, and within our inner self (as distinct from that part of the self which operates on phenomena with our rational tools of understanding).

These intimations are still phenomenal, as they cannot give us *knowledge* of the noumenon itself, and this for several reasons. All our intimations are experienced in time, which Schopenhauer believes to be a purely phenomenal concept. Furthermore, what we believe to be intimations may not be such at all. We may have a very inadequate, or indeed, a wholly deceptive understanding of the intuitive processes which are involved in responding to the noumenon, and the noumenon may work within us in ways of which we are actually unconscious. Finally, it is impossible for us not to separate ourselves as receivers of the intimations from the intimations itself, and in the noumenon, which is One, there cannot be any differentiation between the perceiver and the perceived.

So we cannot be sure that our intuitions are right or that they tell us a truth, but the fact that some intuitive paths lead us astray is no reason to reject intuition altogether, for they do often lead to truths. These may be on the humble level of the uneducated person about observed phenomena, or they may be at the sophisticated level of the philosopher whose intuition can give him some intimation of the noumenon.

So, we *can* respond to experiences without the rational tools of understanding that had been so important to Kant. The criticism that Schopenhauer had of Kant was that the latter had been too exclusively concerned with the way we apply *con*cepts to our experience, but had paid insufficient attention to the *per*cepts, to the actual experiences themselves, before the tools of understanding had got to work on them. As Schopenhauer put it: "Concepts should be the material in which philosophy deposits and stores up its knowledge, but not the source from which it draws such knowledge."

Kant had always urged us to use the tools of understanding properly, respecting the rules of reason, for only then would we interpret the phenomenal world properly. It was a very analytical approach, and the danger in it lay in the possibility that we miss or even destroy the inner meaning of the experiences that are being analyzed. As Wordsworth would put it,

3 See p. 376 above.

Our meddling intellect
Mis-shapes the beauteous form of things: -
We murder to dissect.

Grasping this inner meaning by direct perceptions, direct insights, direct intuitions – that is the only true source of knowledge. That is the real stuff of philosophy, and the task of philosophy is to refine, enrich and deepen these insights.

These intuitions do not reach us through the senses, or rather they reach beyond what the senses tell us, and can often not be adequately described in words. For Schopenhauer, as for Fichte, art had a special significance. The great artist in the act of creation breaks through into this realm of intuition. He does more than express *himself*: he is taking himself and us into something that is bigger than the self. We hear the music he has composed or see the painting he has created through our senses, but these then transport us into a nonsensory realm which gives us a feeling of at-One-ness with something beyond ourselves; they give us an intimation of the noumenal. We say that such experiences "take us out of ourselves"; we call them "timeless". The artist or the lover of art cannot teach us how to appreciate the work of art by any act of exposition. Formal analysis of a symphony's structure or of a painting's composition may give an intellectual understanding of the work, and some pleasure can be derived from that success, but the structures are only the vehicles through which the deepest meaning of a work of art is expressed – they are not the meaning itself. Schopenhauer was impatient with Kant's attempt to define the canons of aesthetics.[4] The only way we can truly respond to a work of art is by sharing something of the artist's own vision.

The Will

The search for a unifying principle has preoccupied philosophers and theologians for centuries. They have found it in several different forms: for Plato it had been the Idea of the Good;[5] for theologians the idea of God; for Spinoza "God or Nature";[6] for some of the *philosophes* it was reason; for Fichte and Hegel it was the Absolute. Schopenhauer found the unifying principle in what he called The Will, and the title of his most important book is *Die Welt als Wille und Vorstellung* (1818). In its first English translation (1883) this title appeared as *The World as Will and Idea*, but since 1958 it has been less confusingly translated as *The World as Will and Representation.*

Both "Will" and "Representation" need to be elucidated. "Representation" is Schopenhauer's word for the way the world is represented to our senses and intellect – in other words, it is very like what Kant had called "phenomena". As for "Will", Schopenhauer warned us that his use of the word was peculiar, and that it had nothing to do with minds, with conscious volition, or with conscious aims or goals.

> It is always dangerous to use a word with a generally accepted meaning in an unusual way, and is perhaps particularly dangerous in this case, because Will

4 See pp. 378f above.

5 See p. 35 above.

6 See p. 237 above.

> in the meaning of conscious volition has already played a significant role in the past (in the debate about free will from Pelagius to Kant) and will be an important part in the philosophy of Nietzsche.[7]

Schopenhauer's Will has nothing to do with any of these. It is the blind force which is at work in all creation, both animate and inanimate;[8] there is as much Will in the fall of a stone as there is in the actions of a man. The actions of a man are only secondarily dictated, if at all, by his *internal* personal volition – the volition itself is preceded by the *external* and impersonal Will.

> Let us take, for example, the matter of getting married. We think that the young man debates with himself whether to marry, then whether to marry a particular young woman, and whether to have children. If he decides that this is indeed what he wishes and goes ahead, he may think that he has exercised his volition. Schopenhauer maintained that, throughout, this volition was itself actually driven by a Will that was outside of himself and had programmed him to seek a particular kind of wife and to perpetuate his species.

Indeed, one might paradoxically define the Will as an *almost* inescapable destiny which often frustrates our volition and at best moulds it. (The significance of that word "almost" will appear later in this chapter.)

> In a discussion with Frederick Coplestone, Bryan Magee suggested Schopenhauer might have called this force "energy" rather than "Will";[9] and the substitution is tempting, not least because modern physics has introduced the notion of matter as energy (and because we have no knowledge of what generates that energy). Coplestone objected that "energy" is too neutral a word for the grim qualities which we will presently see Schopenhauer ascribing to the Will, and so one might prefer some darker and more tragic expression, like pitiless force. There is also a strong case for saying that where Schopenhauer used the word "Will", the *philosophes* would have used a phrase like "the laws of Nature". It is a law of Nature (here the law of gravity) which determines that the dropped stone should hit the ground; and similarly it is possible to argue that the laws of Nature include a struggle for survival or the drive for creatures to perpetuate their species (which, as we will see, are two of Schopenhauer's central ideas.) If one believes that this struggle is necessarily a pitiless one, then one could say that the laws of Nature are pretty grim, even if one did not use the concept of the Will. But Will is the word Schopenhauer used, and we now have to see what its characteristics are.

Its dominant aspect in living creatures is the instinctual drives which make them do things without reflection or rationalization. Schopenhauer says that instinct is simply Will without rationalization. In the animal world it manifests itself in making webs or nests etc. (one presumes that animals do this without

7 For Pelagius, see p. 111 above; for Kant, p. 376 above; for Nietzsche, p. 477 below.

8 The Will is seen by Schopenhauer so much as the source of everything that he occasionally identifies it with the noumenon: "The Will is the *Ding-an-sich*", he writes. But it cannot exactly be that. True, it lies *behind* the phenomena of which we are aware with our senses, and those who are not aware of that fact will have only a misleading understanding of the phenomena. Schopenhauer as a philosopher could, by using his insight or intuition, see the force that lay behind observable phenomena. But, as in the case of all other human intuitions, its object was in itself phenomenal, bound by human limitations, by notions of time and space etc. So the Will is only the way in which *we* perceive the *Ding an sich*, but as we cannot *know* what the *Ding an sich* is like, the Will, as Schopenhauer perceives it, can only be the way in which the *Ding an sich* appears to our limited human understanding.

9 In *The Great Philosophers*, p. 221, BBC Publications, 1987.

any knowledge of why they do so). He believed that it is the Will that determines the nature of every living being, equipping it with whatever it needs to survive: the talons and sharp beaks of predatory birds, the speed with which animals are equipped to pursue their victims or evade their enemies, etc. Darwin had not yet published his *Origins of the Species*, but the idea that these physical features evolve by random mutation was already circulating, and Schopenhauer thought it beyond belief that the many features which make animals so perfectly adapted to their survival could all be a matter of chances occurring over centuries; they must be part of an overall design. Schopenhaue,r as an atheist, attributed to a Will the notion of design which many religious people had attributed to God.

One reason that Schopenhauer rejected the idea of God was that God is supposed to be loving and caring for the individual. Schopenhauer described the belief in a benevolent God, or in a *divine* purpose, as men's efforts to make life – and in particular death – more bearable, for death is a frustration of the Will as it manifests itself in the individual. The Will tells all creatures that they must live at almost all costs, even at the cost of pain and suffering; its total indifference to suffering is its grimmest aspect. Creatures strive to stay alive under the most horrible conditions, even when, in humans, they hold out no rational hope of amelioration. The body fights for breath (that is, for life) to the last moment, and even after a creature has died a violent death, as when a chicken is decapitated, the organism protests by flapping about for a while, so urgent (Schopenhauer thinks) remains the Will to live.

> This last point could of course be much better explained not by something as fanciful as the Will, but by the reflexes of the nervous system. As for the more "conscious" efforts to stay alive – i.e. the reluctance to commit suicide – *as a generalization*, this is certainly true. There are so many cases where people say "I wish I could die" (and they may have good grounds for having that wish) and yet they draw back from killing themselves. They may claim that they would do so if they had the means to avoid a messy or painful end, and yet, however unpleasant, rationally this should count as nothing against the prospect of a prolonged period of suffering. True, some people do deliberately commit suicide under such circumstances, but they are only a tiny proportion (though enough, I would think, for Schopenhauer to give them more serious consideration than he did). Most people, even in the appalling conditions in concentration camps, strove to remain alive and to postpone what was often the inevitable end. Schopenhauer does offer, as we will see below, some ways in which the wise man can free himself from the Will as he defines it, but, while he has sympathy for suicides, he does not see them as rejecting life as such, but rather as demanding a better life. He thinks that suicide is a mistake. There are better ways, as we shall see, of freeing oneself of the burdens that life brings with it.

The religious teaching that suicide is a sin and a crime (an idea Schopenhauer does not share) is just one of the rationalizations which humans create to justify their submission to the Will, just as the religious teaching of an afterlife was, in Schopenhauer's view, a rationalization of the Will to go on living even after death – it does not allow us to face the idea that the Will to live will be frustrated.

The Will demands that we reproduce, again, at almost any cost. In some animals this is so clear that they perish as soon as their reproductive functions have been accomplished. Humans show some recognition of this imperative to reproduce when they say in the religious marriage ceremony that marriage was ordained to produce offspring, but they also build up the rationalization that we really marry for love – a pretence that quickly fades (he said) once the purpose of marriage has been achieved. Schopenhauer believed that arranged marriages, entered into for unsentimental reasons of breeding, actually stand a better chance of happiness and are less likely to be disrupted by extramarital affairs than marriages entered under the delusion that their basis is the fickle passion of love. The Will's demand for reproduction accounts for men's inconstancy: as far as men are concerned, the Will requires them to father as many children as possible. Women respond to an apparently contradictory aspect of the Will, which insists that it is better for their children, both born and unborn, that their fathers accept responsibility for them, hence the naturally possessive attitude of women towards their spouses.

> An extension of this point might be the drive to procreate even under circumstances where the children (as in some developing countries) are more than likely to have as miserable a life as the parents have had. The argument is that such parents produce so many children in the knowledge that many of them are likely to die before reaching the age where they can support their parents in old age. Schopenhauer would probably have said that this is a mere rationalization of the Will to procreate – a Will which is as careless of the individual human being as it is of individual frog spawns, only a few of which will survive to perpetuate the species.
>
> As far as the contrast between promiscuous men and monogamous women is concerned, we would now think that what Schopenhauer thought was a biological fact of life is actually a sociological one. In Schopenhauer's time, and for centuries before our own, single mothers and their children were hugely disadvantaged in the struggle for survival. In our own time the position of women has become much more independent. Some while wanting children, do not want a husband, whilst other women show the promiscuous tendencies that Schopenhauer seemed to find only in men.

The Will is indifferent to what happens to individuals after reproduction. It cares only for the survival of the species and does not care at all for the feelings or the fate of individual members of the species. (Nor, in a wider sense, does the Will care all that much for any individual species which may go down in its struggle against another species.) This is exactly the point that Richard Dawkins would make so powerfully in 1978 in *The Selfish Gene*, and Schopenhauer believed that this had also been a point made by Plato when he said that only the Ideas or Forms (but not their manifestations in particulars) are significant and eternal. The Will is immensely spendthrift of individuals. We have only to look at the lower forms of animate life to see that millions of individuals are allowed to perish at or near birth: it does not matter as long as a few of them survive to propagate the species. Nor does the Will care any more for human individuals; and all philosophies which attribute some special worth to human beings are merely the result of wishful thinking. To quote Richard Taylor:

> A man is often felled at the height of his power by a bacterium; a civilization is robbed of one of its geniuses by the most trivial tricks of fate; cities are abolished by earthquakes; millions are slaughtered by the caprice of a tyrant... And yet it is shortly as though nothing of importance had happened, the will to live persisting in what remains, quite unabated. Men claim that human life is a unique good, even the image of something divine, in spite of the testimony that is constantly before them. They do not realize, Schopenhauer thought, that this very declaration issues from nothing more than their will to live, which they share with all living things, that this Will has no goal beyond life itself, and that, life always being assured to this will, no individual life has the slightest intrinsic importance or worth. [10]

Moreover, the Will that drives each individual living being is always asserting itself against the manifestation of the Will in other creatures – and this leads to incessant violence, what Tennyson would call "Nature, red in tooth and claw". Human attempts to curb this violence in themselves through the state are exceedingly limited in their effect, because, ultimately, the Will cannot be thwarted: states fight against other states, and even within them their citizens ceaselessly compete with each other and try to do each other down, sometimes within the legal framework, but often enough outside it. Civil war, rebellion, murder and theft are common enough. Schopenhauer could see no kind of beauty or harmony in natural processes; he was eloquent on the huge predominance of evil, passion, and ugliness over goodness, reason and beauty. Beauty exists, but it is ephemeral. Taylor again:

> Flowers appear briefly and wither quickly, the more quickly as they are the more lovely; but the dirt and manure from which they spring endure almost indestructibly... Hideous caterpillars transform themselves at last into nocturnal moths whose loveliness fills us with awe, but so ephemeral is their tenure of life that nature does not even give them mouths and they starve in hardly a few hours... Genius appears, here and there, accidentally among men, but it is forever engulfed in the ocean of stupidity that gives no hint of being accidental or illusory. Indeed a man of genius can be rendered an idiot by the slightest physiological disturbance – a slight unbalance of salts in his blood or the malfunctioning of a small gland; but a dolt cannot be made a genius by all the powers of heaven and earth, so durable is that state.[11]

We might also comment that Schopenhauer has a rather subjective view of ugliness. A religious person, a pantheist or a nature worshipper might not agree that a caterpillar is "hideous" and might see a providential or teleological beauty in its functional appearance.

As a result, we all understand pain and suffering so much better than bliss: our pictures of Hell are so much more vivid than our insipid images of Heaven; and when in literature we come across a totally virtuous character, our reaction is often that this person is, as the saying goes, "too good to be true". The constant striving and battling of the Will (a typically Romantic notion) make real happiness impossible, "Happiness", Schopenhauer wrote, "is simply a temporary cessation of desire", and if it lasts for any length of time, it can lead only to boredom, which Schopenhauer believed to be the acutest form of any suffering.

Whilst many individuals are indeed restlessly ambitious and never satisfied, many others surely are, at a certain point in their lives, content with what they have achieved, happy within their marriage and not looking for other women with whom to perpetuate the species. Nor are all such people suffering from

10 In O'Connor, *op. cit.*, p.372.

11 *op. cit.*, p. 376.

> boredom. Only the body will be forced by the Will, as Schopenhauer has described it, to continue the struggle against death.

No wonder that Schopenhauer's philosophy has become a byword for pessimism. Bryan Magee assures us that there was much zest, relish and enjoyment in Schopenhauer's own life. He also points out that whereas some pleasures suspend desire - for food or sex, for example - for a while, most of us have experienced pleasures much more positively than that, as when we take pleasure in art or love or friendship.[12]

If we are so completely subject to the Will, it follows that the individual can have *almost* no genuine freedom,[13] *almost* nothing like what is traditionally understood by the notion of Free Will. *Almost* the only freedom that Schopenhauer recognizes is, not so much the freedom of the individual, but the freedom of the Will (or drive) within him. *That* freedom is only possible if it is not checked by external frustrations. So our Will to live is free until the moment when it is frustrated by an accident (a car crash, for example) or by the exertion of the Will in another creature to destroy us - the lion which savages you to death by responding to its own Will, or the enemy soldier whose Will is to save his life by taking yours. (His life may not be at stake at all; his Will may simply tell him to seize your land, your property, or your woman.)

If the Will cannot be frustrated except from without, there would seem no point in traditional moral judgments. Yet we do make such judgments, and Schopenhauer explains that the reason for this is that we have Compassion.

According to him, Compassion is one of the three basic motives for human behaviour. The other two are Egoism and Malice.

Egoism is and must be the most fundamental of these, as it is so closely connected with the Will. We would like to see it as enlightened self-interest, and we accept it in others if it is not too nakedly displayed but is clothed in good manners, rules and conventions. We accept the rules and conventions becaus,e without them, life would really be impossible. So competition must be carried on within sets of rules for us to approve of it, but, as long as the rules are observed, we claim for ourselves and grant to others approval when we or they are successful in the competitive activity, even though it always means that someone else is the loser - we may even bestow a knighthood upon them. Nor do we really object that it is unnatural if a rich man passes by a beggar without dropping a coin into his hat.

> Actually, egalitarian movements have had considerable success precisely because they challenge these assumptions.

Malice - hurting people not for one's own advantage, but simply for the sake of hurting - is a motive that Schopenhauer believed was unique to humankind. Although very many human actions are dictated by it - from damaging gossip through mockery and torment of the helpless unfortunate, to the excitement that can draw crowds to public executions - ethical systems regard malice with revulsion, and the reason for this lies in the third of motives for human action, namely, Compassion.

12 *The Philosophy of Schopenhauer*, pp. 241/2.

13 Again the force of the word "almost" will be apparent shortly.

Compassion results from the ability to see others as being the same as ourselves, so that we suffer with them (which is the root of the words "compassion" and "sympathy"). When we feel it, we are piercing the veil of Maya and penetrate to the noumenal world, to the One which lies behind it, and in that One we perceive that everything is part of everything else, and that every person is part of every other person. Compassion is, then, the basis of our morality and of virtue. The Maya is pierced by acts of intuition, not by the deployment of reason, and Schopenhauer differed here from Kant, who had thought that moral laws rested on reason (though he had also stressed that they are also affirmed by our moral *feelings).*[14] Schopenhauer believed that one could no more make a person virtuous by rational arguments than one could make a person an artist by teaching the theories of art; one could only play on whatever sensitivities he already had and get him to develop these.

> Certainly our educational system is designed to sensitize children to the feelings of other people. When efforts are made to train the police to be sensitive to the feelings of ethnic minorities, this is also on the assumption that these sensitivities can be taught. However, Schopenhauer is probably right in thinking that the success of such teaching lies less in rational arguments than in developing feelings that are already there, and that such training would be useless for individuals who have no such feelings. The same is probably true of aesthetic sensitivity as well.

Reason will never tell us that we are all members of one another. Reason merely tells us that the other person is a phenomenon which is different from the phenomenon that is ourself, that the other person is an object and one which we can use for our own (good or bad) purposes.[15] Reason takes the difference between people as a reality, whereas when we have penetrated the Maya, we can see that the differences are an illusion.

To the extent that we have that insight, we have emancipated ourselves *somewhat* from the Will, which is indifferent to the sufferings of others, and now we can see the significance of the word "almost" on pages 404 and 408. It is *possible* to find some room for free will in the traditional sense of that phrase. Schopenhauer thought that we could free ourselves from the Will to an even greater extent than we can by exercising Compassion. We can, if we wish to, reduce the force of the Will still further by exercising our intuition to the utmost, just as the Buddhist can undertake certain exercises to come close to Nirvana.

There are three increasingly effective stages in which this can be done. We have already seen that the arts, and music especially, were, for Schopenhauer, a possible way of transporting us into a realm beyond phenomena where the material things of practical life seem to matter very little. The Will is dampened down, and this may well be the reason why artists are often quite ineffective in practical life, almost strangers to the life and people around them.

14 See p. 375 above.

15 We will see that thought beautifully worked out and expressed by Martin Buber – see pp. 490ff below.

> This fitted in with the romantic notion of the artist, proverbially being willing to starve in a garret for his art. It is doubtful whether even the greatest artists of previous centuries were so impractical or indifferent to worldly success.

Philosophers and poets have often understood the special role of music as speaking to us of another, heavenly world, indeed of it "transporting" us into another world. The special role of music was due to it being the purest and most abstract art of all. All the best architecture, sculpture and painting have abstract qualities – these are what distinguishes a great work of art from the jejune – but they still have to be expressed in terms of phenomena such as buildings, figures, subject matter. Even poetry has, by definition, to make use of words which cannot help being descriptive of phenomena. Music alone can express all the emotions without any narrative being required at all.

> Schelling had already described architecture in general as "frozen music", and Walter Pater would say that "all art aspires to the condition of music". One could argue that with the arrival, in the twentieth century, of purely abstract sculpture and painting, even those art forms have come close to it, but of course, Schopenhauer could not have envisaged that.

The absurdity of plot or the banality of the text that one finds in so many operas or Lieder is overcome as the music conveys depths that the words and plot cannot do.[16]

> Music often does take us out of ourselves, but it does not always take us into elevated states of mind: it can express barbaric states, can indeed "barbarize" its devotees. It can take us into Dionysian frenzies in which we aim to get rid of our normal inhibitions and in which the Will ("red in tooth and claw"), far from being subdued, can actually operate in an even more unrestrained way than it could under normal circumstances. Military music may give expression to the aggressive side of the Will; rock music to its sexual imperatives, and so on.

So music is a way into the noumenal, one stage by which we can free ourselves from the Will. Those people who are capable of making Compassion their guide in life have, as we have already seen, found another way, which is superior to the first stage, because it not only takes us into the noumenal world as the arts do, but takes our fellow human beings there also and provides a basis for morality.

The most difficult, but also the most effective way, is the way of the Ascetic. You may embrace the arts or be compassionate for their own sakes, which would mean trying to negate (especially in the second case) the force of the Will, but these two ways do not take issue with the nature of the Will itself. The Ascetic has become aware that the nature of the Will is so dreadful that he will

16 Bryan Magee has some wonderful pages on all this. He discusses Schopenhauer's ideas on music in *op. cit.*, pp. 181 to 188, and in his chapter on *Schopenhauer and Wagner* (pp.351 to 402, *op.cit.*) he explains the relationship between the philosopher and the composer. He shows that Schopenhauer's theory ran counter to the importance that Wagner had attached to the text as well as to the music in his notion of the *Gesamtkunstwerk*. After Wagner read Schopenhauer in 1854, he became the philosopher's ardent disciple (as much for Schopenhauer's general philosophy as for what he had written about music), and although he did not abandon the importance of the words, in *Tristan and Isolde*, which he began in 1856, uniquely in his work, the words are scarcely necessary at all. Magee's analysis of that opera in terms of Schopenhauer's philosophy is magnificent, and he continues by analysing *The Mastersingers* and *Parsifal* in Schopenhauerian terms also.

make a great effort to give it up, to detach himself from it, to annihilate it.[17] Ascetics in all religions have done so by denying as much as they can the drive to eat, to find an outlet for their sexual urges, to seek warmth and comfort, to escape pain. In trying to escape the Will, they do not go as far as deliberately to commit suicide. Schopenhauer believed that the suicide deprived one of the possibility of gaining the insights that could be achieved by asceticism and was therefore a mistake (undertaken, he thought, in a moment of dementia or despair) but not a crime deserving punishment, as it was in the Christian Europe of his time.

> There have been and are of course non-Christian beliefs which extol suicide when the alternative is (especially) dishonour: the Stoics of Antiquity, the Japanese, etc.

Schopenhauer did not think that it was a crime deserving punishment. He thought it was a protest that life was not more pleasant: if it *were* more pleasant, the suicide would not commit the act. Even in the act of killing himself he would be expressing his longing for the comfort of a phenomenal existence rather than a determination to free himself from phenomenal existence by the discipline of ascetism.

> That is certainly true, even if Schopenhauer would not recognize that many suicides are not the result of dementia or even of despair in the normal sense of that word. Rather, they are the result of a rational and level-headed estimation of what the future has in store.

The ascetic does not wish for a more comfortable phenomenal world. He is hoping by his asceticism to gain insights and to come closer to the noumenal world. If he truly managed to annihilate the Will, he is effectively left with nothingness, and it is to this nothingness, to Nirvana, that the Hindu and Buddhist ascetics have aspired. By a paradox, nothingness and Oneness are the same. It is a mystical vision, and in the end, Schopenhauer espouses mysticism for all that he was not religious in the orthodox sense of the word.[18]

17 This line of argument proves that, although Schopenhauer occasionally described the Will as the *Ding an sich,* he did in fact see the noumenon and the Will as diffent things, as only by annihilating the one could we achieve the other. He calls what we might describe as human volition (what in *normal* parlance is considered the will of which are conscious) in aid against the Schopenhauerian Will which is *outside* ourselves and of which most people are not conscious at all.

18 Strictly speaking, Buddhism is not a religion in the orthodox sense either. It does not have a deity, let alone one which demands to be worshipped or shows an interest in how human beings behave. The conduct and practices which the Buddha enjoined on his followers is designed not to please or worship a God, but to refine the soul. Nor did the Buddha make any claims for himself as a divine figure or as one sent by God, and the offering up of incense before his statues, though a very human response and possibly contributing to the achievement of a kind of serenity, are really not compatible with his teaching.

CHAPTER 35

Søren Kierkegaard

1813 to 1855

There were mystical elements in the philosophy of Kierkegaard also, though, unlike Schopenhauer, he was a devout Christian. In the twentieth century he has come to be seen as the founder of Existentialism,[1] in that, like the existentialists, he taught the need to make a total commitment to a belief (in his case to Christianity) even if reason produces all kinds of arguments on the other side. Like them, also, he laid great stress on the moral importance of "authenticity", and of not accepting unquestioningly the morality of one's surroundings. At the same time there are strong links between him and the mysticism of a much earlier time - that of St John of Bonaventura, Duns Scotus and Pascal.[2]

In his own lifetime, Kierkegaard was largely ignored. For one thing, he wrote in Danish, but even the Danes paid little attention to him. For another, he was a fierce critic of Hegel, when Hegelianism still dominated much of northern Europe's philosophy.

Kierkegaard against Hegel

We have already seen that Fichte, Schelling and Hegel had developed a notion of the Absolute as One, in which God and Man are so completely merged that *in the end,* through the dialectical process (which is a rational process) man's knowledge of God is no more than man's knowledge of himself. Kierkegaard, who had attended Schelling's lectures on Hegel at the University of Berlin in 1841 rejected this idea on the same grounds on which the medieval mystics like John of Bonaventura had rejected the rational structure which had been built up by St Thomas Aquinas. First of all, God and Man are separate, if only because Man is sinful and God is not, and secondly, because he thought that an understanding of God cannot be reached by reason, but only by faith.

> Kant, too, had come to this conclusion, when he had said that we can confidently accept what faith tells us, not because its acceptance is demanded by our reason, but because it is demanded by our *a priori* moral convictions.[3]

1 On the general beliefs of modern Existentialism, see Chapter 40 below.

2 For St John of Bonaventura and Duns Scotus, see p. 145 above; for Pascal, see pp. 232f above.

3 See p. 372 above.

Hegel, rather like Plato, had believed that reality lies in the realm of universalizing ideas: the greater the degree of universalization, the closer we come to the truth. Kierkegaard, on the other hand, put all the importance on the particular and the individual, and above all on the individual's experience, choices and commitments. These were all that mattered. Kierkegaard was totally indifferent to social or political problems. If he wrote about them at all, it was only to mock them, as he did the revolutions of 1848. The causes espoused by the revolutionaries (liberalism, nationalism) seemed to him totally insignificant in relation to what *should* matter to them: their individual spiritual task.

For Hegel, religion was something to be understood, as it were, from the outside, by studying its dialectical development, and because the dialectic was a rational process, the stage that religious ideas had reached at any given time could be explained rationally and in terms of historical development. At any moment, religion is time-bound and does not encapsulate any direct and eternal truth. Kierkegaard found that such understanding was much too theoretical: we understand religion not through detached observation but only through an intensely personal experience. If the understanding is not rooted in personal experience, he thought that acceptance of religion could not be authentic: it would simply be the acceptance of something that has been shaped by others and therefore involves no personal responsibility.

> That would appear to dismiss the notion that one can come to an acceptance of moral or religious responsibility by working things out rationally for oneself. Such working out might very well lead one to reject the notions which prevail in the society at large. Kierkegaard was convinced that the truly religious life had little to do with *knowing*.

Dramatically, he announced that "Truth is subjectivity". There is more truth in a deeply felt subjective position than in an objective position based upon commonly accepted and rational criteria.

> That is, of course, a profoundly dangerous position. If the test of truth is merely the intensity with which one is committed to an opinion, then the quality of the opinion seems to matter little. As Patrick Gardiner puts it, "It would seemingly permit any believer to be counted as in the truth provided only that he was appropriately wedded to his belief and irrespective of what that belief happened to be." [4] That is also a charge that may be brought against modern existentialism, with its greater emphasis on the duty to make a "commitment" than on the value of the creed to which one commits oneself. [5]

Kierkegaard was scathing about the complacent attitudes he detected in the Danish church of his day, whose comfortable and complacent clergy, he thought, never issued any profound challenges to their congregations.

The individual must be authentic. He must always be true to his own lights, rather than automatically accept the conventional beliefs of the collective, of one's class, tribe, nation or epoch – the beliefs of what German existentialists would call *Das Man* or the French would call *Les Autres*. Kierkegaard was deeply critical of "the public"; his contempt for the ideas of the masses was very

4 Patrick Gardiner – *Kierkegaard* (OUP), p. 98.

5 See p. 488 below.

similar to what will be Nietzsche's attitude,[6] although against it he will not set the ideas of an élite *group*, but rather those of each individual who is true to himself.

> Modern existentialists feel that Kierkegaard was drawing attention to a phenomenon which has become much worse in the twentieth century: the mass media, sometimes on their own account and sometimes themselves manipulated by politicians, have produced mass opinion and have tended to homogenize our thought far beyond what was the case in the first half of the nineteenth century.
>
> One might argue that the pressure to conform to *das Man* or to *les autres* had been just as great within the small communities that existed before "mass society" had come into existence. True, the thoughts of small local communities were themselves becoming increasingly homogenized into those of national communities as modernity advanced, but in the older units it had been just as difficult for the individual to be "true to himself" in the Kierkegaardian sense.
>
> Was Kierkegaard part of the revolt against early parliamentarianism? The 1848 revolutionaries in Germany, for example, enacted nearly universal male suffrage. Opponents claimed that this would enfranchise people who lacked education, and were therefore believed not to be able to think for themselves and would as a result be easily manipulated into "inauthentic" mass opinion. We have already seen how little sympathy Kierkegaard had for the 1848 revolutions.

Authenticity is difficult because it demands that we do not drift but constantly make choices. Only through these choices do we truly exist and define who we are – another idea that links Kierkegaard firmly with twentieth-century existentialism. The important choices in life are stark: they do not permit compromises; they are a matter of *Either – Or*, the title he gave to one of his most important works in 1843. The Hegelian dialectic did not satisfy Kierkegaard, for here thesis and antithesis would be resolved in a synthesis, which Kierkegaard saw as a compromise between them. The existentialist dialectic differed from the Hegelian, firstly, in being a move from one mode of existence into a radically different one, and secondly, because the tension does not take the social or historical form as a necessary process; it lies within each individual, and the outcome is by no means ordained as it is in the Hegelian dialectic, but depends on the will power which any one individual exerts in making his choice, for himself alone and not as part of any historical process.

The Existentialist Dialectic

How do we get to the stage where we can exist authentically? Kierkegaard distinguished between three stages of responding to the world, only the last of which produces the commitment which he thought was essential to authenticity. He calls them the Aesthetic, the Ethical and the Religious.

In the Aesthetic[7] stage, man is governed by his senses, impulses and emotions. He wants to enjoy the whole range of emotive and sensory experiences

6 See p. 470 below.

7 Kierkegaard chose this word because the Greek *aesthenomai* means "to feel".

and may use his reason to achieve and maximize his enjoyment, but all this without making any commitments that would provide a centre to his being. The experiences may be elevated or coarse, but in any case, the response is purely to the world as it impinges on oneself from outside. As far as morality is concerned, he tends to be a hedonist. He believes that what we describe as morally good is really no more than what we think will ultimately be conducive to our pleasure, whilst we call morally bad those actions which we believe will ultimately give us pain. Kierkegaard believed that morality was a good deal more than that, and he described someone at the aesthetic stage as living only "in the cellar". Lacking any clear and autonomous moral guidelines, a sensitive person will ultimately become restless and even despairing, and the despair should then force him to make a choice.

Needless to say, Kierkegaard believes that we all have the possibility to choose; we are free agents, and can be responsible for the choices we make. Here, the choice is whether or not to leap into the next stage, the Ethical one. It is characteristic of Kierkegaard that he uses the word "leap": he believed that the change from one stage to another is never gradual, but always sudden, accompanied by a feeling of venture and risk.

In the Ethical phase, man accepts moral standards and obligations, which now become the fixed point of his life. He takes responsibility for himself instead of being governed by what impinges on him from outside. He will work out his moral standards by using his reason.

That is an admirable state to be in; one might think that it would satisfy the demands of authenticity, and many philosophers would think that nothing more could be expected of a human being. To Kierkegaard, however, that state still has two deficiencies.

The first is that the obligations are based on reason, and indeed, on the categorical imperative which commanded that one should wish one's own moral actions to hold good as a principle of universal legislation. Although Kant had, in the *Critique of Pure Reason*, asserted the truth of religion because our mental equipment so profoundly demands it, he had also tried to show, in the *Critique of Practical Reason*, that religious truths were *also* based on reason. Moral obligations are based on reason: that is why God lays them down. Kant had therefore found it impossible to imagine that God might command something that appears unreasonable or something that could not possibly become a general moral maxim, such as the commandment which He had given to Abraham to sacrifice Isaac. He had taken this supposedly divine command as so utterly at variance with morality as to state that we are justified in refusing to believe that biblical story; such a command could never have come from God. Kierkegaard, however, thought that the story illustrated perfectly that Abraham was confronted by a clash between two obligations – the ethical one not to commit murder but to protect his much loved son, and the religious one of following God, not questioning Him with rational arguments, nor even being able to tell himself – and others – that some greater general good would come from the sacrifice (as when Agamemnon sacrifices Iphigenia for the sake of his country). Abraham showed the utmost *faith* in God's commands – and in fact, although he could not possibly have foreseen this, he does not, in the end, lose his son. As the Bible says in another place, "whosoever will save his life shall lose it". If we give up the world, we shall get it back again.

The second deficiency of the ethical stage is that it does not help us at the point when we become conscious of our human weakness; when our Will to act morally and rationally lets us down; when we become conscious of our inherent sinfulness. Again, sooner or later the person who aims at full authenticity will come up against the consciousness of his sinfulness, and when that has fully dawned upon him, he will despair and experience a *Sickness unto Death*, the title Kierkegaard gave to a book he wrote in 1848. To a Christian, this despair is itself a sin, and it can be overcome only by a further act of choice: whether to acquiesce in it or take another leap, the leap into the Religious state.

> Some modern existentialists were also overcome by a kind of despair, a feeling of the "absurdity" of the world, and, in the case of Sartre, an overwhelming feeling of revulsion and disgust in contemplating it. For them, that was another challenge they had to confront and to live with as a reality, not something they could remedy or escape from by embracing another kind of reality.

This last leap is the famous Leap of Faith. Like the medieval mystics, Kierkegaard believed that a knowledge of God can never be achieved by rational arguments, indeed, in faith we have to commit ourselves to what, from a rational point of view, is "the absurd",[8] and for Kierkegaard it implied, among other things, the acceptance, totally *contrary* to reason, of God's incarnation in Christ. No rational proof is needed or could possibly be produced - it is sufficient to "know that my Redeemer liveth".

When we make such a leap and leave the safe shores of reason behind us, we experience a feeling of *Angst* ("dread" is a better translation for this term than "anxiety"), of *Fear and Trembling*,[9] the title of another book he published in 1843. Kierkegaard compares it with the feeling of the baby eagle when it leaves the safety of its nest: nervously, it flings itself into the unknown, but finds itself marvellously buoyed up and sustained. The analogy, however, is not complete. Once the eaglet has found its wings, it no longer has to decide whether to launch itself into the void or whether to stay in the nest. In the Religious mode we do not take just one leap as the challenge and the tensions of the religious life are continuous. There is always the temptation to take it easy, to, as it were, soar around problems, primarily those of the inner life, instead of constantly confronting them, so a new choice has to be made each time between faith and reason, and the leap into faith has to be renewed over and over again. Twentieth-century existentialists will agree with this - the philosophically inclined person must be aware that we constantly define ourselves by the choices we make or do not make. Our capacity to choose is the consequence of our freedom, and "we are condemned to be free".

> There seems to me to be another major difference, however, between the existentialism of Kierkegaard and that of twentieth century. The choice for Kierkegaard was between reason and what is contrary to reason (he might have agreed with the dictum of Tertullian, the second-century Christian theo-

8 The word "absurd" is one we shall find again in 20th century existentialism, though there it carries a much more negative and hopeless connotation than it does in Kierkegaard. See p. 506 below.

9 Again I think "Trembling" may not be the best translation: I would prefer "Trepidation".

> logian: *Credo quia absurdum*) whereas twentieth-century existentialists feel they have to choose between fairly rational but competing ideas. They know that every ideology is open to criticism and that none has the absolute truth, but if one is not to be a moral drifter, one simply has to make a commitment to whatever strikes one as the most reasonable position, yet in the full awareness that no ideology can claim to have all the answers.[10] In a sense, it is even more heroic to commit oneself wholly to what one knows is a flawed idea than to an idea of whose truth one is wholly convinced. This is another difference from Kierkegaard, for he *was* sure the leap of faith was into God's absolute truth. Kierkegaard was totally committed to Christianity in his every thought; a modern existentialist is never *totally* committed to any ideology, but only to action.

We can now see that there may be reasons other than those in the opening paragraphs why Kierkegaard made so little impact in his own time. Unlike his contemporaries, he was not really interested in trying to understand the world, from which he felt alienated. He was focussed on the individual and how to achieve salvation. He would have been understood better in earlier centuries – the age of the mystics and of religious thinkers like Pascal – as he would be again a century after his lifetime. In the meantime, European philosophy took a break from being primarily concerned with metaphysical issues and resumed the more pragmatic approach that had preceded the French Revolution.

10 For more on modern existentialism, see Chapter 40 below.

CHAPTER 36

Utilitarianism

JEREMY BENTHAM
1748 to 1832

In the first half of the nineteenth century, English philosophers were not much taken with the kind of metaphysical theories we have discussed in the last five chapters. Their main interest was in the life of this world and, in particular, in the philosophy that should underlie social arrangements. In this respect they were close to the French *philosophes,* which is particularly true of Jeremy Bentham. The two most important of his voluminous writings were the *Fragments on Government,* published in 1776, and *Introduction to the Principles of Morals and Legislation,* published in 1780. Both works appeared before the French Revolution had broken out, and, although the philosophy known as Benthamism is associated with nineteenth-century England, Bentham really belonged to the eighteenth-century Age of Reason, and his fame was initially established in France. Some of his work was first published there and was originally written in French. His "rational" approach to legislation appealed so much to the French revolutionaries that in 1792, the Convention made him an honorary member. The temper in England during and, for a period, after the French Revolution was antirational, and Bentham did not really come into his own in England until very shortly before his death. We shall see below how, after his death, his disciples would bring Benthamism into the very centre of British social legislation.

The *philosophes,*[1] like Bentham himself, were also influenced by earlier English philosophers, notably by the associationist psychology they had found in Hobbes and Locke. This had held that emotions and moral ideas are formed by association with pleasurable or painful experiences - we call "good" what gives us pleasure and "bad" or "evil" what gives us pain.

> Even if we were to accept that what we *call* good tends to be what gives us pleasure, there is still the question whether we are entitled to say that what gives us pleasure actually *is* good. A Puritan instinctively distrusts pleasure as a snare and a delusion, and he would take duty rather than pleasure as his guide. There is an argument against him, which would say that, if he did not derive pleasure from following a painful duty, he would not do so, and even if he obeyed such a duty by external compulsion rather than by internal motivation, it would be because he calculates that the pain of punishment would be

1 In chapter 28, see, for example, Helvétius (p. 312) and Holbach (p. 321).

greater than the pain of the duty. Some people might regard such assertions as simply playing with words.

Hobbes and Locke had also said that we use our reason to work out what strategies would be useful for maximizing our pleasure and minimizing our pain. Bentham thought that, *in the long run*, one could achieve maximum happiness for oneself only if one lived in a society which is itself as happy as possible. It was therefore in a person's *enlightened* self-interest that he should seek to live in a happy society and under a government that aimed to bring that state of affairs about. He put it like this, "The dictates of Utility are the dictates of the most extensive and enlightened benevolence."

We have already discussed how questionable this idea is,[2] if the word "enlightened" is equated, as it was by Helvétius or by Bentham, with "rational". If, on the other hand, we define "enlightened" as meaning "morally acceptable", then we make morality rather than rationalism as our yardstick. Kant had thought that morality was based so firmly on Reason that its imperatives were categorical – i.e. not subject to debate, but we have seen that there are problems with this position as well.[3] Of course, we all agree that a happy society is preferable to an unhappy one, but clearly some people (members of privileged ruling classes, drug dealers etc.) come, quite rationally, to the conclusion that they can get away with maximizing their own happiness by oppressing, exploiting or victimizing their society. We surely have to base the desirability of a happy society upon grounds which, however difficult to define, are nevertheless quite different from an individual's enlightened self-interest.

Besides, even people who do not set out to oppress or victimize anyone usually manage to live quite happily, both in the short and in the long term, in a society in which other people are unhappy. True, we don't like to live cheek by jowl with misery, so if we can afford it, we move into the prosperous areas of the town where we are not constantly reminded of the unhappiness of others. Nor are we all that willing to sacrifice our own affluence by sharing it with those in miserable poverty. This is exemplified by the ready acceptance of the dictum that charity begins at home. Most of us are ready to make sacrifices for the sake of our immediate family; fewer (either individually or collectively) for the sake of the unfortunate in our society, and fewer still for the sake of the millions who are starving in other continents. How many affluent people are prepared to make, or even to vote for, a really serious reduction of their standard of living for the sake of the more remote members of our society or the world community?

Let us now see how Bentham proceeds after he has established to his own satisfaction that a happy society is in everyone's individual enlightened self-interest. He believed that we shape moral laws solely to support our enlightened self-interest and that there is no other basis for morality, such as Natural or Divine laws, Natural Rights etc. All talk of Rights, he said, was nonsense; and talk of Natural Rights was "nonsense on stilts".

However, to all intents and purposes, he treats happiness as if it were a right. On what other grounds could he advocate and identify himself with policies that have as their aim the greatest happiness of the greatest number?

2 See p. 309 above, where the idea is discussed in general, and p. 314 above, where it is discussed in relation to Helvétius.

3 See p. 375 above.

Nor, in the best *philosophe* style, had he any reverence for tradition as such. The *philosophes* had dismissed any traditions that could not be justified on the grounds of reason.[4] Bentham would sweep them away if they stood in the way of the happiness of society, for this was the only moral yardstick he would recognize.

He then has two further tasks: the first is to define how we can ascertain what makes society happy; and the second is how we actually define happiness.

Knowing that it is impossible to make everyone in a society happy, he decided that we should make as many members of that society as possible as happy as we possibly can. We cannot achieve such an end as private individuals, so we have to bring it about by legislation, and the task of legislation is therefore to promote, "the greatest happiness of the greatest number". This formula, which had first been used by Frances Hutcheson in 1725,[5] becomes the guideline of Benthamite Utilitarianism.

> We note to start with the importance attached to earthly *happiness*. This would have struck thinkers of earlier and more religious ages as quite inappropriate. For them, what we should pursue in this life was not Happiness, but Duty, though we might be rewarded for this in the next world. The idea that earthly happiness is the proper and *rightful* goal of the individual and of society was first promoted by the *philosophes*,[6] so much so that, together with Life and Liberty, the Pursuit of Happiness was one of the inalienable rights proclaimed by the Founding Fathers of the United States. The Founding Fathers did not mention duties. So once again, we see Bentham as child of the Enlightenment.
>
> As for "the *greatest* number", this formula does not do enough to safeguard, and may in fact seriously compromise, the happiness of minorities, and this would be pointed out by John Stuart Mill.[7] However, we must see the formula in the context of its times. The political arrangements of eighteenth-century Europe were entirely organized to ensure the happiness of a tiny privileged class. The idea that the majority of the people had any desire for happiness simply did not enter into the minds of the ruling classes. At best, the rulers were aware that if the masses were too brutally oppressed, they might rise in dangerous revolt, with the result that the happiness of the governing classes might be put at risk. Any attention that might be paid to the happiness of the masses was therefore strictly prudential and not at all based on inalienable rights. Under those circumstances, it is easy to see that reformers like the *philosophes* or Bentham might be preoccupied with the need to assert the right of the "greatest number". And since mass democracy did not yet exist in any part of the world, it is also understandable that they paid insufficient attention to the dangers of oppressive majorities. (Of course, the warnings of Antiquity, such as they could have found in Aristotle,[8] would have provided a useful corrective.)

"The greatest number" could be found simply by counting, but how could one assess whether a piece of legislation contributed to the "greatest happiness"? Here Bentham established the Felicific Calculus. The amount of Happiness can

4 See p. 310 above.

5 See p. 314 above.

6 See p. 309 above.

7 See pp. 429f below.

8 See p. 53 above.

be ascertained by weighing different factors, which Bentham described as Quantity, Intensity, Duration, Certainty, Propinquity, Fecundity and Purity.

> In Bentham's time, this could be merely a theoretical account of the factors that go into happiness as they could not have been calculated precisely. But if computerized forms had existed at the time, the Felicific Calculus might have been put to work something like this:
>
> Everybody (to make sure that we get as close to "the greatest number" as possible) would be issued with a form on which the public is asked to choose between two or more legislative proposals. Under each alternative the public is asked to write a figure from, say, 1 to 5, with 1 representing a minimum and 5 a maximum agreement with the following statements:
>
> Quantity: "This legislation would give me a great amount of pleasure."
>
> Intensity: "The pleasure would be intense."
>
> Duration: "The pleasure would last for a long time."
>
> Certainty: "There is no doubt that pleasure would actually be the result."
>
> Propinquity: "The pleasure would follow in the near rather than in the distant future."
>
> Fecundity: "The pleasure would in turn give rise to other pleasures."
>
> Purity: "The pleasure would not be accompanied by any drawbacks."
>
> When the would-be legislator runs the forms through a computer, he would get a figure for each legislative proposal which would tell him which one of them produced the greatest amount of happiness for the greatest number of people, and should therefore be enacted.

It might be objected (and the objections would in fact be made by John Stuart Mill)[9] that there are other and very important factors that ought to have been included in the Felicific Calculus. They would include the following:

> Quality: "The pleasure is sophisticated rather than crude."
>
> Morality: "The pleasure is consonant with morality rather than being an immoral pleasure."
>
> Equality: "The pleasure is not based on exclusive enjoyment by a small group of people."
>
> Equity: "The pleasure does not contravene principles of Justice."
>
> Dignity: "The pleasure does not violate the dignity of the persons experiencing the pleasure nor does it involve depriving others of the dignity to which they are entitled. "
>
> Liberty: "The pleasure is not achieved at the expense of the liberty of the person experiencing the pleasure nor does it involve depriving others of the liberty to which they are entitled."
>
> Minority: "The pleasure of the greatest number is not achieved at the expense of the rights, dignity, or liberty of the minority."
>
> But even if the Felicific Calculus were extended to include all these, it would still be open to two fundamental questions: ought happiness, however calcu-

9 See p. 427ff below.

> lated, to be the ultimate yardstick by which a person appraises whether a measure is to be enacted or not, and ought the task of government be reduced to making the greatest number of its people as happy as possible? Other criteria may be hard to define precisely, but again, they may have something to do with duty rather than with happiness.

I have already explained why Bentham overlooked the criticism that his theory paid insufficient attention to the happiness of minorities; but in respect of the other factors, he was quite aware of the objections that he should have included them, and he explained why he rejected them:

If he had included the Quality of happiness, he said, that factor would have to be assessed by some outside standard, but he believed that no one had the right to decide that one person's happiness is of a lesser value than another. As he put it provocatively, "Prejudices apart, the game of pushpin is of equal value with the arts and sciences of music and poetry."

> We frequently find people defending this point of view today. They condemn the ranking of the quality of pleasures as snobbish élitism. There is no reason to judge the ecstatic happiness that some people get from football or fox-hunting as inferior to the ecstatic happiness that others get from a fine performance of the St Matthew Passion. They would argue that the same is true when we consider art forms; the pleasure that so-called unsophisticated people get from what sophisticates call Kitsch is on a par with the pleasure that the latter derive from a so-called classic.

As far as Morality, Equality, Equity, Dignity and Liberty are concerned, whilst they cannot be *absolutes*, Bentham readily conceded that their presence often - perhaps more often than not - enhances the happiness of the greatest number, although situations can occur when this is not the case. Morality, by his definition, is no more than a codification of behaviour that is supposed to promote happiness.

> One may feel uneasy about the implications of this position. Suppose that the people were asked in a referendum whether particularly heinous crimes should incur capital punishment – possibly even preceded by torture. It is, unfortunately, conceivable that a majority might respond that this would give them great satisfaction. Logic would force Bentham to say that one has no right to claim that opposition to capital punishment is morally superior to defence of it, and that to assert the contrary was a kind of élitism.

As for Liberty, if people are not accustomed to it or have had bad experiences when experimenting with it, they often happily accept an authoritarian government with which "the greatest number" can identify and under which they feel secure. As long as that is the case, Bentham had no objection to authoritarian governments. However, he knew that such governments, which might begin by working for the greatest happiness of the greatest number, usually degenerate into feathering their own nests at the expense of the people's happiness; they develop "Vested Interests" which, by definition, work against the greatest happiness of the greatest number. In English politics, Bentham had initially been a paternalistic Tory, believing that the country as a whole would be happiest under the guidance of a small, competent, and benevolent ruling class, but in time he came to see that this ruling class was too anxious to protect its own Vested Interests against those of the greatest number, and that made Bentham into a Radical. In practice he was a believer in elected, parliamentary governments, because such governments had, since Magna Carta, been seen (rightly or wrongly) as the guardians of liberty against autocratic rule, and because parliaments take the happiness of their electors into account.

> He then became a supporter of the movement for parliamentary reform, which secured its first victory only in the year of Bentham's death. Even then, the Reform Act of 1832 gave the franchise to a very limited number of people, so that parliament still reflected the wishes of only a small minority. Early Benthamites, like Henry Brougham, would identify the middle class, which was then enfranchised, with "the people": they would regard an extension of the franchise beyond that as likely to lead to "mob rule", which was sure in the end to produce unhappiness. It is easy to see that this line could not be held, and later Benthamites, like the members of the Reform League, would campaign for extensions of the franchise. Given the Benthamite belief that each person is the best judge of his or her happiness, there can be no stopping point until universal adult suffrage makes it possible to see what the greatest number thinks best promotes its happiness.

Bentham opposed Burke's notion that members of parliament were the people's representatives, acting in what they thought was the nation's best interests, but having to give an account of what they had done only once every seven years. Such a theory made it too easy for MPs to develop and follow their own vested interests. Bentham thought that MPs should regard themselves as delegates of the public; that they should closely reflect what the public thought contributed to its happiness; and that, to control the development of vested interests, there should be annual parliamentary elections and the secret ballot (which was not actually enacted in England until 1872).

> Annual parliaments would have been a disaster: the country would be in perpetual election fever and no policies requiring long-term planning, let alone temporary hardship for future benefit, could be undertaken.

We should of course respect the dignity of individuals where possible, but dignity cannot be an absolute criterion, and it may have to be sacrificed in some cases in the interest of the greatest happiness of the greatest number. For instance, you deprive a person of his dignity when you make him a prisoner; the deprivation is indeed part of the punishment, but the punishment is there to act as a deterrent to crime and thereby to enhance the happiness of the majority of law-abiding people.

As far as equality was concerned, that is obviously not a fact of life. Bentham would never agree with the phrase in the American Declaration of Independence that it was self-evident that all men are created equal.

> Nor is it true that *of necessity* equality makes everyone happy. We know that whilst everyone would be happy to be equal with the people above them in the social hierarchy, they often resent the people below themselves aspiring to equality with them. The fact that many people *want* a pecking order partly explains why, even after the establishment of universal suffrage, socialist parties have so often been rejected at the polls.

Bentham did believe that if legislation proceeded on the assumption that men *were* created equal, the result was likely (although not certain) to produce more happiness than if the underlying assumption was that men were not equal.

Similarly, while Bentham would not have agreed with Locke that there was a Natural Right to property, he thought that legislation which incorporated the inviolability of property would, by preventing insecurity, be liable to produce more happiness than unhappiness, even among the "greatest number" who had very little property or none at all.

Does the history of socialism bear this out?

Bentham thought that while a government was under an obligation to maximize Happiness, it was not its function in any other way to make individuals or society "morally better": that would imply that there were criteria other than happiness, the only one he would recognize, by which to regulate their behaviour. A person was entitled to be his own judge of happiness and to pursue this, so long as his behaviour did no harm to others and so diminish their happiness. On those grounds he was against laws to control drunkenness: a drunkard's pleasure in being peacefully drunk was to be respected because others were not harmed by it. If a drunkard becomes involved in a fight, the state may prosecute him for fighting; it may not interfere with his choice to be drunk.

Against the argument that it set a bad example to others, Bentham argued that one must allow those others the freedom to decide for themselves whether they would be happier or not to follow the example. He does not seem to have given much thought to the misery a drunkard often inflicts on his family by drinking away the wages that, if spent on his wife and children, would improve their lives and so increase their happiness. He would certainly have disapproved of what has recently been called "the nanny state". The invention of that word by Bernard Levin was a brilliant stroke; a nanny treats us like children and is supposed to make us do things for our own good, whether or not we realize or like it. A nanny state does not trust us to make our own decisions where nothing except our personal safety is concerned, so it not only urges, but actually forces us to wear seatbelts and crash helmets for our own safety. Some people think that this is a legitimate function of the state, others, who dislike that kind of interference, show their dislike by referring to the "nanny state".

Altogether, Bentham personally believed that, in the interests of the greatest happiness of the greatest number, the functions of government should be rather limited. However, it is clear that, once the greatest happiness of the greatest number is made the essential criterion by which legislation should be judged, it is perfectly possible to disagree with Bentham that the criterion is best met by limiting the functions of government, and indeed, after his death his disciples tended to advocate the extension of government precisely on the grounds that this would contribute most to increase general happiness.

In 1830, two years before Bentham's death, the Whig party came to power, and Whig governments were much influenced by a group of civil servants headed by Edwin Chadwick, who was Bentham's secretary during the last three years of the philosopher's life. Chadwick and his friends believed that, to promote the greatest happiness of the greatest number, the state must be rather more active than Bentham had envisaged. It must, through factory legislation, protect young children from exploitation.[10] Bentham, like a good disciple of the Enlightenment, had always stressed the importance of education. The better a person was educated, the better he was able to judge his enlightened self-interest and therefore to give a more valuable response when he was exposed to the Felicific Calculus. The later Benthamites all agreed with the promotion of education, partly because this would enlarge the possibilities of happiness, but also because a literate workforce was more *efficient* than uneducated labour. Efficiency, in Chadwick's book, was highly conducive to the happiness of society, and efficiency, he thought, would often require a degree of centralized control by the machinery of the state. Chadwick and his backers from the industrial middle class exhibited the most deplorable aspect of Benthamism by being prepared to make minorities extremely unhappy in the cause of efficiency. The most striking example of this was the Poor Law Amendment Act of 1834, which was designed to make the receipt of poor relief dependent on going into the workhouse, where conditions were made deliberately so harsh that people would prefer to seek the most underpaid work rather than to suffer from imprisonment in the workhouse. The result, Chadwick claimed, would be to drive the workshy into work, to drive down unemployment and so to reduce the cost of outdoor relief that had fallen so heavily on the rate payers. The result would be that society would function more efficiently, and therefore more happily, for all concerned. The literature of the time shows clearly enough what a huge price in unhappiness was paid by the minority who, for one reason or another, could not avoid the degradation of the workhouse.

This harshness was not necessarily implicit in Benthamism. On the contrary, in later years the workhouse system would be first softened and then abandoned on the grounds of the misery it created for those who were its victims. It also came to be realized, on good Benthamite lines, that the greatest happiness of the greatest number could not be achieved if the upper and middle classes were the only ones who had the vote, so that parliament would represent their vested interest. They also believed that privilege stood in the way of the greatest happiness of the greatest number, so there would be attacks on the privileged position of the Church of England and on commissions in the Army or the Civil Service being bought or secured by influence rather than by competitive examination. Above all, the extension of the franchise was pressed for with Benthamite arguments (among others). The same arguments can be adduced for the redistribution of incomes and for what we call "the welfare state", and the underlying assumption of socialism, too, is that its realization would increase the greatest happiness of the greatest number.

So, in one way or another, this Benthamite criterion, building on the late eighteenth-century notion that the Pursuit of Happiness is one of the inalienable Rights of Man, has permeated our societies ever since Bentham's time. Every social reformer will base his case on it. Even modern dictatorships no longer fall back for their justification on Divine Right, but tend to claim that

10 This group of Benthamites still drew the line at protecting adults from exploitation. Their argument was that adults freely entered into the contracts of employment that were on offer, and so the state should not interfere. J.S. Mill would draw attention to the obvious fact that, though people would be happier to work for a pittance than to starve, such exploitative employment contracts were usually not entered into freely at all, and that adults needed the same protection from the state as children did.

they can produce the greatest happiness of the greatest number; and they go to much trouble to base their authority on plebiscites, even if they have to rig them. As De la Rochefoucault once put it, this kind of "hypocrisy is the tribute that Vice pays to Virtue."

To John Stuart Mill, it had become clear that Benthamite theory had serious flaws which he set out to remedy.

JOHN STUART MILL
1806 to 1873.

John Stuart Mill's father, James Mill, was a close friend and ardent disciple of Jeremy Bentham's, and he brought up his exceedingly precocious son most rigorously in rational and Utilitarian principles. The boy was started with Greek at the age of three, and by the age of eight he had "read" most of the great Greek writers. Then, between the ages of eight and twelve it was the turn of Latin and the Latin classics. Throughout his childhood, the boy was trained in logic. On Socratic principles, he was never told anything that he could not work out for himself. Alongside all this he was taught science, mathematics, history and, by means of his father's lectures on the subject, political economy. James Mill had also written a History of India, which his son saw through the press at the age of thirteen. By that time he was also required to teach his younger brothers and sisters for six hours a day. However, he was never exposed to poetry or imaginative literature, which his father distrusted as not being sufficiently rational.

It was perhaps not surprising that in 1828, at the age of twenty-two, the young Mill had a kind of breakdown, perhaps caused not so much by the strain to which he had been subjected but by the "sacrilegious" doubts that had gathered within him about the validity of the rigid principles on which he had been reared since infancy. In particular, he had begun to question whether analyzing all feelings simply in terms of their association with pleasures and pain did not, in the end, destroy the feelings themselves. He feared that this might have happened to him, that he might have been left as little more than a soulless automaton, so he experienced an immense relief when now coming across, and then seeking, literature to which he could respond emotionally. While he still believed in the importance of happiness, both for the individual and society, he now thought that happiness has more components than could be pinned down by the mechanics of Bentham's Felicific Calculus, and that indeed, it was unlikely that it could be found by aiming so directly and crudely at it. In any case, he thought that it was not possible to make the calculations which were at the heart of Bentham's scheme. Above all, however, he could not accept that Utility as Bentham had defined it (as "the greatest happiness of the greatest number") could be regarded as the ultimate yardstick by which social arrangements and legislation should be assessed. In other words, he thought that the factors which had *not* been included in the Felicific Calculus - Quality, Dignity, Liberty, and Minority Rights - have ultimate values which far exceed the value of happiness as the Utilitarians conceived it.

On the issue of Quality, Mill argued that it was absurd to say that this was so much a matter of personal judgment that no objective standard could be attained; anyone who had sampled both superior and inferior pleasures could tell the difference.

> "Anyone"? A person with what we call "educated" tastes who had sampled both might agree or he might not. Some intellectuals who have experienced both a football match and a study of philosophy might say that the latter is far superior to the former, but there are also intellectuals who enjoy both with equal intensity and would be loath to rank one above the other. Equally, some with so-called "uneducated" tastes who had tried philosophy and gained nothing from it would certainly not agree that the pleasure of philosophy was obviously superior to that of football. I think what Mill should have compared are not the qualities of the pleasure (when he had already said that it was impossible to make the calculations which could measure it) but the quality of the "*product*" that gives the pleasure. Even that is difficult enough, as Hume had found. On the one hand he had admitted that in aesthetic judgments quality could not be an absolute concept, but depended on the eye of the beholder, on the other, he thought the verdict of the "qualified observer" carried more weight.[11] To take an extreme example, an educated person might derive more pleasure from a crude pornographic film than from *Hamlet*, but even he might agree that the Shakespeare play had more quality than the film. One of the tests of that quality might be the durability of the product. Some products are ephemeral both in themselves and in the pleasure they give. What we call "High Culture" has generally stood the test of time – though even here fashions in taste can depose some products of High Culture and bring others that have been excluded at times back within its scope. It is also arguable that the concept of High Culture is defined by an élite. It was, for example, an élite which decided at one time that the Victorians had no taste in art, just as it was a later élite which reversed that verdict. It may be impossible to formulate a clear definition of what constitutes quality in a product. All the same, it seems to me to make more sense to talk about quality in the product than about the quality of the happiness it creates.

If we value the quality of a person's life, then we must also make it possible for that life to have dignity, and of that dignity, an absolutely essential ingredient is liberty. Many people are perfectly happy under a dictatorship, but it is not consonant with dignity that one should value one's liberty so little and lazily acquiesce to dictators making decisions for us in which we should have participated. Indeed, if there was one quality that Mill valued above all others, it was liberty, and *On Liberty* is the title of the short essay of 1859, which is his most famous and most enduring work.

Here, he accepted the Benthamite position that people should be left as free as possible from interference by the state. In chapter 1 he writes:

> The sole end for which mankind are warranted, individually or collectively, in interfering with the liberty of action of any of their number is self-protection. The only purpose for which power can be rightfully exercised over any member of a civilized community against his will is to prevent harm to others. His own good, either physical or moral, is not a sufficient warrant.

This is a famous passage, but it is really quite a vague one, and its import depends on what exactly is meant by "harm to others". One can be sure that Mill supported state action against the grosser forms of exploitation, such as

11 See the lengthy discussion on that point on pp. 298f.

the abolition of slavery and factory acts to limit the hours of child workers. But he defended all kinds of competition and would sanction interference with the economic activities of individuals or organizations only where they involved fraud or force. There is no indication in his writings that he felt for the sufferings of the poor during the Industrial Revolution or that he was aware of the damage that such grinding poverty did to their possibilities of development. He was inclined to rely on the pressure of public opinion rather than on legislation to remedy many abuses, and in general he was suspicious of ,"the great evil of adding unnecessarily to [the government's] powers". He would also leave it to the pressure of public opinion to raise the moral standards in a society. It is not the function of government to legislate on issues of purely personal morality, provided always that no harm is done to others.

Mill explained that his doctrine was meant to apply only to human beings in the maturity of their faculties. It could not apply to children, or, for that matter, to backward societies in which the people as a whole were still immature. Influenced by his father's book on India and by his own career in the India Office at the time, he thought that the "coloured colonies"[12] were not mature enough to enjoy liberty and would do better under despotism, "*provided the end be their improvement*", but such despotism was always to be regretted as falling short of the ideal. Children and colonial people should be raised to the level of maturity when they could be allowed to make their own decisions, and this required education. In the India Office, Mill drew up a famous plan for education in India, and for Britain itself he proposed that the state should require compulsory and universal education.[13]

An overriding respect for liberty also involved a respect for the rights of minorities, and the most important of those rights was the right of free speech: all mankind minus one would not have the right to silence the dissenter. This was vital not only for the dignity of the individual, but also for the sake of truth. Mill had the confidence that in free and rational discussion the truth was bound to emerge in the end, and very often the truth lay in what was initially a minority view; if this were suppressed, the truth would suffer.

> Whilst there are excellent grounds for supporting freedom of speech in terms of rights and dignity, the belief that in free discussion weak arguments will be exposed as such and that the truth is bound to emerge is a typical piece of 19th century liberal optimism. Unfortunately, discussion is not always rational, nor does it always win support by rational means. The nineteenth century liberals did not take into account the power of the demagogue who deliberately manipulates, not the reason, but the emotions of his audience.

Mill was always conscious of how easily straight majority rule could turn into "a tyranny of the majority". This phrase had been coined by Alexis de Tocqueville, whose two volumes, *Democracy in America* (1835 and 1840) greatly

12 The white Dominions had already got "responsible government": Canada after the Durham Report of 1839, Australia and New Zealand in the 1850s.

13 He thought it undesirable that the state should itself provide the education, as that would give it too much power and make education too uniform. The provision of education should be delegated to various bodies (churches, charities, private institutions etc) and the state should be prepared, where necessary, to help with the finance. These were the principles that would be followed in the Education Act of 1871.

influenced Mill. That work was based on the conclusions the author had drawn from his visit to the United States in 1831/2. By then, most of the American states had enacted universal male suffrage. De Tocqueville had seen much to admire in the spirit and in the free institutions of America, but at the same time he concluded that as a result of universal suffrage, the prejudices of the masses, often stimulated by demagogues, prevailed everywhere: the interests of the cultivated minority at one end (and, he might have added, the oppressed black minority at the other end) were simply disregarded. Mass opinion, he thought, held absolute sway and was intolerant of minority opinions. Culture, philosophy, religion and manners were, in his opinion, all debased.

Much of this was grossly exaggerated, but Mill anticipated the same dangers if unadulterated universal suffrage were to prevail in England. In consequence, he wrote his *Considerations on Representative Government* (1861). This proposed certain safeguards against the abuses of democracy. The first check he proposed was a system of plural voting. He believed that, in order to respect the dignity of individuals and to educate them into thinking politically, everyone who could read and write (women as well as men)[14] should be entitled to one vote. In addition, the weight of mature and responsible opinion should be increased (though not to the extent of total domination) by giving additional votes to individuals with certain property or educational qualifications.

> Although this idea runs counter to twentieth-century democratic ideas, one can see some theoretical attractions in it even today. The problem that worried Mill was, and is, a real one. One cannot help but be dismayed by the manipulations of the electorate by slogans, advertising, and some spin-doctoring, all of which tends to oversimplify and play on crude reactions. It must be galling, for example, for someone who really understands complex economic or constitutional issues to have his vote possibly cancelled out by that of someone who has no such grasp of the import or consequences of his vote. Essentially, the argument is that of Plato, who entrusted the affairs of the state to the highly educated only. Aristotle had countered this by saying that the best judge of legislation is not the "expert" legislator (he never thought of *voters*) but the person who has to live under the law.[15]
>
> Moreover, giving extra votes to the wealthy strengthens their capacity to protect their vested interest. Even giving extra votes on educational grounds alone could lead to those who have education preserving their vested interests by obstructing the extension of education to those who do not have it. For that reason they might refuse to vote public funds for the improvement of education, secure as they are in the knowledge that the poor need education to be free, whereas the rich can always buy it. It may also seem wrong that those who are already most privileged, whether through wealth or education or both, should have further privileges added to them by way of a voting system weighted in their favour.
>
> Nor is it true that being educated is necessarily the same as being intelligent. Some educated people can be very unintelligent, whilst some who lack a sophisticated education may still have a capacity for making shrewd judg-

14 Mill's book, *The Subjection of Women* (1869) was one of the earliest texts advocating the of emancipation of women. This was desirable not only on the grounds of equity, but also because he believed that women would have a beneficent influence on politics.

15 For Plato, see p. 23f above; for Aristotle, p. 54 above.

ments on public affairs. Should we therefore weight the vote according to IQs rather than to educational qualification? And even if this were considered to be fair, how is it to be assessed in practice, and by whom?

On many complex issues, educated people are likely to differ among themselves nearly as much as uneducated people do. There is, therefore, no reason to believe that the verdict of the electorate would be significantly different if the opinions of the educated people were given additional weight.

The representation of minority opinions should also be protected by replacing the current electoral system of first-past-the-post by one of proportional representation.

Bentham had proposed the greatest happiness of the greatest number against the background of governments promoting the greatest happiness of a very small number. This had made him pay insufficient attention to the dangers of his formulation for the future, which Mill had to point out: as it stood, it made possible the abuse of the rights of a small number in the interests of the greatest happiness of the majority. Now the same situation could be said to apply to Mill's position on proportional representation. It would deal with the abuse which most concerned him, that the opinions of sometimes quite sizeable minorities could not make themselves heard in a legislature elected on a first-past-the-post system. Had he actually seen a proportional system in action, he might have come to the conclusion that it would often in practice give quite *dis*proportionate influence to minorities who could hold much bigger groups to ransom and in many cases made for weak, unstable and short-lived coalition governments.

Mill also wanted to temper the influence of a mass electorate by reverting to the Burkeian idea that a member of parliament should regard himself as a representative rather than as a delegate (as Bentham had said).[16] Here again, Mill gave additional weight to the expertise and qualifications of a member of parliament, and he thought that no politician of value would consent to be merely a glorified messenger-boy for the opinions of his constituents.

Finally, he thought that a Second Chamber, representing personal merit, was desirable as a counterweight to a House representing popular feeling. He was not radical enough to recommend the abolition of the hereditary peerage, but suggested that a substantial group of *ex officio* worthies should be added to it: the heads of the law courts, former Cabinet ministers, the service chiefs, senior diplomats, former colonial governors, some very senior civil servants etc. In this, as in many other matters, he was ahead of his time, even if his brand of liberalism, now generally called Classical Liberalism, would go out of fashion within a generation after his death and be replaced by Positive Liberalism, whose founder was the Oxford don, T.H. Green.

T.H. GREEN
1836 to 1882

Green's greatest impact was posthumous, when his own notes and those of his students were published as *Lectures on the Principles of Social Legislation* between 1885 and 1888.

16 See p. 243 above for Burke, p. 424 above for Bentham.

The principal difference between Classical and Positive Liberalism lay in their attitude to the state. Mill had believed in *laissez faire* – the function of the state was simply to prevent individuals harming each other. We have seen how suspicious Mill was of extending the powers of the state, for example, in the economic sphere, and he had denied that the state should have any role in shaping the moral climate.

Green, on the other hand, believed that the state *should* advance the moral capacities of its citizens. He wanted to distance himself from the organic theories of the state that drew upon Rousseau and Hegel, and that would be advanced by his own pupil, Bernard Bosanquet (1848 to 1923).[17] These had led to an undue worship of the state, had posited a General Will, and had tended to suggest that the individuals within it only found their true identity as members of the state.

Green was much more down to earth, and had no such mystical reverence for the state, indeed, he preferred to use the word "society" rather than "state", though he focuses on what the mechanism of the state can do to improve society. Instead of the people having to conform to a General Will which expresses what they "really" want, Green stressed that the state should listen to what they "actually" want,[18] and he was well aware how often the state failed to do that. It followed from Rousseau's theory that there was a difference between "actual" freedom (to follow one's impulses, one's short-term interest, and what may be one's "lower" nature) and the "real" freedom (to follow the dictates of one's "higher" nature.) For Green, a person is unfree when he is enslaved, not by his "lower" nature, but by social and economic circumstances which restrict his freedom and prevent him from developing his potential. He may enjoy all the freedoms that the Classical Liberals extolled: freedom to speak, to vote, to organize; and yet may be profoundly unfree because he is fettered by poverty and lack of opportunity. Whilst the state should not dictate to its citizens, it should also aim to advance their moral capacity, and therefore a civilized state should be morally a little ahead of what the general public may want – it should lead rather than follow public opinion.

> Cases where it has done just this would include the abolition of capital punishment, the decriminalization of homosexuality, and laws against racial discrimination at times when a referendum would probably have produced a majority against these measures. Yet these measures have gradually altered public opinion, so that a few years later the opposition against them has greatly diminished.
>
> One might object that Green's theory could be called in aid of theocratic states, who might claim that they were giving a lead to its people to raise their moral standard. However, we must remember that Green was a *liberal*, and liberalism, insisting on freedom of opinion, would rule out a theocratic dictatorship. He would therefore allow the function of raising public morals only to those states that were committed to liberal principles.
>
> By allowing liberal governments to act in advance of public opinion, Green implicitly aligns himself with Burke and John Stuart Mill rather than with Bentham. Bentham had believed that members of parliament were merely delegates, charged with carrying out the wishes of the public in detail,

17 In *The Philosophical Theory of the State*, 1899.

18 For Rousseau's distinction between the Real and the Actual Will, see p. 338. above.

whereas Burke and Mill had maintained that members of parliament should be representatives, chosen because the voters trust their judgment even if that means that occasionally they will differ from the voters.

Above all, poverty, oppression and injustice are hindrances to the development of a person's moral potential, an impediment to his dignity, and severely limit his capacity to live a fulfilled life. Green thought that it was a function of the state to "hinder hindrances". This would mean that it needed to attack poverty, prevent exploitative contracts, extend compulsory education, impose regulations on competition, and enact measures to protect public health. The Benthamites had aimed for the greatest happiness of the greatest number, and to this end they had sometimes sacrificed the liberty and happiness of minorities – we need only remember their Poor Law Amendment Act.[19] Mill and Classical Liberalism had made the liberty of individuals and that of minorities the greatest of all political values, but he had thought too much in terms of formal liberty and had tended to overlook the lack of real freedom (in the normal, rather than the Rousseauist sense of that phrase) that often goes along with it. Green's philosophy could be said to be a synthesis between the two: he cared as much for liberty as Mill had done, but he wanted the greatest freedom of the greatest number. To secure that would mean a more positive role for the state (as the servant of all those individuals, and not as their master) than Mill had allowed.

Something of what Green called for had already been happening before his time. There had been Mines Acts and Factory Acts which had limited the grossest exploitation, first of children, and then of women. The Classical Liberals had acknowledged the need for such legislation to protect some of those who were too weak to protect themselves, but they considered, for example, that adult males entered "freely" into the most exploitative contracts with their employers, and the state should therefore not interfere. Thus, Green pushed forward tendencies that were already making themselves felt. By Green's time the state had already given more rights to trade unions – partly in response to a working-class electorate that was enfranchised from 1867 onwards, partly out of fear of revolution. Green's theories therefore went with the current of history, but his contribution was to give all these measures a moral underpinning: social reform was more than a pragmatic necessity; it was also a moral duty. This view was also held by democratic socialists. Green's ideas would find expression in the Liberal Party of Lloyd George and John Maynard Keynes, but the Liberal Party would go into steep decline, so that it would be left to the Labour Party to carry forward many of Positive Liberalism's ideas.

19 See p. 426 above.

CHAPTER 37

The Notion of Progress

The Industrial Revolution was very largely the result of applied sciences, and it gave a new boost to the desire, already noted during the Enlightenment, to apply the principles of scientific thought to social questions. Auguste Comte in France and Herbert Spencer in England popularized the word "Sociology", putting the study of society on a par with such scientific studies as "Physiology", "Zoology", "Geology" etc., and today many people actually speak of "the Social Sciences", though others might prefer to talk of Social Studies.

The Enlightenment belief in and welcome of progress was also intensified by the Industrial Revolution, which created daily evidence of advances in the prosperity of western societies. The philosophy of Auguste Comte was the first to express the nineteenth-century confidence in progress. When then the scientist Charles Darwin demonstrated that Evolution, itself equated with progress, was not only built into the history of thought (as Vico, Condorcet, Hegel and others had taught)[1] but into physical nature itself, it seemed to support yet further confidence that progress was a Law of Nature, which need only be properly understood and scientifically applied to interpret and speed up the development of society. Herbert Spencer will develop what became known as "Social Darwinism", and Karl Marx will claim to transform Hegelian Dialectical Idealism into a scientifically-based Dialectical Materialism, which is at work in society as the motor of Progress.

AUGUSTE COMTE
1796 to 1857

Comte's philosophy was embodied in a six-volume work, *Cours de Philosophie Positive* (1832 to 1842), and hence is known as Positivism. There followed the four volumes of *Le Système de Politique Positive* (1851 to 1854) in which Comte described what a state run on Positivist lines should look like. Both in its analysis and in its programme for improvement, Positivism reminds us of the Enlightenment and indeed of the principles announced by the philosophers of the Scientific Revolution, like Francis Bacon.[2] We establish positive knowledge by working inductively:[3] we begin with what we observe; we hypothesize a generalization and the generalization is then tested (or verified) by whether

1 For Vico, see pp. 353f above; for Condorcet, pp. 353f above; for Hegel, pp. 391ff above.

2 For Francis Bacon, see pp. 211ff above.

3 For induction and deduction, see p. 212 above.

subsequent experience bears it out. This process of verification is a traditional scientific procedure, and without such verification we can have no positive knowledge.[4]

We cannot use this procedure to give us knowledge of whether God exists or not, and therefore we have to do without God in trying to understand the world we live in.

In principle, Comte thought, we can hypothesize generalizations about the nature of society in the same way that we can about the nature of the physical world, though he admitted that for a long time to come the results are likely to be less precise in the former case than in the latter. The English positivist, Henry Thomas Buckle (1821 to 1862), while realizing that there were practical problems that did not exist in the physical sciences, was nevertheless sure that, by patiently collecting statistics (of which Victorian administrators were becoming enamoured) an ever wider-ranging area of social behaviour could be shown to follow patterns that indicated underlying laws. The heading of chapter 1 of Buckle's *History of Civilization in England* (1856 to 1861) reads, in part, "Proofs of the regularity of human action", and in it he wrote, "I entertain very little doubt that before another century has elapsed ... it will be as rare to find a historian who denies the undeviating regularity of the moral world as it is now to find a philosopher who denies the regularity of the material world."

A problem that neither Comte nor Buckle addressed was the impossibility in history of repeating experiments, a crucial way of testing scientific theories. The scientist can generally create laboratory conditions which exclude variables that could affect the behaviour of the phenomena under examination, however, the huge number of variables in human history can never be eliminated.

These same variables also make predictions in history much less reliable than they are in the sciences (even if those in the sciences also sometimes turn out to be fallible). Some people seem quite unaware of the fact, when talking about "history repeating itself" that it can never do so in any meaningful or comprehensive way. Just one reason it cannot do so is that, if history appears to reveal a pattern that is not considered desirable – say, that the ruling class will always resist pressures from below to the point that it will be overthrown by violent revolution – the ruling class can learn from the pattern of the past to avoid (for example by timely reform rather than by repression) a similar outcome in the future. Perhaps one *can* therefore learn from history, though what exactly one learns is very indeterminate, and there have been just as many examples of the wrong as of the right lessons having been learnt.

The detection of trends or patterns in history (whether linear ones of progress or cyclical ones of rise and fall) is an interesting and often illuminating pursuit, but such patterns as have been found can never have the regularity or reliability of those in the sciences, not least because their detection usually involves a degree of selection that plays down or ignores aspects of history that do not fit into the design.

4 The need to verify a statement in order to talk about it meaningfully is the link between Comte's Positivism and the Logical Positivism of the twentieth century. See p. 550 below.

Comte believed that societies are organisms that, like any form of living matter, have orderly structures and laws of growth and development that can be studied scientifically. To the study of society, Comte gave the name of Sociology. It would show that both order and progress are necessary for the well-being of the organism: order without progress (as during the *Ancien Régime*) dooms a society to petrification and ultimate collapse, whilst progress without order (as during the French Revolution) leads to collapse through anarchy. "Progress remains always the simple development of order."

Like many western European optimists of the nineteenth century, Comte believed that progress was inevitable. History was a story of progress. Societies, like individuals, pass through three stages of development to maturity. The first is the Theological, where explanations are sought in terms of religion. The second is the Metaphysical, where explanations are looked for in abstract forces, like attraction or repulsion ("personified abstractions"), and which culminate in the notion of "Nature". The third is the Positive, which relies on the scientific approach. This does not so much look for *explanations* as for careful *description* of phenomena and their relationships with each other.[5] Comte knew that some theological civilizations had engaged in both metaphysics and science, but he thought that they had subordinated both of these to theology and had rejected any findings that did not fit in with their theological preoccupations. Metaphysical civilizations likewise had often used science to support preconceived notions. Only in the Positive phase were people willing to discard preconceptions, to let the spirit of scientific enquiry lead to wherever it might take them, and to allow a rational construction of society.

With the aid of Sociology, we can not only understand social development, but can, to a very limited extent, control it. The extent must be limited because, broadly speaking, the development is inherent in the laws governing the society and is therefore, to a degree, inevitable anyway. We cannot, therefore, radically change it, but our actions, based on our understanding, can facilitate it, just as actions based on a lack of such knowledge can slow it down.

It is therefore desirable that society should be guided by an élite that understands these laws. Rather oddly, he wanted its ultimate governing body to be a triumvirate of bankers - one connected with agriculture, one with manufacturing, and one with commerce - for such men, he thought, would have the best qualification in sociological understanding - Comte was no democrat.

> We can see how he harks back here to the idea of Plato's philosopher kings. The notion that the best leaders are those who understand social development will be taken up by Marx and Lenin,[6] though their idea that progress needs to be brought about by revolution is absent from Comte's thinking – nor, of course would they put their trust in bankers!

Comte believed that a society which is based on science and industry will necessarily be a peace-loving one, because science and industry, properly understood, demand cooperation.

5 Logical Positivists like A.J. Ayer (see below, p. 551) also claim that philosophy is concerned with accurate description rather than with explanation.

6 For Plato, see pp. 23ff above; for Marx, p. 450 below.

Many people believed this at the time. One of the arguments advanced for Free Trade was that it would lead to specialization. Each country would then produce and export what it did best and would import what other countries did best. In this way, no nation would be self-sufficient; they would all be dependent on others. For example, a country could not afford to fight a war against another on whose iron and steel production it was dependent, nor could a country that had specialized in iron and steel fight against one from which it imported its food.

There is, of course, some truth in this. One of the arguments for creating the European Economic Community was precisely that it would be impossible for countries whose economies were closely integrated to fight a war, but Comte and those who thought like him put the cart before the horse. The desire for peace is not the *result*, but the *precondition* for economic integration; the EEC was founded precisely because, after the Second World War, the politicians of both France and Germany were determined that there should never be another war between them, and *therefore,* they embarked on the close integration of their economies. Countries that want to maintain their sovereignty (which includes the ability, if necessary, to fight wars for their interests) will not pool their economies. In such cases, there will be rivalry rather than cooperation between national economies, and these rivalries may then themselves become a cause for war.

In any case, competition is at the heart of all efficient industrialized societies, and whilst that competition may be peaceful (i.e. remain within the legal framework) it often causes at least as much tension within and between societies as it does harmony.

Also, Comte did not foresee what a significant role the manufacture of armaments would play in the industrialized world. Although that industry argues that armaments are necessary to maintain peace, it is obvious that instead, it generates warlike feelings, and actually stimulates destructive wars.

While Comte saw in science and industry the *practical* progress of society, he also believed that it would bring about moral and spiritual progress. People would see the well-being of humanity as their goal. Aware of the importance for ordinary people of myths, Comte proposed that humanity, which he called *Le Grand Être* (The Great Being), should become the true object of worship. Its priests would expound the laws of sociology; it would have temples and ceremonies to celebrate it; it would have its own saints, the great benefactors of mankind; and the task of education would be to instil reverence for it.

It is interesting how many secular philosophies (Marxism, for example) in the end, copy the religious model. This is in part a calculated strategy to exploit the religious instincts of the masses, but it can also sweep away its very exponents, who, being human themselves, find it hard to draw the line between strategy on the one hand and, on the other, their own instinct to give their passionate beliefs a religious form. This seems to have been the case with Comte.[7]

7 See Frederick Coplestone, *A History of Philosophy*, Vol.IX, pp. 96 to 98. Coplestone suggests that Comte's language suggests that he slipped back from the language of the Positivist stage to that of the Metaphysical stage.

Needless to say of such a religion, the individual finds his fulfilment in subjecting himself to it. He has no rights against it, any "rights" he does possess are granted to him by the society for the latter's well-being. The progress of society "consists above all in substituting duties for rights, in order better to subordinate personality to sociability" and, "nobody possesses any other right than that of always doing his duty." If Positivist education has done its job properly, people will see no conflict between right and duty. We are not far away from Rousseau's distinction between Real and Actual freedom.[8]

CHARLES DARWIN
1809 to 1882

Darwin did not claim to be a philosopher, and was indeed troubled about the conclusions that philosophers and theologians might draw from his scientific work. Even so, his theory of Evolution was to have an enormous effect on philosophy. It has to be said, however, that the philosophical concept of evolution had been in the air since long before Darwin was born. In its modern form it can be traced back to the quarrel in the late seventeenth century between the Ancients and the Moderns.[9] The Ancients had believed that society ought to recapture the achievements of a superior past, whereas the Moderns held that the Renaissance, despite its name, was an *advance* on the past, and the culture of the Scientific Revolution and then of the dawning Enlightenment even more so. From this had grown the concept of organic development and progress in History, which we see developed in various ways by Vico, Condorcet, Hegel, Comte and Spencer. Indeed, Herbert Spencer was to use the word *evolution* to describe this progress in 1858, the year before Darwin's *Origins of the Species* was published. What Darwin did was to reinforce this notion by demonstrating evolution at work throughout the whole organic world. Even in that area, he had been anticipated in 1794 by his grandfather Erasmus Darwin (1731 to 1802) and in 1800 by J.-B. Lamarck (1744 to 1829), though these predecessors had seen adaptation rather than natural selection as the motor of evolution.

Just as Newton's discoveries had then been extended by philosophers beyond the purely scientific field to which Newton had confined himself, so the same now happened to those of Darwin.

The first shock was to religious fundamentalism – the belief that was still lingering even among educated people that the Bible's account of Creation was true. That account had already been shaken. In 1831, Sir Charles Lyell's *Principles of Geology* had shown that the earth was not created in the course of seven days in 4004 BC, as Bishop Ussher had calculated in the 1650s from the genealogies in the Bible, but was millions of years old and had taken many ages to form. Erasmus Darwin and Lamarck had shown that evolutionary changes had taken place in the animal world, but the idea that Man and animals had been separately created had not yet been called into question. Even *On the Origin of Species* had not yet challenged it, but in 1871, Darwin published *The Descent of Man*, and Man was now shown to be part of the evolutionary process, and the

8 See p. 338 above.

9 See pp. 306f above.

human mind a biologically developing tool rather than a divine endowment by God that separated Man from the animal creation.

> Biblical fundamentalists still reject the theory of Evolution, but in due course most churchmen came to terms with it as they had learnt to accommodate themselves to Galileo and to Lyell. Evolution – allied as the notion was with improvement – could be interpreted as God's purpose for His Creation. If He allowed the weak to suffer in the process, we must not question that part of His inscrutable purpose, any more than earlier theologians (predestinarians in particular) had questioned why He should select only a part of His Creation for salvation and the rest for the sufferings of damnation. Such churchmen were certainly driven to accept that the Bible could not be literally true – but then that notion had already received some fatal blows, especially during the Enlightenment.

Eramus Darwin and Lamarck had seen evolution taking place as the result of adaptation: the best known illustration of this was the belief that the long neck of the giraffe was due to the animal constantly stretching up to reach leaves higher up on the trees and being able to pass the gains of this exercise on to the next generation. But an explanation based on Darwin's theory of natural selection would show that *accidental* mutations sometimes result in the birth of a giraffe with a neck that was slightly longer than usual. Such an animal and its descendants would be more successful in reaching the higher leaves than those who had shorter necks. Because they were fitter in this respect, they would stand a better chance of survival, especially when circumstances (like not enough leaves lower down) arose which made it essential to reach the higher leaves, and the shorter-necked species might then become extinct.

The implication of this seemed to be that nature was not the result of God's benevolent design and purpose, but rather of an amoral, random and often brutal struggle for survival, in which success would go not to the virtuous, but to the strongest and the fittest.

This notion of the Survival of the Fittest (a phrase not found in Darwin, but coined by Herbert Spencer in 1864) was crudely translated into philosophy, politics and economics, where it is known as Social Darwinism. In economics, it seemed to make competition part of a law of nature, ensuring that the fittest survived. It was right that those who were less fit should "go to the wall" (whatever that metaphor meant - and it could mean anything from being allowed to perish to being subjugated to serve the needs of those who were the stronger). It would damage the health of the species if the weak were helped by welfare legislation. In politics, Social Darwinism was used to justify Imperialism - the conquest of colonies was the victory of the strong over the weak. Eugenics was very popular in the late nineteenth and early twentieth century. The "unfit" should be discouraged from breeding among themselves lest they become too numerous. Even greater was the danger that they might interbreed with the strains that were "fit" and thereby weaken the latter; racists would say that they would "pollute" the purity of the fitter races. In the end, Social Darwinism even led to the elevation of war itself into a healthy and natural phenomenon - in 1913 the Italian proto-fascist Marinetti would describe war as "the world's hygiene". It was argued that the progress and evolution demanded by nature would be promoted by a battle between the strong and the weak. Hitler would be a particularly articulate and ruthless proponent of this view.

> The crudity of this application of Darwinian theory lay, in part, in that cooperation, certainly within a species and sometimes also between species, has at least as much survival value as conflict. This can be seen when packs hunt together, when ants and termites build together, or in certain symbiotic relationships between species. In human societies, all the greatest advances have been made by teamwork – often between those who are "strong" and those who are "weak". This was realized by Herbert Spencer, even though he himself popularized some of the other applications of Darwinian theory to social policy.

HERBERT SPENCER
1820 to 1903

Herbert Spencer had met Auguste Comte in the 1850s, and had accepted the concept of Sociology from him as a scientific approach to the study of society. He was also looking for a unifying principle that lay behind all phenomena, and he found it in Evolution and Dissolution. We have already seen that it was he who had coined the word "evolution" before Darwin's *On the Origin of Species* had appeared, he initially gave it a Lamarckian interpretation, but would later be persuaded by the Darwinian one. In 1858, he drew up the outline of *A System of Synthetic Philosophy*. He intended, in ten volumes, to apply in detail the notion of evolution to every branch of science, from Biology to Sociology. The first volume, called *First Principles*, appeared in 1862, this was followed, over some thirty years, by volumes on *The Principles of Biology*, *The Principles of Psychology*, *The Principles of Sociology*, and *The Principles of Ethics*.

The most influential of these were the three volumes on Sociology, and, although Spencer believed that societies, just like other organisms, were eventually subject to Dissolution, it is characteristic of the optimism of the Victorian Age that both he and his readers concentrated on Evolution. Concentration on the idea of Dissolution would be left to Oswald Spengler (1880 to 1936) a writer imbued by the pessimism resulting from the defeat of his native Germany in the First World War.[10]

Evolution, he thought, favoured two particular developments; one is that it creates ever larger social groups.

> This was true in the period before Spencer wrote and would continue to be so after his time. The process was, of course, speeded up by technological developments. The railways, for example, brought people who had previously had very little contact with each other closer together; the nations of western Europe are now part of the European Union; countries in eastern Europe, proud of their newly-achieved independence from the Soviet Union are pressing to become part of the European Union, and the culmination of this process is what is appropriately called the World Wide Web, which makes a community of sorts of the entire globe, so that we all become increasingly interdependent.

10 See p. 455 below.

The other development is that in the process of evolution there are increasing differentiations within the group as its members specialize in different activities. This was not a particularly novel insight. Adam Smith, in *The Wealth of Nations* (1776) had already illustrated the benefit of the greater specialization which the incipient Industrial Revolution was accelerating. One of the consequences Spencer foresaw was that class divisions would become steadily less rigid. He could see that skilled workers would have interests that set them apart from unskilled workers, that the self-identification of employed managers would blur differences between employers and the employed, and that this differentiation would increase. In this respect, his analysis was shrewder than that of Karl Marx, who expected the opposite to happen as increasing exploitation of every kind of employee would push them all into working-class solidarity.[11]

The ultimate stage in the process by which social blocks or "collectives" dissolve into more graduated groups will be that the individuals who make up those groups will gain increasing importance. The importance of the individuals, which had always been stressed by the Classical Liberals on moral grounds, was now underpinned by Spencer as the scientific lesson which Sociology taught as an aspect of social evolution. This, in turn, underpinned his belief in *laissez faire* as a characteristic of an evolving society.

Spencer believed that evolution was driven by competition, that this competition was healthy and therefore beneficent, and that it should not be impeded by legal obstacles or even by large-scale (and especially by state-sponsored) charity for the weak and the poor. The Industrial Revolution and its miseries were seen as an inevitable and transient stage to something better.

> The whole effort of nature is to get rid of such, to clear the world of them, and to make room for better ... If they are sufficiently complete to live, they do live. If they are not sufficiently complete to live, they die, and it is best that they should die.

Spencer professed himself a Utilitarian – if we went along with evolutionary ends, we would eventually secure the greatest happiness of the greatest number.

Here we have a deployment of the crudity of Social Darwinism. Elsewher,e Spencer tones down its harshness by stressing that, in due course, as civilizations evolve further, the egoism that seemed to lie at the heart of this philosophy would give way to altruism. He realized that cooperation and mutual aid (so long as these were instinctive and not imposed from outside) were evolutionary qualities that promoted survival, and that these were most likely to be found in industrial societies.

> It is not easy to see how he would define altruism if it excluded large-scale charitable help to the poor!

He stressed that such cooperation and mutual aid must be *voluntary*, for he buttressed his evolution-based defence of l*aissez-faire* with arguments, based on Classical Liberalism, that the individual must be protected against the power of the state. He was disturbed to see the growth during his lifetime of what was then called Collectivism – the theory that the people collectively, represented in institutions (even if these were parliaments) can restrict individual freedoms for the sake of social improvement (social "improvement", moreover, being

11 See p. 450 below.

seen as action by the state to help the weak and the poor). Classical Liberals had always believed in Parliaments, but Parliaments, under the influence of the extension of the franchise to the working class in 1867 and 1884, were now deserting Classical for what would be called Positive Liberalism, which Spencer believed was not true Liberalism at all. He believed that Parliaments were now arrogating to themselves rights that did not belong to them. In a book significantly called *Man versus the State* (1884), Spencer wrote:

> The great political superstition of the past was the divine right of kings. The great political superstition of the present is the divine right of parliaments. ... The function of liberalism in the past was that of putting a limit to the powers of the king. The function of true liberalism in the future will be that of putting a limit to the powers of Parliament.

Such views clearly put him in opposition to the Positive Liberalism advanced by T.H.Green, whose lectures would start being published in the following year.[12]

For all his belief in the state showing the characteristics of an organism, Spencer did not hold the view normally held by exponents of the Organic Theory of the State, which made the individual a subordinate of the state. On the contrary, sharply differing here from Comte,[13] he wrote, "The Society exists for the benefit of its members; not its members for the benefits of Society." That is why mutual help must always be on a freely accepted voluntary basis, but must not be imposed by the state.

It was, as Spencer saw it, part of the evolution of society that it should develop from an authoritarian phase (he called it a "militaristic" or "militant" phase) to a progressive one (which, here following Comte, he describes as "industrial"), "Under the industrial régime, the citizen's individuality, instead of being sacrificed by the society, has to be defended by the society. Defence of his individuality becomes the society's essential duty." The importance of the citizen's individuality could be seen as the ultimate stage of individuation, which has been described above, but where Spencer saw the phase of individualism and *laissez faire* as the goal towards which progress was leading, for Karl Marx, this phase was only an intermediate one.

KARL MARX
1818 to 1883

Marx was first introduced to a philosophy of progress when he went to the University of Berlin in 1836. That university was then dominated by Hegelians, though these were at that time split between the Right and Left (or Young) Hegelians.[14] It will be remembered that the division was over the interpretation of Hegel's dictum that "the Real is the Rational and the Rational is the Real". The Right Hegelians laid the stress on the first part of that saying, concluding that the reality they saw before them was rational, and this made them fundamentally conservative and accepting of the existing situation. The Left Hegelians, stressing the second part of the dictum, had a more dynamic outlook. s the rational process of the Dialectic moved ideas from one stage to the next, so

12 See p. 432 above.

13 See p. 439 above.

14 See p. 392 above.

the material world had to mirror this process and itself move on rather than remain static. Germany was then dominated by the repressive and reactionary Metternich System. This system, when it was set up was, dialectically speaking, the expression of ideas that were antithetical to those of the preceding revolutionary period, but the rational process of the Dialectic had now moved the ideas on to the next stage. The old world was, therefore, no longer rational, no longer "real"; it needed to be transformed so that it would again correspond with the new rational phase that the Dialectic had now reached. The Young Hegelians were therefore in revolutionary opposition to the Metternich System and agitated for new institutional arrangements to correspond with what was now rational. It was with the philosophy of the Left Hegelians that Marx identified himself at the university.

In 1841, the conservative Prussian government purged the Left Hegelians from the universities as dangerous revolutionaries. Marx left Berlin and went to Cologne, in the Prussian Rhineland, where he first contributed to and soon edited the *Rheinische Zeitung*. This was a radical journal with which his friend the socialist Moses Hess (1812 to 1875) was involved. From Hess he took the seminal idea of the primacy of economic factors over purely political ones for understanding a society. This focus on material conditions also made Marx open to Ludwig Feuerbach (1804 to 1827), who had been scathing about the Hegelian notion that it is ideas, operating in an abstract dialectic, that shape the world;[15] on the contrary, he said it is the world that shapes ideas. Marx accepted the materialistic aspect of this theory, but he retained the concept of the dialectic. "Turning Hegel upside down", he saw a dialectic operating in the material world, and in particular in the economic field. Economic processes generated from within themselves problems which, rather like a cuckoo in the nest, eventually clashed, as an antithesis, with the system that produced them. The resolution of the clash was a temporary synthesis which would generate its own antithesis, and so on. At each stage, these material processes shape the ideas of the people that operate them.

> So, for example, the material capitalist mode of production is impossible without creating the material deprivations of a growing working class. In due course, the capitalist mode will be in dialectical conflict with the working-class conditions it has created, and these will then produce the antithetical ideology of socialism.

This view became known as Dialectical Materialism, to distinguish it from Hegel's Dialectical Idealism.

In 1843, the Prussian government suppressed the *Rheinische Zeitung* and Marx moved to Paris, where he edited a new journal, the *Deutsch-französische Jahrbücher*. In France he met two other groups of socialists (the word Socialism was coined in the early 1830s). To these he gave the rather devastating name of Utopian Socialists. One group were the followers of Henri de Saint-Simon (1760 to 1825), F-M-C Fourier (1772 to 1837) and de Sismondi (1773 to 1842). Their socialism, Marx said, was based entirely on their moral objection to social injustice, and they expected the spread of this indignation to bring about changes in society. Marx shared their indignation, but he claimed that it was

15 See p. 391 above.

utopian to believe that mere sensitivity about injustice would ever change a system. What he called his "Scientific Socialism" would inevitably come about in the course of the materialist dialectic, and therefore, a socialist should scientifically study the mechanism and by-products of this process, understand the necessary material conditions which moved society from one stage to the next, and use this understanding to go along with the process and to speed it up at the appropriate time. This might even involve putting socialism on the back burner, if, for instance, the stage a particular society has reached called for a transition from feudalism to a period of capitalism. It would be merely utopian at that stage to call for a socialist revolution.[16]

The importance of choosing the right moment also set Marx at odds with the other socialist group he met in Paris, the anarchists who followed J-B. Proudhon (1809 to 1865) and the Russian (then living in Paris) Mikhail Bakunin (1814 to 1876). The original anarchists wanted to live "without a (central) government" because they believed all central governments to be oppressive; they generally thought that people are happiest if they govern themselves in democratically constituted local communities (or communes) in which most property is communally held. Later in the century, some anarchists became associated with assassinating rulers and politicians associated with brutal repression.

Marx agreed that the aim of socialism was the communal ownership of most property, and he would therefore give the name "communist" to his own movement. But he thought that anarchism was also utopian and lacking in scientific rigour. Destroying central government *in order to* introduce socialism was putting the cart before the horse. At the appropriate historical stage, the state would be needed to establish and consolidate socialism and to defend it against non-socialist enemies. Only at the very end of the establishment of *universal* socialism could Marx envisage the central state "withering away" and society being organized as a series of small self-governing and cooperating communes. By then, all the selfish forces would have been eliminated for good, so that the communes could maintain themselves and would feel no need to compete with each other, with all the aggression that would involve. Since he had attached the word "Utopian" as a derisory label to some of his socialist opponents, it is perhaps ironic that his own picture of an earthly paradise was a Utopian idea if ever there was one! But trying to destroy the state *before* world socialism had been established would simply be a pointless waste of energy. The same was true of assassinations: they would not by themselves bring about socialism, and would most likely result in the replacement of one repressive ruler or official by one who was even more draconian.

In 1845, the French government, at the request of the Prussians, expelled Marx from Paris, and he went to Brussels. There, for the first time, he began to create an international revolutionary organization, called the Communist League, for which, together with his friend and collaborator Friederich Engels (1820 to 1895), he drew up the famous *Communist Manifesto.* This was conveniently completed just before the outbreak of the revolutions of 1848, and so could be issued as a clarion call to the revolutionary working class. The Belgian

16 see p. 451 below.

government expelled Marx on its publication, and he rushed to revolutionary Paris, and from there back to Cologne when the revolution spread to Germany. By 1849, the revolutions were beginning to collapse everywhere on the continent and Marx eventually took refuge in London, where he stayed for the rest of his life.

The *Communist Manifesto* contained the Marxist philosophy in outline, and he spent the rest of his life applying it in many articles and above all amplifying it in the three massive volumes of *Das Kapital*. Volume I was published in his lifetime (1867); in 1885 and 1894 Engels published the other two volumes posthumously from Marx's notes. The principal ideas of this work as are follows.

The economic processes of history are the most important ones. They form the infrastructure of societies and everything else is part of the superstructure erected upon it. The material superstructure will comprise all constitutions and institutions, such as the legal systems, the churches and other social organizations. They will shape the psychology and the ideologies, not only of the dominant, but also of the subordinate, groups, and all the political, religious, social and artistic ideas.

Here are some examples, not necessarily given by Marx himself. For centuries, the dominant group in Europe had been the feudal aristocracy, in which authority came from the top downwards. This structure was mirrored by that of the Catholic Church, its Pauline teaching – that one must obey the powers that be, for the powers that be are ordained of God – was clearly in the interests (both economic and political) of the ruling classes. Those subordinate groups who were not brainwashed by the dominant ideology wanted power to flow from the bottom upwards rather than from the top downwards, and that interest would have found expression in the structure of presbyterian and other nonconformist religions in which the elders – representatives of the congregations – appoint their clergy (called "ministers" rather than "priests", because to "minister" originally meant "to serve" – ministers were supposed to be the servants rather than the masters of their flock.)

If such congregations were in fact encouraged to be socially radical – as, for example, the Anabaptists had been – the ruling classes would do their best to stamp them out. The ruling class will try to control and use the churches to brainwash the people to accept the existing power structure rather than to challenge it, which is why Marx described religion as "the opiate of the people".

The subordinate classes may develop a religion like Methodism when the established Church of England became too obviously an instrument of the dominant class, but its members were scarcely aware that even the teaching of Methodism became a subtle system by which the ruling class could control them by having their ministers preach against revolution, and holding out, just as the established churches did, the promise that there would be rewards in the next world for those who patiently endured their suffering in this one.

For as long as its economic power lasted, a dominant class could create what Marx called a "false consciousness" in the subordinate classes, so that the latter could be brainwashed into accepting an ideology that supported the existing rulers. Challenges to that ideology could succeed only when the economic conditions were right - when they were not, social or religious revolts were doomed to failure.

This is how a Marxist would explain why, for example, an attack on the Catholic Church failed in the fifteenth century, at the time of Hus and Wycliffe, but succeeded in parts of Europe in the sixteenth century. Fifteenth-century England, for example, had a power structure in which the aristocrats who ran the state would install their younger brothers or other close relatives in bishoprics and other high offices in the church. An attack on the wealth or other privileges of the Church would therefore be resisted by the state. The English crown wanted to reduce the power of the nobility, and it took advantage of the slow erosion by wars and civil wars of the nobles' economic power to promote men of humbler birth into the senior positions of the Church. The crown itself, also being in economic difficulties, was now interested in attacking the wealth of the Church and also in syphoning off for itself the money that had previously gone to the Papacy, and the link between the clergy and the nobles had been weakened to such an extent that the laity could be induced to take part in the assault. The laity was also offered a share in the plunder as the crown sold off part of the wealth it had confiscated from the Church.

To justify such an assault, its beneficiaries now promoted the ideology of Wycliffe, which it had previously resisted: that the Church had abandoned apostolic poverty for corruption; that there was nothing in the Bible that would authorize the power of the Papacy or the forgiveness of sins in return for indulgences paid to Rome; that offerings to the saints were superstitions, and that therefore the art forms with which the Roman Catholic Church had induced worshippers to venerate the saints were idolatry and had to be destroyed.

It will be noted that such an explanation rested entirely on material interests and gave no weight to the moral or spiritual issues involved. A Marxist would not deny that there were reformers who were totally sincere in their advocacy of spiritual reform – but ideas, however sincerely held, would never by themselves bring about deep changes in society if "the time was not right", if there were no economic interests to support them, let alone if they ran up against the dominant ones.

And here is an example of how culture is shaped by class (that is, economic) interests. For many centuries, the small ruling classes were steeped in classical texts, for which, as knowledge of Latin and Greek was necessary, the mere possession of classical knowledge was a sign that one was a member of an educated élite, set apart from the masses who had no Latin or Greek. The two kinds of art most favoured by the ruling classes therefore dealt either with religious subjects (which themselves reinforced the support that religion gave to the existing class structure) or to subjects drawn from the mythology of Antiquity. As the young were educated in the classics, they imbibed philosophies that likewise buttressed the notion of hierarchical societies – Plato's *Republic* was after all an élitist one – and the study of the Roman Empire was used to support the imperial and civilizing "mission" of France or Britain.

The rising commercial classes had often not had a classical education, so the newly independent and bourgeois Dutch society produced a great new school of genre paintings, showing ordinary people doing ordinary things (something that we will not find in the work of Rubens, who was working in what we now call Belgium and which was then still the aristocratic Spanish Netherlands.) The bourgeois housewife may not have worked in the kitchens,

> but she often descended below stairs to instruct the household servants, and so took an interest in pots and pans and other objects that became the inspiration of the "still life", another subject in which Dutch painting excelled. Then, when we look at France, we find, alongside the mythological subjects (spiced with frivolous aristocratic eroticism) of a Boucher or a Fragonard, the sober, puritanical "bourgeois" art of a Chardin, which was so close in feeling to the art of the Dutch. Before the French Revolution, Fragonard and Boucher reflected the interests of the dominant social and political group, and Chardin might be said to mirror those of the, as yet subordinate, but rising bourgeoisie, who would, in due course, challenge and overthrow the aristocratic system in France. Such an analysis can be exceedingly crude and schematic, and in fact many of Chardin's genre and still life paintings were bought by aristocrats and monarchs. That does not entirely damage the thesis, however, after all, just as nowadays one can find members of the bourgeoisie who profess or at least toy with socialist philosophies, so there were aristocrats in eighteenth-century Europe who took a more or less serious interest in bourgeois culture. One might say that the bourgeois spirit was infiltrating sections of the aristocracy (and perhaps contributed to weakening it) – but bourgeois it remained, even if aristocrats patronized it.

Political power is a reflection of economic power, and those who hold it will shape the legal system to protect their position. Marx had little patience with the notion sometimes advanced that it is the purpose of the law to protect the weak against the strong: on the contrary, it exists to protect the strong against the weak. Like the state itself, the law is the instrument of the ruling class.

The dominant classes are, however, unable to prevent the economic processes over which they preside from generating the problems which eventually create new and antithetical economic structures.

Marx defined both the old and the new structures in terms of the control of the means of production: land, capital and labour, and he saw the history of that control moving through six phases. The first three were the tribal, the slave, and the feudal phases. The tribal phase is a "communist" phase in that all property (land and "capital" like stores of grain), he thought (rightly or wrongly) is held communally. As tribes go to war with each other, the victorious tribes often enslave the defeated ones. In this way, slave societies come into being, in which masters own the land, the slaves and their labour. However, holding slaves is not always economically profitable, for the master has to provide for them when they are too young, too sick, or too old to be productive. In the next phase, the feudal phase the masters own the serfs, and the serfs have bits of land of their own which they cultivate when they are not needed to cultivate the land reserved for the master, and they are expected to maintain their families from the produce of their strips (though if they cannot manage this, the serf-owner can't exactly allow them to starve because he will need their labour to cultivate his own land.) Marx had sketched out the processes by which these phases succeeded each other rather peremptorily, but he paid considerable attention to the mechanisms by which the next three phases came into existence.

During the feudal phase, the production of goods passed out of the control of the landowners to independent artisans, who made goods not only for the land-based feudal economy, but also for the growing cities and then for national and international trade. As some artisans became manufacturers and merchants, a class of prosperous burghers (the bourgeoisie) developed, whose growth accelerated during the early Industrial Revolution. Some of these bourgeois became so wealthy that, as manufacturers, merchants or bankers, they could lend money even to powerful landowners and monarchs. This was especially so during the so-called Price Revolution in the sixteenth and seventeenth centuries, when, for reasons beyond the scope of this book, prices of manufactured goods rose very fast, but landowners, whose contracts with their tenants were long-term ones, could not raise rents to match. The producers of consumer goods had no problem about raising their prices to correspond with inflation (and thereby to accelerate it), and the balance of economic strength between the bourgeoisie and an increasingly impoverished landed class shifted very much in favour of the former. This development gave considerable economic power to the bourgeoisie, but it was not matched by political power, which remained in the hands of the feudal classes. Eventually, the bourgeoisie claimed political power, too: the productive forces that gave rise to it are the antithesis of those that supported the feudal nobility. The claim was resisted by the feudal classes, and the class struggle developed between the two. This eventually resulted in the violent overthrow of the feudal monopoly, and in the accession to power of the bourgeoisie. This is seen as a temporary synthesis, between the economic forces that had been the antithesis of the feudal structure (the previous thesis) and the state power that had supported that thesis.

> This theory works, more or less, for the French Revolution. By confiscating, breaking up and redistributing the lands of the aristocracy, the Revolution deprived that class of economic and political power so effectively and permanently that even the Restoration could not restore it. The example of a violent overthrow in English history would be the Civil War, but here the outcome was, *in class terms*, not as drastic a shift of control as the theory would have called for, and as the French Revolution had actually brought about. The power of the great English landowners was still considerable right until the end of the nineteenth century, even though they no longer monopolized it, but had to allow the bourgeois classes a significant share in government.

So begins the capitalist phase. As the Industrial Revolution matures, the manufacturing class becomes economically dominant. It owns the capital – the machinery and the funds to support it – but employs rather than owns the labour that produces the goods.

This marks the next phase, the capitalist phase. Capitalism is based on competition, and the way you succeed in competition is by reducing the costs of production. That can be done up to a point by employing capital more efficiently, but when all the efficient capitalists have done that, the only way to reduce the cost of production still further is to reduce labour costs – paying lower and lower wages to those workers they *have* to employ – the process known as immiserisation.[17] (Marx called these workers the proletariat: the cap-

17 In the 1830s and the 1840s ("the Hungry Forties") labour costs were in fact very low: there was a massive population explosion which drove people from the overpopulated countryside into the towns, desperate for work at almost any wage. At the same time, governments favourable to capitalism put every possible legal obstacle in the way of trade unions who might have been able to raise wages somewhat by

italist is called that because he owns capital. The only possessions of the worker are his offspring – Latin *proles* – whom he is often forced to send out to work in order to keep the family at subsistence level.)

Meanwhile, those capitalists who cannot compete will go bankrupt and will themselves be forced down into the proletariat, so that an increasing polarization will take place in the class system; it is the law of increasing misery. Another consequence will be that the impoverished proletariat cannot afford to buy the increasing volume of goods which the successful capitalist can send to the market. The result is overproduction and underconsumption, the essential contradiction within capitalism. There will be mounting unrest. The ruling class will never surrender its power voluntarily, so the capitalist classes will, through their control of the state machinery, become increasingly repressive. Its power can therefore be destroyed only by violence. Increasing repression will eventually create an intense class-consciousness in the proletariat and will destroy the "false consciousness" which the ruling class, through the church, the press and every other kind of social manipulation, has inculcated in the workers. The moment for revolution is approaching, though it is important to judge the moment aright; a miscalculation which leads to a premature revolt can temporarily strengthen the ruling class and put off the moment of its downfall by many years. (Marx thought that this had happened several times in French history: the June Days of the 1848 revolution and the Commune of 1871.)

The downfall, however, is inevitable in the end, though it can be put off for a while by repression (in which case the explosion will be the more violent when it does come) or by incompetent leadership and false consciousness. Conversely, it can be speeded up by revolutionary leaders who understand the process, can teach class-consciousness and can judge when the moment for revolution is right. Even the most brilliant individual is doomed to failure if the time is not right (we have used the example of Wycliffe); and when the time *is* right, it is sure to throw up the leader (say, a Luther) who can give expression to the historical process. Ultimately, it is not individuals, but economic and social processes that shape history. In the twentieth century this will be called the "structuralist view of history" and it will be discussed more fully in the next chapter.

When the overthrow of the capitalist system does happen, the proletariat will seize the machinery of the state, and, just as the capitalists have used the repressive apparatus of state to promote their own interests, so the workers will now use the apparatus to impose their programme; they will establish the dictatorship of the proletariat. This is not yet pure Communism, but the dictatorship will be necessary to destroy all the vestiges of capitalism – the control not only of the infrastructure (the means of production), but also of the superstructure (the ideologies which it taught to the society, through the church, through schools, through art and through the press). Only when all this has been wholly eradicated, when the entire population has been thoroughly permeated with the values of Communism (and when, as later communists pointed out, there is also no longer a threat to a communist state from outside,

stopping workers from undercutting each other.

because all the other states have also destroyed capitalism) – only then can the repressive apparatus of the state be abandoned, and the goal of true Communism – "the withering away of the state" – can be achieved.

An understanding of the process also involves the recognition that no stage in the process can be skipped. Marx believed that a society cannot move directly from feudalism to the dictatorship of the proletariat. First, the feudal system has to be overthrown by bourgeois capitalism, and, therefore, in a feudal society the class-conscious workers need to ally with the bourgeois liberals to bring about the overthrow of the feudal system. Decades will then pass before the new system will mature to the point where it becomes caught up in its own contradictions and the moment has come for the proletarian revolution.

The structure of Marxist thought has been immensely influential. Marx combined the roles of the historian of the past in his analysis of change with that of the prophet and (although he protested that his theory did not depend on it) with that of the moralist. The part of his philosophy which influenced even his opponents was the stress that he laid on economic forces being the main motor of history. In the late nineteenth and early twentieth century, history books giving the background to the French Revolution would begin with chapters on the *philosophes*, followed by chapters on constitutional aspects and only then come to the chapters on the economic background. Today, the economic chapters are likely to come first, in the (usually) tacit recognition that these form the infrastructure, and the other two the superstructure which grew out of it. Even President Clinton, the leader of the most thoroughly capitalist country in the world, when asked what would decide the outcome of the presidential election, answered, "the economy, stupid!"

Many of Marx's prophesies have been heavily falsified by history. Advanced capitalist systems have not behaved in the way in which he expected when he wrote *Das Kapital*. To begin with, the most successful ones have known when to make concessions instead of resorting to repression: the British aristocracy managed, by making concessions to the upper middle class in 1832, to take it into partnership;[18] the middle class used the same tactic with regard to the skilled workers in 1867; the franchise was steadily extended; trade unions won more and more freedoms and were able to raise the standard of living for their members. The Welfare State is not only a powerful antidote to revolution: together with improved wages it also reduced the danger of underconsumption which Marx foresaw. In addition, the capitalist system has devised many other ways – like advertising, the development of credit systems and built in obsolescence – of increasing consumption. This in turn has put more people to work to produce these consumer goods, who then earn more money themselves to spend; this is called the "multiplier effect". So there has been no increasing misery, quite the reverse. Polarization of society has not happened,

18 Nor was this a novel idea in Britain: one of the reasons the country did not have a revolution like that in France was that the British aristocracy had not been averse to making the kind of *Marriage à la Mode* with the merchant class that Hogarth had so famously satirized, while at the same time the younger sons of the aristocracy became commoners, so that the class barriers were not so very rigid.

instead (as Herbert Spencer had anticipated),[19] class consciousness and solidarity has been eroded through the many gradations within all the classes.

Marx began to modify his theory somewhat when he saw that France and Germany had introduced universal male suffrage in 1848 and 1871 respectively and that England had extended the franchise to the skilled workers in 1867. He wrote in 1872 that he could envisage that in these countries the working classes *might* come to power by peaceful parliamentary means, but he never committed himself to this view publicly. Those of his followers who did were called Revisionists. They found themselves locked in a bitter ideological struggle with the orthodox Marxist-Leninists, who continued to believe in violence as the way to overthrow the capitalist system, and for whom "reformist" was actually a word of abuse. Under reformist policies, the workers have indeed, through peaceful processes, won prosperity undreamed of by Marx – but, as we have seen, it is prosperity *within* the capitalist system, which has not been overthrown. Burke had once said, "I would reform in order the better to be able to conserve". The concept of reform was that one would lop off rotten branches to keep the tree healthy. Marx, Lenin, Stalin and their followers were, by temperament, "radical" – that word comes from the Latin "radix", a root – a radical does not want to conserve a system, but to entirely "uproot" it.

> I think that such an attitude is also quite unHegelian. In the dialectical process, a synthesis is not achieved by "liquidating" an opposition, either in theory or in practice, but rather by embracing what is best in thesis and antithesis.

Marx's theory that a communist revolution could take place only in a mature bourgeois society had led him to expect that it would happen first in England or perhaps in Germany. When Russian communists wrote to him for advice, he was first very dismissive of them. Russia, he said, was still a feudal society and had not yet reached the bourgeois state. It would be one of the last European countries in which a communist revolution could happen.[20] Eventually, he was impressed by the dedication of his Russian disciples, and in 1881, in a private letter, he conceded that Russia could perhaps skip the bourgeois phase and move straight into communism – provided that the neighbouring countries had by then destroyed their own bourgeois societies, so that Russia would not have to defend herself against them. This change of mind, too, was never given any publicity, and his followers would split on the issue. The Mensheviks thought the bourgeois phase could not be skipped, while the Bolsheviks only maintained their Marxist orthodoxy by claiming, somewhat against the evidence, that the Russia of 1905 was already a bourgeois state.

These modifications were relatively minor when set against the great increase in working class prosperity. Marx was surely right in essence, Lenin

19 See p. 442 above.

20 Marx did not believe in the revolutionary possibilities of the peasants. Peasants may revolt in despair, they may even secure ownership of their own bit of land, but as soon as they have their own plot, even those with tiny holdings – let alone those with big ones – they cease to be revolutionaries and side with the conservatives in protecting private property. Besides, he thought they were the natural enemies of the industrial proletariate. The peasants are interested in selling the food they produce for a high price and the urban workers demand cheap food. It is therefore easy to enlist peasants for the counter-revolution. It would be left to Mao Tse Tung to show that a revolution could be based on the peasants – which the rulers of the Soviet Union at the time considered to be just one of his heresies.

said to himself, so what explanation could be given for his prophesies not coming true? Lenin found the answer in the development of Imperialism, which he said Marx could not have foreseen. In his *Theory of Capitalist Imperialism* (1916) Lenin said that the polarization was indeed taking place, it was not, however, between the European employers and the employees, but between them and colonial peoples; these were now the truly exploited classes, and the capitalists could make their own workers accomplices in this exploitation. Once the colonial people had been set free and could no longer be exploited, the capitalists would be thrown back on getting their profits at the expense of their own proletariat. The polarization would resume and the revolution to overthrow the capitalist system would at last take place. The Soviet championship of the colonial peoples had the aim of strategically and economically weakening the capitalist states that were ranged against Russia, but in addition, colonial independence was expected to bring about the overthrow that Marx had predicted.

> In this latter hope, Lenin was also mistaken. The independence of the colonies did indeed weaken the strategic position of the former imperialist powers, but it had relatively little effect on their economic prosperity. Political imperialism may be a thing of the past, but economic imperialism is still very much alive. Even if that were one day to come to an end and the trade relations between the developing world and their former rulers came to be on a more equal footing, capitalism would suffer from this no more than it does from trade between the developed nations.

In this section we have seen to what extent Marxism was not only a political theory but also very specifically a theory of history. It is now time to look at some other philosophies of history in the nineteenth and twentieth centuries.

CHAPTER 38

Philosophies of History in the 19th & 20th Centuries

Modern Cyclical Theories of History

The attitude of Comte, Spencer, and Marx to history was that the careful and "scientific" study of social and historical facts should make it possible to discover and formulate some wide-ranging universal laws which governed the course of history. Because they lived in a century that showed many advances in science, technology and humanitarianism, these philosophers were basically optimistic. They were convinced that the laws governing history and society ultimately made for progress.

After two devastating world wars, some twentieth-century historians have been more pessimistic. They still believed in universal laws, but these showed that the course of history was not one of continual advances, but rather of a cycle of rise and fall, progress and decline, such as Giambattista Vico had already described.[1] For Oswald Spengler (1880 to 1936) and Arnold Toynbee (1889 to 1975) western civilization showed unmistakeable signs of decline.

Spengler had begun working on his *Decline of the West* in 1908, but published its two volumes in 1918 and 1922 respectively. By that time, of course, Germany had lost the war. The German public in those years was very ready to be comforted by the notion that the decline of their country was part of the wider phenomenon of the decline of the West as a whole. Critics have sometimes accused Spengler of having written the book with that specific agenda in mind, but when we consider that the book was started in 1908 when Germany had no reason to believe that the two generations of progress would not continue, we must acquit Spengler of any such agenda. It is perhaps more helpful to see his ideas as an example of the pessimism of conservatives who, even before the First World War, saw all traditional structures in society, in philosophy, in the arts and in morals giving way to what they thought were decadent develop-

1 As we have seen, Herbert Spencer had also been conscious of the forces of Dissolution in a society, even though his work focussed on those making for progress. It could be said that Marx, too, for all that he believed that history was a story of progress, had taught that most forms of society carried within themselves the seeds of their own destruction, in the course of which new forms would be born which would themselves go through phases of maturity and decay.

ments. W.B. Yeats was struck by this disintegration, and his poem *The Second Coming* (admittedly written just after the war, in 1919) expressed it in the striking line, *"Things fall apart; the centre cannot hold."*

Spengler had drawn on the course of earlier civilizations to make his point about the decline of the West, but in the end it was contemporary Western civilization that was the main focus of his interest. Arnold Toynbee was much more ambitious. The twelve volumes of his *A Study of History*, published between 1922 and 1961, produced a cyclical analysis of no fewer than twenty-six civilizations. As with Spengler, the implication was that our own civilization was now in the state of decline which had been experienced by the other twenty-five, and again this struck a chord with English readers who saw "decadence" in the manifestations of modernism and who, especially after the Second World War, were painfully aware of the decline of British economic and political power.[2] Of course, no "civilization" (however we define that term) has lasted for ever: in each, by definition, there is a period of growth, of maturity, and of decline. Within these three phases Toynbee recognized "routs and rallies" which may be quite lengthy ones - but the overall pattern will assert itself. Toynbee went beyond description, and detected specific factors that he thought accounted for the rise and the decline of civilizations in general.[3] He may have found a particular explanation when studying one or two such civilizations, but he must then have been looking for a similar pattern when reading about the many others. To that extent, he will have imposed a preconceived notion of the material relating to them, selecting facts that may have fitted the pattern and omitting any that might not. For this and much else, he has been heavily criticized. He defined, in a rather arbitrary and sometimes nebulous way, the civilizations whose rise and fall he described - the units are sometimes as large as "Christian Europe", and sometimes as small as the United Provinces. In particular, anyone who makes generalizations about great sweeps of history and twenty-six different civilizations is likely to make mistakes of omission or commission that are sure to be exposed by anyone who is a specialist in any of these civilizations or periods. The more detailed one's knowledge of any period of history is, the more one has to conclude that the immense variety of factors shaping historical events defies any attempt, in both theory and practice, to bring them within the scope of any valid generalization. Toynbee accused such critics of being so preoccupied with the minutiae of scholarship that they could not see the wood for the trees!

2 Toynbee was not as fatalistic as Spengler had been. In the last volumes he had suggested ways in which the west could renew itself - notably by learning from the civilizations of the Far East, from Buddhism and Hinduism.

3 There is no space here to go into the details of what these factors were, but, for example, he thought that civilizations grew in response to the challenge of hardships such as poor soil or climate which force people to conquer better lands. This may be true, for example, of the expansion of Islam, but conversely, Hindu civilization had prospered because of the immense fertility of the Ganges Plain. He thought that the breakdown of a civilization always begins as the result of internal weakness. This again is often true, but surely not always: Minoan civilization might have flourished for much longer had there not been the catastrophic earthquake which destroyed it, and some civilizations can be described as internally stable and prosperous, not at all in decline, and weak only in comparison with those that overwhelmed it, such as those who were destroyed by the Mongols.

The Romantic Stress on the Particular

Belief in universal laws had been a characteristic of eighteenth-century classical philosophy,[4] but the outlook of many nineteenth-century philosophers of history could be said to have been shaped by the opposition to Classicism, namely by Romanticism. A particular aspect of the Romantics, it will be recalled, was that they valued the particular rather than the universal. They had, therefore, been suspicious of general laws which claimed to apply to history, and in one way or another, they had emphasized uniqueness and difference. The historians who were influenced by this outlook fall into three groups, respectively stressing the uniqueness of each nation; of great individuals; and of each period and of each fact.

The Uniqueness of Each Nation

The father of this school of philosophers, Johann Gottfried Herder (1744 to 1803), has already been discussed in Part II (Chapter 30). The French *philosophes*, it will be remembered, had, in accordance with their general outlook, always laid stress on what all human beings had in common. They had also managed to persuade most of the continent's educated classes that the criteria of a civilized society were universal, based on Antiquity, the High Renaissance and, in its ultimate manifestation, on the culture of seventeenth- and eighteenth-century France. The reaction against this idea had begun with the German *Sturm und Drang* movement in the 1770s. This resented the imposition on Germany of a French culture which was seen as cosmopolitan and standard-setting; it protested against the use of the French language which was so fashionable at the courts of Europe; and it called upon Germans to be proud of their own and very different cultural heritage. In the 1780s, Herder had written his great work, in which he showed that *every* people has an individual culture and national character, expressed in the language of its people.

This idea fitted in with the growth of nationalism throughout the continent, and it led to the writing of nationalistic history. In the end, even the French gave up the idea that their culture was essentially a cosmopolitan one, which happened to be expressed in French only because France was the most developed carrier of that culture. French historians began to look for the roots of their own culture and to bring out the unique character of their own country. The lead in this was taken by Jules Michelet (1798 to 1894), whose poetic and rhapsodic style painted a memorable picture of the course of French history. In Berlin, his contemporary Heinrich von Treitschke (1834 to 1894) was the leading historian of German patriotism. Such historians were imbued with a love of their country. It does not necessarily follow that they denigrated the culture of their neighbours, though when they felt in conflict with them, the dangers of doing so were obvious; they were, after all, avowed champions of their country.

Once championship was avowed as one of the aims of the historian, there was no reason why it should be confined to a nation; it could equally be devoted to a cause. Michelet intended his work to be a passionate defence of the People of France; Augustin Thierry (1795 to 1856) saw his task as writing his-

4 See Chapter 29.

tory to extol constitutionalism, "In 1817 [he was writing in 1820] my predominant concern was to contribute my share to the triumph of constitutionalism. As a result I turned to historical works to find corroboration of my beliefs." His studies then showed him that "this country has never lacked champions of justice and of liberty".

The socialist Jean Jaures (1859 to 1914) likewise put his cards on the table when he wrote, in his introduction to a book openly called *The Socialist History of the French Revolution* (1901 to 1909), "My interpretation of history will ... be marked by both the materialism of Marx and the mysticism of Michelet."

> A modern historian who admitted his partisanship quite so openly would be a little suspect, although of course the commitment of, say, E.P.Thompson (1924 to 1993) in his great *The Making of the English Working Class* (1963) leaves his reader in little doubt about where his heart lies. He engaged wholeheartedly in fighting for the Left in demonstrations, speeches and newspaper articles, and these carried additional weight because he had such a great reputation as a scholar, but he would have claimed that *as a professional historian* he should not allow his partisanship to be as open as Thierry's had been.
>
> At the same time it is widely accepted among contemporary scholars that, although a historian needs to be as fair-minded as he can, it is impossible for him not to allow his outlook to influence the kind of history he writes. Every historian is a child of his time; and tends to focus on aspects of history that appear relevant to the concerns his own society. So revisionism is absolutely inevitable in history. Leaving aside the influence of newly discovered or released documents, every generation brings its own experience to the study of history. It is much more difficult for the generation that lived through the Second World War to write in a detached way about the Nazi period. Anyone, for example, who said that Hitler's economic ideas before the war were not unintelligent would be accused of trying to whitewash him; the man had become so demonized that *everything* he did appears tainted with evil. However, with every succeeding generation the Second World War becomes more distant. Eventually, some of these issues will be less emotionally laden and historians will look with the same *relative* detachment on Hitler with which they look on Robespierre or Napoleon. The generations for whom Robespierre or Napoleon were figures of only yesterday had found that detachment very much more difficult.

For French historians in particular, history was not a dispassionate study. They made no bones about taking sides – indeed they felt that it was their responsibility, through their work as historians, to contribute to the political causes in which they believed. Great French historians like François Guizot (1787 to 1874) and Adolphe Thiers (1707 to 1877) were also leading politicians and indeed Prime Ministers. They were, to use a modern French word, *engagés*, and it is not surprising that the call for *engagement* or commitment would be a characteristic of much French philosophy, from the passionate involvement in current affairs of Voltaire in the eighteenth century, to Michelet, Guizot and Thiers in the nineteenth century and of Sartre in the twentieth century.

If a historian champions a cause so vigorously, he always does so because he takes a moral position towards it, and he will not feel uncomfortable in proclaiming that it is part of a historian's job to deliver moral judgments. This view was most specifically proclaimed by the distinguished British historian, Lord Acton (1834 to 1902). He also called for commitment, though this was not to a particular political cause – we shall meet him again a little later in this chapter as someone who called for the strictest neutrality in the writing of history. How can one be strictly neutral if one feels, as Acton did, that it is the responsibility of the historian to sit in moral judgment on the characters with whom he deals? This is what he said in 1895 during his Inaugural Address as Regius Professor of History at Oxford, "I exhort you never to debase the moral currency or to lower the standard of rectitude, but to try others by the same maxim that governs your own lives, and to suffer no man and no cause to escape the undying penalty which history has the power to inflict on wrong." And he endorsed a saying of the Duc de Broglie, "Beware of too much explaining lest we end by too much excusing."

So, on this view, the historian is a judge – often, as it were, a hanging judge. There are problems about this in any case. What is added to the understanding of *history* by passing moral judgments about it? Why not set out the facts as impartially as you can and then let the *reader* come to whatever moral judgments he feels like making? In addition, there is the fact that the moral judgments of one age are not necessarily the same as those of another. One wonders what moral judgments one might wish to make today on certain social and political attitudes that the good Lord Acton unthinkingly held in 1895 as a child of his time. Of course, today we deplore religious intolerance or imperialism, but a good historian should not project his own moral standards on those periods when most men (and many good men among them, too) saw no wrong in it. What is the point of inflicting on them the penalty of moral execration? It only gets in the way of *understanding*, which is surely the most important task of the historian. We need not *sympathize*, but we do need to *empathize* with people of past ages, to try to understand *their* way of thinking. It may make one feel better to express disapproval of their ideas and behaviour, but that feeling has nothing to do with history.

The Uniqueness of Each Individual

The greatest exponent of the idea that history is shaped by great individuals was Thomas Carlyle (1795 to 1881). In a set of lectures published as *On Heroes and Hero Worship* (1840), he proclaimed that "History ... is at bottom the History of the Great Men who have worked here." He referred specifically to Luther:

> This ... is an age that as it were denies the existence of great men; denies the desirability of great men. Show our critics a great man, a Luther for example, they begin to what they call 'account' for him... He was the 'creature of the Time', they say; the Time called him forth, the Time did everything, he nothing – but what we the little critic could have done too! This seems to me but melancholy work. The Time called forth? Alas, we have known Times call loudly enough for their great man; but not to find him when they called! He was not there; Providence had not sent him; the Time, calling its loudest, had to go down to confusion and wreck because he would not come when called.

We have here, of course, the exact opposite of the *structuralist* view of history which we have discussed in connection with Marx.

I think myself that the structuralist view is a good way of explaining the rise and fall of politicians in a democracy. They are voted into power because they reflect the mood of the times; they fall when they no longer do so. It is rather different with dictatorships. A dictator is sometimes voted into power, so that at that point he, too, reflects his times. Or he may stage a coup, but this, too, will be success-

> ful only if the forces that support it are structurally significant. If he then consolidates his power and becomes absolute, then he can *impose* his view upon the structure of the society, rather than reflect it. It then matters enormously whether the dictator is paranoid and ruthless like Stalin, megalomaniac and insanely racist like Hitler, or relatively sensible and benign, like Napoleon III.

Carlyle, like Michelet, saw history as an art and as a branch of literature. The historian must use his imagination. Of course he cannot give his imagination unbridled rein; he must study the documents and other evidence, but his task is to paint a vivid picture of the past for the general public. The nineteenth century produced a great deal of historical research for its own sake and Carlyle despised the plodding scholars he called Dry-as-Dust.

Naturally, Carlyle was equally opposed to the ideas of the Positivists, and he would have scorned the view advanced by J.B. Bury (1861 to 1927) in his Inaugural Address (1902) as Regius Professor of History at Cambridge, "I may remind you that history is not a branch of literature... History is a science, no less and no more." Bury was specifically answered in the following year by G.M. Trevelyan (1876 to 1962) in an essay later republished, this time without naming Bury, under the title of *Clio, A Muse* (1913). In it ,Tevelyan denied that history could ever be a science like the physical sciences. It has no practical utility like the physical sciences. If historical phenomena "repeat themselves", they do so only occasionally and then only in a very general way and never in exact terms.[5] Most scientific phenomena, however, can be isolated and then reproduced in exactly the same form every single time. History cannot deduce laws of general application, but, even if it could do so, "the deeds themselves are more interesting than their causes and effects, and are fortunately ascertainable with much greater precision". The historian's first duty is, "to tell the story. For, irrespective of 'cause and effect', we want to know the thoughts and deeds of Cromwell's soldiers, as one of the higher products and achievements of the human race, a thing never to be repeated, that once took shape and was." So one function of history is to educate the feelings and to uplift the reader. It "should be both written and read with intellectual passion", and so it must be well written, "History and literature cannot be fully comprehended, still less fully enjoyed, except in connection with one another."

Gibbon would have agreed, and so would Trevelyan's great-uncle, Macaulay, who had written, "I shall not be satisfied unless I produce something which shall for a few days supersede the last fashionable novel on the tables of young ladies." Gibbon, Macaulay and Trevelyan and other great literary historians (like Carlyle and Michelet) were indeed immensely popular and scholarly at the same time. Even so, Trevelyan's essay was something of a rearguard action; a more austere approach to history was by then in fashion.

The Uniqueness of Each Period and of Each Fact

Unlike those historians who would call history in aid of causes or of morality, there sprang up a school of historians who demanded that the subject be

5 One may, for instance, see similarities in the empires of Napoleon, the Kaiser and Hitler which all failed because they overreached themselves, but then it is easy to forget that there have been other empires as great as theirs which have lasted for centuries.

approached with absolute impartiality, and that each fact and each period be studied without any preconceptions. This school of thought originated in Germany and its most notable exponents were Barthold Niebuhr (1776 to 1831) and Leopold von Ranke (1795 to 1886). In 1824, Ranke coined the famous phrase that the purpose of history was to study *wie es eigentlich gewesen* (approximately translated: "how things actually were" or "what actually happened"). The best way of making sure that we achieved this goal was to go to the archives and other original sources (like artifacts, inscriptions etc.) and to be extremely suspicious of all secondary authorities which were likely either with conscious or unconscious preconceptions to distort it. The most dangerous distortion came from judging an earlier period by the criteria of a later one. As Ranke put it, each period is, *"immediate to God"* – we should consider it for its own sake. History should neither judge the past nor instruct the present for the benefit of future ages. "The strict presentation of the facts, contingent and unattractive though they may be, is undoubtedly the supreme law."

When we describe the connection between facts as contingent (from the Latin *tangere,* to touch), we mean that it is not "necessary", governed by some inescapable law. A contingent connection can be a purely chance or random one.

For example: a handful of rulers happened to die without direct heirs, and as a result a series of very disparate lands – Austria, Hungary, Bohemia, the Netherlands, and Spain – found their destinies knitted together under the Habsburg dynasty. This would not have happened if some of those rulers had lived to have children of their own, and the history of their countries and indeed of the whole of Europe would have been radically different.

In a famous phrase (1935) H.A.L. Fisher (1865 to 1940) was to claim that the historian, "should recognize in the development of human destinies the play of the contingent and the unforeseen". He had been unable to discern in history, "a plot, a rhythm, a predetermined pattern ... only one emergency following another as wave follows upon wave".

It seems absurd that one should have to choose between two philosophies of history: one that maintains that all causes in history are contingent, and one that claims that they are all necessary. If Fisher really could not detect certain influences on history which are inescapable (economic trends seem to me to be an example), he would seem to have been excessively blinkered. On the other hand, to deny the role of chance events (unexpected deaths, natural disasters like the earthquake that destroyed Cretan civilization, diseases like the Black Death, herrings unaccountably moving their spawning grounds away from the North-West coast of Europe and so destroying the prosperity of the fishing trade there) seems to be equally obtuse.

In fact, both Ranke and Fisher knew that it is not really possible to write any history unless the historian can discover and set out a connection between contingent facts which, while not exactly necessary – the possibility of alternative connections is always there – does reveal what Ranke called *"the unity and progress of events":*

We see before us a series of events which follow one another and are conditioned by one another. If I say 'conditioned', I certainly do not mean conditioned through absolute necessity. The important point is rather that human freedom makes its appearance

> everywhere, and the greatest attraction of history lies in the fact that it deals with the scenes of this freedom.

When he talks about "human freedom", Ranke is thinking of individual quirkiness or decision-making as contingent causes in history. If only Stalin had not been so paranoid, the argument would run, the history of the Soviet Union would have been different. Germany lost the Second World War because Hitler not only chose to attack the Soviet Union, but compounded the error by choosing to declare war on the United States after Pearl Harbour when he was under no obligation to do so. He therefore had to fight the United States who would otherwise have concentrated exclusively on the war against Japan and might never have considered fighting a war in North Africa or in Europe.

It should be clear from what has already been said that it is not only "human freedom" that impinges contingently on history: so do phenomena like disease, natural disasters etc.

Ranke's approach was immensely influential. So we find Lord Acton, as editor of that great collaborative work, *The Cambridge Modern History* (1899), including the following injunction in the instructions to his international team of contributors: "Our scheme requires that nothing shall reveal the country, the religion, or the party to which the writers belong... Our Waterloo must be one that satisfies French and English, Germans and Dutch alike; ... nobody [should be able to] tell, without examining the list of authors, where the Bishop of Oxford laid down the pen, and where Fairbairn or Gasquet, Liebermann or Harrison took it up."

Such impartiality and fairness are certainly goals to which most reputable historians aspire, but they do not have the confidence of a Ranke or an Acton that this can be achieved. For one thing, they will be almost as suspicious of original sources as they are of secondary ones. One can establish what an original source says, but it may itself not tell the truth, and could have a conscious or unconscious agenda of its own. For another thing, "the unity and progress of events" do not establish themselves out of all those contingent facts: they have to be arranged by the historian. He will have his own view about which relationships are significant and which are not, and is likely to pay insufficient attention to whatever does not fit in with the "unity" that he claims is there. So the modern historian is much more aware than were Ranke or (in the extract above) Lord Acton[6] of the impossibility of complete objectivity.

Empathy

Historians do try to be as impartial as they can be, and they also try to respect Ranke's doctrine that each period is autonomous and must not be judged by the criteria belonging to a later period. The idea was not new: Vico, in the eighteenth century, had already made that point.[7] It means that the historian has to try to immerse himself as best he can in the thought-world of the period he is studying, and some nineteenth-century historians developed this idea further. Thus, N.D. Fustel de Coulanges (1830 to 1889) in his Inaugural Lecture as Pro-

6 It will not have escaped the reader that the Lord Acton of the 1895 Inaugural Lecture (see p. 459 above) preached a message very different from that sent by him as editor to his contributors only a very few years later.

7 See p. 354 above.

fessor at Strasbourg (1862) made the rather Hegelian point that one must study the thought of a period before one can understand its institutions. This could have been taken as a criticism of the Marxist view that one can deduce the nature of the thought from an examination of the institutions, which often leads to misunderstanding of the latter, such as Fustel de Coulanges thought had misled Napoleon when he copied the institutions of Antiquity (Consuls, Senators etc.) without really understanding the spirit that had animated them in Ancient Rome.

An extension of this idea would criticize the notion that one can export the institutions of a colonial power to newly independent colonies. Parliamentary institutions that have grown out of the thought-world of Britain will look very different when they are bestowed as a parting gift by the outgoing imperial power on former colonies whose thought-world is very different.

The German Wilhelm Dilthey (1833 to 1911) coined the word *Geisteswissenschaft* (study of ideas). He said that only by steeping himself in the ideas of a period can the scholar achieve that *Erlebnis* (experience) that is necessary for the true historian. That idea was taken further still by Benedetto Croce (1866 to 1952) and by R.G. Collingwood (1869 to 1943). Collingwood wrote that, in the last resort, "all history is the history of thought"; any history that neglects this is mere chronicling. He elaborated:

> If you can enter into the mind of [neolithic] man and make his thoughts your own, you can write his history, and not otherwise. If you cannot, all you can do is to arrange his relics in some kind of tidy order, and the result is ethnology or archaeology, but not history. Yet the reality of neolithic man was an historical reality. When he made a certain implement, he had a purpose in mind; the implement came into being as an expression of his spirit, and if you treat it as non-spiritual, that is only because of the failure of your historical imagination.

In this way, history becomes the recreation of past thought-processes in the present, and it is in this sense that Croce wrote that, "all history is contemporary history". We have to *escape* from the present if we want to write properly about the past.

Many historians believe that is impossible, and if they were to agree with Croce's phrase, it would be because for them it would mean the very opposite of what Croce had meant. To them, all history is contemporary in the sense that it tells us about the preconceptions which a historian is bound to bring to the study of the past, so that in some sense it becomes a reflection of *his* present. We can learn nearly as much from reading a history book about the ideas that were contemporary with the historian as about the period of which he is writing. This was a point made by E.H. Carr (1892 to 1982) among others. We have already seen it illustrated among the historians who are openly committed to a cause – we have seen how, in a more democratic age, historians like Michelet have taken an interest in the lives of ordinary people and broadened the subject, which had previously confined itself largely to the political history made by kings, ministers, prelates, generals and the like, out into social history. Then the victory of Marxism in the Soviet Union made a growing number of historians, whether committed to Marxism or not, concentrate on analyzing economic factors in history. Sometimes such broadening is not so much a case of championing causes as of establishing the earlier history of aspects that are of particular interest to the present. All institutions were undergoing great changes in Victorian times, and this is perhaps reflected in studies of the functioning in the Middle Ages of the administration by T.F. Tout (1855 to 1929), of the legal system by Frederick Maitland (1850 to 1906), and of parliament by William Stubbs (1825 to 1901).

The way in which the history of Parliament was written came under special examination by Herbert Butterfield (1900 to 1979). Macaulay's famous five-volume *History of England* (1849 to 1861) actually confined itself to the reigns of James II and William III, and it celebrated the Glorious Revolution for making England safe for parliamentary government. Although many Tories had taken part in that achievement, the Whigs (of whom Macaulay was one) looked back on 1688 as an essentially Whig revolution. Although the Crown still held and exercised very considerable prerogative powers under William III, the Revolution laid down the basis on which future parliamentary sovereignty would rest. By the time Macaulay's History was written, the power of the Crown had been so thoroughly eroded that one could legitimately speak of the sovereignty of Parliament. It was with that perspective that Macaulay treated the history of those two reigns. Any resistance to that development met with scant respect, both for what it stood for and, more importantly, for having been a losing cause. It was Butterfield who labelled this way of writing history as "the Whig interpretation of History" in a little book of that title in 1931. Here he pointed out the danger of writing history, consciously or unconsciously, solely with a view to what contributed to the present, and of neglecting, if not maligning, what one might call "lost causes". It leads to a possible underestimation of what lost causes have contributed to the shaping of the winning ideas, and it may distort the history of those periods when it was not at all certain which were the winning and which the losing causes. In any case, the historian should try to analyze even "losing" causes with the same care and empathy as the others.

> It may not be totally irrelevant to consider that, in Butterfield's lifetime, there was some disillusionment with the failure of parliaments to deal with economic crises. E.M. Forster (1879 to 1970) could raise only Two Cheers for Democracy;[8] if there were some qualifications about the virtues of parliamentary democracy in the twentieth century, there was perhaps some interest in the more authoritarian approaches to the politics of the seventeenth century.

So history is not something "out there"; even for the most conscientious historian there is bound to be a subjective element within it. Of course, we ought to try to be as scrupulous as we can be. Accepting the subjective element does not mean that we have absolute freedom to make of history what we will.

In that sense, the historians we have discussed convey a different atmosphere from the existentialist thinkers who will be the subject of the following chapters. The latter are concerned with the decisions we make in our own life, and they stress that in that area we *do* have complete freedom and that we need to embrace this positively. We have the responsibility to *be* subjective, to shape our own life as we wish it to be lived - but then the existentialists are dealing with individuals, and not with history.

8 The title for a collection of essays he had written from 1936 onwards.

CHAPTER 39

Nietzsche and Bergson

FRIEDERICH NIETZSCHE
1844 to 1900

Nietzsche was born in Röcken, in Prussian Saxony, where his father was a Lutheran pastor. At school Nietzsche was already a brilliant classical scholar; he studied at the Universities of Bonn and Leipzig, and in 1869, aged only twenty-four, he became Professor of Classical Theology at the University of Basel. He volunteered to serve as a medical orderly in the Franco-Prussian war of 1870/71, but he had been sickly since childhood,[1] and after six months he had to leave the army, returned to academic work in Basel, and took Swiss citizenship.

Dionysianism and Apollonianism

Nietzsche quickly damaged his reputation with most of his academic colleagues with his first book, *The Birth of Tragedy*, published in 1871. Its vivid prose was felt to be unscholarly, and he challenged the prevailing notion that the most admirable aspect of the culture of Ancient Greece was the "noble simplicity and serene grandeur"[2] it had displayed in fifth century Athens. Worst of all was the way in which Nietzsche used his account of Greek antiquity to make strongly controversial statements about Christianity and other aspects of the culture of his own time.

Nietzsche had lost his religious beliefs at the age of sixteen, soon after his confirmation. While he was at the University of Leipzig, he had discovered the philosophy of Schopenhauer. Schopenhauer had said that even those who have lost their religious faith can, through art, and especially through music, escape for a while from the misery of earthly life and have a glimpse of the transcendent.[3] Nietzsche did not have much use for the notion of the transcendent, but he shared with Schopenhauer the longing for escape - not so much from a world that was miserable and full of suffering (he believed that suffering was

1 It is not too fanciful to see him compensating later for his own physical weaknesses by creating the ideal of the Superman, the Hero - and though, as we shall see, these ideals are not specifically physical or military, they do carry an overtone of the prowess to which Nietzsche's health did not allow him realistically to aspire.

2 The phrase had been coined by Johann Winckelmann, the influential archaeologist and art historian, in 1765. Matthew Arnold, a contemporary of Nietzsche's, still spoke the same language as Winckelmann when he claimed that "the pursuit of perfection is the pursuit of sweetness and light". (*Culture and Anarchy*, 1869).

3 See p. 409 above.

something to overcome, not to be escaped from) as from what was humdrum, savourless, sterile in its rationalism and ignoble. It was from this point of view that he examined the art of Greece.

He identified two strands in all the arts, which he called the Dionysian and the Apollonian. The Dionysian element is the earliest. Under the influence of its rites, worshippers abandon themselves to what is intoxicating, both literally and metaphorically. Dionysus was, after all, the god of wine, and under its influence we lose the inhibitions of reason; our "natural" self comes into its own. The worshippers of Dionysus are taken over by the life force, by wild (creative and destructive) urges,[4] so that they cease to be artists (*Künstler*) and themselves become works of art (*Kunstwerke*); they lose their individual identity and become as one with the stream of life. In their ecstasy, they embrace not only the joys, but also the terrors of life – they "triumphantly affirm existence in all its darkness and horror". They feel god-like: everything is possible, and they break through all limits and frontiers set by everyday life. It is all a long way away from Winckelmann's "noble simplicity and serene grandeur".

It is clear that throughout his life Nietzsche felt a deep emotional identification with the Dionysian element, as one would expect of someone who was essentially of a romantic rather than a classical disposition. Nevertheless, as a literary craftsman himself, he knew that these outpourings must be moulded, and it is the task of the later, Apollonian strand in art to do that. Ideally, the Apollonian element does not want to destroy the vitality of the Dionysian one, but it aims to channel and so in a sense restrain it in order to give it some shape. This requires some detachment, some control, a sense of moderation and a use of reason, but, if the Apollonian element is *properly* used, the sheer diffuseness of the Dionysian element is concentrated, and the resulting work of art should become more powerful and more telling. The balance between the two elements is a delicate one; in Greek drama the process of striking it had begun with Homer (ninth or eighth century BC) and Nietzsche believed that it had reached perfection in Aeschylus (525 to 455 BC) and in Sophocles (496 to 404 BC).

Then, according to Nietzsche, the balance was destroyed by the influence of Socrates (470 to 399 BC) and of Plato (428 to 347 BC). He thought that it was already no longer present in the last of the three great Greek tragedians, Euripides (484 to 406 BC). Socrates and Plato were no longer receptive of the Dionysian element – indeed they distrusted it, we have only to see how suspicious Plato was of the theatre and how he would have censored certain kinds of music.[5] Myths, which in the Dionysian culture were experienced as part of an ecstatic religious ritual, were now the object of rational analysis, and were regarded by Plato, as at best, a useful tool of social control. The incessant critical and questioning techniques of the Socratic-Platonic approach sucked the life out of man's contact with his inner self, and became, in a favourite phrase of Nietzsche's, "life-denying". This was reinforced by the way in which Plato claimed that this life is but a pale and imperfect shadow of the perfection stored up in the transcendent world of Ideas.[6] Nietzsche's contemporaries saw Socra-

4 We think of the relationship between drunkenness and violence.

5 See pp. 28ff.

6 See p. 32 above.

tes and Plato as the greatest of the Greeks. Homer was widely read, of course, but was generally seen as an inferior, because a more naïve dramatist than his illustrious successors. Nietzsche challenged this view by exalting the merits of Homeric and pre-Socratic Greece over the Socratic and post-Socratic period.

> This valuing of the earlier, more "primitive" or archaic aspects of art was of course also in tune with general Romantic thought,[7] and it has greatly widened our modern appreciation of art. Shortly after Nietzsche's death, Picasso taught us to see, for example, African art with new eyes.

Nietzsche believed that European culture has suffered from life-denial ever since the time of Socrates and Plato. Life-denial, Nietzsche thought, was central to Christianity with its insistence that man's natural instincts were sinful and needed to be subdued, and its rejection of this world for the next. Moreover, although the Age of Reason had done much to undermine the teaching of Christianity, it had then presented its own arid rationalism as a substitute.

Nietzsche then narrowed his focus still further, to the Germany of his age. It, too, was suffering from the life-denying disease. Education in Germany was too rational, too much imbued with the scientific spirit, too specialized, but help was at hand - in the music of Richard Wagner.

Nietzsche had met Wagner in 1868. Both men shared Schopenhauer's exalted view of the role of music, and now Nietzsche fell under the spell both of Wagner's music and of his message. After the failure of the 1848 revolutions in which Wagner had taken part, the composer had become disillusioned by politics, and preached in all seriousness that society cannot be transformed by politicians but only by artists.[8] He himself offered salvation by rescuing music from the commercialized triviality of his time and by creating in his music dramas the fusion of all the arts (the *Gesamtkunstwerk*) and the mythic and communal power of the drama of ancient Greece.[9]

By the time Nietzsche was writing *The Birth of Tragedy*, Wagner was in the middle of the *Ring* cycle. That music struck Nietzsche at the time as having the perfect blend between Dionysian passion and Apollonian control; the content, like that of some of Wagner's earlier operas, was a celebration of myths whose heroes and heroines life-affirmingly broke through conventional constraints and divine commands. Wagner had provided Germany with the possibility of a spiritual awakening, and after that it would be the mission of Germany to give a cultural lead to the rest of the world.

Nationalism, Germans and Jews

Would the Germans understand this mission and the nature of the leadership Nietzsche hoped they would provide? About this he was very pessimistic. True, after unification in 1871 there were many in the country who believed in the leadership of Europe, and who claimed that the victory represented the superiority of German culture, but Nietzsche believed that 1871 was only the victory of the German state, and he thought that the nationalism which fol-

7 See p. 326 above.

8 *Das Kunstwerk der Zukunft (The Artwork of the Future)*, 1849.

9 See Bryan Magee - *Wagner and Philosophy*, p. 86

lowed that victory was the very reverse of the culture he had in mind. This Prussian who had become a Swiss citizen in 1870 had no love for nationalism. On the contrary, he detested it and disdained a state which encouraged it. For the Germans of his time, taken *en masse*, he had nothing but contempt:

> One pays heavily for coming to power: power makes stupid. The Germans – once they were called the people of thinkers: do they think at all today? The Germans are now bored with the spirit, the Germans now mistrust the spirit; politics swallows up all serious concern for really spiritual matters. *Deutschland, Deutschland über Alles* – I fear that was the end of German philosophy.[10]

The Germans were intoxicated by nationalism, an emotion of the masses and of the herd which Nietzsche so despised. Throughout his life he looked for élite *individuals* who were free of the herd mentality: he did not believe in superior qualities of nations or of races.

German antisemitism he described as "the instinct of a people whose type is still weak and indefinite".[11] In any case he rejected antisemitism. It was a despicable herd-emotion and an example of *ressentiment*.[12] Moreover, he respected much of what the Jews had contributed to civilization: they had preserved the "ring of culture" that connected modern Europe to ancient Greece; they had produced "the noblest human being [Christ], the purest philosopher [Spinoza], the mightiest book [the Hebrew Bible], and the most efficient moral law of the world".[13] Under their kings the Jews of Biblical times showed many of the heroic qualities which he admired;[14] only when the priestly period began (Nietzsche associated it with Isaiah), and especially after the Diaspora, were they forced into the meekness of turning the other cheek, which Nietzsche so despised when the Jews who became Christians incorporated it into their teaching. He also admired those Jews of his own time who had emancipated themselves from the slave religion which Judaism had become, had adopted none of the contemporary herd-ideologies – German nationalism, Zionism, or Socialism – which Nietzsche despised, and had instead created their own values.

Nietzsche, like the Nazis, was an advocate of eugenics, a notion that, when applied to humans, is rightly very suspect today, but was quite widely held by intellectuals in Nietzsche's own time. (They were worried that the poor and ignorant – and therefore *ipso facto* the weak and degenerate – would outbreed and swamp the educated classes.) The Nazis approved of such sentences as "the species requires that the ill-constituted, weak, degenerate should perish".[15] Nietzsche does not discuss how this should be achieved. It sounds as if he believed that nature would do the job, as the weak naturally go to the wall –

10 *Götzendämmerung*, 1888.

11 *Beyond Good and Evil*.

12 For *ressentiment* see below, p. 473.

13 In *Human, All Too Human* (1878 to 1880)

14 In *Beyond Good and Evil* (1886) he would write: "In the Jewish Old Testament ... there are human beings, things and speeches in so grand a style that Greek and Indian literature have nothing to compare with it. With terror and reverence one stands before these tremendous remnants of what man once was."

15 *The Will to Power*, jottings of 1887, organized and published posthumously by Nietzsche's sister. We shall discuss below how we should estimate these notes, which he wrote down in the feverish state that preceded his mental breakdown in the following year, from which he never recovered.

but then in other places, as we shall see below,[16] he specifically rejects the notion that nature sees to it that the fittest survive.

Animal breeders know that breeds can often be improved by introducing a desirable strain from another breed, and what would have particularly upset the Nazis is that Nietzsche advocated that the best Germans and the best Jews should intermarry, "It would be quite interesting to see if one could not add or breed to the hereditary art of commanding and obeying [of the Junkers] the genius of money and patience, and above all some of the esprit and intellect [of the Jews, to produce] the breeding of a new caste which would govern Europe."[17]

> So there can be no doubt that he would have deplored the antisemitism, the vulgarity and the state worship of the Nazi regime, though the Nazis were to claim Nietzsche as one of their own. This is due partly to the fact that his sister Elizabeth Förster-Nietzsche (1846 to 1935) became his literary executrix after his death. At that time she already had a proto-Nazi ideology,[18] in accordance with which she edited and often forged or re-wrote her brother's works, some aspects of which she suppressed altogether. When the Nazi party emerged, she would become an enthusiastic supporter. The Nazis then perverted some of Nietzsche's ideas still further to justify their brutal practices and racial theories. For years, Nietzsche became associated with Nazism. His contempt for democracy and for socialism also did not endear him to the postwar world, nor did his admiration for virtues that are most immediately associated with militarism. At least now he has been rehabilitated as someone who would not have had any truck with the most repellent aspects of Nazism.

Nietzsche found to his dismay that Wagner espoused this vulgar nationalism and antisemitism. Wagner compounded the offence with the ideas in *Parsifal*, the opera on which he had started working in 1877. Nietzsche saw it as a Christian allegory and a sell-out of the joyous paganism of the *Ring*. That year, the friendship between the two men came to an end. In 1888, Nietzsche would publish *The Case of Wagner*, in which he condemned the work of his former friend as decadent He was also critical of its musical language: the Apollonian element was too weak and Nietzsche had come to describe it as a formless "anarchy of atoms".[19]

"Everything is False"

The Birth of Tragedy had set out to be an appraisal of Greek culture, and then became a vehicle for certain philosophical attitudes and reflections on the state of German culture. The former were not particularly original in themselves,

16 See p. 472 below.

17 *Beyond Good and Evil* (1886).

18 In 1885 she had married the rabidly anti-Semitic Bernard Förster, who, in 1881, had organized a petition with 267,000 signatures to Bismarck against the Jews. Nietzsche had written to her that by this marriage she had "gone over to my antipodes". In 1886, Bernard and Elizabeth, despairing of Germany, had gone to Paraguay to found there a purely Aryan colony called Nueva Germania. Bernard committed suicide in 1889 because the colony was heading for failure, and after it finally went bankrupt in 1891, Elizabeth returned to Germany.

19 Nietzsche repeated many of his criticisms in *Nietzsche Contra Wagner*, the very last work he wrote before his mental collapse in 1888. So both his first and his last book were written under Wagner's influence.

restating, as they did, the old Romantic response to an excessive concentration on reason. In *Human, All Too Human*, written between 1878 and 1880, Nietzsche engaged more specifically with philosophy and began to lay the foundations for his own idiosyncratic position.

Nietzsche rejected the whole tradition of distinguishing between the world and our perceptions of it. The latest manifestations of this school of thought had been the philosophies of Kant and of Schopenhauer, with their notion of a noumenal reality lying behind phenomenal appearances. Nietzsche, at this stage of his life, declared that such metaphysical statements have no validity – and then promptly made a metaphysical assertion of his own: we could never grasp reality because its essence was a perpetual Becoming, therefore a constant flux.[20] Human nature tries to master this Reality by turning Becoming into Being, but we can do this only by imposing artificial patterns on the flux, and then proclaim these patterns as truths. The patterns themselves are based on our experiences, for these are all we have to go on, but people's experiences differ, so they cannot provide a standard of truth. Nietzsche rejected the notion that we can accept the experiences which most of mankind has had to give us an indication of the truth, as he thought of the majority as a "common herd"; he despised any view of the truth that might depend on their experience. No, "everything is false", Nietzsche proclaimed challengingly. We make our own truths for our own purposes (an idea which at the time he called *Perspectivism*). All our ideas are merely "fictions" which we need for our survival, and, as he will argue later,[21] the common herd will need fictions for its survival which are very different from those needed by nobler individuals.

However, we all, herd and masters alike, find certain of these fictions so useful and indeed so necessary in practice, that they tend to become unquestioned assumptions. These include the laws of causality, the laws of logic, and certain scientific hypotheses. So, "Truth is that sort of error without which a particular type of living being could not live."

> That had been argued by Hume, when he said that there is no philosophical reason for accepting such notions as cause and effect, but that in practice we could not manage our lives without them.[22]

With his philological training, Nietzsche was also aware that many assumptions become so deeply embedded in our very language that we can only speak in forms which assume truths that do not actually exist, "A philosophical mythology lies hidden in language, and it breaks out again at every moment, however careful one may be."

> Already Nietzsche has proved himself to be a seminal thinker. The ideas in this book will have resonances long into the twentieth century. The idea of flux not only dates back to Heraclitus, but forward to Henri Bergson's *Creative Evolution* of 1907. The concept that we fashion our own truths will be at the

20 One could assume that Kant's *Ding an sich*, though we could not perceive it directly, was nevertheless stable, as the categories through which we interpret its signals produce fairly stable results – see p. 370 above. For Schopenhauer, the ultimate reality was an ever striving Will – p. 403 above – which was a little closer to Nietzsche's dynamic view of reality.

21 primarily in *Beyond Good and Evil*, 1886 – see p. 475 below.

22 See pp. 288f above.

> heart of twentieth-century Existentialism, and his perception that our thoughts are to a large extent conditioned and limited by our linguistic equipment will be developed in various ways by Bertrand Russell, linguistic philosophers like John Searle, and by structuralists, especially Noam Chomsky.[23]

Nietzsche was by now thoroughly out of tune with the academic orthodoxies of his time, and he continued to suffer from bad health. In 1879 he resigned his Chair and began a life of restless travelling. From 1881 onwards, the base to which he returned from his journeys was the Swiss mountain village resort of Sils Maria. His writings broke still further away from the style approved by academics. He resorted increasingly to aphorism instead of formal argument or exposition, and he never earned any money from the books that poured out from his pen: *Human, All Too Human* (1878 to 1880); *Daybreak (Morgenröthe)* (1881); *The Joyous Science (Die fröhliche Wissenschaft)* (1882); *Thus Spake Zarathustra* (1883 to 1885 – printed privately); *the Genealogy of Morals* (1887); and the notes for the posthumously published *The Will to Power* (1885 to 1888).

The Superman

In *Thus Spake Zarathustra*, written between 1883 and 1885, Nietzsche considered how certain individuals can transcend what is "human, all too human".

> There is a certain inconsistency in Nietzsche in what it means to be human. In *The Birth of Tragedy* he had given the impression that the Dionysian element was a valuable part of human nature, to which we ought to be true. It was not "all too human"; it was not something we ought to overcome; and he had condemned Socrates and Plato for trying to smother it. In *Zarathustra*, he preached that we do need to transcend our basic human nature, which is now identified with the urge to conform and with an abdication from the duty we have to think for ourselves and fashion our own morality.
>
> Of course, there are dangers in being "true to yourself" – a danger we find in all existentialist philosophy. The self to which you are summoned to be true may be noble, but it may also be vicious. On the surface, we all approve of Polonius' advice to Laertes in *Hamlet*: "This above all, to thine own self be true." But it has been suggested that an Elizabethan Christian audience would immediately have recognized the pernicious nature of this advice: because Original Sin is an inescapable part of ourselves, we ought to be true not to our fallen nature, but to God. As we shall see, however, Nietzsche thought that God was dead and that therefore there can be no prescriptive morality and, for better or for worse, we have to shape our own.

The English translation for the name Nietzsche gave to a person who can transcend what is "all too human" is "Superman"; the German was *Übermensch*, that is, someone who has *überwindet* (that is, has "overcome") what is herd-like within himself. For Nietzsche, perhaps, not only what was herd-like: there was the handicap of his frequent ill-health; his love-affair with Lou Andreas-Salomé had collapsed – the book has been interpreted as auto-therapy, an effort to "turn his will to health, to life, and the Will to Power". He wrote it in Sils Maria, the imagery in the book is that of the man who has painfully scaled the

23 For Heraclitus, see chapter 1, p. 7; for Existentialism, see chapter 40, *passim*; also p. 479 for Bergson; p. 530 for Russell; and p. 601f for Chomsky.

heights, but then breathed the pure air at the top, where he understands what is "beyond good and evil" (the title of his next book). He descends as a prophet to the puny world below, which does not understand him.

The Superman is offered as a myth, a goal of human aspirations. Nietzsche does not think that anyone has yet become a Superman - even the best people in the past have been "human, all too human".

> *Up to a point*, there is a certain parallel in Christianity. For the Christian, the goal of human aspiration is to be Christ-like, but, although some people come nearer to the ideal than others, none, not even the saints, can be as perfect as Christ. Our fallen nature condemns even the best of us to be "human, all too human". Nietzsche praises several people in the past for having shown *some* of the qualities incorporated in the notion of a Superman, including even Socrates and Christ, whom he fiercely criticizes for other characteristics (see below). The *difference* in this respect between Christianity and Nietzsche is that Christianity not only demands that everyone should be as Christ-like as possible, but morally condemns those who cannot live up to this standard and inculcates guilt in those who fail. Nietzsche makes no such demands, and he thinks that guilt is an ignoble emotion which those with a master mentality (see below) never feel.

Nietzsche does not believe that a race of Supermen will come into existence in the course of evolution. On the contrary, he feared that humanity as a whole was far too complacent to aspire to the ideals. In any case, he did not believe, as some neo-Darwinians like Herbert Spencer did,[24] that evolution and natural selection were engines of social progress. Rather, he thought that history had regressed, from a world that accepted that some people were superior to others and respected the principle of aristocracy (even if it was contaminated with the hereditary principle in which Nietzsche did not believe) to one that increasingly, through democracy, was based on the idea that everyone was of equal worth, and that the weak should be helped instead of being allowed to go to the wall - an idea which gave collective strength to the mediocre, "Taken individually, the members of the majority may be inferior, but when grouped together under the influence of fear and the gregarious instincts, they are powerful."[25]

Another reason that Nietzsche did not believe in continual progress lies in his strange theory of Eternal Recurrence. The world is made up of a large but finite number of combinations of forces and elements. Because their number is limited, eventually combinations will recur, and the cycle of history will be repeated in perpetuity and, as Nietzsche had already made clear in *Die fröhliche Wissenschaft – The Gay Science* (1882), not just in the general terms in which some people maintain that "History repeats itself", but *in every particular.* If this theory were true, one might conclude that all human striving is basically absurd - and that the world is absurd is indeed a theme which some twentieth-century existentialists will take up.[26] Nietzsche and the existentialists agree that this absurdity is a challenge; it is the herd which would find such a notion debilitating and reducing life to meaninglessness. Members of the herd would either

24 See p. 442 above.

25 Coplestone, *op.cit.*, Vol.VII, p. 412,

26 See p. 506 below.

refuse to entertain it, or, if they were persuaded by it, they would lament, look for a better world elsewhere, regard this life as a kind of disease, or sink into apathy. The Superman accepts the idea: he will never cringe, never say "nay" to life, but will say "yea" to everything it throws at him, the sufferings as well as the zest.[27] He finds his life exhilarating as it is (quite irrespective of any notion of progress) and so his philosophy (*Wissenschaft*) does not fill him with gloom, but with gaiety (*Fröhlichkeit*).

What are the other aspects of the Superman *ideal*? He is an individualist and a law to himself, and he does not conform to the conventions of the herd, especially when these would curb the instinctual life.

> Nietzsche has little respect for the idea that without general moral codes, such as, for example, the Ten Commandments, society could hardly exist. They are of course often flouted, but it is in the general interest of society that we should not, for example, kill or steal. By and large, Nietzsche had a contempt for "society"; he readily equated it with the mass which demands conformity.
>
> Nietzsche hated mass conformity, whether it was demanded by public opinion or by state imposition. He would therefore have been radically at odds with the conformity that the Nazis would demand. It is true that the Nazis removed many curbs on the instincts, though Nietzsche would have described many of those as unworthy herd instincts and based on envy and resentment. Nevertheless, it must be admitted that the Nazis also exalted many of the instincts he did value:

The Superman will be brave and heroic; he is ready to live dangerously; he will not try to protect himself from suffering; he will accept conflict with joy.

> One's first associations with such ideas are physical ones, but they need not be so, and Nietzsche did not mean them to be thus limited. Someone who stands up for his ideas in the face of deadly persecution is heroic even if he does not physically fight for them – such a person is certainly living dangerously and does not protect himself from suffering. One can also enter with joy into a conflict of *ideas*. Not for Nietzsche the evasive "let's agree to disagree", let alone any compromise over one's principles for the sake of peace or even of power, that would betoken, he thought, a flabby weakness which is unworthy of a Superman.

The Superman may be ruthless, with the natural cruelty of the eagle who follows his instincts by pouncing on the lamb, and he will not indulge in the weakness of pity. Pity, in Nietzsche's view, was merely a hypocritical mask for a feeling of superiority over the person who was the object of it. (It was not, of course, the feeling of superiority to which he objected, but the hypocrisy.)

But the Superman will never inflict cruelty out of hatred or vindictiveness, for he never bears grudges, never feels resentment (*ressentiment*), and never harbours revenge

> though of course he may plan to reverse a defeat. It is the spirit in which he does it that matters: it must not be done in the spirit of vengeance but with the joyous resumption of the battle.

27 There is a slight difference between Nietzsche's response to the absurd and that of the Existentialists. The latter called on us to respond to the Absurd with a grim stoicism – which had about it none of the joy with which even the absurd is welcomed by the Nietzschean Superman.

The Superman will not gloat in victory, and he may be generous to the defeated, but his generosity will come out of the knowledge of his strength, and not out of Christian duty.

As has already been said, it is a misconception that Nietzsche praised these virtues only in their military form, for he held that they can equally be intellectual ones. There is also the Superman who displays a heroic intellect. In *Beyond Good and Evil* (1886), Nietzsche lists 125 individuals whom he admired as "higher men".[28] They do include great military figures like Julius Caesar and Napoleon, but more than a hundred of them were writers: they include Luther, Spinoza, Kant, Schopenhauer, Goethe, Shakespeare and Darwin. There are passages in Nietzsche's work in which he speaks highly even of Socrates and of Jesus. Much as he despised their teaching,[29] he admired them for their lack of resentment.

Master Morality and Slave Morality

The Superman, as we have seen, is a law unto himself. Nietzsche has already told us that truth is something we make for ourselves. The same must therefore be true of morality, and here Nietzsche clearly differed from Kant's belief that moral precepts are *a priori*, invariant and absolute.[30] Moral rules, he says (not very originally) are made by groups to support their interests. Essentially, there are two kinds of moral systems: that of masters and that of slaves. Each group uses the words "good" and "evil" for its own end – though masters prefer to talk about "bad" (*schlecht*) rather than "evil" (*böse*) moral attitudes. It is only slaves who have a notion of sin, who want to inculcate feelings of guilt, and who therefore speak of evil.

> Nietzsche does not *blame* slaves for having a slave morality. They are no more evil because they have a twisted moral defect than cripples are evil because he they have a twisted physical one. Slaves are true to their own slave nature, just as the masters are true to theirs. Of course, he thinks that the master morality is superior, just as a good physique is superior to physical deformity. Zarathustra, as a preacher, tries to convey this to the masses. He may succeed in inspiring a few and lifting them out of the herd, but the majority not only *will* not hear him, but actually *cannot* hear him, tied down as they are by their true nature as slaves.

Those who follow slave moralities have a very poor view of human nature, and assert that we live in a fallen state. They regard all our natural appetites as dangerous temptations. The master morality does not, as we have seen, necessarily condemn cruelty and aggression against the outside opponent or weakling, but slaves wallow in guilt, which is cruelty and aggression turned inwards; it can be alleviated only by looking out for worse "sins" in others.

28 The phrase is a reminder that Nietzsche did not believe that anyone had actually ever attained the full ideal of the Superman.

29 He was contemptuous of Jesus' exhortation to meekness, turning the other cheek etc but St Paul had gone further still, by waging a life-denying war against human instincts and by focussing on Jesus' death on the cross rather than on his life.

30 See p. 374 above.

> At best, the Puritan acknowledges his own sinfulness, but instead of that making him more generous to other sinners, he is particularly hard on those whose sinfulness exceeds his own. At worst, he sees the mote in the other's eye, but not the beam in his own.

Slaves interpret all suffering as a divine punishment, and invent a god before whom they can abase themselves. The very concept of such a god is life-denying, so that a life led according to such false notions is essentially an inauthentic one.[31]

Where master morality is based on the strength that the masters have, slave morality is based on their own weakness. Slaves extol their own meekness and humility, and are full of resentment against those who have what they themselves would want, but do not have. Because they are poor, they criticize wealth; because they are weak, they decry power and strength; because they are forced to be humble, they excoriate pride; and because it is dangerous for them to express their own strong feelings, they demand control over passions.

The tragedy is that, through Christianity, the slaves have managed to get the master-types to accept their false values: there has been what Nietzsche called a *transvaluation of values*, by which those who espouse the slave morality have become the masters, and the weak have actually become the strong. The new masters are now doubly inauthentic, as they still profess and impose upon their subjects the unnatural faith in meekness and humility as virtues, but they themselves do not practice what they preach. Ostensibly, they profess a creed that condemns "the world" as a fallen world and that denounces, for example, force and pride. At the same time, however, they engage in the profoundly anti-Christian activities that have always been required of rulers, "What is it that Christianity calls 'the world'? To be a soldier, a judge, a patriot; to defend oneself; to look to one's honour; to seek one's advantage; to be proud: every practice of every moment, every instinct and every valuation translated into action is today anti-Christian."[32]

> On the face of it, Nietzsche should rejoice that even the "Christian" rulers should do what the master morality has always prescribed, but, as we have seen before, he detests hypocrisy and attaining one's end through lies, deviousness, deceit or guile. These are the weapons of cowardice and of the slave. Nietzsche's model is the frank hero figure of a Siegfried, who is particularly scornful when he catches Mime out in a lie.

The Death of God and the Open Sea

In earlier periods, men at least genuinely believed in God and His commandments, in Jesus and the Sermon on the Mount – and their confessions that they were miserable sinners were sincere. Now, after the Age of Reason and the Age of Science have done their work, belief in God is decaying. More than two generations earlier, Schopenhauer had described the nineteenth century as, "an age in which religion is almost entirely dead". In the next generation, Heinrich Heine had said, "Our heart is full of terrible pity. It is the old Jehova himself

31 The importance of living life authentically is important to all existentialist thought, from Kierkegaard to Sartre.

32 *The Anti-Christ* (published posthumously in 1895).

preparing for death... Can you hear the ringing of the bell? Kneel down, they are bringing the sacraments to a dying God." Now Nietzsche adds, "The greatest event of recent times - that 'God is dead' ... is beginning to cast its first shadow over Europe."[33]

Faith in God and Christianity had underpinned almost every value system in Europe, from feudalism to democracy and socialism. Therefore, the loss of faith in God entails a loss of faith in all values,[34] and so leads to Nihilism, which can be either active or passive. Passive Nihilism is resigned to the purposelessness of existence. Nietzsche believed this was the case with those who substituted a belief in scientific materialism as an alternative to a belief in God. Scientific materialism, reducing us to a bundle of mechanical reactions, deprives humans of all dignity and allows no place for spiritual values. Like religion, it inculcates a feeling of human worthlessness and it is therefore merely a "shadow of God".

Active Nihilism sets us free, for better or for worse, to shape our own value systems. Again he calls out, "Nothing is true; everything is permitted." The quotation is from Dostoevsky, but of course, Nietzsche did not believe that there were now no values. As we have seen, personally he had very clear ideas of which values he thought were noble and which were not. But it is up to each one of us to work out our own, and then, by living them, to make ourselves the kind of person we want to be. It is the kind of challenge which is gaily embraced by those who have the courage. The passage quoted above from *Morgenröthe* continues, "At last the horizon lies free before us, even granted that it is not bright; at last the sea, our sea, lies open before us. Perhaps there has never been so open a sea."

This is a truly existentialist theme: absolute freedom entails absolute responsibility for ourselves in a terrifying but exhilarating solitude. As Arthur Danto comments, "If the world is of our making, so to speak, and if there is no other world than this, we can make another one and remake ourselves along with it."[35]

The Will to Power

In January 1889, Nietzsche suffered a mental breakdown from which he never recovered. After a brief stay in a clinic, he was cared for in the home of his mother and then, after her death in 1897, in that of his sister. As we have already seen, Elizabeth Förster-Nietzsche made herself the guardian, not only of her sick brother, but of his literary work.

From 1885 to 1888, Nietzsche had made notes for a book to be called *The Will to Power*. Elizabeth organized these jottings and others from his notebooks, and published the work in 1901, the year after Nietzsche's death. It must be uncertain whether he would have published it himself - he is on record as having repudiated some of the ideas in those notebooks - or, if he had published, what shape he would himself have given to the final work, what he would have

33 *Morgenröthe (The Dawn)*, 1881.

34 Nietzsche was not always consistent: elsewhere he rails against the continuing influence of faith in democracy and socialism, which have survived even when their original religious inspiration had not.

35 In D.J. O'Connor - *A Critical History of Western Philosophy*, p. 397.

omitted and what he would have added. We also know that Elizabeth was a highly suspect editor with an agenda of her own. In later years, those commentators who were sympathetic to Nazism, as Elizabeth herself was, considered *The Will to Power* the most important of Nietzsche's works. Although it has often met with distorted interpretations, we do know that Nietzsche had for long engaged with the Schopenhauer's philosophy of the Will; and we may regard at least parts of this posthumous work as authentic.

Like Schopenhauer, Nietzsche attached great importance to the Will as the defining trait of all living matter, but his interpretation of this phenomenon differed greatly from Schopenhauer's. In Schopenhauer, the Will was in the service of something still more basic: the survival of the individual and that of the species.[36] Nietzsche believed that the Will to Power was absolutely primary; survival was *"merely an indirect and frequent consequence of this"*, and life was indeed often sacrificed for it.[37] For Nietzsche, life was not a struggle to survive, but to *prevail*. In that struggle, the Will does not present us with the imperative to survive, on the contrary, it makes the Superman prepared to confront death and to forfeit his life. Less dramatically, Nietzsche's Will is seen in efforts to subdue the environment, in the work of artists, philosophers and scientists to master problems, and not least in mastering oneself.

In Schopenhauer, the Will is an impersonal force external to Man, which drives him in ways which, in general, he has no control over. Schopenhauer is a pessimist: the Will is a source of much pointless suffering, and it can be escaped only through a great effort of Asceticism, which is a denial of ordinary human nature and an escape from practical life. When we have escaped the Will, we are also capable of that Compassion which perceives others as being the same as ourselves.[38]

For Nietzsche, the Will is not something outside ourselves, for that would make us mere instruments of it. On the contrary, the Will is an instrument for us to use, not to be used by. It is entirely personal, and our health requires that we assert it joyfully, rather than aspire to escape from it. If there is suffering, it, too, must be embraced in the same spirit as part of life. The Will is a source of joy, of strength, and of achievement.

Compassion, for Nietzsche, was not a virtue, but a weakness. The Will to Power has an inherent ingredient of cruelty, in the strong and in the weak alike. In the strong it shows itself in an element of what we call barbarity, "One cannot fail to see at the core of all these noble races the animal of prey, the splendid blond beast prowling about avidly in search of spoil and victory."

> This famous quotation actually comes from one version of *The Genealogy of Morals* (1887),[39] and with its references to "race" and "blond beasts", it seems tailor-made as a self-description of the Nazis. Commentators have taken the

36 See pp. 405f above.

37 This need not be a contradiction of Schopenhauer. As we have seen, Schopenhauer believed that the Will was interested, not in the survival of the individual *so much as* in that of the species, for which individual members of it frequently do sacrifice themselves.

38 See p. 409 above.

39 Here the translation is by R.J. Hollingdale in *A Nietzsche Reader*, Penguin Books, 1977.

phrase "blond beast" to be a poetic reference to lions, rather than to Aryans,[40] and two lines later in this passage, Nietzsche enumerates the "distinguished races" he had in mind: *"the Roman, Arabic, Germanic, Japanese nobility [sic], the Homeric heroes, the Scandinavian Vikings"*. He clearly does not mean race in the Nazi sense that applies to an entire nation, rather he applies it to a race of, say, Roman heroes living among a race of Roman slaves. What is implicit in Nietzsche's views is that some *societies* (rather than "races") are more likely than others to provide the setting out of which a group of superior individuals may emerge, even if the mass in those societies remained inferior. Nietzsche did not trouble to provide an analysis such as a more sociologically inclined philosopher, like Marx, would have provided; but he would have thought that the ethos and education in the Roman Republic was more conducive to the development of superior beings than a society in which the dominant teaching was based on the Christian "slave morality" he so despised.

It is clear that Nietzsche does not regard cruelty with distaste; he simply takes it as a fact of life, even as something that, in its natural state, gives life something of its savour. We should embrace what we are: in *The Gay Science* he summons us to the *amor fati* – the joyful acceptance of our fate. We cannot eradicate the cruelty. If, through Christianity for example, we try to suppress it, we are bound to fail. The cruelty will merely take on unnatural and unhealthy forms. We will simply turn inwards, against ourselves, and what was a source of strength then becomes a source of weakness, as we fight against our true nature.

This is just one of Nietzsche's insights that interested Freud, for whom repressed aggressive impulses turned inwards and lame our psychic strength. Of course, unlike Nietzsche, Freud believed that aggressive impulses need to be resolved or sublimated rather than be acted out, displaced, or repressed.[41]

Conclusion

Some of Nietzsche's ideas, even if purged of Nazi distortions, are repellent to the modern liberal mind. However, there is no doubt that he has much to say to our time. Our range of aesthetic appreciation of art has been greatly widened by what he had to say. He had important things to say about the messages that often lie hidden in the language we use. When we witness the intoxicated nationalism which has brought, and still brings, so much misery to the world, we respond to his contempt for the mass emotions which it engenders. His "realism" is often crude and repugnant, but his unmasking of hypocritical cant is still immensely refreshing. There is also something attractive in an attitude that says "yea" to life, however challenging it is, and in a stoicism that wears not its usual dour face, but a joyous one.

40 In another translation of what is clearly a different version of *The Genealogy of Morals* by Francis Golffing, (Doubleday, 1990), the passage reads: "Deep within all these noble races, there lurks the beast of prey." No references to blondness here; but then, some 18 lines later: "The profound and icy suspicion which the German arouses as soon as he assumes power (we see it happening again today) harks back to the persistent horror with which Europe for many centuries witnesses the raging of the blond Teutonic beast (although all racial connection between the old Teutonic tribes and ourselves has been lost)."

41 See p. 586 below.

His rejection of absolute morals was not original, but is now more widely shared than it was in his time. He challenges us, in a world of crumbling certainties, neither to seek shelter in worn-out creeds nor to become what he calls "passive nihilists", but never to forget that it is incumbent upon us to stand on our own feet, to fashion our own ideas and then to live up to them. We have noted the risk that the ideas we form and the actions we base upon them may be what most of us would describe as ignoble and even wicked rather than worthy of respect. In particular, we may not share Nietzsche's own views about the kind of life that a noble individual will carve out for himself, but his call that we must think for ourselves and not simply follow the herd is more important than ever in a world in which politicians and advertisers use every trick they can to create dumbed-down mass opinions. These issues will form the bedrock of twentieth-century Existentialism.

HENRI BERGSON 1859 to 1941

While Nietzsche stimulates thought and commentaries to the present day, the name of Henri Bergson is now almost completely forgotten. He had much in common with Nietzsche, although his range was not as great nor was his message as provocative. Yet he was very influential in his time. He was perhaps the last great representative of nineteenth-century Romanticism. His ideas, like Nietzsche's and those of earlier Romantics, were picked up by the early fascist movements, and, although he was born a Jew, his name was initially on a German list of eminent Frenchmen who were not to be molested during the Occupation.[42] So, like Nietzsche, he fell into disrepute after the War, but, unlike him, he has not benefited from a later re-evaluation. This is ironical, because, even after re-evaluation, much of Nietzsche's work remains pernicious, whereas Bergson did not write anything about politics, and his ideas do not actually invite dangerous social or political attitudes. Rather, they form, in some respects, a bridge between early and later existentialism, between Kierkegaard and Sartre, and therefore, they seem to have an interesting place in the history of philosophy.

One central notion of Bergson's goes much further back than Kierkegaard to Heraclitus (*ca.* 500 BC).[43] Like that ancient Greek, Bergson believed that the reality of the world consists of perpetual Flux and Change. This has no teleological purpose.[44] It is so continuous that our intellect finds it impossible to get a grip on reality, so much so that, according to Bergson, the intellect "is characterized by a natural inability to understand Life". However, the intellect is only one way in which we understand the world. The others are instinct and intuition. These two differ in that instinct is incapable of reflecting on itself, whereas intu-

42 Towards the end of his life, Bergson had been drawn increasingly to Roman Catholicism, but, in a wish to show solidarity with other Jews during the Nazi period, he did not convert. In December 1940 the Nazi authorities in Paris ordered Jews to register. He was offered exemption, but refused it. Though already sick, he queued for several hours in the bitter cold, which contributed to his death from pneumonia shortly afterwards.

43 For Heraclitus, see p. 7 above.

44 But see note 49 below.

ition can do that. The intellect may accumulate a mass of information; but often it is the intuition which makes it all "fall into place" – something that has been experienced by many creative individuals. On other occasions, the intuition understands reality with "immediate consciousness", without any previous analysis. Its insights have some of the qualities of mysticism as they are difficult to explain in terms of a precise or wholly rational vocabulary. So we have to express them in imagery and metaphor, to which Bergson, like Nietzsche, had frequent recourse.

Bergson calls the unbroken continuum of time within which flux is constantly at work *Durée* or Organic Time. For the purposes of *action*, Flux and Change are unmanageable, but we need to act, so we *need* to use the intellect to carve up Organic into Mathematical Time, which consists of one separate instant followed by another. Bergson says that we should remember that what the intellect produces in this way is artificial.[45] The action of the intellect is *cinematographic*: a film that gives the impression of movement and change, though each of its individual frames is frozen and still. It is intellect which produces Zeno's paradoxes of Achilles and the Tortoise, and, even more to the point, of the apparent inability of an arrow to be in motion because at any given moment it is frozen in a particular position,[46] but intuition knows better.

> Actually, it is precisely the intellect which has, through the Infinitesimal calculus, shown up the fallacy of Zeno's arguments, and it is the intellect which can deal with the phenomenon of change.

Similarly, in approaching a work of art, like a symphony, intuition grasps it as a whole and understands the creative process that gave birth to it. Intellect, on the other hand, will analyze it as a succession of notes or phrases in time. In the process, according to Bergson, it runs the danger of losing the essence of the work of art. Like most Romantics, Bergson would have agreed with Wordsworth's lines that by using our "meddling intellect ... we murder to dissect."[47]

> This is, of course, an extremely narrow way of defining the true appreciation of a work of art. Most people benefit enormously from having a work of art analyzed for them by a teacher or a book. Analysis can sensitize a reader of Shakespeare to the resonances and references of a particular phrase. The symbolism of a painting may escape a viewer if it is not analyzed for him. The artists themselves have to learn and to a large extent depend on the analysis of structure and on examples from the past that they are taught at academies.
>
> Certainly that is not all that makes for a great work of art: one can follow all the rules of composition and deliberately load words with a variety of symbolic meanings and yet produce a mechanical and clod-hopping piece of work. A great artist has to transcend techniques. Often, he carves out techniques for himself which run counter to the orthodoxies he has been taught, and that transcendancy *sometimes* defies analysis and appeals directly to what

45 There is a similarity here between Bergson and Hume – see p. 288 above. Hume had argued that, philosophically speaking, the notions of Cause and Effect are untenable, but we cannot live our lives without assuming that causes have effects. Similarly, Bergson says that, from a philosophical point of view, the intellect cannot understand reality, but we have to act as if the intellect had a grip on it.

46 See p. 8 above.

47 The point had been made by Schopenhauer – see p. 402, above.

Bergson called the Intuition. More often than not, however, analysis can get to the heart of what a work of art is about.

The use of Logic by the intellect is akin to its use of Mathematics in breaking down our observations into separate units. Science is a product of Logic and Mathematics. Its reduction of experience into separate parts, its reassembling of these parts so that one part is seen as *causing* another, leads us into seeing mental and physical experiences as causally determined. Only when we use our intuition are we truly conscious of free will. The weaker our intuition, Bergson thinks, the more we are governed by Determinism.

What presumably underlies this idea is that philosophies based on science have in fact tended to see mental processes as similar to physical ones, to see them influenced by the forces of attraction and repulsion etc., and therefore to lead to Determinism. Rightly or wrongly, over a large part of our lives we feel "intuitively" that we are free to make choices and can exercise our Will. If we value the freedom of the will, we will trust our Intuition rather than what science, the product of our Intellect, may tell us. This is quite a common human *feeling* and, as such, much valued by Romanticism.

It is, however, difficult to see how, if our intuition shows us that we are part of a continuous flow of change, we should feel that we have any freedom within that relentless current.

Bergson admitted that science has its uses, but by artificially carving its objects of study out of reality, it can tell us nothing about reality, which is the subject matter of philosophy. Science and philosophy therefore have nothing to do with each other: they are totally different pursuits.

This is, of course, one reason why Bergson is completely out of fashion now, especially in the Anglo-Saxon world. From the seventeenth century onwards, all major English philosophers have aimed to make philosophy compatible with scientific thought. Some, like Herbert Spencer, had acknowledged the existence of the metaphysical (he had called it the Unknowable) without entering into it, others, like Bentham, had had little hesitation in describing metaphysics as "nonsense on stilts" and unworthy of being considered a valid part of philosophy at all. All of them (and their heirs, the Logical Positivists)[48] would agree that their philosophy had nothing to contribute to metaphysics. Bergson, on the contrary, held that philosophy had nothing to contribute to science. Considering the centrality that science has achieved in our culture and the way it has forced philosophers to grapple with its methods, findings and effects, it seems positively perverse to claim that philosophy can, or should, ignore it.

Bergson said that the driving force behind the constant Flux and Change was Creative Evolution – the title of his best-known book of 1907. The title sounds Spencerian, but we have already seen that Bergson had nothing in common with Positivism, and its claim to be a social *science*. Nor was Evolution either a matter of purposive adaptation (as in Lamarck) or of chance variations leading to progress (as in Darwin). Rather, it was a constantly creative urge or Life Force, which Bergson called the *élan vital.*

48 see p. 551 below.

He went on to describe the world as consisting of a clash between this Life Force and Matter. The Life Force was striving ever upwards towards unity, but Matter impedes this by striving downwards and towards separation.[49] Bergson uses the metaphor of a fountain to explain this notion: Life is the jet, Matter is the drops which are falling back. Life is continuing change and evolution, and Matter is represented by something preserving itself instead of going on evolving; as something fixed. The Life Force has had Man evolving from monkeys, but monkeys still exist – they are the drops that have fallen back.

> No wonder Bergson's philosophy had nothing to say to science! The notion of the *élan vital* inspired the Vorticists and Futurists, and also Bernard Shaw. It also made Bergson popular with fascists, who saw themselves as representing movement and dynamic change.

Morality and Religion

In a late work of 1932, *The Two Sources of Morality*, Bergson distinguished between a *closed* and an *open* morality, and also between a *static* and a *dynamic* religion. Closed moralities and static religions create obligations through social pressures. They are reinforced by myths to secure social cohesion and to protect them against scepticism.

An open morality and a dynamic religion are found among great individuals. Their codes are higher and more universal than those of any particular society. They spring from the contact of these individuals with "the free creative force of life itself"; their source is therefore essentially mystical.

This mysticism, "is presumably a participation in the divine essence". It is the only way in which we can know about God, and the mystical experience of participation in the eternal flow of life, "adds probability to the belief in the soul's survival after bodily death". The formulations are cautious, but we have already seen how, towards the end of his life, Bergson was increasingly drawn towards Roman Catholicism.

> With his distinction between an open and a closed morality, Bergson links to the Existentialist tradition, with Kierkegaard's rejection of *Das Man*, with the contempt of Nietzsche's Superman for mass conformity, with Heidegger's and Sartre's stress on authenticity.[50] It is to twentieth-century Existentialism that we must now turn.

49 It is difficult to square the notion of *striving* (either upwards or downwards) with Bergson's denial that there is anything teleological in the processes of Flux and Change.

50 For Kierkegaard, see p. 414 above; for Nietzsche, p. 470 above; for Heidegger, p. 498 below; and for Sartre p. 508 below. But note none of these would propound a *universal* morality: each person has to carve out his own.

PART SEVEN:
THE TWENTIETH CENTURY

CHAPTER 40

Twentieth Century Existentialism

Some Basic Concepts[1]

The three giants of twentieth-century Existentialism are Martin Buber, Martin Heidegger and Jean-Paul Sartre, but we have already seen that the thought of Søren Kierkegaard, Friederich Nietzsche and Henri Bergson included some of the characteristics of the philosophy.

In several respects, Existentialism is an outcrop of Romanticism. It is therefore strongest in Germany and France which have had a strong romantic philosophical tradition, and weakest in the Anglo-Saxon countries where philosophy has mostly taken the pragmatic line. It is true, of course, that England has had her romantic poets, artists and writers, but only one of these (Coleridge) was also a philosopher, and he hardly ever figures in books on English philosophy. French philosophy did have a strong rational tradition stemming from Descartes and continued by the Enlightenment philosophers and then by Comte and the Positivists, but from Rousseau's time onwards there was a rival romantic tradition which extolled the feelings rather than the intellect. In Germany, Fichte, Schelling and Hegel launched a modern form of mysticism, which also essentially appeals to the feelings rather than the intellect. Another aspect of German philosophy, from Kant through Fichte, Schelling, Schopenhauer and Nietzsche, laid stress on the importance of the Will; this element also plays a big part in Existentialism.

One of Existentialism's central theses is that we relate to the outside world primarily through our feelings, though its exponents differ about what these feelings tell us. Optimists like Buber and Heidegger say that the truest understanding of the world comes through feelings like joy, love and confident acceptance. Sartre is more pessimistic: the feelings he experiences when confronting reality are those of boredom, nausea and alienation and the anxiety (*angoisse*) he feels in this confrontation is about the absurdity and nothingness of the world. Kierkegaard and Heidegger also describe anxiety and dread, but for them it is a summons to exert their Will and to escape from the apparent emptiness of the world into a more meaningful existence.

Knowledge of the most important things in life is not reached by intellectual analysis or a grasp of theory, but by unmediated awareness, by feelings and by

1 Many of the ideas in this introduction come from John Macquarrie's *Existentialism*, Penguin Books, 1973.

active engagement. This is how we get to know another person; it is how we perceive a work of art or of craftsmanship; it is how we experience religion. We find it difficult and sometimes impossible to describe any of these encounters in analytical or theoretical language, and when we try to do so, their essence often escapes us and we are left with arid formulations. If, as the churches have done in respect of articles of faith, we attach too much importance to these verbalizations, we substitute obeisance to fetishes and superstitions for the transcendent understanding of religion. The often meaningless verbiage in which especially abstract art is so often discussed by critics is another case in point.

Existentialism arises out of temperament. Its exponents *begin* with an intense awareness of existence of oneself and of the relationship between that self and that which is not oneself. This awareness does not need any rational analysis; it is simply accepted. Some people do not have it, their sense of individuality has been blunted and temperamentally they do not differentiate themselves from other people, rather, they see themselves (or have learnt to do so) as part of a group and absorb without much reflection the values of the group. They behave a bit like sheep or like ants. Such people can never be existentialists. In the vocabulary of existentialism, they live "inauthentically" - they do not base their lives on choices, indeed, they do not really *exist* at all.

> If one is engaged in sociological studies, one sees the individual as a specimen of a group, but sociological thinking – however necessary it may be from time to time as a *tool* for governments and other kinds of planners – is not existentialist thinking, because it does not see the individual as a unique, autonomous and responsible being. The existentialists see the particular as far more significant than the universal – another link with Romanticism.

In all periods of history, the social forces that mould people's thinking have been very strong, but techniques in modern society have intensified this tendency. Automation, computerization, mass production, the mass media, and the pervasiveness of political propaganda all conspire to mould us into herd-like patterns, and make it harder to forge an authentic existence for ourselves. They constantly tempt us to surrender our existence to others, to let them decide for us, to adopt conventional behaviour and morality. (This does not mean that we *have* to reject the conventions. If we have examined them for ourselves and have then decided that we agree with them, we can accept them without losing our authenticity, it is only unexamined acceptance that is incompatible with it.)

The dangers to our true existence and to making free and responsible choices do not come only from outside ourselves. Our autonomous decision-making can be undermined just as easily by our own bodies, by addictions, by our sex drive, or by impulses such as greed or fear.

> This is very close to the Pauline concept that we cannot have "perfect freedom" so long as we are "enslaved to sin".[2] Our "higher self" aspires to perfect freedom; our "lower self" is represented by our servitude to sin. For "perfect freedom" the existentialists would substitute the word "authenticity", and if they did not speak in terms of "sin", they nevertheless recognized that we can be enslaved, not only by external pressures from *les autres*, but also by drives

2 See p. 338 above.

> *within ourselves* – whether physical or psychological – that prevent us from being authentic.

Existence also implies a confrontation with what is not oneself, with the existences of other people and things. It is an intense awareness that the individual is part of a bigger world into which he is "thrown". If there is no confrontation, the result is the conformity against which existentialists strive so hard. In Sartre, the confrontation is an adversarial relationship, but it need not be so. In Buber and Heidegger, the confrontation is not, in principle, an adversarial one, and the more neutral word "encounter" is really a better one to use. The encounter should enhance one's relationship with fellow human beings and with nature, and should prevent one from using them instrumentally. In such encounters, human beings validate each others' existence.

> A strong human being, with his or her own feeling of self-worth and dignity, is not dependent on such validation, but we so often see how a *denial* of validation can cripple many people – how, for example, for many years black people had been taught to internalize the view that white people had of them. It would take a campaign with the slogan "Black is Beautiful" to anchor them in a sense of self-worth. If people of despised minorities do have a sense of self-worth, it arises to some extent out of being validated by people of their own kind – but even more importantly by having been validated by their parents. A child that is not valued for its own sake by its parents, that is treated merely "instrumentally", will find it extremely difficult in later life to have a sense of self-worth.

In a Buberian-type encounter, instead of using or trying to control each other, people accept and open themselves up to each other, as, paradigmatically, they do in a caring sexual relationship. Such acceptance is not conformity and in no way diminishes one's commitment to authenticity. Kierkegaard, however, had felt that other people - even the fiancée whom he loved - could be a hindrance to his "true" existence, for a loving relationship would demand a commitment which might take him away from his overriding responsibility to be authentically true to himself. In this respect, he shared the outlook which teaches the Roman Catholic clergy to see families as a possible hindrance to their total commitment to God and to their parishioners. As a result, Kierkegaard had broken off his engagement. Sartre went even further: he thought that instrumental relationships with others were unavoidable. He made commitment (*engagement*) a key concept of his philosophy, but the commitment was to ideas and not to people - as the story of his relationships bore out.

Commitment to an idea is not enough, it must result in action. Through his actions Man continually makes himself. Actions are central to existentialists that they say that Man is defined, not by what he *is*, but by what he *does*, by what he chooses to do, by what he commits himself to. What is more, choices have to be continually renewed, perhaps even altered. Needless to say, alterations must not be light-hearted or opportunistic, any more than the abandonment of a friendship, a marriage or a vocation can be a trivial matter. They must be the result of serious examination and much heart-searching. Self-deception is only too easy, and we may think we have searched our hearts when in fact we are yielding to urges or to convenience. Such self-deception is called "bad faith" (*mauvaise foi*) and is incompatible with authenticity. All *true* choice is painful and implies renunciation of what is not chosen, and to act upon it requires an act of Will – what Kierkegaard had called a Leap of Faith and Heidegger called resolve (*Entschlossenheit*). The emphasis on Will is another link between the Existentialists and Romanticism.

For existentialists, authentic choice is the more difficult because they recognize that there are no *universally accepted* criteria which will help us to make the choice. We are forced to fashion our own criteria in the knowledge that they are personal to ourselves. This in turn implies a recognition that they are relative and cannot be absolute. The most important choices and criteria for the existentialist are moral ones, but when we make them, we do not have the comfort enjoyed by other people who believe (often in an unexamined and therefore inauthentic way) in absolute moral certainties. Commitment to criteria that we know to be relative is essential for the existentialist. It is not good enough to say that, because we know our criteria to be uncertain ones, we had better not commit ourselves to them. That would lead to a moral vacuum which is incompatible with human dignity. We would be like the proverbial donkey who starves to death because he is unable to decide from which bale of hay to feed himself. So we must make commitments to causes without the comforting blinkeredness that does not see their weaknesses. Thus, an existentialist Christian will readily admit that there are good arguments against Christianity, and yet on balance he thinks that those for it are stronger *for him*. He will therefore commit himself to Christianity, as Kierkegaard had done when he took the Leap of Faith and accepted God's incarnation in Christ in full awareness of all the arguments against it.[3]

If we make an existential commitment to religion, some choices are easier, as we accept religious commandments as being binding upon us. Of course, it does not solve all the problems of choice. Religious commandments may conflict in certain situations, so that even a truly religious person may have a struggle to work out what his religious duty may be.

There can be existentialist democrats, who, being able to give only two cheers for democracy, will nevertheless commit themselves to its defence.[4] One can even describe Heidegger as an existentialist fascist. It is inconceivable that he should have swallowed the Nazi ideology whole, but Nazism entertained enough concepts that resonated with his own which led him for a period, with apparent conviction, to commit himself to the Nazi cause. Sartre was an existentialist communist: he made a commitment to the communist cause during the war and also often after it, not because he believed in the infallible truth of communism, but because the alternatives (fascism, imperialism) seemed to him worse, and because it struck him as an unworthy position to fastidiously stand aside from the struggle and say, "a plague on both your houses". Such authentic choices are often difficult; we may find it easier "not to choose." However, "not choosing" to make a choice is itself choosing not to choose, and thereby actually choosing to help the worse cause to prevail. So, we cannot

3 See p. 417 above.

4 One is also reminded of Churchill's dictum in 1947: "It has been said that democracy is the worst form of government except all those other forms that have been tried from time to time." Even Churchill could have been called an existentialist democrat.

escape making choices. Nothing within us is determined *for us*. We are, as Sartre put it, "condemned to freedom", forced only to exercise our inner freedom. The only question is whether we do so in good or in bad faith.

> Needless to say, the existentialists believed that we have a large amount of free will, and they rejected determinism. The determinists say that any decisions we make are determined by the complex field of force, within which we find ourselves. Some forces (attraction or repulsion, conditioning by upbringing or by our genes) pull or drive us one way, while other forces pull or drive us in another. We respond to these in the way in which, say, a piece of metal filing behaves in a gravitational field. There are times when we feel that our behaviour is not a matter of choice; that, we "can't help ourselves", but at other times we feel that our behaviour is a matter of our choosing. If we were merely like metal filings, we would not experience the difficulties of making choices. The metal filing in a field of magnetic force doesn't dither about which way to move, the way that we do, doesn't struggle the way we have to do, to make up its mind. The fact that an authentic moral choice is often so difficult, the fact that we have to struggle, seems to suggest that our Will is involved, that we do have a choice, and that therefore there is at least an element of free will. That is part of the existentialist position.

Of course, our *outer* freedom is limited by external restraints, which Heidegger and Sartre called "facticity". A prisoner cannot escape his chains, but he does, however, have a free choice about how to behave in that situation. He can choose whether to defy or to obey his gaoler, whether to keep himself mentally and physically alert or whether to sink into apathy or despair. In some ways, we may even be "imprisoned" by aspects of our own make-up which we cannot change. To a strictly limited extent then, the influence of one's past can also be accepted as facticity. There are some influences which have moulded us since childhood and we find it almost impossible to escape – though the word "almost" allows for the possibility that, with a sufficient exertion of the Will to be authentic and to escape *mauvaise foi*, we *could* overcome whatever handicap these influences represent.

The ultimate facticity which we have to accept is death. Those who believe in an afterlife do not see death as the end of our real existence, but merely as a passage from one kind of existence to another. Such a belief has its own philosophical implications. Neither Heidegger nor Sartre believed in an afterlife, but they drew very different conclusions from their belief that death is the real termination of our existence. Heidegger believed that, properly understood, death can add to the meaning of life, whereas Sartre believed that it showed up life's meaninglessness.

MARTIN BUBER[5]
1878 to 1965

Martin Buber, the son of a wealthy banker and Jewish religious scholar, was born in Lemberg (Lvov, Lviv) which, at the time, was part of Austrian Galicia. He attended the universities of Vienna, Leipzig and Berlin. While in Vienna, he

5 I owe much of this section to the fine chapter on Martin Buber in Nathan A.Scott Jr's *Mirrors of Man in Existentialism*, Collins 1969.

took up Zionism and edited a Zionist journal, *Die Welt*, and in Berlin he started a Jewish publishing firm with a strong Zionist list; but for him, political concerns were never the most important. In 1904, he withdrew from Zionist activities and publishing for five years to study the Jewish mystical sect of Hasidism, among whose characteristics is an emphasis on the hallowing of everyday activity and the injunction to respond to God's world in a spirit of joy. At this time, he also read Kierkegaard, and was much influenced by the nature of his religious faith and by his stress on commitment and authenticity – though joy is hardly something one associates with the author of *Fear and Trembling*. Nor, as we will see, would Buber share Kierkegaard's extreme individualism, the fear that human relationships can get in the way of relationships between Man and God.

In the 1920s, together with his friend Franz Rosenzweig (himself an existentialist philosopher) he made a new German translation of the Hebrew Bible. It was intended to bring out the original resonance of the Hebrew, which they felt had been lost in earlier translations. This interest in the lost overtones of an early language is something that Buber shared with his contemporary Martin Heidegger.[6] Both men believed that the world is at best impoverished, and at worst misled, when we lose touch with the truths embodied in the original coinage of words.[7]

From 1923 to 1933 Buber held the Professorship of Jewish Philosophy, which had been specially created for him, at Frankfurt. During this time, he wrote his two most famous books, *I and Thou* in 1923, and the collection of essays which appeared in 1947 under the title *Between Man and Man*. He emigrated to Palestine in 1938, where, until his retirement in 1951, he was Professor of Social Philosophy at the Hebrew University in Jerusalem. As one would expect from a philosopher who taught the importance of opening oneself up to others and of not using others instrumentally, he was a leading advocate of dialogue between Zionists and the Arabs, and a critic of those Jews who had no wish for such encounters, had no respect for the Arabs as people like themselves and regarded them as simply an obstacle.

"In the beginning is relation", wrote Buber. No such thing as "I" exists in isolation. Existence from beginning is an encounter (*Begegnung*) and a relationship (*Beziehung*) of the "I" with the world. They have to take one of two modes, which Buber calls *I-Thou* and *I-It*. The hyphen is important: it is meant to drive home the point that we are not talking about the existence of a separate "I" which may (or may not) choose to enter into a relationship with the existence of a separate "Thou" or a separate "It". Neither can exist *at all* without one of those relationships, so the only existence there can be is of I-and-Thou or I-and-It.

In modern English we use the word "you" when we address other people, and keep "Thou" only for addressing God (though many modern clergy think

6 See below, p. 496.

7 For example, when Moses asks God how he should answer those who want to know God's name, God replies (Ex.3:14): *Ehyeh-Asher-Ehyeh*. The meaning of those Hebrew words has been much debated among Biblical scholars, but it is normally translated (e.g. in the King James Bible) as "I AM THAT I AM". Buber and Rosenzweig felt that the original Hebrew carried the force not only of a mysterious name, but also that of a mysterious presence, and so they translate the phrase as "I am there such as I am there". "Thereness" (*Dasein*) will also be a central concept for Heidegger – as indeed it is for all existentialists.

they can make prayer more "accessible to the ordinary person" by using "you" in prayers to God also). In German, the word "Du" is used both to address God and to address a person intimately. The early translations of Buber into English, like that by Ronald Gregor Smith in 1937, translate Buber's "Du" as "Thou" throughout. Walter Kauffman's translation of 1970 uses "I-you" when Buber is specifically talking about a relationship of one person with another, and "I-Thou" when Buber speaks of the relationship with God. Buber did believe that God, "is the great silent partner of every human dialogue into which we enter".[8] Buber himself wrote: "In each Thou we are aware of the breath from the eternal Thou: in each Thou we address the eternal Thou." I think that Smith's translation reminds us that Buber tells us that we must *first* work on I-Thou relationships with people, then God will be present also. If we do not have an I-Thou relationship with people, God cannot be present.

> Buber would have had little sympathy with hermits and those ascetics for whom close relationships with people are an obstacle to their relationship with God.

I-It describes an existence that is an instrumental relationship, one of use or manipulation. We find it, for example, in science, technology, commerce, advertising and administration. We use all these activities for our purpose, they are necessary for life and quite legitimate – though, as we shall see, it is possible and desirable that even in these areas we can sometimes show the reverence that is part of an I-Thou existence.

However, when we come to dealing with other people (and occasionally even with aspects of the natural world) we need the "I-Thou" relationship. Here we are engaged in dialogue: we are addressed, are willing to listen, are invited to make a response, and accept the invitation. In this way, we confirm one another's humanity. This is important not only in one-to-one relationships, but in relationships between groups of people, when very often the tendency for stereotyping and depersonalizing the members who make up the group is especially strong. When one administers a group (in government or in business) there must be, as we have seen, a large element of I-It, but if I-Thou never enters it, the citizens being governed or the workers being employed are likely to feel alienated through being treated in a way which disregards their humanity.[9]

It is easy to treat people in an I-It way, to regard them merely as objects to use or manipulate, to see them just as obstacles in your way or as targets upon which to vent your frustrations, anger, cruelty or the impulse to dominate. In such cases you do not open yourself up to them, you do not listen to them, and you deny them the possibilities of opening themselves up to you. This can, of course, be extremely damaging to their development. If we have extensive experience of our humanity not being confirmed by others, we tend to become less than fully human ourselves, with very low feelings of self-worth, aggressive feelings turned outwards or inwards, possibly suspicious of good inten-

8 Nathan A. Scott – *Mirrors of Man in Existentialism*, p. 209

9 For an extreme expression of employers using their employees in an instrumental way, note how the Victorian employer often referred to his workforce as consisting of so many "hands". He was not interested in the worker's "soul", in his individual life, but merely thought of him providing the hands which were the instruments of his production. The word has gone out of fashion, but, alas, the concept still survives in many a business or industrial concern.

tions when we come across them elsewhere and then rebutting dialogue that may be offered.

So an I-It relationship with people can regrettably replace what should be an I-Thou existence. Less regrettably, the I-It relationship which we normally have with what is not human can become an I-Thou relationship with the natural world. We then look upon that world not simply as something to study scientifically (it will be remembered that Buber had thought our relationship to science is usually instrumental), let alone as something to exploit for our own purposes. Instead, we allow nature to address us, we treat animals with respect and allow even trees to "speak to us" in some mysterious way.[10] This idea probably also stems from Buber's study of Hasidism, where every part of God's world is a manifestation of Him, and we have seen that, in fact, Buber sees God as present in every I-Thou relationship.

EDMUND HUSSERL
1859 to 1938

Edmund Husserl was primarily an epistemologist,[11] coming to philosophy via psychology, rather than an existentialist, but he had some influence on his pupil Martin Heidegger, and so a brief section on Husserl is appropriate here.

His most important book was *Logical Investigations*, published in two volumes in 1900 and 1901. He began as Descartes had begun, with the question of what we can be sure of. For Descartes that had been the fact that we think (have consciousness) and therefore that we exist. Husserl pointed out that consciousness is inseparably consciousness of something, and that we can never in practice distinguish between consciousness and the content of consciousness. His link with existentialism is the idea that we cannot separate subject and object; they are integral parts of one another. There is not even a self which has consciousness – the self is both itself and at the same time the content of consciousness.

Husserl followed Kant in calling that of which we are conscious "phenomena". Kant had believed that phenomena are signals sent out by something outside ourselves, by the noumenal *Ding an sich*, but that we have no certainty that our receiving apparatus receives those signals correctly. Husserl was closer to Fichte and Schelling. If we have no knowledge of what the *Ding an sich* is, we have no reason for thinking that it exists, so for Fichte and Schelling, the world in our minds is the only world there is. Husserl would not commit himself to dispensing with the noumenal world in such a cavalier manner. He merely said that if it exists, we have to "bracket it off". The fact remains that consciousness-and-its-phenomenal-content is the only thing we can study.

If in practice we cannot separate consciousness from its contents, it should be impossible to give consciousness any role in shaping its contents – or, if we do give it such a role, we could not study that function. This was not the line that Husserl took. He maintained that the content of consciousness is *intentional* (from the Latin *intendere*, meaning "to aim"). The contents or phenomena are

10 It is, I think because Buber and Heidegger, grew up in a German environment that both men have a special reverence for trees. The forest (*der Wald*) has always played a special role in the German romantic imagination.

11 Someone who is interested in the theory of knowledge: how do we know what we think we know?

shaped by consciousness. He wrote, "My consciousness is not a passive registration of the world, but actively constitutes or 'intends' it."

Consciousness organizes its content into systems of what Husserl calls "essences" - rather confusingly so, as the word had been used in a quite different sense by Aristotle and by medieval philosophers. Husserl applies it to what we group into systems of mathematics, aesthetics, religions, etc. We give names to the systems and to the phenomena we organize in this way. This means that the systems and their contents have no prior or independent existence - very much the position taken by the medieval Nominalists against Plato and the medieval Realists.[12]

> The notion that thoughts come first and that the language in which we express comes afterwards will be challenged later by Structuralists, who stress how dependent we are on our language for what we are capable of thinking.[13]

Because all we can study are the consciousness-and-its-contents, and because we have no way of correlating the contents with anything that exists outside consciousness, we can study phenomena only in terms of how they relate to each other within consciousness, rather than how they might relate to any external world, which, as we have seen, we have to "bracket off".

From this, it follows that dreams, fantasies etc. have the same status as rational thoughts or perceptions. We cannot know that what we call rational thought has any better foundation in the outside world than fantasies. If we dismiss fantasies, it is not because they do not correspond to reality, but because they do not relate satisfactorily to those other contents of our consciousness which we have shaped to form a coherent overall system that is closed to dreams and fantasies.

MARTIN HEIDEGGER
1889 to 1976

Introduction

In a book called *Philosophy and Living*, one has to address a question about Heidegger's life before considering his philosophy. Heidegger had an unsavoury political past, which is well documented, especially in Hugo Ott's political biography of him.[14] He was a member of the Nazi Party, and in April 1933 he became Rector of Freiburg University after his predecessor, a Social Democrat, had been forced to resign from that post by the Nazis. He supported the *Führerprinzip* for the running of universities collectively and individually. He made pro-Nazi speeches, extolling, "the inward truth and greatness of National Socialism", and he supported the *Gleichschaltung* of the universities by which they were purged and integrated into the totalitarian state. Although he is not on record for any public antisemitic speeches, there are private comments on record as early as 1929 in which he complains about the Jewification ("*Verjudung*") of German culture. He had dedicated his most important book,

12 For Aristotle on essence, see p. 45 above; for Nominalism, chapter 14.

13 See p. 600 below.

14 Hugo Ott - Martin Heidegger: a Political Life. English translation Harper Collins, 1993.

Being and Time (1927), to his teacher, friend and patron, Edmund Husserl, yet he remained silent when Husserl was attacked for his Jewish origins and dismissed from his emeritus professorship at Freiburg in April 1933. He also denounced a colleague and recommended his dismissal for having been a pacifist in the First World War. It is true that he was critical of the cruder Nazi academics and students who had "forgotten" the "inner truth of National Socialism" and who claimed that his philosophy was too woolly, eccentric, and hair-splitting. One of his Nazi denigrators even described Heidegger's careful distinctions between apparently related concepts as Talmudic (!). These men were influential with Alfred Rosenberg, whose satrapy included a say over educational policy and appointments and who was regarded as the leading exponent of National Socialist philosophy, and in April 1934, Heidegger resigned his Rectorate. The authorities began to supervise his lectures, though the local Nazi Party described him in 1938 as, "an exemplary party member". After the war he was banned from teaching by the de-nazification commission – the ban lasted until 1951. During his life-time, Heidegger never excused himself in public for what he had said and done, never spoke about the Nazi period, did not repudiate the pro-Nazi speeches he had made and never referred to the Holocaust. It was only after his death that, in 1983, his apologia – *The Rectorate, 1933 to 1934: Facts and Thoughts* – was published. Ott shows that it is full of factual inaccuracies.

This life story has persuaded some people to condemn his philosophical work – either out of hand, or by seeing in it the germs of pernicious Nazi ideas. Heidegger becomes a rather extreme example of a man whose lifestyle has been held by some to rob his philosophy of any real value – rather as some people have dismissed Rousseau's thoughts on education because he had left all his five children at the door of a foundling hospital.[15] In the latter case, I have commented that this is not a very sensible way of looking at ideas; people whose personal behaviour is unworthy do sometimes produce very valuable ideas. We should take these ideas on their own merits. We should exclude considerations relating to the personalities of their authors, and, while it is legitimate and important to draw attention to how the ideas have given rise to pernicious ideologies, we should remember that very often these ideologies are an unwarranted extrapolation from the original ideas, unintended by their author. One can certainly argue that this latter point would hardly apply to Heidegger. Although in his philosophical works there is nothing directly about politics (nothing, for instance, that can be taken as advocating the *Führerprinzip*, totalitarianism, or racial intolerance) he had, in several speeches, identified himself with Nazi ideology. I believe that Heidegger supported the Nazi Party largely because part of its rhetoric chimed in with the non-political philosophical ideas he had already put forward. It was these he recognized as, "the inner truth of National Socialism"[16] and they were to be distinguished from the crude excrescences and extrapolations that made Nazism so detestable, and which find no expression in his philosophical work. He should certainly have dissociated himself from them. His failure to do so, his support for and praise of the

15 See p. 340 above.

16 He even retained this phrase, from a lecture he gave in 1935, when he reissued its text in 1953.

system as a whole, his ambition, opportunism and lack of fundamental decency were severe human failings. He may even have been a genuine believer, swept away by the mass hysteria of the time, which would be just as deplorable. None of this, however, was an essential or integral part of his work as a philosopher. This has been recognized by writers, some of whom, like Sartre (who had been in the French Resistance against Nazism) or Hannah Arendt (the Jewish refugee, who had once been Heidegger's lover) have contributed to his rehabilitation as an important thinker. No writer is as unsparing a critic of Nazism as George Steiner, yet his masterly little book on Heidegger [17] brings out how frequently his thought can speak to our concerns and experiences, and how suggestive and profound are many of his metaphors.

Being

It was Heidegger who first showed the intense awareness of Being. He had that sense of awe which we will occasionally find in a small child which marvels that things should be rather than not be, and which is disturbed by the possibility that they might not be, that there might be Nothing. Sartre would inherit this feeling and indeed, would use it as the title of one of his books, *L'Être et le Néant* (1943). When philosophers see an object, say a rose, they ask themselves questions such as "What is the Idea of a rose?" (Plato) or "What is the essence of a rose?" (Aristotle) or "is the word 'rose' merely the name we give to a cluster of sensations?" (medieval nominalists) or "What are its primary and secondary qualities?" (Locke). A poet may talk about the symbolism of the rose; a botanist will be concerned with classifying what kind of a rose it is. In all these cases we concentrate on something other than the word *is*. Historically, the word has been reduced to a mere "inert piece of syntax".[18]

Yet, when languages first arose, each of the various forms of the verb "to be" had its own resonance which today we have completely forgotten. Only etymologists have some notion of it. Heidegger attached great importance to etymology. He constantly dug back to the roots of a word, especially in the Greek and German languages, because these roots contained meanings which he tried to recover. The verb "to be" is unique in western European languages in that, unlike all other verbs, it has three different roots, each of which once carried a different resonance. There is the Indo-European *es*, which initially meant "living": it lies behind *is, est, ist*; the Indo-Europeam *bhu* meant "emerging" or "standing autonomously", and it lies behind *fui, be, bin,* and *bist*. Then there is the Sanskrit *vasami*, meaning "to dwell, to linger, to belong to", and this lies behind *Wesen, gewesen, was, war, sum, sommes* and the Latin suffix *-am* used in past tenses. When each of these roots came to be fused in so many languages into being merely the expressions of tense, we forgot their potency and can no longer pick up the vibrancy of the "thereness" that these words representing Being convey.

This is one example of how we ought to attend to what language has to tell us. "Language", Heidegger tells us, "is the house of being. Man dwells in this

17 George Steiner - *Heidegger*. Fontana Press, 1978. I am greatly indebted to his lucid exposition of Heidegger's difficult and often cloudy philosophy.

18 Steiner, p. 42.

house." Our thinking is shaped by it. Again, Heidegger used German etymology to drive home his point, *"Denken ist Andenken"* – Thought is remembrance of the language. The German word for "pondering" or "reflecting" is *Nachdenken*, whose etymology is "thinking after", meaning that thinking comes after the reception of the original message which Being sends out. When we lose the original meaning that a word once had, we are sadly impoverished; conversely, we are enriched when we recover the original meaning.

> There is a school of thought today which urges us to accept that a language constantly changes and evolves, and that it is pedantic to try to preserve its original meaning. We simply have to accept, to use an example that would have been very meaningful to Heidegger, that the word "awful" has simply come to mean either "very" (as in, "I am awfully sorry") or "terrible" (as in "it's an awful shame"). Not only has the original meaning – to describe something that fills us with awe – been almost wholly lost, but when we do try to use it in its original meaning, it becomes faintly embarrassing or even risible. Is that not a sad loss? And does not the present association of the word "gay" make it difficult to use it in its original, and rather charming, meaning?

We should therefore gratefully acknowledge that the original sources of words can teach us something of which we have been unaware, so here comes another play on words, *Denken ist Danken*: "to think is to thank". Here is another one: to think is to at-tend on Being, to tend and treasure it; our role is to be the loving shepherd of Being (*der Hirt des Seins*).

The "thereness" (*Dasein*) of Being precedes our perceptions of it. When we start analyzing it, our language embodies the truth that in the analysis we know it (or rather, in part know) again, or "re-cognize" it. The initial cognition, because it is of the essential Being, is of something that is always much more than any subsequent analysis can convey. Music is so much more than the notes we perceive, poetry so much more than the words which make it up, a painting so much more than the pigment and canvas; in a great painting (Heidegger cites Van Gogh's *Boots*) more even than its analyzable content. The same is true of some concepts - for example "a nation". To Heidegger, the term conveys the "thereness", the Being of something which precedes, transcends and even defies any definition or analysis we make of it.

> Note how difficult it is to be precise about the meaning of "British", for example. This difficulty goes beyond the fact that the word may mean different things to different people. Even an individual who thinks he knows what it means for him will have trouble defining it exactly, yet it is a deeply meaningful concept. The concept itself sets up resonances, even if these vary from the narrow-minded and bigoted to the cultured and sophisticated.

If we want to understand a thing deeply, we must not impose an analysis on it. Heidegger enjoins what he calls *Letting-Be*. We need to open ourselves up to what it has to tell us, remembering Wordsworth's warning that we will "murder" it if we "dissect", and rejecting Francis Bacon's stance that "we put nature on the rack to compel it to answer our questions". Rather than demanding answers, we need to let the Being of something strike a chord in us, so that we are in "ac-cord" with it. Sure, we can ask questions in an analytical way - science would be impossible without it.

In many respects, progress in science has depended on our being able to discriminate analytically; a thing is this and not that. But even here we can go too far, as scientists themselves have discovered. For example, we used to believe that certain phenomena fell into the field of Biology while others fell into that of Chemistry. Now the new science of Biochemistry shows that such discrimination reduces our capacity to understand the phenomena we are studying.

In Heidegger's view, the answers a scientist *qua* scientist receives to his questions are generally not very significant from a philosophical point of view. The answers to analytical questions generally achieve at least a temporary consensus and, for the time being at any rate, they therefore settle a matter. Once settled, they become, for Heidegger, of secondary importance philosophically and occupy a lower place in the hierarchy of problems that should be entertained by philosophers. They are "in-essential" in that they do not address the essence, or Being, of whatever they investigate. There are many things in life that can be questioned (are *fragbar*), but for a philosopher only those questions are *worthy* of being asked (are *fragwürdig*) which humbly seek to respond to the mysterious, multi-layered and inexpressible meanings of Being.

We are reminded of the suspicion of the search for factual knowledge by medieval pre-Thomist theologians[19] and of the preference for intuition over analysis by the Romantics. Often the approach of Heidegger seems to be that of a mystic.

The distinction between the two approaches to nature – the asking and the listening – is perhaps somewhat artificial. Many scientists would say that they listen as much as they ask, and that, unless they ask some questions, they might not know what to listen for. Some philosophers tend to polarize issues. They do this generally because they want to combat what they think is the prevailing element in the culture of their time, and in Heidegger's view the prevailing culture in twentieth-century society was excessively dominated by science.

As for our own Being, this, of course, also precedes analysis. According to Heidegger, Descartes' *Cogito ergo sum* has it exactly the wrong way round. On the contrary, I am, therefore (being a member of the human species) I think.

In a sense that is obvious, one would imagine that in some sense even Descartes would have agreed with it. We can assume that Descartes knew "intuitively" that he existed before he coined the aphorism, but that he felt the need to provide a rational basis for that intuition (and for the whole logical edifice he erected upon that statement). The Cartesian outlook prides itself on logic, on the use of reason, and on the close analysis and tightly constructed arguments which all this involves. The aim of Cartesianism is to achieve knowledge that is as precise and certain as the knowledge we get from mathematics – but that was precisely the kind of knowledge that Heidegger thought was at best *fragbar* and at worst missed the truth altogether because it had "murdered to dissect". In any case, that little phrase, *cogito ergo sum*, had become a kind of mantra, a basis for a particular philosophy of life which Heidegger wanted to dethrone in favour of one that listens to nature rather than tries to analyze it.

19 see p. 104 above.

Being comes before knowing, and very often knowing is directly – that is, not through the mediation of focussed thought – in touch with the Being of something other than ourselves. This is most obvious in what Heidegger calls "primordial understanding". The phrase implies that this kind of understanding precedes intellectual thought or analysis. Examples he gives include the intuitive ways in which an artist uses his brush or pen, a craftsman his tools, a sportsman his equipment, a rider his horse, or a driver his car. Each understands and is in touch with the Being of the thing he uses.

They are of course all *learnt* actions, and in that sense not primordial at all. Nor does learning necessarily result in such intuitive being-in-touch. Some people will never learn it at all, will always be clumsy, will never have the satisfaction of, as it were, "swinging" with the thing they use. Others acquire, by learning and repetition, the habit of achieving a reasonable result, but with some people there comes a critical point when they reach a stage of harmony with the things they use that is more the result of an attitude of mind than any amount of learning or practice. Here one might well recognize what Heidegger meant by being in touch with the thing's Being. This is one theme of Robert M. Pirsig's thought-provoking philosophical novel *Zen and the Art of Motorcycle Maintenance.*

Das Man

"Being" is always "Being-With". We are an integral part of the world, and, as far as other human beings are concerned, our "Being" is naturally a socialized Being.

Compare Aristotle's dictum that "man is a political [meaning social] animal".[20]

The easiest and most natural thing for a socialized being to do is to conform to what others are doing. Sartre will refer to those others as *les autres;* Heidegger uses the expression *Das Man. Man* is the German equivalent of the English "one" in such expressions as "that's the way one should behave".

One might think that conformity (if it is not the result of a rationally analyzed strategy for "getting on") is almost intuitive, and in what we have seen so far, Heidegger saw the intuitive approach as more valuable than the analytical one. Of course, this is not the line that he takes on conformity. Like all existentialists he tells us that we must rise above this natural inclination; we must be authentic and take responsibility for our own actions. When we discover that our adhesion to *Das Man* is "ungrounded" (that is, not rooted in our authentic decision-making) we no longer feel comfortable in the world we have inhabited so far. We will experience *Unheimlichkeit* – translated as "discomfort", but the etymology of the German word actually implies that we are no longer "at home" in that world. Thereafter, we will first experience the fear (*Furcht*) of leaving the comfort of conformity, the worry about what other people might think of us if we behave in a way they think is unconventional, and indeed, sometimes the fear of being discriminated against or even persecuted for speaking our mind. *Furcht* is really a kind of cowardice. In some situations, relatively little courage is theoretically required to behave authentically, whereas in others, very great courage may be called for. In both kinds of situations, however, we are con-

20 See the discussion on p. 51f above.

fronted with the *choice* of whether to draw back and continue to live inauthentically or whether to accept responsibility for ourselves and (since Being is also Being-With) for our relationship with others. If we exercise our Will and show the resolve (*Entschlossenheit*) to choose responsibility and authenticity, we will initially experience another kind of fear: the dread (*Angst*) about what we should now do to be true to ourselves. It is the *Angst* to which Kierkegaard had referred when he had called his book *Fear and Trembling*, and when he had compared us to the baby eagle leaving its nest and casting itself into the void,[21] and, as it was for Kierkegaard, this *Angst* is creative - it leads us to take trouble (*Sorge*) to work out what is really authentic for us.

Again, because Being is also "Being-With", responsibility towards oneself also involves responsibility towards others. Obviously, detaching oneself from *Das Man* does not mean detaching oneself from society; on the contrary, it requires active awareness of and involvement with the "Beingness" of others. Heidegger here has the same idea that Buber had expressed in the concept of the "I-Thou" relationship, as opposed to the "I-It" relationship which treats others merely instrumentally.[22]

More about Language

The person who has repudiated *Das Man* can often be identified by the kind of language he uses. He will not use jargon, clichés, or empty phrases, which indicate shallow thought and superficial understanding. Heidegger calls this kind of talk *Gerede*, the German word for "chatter". Authentic being expresses itself in a thoughtful use of language. Heidegger says that only such language merits being called *Rede* (speech). It is to be found in its most freshly-minted form among great poets. A poet scarcely *wills* a poem, it comes to him because he opens himself up to Being. The German word for poet is *Dichter*, and the root of this word is *dicht*, meaning dense, condensed. A great poet packs a world of meaning into a single word or phrase, and is best qualified to express thereby the multiplicity of resonances of Being. The poet and other creative artists do not literally create something that was not there before. German etymology is again called in aid to explain: the German for creation is *Schöpfung*, but the original and basic meaning of *schöpfen* is, "to draw up from a well", the creative artist draws on what is already present in the wells of Being and so makes it accessible to the reader or spectator who then, too, can re-cognize it by letting Being speak to him. Heidegger admired the poet Hölderlin, who had said, "poetically, man dwells on this earth", meaning that if he dwells in any other way, he is merely skimming the surface of life.

> Here again, the suggestion is that it is intuition rather than analysis which makes us respond to a work of art – a view we have already met in Bergson.[23] The poet *may* not think in analytical terms when he is writing his poem. If it has many layers of meaning, they *may* spring intuitively from his unconscious. Even here we may succumb to an overly romantic vision of the creative pro-

21 see p. 417 above.

22 See p. 491 above.

23 See p. 480 above.

cess. Perhaps Edison greatly exaggerated when he described genius as one percent inspiration and ninety-nine percent perspiration, but the working and re-working of any poem by its author might suggest that a certain amount of analysis is involved in the final version. (Heidegger would presumably counter this by saying that the re-working is due to the poet's awareness that the first draft did not express satisfactorily enough what he had heard when he had opened himself up to Being.)

Certainly the minds of many students have been opened to the resonances of poetry by a good teacher. Can we really not benefit by having a work of art explicated to us, being helped to see it in a many-layered and more profound way?

Death

"Being" is not only "Being-With"; anyone who is in touch with "Being" realizes that it is also "Being-towards-Death". The inauthentic way of dealing with death is to avoid thinking or talking about it on the grounds that this is morbid. Once again, the person who would be authentic is likely to go through the stages of *Furcht* (the fear of what *das Man* will think of him if he breaks this convention), *Entschlossenheit* (resolve to break it), *Angst* (the dread involved in deciding what to do next), and *Sorge* (the trouble we take to work out what is now incumbent upon us).

The *Furcht* may take several forms, and one is the fear of other people thinking that it is morbid to talk about death. (Incidentally, we ought to remember that in Heidegger's time, there were many more social taboos about what could be talked about – whether it was sex or death – than there are today.) The other form it may take is our fear of death itself. Because we are frightened to confront the issues it poses, we avoid talking about it, but these *Angst*-provoking issues ought to be confronted and not evaded.

Moreover, this grappling with the issue is really something we ought to do throughout our life, not just as we draw towards its end. It is probably more difficult to be philosophical about death on our death-bed if we have never been philosophical about it beforehand. Psychotherapists tell us that in many situations what they call preliminary "worry-work" (i.e. *Angst*-work) will help us to cope better with the dreaded crisis when it comes, and this is all quite hard work. George Steiner puts it thus, "An authentic death has to be striven for." If we have striven for it, perhaps we will not, when the time comes, "rage against the dying of the light", complain about the pointless suffering and bodily indignities that we may have to endure, but rather meet it with resignation and acceptance.

Nathan A. Scott puts it like this: with *Angst*, the individual is now, "entrained towards a truly authentic lucidity, the kind of lucidity that will enable him to discern the relative triviality of the concerns to which the daily round is normally devoted and that will prompt him to undertake such projects as may give some really high significance to his human career."[24]

This is, of course, an old truth, particularly for religious people. "Lay not up for yourselves treasures upon earth, where moth and rust doth corrupt ... but lay up for yourselves treasures in heaven" (Matthew 6:19-20). And this is urged upon us as a life long outlook. Throughout our lives we ought to prepare our-

24 Scott, *op.cit.*, p. 97/98.

selves for what, in the end, will make for a "good death". Wealth and power you cannot take with you; the treasures "in heaven" (Heidegger makes no commitment to the afterlife in the religious sense) are things like lifelong honesty, integrity (i.e. authenticity), or *Sorge* for our responsibility to ourselves, to others and to the environment. It is true that only in deathbed repentance do many individuals realize that they have wasted their lives on inessentials or that they have lived unworthily. It is of course arguable whether it is only the awareness of death at the end of life which gives a person such a sense of proportion. It is more likely to be one's moral constitution than a consciousness of mortality. At the same time there are many people who, fully aware of their impending end, continue to attach great importance to their earthly treasures and spend much of their lives arranging for their wealth or their power to be passed on to their children.

Time

Our death is an event in time, and this leads Heidegger to draw a distinction between authentic and inauthentic time. If we live in inauthentic time, we take each moment as it comes, without relating it to what came before or what will come afterwards. If we live in authentic time, we are strongly aware of the interrelationship between past, present and future. As the German word shows, the past (*Gewesenheit*) is not finished when we are in the present, it continues to have its own *Wesen* – the German word for Being. The German word for the present is *Gegenwart*, whose etymological roots are *warten* (to wait) and *gegen* (towards). Our present is therefore a Waiting for the Future, and so loses its significance if it is detached from the Being of the past or the goal of the future. If we look at the past in isolation and become excessively preoccupied with it, we are so locked into the past that we cannot respond to change. If we fix our attention upon the future without understanding that it has a connection both with what is and with what was, we are likely to see it in the unrealistic terms of Utopianism. We cannot understand the present if we have no sense of perspective, both in the literal sense that we cannot see its links with past and future, and also figuratively, in that we attach overwhelming importance to what is only fleeting and fashionable (fashion being a typical product of *Das Man*.)

Another very apposite application of this is the ecological one. A generation that lives only in the present will not be prepared to make the necessary sacrifices to ensure that future generations will not be bearing the full brunt of, say, global warming or deforestation. It is all so obvious, and yet we see every kind of resistance from those for whom present comfort and convenience or present profit are the only things that matter.

A due respect for the past would involve careful thought (which is not always given) that, when we make necessary changes to past traditions or constitutions, we do not throw out the baby with the bathwater. I think Heidegger would have agreed with Burke's majestic statement that society is "a partnership not only between those who are living, but between those who are living, those who are dead, and those who are to be born."[25]

An authentic concept of time is therefore important not only for the individual, but also for society. Heidegger gave this notion a particularly historical appli-

25 See p. 343 above.

cation. Just as an authentic individual lives not only in the present but sees it as an integral part of the past and the future, so an authentic people or *Volk* should be aware both of its history and of its destiny.

The word *Volk*, it will be remembered, had been a key concept for Herder.[26] He, too, had attributed authenticity to the *Volk*, as distinct from the inauthenticity in the ruling classes who chose to speak in a language (French) different from that of their people and who valued French literature above the ancient native literature of their country.

> Today, ironically, it is French intellectuals who are alarmed by the intrusion of foreign words into their language. They feel particularly touchy about this perhaps precisely because French culture had once dominated the continent.

The *Volk* had therefore become an essential part of the vocabulary of German nationalism - the Nazi party was *völkisch* through and through. Hitler made much of the past of the German *Volk* and of the future which was summoning it to its destiny, and Heidegger recognized in the Führer's rhapsodic invocations of the word an expression of his own philosophy. Herder had urged every *Volk* to be true to its own native traditions, but there had been no suggestion in his writings, as there was in Nazism, that one *Volk*'s traditions were superior to those of another. Heidegger may not have trumpeted the superiority of German culture, but we have already seen that he believed that there was something very special about the German language - no other, except Greek, was so profound or reverberated with such insights into meaning.

National Socialism had other features which chimed in with what Heidegger had already written. When the Nazis inveighed against rootlessness and extolled the notion of *Heimat*, Heidegger saw therein the value he attached to being rooted in Being, to feel "at home" in the world. Hitler also constantly used the word *Entschlossenheit* (decisive determination or commitment) for his determination to make radical decisions, and here, too, he used a term that had a special meaning for Heidegger. Heidegger also responded to the Nazi claim to see archetypal virtues in the craftsman and the farmer. George Steiner describes Heidegger as "an agrarian through and through".[27] He had the romantic's admiration for the man who has an empathy for his tools and for the soil. He believed that in the countryside there are more authentic individuals than in the cities, where *Das Man*, through mass culture, exerts much more influence.

> This glorification of the sturdy independent thinking (i.e. authenticity) of the peasant, who may not have much education, but in his communion with nature has a wisdom beyond that of the superficial town-dweller, ignores that the peasant was at least as much under the control of his society and the indoctrination of the priests as any town-dweller. Nevertheless, we have here a *topos* much beloved by romantics, who see the countryman as a reflective and sturdy individualist, and play down the pressure that a village community often exerts over its members. The *topos* was popular in the late nineteenth century and in the twentieth century among those sections of society who

26 See p. 356 above. See also the discussion of the *Sturm und Drang* movement which had slightly preceded Herder, p. 326 above.

27 Steiner, *op.cit.*, p. 141.

> were finding it difficult to come to terms with "modernism" – the development of industry and urbanization, and the "rationalization" of many aspects of society. That soil produced both Heidegger and the Nazi propaganda extolling the virtues of the land and of the peasants who worked on it.

The countryman is in tune with nature, with the field and the forest, the *Wald* that is such a potent image in the German romantic imagination. Heidegger had always used metaphors from fields and forests, increasingly so as he grew older.[28] One of his later books (1950) was called *Holzwege* (Paths in the Forest). The image was that a search for the truth is like following paths in the forest towards a clearing (the German is *Lichtung*, with the etymological root of light) at the centre.

Heidegger was a philosophical ecologist. In a pre-mechanized society, farming was a way of *giving* to nature by sowing and *accepting* from nature by harvesting. It was a *vocation* – that is, a response to nature's call. Modern farming is a form of *enslaving* nature, forcing what we call technology upon it, and forgetting that the original meaning of the Greek *techne* (so Heidegger tells us) was not just skill but, "bringing into true being what was there". Instead of farming remaining a *vocation*, it has become a *provocation* to her – it treats nature as a mere object. The German word for an object is *Gegenstand*, whose etymological root is "stand against".

> In this context, it is significant to compare Nazi and Soviet propaganda paintings of the farming life. The Nazi farmer was always shown using ancient farming implements – the spade, the plough and the scythe. Soviet art gloried in the tractor, and Soviet planners were clear that they believed in Man's mastery over nature. Soviet films also revelled in the power of industrial machinery. A Heideggerian opponent might say that it portrayed Man having lost his individuality and being shown as a mere extension of the machine. Of course, one need not be a Heideggerian to make this interpretation, it could equally be made by left-wing critics of capitalism, such as Charlie Chaplin so memorably made in the film *Modern Times*.

Heidegger went back as far as Plato and Aristotle to see the origin of our alienation from nature. Plato had taught that everything in this world was but a pale or distorted reflection of Ideals laid up in Heaven. In Heidegger's opinion that was bound to alienate humans from nature rather than to integrate them with it. Moreover, through Neo-Platonism this notion entered Augustinian Christianity, which also taught the unimportance of this world compared with the next. Only with Thomism did Christianity endow concern with this world with respectability – and at the beginning of his academic career, Heidegger had been a Thomist. Aristotle was more interested in this world, but his influence was pernicious also. His zest for analyzing nature into its different components was the beginning of that destructive analysis, that murderous dissection of which Wordsworth was to speak. In their different ways, Plato, Aristotle and St

28 Some commentators have seen in his later philosophy a *Kehre* (a turning or even a reversal) – paying less attention to the nature of Man and the problems of individual authenticity and more to the wider Nature in which Man is rooted. Heidegger himself rejected the notion of a *Kehre*, saying that the later phase was an organic development and extension of the earlier one.

Augustine all contributed to *alienating* us from Being and from nature instead of integrating us with it.[29]

The modern manifestation of technology reflects the Will to Power, which had been so extolled by Nietzsche. It is the attempt to master and *control* the world instead of attending to it. It brings results, of course - we have wrested from nature much that contributes to our wealth and power - but we pay a heavy philosophical, psychological, and societal price for this gain. The philosophical price is that we have become, according to Heidegger, "homeless on earth", alienated from nature's Being. The psychological price is living under the threat of technology escaping from our control. When we split the atom, we let a genie out of the bottle, and it may destroy us. Nature will revenge itself upon us in the form of climatic catastrophes as we cut down the precious forests and take no care to give as well as to receive.

> One can imagine what he would have said about the feeding techniques that have brought the scourge of BSE, not only upon cattle but then also, as CJD, upon humans. What would he have felt about battery farming or the terrible consequences that may follow from our experiments with genetic modification?

Though Heidegger was certainly a romantic and in his political allegiance a fascist, one does not have to be either a romantic or a reactionary to accept that in his philosophy he addressed some of our deepest concerns. His call to authenticity, a secular form of injunctions contained in many religions, is doubly important in an age when religious teaching has declined and the pressure for conformity, exerted by the mass media, is arguably greater than it has ever been. However, partly because of the obscurity and difficulty of his style, partly because his play on German words is particularly difficult to translate into English, and partly because of his unsavoury political reputation, it is not Heidegger's name that first occurs to one when one thinks of Existentialism, but that of Jean-Paul Sartre.

JEAN-PAUL SARTRE
1905 to 1980

Introduction

If many people are put off by Heidegger's connections with Nazism, Sartre's anti-fascist credentials present no such obstacle. After the war, Heidegger could take no part in public life and secluded himself rather self-consciously in his cottage at Todtnauberg, in the midst of the Black Forest. Sartre deliberately lived in the glare of publicity. He was a tireless participant in left-wing causes and demonstrations, and, in 1948, formed his own short-lived political movement - the *Rassemblement Démocratique Révolutionnaire*. Unlike Heidegger, he was not much interested in the past, but lived intensely in the present. The *avant garde* journal he founded in 1944 and edited for the rest of his life, significantly called *Les Temps Modernes*, was immensely influential. He wrote sparkling plays and novels and those who found the text of his academic

29 For Plato, see p. 32 above; for Aristotle, p. 47 above; for Augustinianism, p. 104 above; and for Thomism, p. 132 above.

philosophical works forbidding could catch the flavour of his ideas in these intellectually less demanding works. At his favourite Café des Flores in the Quartier Latin he was accessible to writers and students. He championed the young; the message conveyed by his bohemian life-style was popular among them, and the students of 1968 regarded him as their guru. He also spelt out in much more concrete and practical terms than Heidegger had done the demands and problems of commitment and authenticity, and this, too, made his treatment of existentialism more accessible. The word "existentialism" had been used to describe a certain kind of philosophy before it was used by Sartre,[30] but it was Sartre whose work gave it currency with a wider public.

Alienation from the World

While Sartre's thought has something in common with Heidegger's, there are also major differences between the two. For Heidegger, the word existentialism was so much identified with Sartre and his followers that he repeatedly objected to it being applied to his own philosophy. He contemptuously dismissed Sartre's *L'Être et le Néant* as *Dreck* (muck). It is a strong expression, but one can see why that book revolted him.

Like Heidegger, Sartre was very conscious of the Beingness of things in the world, as he was of the Nothingness that precedes our Being. (His notion of this Nothingness will be discussed presently.) But Heidegger (like Martin Buber) had seen the consciousness of Being-With as an intimate and enriching fusion between the subject and the object, between oneself and the things in the world. Sartre returns to the Cartesian tradition in France, to the notion that consciousness (the mind) is separate from matter (the Being of other people and things in the world). Moreover, Buber and Heidegger had criticized us if we treat the Being of other people and things as objects. Buber had described this undesirable relationship as *I-It*, and Heidegger had made play with the German word for object, *Gegenstand*, which nicely conveys a hostile confrontation between the subject and the object. Both had taught that we escape this sterile or hostile relationship if we understand Being correctly. Sartre, at least in his early years, believed that such an escape is impossible. The "others" - things, people - are quite naturally alien to us, and the individual is doomed to be the Outsider - *L'Étranger*, the title of a novel by the existentialist writer Albert Camus. Buber had urged upon us an *I-Thou* relationship in which we accept and open ourselves up to each other, as we do especially in loving relationships. Against this, Sartre saw us as fundamentally lonely, and as compelled either to treat others as objects and to impose ourselves on them (which he called sadism) or to accept being regarded and treated as objects when others impose themselves on us (masochism). In *L'Être et le Néant* (1943) he could visualize no other relationship, from which results one of his most famous sayings (in the play called *Huis Clos* - No Exit, 1944) that "Hell is other people."

If the confrontation with people is unpleasant, then that with things is equally so. Heidegger's response to the Being of things was a sense of wonder. Sartre's is first of all a sense of alienation and absurdity which fills him with a

30 The Oxford English dictionary finds its first use in German in 1919, its first use in English was not until 1941.

fear that is neither Heidegger's *Furcht* nor his ultimately creative *Angst*. Sartre cannot see any logic that would account for the "thereness" of things, that would give them a grounding, and in that sense, behind the world appearances there is Nothing (*Néant*). There is no more reason for objects to exist than there is for oneself. Everything is simply "thrown" into this world. The notion of being "thrown" is also to be found in Heidegger, but in his philosophy we, other people, and things are all thrown into the world as an *integral* part of it, with the potential for the Being of all these parts to "speak" to each other in mutual spiritual harmony and enrichment. For Sartre, there is no integration, just a brutal casualness. The world is totally indifferent to the individual, and the fact that it all ends in death merely underlines the irrationality, the meaninglessness, the absurdity [31] of it all. It makes existence – our own and that of everything else – "superfluous".[32] On the face of it, that belief should make all our painful efforts to be authentic pointless, but, as we know, that was not the position Sartre took. He would have agreed with the Spanish philosopher Miguel de Unamuno (1864 to 1936) that, "If it is nothingness that awaits us, let us so act that it shall be an unjust fate."[33]

Sartre cannot see even temporary beauty in the world, on the contrary, in contemplating it, he experiences a sense of nausea. The image of nausea is used in *L'Être et le Néant*. Five years earlier, in 1938, it had been the theme of his novel, *La Nausée*. In it, the central character has a positively schizoid view of the objects around him – his own hand, a seat in a railway carriage, trees in a park – seeing them as slimy, sticky and disgusting. (It may be the revolting vividness of these images that made Heidegger react to them with the word *Dreck*.)

Choosing

One might think that all these sweeping statements about the world are not a matter of philosophy, but of Sartre's individual psychology (not to call it pathology), but now come the philosophical questions, questions involving analysis, definition, and ethical responses. If the world is such a bleak place, what is there for us to do in it? Does it not drive us to despair? Why not commit suicide? It is in his answers to these questions that Sartre has something important to say to people of a less gloomy disposition. As he says in his play *Les Mouches* (1943), "Life begins on the other side of despair."

Many philosophers from Aristotle onwards [34] have looked for the *essence* of Man and of things. The essence of something is that by which we identify and *define* a thing, so that, for example, we recognize the continuity of a particular human being between babyhood and adulthood. Essence is therefore present during the whole lifetime of that human being. The development from baby-

31 Colloquially, we use the word absurd of something that makes us laugh. That is of course not the sense in which Sartre and Camus use it. They stick closer to the root of the word, the Latin "absurdus" initially referred to sounds that are so muffled (cf. the French "sourd" meaning "deaf") that they reach us as a meaningless jumble.

32 We remember that, for Heidegger, a proper awareness of the inevitability of death should *protect* us from the absurdity and meaninglessness of much with which we normally fill our lives. It should precisely help us to lead a really meaningful life.

33 Unamuno – *The Tragic Sense of Life*, p. 263

34 For Aristotle on Essence, see p. 45 above.

hood to adulthood is predetermined by the entelechy inherent in essence (though it can be thwarted or impeded by outside circumstances like a fatal accident). This idea of essence is largely physiological, but Sartre uses the word in an entirely psychological sense, to express what sort of a personality one is, which is defined by what choices we make in life. So for him, we have no essence or identity when we are born - only existence. In *Existentialism is a Humanism* (1946) he writes "Existence precedes Essence ... Man first of all *exists*, encounters himself, surges up in the world - and *defines himself* afterwards. If Man as the existentialist sees him is not definable, it is because to begin with he is nothing. He will not be anything until later, and then he will be what he makes of himself."[35]

> This is clearly at the opposite pole of the view that man is shaped essentially by the effect his environment has upon him. We admittedly have certain faculties (of understanding, of temperament etc.) with which we then handle these experiences. An existentialist will lay the strongest possible emphasis on the power of these tools, while some schools of psychology stress the overwhelming importance of the environmental influences from infancy onwards.

Sartre insists that, within certain limits of external constraints (the "facticity" we shall discuss presently) Man shapes himself. He is free to choose what kind of a person he wants to be, and it is how he uses that freedom of thought *and then how he acts upon it* that defines him. It is not what we think or preach that defines us, but what we do, "By their fruits ye shall know them" (Matth.7:20).

> The faculty we use when we make choices and act upon them is will power. This implicit stress on the importance of the Will places Sartre squarely within the Romantic tradition, as exemplified especially by Nietzsche.[36]

That freedom is an inescapable condition of Man. It is often a burden because significant choices are always difficult to make, and very often we claim that we have no choice, are not really free at all. Even refusing to make a choice is choosing not to choose, and we have to accept responsibility for what flows from that decision.

> If, for example, as the result of our abstention in an election – either because we dislike all the candidates or because we cannot be bothered to vote – an extremist party (say) wins which might not have won if people like us had not abstained from voting, then we are *responsible* for the victory of that extremist party.

We are therefore totally responsible; there are no excuses. Sartre insists that "Man is condemned to be free".[37] Therefore, if we say that we are not free, that we have no choice, then we are, for whatever reason (cowardice, ignorance, the desire to conform to *les autres*) deceiving ourselves and are guilty of inauthenticity or of what Sartre called "bad faith" (*mauvaise foi*).

35 Note that the word "essence" comes from *esse*, to be. Sartre, as an existentialist, shares Heidegger's interest in "Being". Before we acquire Being in the Sartrean sense, we are, as he says, "Nothing". (His main philosophical book is called "Being and Nothingness.") Of course we cannot take the word "nothing" literally, because after all, as soon as an embryo or a new-born baby exists - even if it does not yet have essence in the Sartrean sense - it is after all "something"!

36 See pp. 476f above.

37 *Existentialism is a Humanism.*

> Sartre's companion, Simone de Beauvoir, was an existentialist, too, but she pointed out that one cannot accuse someone of bad faith if one has no awareness of the freedom one has. This would apply to children and also, she maintained, to most women at that time – though in her feminist book, *Le Deuxième Sexe* (1949), she did her best to illustrate and emancipate women from this state of affairs. Until they were emancipated, they were more victims of deceptions (she called them *mystifications* – what we would now call "brain-washing") imposed on them by others than of self deception or "bad faith". It was not their fault if they fell victim to these deceptions, any more than Marxists thought it was the fault of the workers that many of them had been brain-washed into "false consciousness".[38] Just as a committed Marxist sees it as one of his functions to awaken the workers from their false consciousness, so Simone de Beauvoir saw it as hers to awaken women from *mystification*.
>
> Yet, in 1949, no French woman, whether she agreed with it or not, could really be in ignorance of the feminist case; the injustice of their position must have rankled with most of them at least at some times in their lives. They, too, therefore, had a choice of whether to submit, or to run the risks that many feminists did run if they rebelled. The risks were, after all, on a different scale from those run by Afghan women who would like to rebel against the Taliban. In their case, the constraints are so overwhelming that one can really speak of massive facticity (see below), akin to the facticity of the chains which bind a prisoner.
>
> Sartre could never have accepted the weakening of his call to authenticity by invoking "mystification" as an excuse, either for women or for children. Children, too, have, from very early on, to choose between obedience and rebellion, and if, in the end, women and children internalize the standards imposed on them to such an extent that they take these standards as given, that is not really different from the internalizations that adult males often make of social norms. This *can* of course be a matter of authentic decision-making, but we know how often it is merely the path of least resistance to the demands of *les autres* and is therefore *mauvaise foi*.

Sartre gives several valuable examples of what good faith and authenticity demand. For instance, there are some judges who are privately opposed to the death penalty, but who feel that, in a country where it is mandatory for certain offences, they have no choice but to impose it. Not so, says Sartre, they have the choice to resign from the judiciary. Of course, it could be a painful choice to forfeit the prestige and pay of the position, and possibly to inflict hardship on their families, but it would be bad faith to say that they must obey the rules of their profession. It goes without saying that he would never accept the defence of Nazis who said that "they were only obeying orders". In cases where comrades have been betrayed after torture, it is never right to say, "I couldn't take any more" - only that, "I chose not to take any more". A Frenchman who would not defy the Gestapo because he was concerned about what would happen to his family if he were caught and executed, should not say, "I couldn't help putting my family first", but should say instead, "I chose to put my family first" - and Sartre would then have accepted *and respected* this choice as authentic.

38 See p. 450 above.

This philosophy made Sartre explicitly take issue with the Freudian view that there are choices which stem from our unconscious, over which, as a result, we have no control and for which we therefore cannot be held responsible.

> It is obvious that in the age-old debate between Free Will and Determinism, Sartre was firmly on the side of Free Will. He would have been aware that he could not refute all the determinist arguments against it, but he thought that the case for Free Will was stronger, and therefore he would make an existential commitment to it – just as an existentialist Christian would commit himself to Christianity while acknowledging the strength of the arguments against it.
>
> Now a commitment to Free Will is on the Romantic side of the Romantic-Classical divide. Free Will is basically something we *feel* we have; we simply assert it, as it were, with our heart. Determinism, however, at least in its modern form, is a by-product of science and ratiocination: we assent to it largely with our head. Once again, existentialism shows itself as basically a romantic philosophy.

If one believes in God, the decision about what God would have one do is difficult enough. Sartre was an atheist, and an atheist existentialist can obviously not rely on religion to help him to make moral choices. We are, he says, "abandoned" (by whom or by what?) to our own resources.[39] The religious person tends to believe in values that are absolute (though this is not true of the religious existentialist).[40] As Sartre believed that there were no absolute criteria and that every ideology has weaknesses which can be fairly exposed by its opponents, he also thought that invoking any such criterion as a justification for a course of action was a device to shuffle off responsibility, and was therefore another example of inauthenticity.

One imagines that Sartre's experience during the Nazi occupation of France had much to do with this position. Though he was always on the Left, he was never an orthodox Marxist. (His view that the individual was a lonely and non-social being would not be compatible with Marxism). Nevertheless, despite his recognition of what was wrong with communism, he made a commitment to the communist cause, both during and after the war, because he saw the communists as the only *effective* opponents of fascism and imperialism. Fastidious abstention from such a commitment was a luxury one could not allow oneself during the Occupation because it would effectively strengthen the fascist cause.

Even such a commitment to the Resistance might clash with other commitments. He gives the example of the pull on a young man between, on the one hand, leaving France to join the Free French in England and, on the other, the demands of a much loved and dependent elderly mother whom he would have to leave behind. No formula can resolve the anguish (*angoisse*) caused by such a clash between one right cause and another, and yet a choice between them is inescapable.

> Here again, Sartre rejects the determinist view of such a situation. The pure determinist would say that the outcome would be the result of whichever motive exerted the stronger "magnetic" pull (itself the result of the son's earlier

39 cf. Nietzsche, p. 476 above.

40 See the introduction to this section, p. 488 above.

experiences),[41] the son could not help being attracted by the more powerful magnet. Choice (the result of Free Will) did not really come into it. After all, our education is usually designed to strengthen our will power. If there is within us a strong component to be, say, aggressive, we are encouraged from childhood onwards to exercise our will power and to tame that instinct (i.e. to counteract the force of that particular magnet) and not to be unacceptably aggressive. The assumption is that the "magnet" is strong, but not irresistible. If we were to recognize it as irresistible, then educational efforts to strengthen the will would simply be a waste of time.

So Sartre insists that the son is free – is, indeed, *compelled* to be free – to make the choice between these painful alternatives. If, for example, the son decides to stay in France, he should not say that loved his mother so much that he really did not have a choice, that would be *mauvaise foi*. Instead, he should say that he *chose* the course he took. Besides, denying our *ability* to choose is accepting a *degrading* description of the human condition. The existentialists say that we are called upon to make something dignified of our life.[42]

It will be noted that there seems to be a contradiction between the examples we have been discussing (all of which involve some commitment to causes or to other people) and his early insistence, in *Nausea* (1938) or in *Huis Clos* (1944), that we are lonely and alienated from the world, and that our relationships with other people must be based on antagonistic confrontation. But in *Existentialism is a Humanism* (1946) he recognized that deep down we know that other human beings are as human as we are. To treat them simply as objects is a denial of that recognition, and is therefore untruthful and inauthentic.[43] If I am condemned to freedom, then so is my neighbour, and I need to acknowledge his freedom as much as I do my own. Commitment to personal authenticity therefore demands a commitment to other individuals (even *though* we are doomed to relate to them either "sadistically" or "masochistically")[44] and, by extension, to causes that protect both our freedom and theirs in public life.

We often experience that apparent contradiction in our own lives. Other individuals may repel us, and yet we may scruple to deprive them of their freedom.

Sartre had declared that no values are absolute, so one might think that freedom was a value to which he was only existentially committed, but he *defined* one component of existentialism as an acceptance that we must accept not only our own freedom, but also that of others. From this it must follow that it is impossible to be an existentialist and at the same time espouse a philosophy that denies the importance of freedom. One could therefore not be an existential fascist, for example. We have seen in the introduction to this chapter that one could be an existential Christian: such a person would acknowledge that he could not refute arguments against Christianity, but he would think there is more to be said for Christianity than against it, and he would therefore make an existential commitment to Christianity. For Sartre, this line of thought could

41 See p. 489 above.

42 Cf. Unamuno, p. 506 above.

43 Sartre – *What is Literature?*, 1949.

44 See p. 505 above.

not apply to "existential fascism", for whereas an existentialist Christian could accept his own freedom as well as that of others, the fascist denies the importance of the freedom of others. We might note here in passing that Sartre's conception of Freedom was a straightforward "classical" one. He had no truck with the pernicious Rousseauist notion espoused by fascists that real freedom consists in obedience to the "General Will".[45]

So in this instance Sartre found himself, for once, on the classical side of the Romantic-Classical divide.

For one thing, of course, he would have thought that obedience to the General Will was, after all, an acceptance of the demands of *les autres*. Sartre is an individualist. For Sartre, his commitment to freedom meant supporting socialism – democratic socialism wherever possible, but hard-line Marxism or Maoism where these stood the best chance of achieving freedom from fascist, imperialist or capitalist oppression.

One might argue that hard-line Marxists and Maoists had as little respect for "classical" freedom as fascism did. Indeed, Sartre, even while he marched with such people when they were fighting capitalism or imperialism, did speak out against their dictatorial practices and, for example, came out strongly against the Soviet intervention in Hungary in 1956. He acted with them when he thought they were right, and he opposed them when he thought they were wrong. Doubtlessly, he would have experienced *angoisse* from time to time in deciding which course of *action* he should commit himself to, but not for him the fastidious squeamishness which prevented some opponents of fascism from taking part in any communist-led demonstrations against it. Sartre would never be like the indecisive donkey between the bales of hay.[46]

Facticity

Sartre, like Heidegger, accepts that there are certain external and genuinely inescapable constraints on our freedom. These were described as "Facticity". The chains which fetter a prisoner are facticity. Clearly he does not have the freedom to escape his chains, but even in prison he has the choice of whether to defy his jailers, to plan escapes, to despair or to accept. One's make-up can also be part of that facticity. One's choices may, for example, be restricted by one's lack of intelligence, talents, or health. Under certain circumstances it could be bad faith to deny one's make-up, for instance, if one entertains extravagant ambitions to be an artist when one really has no talent.

These cases are difficult to decide. On the one hand, Hitler could persuade himself that he had great artistic gifts when, in the eyes of real artists, they were only mediocre. On the other, Van Gogh's confidence in his own talents was not recognized by other artists in his lifetime, and yet no one could now claim that he had gone in for self-deception.

Sartre also illustrates a dilemma about homosexuality. Is one's acceptance that one is a homosexual a recognition of facticity and therefore an example of good faith? Or is it bad faith to assert that one cannot help giving in to one's homosexual urges?

45 See pp. 335ff above.

46 See p. 488 above.

Sartre calls on each individual to be honest with himself. Very often the outside world cannot judge whether a person is acting authentically or in bad faith. In the case of homosexuality, for example, only the person concerned can tell whether his condition represents facticity – a "given" within which he *has* to operate, so that he could no more escape it than a prisoner can escape his chains – or whether it is something he could resist if he made the choice to resist it.[47] In the latter case, the choice is authentic only if the individual decided *for himself* whether to act out his homosexuality or to repress it. If his decision to repress it is made *merely* in response to the pressure of society (and in Sartre's day, that pressure was enormously greater than it is today), then he is simply conforming to *les autres* – and we know that an action cannot be authentic if it represents simply automatic acceptance of *les autres*. This again is something of which only the individual concerned can be the judge. Sartre himself does not sit in judgment over what an individual does, for he is not in a position to do so, he merely calls upon the person concerned to sit in *honest* judgment over his own motivation and behaviour.

Conclusion

So we see that the view which Sartre presented of the total alienation of the individual from his environment did not lead him to total nihilism. He erected on top of it a structure of commitment, although we live in a world in which all values were relative. His notion of alienation may have been expressed in extreme terms, but there was (and is) enough of a feeling of alienation in western societies for many people to recognize in that part of his work something of their own estrangement from their surroundings. Arguably, there are more amateur and professional philosophers who are troubled by the disjunctions that Sartre saw in the world than there are those who are seized of the potential harmonies which had inspired Buber and Heidegger. However, Sartre's greatest influence lies, I think, not just in portraying the world as a bleak and repellent place but in the way in which, despite that, he summoned us (as Buber had done from a much more benign view of the world) to a recognition of responsibility towards ourselves and to others. He does, in the end, stand for something positive. He has shown us, at a time when relativism has made us more confused than ever about morals, how we can nevertheless make a defensible moral stand and live with integrity.

The existentialists were concerned with the meaning of our lives. In later chapters we will be dealing with some other thinkers who have this same interest, but before then we will have to look at philosophers who are more interested in the meaning of words.

47 Today, many homosexuals will deeply resent the comparison made here between being a homosexual and being in prison. They have made an authentic choice to act as homosexual and have resisted any pressures there may be from *les autres*. During most of Sartre's lifetime, however, the majority of homosexuals would have considered their own inclinations to be highly problematic.

CHAPTER 41

Twentieth Century Pragmatism

Introduction

Towards the end of the nineteenth century, Americans began to make an important contribution to the history of western philosophy (just as they did in other cultural fields, like literature and painting). Indeed, one may say that there is a largely English-language sequence of philosophy which begins with them, runs through the philosophers based in Cambridge (England) – Moore, Russell, Wittgenstein – and ends with Logical Positivism[1] and Linguistic Philosophy. It is called Analytical Philosophy because it focussed largely on analyzing the way we use language. It is therefore sharply differentiated from its contemporary, the continental school of the Existentialists, which centred on Man's relationship with his environment. The analytic philosophers were concerned with the Word, while the European continentals were concerned with the World.

One might think that a philosophy concentrating on the meaning of words would be easier to understand than one which deals with the sometimes cloudy concepts of the existentialists, but in fact it will be much more difficult. If we do not understand exactly what Heidegger meant by "Being" or Sartre by "Nothing-ness", we may nevertheless feel that we understand the kind of psychological states they describe because we have experienced aspects of the "human predicament" ourselves. To pin down how exactly we use language is an altogether more rigorous activity. Again, this might surprise us. A key phrase which the philosopher C.E.M. Joad popularized in the famous radio broadcasts of the Brains Trust during the 1940s was: "it all depends on what you mean by ..." That is a very useful phrase in a discussion on, say, "democracy" or "God", or in drawing fine distinctions between "freedom to" and "freedom from". We can therefore see in the expression a connection between Philosophy and Living. It is not always easy to see that link when professional philosophers discuss "meaning", the debate is often so technical that it may

1 Admittedly Logical Positivism began in Vienna, but it was A.J. Ayer's *Language, Truth and Logic* which popularized it in England. Besides, the Nazis destroyed Vienna as a centre of Logical Positivism. One of the leaders of the Vienna Circle, Rudolf Carnap, had emigrated to the United States in 1936 and taught his philosophy at American universities. Logical Positivism was, therefore, transplanted into the receptive Anglo-Saxon world. In England, Ayer saw himself as resuming the British analytical tradition which had culminated in Hume and then had been swamped by the influence of Kant, Hegel and other continental philosophers.

strike one as having only a very remote bearing on attempts to elucidate the meaning of a term we use in everyday discussion. This is why continental existentialism has had a much bigger impact on the educated general public than has the twentieth-century philosophy, which is largely associated with the Anglo-Saxon tradition. The professionals in this latter group were not at all troubled by this. They wrote for each other as professionals. If they had expository gifts, they were happy to use them, as A.J. Ayer did on the media, or Bertrand Russell in a series of books on current moral or political topics, but it was not important to them whether their technical philosophy was understood by non-professionals. John Dewey was the only one of them who, in theory and practice, applied his philosophy to political, social and educational issues.[2] The others thought, in Wittgenstein's famous phrase, that "Philosophy leaves everything as it is", its task is simply the *descriptive* one to elucidate the way we use words, not the *prescriptive* task of suggesting how people ought to live.

Because of what this book is trying to do – to show the link between Philosophy and Living – it will select only a few of the key ideas of these philosophers and will not be trying to do justice to their technical sophistication. Even then, it may be hard going.

CHARLES SANDERS PEIRCE
1839 to 1914

C.S. Peirce began his career as a physicist and astronomer, and the only book that he published in his lifetime dealt with astronomy. He earned his living working with the United States Coast and Geodetic Survey. His experimental work in Geodesics won him renown and led to him being elected to the National Academy of Sciences. He produced several papers for them, about a third of which were on logic, which was becoming his main philosophical interest. He held brief university appointments, at Harvard (1870/71) and at John Hopkins University (1879 to 1884). He did not get on with his academic colleagues, and when he inherited a small bequest in 1887 he retired, aged only forty-eight; it was in retirement, and in increasing poverty, that he produced most of his philosophical work. Very little of this, however, was published in his lifetime, and only relatively few people knew of it. Among them was his friend William James. James was much more successful in public academic life. He had become Professor of Philosophy at Harvard two years before Peirce retired. He did his unavailing best to secure academic posts for Peirce, and helped him financially, but perhaps the most important thing he did for his friend was to acknowledge his debt to him when he published his own book, *Pragmatism*, in 1907. The title itself was a tribute to his friend, who had given this name to an aspect of his philosophy in a series of articles he had published thirty years earlier. Peirce, however, did not agree with the direction in which James had taken his ideas, and renamed his own system "Pragmaticism". Even with the publicity that James had given to Peirce's ideas, it was not until 1931 that a beginning was made on publishing what would be the eight volumes of Peirce's Collected Papers.

2 Bertrand Russell's undoubted *engagement* in social and political matters had little to do with his philosophy (and the same is true of Noam Chomsky). No layman can cope with Russell's strictly philosophical writings, some of which – like his work on logic – involves higher mathematics!

The word "Pragmatism" comes from the Greek *pragmatos*, meaning a deed or action. It is related to the stem from which we get the word "practice". It is, Peirce said, by seeing how an idea (a statement of fact, or a theory, or a belief) works in practice, by seeing what are its sensible effects or consequences, that we ascertain its meaning. He wrote, "In order to ascertain the meaning of an intellectual conception, one should consider what *practical* consequences might *conceivably* result by necessity from the truth of that conception; and the sum of these consequences will constitute the entire meaning of that conception."[3]

We should consider what we *can do* to demonstrate the meaning, or what results *could do* so. For example, the meaning of the statement, "this stone is hard" can be explained (and be explained only) by describing the consequence of the pressure we *actually* exert or *could* exert on it, or else by showing the results of carrying out other actions with it, like, for example, using it as a weapon or a missile ("the sum of these consequences") the results would differ from those of such actions when carried out on or with a soft object, like a pat of butter.

> Needless to say, the word "hard" would often be too general to make the meaning clear, and it may have to be refined. For example, some stones are harder than others and a small stone might have a different effect from a large one, and so on. A piece of butter that has just come out of the deep freeze might be used just like a stone as a missile. So one might have to define the word "hard" more closely – perhaps we should use the words "very hard" as opposed to "fairly hard", or one might even have to use a scientific formula to describe the degree of hardness. None of this, however, would affect the argument, we would merely describe the meaning of the word "very hard" by showing what we can or could do with a very hard object that we could not do with an object that was only fairly hard.

The meaning of a statement of belief is to be assessed only by the results that flow or could flow from it, and from this it follows that two statements that in practice have the same outcome must have the same meaning. Coplestone illustrates the point thus:

> If one man says that he believes that there are other persons beside himself while another man says the opposite, and if we find them acting in precisely the same way by talking with others, questioning them, listening to them, writing them letters and so on, we naturally conclude that, whatever he may say, the second man really has exactly the same belief as the first man, namely that there are other persons beside himself.[4]

That was certainly a new way of disposing of solipsism! In fact, as Hume had pointed out, however strong the philosophical case for solipsism might be, one cannot possibly base one's life on that belief.[5] One can therefore find no *meaning* in solipsistic statements, as we cannot verify them by observable results or imagine any way in which they *could* be thus verified. Peirce is the father of the *Verifiability Theory of Meaning* which will be made famous by the Logical Positivists.[6]

3 The italics are mine.

4 Frederick Coplestone – *A History of Philosophy*, Vol. VIII, p. 315.

5 See p. 288 above. For a definition of solipsism, see p. 280, note 12 above, and for a discussion of the concept, pp. 283f above.

6 See pp. 550f below.

Peirce was primarily interested in eliciting what a statement might *mean*. One might stop there, without going on to ask whether the statement was also *true*. For example, someone might make the statement that no foreigner can be trusted, and indeed, he never does show any trust in even the most honest of foreigners. If we can show a correspondence between, on the one hand, what he says he believes and, on the other, the practical way in which he acts in accordance with that belief, then, *pace* the argument in the paragraph before last, we can reasonably say that we have understood the *meaning* of his statement.

But we find it hard to stop there. We want to verify not only its meaning, but also whether it is true; and we do that by applying other tests of verifiability, which would quickly show that some foreigners are totally trustworthy.

So when a statement has been or could be subjected to this second kind of verification, it becomes more than merely meaningful, it also enjoys the *temporary status* of being true. To go back to the earlier example, we can verify in the second way that a stone of a given size and density thrown with a given force will break a window whose glass is of a certain thickness. However, that statement will lose the status of being true if subsequent observable results can prove it false. A new type of glass may be invented which, though of the same thickness as that which had previously shattered, has been reinforced so that it does not break. We should always be on the lookout for results that may falsify or modify statements that have been taken as true, as is constantly happening in science. This aspect, which Peirce called *Fallibilism*, is a forerunner of Karl Popper's *Falsification Principle*.[7]

Although Peirce recognized that much of what we believe to be true is subject to falsification or modification, he did see an evolutionary process at work in the world and believed that the "temporary" truths we hold at a given time are stepping stones towards an objective truth, "independent of ... any man's opinion of that subject". Coplestone says, "We must conceive absolute and final truth as the ideal goal of enquiry. This ideal stands eternally above our struggles to attain it, and we can only approximate to it."[8]

Peirce applied this notion of an absolute and final truth not only to statements of the kind that scientists are interested in, but also to ethics. At various times he did in fact describe ethics as "the science of right and wrong", or as "the science of ideals", and if ethics is to be conceived as a science, then it will share with science the Peircean assumption that it, too, progresses towards, without ever reaching, a permanent and immutable truth.

> Some people might be attracted by the idea that there is an absolute truth in science, to which we all aspire. After all, despite the occasional backsliding or going off on the wrong tack, the progress of science has been very solid, demonstrable and impressive. Over the centuries we have learnt more and more about the way nature works, and by rational extrapolation, and not just by faith, we are tempted to assume that we approach ever closer to discovering the ultimate truth, even if we will never quite get there.
>
> It does, however, seem to require faith (literally so) to perceive a final truth in ethics. There are no agreed criteria by which to judge even temporary ethical

7 See p. 557 below.

8 *op. cit.* p. 308.

> truths. Human nature, in all its complexity, constantly pulls us hither and thither and clouds any clear assessments of ethics; regressions have been more frequent and far more savage in ethics than in any backsliding in science.
>
> Peirce (and James after him), did have faith, and perhaps that is why they would have seen the distinction between absolute truths in science and in ethics as differences in degree rather than as differences in kind. Peirce thought that there was an objective basis to morality, which was above and beyond the morality which arises in the context of society at any particular time, and he had the faith to believe that, harder though it is than in science, ultimately the world community will reach consensus on ethical matters also.

All this is thoroughly Platonic and metaphysical. Peirce derided much metaphysics as "meaningless gibberish", but he had no intention of rejecting metaphysics altogether, and in this he would differ from the Logical Positivists, who thought that *all* metaphysical statements were meaning-less.[9] Peirce believed, for instance, in a theistic God. The Platonic outlook led to it. Moreover, as a logician, he accepted some of the logical arguments that had been used over the centuries to prove the existence of God. In a self-avowedly Hegelian way, he saw God as the goal to which all the different evolutionary processes in the world aspired. For Peirce, the Platonic and Hegelian approach was strengthened by an experiential one – he was unwilling to discount the experience that believers (himself included) had of God.

Some beliefs about God certainly led to observable results. So we must describe as at least *meaningful* the two propositions "I believe in God" and "my belief in Him leads me to act in a certain way". They may lead the believer into being, say, charitable and peace-loving. (And of course we know that some are led by their belief into being harshly judgmental and militant.)

Like all meaningful statements, these must now be tested for truth. We have seen that Peirce thought he had reasons to think that the statement "God exists" was true. The connection between the belief and subsequent conduct was also often verifiably true. There is, of course, at least one link between the first and the second proposition, whose truth is not only not obvious, but is also not subject to verification or falsification. The full chain might run something like this:

1. "God exists"
2. "He commands us to be charitable and peace-loving"
3. "Because of His command, I act in a charitable and peace-loving way"

Peirce made no philosophical commitment to the truth of this middle proposition. As we shall see, William James found grounds for finding truth in both the first and the second (and therefore also in the third) proposition.

WILLIAM JAMES
1842 to 1910

William James (the elder brother of the novelist Henry James) was trained as a doctor, and his first appointment in his lifelong stint at Harvard was as Instructor in Physiology (1872). From physiology he turned to physiological psychology (1876). This was a new approach in American universities, where

9 See below, p. 551.

psychology had been considered from the philosophical and theological point of view, but not as a branch of physiology. He set up the first psychological laboratory in the United States and started work on a textbook which eventually took the form of the two-volume *Principles of Psychology* in 1890. By then, his interests had long moved to the psychology of religion and then to philosophy proper. Whilst not himself religious in any theological sense, he had great empathy with religious feeling. The work he did in this field found its most famous expression in a series of lectures in Edinburgh, which were then published as *The Varieties of Religious Experience* in 1902.

Perhaps it was the tension between his scientific training and the feeling that there was something "in" religion that turned him to philosophy. A year after he began to lecture on the subject, he was made Assistant Professor of Philosophy in 1880 and full Professor in 1885. From the beginning he was influenced by Peirce, and in 1907 he summed up his own philosophy in *Pragmatism.*

We have already seen that Peirce dissociated himself so much from James' version that he now described his own philosophy as "Pragmaticism". One reason for this was the sweeping, one may even say crude, way in which James often expressed himself in books and lectures. Certainly, the sensational manner in which James defined the truth, and the metaphor of cash value which he frequently uses, jar on our sensibility and may offend our feeling for the dignity of truth.[10] Where Peirce had stressed that the truths we believe in are temporary, aspiring towards an absolute truth in an evolutionary manner, James said, much more broadly, "The true is whatever proves itself to be good in the way of belief"; "An idea is 'true' so long as to believe it is profitable to our lives"; "Our obligation to seek truth is part of our general obligation to seek what pays" and:

> Truth lives, in fact, for the most part on a credit system. Our thoughts and beliefs 'pass' so long as nothing challenges them, just as bank notes pass so long as nobody refuses them. But this all points to face-to-face verification, without which the fabric of truth collapses like a financial system with no cash-basis whatsoever. You accept my verification of one thing, I yours of another. We trade on each other's truth. But beliefs verified concretely by somebody are the posts of the whole superstructure.

Note that he says only "by somebody", it is not necessary that they be verified by everybody.

10 We must remember that James was an American and was writing for an American public. Americans (as a generalization) were and are much more ready to discuss money openly than Europeans were. They have none of that aristocratic attitude that to show an interest in money is somehow sordid. Europeans are still influenced by what was originally an aristocratic attitude, which thought it bad form if at a social gathering one asked a new acquaintance how much money he earned; apparently Americans do not suffer so much from this inhibition. So it is unclear whether, when James so frequently compared the truth with cash values, he was speaking as he naturally thought, or whether, eager as he was for a large public, he chose striking phrases and financial metaphors because he knew that the American public would readily respond to it. His wish to address a large public may also have something American and democratic about it: philosophy should not be pursued in an ivory tower. Some European philosophers have been accused of living in an ivory tower, but they would scarcely take that as a criticism, philosophy is an academic discipline, and it is vulgarized if too much of an attempt is made to make it accessible to a wider public. If an Oxford philosopher compared truth with "cash values" in the way that James did, I fancy that his colleagues would be appalled. Perhaps that kind of élitism was alien to James, but his occasional slapdash "sound bites" certainly detract from the precision one should expect from a philosopher.

If we strip away the brash metaphors drawn from economic materialism, James is not saying anything that has not been frequently said in relativist philosophy before, from the Sophists onwards,[11] that there can be no notion of final truth, that all truth is subjective and is therefore dependent on us. We make our own truth, and we accept it as such for as long as it works to our satisfaction.[12] There is, therefore, an intimate connection between something being "true" and it being "useful" (or rather "temporarily true" and "temporarily useful"). In the physical sciences, at any rate, that is a very respectable position to hold, though perhaps some questions arise when we try to extend it to moral or ethical matters.

James made no distinction between scientific and ethical "truths". He wrote that, "we can say [of an idea or belief] that 'it is true because it is useful' or that 'it is useful because it is true'. Both phrases mean exactly the same thing."

> This is certainly not the way in which we normally use the word "useful". To give an example, in wartime it may be useful to think of the enemy as not being really human, but that hardly makes that useful belief true. Alternatively, people in the Middle Ages believed it to be true that the earth was flat and that one would fall off it if one sailed beyond its edge. That was hardly a useful belief – except in so far as it was what everybody else believed, and to challenge it might have caused the challenger to be treated as mad or heretical. Nor does the so-called "Wild Duck" syndrome (the compulsion to speak the truth at all times) make for a particularly useful social life. If the Gestapo demands of a householder whether he has seen someone they are looking for, it will undoubtedly be useful for him to persuade them that he saw that person fleeing into the woods instead of admitting that he is hiding in the cellar, but it does not make his statement true.
>
> Two of the above examples come from ethics, and we might note here James' radical difference from Kant, for whom ethical criteria had been categorical imperatives, and had to be totally separated from prudential considerations of "usefulness".[13]

In more cautious passages, James said that for a statement to be true it needs to agree with reality, but he believed that we make our own reality by making a selection from the world around us. The world bombards us with billions of impressions. The selection we make from these and the truths we build upon this selection are *subjective* and depend on what we are looking for or are interested in. Truth is a property of certain of our *beliefs*, not of *things*. As James wrote, "Realities are not true; they are; and beliefs are true of them." The selection we make will not always be the same. when our interests change, the selection we call reality changes also. The "knowledge" we have of "reality" is therefore not something we have, but something we make.

> Now this is what Kant had also said,[14] though for Kant the tools of understanding with which we make this phenomenal "reality" [15] were "high precision"

11 See the discussion on the Sophists, pp. 13f above.

12 I prefer the word "satisfaction" to the Jamesian one of "profit" or "advantage".

13 See pp. 374f above.

14 See p. 364 above.

15 I put the word "reality" into inverted commas, as for Kant the phenomenal world was not reality at all. That word was reserved for the unknowable *Ding an sich,* and this was not a concept James shared.

tools which, properly used, should produce definite results in the phenomenal world. If they produce results that subsequently have to be revised, that was because they had not been deployed properly. When James says that we select from the world what we then call "reality", he does not, as Kant did, commit himself to so rigid a view of what the phenomenal world is like if it is *properly* examined by our tools of understanding.

All the same, James does provide us with a certain discipline when we try to establish truths, however temporary, in the physical world. Even if we have made our own physical "reality", there are certain tests which we can carry out to see whether theories relating to that "reality" work. The tests are also subject to appraisal by the scientific community (which is well aware that it may have to alter its view of "reality" in the light of new discoveries). So, when James says that for a statement to be true, it needs to agree with "reality", that will not greatly trouble us as long as it refers to the physical world. As we shall see shortly, it is when he says the same of truths in the realm of ethics that certain misgivings must arise.

As far as the physical world is concerned, we might well agree with James when he wrote, "To 'agree' in the widest sense with a reality can only mean ... to be put in such working touch with it as to handle either it or something connected with it better than if we disagreed. Better either intellectually or practically." He made a similar statement 146 pages later in *Pragmatism*: "The 'true', to put it very briefly, is only the expedient in the way of thinking, just as the 'right' is only the expedient in the way of our behaving. Expedient in *almost* any fashion ..."

The italics are mine, to draw attention to the sheer looseness of definition here. Is he covering himself for a situation like, perhaps, telling the truth? It could be expedient in a situation to tell a lie, and James may have felt that he cannot really say that under those circumstances it is right to tell a lie. I think there are so many and countless situations like this that they are scarcely the *exception* that would warrant the words "in almost any fashion". There would seem to be more justification for attaching the word "almost" to the relatively *few* occasions when it would be right to tell a lie.

But the last words I have quoted are immediately followed by two other important qualifications, "... in the long run and on the whole, of course."

In this second passage there is no doubt that he extended to "right" (that is an ethical concept) the same criterion that he had applied to "true": both are *defined* in terms of expediency.

It is in the ethical field that the qualification " ... in the long run and on the whole" is most necessary. A successful burglar might very well assent to the truth of the statement that "I have the right to steal", because it has worked for him. By adding the qualification "in the long run", and, "on the whole", James moves us away from the temporary and the individual. "In the long run" the thief may well be caught (but what if he is not?) and "on the whole" it is bad for society if burglary is regarded as a right.

But even with the qualification, there are still problems and dangers in the theory. First of all, one surely has to ask the question "expedient for whom?" What is expedient to one group of people may not be so for another, especially where ethical questions are concerned. The statement "property is an inalienable right" is expedient and therefore true for property-owners, but inexpedient and untrue for those who believe it is right for the state to redistribute property. The phrase "in the long run and on the whole" will hardly settle this disagreement, because each group will interpret that qualification in its own interest.

James, like any relativist, would not disagree, he would simply reaffirm that truth is subjective, and that any hankering after some way of establishing absolute criteria for truth is vain. Surely the fact that there are no absolute criteria for truth does not mean that there are absolutely no criteria for truth. We are obliged to be as accurate as we can possibly be, to free ourselves as much as possible of vested interests, whether these are psychological, economic, or political. Our education should be, and in many ways is, designed to alert us to the necessity to be accurate and clear-eyed, and to be on our guard against being led astray by emotions, prejudices, or vested interests. In science, as we have seen, there are at least the temporary truths, tested and accepted as such by the scientific community until they are shown to have weaknesses or errors in them. In ethics such a consensus of what is "right" is admittedly harder to come by, but most people would question whether that means that "anything goes", and that so long as it is expedient, even "in the long run and on the whole", any behaviour can be described as ethically right.

It has been rightly argued that James' formulation provides no safeguard against self-deception, against yielding to any practical or emotional interest we may have in believing a statement to be true (or, for that matter, in believing a statement of inconvenient truths to be false because we cannot see how it could be "profitable" to our lives). As H.S.Thayer writes, "Standards of veracity go slack on the very occasions on which, ordinarily, they need the tightest rein, where passions and personal interest are most in play."[16]

Thayer says that, "James later regretted the license that [his] loosely stated condition of workableness seemed to permit". He obviously did not want people to indulge in self-deception, but it is difficult to see where in practice one would draw the line between an ethical idea being based on self-deception and one based on unconscious, or even on conscious, self-interest.

One dramatic application of the saying that a belief is true because it is useful is to religion. James thought (as his theory forced him to say) that all those beliefs in God are true that have consequences useful to life. He wrote in *Pragmatism,* "On pragmatistic principles, if the hypothesis of God works satisfactorily in the widest sense of the word, it is true." He thought that the consequences of an active belief [17] in God or in the Absolute were beneficial, "Of two competing views of the Universe which in all other respects are equal but of which the first denies some vital human need while the second satisfies it, the second will be favoured by sane men for the simple reason that it makes the world seem more rational."[18]

Note the word "seem", which leaves open the question whether a view actually *is* more rational.

Here again, of course the problem arises of who is to judge whether the belief is beneficial, even in "the widest sense of the word". The presumption is

16 In *A Critical History of Western Philosophy*, ed. D.J. O'Connor, p. 451.

17 James pointed out that whenever he talked about religious beliefs, he meant "live" beliefs - that is, beliefs which involved a willingness to act on them. He was not interested in tepid or merely formal acknowledgment of beliefs, which had no real bearing on the way that their holders behaved.

18 William James - *The Meaning of Truth.*

that every believer finds his belief useful in this way, though even that is surely not always the case. True, some people find their faith inspiring them to good or noble acts; others find it comforting – if it tells them that they are loved, for example, or if they find themselves bereaved. But what about those who believe that they are sinners and as such are doomed to eternal hell-fire? In their eyes that might be a perfectly rational belief, and preachers of such a doctrine might argue that it is a beneficial belief ("on the whole and in the long run, of course" !)) because it is an incentive for people to behave well, but it is scarcely beneficial for the person who is terrified each night for the fate of his immortal soul. Would James answer that such beliefs, because they are not beneficial, are therefore by his own criteria untrue? And what about religious beliefs which may make men feel very self-righteous because they have the truth? They believe that this is beneficial to them, especially if they have power, but what if they are led by this same belief to persecute nonbelievers or to suppress advances in knowledge?

Then there is the question of defining what "a vital human need" might be. For some people it is a vital need to worship, not necessarily God, but idols (assuming that God is not an idol) or dictators. Next, there are many sane men whose vital human need is to confront the world in all its indifference to what we call rational considerations; in its wastefulness and in its amoral aspects. To say that all these beliefs about God (or beliefs in the nonexistence of God) are "true" is simply an abuse of the word. Better to stick to the tautology that what is useful for someone is useful for that person!

We have here a particularly striking example of how a relativist philosopher who wants to express himself carefully and clearly should never use the word "true" when discussing ethics or religion without at least adding every time "for the believer". With that addition, it might be possible to argue that an atheist or an agnostic finds his position "beneficial" in that he is not fobbed off from confronting the world as it is by what he would describe as false comfort.

It may not be quite so necessary to add "for the believer" when we are discussing whether a belief in a scientific statement is "true", because we have already seen that there is at least some checkable correspondence between what we believe to be true and the "reality" we have selected. Belief here is close to "knowledge": we can test and therefore know that there is such a correspondence. A Logical Positivist like A.J. Ayer will have a point when he says that ethical and religious statements, while they may be important, are from a philosophical point of view emotive and not factual.[19]

This is not to deny that when it is expressed more precisely than it was by James, there is much to be said for the pragmatic outlook. Today, few thinkers would believe that there were absolute criteria in anything – not in art, not in ethics, not in religion, nor even in science.

This is often uncomfortable, but, as Nietzsche and Sartre had pointed out,[20] the modern world has to have the courage to live with that, and we have to do our best to carve out for ourselves some standards, in good faith, to which we commit ourselves, even if we know that they cannot give us the comfort of being absolute. It is interesting that in this respect, although the Pragmatists were interested in the word while the Existentialists were interested in the world, their views show some convergence, especially when the Pragmatists

19 See p. 551 below.

20 For Nietzsche, see p. 476 above; for Sartre, p. 509.

go on, as we shall see Dewey doing, to draw conclusions from their analysis of meaning to social and moral dimensions.

JOHN DEWEY
1859 to 1952

Dewey, like Peirce and James, began by defining truth as something that works, but he later became more cautious, and, when something is seen to work, he preferred to speak of "warranted assertability" rather than "truth" having been reached.

His primary interest was in analyzing what induces us to discover what it is that actually works. It is not something we ever ask until we are confronted with a situation that is "doubtful" - when we are not sure how we should respond to some situation in the environment.

A lesser known version of Descartes' "I think, therefore I am" was "I doubt, therefore I am". Dewey did not agree that our thought processes begin with doubting. He says robustly, "We are doubtful because a situation is inherently doubtful. Personal states of doubt that are not evoked by and are not relevant to some existential situation are pathological."

Even when a situation *is* inherently doubtful, we may still simply accept it, either because we do not yet recognize it as such, or out of habit, or because existing power structures have conditioned us not to ask questions. The awareness that there is a problem is uncomfortable, and inquiry is an *instrument* to *change* that situation. (The name that Dewey gave to his philosophy was "Instrumentalism". It is a form of Pragmatism, because it holds that all inquiry, whether in science, politics, or morals, has a practical function, related to action or potential action, and to making things work satisfactorily.)

Of course, we still have the problem of who is to decide whether something works satisfactorily. For one thing, this depends on the aim of the enquiry. For example, the aims of an authoritarian ruler are clearly different from the aims of a liberal one.

The first stage of inquiry is a formulation of the problem; next one asks oneself how to approach it with a view to a solution. The various approaches are then tested by experiment; and if the tests are successful, the problematical situation has been resolved, at least for the time being, and a "warrantable assertability" has been achieved.

"Warrantable assertability" may be a ponderous phrase, but is greatly preferable to "truth" or even "temporary truth".

Some problems relate to purely private concerns - for example, "what should I do to make myself less disliked by my colleagues?" but others are in the public domain. These include, for example, scientific, political, or ethical problems. When an individual produces a resolution with warrantable assertability, and that resolution is challenged by others, then there is still a doubtful situation. Inquiry into the problematical situation then becomes *a communal activity.* As long as the community shares in this enquiry, it binds that community together; "in inquiry men achieve cohesion".[21]

Of course, this does not happen when one group of people declares the question settled and tries to close off further inquiry by other groups. One reason (though not, of course, the most important one) that science has made such progress is that the scientific community really *is* a community, engaged in a joint enterprise of open-minded problem-solving, testing etc. Dewey believed that moral and social problems would also greatly benefit from this approach, and experience suggested to him that democratic societies offer the best chance of freedom of inquiry and experiment.

We are reminded that "warranted assertability", even if agreed by the community, is only a staging post. Again, this is true of every aspect of human thought, be it scientific, social or moral. No resolution of a "doubtful" situation is permanent, and sooner or later a further inquiry is called for. (Dewey was influenced by Hegel's insight that every solution, formulated in a thesis, will throw up an antithesis.) Like Peirce, Dewey believed that there was a never-ending evolutionary process at work in the world, and that the ultimate purpose of all inquiry was to facilitate growth and development. If we ask "evolution, growth, development towards what?", Dewey does not, as Peirce did, posit some "absolute and final truth as the ideal goal of enquiry ... [an] ideal [which] stands eternally above our struggles to attain it". So, as far as morals are concerned, the goal or end of morals is not for him some morality which transcends all our experiences of it. All we know is that there is growth, and so, he writes, "Growth itself is the only moral 'end'".

Let us first notice that he puts the word "end" into inverted commas. By doing this, he is indicating that he does not actually think there is such a thing as an end or a goal; the process by which truth evolves is not teleological.[22] He is using the word "end" rather carelessly, it would have been better had he written that growth or evolution is a moral process.

However, that statement is also problematical. Was evolution, as Darwin described it, a *moral* process? Was it not, rather, merely a description of genetic change that made it easier for an organism to adapt to an environment? The pragmatists are right when they say that, largely, growth and development in the sciences help us to cope better with the environment; it is therefore a "good" thing, but to go from there to saying that it is therefore also a "moral" thing is something of a "leap of faith". At the very least, Dewey would need to clarify what he means by "moral". After all, we do not all agree which actions are moral and which are not. How, then, do we decide the meaning of the word? That, as we shall see in the next section, is one of the questions with which G.E. Moore was to grapple.

Evolution in the sense of adaptability to the environmment may produce behaviour that we could easily describe as "immoral". The Catholic Church, for example, would describe as immoral the adaptation to contraception, to human cloning, or to certain economic developments which depersonalize the individual. In lawless countries, adaptation will lead great swathes of soci-

21 Thayer, in O'Connor, *op. cit.*, p. 460.

22 Teleology is the notion that the real nature of something lies not in what that thing is at its beginning or at an intermediate stage, but lies in the goal it is intended to achieve: the real nature of the acorn lies in the oak-tree it is intended to become.

ety to indulge in survival strategies which one could, by no stretch of the imagination, describe as "moral". At the very least, one will have to fall back on the Jamesian let-out "in the long run and on the whole, of course". *In the long run* we might indeed come to the conclusion that society suffers too much from contraception, cloning, or brutal survival tactics, and that what we have here is not evolutionary change at all but morally regressive change.

Anyway, for Dewey the solving of problems by enquiry and testing is not merely pragmatically useful (though it is that), but also has a moral value, as has the evolutionary process of which it is a part. So he would not have agreed with those who say that problem-solving and evolution in themselves are neither moral nor immoral, but merely "value-free", and who would argue that questions of morality only come into play when we decide how we use the results of our enquiry. Dewey's ascription of a moral end to growth and evolution is an optimistic and perhaps even a religious assertion that cannot be proved to be true in any normal way.

Dewey, more than most philosophers who are primarily interested in the meaning of words, was ready to make some concrete proposals about how we could create a better society. We have already seen that one test he would apply to society was whether it facilitated inquiry and growth. Democracies, he thought, did this. He was critical of Utopias and of any rigid theories about the state. We must not work from theory to practice, as, for example, socialist or capitalist theorists do. Theories are too general for the specific problems we have to solve. When we try to solve them, the application of theories usually does not assist inquiry, but closes it, "They are not instrumentalities to be employed and tested in clarifying concrete social difficulties. They are ready-made principles to be imposed on particulars."

We have seen that Dewey held growth to be a moral process, and so it is not only in our pragmatic interests to promote that growth, it takes on the flavour of a moral duty, too.

Above all, Dewey attached great importance to education. His books *The School and Society* (1899) and *The Child and the Curriculum* (1902) would be influential texts on progressive educational theory for decades after they were written. Their theme was that growth was frustrated by mere instruction and by rote learning. Instead, children should be encouraged to participate in the processes of inquiry and of democratic communal living that contributes to an open-minded society and encourages its moral growth. He had become Professor of Philosophy at the University of Chicago in 1894, and there he set up a Department of Pedagogy and founded a number of "Laboratory Schools", which he headed between 1896 and 1904, to test out these theories.

GEORGE EDWARD MOORE
1873 to 1958

Like the American Pragmatists, the Cambridge philosopher G.E. Moore was primarily interested in the analysis of meaning. In the course of this analysis he developed the idea that to find out what a word means, we must examine how it is used. For example, there is no one meaning of the word "democracy". For some, it has meant that the majority of people have the right to impose their will on the minority; others would say that that is not democracy at all, but the dictatorship of the majority. For them, democracy needs to take the interests of all people into account. So if we are arguing about democracy, we will get nowhere until we have ascertained how each side uses the word. [23] That is only common sense.

So G.E. Moore elevated common sense into a principle of philosophy. In an essay of 1925, *In Defence of Common Sense,* he expressed puzzlement that so many philosophers could come to conclusions which were quite contrary to common sense perceptions. Parmenides had seemed to prove that all change is illusory, and Zeno that Achilles can never catch up the tortoise;[24] solipsists argue that we cannot be sure that any object exists; David Hume had claimed that we cannot be sure that the sun will rise in the east tomorrow; Hegel had asserted that thought and reality are one; the Hedonists had maintained that good and pleasure are identical.

Moore placed reliance on the truth of common-sense statements under certain conditions,

They must command universal acceptance, such as "there are tables", or we *have* to believe them even if we have other beliefs that are incompatible with them. Hume had written, in effect, that his philosophy forced him to believe that there is no such thing as a necessary connection between cause and effect, and yet he had to act in life as if there were such a connection. He should therefore put his trust in the truth of the latter belief even while he was also convinced of the contradictory truth of the former.

Philosophical theories that do not meet these conditions must be further discredited if, in the course of describing them, we are forced to use language that is incompatible with the theory. Moore's contemporary John McTaggart had denied the reality of time (thus already falling foul of the first and second condition) and yet he had used phrases like "what we *constantly* believe". Hume had questioned whether we have a mind (on the grounds that we can never experience it directly, but only the thought of thinking), whether objects exist apart from our perceptions of them, and whether there is any continuity in the self, yet he could not avoid using the words "mind", "object" or "I".

While Moore accepted common-sense statements as true, he accepted that he could not *prove* them to be so, but then he thought that, for all their ingenuity, philosophical arguments like those of Parmenides or the solipsists, could also not be proven to be true, as experience so clearly showed the opposite. Therefore, we have the choice between ingenious but unbelievable statements on the one hand and common-sense and believable statements on the other. Under those circumstances, we do best to settle for the common sense ones. *Analysis* of common sense experiences may be a problem, but their *reality* is not.

Some readers may be heaving a sigh of relief at this point; it may confirm for them that their bewilderment at some philosophical conclusions is quite justifiable. "Thank goodness," they may think, "at last we have here a philosopher of common sense who hasn't lost touch with living", but even those readers must accept that, when we move from philosophy to science, we have to accept

23 Note, again, Joad's mantra, "it all depends on what you mean by ..."

24 For Parmenides and Zeno, see p. 7f.

many statements as true which, dramatically and irrefutably, run counter to common sense and are deeply counter-intuitive. Bryan Magee gives several obvious examples of this.[25] Is it common sense that matter consists in the last resort of energy? Is it common-sense that an object we think of as stationary is in fact standing on an earth which is moving at great speed through the universe and rotating rapidly at the same time? Given these examples, why should we assume that common sense is capable of telling us the truth about this world?

Common sense tells us that objects do not exist in the mind, but exist independently, irrespective of whether they are perceived or not. They present to the mind sense data (shape, colour etc.) which the mind receives as sensations. Moore believed that the sense data were objectively present in the object (a coin has the quality of being round and gold) irrespectively of whether anyone was perceiving them. How is it, then that the sense data differ when the object is seen from a different angle or in a different light? Does that not suggest that the sense data are in the mind and not in the object? Can one object "have" conflicting sense data? Coplestone writes, "These are the sort of problems with which Moore grappled on and off throughout his life. But he did not succeed in solving them *to his own satisfaction*".[26] Moore readily acknowledged the strength of the criticisms levelled against his theories, but he would then proclaim an "inclination" to remain with his original one. On one occasion, he wrote of an opposing point of view, "I am inclined to think that this is so, but I am also inclined to think that it is not so; and I do not know which way I am inclined most strongly." The occasion for this particular confession was his response to a criticism of the ethical theory which he had put forward in his *Principia Ethica* of 1903. We have already seen that in his *Defence of Common Sense* of 1925 he acknowledged that analysis of some common-sense ideas may be a problem. In the earlier book he had gone further. Some concepts, he said, cannot be analyzed at all. Among these he included the concept of "good". He denied that it could be analyzed into meaning "pleasurable", for example, as hedonists do. That would make "good" a subjective concept – what is pleasurable to one person is not pleasurable to another. Again, like sense data, goodness is not dependent on us, but is objective, just as the concept "yellow" is an objective one. Both are directly perceived, the one by the physical eye, the other by the "moral" eye. In line with his later approach to common-sense truths, he claimed that good was recognizable without being definable.

> In many instances, that seems to be true. Why, for example, do so many people shrink from the idea of killing handicapped children at birth? Of course, some doctors do quietly do this, but they have to be careful not to be found out. Why do they have to be so careful? Because the law forbids it. Why does the law forbid it? It is surely not chiefly because it is the thin end of the wedge and might lead to the killing of, say, babies of the "wrong" sex. One cannot argue that the killing of deformed babies will either logically or in practice lead to the killing of babies of the wrong sex. The reason for the law is that most people see with their "moral eye" that killing deformed babies is just wrong, and that

25 Bryan Magee – *Confessions of a Philosopher*, pp. 42 to 43.

26 Coplestone, op.cit., p. 422. My italics.

> feeling or intuition – not any form of rational argument – is the bedrock on which the law rests.[27] It also makes possible the apparently illogical position that it is unacceptable to kill a deformed baby, but acceptable to kill human beings in war time.

There is the obvious problem that not everybody agrees on these questions, and Moore's theory seems at odds with what he said elsewhere about the meaning of words – that meaning is made clear by the way the word is used. Take, for example,[28] one person who believes that it is ethically good to facilitate euthanasia for a sufferer who wishes to be put out of his misery, and ethically bad to allow him to continue to suffer. Another person might take the exact opposite view that it is ethically good to allow nature to take its course and ethically bad to end life by euthanasia. Is one of these statements true while the other one is false? Or do these two use the words "good" and "bad" in a different way and therefore the words have different meanings? Moore was "inclined" to think that the protagonists of the two statements had the same objective but indefinable notion of the meaning of "good", but that they differed in how best to apply it to the situation of the man who asked to have his life ended; he was also "inclined" to think, in the face of criticism, that the word "good" had a mere emotive meaning and was therefore subjective.

The reader wedded to the idea of common sense might at this stage ask what is the importance of a philosopher who can't make up his mind. Moore's importance lies partly in his formulation of the notion that the meaning of words is to be deduced from the way they are used. This idea would be examined more systematically by Wittgenstein, for example, later in his philosophy.[29] Beyond that, Moore's defence of common sense gave him an enormous following (even if in a modified form) among philosophers, and certainly among that part of the public which knew little more of his work than the title of his book.[30]

Moore's indecision and reversals of opinion are characteristic of several other twentieth-century philosophers. Frederick Coplestone characterizes Moore's work as "thinking aloud, so to speak".[31] We will find others doing the same. Bertrand Russell would change his mind many times; Wittgenstein (like Heidegger) was considered to have produced two different philosophies; A.J. Ayer would cheerfully confess in later life that nearly everything he had written in *Language, Truth and Logic* was false. Following their opinions, and their subsequent honest doubts about them, involves us, too, in a philosophical voyage, and in philosophy, as in much else in life, "the journey and not the arrival matters."

27 We are reminded of Hume's dictum that "Reason is, and ought to be, the slave of the Passions."

28 The example is mine, not Moore's. Moore's was the assertion of whether it was right for Brutus to have stabbed Caesar.

29 See pp. 544f below.

30 Magee, *op. cit.*, p. 42, describes "this enthronement of common sense as an intellectual catastrophe ... the metaphysics only of the insufficiently seriously reflective".

31 Coplestone, *op.cit.*, p. 414.

CHAPTER 42

Bertrand Russell

1872 to 1970

Bertrand Russell's most towering achievement in philosophy was in an area that had no possible connection with living. Indeed, Ray Monk, in his biography,[1] several times implies intriguingly that he escaped into the cold regions of the philosophy of mathematics when life was too much for him. He deserted them when he fell passionately in love with Lady Ottoline Morrell, and retreated back into them when that relationship came to an end. In 1900 he wrote to a friend, "The world of mathematics ... is really a beautiful world; it has nothing to do with life and death and human sordidness, but is eternal, cold and passionless." This world had fascinated him since his orphan childhood, spent in the home of his grandparents, Lord John Russell (the former prime minister) and his pious and controlling wife.

> The idea that the truths of Mathematics were particularly pure and undiluted had, of course, been held by philosophers in the past – by Pythagoras and Plato for example. For Plato, a study of mathematics had been the best training for a study in eternal truths, which is why he had inscribed over the entrance of his Academy that "no one without a knowledge of Geometry may enter here."[2]

Philosophy and Mathematics

When Russell began to investigate the nature of mathematics, he first accepted the idea of Kant, that mathematics is a human construct, depending on our intuitions of space and time, but without any certainty that they correspond to reality, *das Ding an sich*.[3] Kant had been aware that our conceptual apparatus often delivered ideas that could not be reconciled with each other and produced what he had called "antinomies",[4] even in the field of mathematics.[5] They could not exist in the *Ding an sich* (and Hegel had said that such apparent contradictions would be resolved only in the Absolute). A number of Russell's

1 Ray Monk - Bertrand Russell: The Spirit of Solitude (Volume I of the biography), 1996.

2 See p. 35 above.

3 See pp. 365f above.

4 See p. 371 above.

5 I am afraid I know too little about mathematics to explain examples of such antinomies.

contemporaries (the mathematicians Karl Weierstrass, George Cantor and Giuseppe Peano) had already produced highly technical theories claiming that the problems of antinomies arose only because they had been incorrectly formulated. These theories eventually convinced Russell, and he then produced his own formulations.

As long as antinomies existed in mathematics, it was difficult to see them as part of reality, independent of human constructs, and one can understood the temptation to see them resolved in an unknowable *Ding an sich* or an Absolute, but the new ideas made it unnecessary to postulate these metaphysical unknowables. Russell now concluded that numbers, temporal and spatial relations, and the logical deductions in mathematics are not just human constructs but are real and objective. He set out his new theories in *The Principles of Mathematics*, published in 1903, and this established his fame as a philosopher of mathematics.[6]

In 1901 he had begun to collaborate with another Cambridge mathematician, Alfred North Whitehead, on a massive work, the *Principia Mathematica*. It was published in three volumes between 1910 and 1913. It was the crown of his achievement, though only specialists can understand it.

Russell also made some highly technical contributions to mathematical logic, which are quite incomprehensible to the layman. All mathematics were based on logic alone, but to Russell, logic represented the very essence of *all* philosophy. The trouble is that, whereas in mathematical logic the terms used are extremely precise, they are often extremely imprecise in non-mathematical logic. Moore had already said that we can work out the meaning of a word in any given statement by studying the way the word is used. As we have already seen, the words "democracy" or "good" can mean one thing to one person and something quite different to another. Russell agreed with this, but thought that something more precise was needed than a general statement like "it all depends on what you mean by...". Moreover, it is not just about broad concepts like "democracy" and "good" which mean different things in different settings. Take, for example, the humble little word "is" in the following sentences, in each of which it means something different:

In "2 x 2 is 4", it indicates a result.

In "Socrates is a man", it indicates identification.

In "a thief is someone who steals", it indicates definition.

In "it is raining", it indicates tense.

In "this picture is beautiful", it indicates opinion.

In "the flag is red", it indicates description.

6 The development of this text was characteristic of what happened to many of Russell's ideas. He had found flaws in his first draft of 1900 and had then produced a second draft in 1902 when he discovered that the German mathematical philosopher Gottlob Frege (1848 to 1925) had come to similar conclusions in his *Grundgesetze der Arithmetik* ("Fundamental Laws of Arithmetic) published in 1893. He then found further flaws, both in his own and in Frege's arguments (which Frege accepted). Russell's own published 1903 version did not satisfy him either – he had discovered a paradox in it which became known as Russell's Paradox, and which he did not solve to his own satisfaction until 1905.

Even the word "the" can have more than one meaning:

"Charles I was the (i.e. only possible) father of Charles II.

"Charles II was the (possibly one, but also possibly one of several) son of Charles I."

It is possible that such imprecisions might vitiate a logical argument. Again the meaning of the words depends on the way they are used. If only ordinary language could have the precision of mathematical language!

So Gottlob Frege had designed, in a text of 1879 called *Begriffschrift* (literally "Text dealing with Concepts"), a language of largely mathematical symbols which could be applied to a chain of logical statements and would avoid such ambiguities. An Italian team under Giuseppe Peano had developed a less cumbersome form of this *symbolic logic;*[7] Russell and Whitehead had refined it still further and had used it in the *Principia Mathematica.* Russell now thought that symbolic logic would help to elucidate whether a proposition was true, false or meaningless. It was, for instance, a way of ascertaining that a proposition like "the present king of France is bald" was a meaningless statement (since there *was* no present king of France). From this example, one might conclude that a gigantic philosophical sledgehammer was being wielded to crack a nut which did not even have a shell. Indeed, it is hard to think that the use of symbolic logic has made any difference whatever to the way even a very rigorous argument among intelligent laymen might be conducted.

We shall see in a later chapter that the Logical Positivists, contemporaries of Russell's, thought that all that philosophy could do was to test whether statements were true, false or meaningless. Once a proposition had been verified as true, the task of the Logical Positivist ended – he was not interested in making further deductions that would lead from a true statement to conclusions about the world. Only if such conclusions were embodied in new propositions would a Logical Positivist be prepared to examine the meaning of the new proposition to determine whether it was meaningful and, if so, whether it could be verified or falsified.

Here, Russell parted company with them. Though he had devoted much of his energy to establishing a linguistic analysis, he thought that it could never be an end in itself, but was only a tool with which to understand and interpret the world. That is what the scientist does, and Russell was very interested in science. The English Logical Positivists claimed to be "scientific" in their approach, but, unlike their colleagues, the Austrian members of the Vienna Circle, most of them had been educated as classicists and were actually quite ignorant of science. Russell, however, did study the latest developments in science, and as early as 1912 he turned from the philosophy of mathematics to the philosophy of science.

The timing of this change was not accidental. In the first place, creative thinking about mathematical logic is particularly taxing intellectual work, and after ten years' work on the *Principia Mathematica,* Russell, then aged forty, was exhausted. Then, in 1911, the young Ludwig Wittgenstein arrived in Cam-

7 As a total layman, I am not able decide between Monk's opinion that Frege's Logical Symbolism is "more cumbersome and more difficult to grasp than Peano's" (*Bertrand Russell: The spirit of Solitude,* p. 153) and A.J.Ayer's, that Peano's was "a less efficient system than Frege's" (in Bryan Magee – *The Great Philosophers,* p. 308.)

bridge to become Russell's pupil. Wittgenstein had a fierce passion for technical philosophy which Russell no longer possessed, and by 1912 Russell saw Wittgenstein as more creative in mathematical logic than he now was. Wittgenstein noticed certain inexactitudes in the proofs for the third volume of the *Principia*, and the older man entrusted him with correcting the proof sheets. Russell thought that his student would merely improve his formulations; instead, it soon became clear that Wittgenstein challenged some of the very foundations on which the work rested. Russell was devastated, but was convinced that Wittgenstein was right. For the next five years he did no further serious work in mathematical logic, and when he returned to the subject in 1918, he had taken on board Wittgenstein's criticism of his earlier work. He formally acknowledged this debt in his lectures on *The Philosophy of Logical Atomism* (1918).

Russell now saw a word, a symbol or a proposition standing for something *in the world*, so that logic is now no longer just a way of analyzing *language and propositions* for meaning, but of analyzing the *world*. Propositions, after all, are not self-contained, even mathematical propositions are statements about something outside of themselves. At its simplest, 2 + 3 = 5 means that if you take two apples and add three apples, you have five apples. To the layman it seems quite obvious, but that this is a far more complicated notion than it may seem (and that it was rather different from Wittgenstein's view) is made clear by Monk.[8] Again, the arguments are highly technical, but the shift is significant because it brings Russell out of the rarified sphere of ideas which seem to have little or no bearing on Life into an area which touches on the thoughts and activities of people who are not professional philosophers, logicians or mathematicians.

Philosophy and Science

At the time when he had concluded that only mathematics provided eternal truths, Russell had drawn a distinction between philosophy, whose truths should be able to stand the test of time, and science, which – relying as it does on experiment, measurement and the formulation and testing of hypotheses – is always on the move, always subject to revision, and therefore not a basis upon which philosophy could rest.

Of course, by any standards this was historically an exceptionally narrow definition of philosophy. Even before Plato, it had been part of the philosophy of Heraclitus that there is no such thing as permanence – everything is in perpetual flux.[9] True, Plato himself, as we have seen, had stressed the eternal truths and purity of mathematical thought, and had shown no interest in investigating those areas which would become the subject of science. From Aristotle onwards, however, many philosophers have considered science as coming within their purview. Indeed, from the seventeenth-century Scientific Revolution onwards, the impact of science on philosophical thinking has been profound.

8 Monk, *op. cit.* pp. 517 to 519 for the lectures and pp. 547/8 for the differences with Wittgenstein.

9 See p. 7 above.

In due course, Russell would himself come to the conclusion that philosophy had a wider remit than he had originally given to it. At the very least, it has something to say about the principles which justify scientific *inferences*, even if these inferences are only temporary. In his mid-seventies, in *Human Knowledge* (1948), Russell would work out what these should be. In essence, they amount to the common-sense idea that if a number of things show something like a repetitive pattern, we are entitled to build up scientific theories on that basis. Of course, the validity of these principles cannot be proved: they are "extralogical". The theories that we build upon them have to be tested, and even then they are provisional, and provide probabilities and not certainties, but they work. Though our inferences are conscious and intellectual, they are not unlike the instinctive inferences made by animals, and, as in their case, they are biological- psychological in origin.

In the end, Russell came to believe that, provisional though the truths of science are, those of philosophy are even more so. By now he had quite abandoned his earlier and very narrow definition which had philosophy concern itself only with truths that could stand the test of time. He now went so far as to say, "whatever can be known, can be known by means of science",[10] and "what science cannot discover, mankind cannot know".[11]

> Should he instead have said, "whatever can be *proved* can be proved by means of science"? For him, something that cannot be proved, cannot be *known*, it can only be an *opinion*. So, for example, ethical or aesthetic propositions cannot be proved in the way that mathematical or scientific ones can be. In that sense, we cannot *know* that "Stealing is wrong" or that "Bach was a great composer".

The two pronouncements of Russell's quoted above were made late in his life, but they are an extension of a comment he had written as early as 1918:

> A great many philosophical questions are, in fact, scientific questions with which science is not yet ready to deal. Both sensation and perception were in this class of problems but are now, I should contend, amenable to scientific treatment and not capable of being fruitfully handled by anyone who chooses to ignore what science has to say about them.

Science, therefore, pragmatic and temporary though its conclusions must be, had made many philosophical problems obsolete, and it had done so in a piecemeal fashion, tackling problems one by one. This, Russell thought, should also be a model for philosophy, which should not *aim*, as metaphysicians do, to work out some system that embraces all reality. Nevertheless, careful work in philosophy, as in science, was likely to *reveal* that apparently disparate areas of enquiry eventually produce results that cohere in increasingly unified systems.

The task of philosophical enquiry is to pose problems to which there are no answers. To some of these, science will in time bring solutions, as the passage just quoted assumed. "Philosophical speculation as to what we do not yet know has shown itself a valuable preliminary to exact scientific knowledge."[12] The next stage in Russell's outlook was the realization that there will be philosophical problems which science will never be able to resolve. Indeed, "Almost

10 Russell – *A History of Western Philosophy*, (1946), p. 863.

11 Russell – *Religion and Science* (1935), p. 243.

12 From an essay in Russell – *Logic and Knowledge*, ed. by R.C. Marsh, 1956

all the questions of most interest to speculative minds are such as science cannot answer"[13] and if we dismiss such questions on these grounds, we would grievously restrict our mental horizons and, "human life would be impoverished".[14] Having widened the scope of philosophy from mathematics to science, he now widened it still further. The philosopher rightly concerns himself with those profound questions which science cannot answer now, and which it may very well never be able to answer. These are, for example, problems of ethics or of aesthetics.

> It has since been argued that science, in the form of theories of evolution for example, might have at least something to contribute to the "solutions" of ethical problems, and that we would be foolish to ignore that dimension. Mary Midgley, for example, has addressed this question in her book *The Ethical Primate* (1994). To the best of my knowledge, no such contribution has yet been made by science to a better understanding of aesthetics, and one wonders whether it ever could do so. (I suppose we have to admit to the possibility that it might do so one day, after all, who would have thought a century ago that it would ever have anything significant to say about ethics?)

Some Logical Positivists had dismissed ethical statements as philosophically meaningless as they could not be verified.[15]

In his confidence in science and the scientific method, Russell appears as a Positivist,[16] but he disagreed with the Logical Positivists. In 1959, at the age of eighty-seven, he wrote of them:

> The new philosophy [of reducing philosophy to the study of language] seems to me to have abandoned, without necessity, that grave and important task which philosophy throughout the ages has hitherto pursued. Philosophers from Thales onwards have tried to understand the world ... I cannot feel that the new philosophy is carrying on this tradition.[17]

Philosophy and Ethics

Concern with ethics was clearly one of those "grave and important tasks", which Russell would not dismiss as "meaningless". But his view on ethics, like his views of many other subjects, changed in the course of his life. In *Philosophical Essays* (1910) he accepted the view of G.E. Moore that "good" and "bad" were objective qualities,[18] and he expressed it even more starkly than Moore had done, "Good and bad are qualities which belong to objects independently of our opinions, just as much as round and square do."[19]

The argument was that if we define a good action as one that leads to good consequences, we have to ask why we call the consequences good, and if we

13 *A History of Western Philosophy*, p. 10. Russell was 73 when this book appeared in 1945

14 Russell – *Unpopular Essays* (1950).

15 See pp. 551f below.

16 See pp. 435f above.

17 Russell – *My Philosophical Development*.

18 see pp. 527f above.

19 From the date of this statement it is clear that even when Russell was in his first phase, of thinking that philosophy should concern itself only with the permanent truths that lie in mathematics, he did some thinking about ethics. The interesting thing about his 1910 view of ethics is that he gives to ethical qualities something of the wholly objective nature that mathematics had.

say they are good because they are pleasurable, we have to ask why it is good for them to be pleasurable. In the end we find that good is indefinable. Russell believed that most people are in agreement about the meaning of "good", and that differences between them are differences about how to achieve them.

We have seen that Moore himself, while "inclined" to this view, was similarly "inclined" to accept the opposite view, that the word "good" had emotive meanings and was subjective. Certainly, Russell came to move away from the position he had held in 1910. By 1927, in *An Outline to Philosophy* he had taken a view, which was much closer to traditional hedonism, that the expressions "good" and "bad" derive from our desires and aversions and are therefore subjective. It is not possible to convince someone who does not have an aversion either to cruelty itself or to the consequences that can be shown to flow from cruelty that cruelty is bad.

We can see what a long way Russell had moved from his original positions and interests. In the 1920s he had already ceased to think of mathematics as the purest kind of philosophy there is. By the time he was aged eighty-seven, he no longer even believed that there was something sublime about the truths of mathematics. "I have come to believe", he wrote in *My Philosophical Development*:

> though very reluctantly, that it consists of tautologies.[20] I fear that, to a mind of sufficient intellectual power, the whole of mathematics would appear trivial, as trivial as the statement that a four-footed animal is an animal... I cannot any longer find any mystical satisfaction in the contemplation of mathematical truth.

"The Picasso of Modern Philosophy"

Russell's readiness to re-examine not only the intense significance of mathematics, but many other opinions that he put forward (sometimes, like G.E. Moore, expressing reservations about them even while he propounded them) had caused C.D. Broad to say of him in 1924, "As we all know, Professor Russell produces a different system of philosophy every few years." Other commentators have defended him by saying that, though his conclusions often differed, there was a consistency in the analytical manner in which he arrived at them. In 1941, reviewing Russell's *An Inquiry into Meaning and Truth* (1940), A.J. Ayer strikingly described him as, "the Picasso of modern philosophy [who] has expressed himself very differently at different periods, and in each period he has exerted deservedly great influence and aroused extravagant hostility."

20 What Russell meant was that mathematics does not really tell us anything that is *new*, what it generally does is work out a proof of something that we know already. Consider the example of the theorem of Pythagoras that the square of the hypotenuse (the longest side) of a right-angled triangle is equal to the sum of the squares of the other two sides. In the case of a right-angled triangle whose sides are respectively 3, 4, and 5 inches long, Pythagoras (and probably other geometers, too) had observed that 3 squared plus four squared equals 5 squared. The theorem does not discover this fact, it merely works out or proves why this should be so. No wonder that setting out such a proof begins with the line "RTP" ("Required to prove") and ends with the letters QED (*Quod erat demonstrandum*). It is known from the beginning what needs to be, not newly discovered, but explained. The seventeenth-century mathematician Fermat had observed certain qualities of prime numbers, and posed for mathematicians of future generations the problem of how to explain why they should have these qualities.

Neither his influence nor the hostility towards him was confined to philosophers. In books, lectures, articles and broadcasts for the general public he had advocated the radical, rationalist and anti-religious views of his time. In these he expressed himself with a clarity of style that won him the Nobel Prize for Literature in 1950. His *History of Western Philosophy*, dashed off in 1946 when he was in his mid-seventies from notes for his adult education classes, became a best seller, and is probably still the most widely-read single book on the History of Philosophy.[21] He also had progressive views on education, and he founded and ran a school in which his theories were put into practice, sometimes to the scandal of more traditional educationists. He involved himself passionately in public affairs when he thought that morals and ethics were involved. His activities as a member of the No Conscription Fellowship during the First World War landed him in prison for six months in 1918. After the Second World War he headed the Campaign for Nuclear Disarmament as its President (1958). In 1961, at the age of 89, he took part in a sit-in for that cause, and he went to prison again.[22] In 1966, together with Sartre, he convened a number of personalities hostile to the American role in Vietnam to form an "International War Crimes Tribunal".

In his earlier years, when Russell had dealt with the philosophy of mathematics and with symbolic logic, non-specialists could not understand what he had to say; it was far too difficult. Nor were they interested in the problems with which he was grappling. In his later years, when he addressed himself so lucidly to questions in which the public was also interested, he was not particularly original or profound. When progressives read his works, they were often able to say, "that's just what I think, though I couldn't have put it as well as he has". Professional philosophers dismissed much of his later work, but by the general public he was widely regarded as a sage.

21 Bryan Magee, in his *Confessions of a Philosopher*, pp. 182 to 183, is rightly scathing about it, calling it: superficial and flippant.

22 The sentence was for two months, but he was released after seven days in view of his age.

CHAPTER 43

Ludwig Wittgenstein

1889 to 1951

The intense young man who arrived in Cambridge in 1911 to study under Russell was the youngest son of Karl Wittgenstein, an immensely wealthy and cultured Viennese industrialist who had made his fortune in engineering and the steel industry. Ludwig was educated at home until the age of fourteen, and his intellectual guide during adolescence was his sister Margarete. Like the whole family, she was intensely musical and artistic. She also had an interest in philosophy, and especially in that of Schopenhauer, who had written so eloquently about music as giving us access to the world that lies beyond phenomena, a transcendent world whose nature cannot be conveyed in words at all.[1] Wittgenstein then and later made a close study of Schopenhauer. He never mentioned him in his own writings, and it was only in the 1960s that commentators detected the influence of Schopenhauer on his thinking.

Karl hoped that Ludwig would go into the family business. Ludwig, anxious to please his father, proclaimed an interest in engineering for which, he confessed later, he had neither taste nor talent. So, in 1903, at the age of fourteen he went to a *Realschule* (a school with a vocational rather than a classical curriculum) in Linz.

Because Wittgenstein's career as a philosopher is associated so largely with England, the cultural influence on him of *fin de siècle* Austria had been largely overlooked until the appearance in 1996 of Allan Janik and Stephen Toulmin's *Wittgenstein's Vienna*. They make the point, among others, that engineering courses in German-speaking lands had a much stronger basis in theoretical physics than they had in English-speaking countries. The leading Austrian physicist at the time was Ernst Mach (1838 to 1916) who was also an influential philosopher. He taught that the task of the scientist is merely to measure and to describe; that all theory is suspect, and all metaphysical concepts are nonsense. He took the Humean view that sensations are the only elements of experience, (though there might be a reality beyond what appears to the senses) and he rejected the idea that there was an ego that held them together. Toulmin called Mach "the godfather of Logical Positivism, if not its chief progenitor". The

1 See p. 403 above.

Vienna Circle, where the philosophy of Logical Positivism began, was originally called the Ernst Mach Society.

Wittgenstein was therefore exposed to such philosophies of science as well as to the mystical philosophy of Schopenhauer. He will also have been influenced by the austerity of the cultural *avant garde* in prewar Vienna. Its practitioners – architects like Adolf Loos,[2] composers like Arnold Schönberg – and its theoreticians – Karl Kraus, Fritz Mauthner – all thought that art should be stripped down to its bare essentials. Architecture should be free of ornamentation, composers should eschew programme music or an overt appeal to extrinsic emotions. Extremists believed that even literature would somehow be polluted if it was not stripped down to pure form.

All the intellectuals in prewar Vienna had known each other and affected each other's ideas. Wittgenstein was part of this circle, and Janik and Toulmin suggest that his philosophy can be seen as addressing these issues rather than the issues that concerned Russell and Moore. We shall see that the way he would present his own thoughts could not be more austere and stripped down.

In 1906, Wittgenstein went to the University of Berlin to study engineering and in 1908, at the age of nineteen, he moved to Manchester to study aeronautics. There he developed an interest in the philosophy of mathematics. He planned to write a book on it, and in 1911 sought and secured an interview with Frege at his home in Jena to test out his ideas. Frege did not think much of them, but he saw that Wittgenstein could profit from studying under a philosopher of mathematics, and suggested that he should go to Cambridge to hear Bertrand Russell's lectures there. Wittgenstein did that. The lectures were really seminars, attended by only a tiny handful of students. Wittgenstein not only dominated the seminars, but badgered Russell after them. Russell was quite indulgent of him, though initially he was not convinced of his ability, until, in 1912, Wittgenstein asked Russell to read a manuscript, and Russell was very impressed. On the strength of that, Wittgenstein gave up his work in Manchester and enrolled at Trinity College, with Russell as his supervisor. G.E.Moore was also very impressed by him. As we have seen in the last chapter, Russell felt exhausted at that time by the work he had been doing on the *Principia Mathematica,* and he recognized in Wittgenstein the "son" who could take his work further. Wittgenstein soon began to challenge Russell's ideas, not only on the philosophy of mathematics, but also, devastatingly, on the new work (still very technical) that Russell was doing on the Theory of Knowledge.

Wittgenstein was on a visit to his family in Vienna when the First World War broke out. He volunteered to join the Austrian army (not out of patriotism – he corresponded with his friends in England via neutral countries throughout the war – but to test himself). After being decorated several times for bravery on the Russian front, he was transferred to the Italian front when Russia had been knocked out of the war in March 1918. There, at the very end of the war, his section of the army surrendered to the Italians, and he became a prisoner of war.

2 Wittgenstein himself, in 1926, designed a house for his sister Margarete which lacked all external decorations, dispensed with carpets and curtains, was lit with naked light-bulbs hanging from the ceiling – but had exquisite proportions.

During all these campaigns he had been working on the philosophical ideas he had been developing at Cambridge. Not long before his transfer to the Italian front, he had completed the first draft of the *Tractatus Logico-Philosophicus,* and from his prisoner-of-war camp he sent copies of the manuscript to Frege and to Russell. Neither of them really understood them. This was due in part to the extreme compression with which Wittgenstein expressed his ideas. Russell had complained in 1912 that Wittgenstein should not simply state what he thought, but should also provide arguments for it. Wittgenstein had replied that argument would spoil its beauty and that he would feel as if he were dirtying a flower with muddy hands! [3] The *Tractatus,* less than eighty pages long, takes the form of numbered notes, which are sometimes just single aphoristic sentences. All the same, Russell wrote a foreword to the *Tractatus.* Even then it took until 1920 before a German publisher could be found, and until 1922 before an English translation, made by Frank Ramsay, a brilliant young undergraduate, appeared. In the following year Ramsey (still only 20 years old), published a review of the book in *Mind,* and this gave it instant recognition as a work of great importance.

The Tractatus Logicus-Philosophicus

The basic concern of the *Tractatus* was to work out the relationship between meaning and truth. A sentence is meaningful if it has a close correspondence to possible or actual facts in the world *and can make a clear picture of them.* It is to be noted that the picture is not *passively received* (what in German is called a *Vorstellung*) but is *actively made* (in German: *Darstellung*) – i.e. it is a human construct – and we then put it into words. Both our picture of the world and the language in which we express it are therefore a product of the world. We then turn both picture and language back on the world and read off reality from them.

> In this respect, Wittgenstein seems to be close to Kant, the first philosopher who said that knowledge is not something we receive, but something we make. This knowledge, he had said, is then applied (correctly or incorrectly, depending on the accuracy with which we deploy our tools of understanding) to an understanding of the phenomenal world.[4]

Every *meaningful* sentence, then, corresponds to a *possible* fact, and every *true* sentence refers to an *actual* fact.

> The sentence "the earth is flat" is a meaningful sentence, because we can picture the idea of a flat earth, as people did in the Middle Ages, but it is not an actual fact.
>
> Using this criterion would also make sentences like, "God is in His Heaven" at least *meaningful*, because simple people can certainly form a picture of God and of Heaven – indeed, they were helped to do so by religious artists.

A sentence which cannot correspond to a possible fact in the world is *meaning-less* from a philosophical point of view. And here it is important to note that Wittgenstein took the word "picture" to mean a representational picture and

3 Ray Monk – *Ludwig Wittgenstein: The Duty of Genius,* p. 54

4 See p. 369 above.

excluded any other kind, like an abstract picture. Kant's phenomenal world was a world of appearances, and appearances can be pictured.

> Even so, Wittgenstein cannot have taken the word "picture" (*Bild*) absolutely literally: he must have included among appearances not only those phenomena which appear to the sense of sight, but also those which appear to the other four senses. The statement, for example, "the baby is crying" corresponds to a possible or an actual fact, and must therefore be meaningful even if the representation (*Darstellung*) in this case is auditory rather than visual.

Anything of which we cannot form such a representation (statements about ethics, aesthetics, or religion, for example) lies "outside the world" because we cannot make pictures of such statements: they are therefore "meaning-less" from a philosophical point of view.[5]

> By religion, Wittgenstein must have meant *not* the belief that God was in His Heaven which, as we have seen, represents a possible fact of which people could form a picture, but rather the beliefs that flow from that, such as He wishes us to obey the Ten Commandments, for example. True, we can picture Moses going up on Mount Sinai and God telling him there to inscribe the Commandments on the tablets of stone, but that is not really a religious statement in Wittgenstein's eyes. The religious statement would be that it then became an *obligation* to obey the commandments, and of that religious obligation we cannot form a picture. It therefore lies "outside the world".

Wittgenstein described subjects that are "outside the world" as "transcendental". "Ethics is transcendental", he wrote, and also, "Ethics and Aesthetics are one and the same."

> Note, incidentally, that this identification between ethics and aesthetics attributes to aesthetics a *moral* quality. Compare this with the view of, for example, Oscar Wilde in the previous generation, for whom aesthetics was wholly autonomous. The slogan was "Art for Art's sake", and art has nothing to do with morality. The aesthetic circle of which the young Wittgenstein had been a member in Vienna had seen it as a moral duty that art be "honest", which to them, as to Wittgenstein, meant that it had to discard all ornamentation (associated in his mind with the bourgeois display he had seen in his father's house) and programmatic agenda.

But *philosophy* cannot deal with ethics, aesthetics or religion.

> An ethical or aesthetic statement cannot be said to be "true" in the sense in which a scientific statement can be so described. It is impossible to get the kind of consensus about ethical, aesthetic or religious questions that we can hope to achieve in science (at least at any one time, until new discoveries are made which then in turn command consensus). Wittgenstein, with his scientific training, thought that philosophy ought to follow the scientific model; consensus ought to be the aim of philosophy, too. A subject on which no such consensus was possible lay outside the field of philosophy proper.
>
> Now there are some people who rebel against such a narrow and exclusive definition of what philosophy is about. For many layman, philosophy means the pursuit of *wisdom* (in Greek *sophia*, which is actually part of the word philosophy) rather than of *knowledge*. That is as one-sided a view of what phi-

5 This is an extraorindarily arbitrary definition of what is "meaningful" and what is "meaning-less"; I have postponed a discussion of this point to the chapter on Logical Positivism, see p. 551 below.

> losophers do as is the view that they are concerned only with knowledge. Probably most philosophers have pursued both knowledge and wisdom. Even before the Scientific Revolution many philosophers have sought knowledge of the kind that a scientist does: *how* does the mind work? *what* is the nature of sensation? Such questions look for answers that are *de*scriptive, and since the Scientific Revolution, the scientific model has been very influential in philosophical thinking. *In addition*, however, many philosophers have also been interested in moral and ethical questions: what is the nature of obligation? They ask not only what is, but also what ought to be.

Wittgenstein belonged to the tradition in philosophy which did not regard metaphysical statements - so important a component of ethics, aesthetics and religion - as a proper subject for philosophical consideration.[6] Some thinkers in that tradition dismiss metaphysics rather scathingly (Hume, Bentham or the Logical Positivists, for example) as not being *worthy* of serious thought. Wittgenstein at this stage did not believe this. He did think that *philosophy* must deal with and express itself in *rational* (that is, non metaphysical) language. He was well aware that there are other kinds of languages - poetic language, for example, however, he felt he could not discuss them in the *Tractatus*. Nevertheless, he knew from the beginning that questions of ethics and aesthetics were important, indeed, he had put off one potential publisher by saying that what the book did not contain (a discussion of ethics) was more important than what it did. In the end he closed the book with the famous sentence, which was so misunderstood by the Logical Positivists:[7] "What can be said at all can be said clearly; and ... what we cannot speak about we must pass over in silence."

In the meantime, Wittgenstein concentrated on clarifying what *can* be said clearly. The sentences we ordinarily use, even when we are describing phenomenal rather than transcendental matters, are often too complex to reveal their underlying logical structure. So he agreed with Russell that mathematical logic was a useful tool to make sure that we are not misled, for example, by words which look the same, but actually play very different roles in the structure of sentences. [8] Whereas Russell believed that, once that had been done, we have a better grasp of the *world*, Wittgenstein insisted that we merely have a better grasp of the meaning of a *statement*, so that we become clearer about the picture it presents of the world. If the picture corresponds with an actual fact, it is that correspondence, and not logic as now clarified, which tells us that a statement is true. Wittgenstein thought that neither mathematics nor philosophy could deduce anything from the world: "In philosophy there are no deductions: it is purely descriptive."[9]

> This seems an odd thing to say, compatible with a view of "truth" that is so extremely relative that even an out-and-out relativist would not normally hold

6 In this respect Wittgenstein (like the Vienna Circle of Logical Positivists) differed sharply from much of the German philosophical tradition which, from Hegel onwards, was exceedingly metaphysical in its interests. The Anglo-Saxon tradition of philosophy has, on the whole, shown relatively little interest in metaphysics. In that respect Wittgenstein at least spoke the same *kind* of language that he found in Cambridge.

7 see below, p. 551.

8 See p. 530 above.

9 This sentence appears in *Notes on Logic*, a typescript which he wrote for Russell in 1913.

> it. To take once again the statement "the earth is flat": people who held that belief in the Middle Ages would certainly have thought that it corresponded with the world, and so the picture and statement of a flat earth was true for them; but it was still not a true statement. The statement that the earth is round was arrived at by logical *inductions* from certain observations that had been made and from certain inconsistencies that could not be squared with the idea that the earth was flat. When Columbus, acting on these deductions, had provided "experimental support" for the statement, people formed a new picture of the earth in which the earth *was* round; and subsequently new logical inductions from inconsistencies came to the conclusion that the earth was actually not completely round but slightly flattened at the poles; and so yet a third picture came into being. But surely nobody would deny that the second picture was truer than the first, even if the third picture showed (to those who were aware of it) that the second picture was not 100% true.

Between the Tractatus and Philosophical Investigations

When the *Tractatus* was finished, Wittgenstein thought he had nothing further to say about philosophy. After his release from the prisoner of war camp in Italy, he returned to Austria, became a village schoolmaster, then a gardener in a monastery; and then spent some time designing the house in Vienna for his sister Margarete to which reference has already been made. It was during this latter period, in 1927, that Margarete introduced him to Moritz Schlick, Professor of Philosophy at the University of Vienna. In 1924, Schlick had founded a group of philosophers which later became known as the Vienna Circle and which developed the ideas of Logical Positivism. After the *Tractatus* had been published, Schlick had been one of the first to read it in Vienna, had seen its significance, and had lectured on it. The book had been much discussed by the Vienna Circle who saw its author as a kindred spirit. Wittgenstein now attended some of its meetings. At one of these, at around the time in 1929 when the Circle was producing the Manifesto which defined their stance, they were discussing how to define a meaningful statement. Wittgenstein had said that we could test that by considering how we would verify whether it was true or false.

> For example, a statement like "this container is round" is a meaningful statement because we can form a picture of a round container. We can also have a picture of a square container. Whether the container is round or square can be ascertained by measurements. If by applying these measurements to the container in question we can see that it is in fact a round and not a square container, we have established not only that the statement "this container is round" is meaningful, but also that it is true, because we have verified it.

Monk tells us that the Vienna Circle henceforward referred to "Wittgenstein's Principle of Verification", and that "so enthusiastically was it adopted by the members of the circle that it has been regarded ever since as the very essence of logical positivism".[10]

Wittgenstein later said that he had never meant this Verification Principle to be the only way in which one could establish whether a proposition was *impor-*

10 Monk, *op. cit*, p. 286/7.

tant. The Circle had fastened on this aspect of the *Tractatus*, but had misunderstood what he had meant by its famous last sentence, that "what we cannot speak about we must pass over in silence". The Vienna Circle had a very reductionist point of view: they believed that philosophy could concern itself only with the technique of analyzing what a statement could mean and with how the truth of a statement could be verified by sense observation. The members of the Circle had a scientific or mathematical background, and for them, typically, meaningful statements were of the kind made by scientists, and typically the way scientists tested their statements was by verification. So they had the same confidence in the scientific method that Comte and the nineteenth-century Positivists had, hence the name Logical Positivism. Statements and beliefs that were not amenable to these techniques were simply not worth a philosopher's attention, and when they had read in the *Tractatus* that subjects like ethics, aesthetics and religion could not be the subject of philosophy, they were perfectly happy to see the realm of philosophy thus circumscribed and felt no regret about "passing over in silence" those areas about which, as philosophers, we cannot speak. They really did not think them important.

But, as we have already seen, Wittgenstein had felt all along that what could find no place in the *Tractatus* was more important than what was in it. As Toulmin strikingly puts it, "Wittgenstein's silence in the face of the 'unutterable' was not a mocking silence like that of the Positivists, but rather a respectful one. ... The positivists thought that Wittgenstein was concerned with the foundations of knowledge, whereas in fact he was concerned with the nature *and limits* of language. ... It is a mistake to see him even as a linguistic philosopher... Wittgenstein was undoubtedly concerned with language and with the manner in which language operates within our lives; yet he never saw this as the self-sufficient subject matter of philosophy."[11]

Wittgenstein had come to feel that now he did need to speak about the things about which he had previously remained silent. The Circle might have picked this up soon after he had first attended their meetings; he would sometimes read mystical poetry to them without commenting on it (perhaps once again he felt that any explanation would be like dirtying a flower with muddy hands). He said he could even imagine what St Augustine, Kierkegaard and Heidegger meant in some of their mystical-sounding utterances.[12]

At the persistent urging of Bertrand Russell, Frank Ramsey and John Maynard Keynes, Wittgenstein returned to Cambridge in 1919, and in 1930 Trinity College made him a Fellow. For the rest of his life he worked on notes for lectures and for a new book. His lecture notes circulated as bound note books (the Blue Book, covering his lectures in 1934/5, and the Brown Book for those 1934/5) but he was extremely reluctant to consider the notes definitive or in the right order.[13] However, he discussed them exhaustively with his friends,

11 Janik & Toulmin, *op. cit.*, pp. 220 and 221.

12 Monk, *op. cit*, p. 283.

13 During the Second World War, Wittgenstein left Cambridge to work, first as a porter in the pharmacy of Guy's Hospital and then as a laboratory technician in Newcastle. He returned to Cambridge in 1944, but resigned his professorship there in 1947. For most of the rest of his life he lived in remote areas of Ireland and Norway, where he continued to work on his notes. He died (in a friend's house in Cambridge) of cancer in 1951.

so that they could publish them after his death – he was haunted by the thought that he had not much longer to live. All the work which he did after 1930 was published in book form only posthumously, the main work appearing in 1953 under the title *Philosophical Investigations.*

Philosophical Investigations

Whereas in the *Tractatus* Wittgenstein had focused on the logical structure of a statement and on how to test its meaning for truth, in *Philosophical Investigations* he had come round to G.E. Moore's idea that we could best understand the meaning of a statement by examining how the words in it were used.[14] He abandoned the metaphor that language was a picture of the world rather it was a tool fashioned, within limits, on an *ad hoc* basis, according to the actions which we wanted to perform.[15]

"Within limits", because we are usually not free to devise our own meaning, or if we do, we can communicate with others only to the extent to which they accept the meanings we have devised. Examples might be a parent's acceptance of baby-talk, or the public's acceptance of an advertiser's neologism or of a slang word which hitherto had meant something quite different, or the percolation of a new technical term, like Freud's "super-ego", first into the language of professionals and then into common parlance. Language is *socially conditioned,* and society teaches us what meanings to attach to words in different situations. Also, over time, the meanings society attaches to words can change: we have only to think, for example, of what has happened to the associations of words like "nice", "awful" or "gay".

The meaning of the word in each situation is governed by socially constructed meanings. The language in each situation has its own rules, and it is according to these *different* rules that we have to play the *language game.* In the same way the rules which govern the use of the ball in a game of Association Football differ from those that apply in Rugby football. Wittgenstein now saw that in the *Tractatus* he had made "the characteristic mistake of twentieth century intellectual life [which] was to try to treat all intellectual endeavours as if they were attempting to be like science".[16] He had attached only one meaning, one set of rules – those that operate in the game of science – to all language. He did not repudiate what he had said about language when it is used in the game of science; but he had not paid attention to language when it is used in another kind of game in the *Tractatus.* He now saw it as the task of philosophy to elucidate by which rules the language game is being played in any particular situa-

14 See p. 525 above.

15 Wittgenstein thought this was true even of mathematical language; we choose to give a particular meaning to words or symbols. 2 + 3 = 5 in one language (where the numerical system uses base 10) will be the same as 10 + 11 = 101 (where the binary system is used – and has to be used if we wish to perform certain calculations electronically). The actual quantity of objects in the real world is unaffected by whatever system of notation we choose to use. If someone were to hold up first two fingers, then three fingers and were then to say that altogether he was holding up six fingers, that would be acceptable if it were generally understood that the symbol we attach to the sum of 2 + 3 is "six" or "6". However, this is not the way the word or symbol *is* used, so if a person were to say that 2 + 3 = 6, he would either be making an elementary mistake in his addition or he would not know that the generally accepted name for the sum is 5.

16 The words in quotation marks are John Searle's description of Wittgenstein's later view.

tion, and in the process to clear up any problems that would arise out of getting the various conventions mixed up with each other. Presumably, therefore, we need to italicize one of the words in another famous sentence of Wittgenstein's famous lapidary sentences, "Don't ask for the *meaning*;[17] ask for the use."

If we do that, and distinguish one use or convention from another, he thought many apparent problems in philosophy would disappear, and that this prescription would, "show the fly a way out of the fly-bottle."

The walls of the bottle against which the fly had been bumbling were apparently conflicting views of what a proposition could *mean*. The task of the philosopher was merely to free it from *that* dilemma. What the fly would do once it was out of the bottle was of no concern to the *philosopher;* it is not *his* task to adjudicate between the different conventions or to examine which of the various possible meanings might be the true one. This does not mean that the questions we ask about the *truth* of propositions are unimportant; Wittgenstein would agree that these questions are profoundly important for each individual, but he thought that they were not questions that could be answered *philosophically*. All the philosopher can do is to show that the rules of one language game (like that of science) cannot be applied to a situation in which another language game (like that of religion) is being played.

When there is confusion about the game being played, the result was a "puzzle" which philosophy had to disentangle. That was all that philosophy could do. It could not solve "problems" that might present themselves when the disentanglement had taken place. Where in the *Tractatus*, Wittgenstein had written that, "in philosophy there are no deductions: it is purely descriptive", he now stressed again that, *"Philosophy leaves everything as it is."* He still had the same restrictive view he had in the *Tractatus* that the concern of philosophy was solely with language. He was now examining, for example, the language used in ethics, which had been excluded from consideration in the *Tractatus*, but he still rejected the idea that philosophy had anything to contribute to the solution of ethical *problems* once we had clarified the meaning of an ethical statement.

In a sense his view, though easier to understand, was now even narrower than it had been in the *Tractatus*, for in the earlier work he had *started* with examining whether a statement was meaningful, but had then *gone on* to describe the conditions under which a meaningful statement could also be said to be true. This latter aspect could be tested when the only game that was acknowledged was the "scientific" game, but no test is available to ascertain the truth when the statement is an ethical one. So all a philosopher can do when examining statements like "it is wrong to steal" or "this picture is beautiful", is to elucidate what exactly the speaker means by words like "wrong", "steal" or "beautiful". It is not his job to pronounce on whether stealing is in fact wrong or whether a picture is in fact beautiful.

Many philosophers continued to object strongly to Wittgenstein's assertion that there were no "problems" in philosophy, but only "puzzles". This was the issue in the famous incident at the Cambridge Moral Sciences Club in 1946 when Wittgenstein, who was the Chairman, is said to have threatened Karl Popper with a poker. Popper had come to the Club to assert that there were

17 (because there is no *one* meaning of any word)

indeed philosophical *problems* of all kinds – ethical, political, but also technical ones relating to notions like cause and effect, infinity, and probability.[18] Of course, Popper accepted that elucidating the meaning of language was important, but it could never be the be-all and end-all of philosophy. On the contrary, an understanding of the meaning of language was merely a necessary preliminary before one could tackle what were the real problems in philosophy.

Even when the philosopher has confined himself to the role Wittgenstein had allocated to him – that of disentangling "puzzles" and of elucidating the rules according to which any given game is being played – it does not follow that everyone can see and understand those rules. For example, it is not difficult to establish that humorous statements have their own convention, but a person lacking a sense of humour will not see the joke. A person without a sense of poetry may realize that poetic meanings are different from prosaic ones, but he will not be able to make sense of the former. These people will be like those for whom music is just a noise or just a series of notations and cannot understand its inner meaning. In fact, Wittgenstein said, "understanding a sentence is much more akin to understanding a theme in music than one may think".

We need to be able to observe other people fairly carefully to understand what a particular statement may mean to them. Sometimes we can deduce this from another person's tone of voice, from his body language or from whether he smiles or frowns while making a statement. From such signals we should, for example, be able to tell when someone says, "I am afraid", whether he is expressing fear or is merely apologizing for, say, being late or not understanding. In such cases the person saying "I am afraid" at least knows the meaning he is intending to convey.

There are also cases where the deeper meaning is hidden even from the speaker, as Freud had pointed out. The unconscious plays a game with rules that are often different from those of conscious behaviour, and the overt meaning of what a person is saying may be quite at odds with a hidden meaning. This can make life quite difficult for that individual, and a therapist can sometimes help by bringing to light latent confusions from which a patient may be suffering. Wittgenstein in fact sometimes likened the task of the philosopher to that of the therapist: both clear up often unconscious misunderstandings which make us confused.

Wittgenstein also knew that many people, by using their experience or intuition, understand the rules of these language games without needing the help of philosophers. The ordinary man sometimes understands things better than does the professional philosopher.[19] Wittgenstein produced a theory of language games, but no theoretical skills are needed to play them. Logical analysis is not necessary for playing the game. Someone who can play the game of mathematics does not need Frege's or Russell's analysis of mathematics to play it with confidence. In fact, the whole longing for theory was merely an example of "the craving for generality" that lies behind the efforts of scientists.

18 For an entertaining book about this incident, see David Edmonds and John Eidinow's *Wittgenstein's Poker*, (Faber & Faber, 2001)

19 cf. G.E. Moore, p. 526 above.

This, for Wittgenstein, was true of philosophy itself. When he had been writing the *Tractatus* it had been the sheer abstruseness of his philosophy which had made Wittgenstein doubt the value of what he was doing. He now worried about what, in the end, might be the difference between philosophy and common sense – a question that G.E.Moore had also addressed.[20] Eventually, he did find a humble use for philosophy. It is true that the mere elucidation of what is meant by a proposition – the sole task of philosophy as he saw it – is, by comparison, less grand than building theories about the world. He wrote, "What we find out in philosophy is trivial; it does not teach us new facts, only science does that. But the proper synopsis of these trivialities is enormously difficult, and has immense importance. Philosophy is in fact the synopsis of trivialities." It should not aim to build structures or systems such as scientists do. "Philosophy is not, like science, building a house. Nor are we even laying the foundations of a house. We are merely 'tidying up a room'."[21]

Wittgenstein was now free to say something about Ethics and Religion, subjects which, in the *Tractatus*, he had felt compelled to keep silent about. Clearly an understanding of religious or ethical utterances now depends on experience. They are not "bad" scientific statements; they speak a language of an entirely different kind. The experiences they try to express run up against the very limits of ordinary language. They cannot be proved either right *or wrong* by analysis, so the atheist, who finds no "evidence" for religion, and the believer, who wants to produce "proof" of religion, are both wrong. He is reported as having said to a friend that "Russell and the parsons between them have done infinite harm, infinite harm."

"Evidence" and "proof" are part of the discourse of science, and just as whether someone has an understanding of music is shown by how he responds to it and not by how he analyzes it verbally, so we can see the meaning he attaches to religion not by what he says about it, but by how he lives his life.

Conclusion

If, as laymen, we trouble to think about the way we use words, we would find Wittgenstein's second philosophy much closer to what we are conscious of doing than his first, which is not only very difficult and technical, but also seems to have little correspondence with our experience of living. A whole nation once responded to Joad's mantra, "it all depends on what you mean by ....", which could be said to be a very simple way of saying, with Wittgenstein, that we have to understand the context in which a word is used or the language game is being played. The second philosophy is therefore much easier to understand – so much so that Russell thought that, "the later Wittgenstein seems to have grown tired of serious thinking and to have invented a doctrine which would make such an activity unnecessary". This accusation would be true only if we were to equate "serious thinking" with the attempt to formulate a theory which expressed a testable truth about the world – and there is no need to limit "serious thought" in this way.

20 See p. 528 above.

21 Monk, *op. cit.*, p. 299.

The philosophy of the *Investigations* has influenced many thinkers since. It was taken further by a group whose work is known as linguistic philosophy. The most important people associated with this are J.L. Austin (1911 to 1960), Gilbert Ryle (1900 to 1976), Peter Strawson (born 1919) and John Searle (born 1932). The first philosophy of the *Tractatus* also had an influential progeny, as we have seen. Wittgenstein had, from the first, believed that the *Tractatus* was an inadequate way of dealing with experience, and had later thought that it was not only inadequate, but in some respects actually false. Neither of these beliefs troubled the Logical Positivists, who, as we have seen, saw themselves as applying its principles. It is now time to look in more detail at this school, to which several references have been made in this chapter and the last.

CHAPTER 44

Logical Positivism

As has already been said, the movement known as Logical Positivism began in Austria, where the German-born Moritz Schlick (1882 to 1936) founded the Vienna Circle in 1924. Its most important members were Rudolf Carnap (1871 to 1970), also German-born, and Otto Neurath (1882 to 1945). The Circle consisted mainly of philosophers who had been trained as scientists and mathematicians. They were in revolt against the cloudy mysticism and metaphysics that had dominated German philosophy since the days of Hegel, Fichte and Schelling, and that was still alive in the work of Heidegger, who was of the same generation as the members of the Vienna Circle. Instead, the Circle wanted to apply the disciplines of science and mathematics to philosophy. By 1929, they felt their approach and ideas had been sufficiently defined and consolidated to be expressed in a manifesto, *The Scientific Conception of the World: the Vienna Circle*, drafted, in the main, by Neurath.

We have seen the brief and occasional participation of Wittgenstein in the Circle between 1927 and 1929, and the reason why he distanced himself from it.[1] During 1932 and 1933 the Circle's meetings were attended by another visitor, the twenty-two year old A.J. Ayer (1910 to 1989), who had just passed his Finals with First Class Honours at Oxford. As an undergraduate, Ayer had felt out of sympathy with the metaphysical tradition in philosophy which was then still dominant in Oxford. Instead, he had been attracted by Hume and by what was happening in Cambridge, under Russell and Wittgenstein. He had read the *Tractatus* and wanted now to study further under its author, but his tutor suggested that he should go to Vienna and study under Schlick instead. He returned from Vienna as an ardent disciple, and in 1936 brought Logical Positivism to the attention of the English-speaking world in a book which achieved instant fame: *Language, Truth and Logic*. Logical Positivism seemed to fit much better into the English philosophical tradition dating back to Hume than it did into the Hegelian heritage of Germany.

The contempt of the Logical Positivists for German philosophical mysticism had aroused the ire of German-Austrian nationalists. This had made Austria an uncomfortable place for the Vienna Circle even before the Nazi takeover in 1938. Neurath had been travelling in Russia at the time when Chancellor Dollfuss was murdered by Austrian Nazis in 1934. He never returned to Austria, instead, he went to Holland and escaped from there to England in 1940. Carnap held an appointment in Prague from 1931 to 1936, at the end of which time he emigrated to the United States. When a mentally deranged student

1 See pp. 542f above.

assassinated Schlick in 1936, the right-wing press extolled the deed as a protest against Jewish and un-German philosophy (though Schlick had no Jewish ancestors at all. Carnap and Neurath are not mentioned in the *Encyclopaedia Judaica*, from which I take it that they were not Jewish either.) After the Nazi takeover, most of the remaining members of the Circle emigrated. The only philosophy the Nazis tolerated was a bastardized romanticism,[2] and so the torch of Logical Positivism and of its derivative, Logical Empiricism, passed to the English-speaking world.

When we consider the main principles of Logical Positivism, we can see how close they are to the ideas of the *Tractatus*. At the time neither the Vienna Circle nor Ayer made the kind of reservation that was implied in the last sentence of the *Tractatus*.[3]

Meaningful propositions are of two kinds: analytic and synthetic. A meaningful analytic proposition rests on generally accepted definitions, like "2 + 3 = 5", or "Mr X is an atheist who rejects a belief in God." The truth or falsehood of these propositions is essentially tautological; they simply unpack the meaning of the words in the proposition. The propositions given here can also be shown to be *true*, whereas such propositions as "2 + 3 = 6", or "Mr X is an atheist who believes in God", though meaningful, can be shown to be false because they ignore the generally accepted definitions of the words employed.

A meaningful synthetic proposition, such as "there are three railway stations in this town", is capable of being verified or rejected by sense-observation. Again, if in fact there are only two, the statement is still meaningful (because, as Wittgenstein would have put it, it corresponds to a *possible* picture) but observation would prove it to be false.

The observations we do make are "atomic", meaning each is philosophically discrete, separate from any other observation. For example, we can verify in several particular instances that gases expand when they are heated, but we cannot possibly verify that *all* gases *always* expand when heated. We do make links when we see a succession of recurring and verifiable individual instances, but, as Hume had long ago pointed out,[4] these connections are not philosophically "necessary" ones. Any conclusions and expectations we base on them are philosophically provisional. The philosophy of science had long been based on verification by sense observation[5] and on accepting the provisional nature of the

2 It will be remembered that Heidegger, who was a contemporary of the Logical Positivists, was for a time the Nazis' favourite philosopher – see pp. 493f above. There could hardly be a greater contrast than the one between Heidegger's interest in the widest resonance of words – see pp. 495f above – and the Logical Positivists' astringent attitude towards them.

3 See p. 541 above.

4 See p. 288 above.

5 This observation has to be taken in its broadest sense. We might say that sense observation would tell us, for example, that the earth is stationary, but other sense observations suggested to Galileo that the earth must in fact be moving. The proposition that the earth does move can then be verified, not by direct sense observation of the earth moving, but by the fact that the conclusion that it must be moving can be confirmed by those other sense observations. This would also deal in reverse with the other objection that is sometimes raised that there are some things in science, such as the behaviour of electrons that are not verifiable by sense-observation at all. However, some features that scientists have observed have led them to conclusions about the behaviour of electrons which are then borne out by other observable results. So they provisionally accept that electrons do these unobservable things – until they observe phenomena that would suggest that their provisional theory should be modified or abandoned.

conclusions, and, as has already been said, the Logical Positivists believed that the methods of science should be the model for the methods of philosophy also.

A proposition which can be neither verified nor falsified by sense observation is philosophically "meaning-less". All metaphysical propositions fall into this category, and Ayer rather brashly implied that therefore it was a waste of time to study much of the philosophy of the past. Most of it cannot convey any knowledge - only beliefs and emotions.

> This view, which we first came across in Wittgenstein's *Tractatus*,[6] seems an extraordinary limitation of the word "meaningful". Until then, ethics, aesthetics and religion had been universally recognized as branches of philosophy. Histories of philosophy have chapters about them. Most of the great men we call philosophers had concerned themselves with these subjects, and, hugely influential as Wittgenstein's view was, even now almost everybody would still think of these thinkers as philosophers. Nevertheless, the Logical Positivists thought that most of the philosophers of the past were not worth studying, and where they had control over university philosophical faculties, they excluded them from the syllabus.
>
> We also have here a total divergence from the normal use of the word "meaningful". We may or may not agree with the statement that a particular painting is beautiful, but we certainly understand what a person means when he makes such a statement, and it is therefore meaningful in the normal sense of the word.
>
> It is also significant that when a scientist finds that a particular word has too wide or too vague a meaning for his purposes, he will coin a new technical word to avoid confusion. The Logical Positivists wanted philosophy to be like science. All the more reason, then, why they should have found a new word – or at least attached an adjective like "verifiably" to the word "meaningful" – to mark the distinction between a meaningful proposition that can be verified and one that cannot.
>
> As it is, the banishment of unverifiable propositions from philosophy is as unwarranted as it would be for a cubist to deny that impressionist painting is an art form. No cubist would do that. If he calls himself a cubist, it is simply because he wishes to practice that particular art form rather than another one. At most he might go as far as to claim that the impressionist vision is more (shall we say) "superficial" than the cubist one, so that, in his opinion, cubism is in some sense "better" art than impressionism.
>
> So while it is perfectly legitimate for the Logical Positivists to *prefer* what is called "analytical" philosophy to "metaphysical" philosophy, to go beyond that is surely as intolerant as it is arbitrary. The later Wittgenstein of the *Philosophical Investigations* recognized this. In that book he moved from considering the relationship between meaning and truth to examining that between meaning and use. To understand meaning, we need to discover the rules by which different language games are being played. So the very word "meaning" means one thing when it is mentally prefixed by the adjective "verifiable" or "scientific", and something else when it is mentally prefixed by "unverifiable", "artistic", "ethical", or "religious".

The Logical Positivists thought an ethical statement, like "killing is wrong", needed to be reformulated to bring out what was really meant, but they differed among themselves about the actual reformulation. Carnap rephrased

6 See p. 541 above.

them as imperatives, "killing is wrong" is saying no more than "do not kill", and imperatives are not subject to being verified. They are therefore philosophically meaning-less. "A value statement is nothing else but a command in a misleading grammatical form. It may have effects on the actions of men ... but it is neither true nor false. It does not assert anything and can be neither proved nor disproved."

Ayer rephrased ethical statements as expressions of emotions. So, "killing is wrong" simply means "I disapprove of killing". It might be possible to verify whether a person *really* disapproves of killing. For example, many people who claim that killing is wrong might nevertheless approve of "just" wars, of capital punishment for certain offences, or of euthanasia. It does not need a linguistic philosopher to point out to such people that they are talking sloppily if they make the unqualified statement that killing is wrong, but it is not possible to verify that the emotion itself *makes* killing wrong. So he, too, believed that "killing is wrong" is a meaning-less statement:

> If I say to someone, 'You acted wrongly in stealing that money', I am not stating anything more than if I had simply said, 'You stole that money'. In adding that this action is wrong, I am not making any further statements about it. I am simply evincing my moral disapproval of it.

Only Schlick was prepared to rephrase moral statements so that they were neither mere expressions of disapproval nor mere imperatives. He held that they could be rephrased as propositions about the world that *were* empirically verifiable, at least in theory. "Killing is wrong" could be said to mean, "human beings generally want to live in peace, and this is best achieved by not killing one's neighbours". Whether it is true that human beings generally want to live in peace could be ascertained by, say, polling a population (or at least a representative sample of it) on the question, and then one could also examine the truth or the falsehood of the second component that the best way to achieve the aim of living in peace was in fact a general prohibition of killing other people.

> That is essentially a kind of Utilitarian argument.[7] The Utilitarians thought they had found a kind of scientific basis for morals, they had argued that we describe as "good" whatever is conducive to the greatest happiness of the greatest number, and Bentham had devised the Felicific Calculus which was designed to work out (or verify) whether a given course of action was "good" in that sense.[8] In chapter 36 we noted a variety of objections to utilitarian ethics, for example that it is far too sweeping a statement (and easily empirically disprovable) that human beings generally do want to live in peace or that, even if they do, they agree that a prohibition of killing (criminals or aggressors) is the best way of ensuring that they can live in peace. More questionable still is the assertion that what is morally right is what gives the greatest amount of happiness to the greatest number, as this view often rides roughshod over the legitimate rights of minorities.[9]
>
> So there are serious problems with Schlick's utilitarian ethics, but at least he was trying to include ethics within what the Logical Positivists considered philosophy, whereas Carnap and Ayer could find no place for ethics in philosophy proper at all.

7 See pp. 421f above.

8 See pp. 421f above.

9 See p. 422 above.

The views of Carnap and Ayer were considered shocking by many of their contemporaries because they seemed to downgrade the importance of ethical questions. In fact, they did not deny that ethical or moral statements register genuine and *important* moral standpoints, nor did they claim that these were simply arbitrary. As individuals they did in fact have political and social commitments towards which they took a position similar to that of the existentialists – one may not be able to make a philosophically watertight case for an ethical stance, but one still has to make a stand for what one believes in.[10] However, one must be sure not to claim any *philosophical* justification for the "truth" of such a stand.

Here we are again at one of the central concerns of this book, the relationship between Philosophy and Living. The existentialists believed that their call for commitment was part of philosophy, that the most important part of philosophy is to be a guide to living. Logical Positivism, on the other hand, is one of the philosophies that deny that philosophy has that function. Instead its only role is to examine the meaning of statements, but not the meaning of life. Philosophy is not a doctrine: it is an activity.

In an essay of 1954, *On the Analysis of Moral Judgments*, Ayer allowed the obvious, that the way the word "meaningful" had been used in his earlier work was not the way that word is usually used, and that statements that are neither analytical nor synthetic can be "meaningful" if that word is used in its normal and wider sense. All the same, he maintained, it would make for greater clarity in handling different kinds of statements (factual or logical on the one hand, metaphysical, poetic or ethical on the other) if we distinguish between the kind of "meaningfulness" that each of them has. This comes rather closer to Wittgenstein's *Philosophical Investigations*, which had just been published in the previous year, than to the *Tractatus*: for in the *Investigations* Wittgenstein had urged the reader not to ask for the meaning, but to ask for the use. Ayer's concession meant what Wittgenstein had meant: if the philosopher can elicit the language game that is being played, it would make for greater clarity in handling different kinds of statements. There is still, however, a disagreement between the *Investigations* and the Ayer of 1954: the latter still believed that in the language game that he was playing (the one that confined the word "meaningful" to analytical or synthetic statements), there were tests by which he could ascertain whether such statements were true or false. We have seen that Wittgenstein had disclaimed for his philosophy the ambition to say anything about the truth of the statements made in the course of the various language games: his task was merely to clarify what kind of language was being used, not whether that language expressed any truth.[11]

Wittgenstein was not the only famous philosopher who had engaged in debate with the Vienna Circle and had then found himself in disagreement with them. Karl Popper, too, had attended their meetings: his criticisms of their whole approach had Neurath describe him affably as "the Official Opposition". It is to him that we must now turn.

10 See p. 488 above. Though the Logical Positivists, when they spoke in their non-philosophical capacity, found themselves in a stance similar to that of the Existentialists, we must remember that they never thought that Existentialism, with its strong concern with ethics and its metaphysical basis deserved to be called a philosophy.

11 See p. 545 above.

CHAPTER 45

Popper and Kuhn

KARL POPPER[1]
1902 to 1994

Popper and the Vienna Circle

Karl Popper, who was originally a school teacher of mathematics and physics, had some friends in the Vienna Circle, which, as will be remembered, was made up largely of philosophers with a mathematical or scientific background, but he was never invited to join the Circle. Its chairman, Moritz Schlick, recognized Popper's qualities, but he had enormous respect for Wittgenstein (even though Wittgenstein thought that the Vienna Circle had misunderstood him) and he was offended by Popper's openly expressed contempt for Wittgenstein's ideas. In 1932, Schlick walked out of a meeting in protest at Popper's remarks about Wittgenstein. Otto Neurath described Popper as "the Unofficial Opposition" to the Vienna Circle.

Popper's disagreement with Logical Positivism seems, at first sight, not to be a very profound one. The central point for the Logical Positivists was that for a proposition to be meaningful it must be capable of being confirmed or rejected by sense observation. They called the process of confirmation "verification", a name which suggested that confirmation proved the statement to be true. As men with a scientific training, the members of the Vienna Circle were perfectly well aware that any truth established by sense observation must be philosophically provisional, and that later observations might force them to modify or even abandon the truth-status of a proposition that had been "verified". This is why they had taken care to say that verification was possible only for "atomic" propositions.[2] Therefore, when Popper said that verification in the strict philosophical sense is impossible and that any theory is potentially subject to being falsified by later sense observation, they could scarcely disagree. So they initially thought that what Popper called the technique of "falsification" (see below) was merely a refinement of their tests of "verification" (which did not prevent them from continuing to use their own formulation).

The differences between them and Popper ran deeper than this, however. We have seen that it took Ayer until 1954 to admit that the word "meaningful"

1 In this chapter I am deeply indebted to the brilliant analyses of Popper's ideas that are to be found in two works by Bryan Magee: his little book on Popper in the Fontana series of Modern Masters and *passim* in his *Confessions of a Philosopher.*

2 See p. 550 above.

had been used by the Logical Positivists in a much narrower sense than it usually carries. In the early days especially, they had drawn a sharp distinction between meaningful and meaningless propositions, or between propositions that made sense and those that made "non-sense": in each pair the first type of proposition could be verified or disproved, whereas the second could not; and if the second type could not be verified, then, if such a proposition has been described as meaningless, it could not be said to be true. Popper believed that statements which the Vienna Circle considered "meaningless" or "non-sense" could nevertheless be true or contain an element of truth. It was merely that any truth there might be in the statement could not be tested in the empirical way in which we test scientific statements. Therefore, he thought the important distinction to be made was not been sense and non-sense, but between science and non-science.

There was also another difference: the Logical Positivists and Popper were basically interested in different things. Although they had a scientific background and indeed, as individuals had concerned themselves with the philosophy of science, the Vienna Circle concentrated not on that, but on the philosophy of language. One might almost say that whereas they had moved from science to language, Popper made some trenchant points about language, and then moved on to science. He had been sufficiently interested in language to show that, for people claiming to deal with precise meanings, they had used the word "verification" much too loosely, but he had never seen language as more than an instrument with which we can examine the real world. Besides, he pointed out, the proposition that a statement is meaningless unless it is either analytical (and so tautologous) or synthetic (and is subject to verification or falsification) itself fails both these tests, being neither tautologous nor verifiable or falsifiable.

Having made this point about language, he moved on to develop a philosophy of science (and then, later, a political and social philosophy). His main interest was not just in what one could say about the *word*, but about the *world*. He did not believe, as Wittgenstein did, that, "philosophy leaves everything as it is". Bryan Magee recounts two brilliant metaphors which express Popper's view of the men who attribute excessive importance to ascertaining what language could mean: "One is that they are like a carpenter whose uses his tools all the time on one another ... but never carries out any other task with them. The other is that they are like a man who sits all the time polishing his glasses but never puts them on his nose and looks through them at the world."[3]

> Of course, it is important to make sure that the lenses of your glasses are polished (i.e. to use language with precision), that is an elementary requirement for all philosophical enquiry. Obviously, if the lenses of the spectacles are smudged or poorly focused, it will vitiate the attempt to see the world clearly and to make significant statements about it.

Later, when Popper looked at the world, he would feel impelled to examine wider social problems (for instance, about what makes a good society and problems about the interpretation of History) but in his earlier work he still spoke primarily as a philosopher of science.

3 *Confessions of a Philosopher*, p. 91.

The Logic of Scientific Discovery

In 1935, Popper published his theory about the philosophy of science in *Die Logik der Forschung,* which was not widely known or influential until, twenty-four years later, an English translation, *The Logic of Scientific Discovery,* appeared. By that time, Popper (who, like Wittgenstein, had come from a baptized family of Jewish origin) had long left Austria. In 1937, noting the steady rise of antisemitism in Austrian universities and anticipating a Nazi takeover, he had emigrated to New Zealand, where he taught at Canterbury University College. There he wrote *The Open Society and its Enemies* whose publication in 1945 made him famous with the general public (and which will be discussed below). In 1946 he came to England. At that time Cambridge philosophy was largely dominated by Wittgenstein, and Oxford philosophy by Ayer. So there was no love lost between Popper and either of these universities. In 1949 he took up an appointment as Professor of Logic and Scientific Method at the London School of Economics (which suggests that his principal philosophical interest was still in science rather than in the social field) and he remained there until his retirement in 1969. In 1957 he published another book on a non-scientific subject, *The Poverty of Historicism.* It was only then that his publishers ventured on the English translation of *The Logic of Scientific Discovery* (1959) and that the general public became familiar with his famous "Falsification Principle".

The not very original starting point of Popper's philosophy of science was the reminder that a statement might have been "verified" millions of times, but that one single sense observation would suffice to call it into question. At a very elementary level there are statements like "swans are white", which was falsified when black swans were found in Australia. Another example is the statement that "water boils at 100°C" is serviceable enough for most purposes at sea-level, but when it was observed that in closed vessels or at high altitudes the boiling point is lower, the statement has to be modified to read, "water boils at 100°C in open vessels at sea-level". We then have to try to work out *how* this difference can be explained, and how to reformulate the original theory to embrace the wider range of phenomena we have observed. In this case it is achieved by working out a formula that will link the boiling point of water with air pressure and other variables.[4]

The statements about swans and the boiling point of water are both non-theoretical statements. The theoretical example that had impressed Popper, and had first led him to formulate his philosophy, was an observation made during an eclipse in 1919 which confirmed Einstein's theories on the curvature of light and did not fit Newtonian theories that appeared to have been "verified" for over 200 years. This falsification did not altogether nullify Newton's theories, which were still "true" in terms of what could be observed with the equipment that was available in Newton's time and right into the twentieth

4 Thomas Kuhn suggests, in *The Structure of Scientific Revolutions*, p.147, that the distinction between verification and falsification is an artificial one, in that both the falsifying instances (the black swans or the boiling point of water at altitudes) and the theory that would replace the earlier one are in need of at least temporary verification. We should therefore be talking about the "verification-falsification" principle. (As the falsifying instance has to be verified, would it not have been better to talk about the "falsification-verification" principle?)

century, and the theories are still serviceable *up to a point*. But new instruments showed that they were not *absolutely* true, as people had believed; that, on the scale of what was now observable, they needed to be modified – or, in this case, actually rejected because *on this macrocosmic scale* Newton's and Einstein's theories could not both be true. An explanation had to be found for the way light behaves that would account both for Newton's and Einstein's observations.

> Popper has perhaps been most associated with the explanation of how existing theories come to be *modified* by taking hitherto unnoticed phenomena into account. But Popper was very well aware that many important developments in science do not modify but completely shatter existing theories. These will be the scientific *revolutions* or "paradigm shifts" in which Thomas Kuhn was most interested – see the next section.

Popper challenged the prevailing view of scientific progress:

1. the scientist begins with a series of observations
2. from these he makes certain inductions which lead to the formulation of a hypothesis
3. the hypothesis is then tested (i.e. verified)
4. a "law" is then formulated
5. this law then suggests new lines of observation and research.

Popper questioned the first and second steps of the supposed process of making progress. These assume that observation precedes induction and hypothesis. He argued that frequently we already have a theory which suggests to us what we should observe and then informs the interpretation of the results of the observation. The danger of this is that one is tempted to look for evidence supporting the hypothesis and brush aside any observations that do not fit it. He also argued that, historically, most progress has depended, not on the fifth step, but on scientists coming across something that did not fit in with a theory as it stood, trying to find out *why* it did not fit, and then modifying or abandoning the old theory. This has led to such fruitful results that, instead of relying on innumerable examples that would verify the old theory, one should be actively *looking for* examples that would falsify it.

The Open Society and its Enemies

Because every true scientist knows how important a role falsification plays in making progress, he will welcome criticism even of his own theories (an assertion that would be heavily qualified by Thomas Kuhn)[5] and Popper said that what was true of science should be true in all spheres of life. Of course, he was quite aware that testing for accuracy or inaccuracy of a theory is much easier in the physical sciences than in the social sciences. The physical scientist can repeat experiments, and he can much more easily isolate the factors he is studying than is possible in the social sciences, given the innumerable factors that influence any particular situation, problem or solution. What *is* as possible in the social sciences as in the physical sciences is an open-minded approach, a

5 See p. 564 below.

readiness to accept criticism, and a willingness to make experiments. Unfortunately, whereas he believed that these qualities are predominant in the scientific community, they are far less in evidence in society in general. This was the basic thesis in two of his later books, *The Open Society and its Enemies* (1945) and *Conjectures and Refutations: the Growth of Scientific Knowledge* (1963).

An Open Society is one that, like the scientific community, understands the value of criticism and puts no obstacles in its way. It tolerates the posing of problems, the asking of awkward questions and the advocacy of possible solutions. The case for an Open Society is not merely a moral one; such a society will also, in the long run, be more efficient than one in which the authorities propagate an ideology which may not be questioned from outside and is only very occasionally questioned from within.

> In this respect, Popper has the same view as John Stuart Mill had had. Mill believed in freedom of speech and criticism because he was confident that in such cases good arguments will eventually drive out bad ones. On p. 429 above, it has been suggested that this view might be a typical piece of nineteenth century liberal optimism and did not make sufficient allowance for demagoguery.
>
> *The Open Society* was published in the year in which the democracies had been on the winning side against Nazi Germany. This might have appeared to be a demonstration of the superiority of open societies over closed ones, and indeed, economic historians like Richard Overy have since shown that the vaunted and dreaded "efficiency" of the Nazi state has been greatly overrated. However, the equally authoritarian Soviet system had contributed considerably to the defeat of Germany. (True, in the long run, the Soviet system would also collapse as the result of the rigidities imposed upon that society.)

In modern times, many authoritarian governments have imposed an all-embracing blueprint on society. The economy, education etc. should all be centrally planned. As a result any mistakes affect the entire society. In both open and closed societies, any plans are likely to have some unplanned and unforeseen outcomes. Whenever mistakes are found in such planning, the people who made them, in any society, will usually be those most resistant to acknowledging them.[6] In an Open Society there are regular mechanisms for peacefully replacing such people. In a closed society that is not possible. Instead, the excuse is often proffered that there is nothing wrong with the theory, but that it is just not being properly implemented in practice. Failures are then ascribed to incompetence, and more often to malignancy and conspiracy. The people held responsible are purged, and the more ruthless the purge, the more the authorities diverge from the original idealistic blueprint, and the more the basic causes for failure are left undiagnosed. If there is such a resistance to necessary change, when, in the end, it does come, it is unlikely to be peaceful, and a violent revolution takes place. Unfortunately, violent revolutionaries then tend to impose blueprints of their own.

6 Popper had thought, as we have seen, that scientists are sufficiently open-minded to welcome corrections, and here his emphasis had been rather different from Kuhn's. When it comes to politicians or social planners, Popper and Kuhn seem to be in agreement that those groups tend to put up resistance when their work is challenged.

Popper will have none of the excuses proffered by the creators of blueprints when practice does not live up to theory – as in science, if things don't work out in practice, there is something wrong with the theory. Democratic societies do better because they generally do not go in for imposing an overall blueprint. Instead, they tend to go in for piecemeal social engineering, so that if the results falsify expectation, amendments or improvements are relatively easier to make. The emphasis for Popper was always on trying to solve problems that present themselves, or, as he put it, aiming to minimize unhappiness, rather than trying to maximize happiness. We can do something to minimize unhappiness because we know what makes people unhappy, but he thought we did not know how to make people happy. "Instead of the greatest happiness for the greatest number, one should demand, more modestly, the least amount of avoidable suffering for all; and further, that unavoidable suffering – such as hunger in times of unavoidable shortage of food – should be distributed as equally as possible."[7]

> Magee rightly points out[8] that one can aim for a little more than that. We do know how to increase happiness by, for example, making public provision for the arts, sport facilities etc. (He also includes under this heading provision for education, housing and health, though one could surely argue that all we know is that their absence creates actual unhappiness.)
>
> One might also argue, as a revolutionary would, that piecemeal tinkering with a rotten structure is useless, and that in any case some societies are so rigid that they resist even relatively minor improvements. In such cases it is hopeless to rely on evolutionary change; what is needed is what Kuhn called a "paradigm shift",[9] and only the radical destruction of the old structures will do. Popper's temperament was all for evolution, but he would have realized that there are circumstances when revolutions are, if not philosophically, then at least in practical terms, inevitable. However, in such cases the new system that is put in place, almost invariably based on an ideological blueprint, will soon show the resulting distressing consequences.

Are there any limits to what an open society should tolerate? Popper could see only one circumstance under which it was entitled to suppress opposition. That was when the opposition's programme was to close down the open society or to stifle the freedoms for which the open society stood. These freedoms were not only political (freedom of speech or organization), they could also be economic (when they led to the exploitation of the weak). The state has a right to limit these abuses – too much as well as too little freedom can imperil freedom. In 1988 he wrote, "We have need of liberty in order to prevent the abuse by the State of its power, and we have need of the State to prevent the abuse of liberty" and further, "Too much as well as too little freedom can imperil freedom." Popper knew that it was a delicate business to draw an exact line. It could not be defined by any theory,[10] that would run counter to his general phi-

7 *The Open Society*, Vol.I, p. 285.

8 in his book in the Modern Masters series, p. 86

9 See p. 565 below.

10 Isaiah Berlin had a very similar outlook in this respect – see p. 572 below. He stressed that many values of necessity conflict with each other, and that there has to be some kind of trade-off between them: in this case between the right of free speech and the right to protect free speech.

losophy that problems are best dealt with on an *ad hoc* basis rather than by any formula.

> One has to weigh up, for example, whether one does more harm than good by banning political parties whose programme is to establish a dictatorship. There would certainly appear to be a moral entitlement for a democracy to ban parties whose avowed programme is to use the democratic process to destroy democracy once they are in power. When the Nazis were in opposition, they had made no bones about "holding their noses" while they took part in parliamentary elections, even though they vowed to end parliamentary talking shops once they were in power. Stalinists, too, made it clear that, once in power, they would establish a *dictatorship* of the proletariat.
>
> It is a moot point whether a democracy should actually invoke its moral right to ban parties with such an avowed programme. In Britain, where a democratic society is firmly based, such a step has generally been felt to be unnecessary and possibly, by driving the banned parties underground, even counter-productive. It has generally been felt that the best way to cope with extremist parties is to enforce the existing laws against violence, incitement to violence, or threats to public order. Yet Popper must have remembered that the Weimar Republic might have been saved if the Nazi party had been declared illegal, and the threat it presents to German democracy even today is felt to be grave enough for the party to be banned there.

Popper divides the enemies of the open society into two groups, and each of the two volumes of the *Open Society and its Enemies* deals with one of them. The first are conservatives who are alarmed by anything that would undermine their values. Their prototype was Plato. The second are Utopians, radicals who aim at a perfect society and then want to freeze it. Here he took Marx as a prototype.[11] Both are unavoidably led into dictatorship.

He thought that Marxism had another defect. It was one of those theories of society which purport to be "scientific" and yet have built into them a component by which any criticism is invalidated in advance. When Marxists were confronted with ways in which the theory had already been falsified,[12] the cruder proponents dismissed the arguments as merely an expression of the reactionary class-interests which Marxism had laid bare.[13] The subtler ones, like Lenin, tried to keep the basic system intact by trying to accommodate the objections within it. For example, at one time, in the early stages of the Industrial Revolution, the misery of the working class was, for a generation or so, intensified. From this Marx deduced the law of increasing misery within capitalism. When the standard of living of the working class slowly improved towards the end of the nineteenth century, Lenin put this down to Imperialism. Conditions only improved because the working class benefitted from the increasing misery of the colonial peoples. An alternative view was that trade unions had secured better terms within the capitalist system because, to some extent, the enormous wealth which the system produces has trickled down

11 Plato's *Republic*, though enshrining conservative values, also presented a Utopia.

12 See p. 451 above.

13 The same reaction could be found in another "ideology" which Popper criticized, that of psychoanalysis, because criticism of its theory was often interpreted as the kind of psychological denial mechanism with which insecure people resist unwelcome truths.

to the workers. However, such factors would not fit into the basic system and were therefore not considered.

A further basic flaw Popper detected in Marxism was "Historicism", to which he devoted another book, *The Poverty of Historicism* (1957). It is the idea that it is possible to detect laws in history which make predictions possible, which in turn implies historical inevitability. All earlier such predictions had been falsified by events. In evaluating a situation, we must always start from where we are, rather than see it in the context of an abstract goal.

Popper did not deny that Marxism, and psychoanalysis also, might still have valuable insights, but they cannot be tested empirically as they now stand. Some of the Freudian insights he compared to myths; and *"a myth may contain important anticipations of scientific theories"*.[14] As an example he gave the theories of Empedocles about how the four elements combine with or are separated from each other by Love or Hate, how some of these combinations were the result of chance, and how, of those, only a few were capable of surviving. One can see in this the foreshadowing of scientific theories (like that of evolution being the result of random mutations) which could be tested empirically. Statements that were *in principle* untestable, like those about ethics, aesthetics and religion, important and meaningful though they could be, did not interest him as a philosopher. There is no indication in his work that he would have agreed with Wittgenstein or the later Russell that it is precisely those questions which are philosophically the most important ones.

Objective Knowledge

In 1972, in a book called *Objective Knowledge: an Evolutionary Approach*, Popper offered a new solution to the question of the relationship between the material world and the perceptions of our mind. At one extreme there had been Descartes, who had believed that there was an objective world outside the mind and independent of it; at the other extreme Hume had said that we can be sure only of mental processes and have no philosophical evidence that there is an outside world at all. Kant had offered the intermediate position: there is an outside world (*das Ding an sich*) which sends us signals, but that these have to be interpreted by the tools of understanding that we have; we can never know whether the interpretation gives us an accurate picture of the outside world.[15]

Popper saw three worlds. He accepted that there was an objective world of material things which he called World 1. Then there is what he called World 2. This is the world we create subjectively and more or less individually, as when we *develop* a system of describing or interpreting World 1, for instance through language and through science. It also involves *fresh-minting* moral or aesthetic judgments, religious opinions, political theories. There is also a World 3. This world has been created by our minds, but, once created, has assumed an objective existence of its own. Thus, for example, the elementary language of mathematics is a human construct, but once it has been constructed, we find that it yields implications that are so far from having been in the minds that had con-

14 *Conjectures and Refutations.*

15 For Descartes, see p. 222 above; for Hume, p. 288 above; for Kant, pp. 365ff above.

structed it that they often remain hidden, sometimes for centuries, and are discovered only with great difficulty. One example he gives relates to prime numbers. When numbers were constructed, they were not constructed with the intention that some of these numbers should be prime – that is whole numbers (integers), like seven or eleven, which cannot be divided into other integers other than by one or by themselves – while others should be composite, like nine, which can be divided into other integers. In 1742, it turned out that their indivisibility is not the only characteristic that prime numbers have, when Christian Goldbach discovered that every even number can expressed as the sum of two prime numbers, thus, for example, eight can be expressed as the sum of five and three.[16]

Rather more flexible than mathematical language are other parts of language, but they are not infinitely flexible. Once a language or a grammar has been constructed, it represents a fairly objective reality which confronts a child as it grows up, or someone trying to learn a foreign language. True, Wittgenstein had shown that the meaning of a word depends on the language game that is being played, but then the language game itself has to be learnt by the child or the person who wants to understand another language. The language and its uses become even more solidly objectified when they are "encoded" in World 1 objects like dictionaries or books of grammar. In fact, all information of whatever kind that we find encoded in books, in computers, in images etc. and that we allow unquestioningly to influence our lives and thoughts – all that is the kind of objective knowledge[17] which Popper finds in World 3.

Social structures have the same characteristic. Originally man-made, they acquire a presence that shapes us rather than being shaped by us. They, too, are "encoded" in legal systems or in custom.[18] Similarly, belief systems, customs, moral and aesthetic standards are originally man-made, but influence people who had no part in the making of them.

> World 1 objects could really be subdivided into those that are man-made (like chairs) and those that are not (like rocks). There does not seem to be much difference in kind between the man-made objects in World 1 and the man-made creations which become World 3. An original chair[19] was first a design in the chair-maker's mind. Subsequently, it has an objective presence which confronts us, and, like a World 3 object, it can be changed. We could, for instance, reshape its arms if the original arms are somehow uncomfortable.

16 This is known as Goldbach's *Conjecture* – a nice touch in the name, allowing for falsification in future. No one has ever been able to demonstrate why the theory is true: according to the *Encyclopaedia Britannica*, it has been tested for all even numbers up 100,000, where it has been found to fit, but because it has not been tested for numbers beyond that, there is always the possibility that one might find an even number for which it does not fit.

17 In this area it is important to distinguish between two meanings of the word "objective". When Popper describes the contents of a book as objective, he means that the contents have a presence which is independent of whether the book is read or not. The other meaning of "objective" is "undistorted by prejudice", and of course Popper does not use the word in that sense, but in the technical sense in which it has been used by philosophers since the days of Aristotle.

18 There is something Hegelian in this idea. Hegel described social structures as ideas solidified in the world.

19 I use the word "original" deliberately. A mass-produced chair owes its origin to a World 3 object: a design which was once in a draughtsman's mind but has been "encoded" in a pattern-book.

When we confront such presences and we wish to change them, we often speak of running our heads into brick walls, so solid and immovable do they often appear to be. Of course, they do change over time. A body of knowledge (whether of science, history, or anything else) is objective in the sense that it comes to stand outside of a subjective mind, but that body evolves, as do the objective presences of language, social structures, belief systems, moral and aesthetic standards. They do so because they throw up problems or because new needs are felt, and we have already seen that the existence of problems is an incentive to find better solutions. We will also remember that Popper believed that the best solutions are piecemeal rather than based on preconceived blueprints, and gradual rather than sudden and sweeping.

Here, much depends on the spectacles through which one looks at social change. Are the changing attitudes to sexual questions or to punishment which we have seen in the last generation or two gradual or revolutionary?[20] Or could we say that they have been both? Perhaps we can be helped to approach this problem by studying Kuhn's theories of how, and over what period of time, paradigm shifts take place.

THOMAS KUHN

1922 to 1996

As the title of his best known book, *The Structure of Scientific Revolutions* (1962), suggests, Thomas Kuhn also concerned himself with the question of how a body of knowledge comes to change over time, though his answers differ somewhat from Popper's.

Popper had challenged the notion prevailing in his time that good science relies on verification. For him, progress is made by looking for falsification of existing theories, and any scientist worth his salt is interested in scientific progress and therefore welcomes falsifications. Kuhn's contention was that the scientific community was inherently resistant to the process of falsification. "Normal science", he maintained was extremely conservative. It worked within a given conceptual framework or set of beliefs which are shared by the entire community and in which entrants into it are trained. He called this set of beliefs a paradigm (from the Greek *paradeigma*, meaning "a pattern"). The paradigm embodies rules, standards and assumptions within which to carry out further research. According to Kuhn, the scientific community is confined by paradigms to a mental straitjacket which makes it conservative, rigid and resistant to change.

Needless to say, many scientists have strongly objected to this description of the setting within which they work.

As long as a paradigm holds, there is no serious disagreement between scientists; they feel certain about what they know. That certainty is reinforced to the extent to which the paradigm has a predictive value — predictive in the sense

20 In aesthetics, it seems to me, there is no question but that changes have been self-consciously revolutionary, especially after the Impressionist period. In no way can the developments of Cubism, Dadaism, Abstract Art or Conceptual Art be seen as evolutionary. The same might be said of some developments in Literature and in the Theatre. But then artistic ideas, in my view, differ from other ideas in society in that they do not present good or harmful solutions to the problems of how we should live.

that further research within it produces results that fit into the scheme, extend its scope and precision, fill in gaps (Kuhn calls this "solving puzzles" in the sense that we talk about jigsaw or crossword puzzles – the metaphor assumes the unwarranted optimism that the missing pieces *will* fit into the scheme) or perhaps even refine it. The paradigm also suggests the directions in which future research might go. An example would be cancer research: scientists know the causes of some cancers, but not of others, yet scientists think they know what kind of causes the unexplained cancers would have.

So paradigms "work until they cease to work", until, that is, anomalies occur. When they do, there are three possible approaches to them:

1. They will initially be seen as "puzzles" rather than as "counter-instances", and the expectation is that they can be solved by refining the existing paradigm. In the process, Kuhn said, there is the danger of unduly forcing them to fit into the established framework.

   This is anyway a natural human tendency, outside as well as inside science. The psychological theory that explains this is called *Gestalt* psychology. The German word *Gestalt* means a shape or form: we tend to be thrown when we come across an experience that does not fit into our previous ones, and if at all possible we make the new ones conform to the shape of the old ones. In this way we often misunderstand or misinterpret the new ones.

   If they are genuine counter-instances, their incorporation into the paradigm will throw up new anomalies.

2. The scientist may honestly recognize that the existing paradigm cannot explain the anomalies with the intellectual tools that are available to it. The anomaly is then set aside, perhaps for a future generation to work on. That has happened more often in the history of science than is commonly realized. Almost from the beginning scientists noted, for example, observations that did not fit in with Newton's laws. In the overwhelming number of such cases they found so much predictive value in Newton's paradigm that they were content to put the odd anomaly aside.

3. Someone has an intellect powerful enough to suggest a new paradigm. Kuhn said that usually this is someone who is very young or very new to the field, and who is therefore not conditioned by the disciplines of the old paradigm.

When the old and the new paradigms are incompatible, there follows a period during which they have to battle it out and the one that is fittest to account for the world will survive. We then have what Kuhn called "a Paradigm Shift", which, in the field of science, is called a Scientific Revolution.

The period of struggle can be quite long, if the old paradigm has institutional and/or non-scientific vested interests to back it. Thus, for many years the Catholic Church backed the Ptolemaic picture of the universe, by which the earth is at its centre. The vested interest was not simply scientific, it was also theological because the Church could not accept that God should have sent His only begotten Son anywhere but to the centre of the universe. The Copernican heliocentric theory was therefore theologically unacceptable, and was proscribed.

Paradigm shifts can have a momentous effect over many fields of science (as they had in the case of Copernicus, Newton, Darwin or Einstein) or they can be limited to quite a small section of science without other scientists being affected by it. In either case, the change will be revolutionary rather than cumulative.

Kuhn used his theory to challenge the notion, which he says is often implied in science textbooks, that scientific progress is organic, evolutionary, linear or cumulative. This is true of the filling out and refinements that take place *within* an existing paradigm, but the establishment of a new one is revolutionary rather than evolutionary; the break is a radical one and quite new rules and perspectives are established. But when textbooks refer to the work of past scientists, they *select* only that part of their work which is still considered useful. This necessarily detaches it from the context in which it was created. A *history* of science would bring out the revolutionary aspect, but the *textbooks,* which are all that students of science are required to study (unlike students of literature or history, they are never required to study original texts) make the progress seem cumulative.

Here again some scientists have protested that Kuhn overstates his case. They agree with Kuhn that, because history has been and will continue to be full of paradigm shifts, there can be no absolute truth in science, but they point out that many scientific and mathematical concepts can safely be taken as resistant to all paradigm shifts and therefore to be true. They also draw attention to largely descriptive sciences – geology, for example – where advances in knowledge take the form of refinements or even major corrections, but which can easily be handled within existing frameworks and hardly call for revolutionary paradigm shifts.

Paradigm Shifts Outside Science

Although Kuhn confined himself to a theory of how science advances, his notion of paradigm shifts has caught on in a big way in areas that have nothing to do with science as such. Historians have long been conscious of the breakdown of old frameworks and the revolutionary changes that then follow. Some historians now use the words "paradigm shift" to describe this process.

Hans Küng's books on the historical developments of Judaism (1991) and Christianity (1994) are organized explicitly in terms of paradigm shifts. Just one example of a paradigm shift in Christianity was effected by St Paul when he set out a theology that sharply divided Christianity from Judaism. Before this split, Christianity had been a sect within Judaism.

We might note in passing that paradigm shifts outside science are possibly easier to bring about than within science. Kuhn had said that one difficulty of getting a *scientific* paradigm shift accepted is that it has to be accepted within the closed scientific community. The revolutionary scientist cannot appeal to those outside the community because the outsiders simply do not have the expertise to decide whether the revolutionary scientist is right or not.[21] When St Paul produced his paradigm shift, he successfully appealed to people out-

21 I am leaving out of account here the following that some unorthodox and even "quack" scientists sometimes have with the general public when they promise them cures for certain medical ailments. Alternative medicine is a case in point. This may be accepted by the general public out of superstition, but there are occasions when it is accepted because it really works, and possibly better than orthodox medicine.

side the theological Jewish establishment who, for the most part, had no theological expertise at all.

Karl Marx likewise could appeal to people outside any establishment. His theory that the *primary* forces that shape history are economic ones eventually produced another massive paradigm shift. For a time it could almost have been said that "we are all Marxists now", as even conservative historians had to take on board economic explanations for historical developments. The Marxist paradigm dominated until the collapse of the Soviet Union, when it lost supporters even on the Left.

There have been major paradigm shifts as the theories of Freud percolated into attitudes to the upbringing of children, to education, crime, sexual behaviour and much else besides.[22] In art, a major paradigm shift established itself when it became accepted that a painting does not have to bear a resemblance to anything the eye actually sees. That opened the floodgates to a variety of revolutionary movements in art, like Cubism, Dadaism, Surrealism and abstract art of all kinds.

Sometimes, individuals have been as important in sociological paradigm shifts as Kuhn maintains they are in scientific ones; at other times it is hard to attribute a shift to one particular powerful intellect rather than to changing conditions in society, like, for example, industrialization or effective contraception.

There are countless assumptions that went almost unquestioned in the past that are now almost universally discredited in society at large: the legitimacy of slavery; the subordination of women; the sinfulness of various kinds of sexual behaviour; to name but a few.

In religion, the stories and commandments set down in sacred books formed the unquestioned framework of belief, law, and rituals for centuries, and they worked – until they ceased to work. So-called fundamentalists[23] continue to take the Bible stories literally while other religious people have made the paradigm shift to treat the stories as myths that might embody valuable and lasting insights, but which cannot be accepted in their literal sense, and of course, more people than ever before have turned away from religion altogether. Those like, for example, the so-called religious fundamentalists, for whom a paradigm shift is so painful that they cannot make it at all appear trapped in a time-warp; they often cut themselves off from a world which has accepted the new paradigms and retreat into deliberate isolation (though in some cases they manage, at least for a time, to enlarge their sphere by force or intimidation). Institutions which maintain the old paradigms may slow down the acceptance of new ones, but they gradually lose their influence (unless, again, they have the physical force to hold down the new ones and are prepared to use it.)

There is a danger of using the words "paradigm shift" too loosely. When Kuhn used it, he applied it to *revolutionary* developments in science, and he specifically would not accept it for the *evolutionary* developments of "normal science". Outside the sciences it is often debatable whether the shifts are rev-

22 See pp. 585f below.

23 Most of us have some fundamentalist beliefs, and there is nothing wrong with that. I deplore the way the word "fundamentalist" is used to describe people who believe in the literal text of their sacred books. I prefer to call such people "literalists". Many people with fundamental, or literalist, views are perfectly peaceable in their relations with others; and it is equally regretable that the word "fundamentalist" now also often carries the meaning of religious people who are intolerant and who would like to impose, by force, their views onto others, and who should, more properly, be called "religious fanatics".

olutionary or evolutionary. Take the change in the position of women in western societies, for example. When a woman now in her eighties reflects how different the position of women is today from what it was when she was a child, the change may indeed seem revolutionary. However, the emancipation of women has been a gradual and evolutionary process. In England it began in a small way during the premiership of Gladstone when women were allowed to retain some rights over the property they brought into marriage, and gathered pace as women won the vote, could receive a university education, and as sex discrimination in employment was made illegal. There are many similar situations in which change has both an evolutionary and a revolutionary aspect, and in which it is perfectly possible – and indeed desirable – to identify the processes of change and reaction to change without adding a spurious gloss of profundity by invoking the concept of paradigm shift.

CHAPTER 46

Isaiah Berlin

1909 to 1997

Isaiah Berlin was born in Riga, then part of Imperial Russia. He had come to England with his family after the Russian Revolution. He eventually went to Oxford, did brilliantly as an undergraduate, and after his graduation in 1932 became first a philosophy tutor at New College and then a Fellow of All Souls. He was initially a part of the Logical Positivist circle around A.J. Ayer. Berlin was never convinced by the claim that all meaningful problems of philosophy arose out of linguistic confusions, or that statements that could not be verified empirically were therefore meaningless. In a paper of 1939 entitled *Verification* [1] he made technical criticisms of the principle of Verification, but by then he also had a wider view than had the Logical Positivists of what philosophy was all about. He had already been disturbed by their complete lack of interest in the thought of past philosophers. In 1933 he had been asked by the Warden of New College, who was editing a series of short books in the Home University Library, to write a volume on Karl Marx, and in the course of this work, Berlin had become increasingly interested in the ideas of the past, in their historical context, and *in the influence they had on what people actually live by*. When, in 1946, he returned to Oxford from war work he had done in the United States, he abandoned so-called "pure philosophy", and turned instead to the history of ideas, a subject which he virtually created.

> Some philosophers believe that from this time onwards, Berlin ceased to be a philosopher at all. Anthony Quinton described him as "superficial" and "not a philosopher *in the academic sense*"[2] We come back again to the purpose of the present work, which is opposed to such a narrow concept of what philosophy – or even "academic philosophy" is. For many of the greatest philosophers of the past – Plato, Aristotle, Aquinas, Kant – the question of how we ought to live has been an integral part of their thought. Others, like Hobbes and Locke, have not drawn such a sharp line between philosophy and living, even if they dealt with "technical" philosophy in some books and with applied philosophy in others. Nietzsche is generally considered to have been a philo-

1 This can be found in a collection of his essays published in 1978 by H.H. Hardy under the title *Concepts and Categories*. Most of Berlin's work has been in the form of lectures or papers, and it has been the life-time work of H.H. Hardy to edit these and publish them in collections of essays arranged according to subject matter in a series of volumes which is still not complete.

2 In a 1998 *Times* review of Michael Ignatieff's biography of Isaiah Berlin. My italics.

> sopher, and he was concerned almost entirely with how people ought to live. It seems peculiarly arrogant to reserve the word "academic" for the kind of philosophy which tends to monopolize research areas in university philosophy departments at the moment, and to deny it to serious thinkers who try to throw light on how we ought to live our lives. We shall also see presently another reason why the likes of Lord Quinton dismiss Berlin as "superficial". It seems to me that they want to see – or at least to aim for – unambiguous answers to philosophical problems. Berlin showed that these are simply not available, that we have to live with ambiguity, and that the most important problems in living cannot be "resolved" by scientific analysis. Bertrand Russell and Wittgenstein had been fully aware of this, but had not felt capable, *in their role as philosophers*, to say anything about them. They, too, had a very restricted view of what philosophers could speak about. Berlin knew that philosophers in the past had addressed themselves to finding the meaning of the world. At the very least he was undertaking a philosophical task by investigating and explaining their work. He then drew certain conclusions on the nature of value systems, an activity which surely merits being described as philosophical – even if, modestly, he did not think that he had himself made important new contributions to philosophy.

Anyone who studies the history of ideas will of course be struck by the fact that value systems are relative; the values that are paramount for one person or one society are not paramount for another. Berlin went well beyond this historical observation. He thought that no individual or society should erect a system which gives paramountcy to one particular value over others that are just as important, but that necessarily collide with it. We rightly attach great importance both to liberty and to equality. A system which is wholly dedicated to liberty must sacrifice equality, for under such a system men must be free to do things which will result in inequality. Conversely, a system wholly dedicated to equality must interfere with liberty – and even then there is a clash between a system dedicated to equality of opportunity and one committed to equality of outcome; both are valuable, but they are incompatible with each other. If an equal outcome is fixed, then the opportunities that would lead to an inequality of outcome must be restricted; if everyone is given equal but unfettered opportunities, there will be no equality of outcome.

There is also a tension between Positive and Negative Liberty, which Berlin addressed in a lecture in 1958 entitled *Two Concepts of Liberty*.[3] This was a statement of the distinction which Liberals had been making at the very end of the nineteenth century, when the Classical Liberalism of John Stuart Mill gave way to the Positive Liberalism of T.H. Green.[4] At the time when he gave his lecture, Berlin leaned strongly towards the Classical position and Negative Liberty which put the emphasis on freeing the individual as much as possible from being told what to do by outside authorities, and to give him as much opportunity as possible to govern himself. Of course, for many people that freedom must be rather theoretical. By itself, it will do little or nothing to relieve poverty, and, though some people do have the capacity to pull themselves up by their own bootstraps, most of those who live in poverty have little ability to develop

3 Published in the collection *Four Essays on Liberty*.

4 See p. 432 above.

themselves. To remedy this, there arises the call for the state to provide the possibilities for enlarging the freedoms which negative liberty alone cannot provide for the poor. However, Negative Liberty involved restricting the activities of the state, Positive Liberty meant enlarging them and surrendering some of the negative freedoms which had been the hard-fought gains of Classical Liberals. Berlin was nervous about this as he knew how easily the surrender of powers to the state can lead to oppression and how the state can claim to exercise great power in the name of democracy, when democracy is defined in terms of numbers rather than in terms of the right for individuals to make their own decisions. Very often, the state went further, claiming that it knew what the people "really" wanted, as opposed to what they actually wanted. In Rousseau's terms, the state would adopt the role of the interpreter of the "General Will", which gave it the right and duty to force people to be free, or in Marx's, to free them from "false consciousness."

Towards the end of his life, in an interview with Steven Lukes,[5] Berlin admitted that, whilst in his lecture he had pointed out the dangers of Positive Liberalism, he had neither done justice to the idealism that could lie behind it, nor had he sufficiently developed the horrible sufferings of the poor which were the consequences of *laissez-faire* Negative Liberty. This admission pointed up that we have here another unavoidable collision of values. Such conflicts, it must be repeated, are between values that are important. The difficult conflicts are not between right and wrong, but between right and right, and the collision between them can assume tragic proportions for individuals, as is brought out in the plays of Sophocles. Berlin was a liberal, but he did not share the idea of many liberals that conflicts can be *resolved* through rational discussion - the best that society can do is to *manage* them. We have to accept a *pluralism* of values, not only in the abstract, as when a philosopher observes that there are many values, but in the concrete, in the way we live our personal and social lives.

Pluralism asserts that no value is absolute, and on the surface this looks like relativism, but there is an important difference. Relativism will generally make no moral judgments between different value systems, and often claims that they are merely socially determined. Berlin saw some values - liberty and equality, justice and compassion, tolerance, loyalty - colliding though they often are, as having a universal moral character. On what grounds can one describe any moral values as universal? Berlin said that they enter so deeply into what it means to be human that someone who lacks them is not regarded as "fully a man at all", "I shall begin to speak of insanity and inhumanity".

> It is such statements as these that have brought the scorn of some professional philosophers down upon Berlin. It is certainly lacking in philosophical rigour and merely dogmatic to describe anyone who is unjust, intolerant or disloyal as "insane" or even as not "fully a man at all". Sadly, it is only too obvious that "being human" frequently means giving vent to the human urges to injustice and intolerance. One might even argue that human nature in the raw is intolerant, and that tolerance and justice are hard-won victories over human nature.

5 *Prospect*, October 1997.

It is also excessive to think of people who do not agree with Berlin's values as "insane". It even reminds us uncomfortably that the Soviets used to treat people who disagreed with them as insane. (Berlin would of course have been horrified that anyone should make such a comparison.) I personally think that the values that Berlin cherishes are precious and *ought* to be universally held, and I regret that they are not, but he really should have known better as a philosopher than to dogmatise in this way about what it means to be human.

What are the practical implications of pluralism? What do we actually do when confronted by a collision of ideals? Clearly, to look for an absolute formula to guide us through the problem of pluralism would be a contradiction in terms. So we have to keep the values in a *pragmatic* balance, and we must accept trade-offs between them, even though every trade-off involves loss and a genuine sacrifice of desirable ends. Trade-offs are necessary in our personal life, and each individual has to choose how to deal with conflicting values in his or her own life. Trade-offs are also necessary in social and political life: each society has to decide how to balance conflicting values within it. The alternative to a willingness to make trade-offs in society between desirable ends is the imposition of one value system on those who hold a different one. Berlin found this not only philosophically problematic, but, because it involves lack of tolerance, morally unacceptable.

Is there some lack of philosophical rigour here, too? I don't suppose he was really suggesting that a democratic government has to make a trade-off with its opposition? There is certainly a clash between, for example, socialism and capitalism, each of them enshrining important values: social justice for the one and freedom from government control for the other. While it is desirable that government and opposition should seek as much common ground as possible, a democratically elected socialist government, for instance, must surely be entitled to put its legislative programme into effect, even if the opposition would call such a programme divisive.

Berlin would certainly have insisted that such a government should not claim that its values are the only possible ones. It should show some *respect* for those of a democratic opposition, and above all, it must itself remain democratic, that is, it should continue to allow opposition groups freedom of speech and organization.

The philosopher can *illuminate* the collisions between values, but he cannot *prescribe* what trade-offs we should make. Of course, we must be as rational as we can in making these choices, but as reason can give no absolute answer when balancing out the claims of conflicting values, ultimately the choices we make will rest on our emotional commitments.

"Commitment" is an important concept in Existentialism. Was Berlin therefore an existentialist? In one interview [6] he said "In a sense I am an existentialist – that's to say I commit myself ... to constellations of certain values." In another one[7] he used the more modest and homely phrase that he "plumped" for them; that he came off the fence.

6 with Steven Lukes, *Prospect*, October 1997.

7 with Michael Ignatieff, May 1995

> I suspect that Berlin, who urged the necessity of trade-offs between desirable but incompatible values, felt a little uncomfortable with the notion of commitment: it is *possible* to be committed to a trade-off, but commitment seems to sit uncomfortably with the sacrifice you have had to make in the process.

The existentialist's choice is made in full awareness of the fact that his commitment cannot be one to an absolute truth, but I sense an important difference between Berlin and an existentialist. Once the latter has made a commitment to an idea, he is also committed to action; and, as Berlin wrote in an essay of 1964, it is difficult to be an activist if one realizes what choices are open to one – or, he might have added, if one constantly examines what is on the other side of the fence.

We have seen that one value that was very important to Berlin was tolerance, and he believed that in order to be tolerant, the quality of empathy was enormously helpful. His own capacity for empathy was indeed one of his strongest traits. His virtue as a historian of ideas was his ability to enter the thought world of other thinkers, and he was almost more interested in the ideas with which he personally disagreed than he was in those he shared. So it may not be a coincidence that, although he was committed to "constellations of certain values", he never felt that he must speak out on political issues of his time, let alone take as active a part in campaigning as, for example, Sartre did.

The one exception to this was his support for Zionism – though even then he declined the invitation of both Weizmann and Ben Gurion to play an active part in Israeli politics. His Zionism was largely due to the feeling that the Jews must have a place in which they can be free and in which those who want to live a purely Jewish life without the pressure of Gentile surroundings can do so.

Beyond that, Berlin, deeply cosmopolitan though he was himself, was one of the few modern liberals who had some respect for nationalism.

> In the first half of the nineteenth century, nationalism and liberalism had, for the most part, gone hand in hand. Most European monarchs were repressive autocrats who suppressed nationalism. Liberals wanted parliamentary governments to express the wishes of an electorate, and they believed that the electorate wanted nationalism. Nationalists, for their part, supported liberalism because they believed that only through parliamentary governments could they achieve nationalism. In the second half of the nineteenth century, for a variety of reasons, liberalism and nationalism tended to part company, and in the twentieth century they have often become polarized. Nationalism has generally applied force to those who hold values held to be incompatible with national culture – in other words, they have rejected pluralism. As a result, most modern liberals are hostile to nationalism.

Berlin greatly admired Vico and Herder,[8] who had brought out, against the universalism of the *philosophes*, that the different nations of Europe had individual characters which ought to be respected. In the eighteenth century, neither Vico nor Herder had envisaged the intolerant nationalisms of the nineteenth and twentieth centuries. They had envisaged, as it were, a pluralistic Europe, in which nationalities respected each other's rights just as, in a pluralistic society, individuals would respect each other. Berlin was well aware

8 See pp. 353f above for Vico; pp. 356f above for Herder.

how oppressive nationalism could be, but for him, national self-identification was a part of human nature. On those grounds he was sympathetic to national liberation movements from colonial oppression, though he also warned that they were often as hostile to individual liberty as the oppressors had been. He supported the Zionist cause, but he also had sympathy for Arab nationalism and spoke out at the end of his life for a Palestinian state alongside the Jewish one. *Within* any state or empire, cultural pluralism was important, and it was as wrong to suppress it as to suppress any other kind of pluralism. He knew, of course, that nationalist values will collide, but as with other value-conflicts, a pragmatic trade-off will be necessary in a tolerant world community.

> This will be true of societies as well as of individuals. It is easy to say that in any society there has to be respect for minority cultures, but there may be situations when the values of the majority and the minority culture collide in major and unavoidable ways. In that case only a pragmatic trade-off between both the majority and the minority culture can avoid a poisoning of the society or an explosion into destructive violence. An individual, too, may find himself heir to colliding cultures, and may find the solution in a personal trade-off which may be painful. How much of one culture is he prepared to give up for the other?

Berlin's sympathy for nationalism was part of the fascination he felt for Romanticism. Many of his essays deal with Romanticism or with the Enlightenment against which it was a reaction. The title of one of the volumes of Berlin's collected essays is *The Crooked Timber of Humanity*, which is taken from a saying by Kant, "Out of timber so crooked as that from which man is made nothing entirely straight can be built." That expressed Berlin's reservation about the Enlightenment assumption that for all questions there must be one true answer, to be discovered by using reason. Because reason tries to discover general laws, what most interested the philosophers about human beings was what they had in common rather than their cultural variety or anything else that made them different from one another. This led them to the view that, if people used their reason, they would "really" all have the same goals; that these goals were not really in conflict (betraying a lack of awareness of, for instance, the tensions between Liberty, Equality and Fraternity) so that any failure to recognize them must be the result of miseducation which had to be corrected, if necessary by imposition.

> This is, of course, a caricature of the Enlightenment. Though the *philosophes* believed in reason, they were well aware that reasoning led people to very different conclusions, and in fact all the *philosophes* frequently drew attention to the relative nature of value judgments. They could hardly do otherwise, as they differed so much among themselves about the prescriptions they offered for a rational organization of society.[8]

By contrast, the Romantics understood that values were historical (because people were rooted in their history) and contradictory (because human nature was inherently contradictory). For them, the challenge was not the discovery of their nature as something static, but as something they could shape for themselves. In his earlier years, while he was focussed on the eighteenth century, Berlin was less conscious than he would be later of the dangerous excrescences

8 See Chapter 28.

of Romanticism in the twentieth century: the exaltation of irrationalism, the self-creation that might result not only in a Beethoven but also in a Hitler, or the self-expression which in national groups so easily led to the denial that other groups, too, have the right to express themselves.

Berlin never abandoned the Romantic idea that we are choice-makers, and that the choices we make are sufficiently free to discount the idea of Historical Inevitability,[8] whether in the form of inevitable progress (such as we find in the works of Positivists and Marxists) or in that of inevitable cycles (as with Vico, Spengler, or Toynbee). They all see history as a science, following inexorable laws which make it pointless to oppose them, not only from a practical point of view but – what is even more pernicious – from a moral one: if inevitable forces are responsible for the course of history, then the responsibility is not ours. History is not even that of the great tyrants in history, who are seen as mere vehicles for inevitable historical processes, and it is therefore pointless to hold them morally responsible, or to bestow praise or blame on them for anything other than whether they cooperated with or tried to withstand the predetermined course of history.

These issues have been discussed in Chapter 38. Berlin's view was to some extent that of Carlyle when he opposed the views of the Positivist historians of his time. What Berlin adds to the Carlylean view is, in the first place, a greater sophistication. In his long essay he also carefully sets out the degree to which our moral judgments must consider that historical figures have to operate within the real alternatives that are available to them at the time:

> We shall not condemn the Middle Ages simply because they fell short of the moral and intellectual standard of the révolté intelligentsia of Paris in the eighteenth century... Or if we do condemn societies or individuals, [we should] do so only after taking into account the social and material conditions, the aspirations, codes of value, degree of progress and reaction, measured in terms of their own situation and outlook...[9]

Berlin also adds to Carlyle – and, for that matter, to Popper's condemnation of Historicism[10] – the specifically moral dimension. Carlyle's was the gut reaction of a hero-worshipper against Historicism; Popper condemned it on the coolly scientific grounds that the predictions in which historicists indulge have regularly been falsified by events. Berlin's essay also shows that Historicism is empirically unsupportable; beyond that he strikes the note which we heard in Lord Acton's dictum that, as moral human beings, we *ought* to exercise moral judgment when we look at the past.[11] Acton had spoken from the moral certainties of a believing Catholic. Berlin, with his awareness that values must collide, could not share the moral absolutes of Acton, but he shared with the existentialists the conviction that moral commitments are required of us. A refusal to make them is a denial of an essential part of human nature. It must make us less sensitive to moral issues, it damages us as individuals, and it has a sinister influence on society.

8 *Historical Inevitability* is the title of a lecture Berlin gave in 1953, and it appears in the collection published as *Four Essays on Liberty.*

9 Taken from p. 102 of *Four Essays on Liberty*. See the whole passage, pp. 101 to 103.

10 See p. 562 above.

11 p. 459 above.

CHAPTER 47

Freud and Jung

Introduction

Freud and Jung did not regard themselves primarily as philosophers. Both came from a medical background, became interested in nervous diseases, developed theories about their origin and cure, and founded schools of psychotherapy. But the pictures they presented of the human condition had major philosophical and cultural implications and a considerable influence on attitudes to life. They showed that forces in our unconscious are enormously strong; that the hold that pure reason has on us is very fragile and that very often, when we think we are reasoning, we are actually only rationalizing, using (or rather abusing) our reasoning powers to justify behaviour which is actually dictated by our unconscious.

Very often it is the tension between the clamouring forces of the unconscious and the views which are held by our conscious mind which makes us ill (neurotic). If we are to regain our health, we must bring the contents of the unconscious into consciousness: as long as they remain in the unconscious, we can have no purchase on them. We cannot (says Freud) disarm them by looking at them rationally, nor (says Jung) can we fully benefit from the non-rational wisdom that often lies unrecognized in the unconscious. The function of psychotherapy (Freud called his technique psychoanalysis and Jung called his own method analytic psychology) is to help the patient to gain access to the unconscious, to interpret what he finds there, and to relieve or dissolve the tension that had caused the neurosis.

SIGMUND FREUD
1856 to 1939

For Freud, there were three basic forces which shaped our personality: he called them the Id, the Ego and the Superego.

The Id is the bundle of urges or drives which is all a child has when it is born. Initially, these urges are mainly the urge for food, and the aggression it feels when that urge is frustrated. The frustration may be very short-lived – the baby may have to wait five or ten minutes before it is fed – but as it has no concept of time, even a short delay is felt to be very threatening, and the urge is felt with an intensity that an adult may find hard to remember. Soon after that comes the urge to eliminate perceived rivals in the bond the child has with the supplier of food, the mother. The child wants a monopoly on its mother's attention, on which, however, the father and siblings also have a claim, and so these often become objects of the child's resentment. In later life, additional urges make themselves felt: the sexual urge which develops during puberty, and urges related to avoiding frustrations, and, notably, urges to control and dominate the environment (and also, of course, to investigate it, though I am not aware that Freud made anything much of inborn inquisitiveness).

The Ego is the seat of the developing intelligence which learns, by experience, what outlets of the Id the world makes possible. The Ego may be involved in finding safe and indirect ways of satisfying the drives by processes which I will describe later. Note that the Ego distinguishes only between strategies which work and those which do not; it does not distinguish between strategies which are "moral" and those which are "immoral", so the Ego *by itself* would accept an undetected lie or an undetected theft as a successful strategy.

The Superego makes the distinction between those expressions of the Id and the Ego which are acceptable and those which are not. Children learn this to some extent from parental or possibly other environmental reactions, but also from an internal fear that they may destroy, by their aggression, the people they need and love. (Freud thought that children have an idea of their own omnipotence. If, for example, they feel anger against a parent and then the parent falls ill or even dies, many children will think that their own aggressive feelings have been responsible for this, and then experience guilt.)

> Here, as very often elsewhere, one might ask what is the evidence? How do we know that small children have an idea of their own omnipotence (especially as this seems to be at variance with consciousness of their vulnerability to aggression)? Freud claimed that in the course of treatment such memories have been recovered. Among the attacks on psychoanalysis is the charge that sometimes false memories are suggested by the analyst.

A child also fears that the parents will respond to its own aggression by aggression and annihilation on their part (even though loving and understanding parents have contemplated no such response).

Uncontrolled expressions of the Id and the Ego are therefore accompanied not only by fear, but also by guilt, and by attempts to escape this fear or guilt by repression.

The operations of the Superego and of repression are mostly not conscious acts of the mind, but are unconscious. It is, however, impossible to destroy such negative feelings: they are pushed by repression into the unconscious part of the mind, from where they will attempt to push their way back into consciousness. This attempt is met by strategies, again unconscious, of various kinds.

One strategy is to repress the feelings even more fiercely, but this merely strengthens the effort of the countervailing repressed forces to break out. The steadily intensifying conflict absorbs and locks up a huge amount of psychic energy. If the repressed forces cannot break out in *any* form, the result will be a crippling inactivity to grow, and the creation of the most acute neuroses.

> It is interesting to apply this notion to political repression as well. Many dictatorial regimes find themselves committed to fiercer and fiercer repression; they seem to become increasingly afraid of the forces they repress, and indeed often do increase them by doing so. The police state often locks up an enormous amount of a society's energy which could instead have been used for the greater health of that society.

The psychic tension may even result in bodily symptoms for which no physiological causes can be found. In a famous early case in which Freud was involved, a patient's arm was paralysed and was freed from paralysis only when the guilt which the patient felt for the desire to strike a relative had been elucidated. It is largely due to Freud that the concept of psychosomatic illnesses has become *widely* known, though of course, like the whole notion of the unconscious, it had been intuited by poets, by philosophers, and by doctors long before – this was repeatedly and readily acknowledged by Freud.

Freud suspected that ideas might be linked with other ideas or with bodily symptoms by some neurological pathways in the brain which medical science had not yet discovered; he thought it possible that one day these pathways would be discovered and he did not rule out that they could then perhaps be acted on by biochemical means. In the meantime the lengthy processes of psychoanalysis were the only way of changing obsessional behaviour patterns.

> Such physical pathways in the brain have indeed been discovered since Freud's time. They are connected to each other by synapses; the more often the connection is made, the stronger the electric potential of synapses become. If these organic connections are strengthened by repetition, it becomes harder to break them and to establish new connections. The psychotherapist wants to help a patient to change his thought-processes; he will therefore have to establish and strengthen new synaptic connections. If, in the absence of biochemical means, this is done by a "talking cure", it is not surprising that the process should take a very long time.

Of course, Freud was aware that not only could mental conditions affect the body, but also that bodily conditions could affect mental states. Some mental states, like certain psychotic and schizophrenic states, originated in such severe organic disorders that they were inaccessible to psychoanalytic treatment.

Another strategy of dealing with repressed feelings is to provide a safer outlet for them which the *conscious* mind will not recognize as related to what is being repressed. Examples of this might be, for example: unadmitted hate or fear of the father, which may take the form of hatred or fear of figures that stand for the father; figures of authority; the concept of a God of Wrath (as well as a certain kind of atheism which is a repudiation of God); the concept of the Devil (the result of splitting the father image into a good side – the loving God – and a bad side – Satan); minority groups whom it is safe to hate; fear of animals.

In these and other examples which follow in the rest of the chapter, it needs to be stressed that any one of them may have quite different causes, notice, for instance, that I said "a certain kind of atheism". Of course, atheism need not be the result of a repressed attitude to a father figure at all. Even a lay observer may not find it difficult to distinguish between obsessive, driven atheists and what one might call well-adjusted atheists, or between healthy opposition to, say, dictatorial authority figures and the "chip-on-shoulder" obsessional resentment of every kind of authority.

In the case of the obsessive atheist, the outlet for hatred of the father may be safer and less guilt-ridden, but it does not wholly discharge the intense negative feelings from which it originated: a lot of psychic energy is still locked up;

and the psyche does not really feel liberated. In such cases Freudians say that "displacement" has taken place.

There is a healthier strategy than displacement for dealing with repressed forces, it is called "sublimation". It is possible to turn negative feelings of hatred or fear into positive feelings, and to free energy for creative and constructive activity (which is also often rewarded with social approval, expressing itself in status and respect or even knighthoods or peerages).

It is not suggested that every creative or constructive activity is sublimation rather than displacement: we can perhaps sense a difference between a kind of frenzied, obsessive need to create, as observed in, for instance, a Van Gogh or a Picasso, (let alone the compulsive reenactment, in canvas after canvas, of personal suffering in the works of someone like Munch), and a calmer creativity which one may feel in a Renoir.

The satisfactions derived from sublimation tend to be *reality-based* rather than based on fantasies, and they do not leave the original drive unsatisfied. Compare, for example, the man who is never satisfied or secure with power and compulsively seeks ever more of it, with the confident and fulfilled achiever whose goals are generally limited and who may be chosen for advancement (which implies social approval) rather than seeking it.

> In the case of artists, their biographies often seem to reinforce the impression we get from their works. Van Gogh was in fact an unhappy and disturbed man; Picasso's compulsive dismemberment or mutilation of women on canvas has some relationship with the ruthless way he treated the women in his life; Munch felt an almost unbearable tension about women, whom he saw as both desirably seductive and terrifying as the bearers of sexually transmitted diseases. On the other hand, Renoir was happily married and seems to have felt the serenity and *joie de vivre* which we feel in his art. Mahler's personal life was full of unsatisfied longings which were not appeased by his appointments to prestigious posts in the musical world, and much of his music seems to express this. Bach, however, seems to have had a happy family life whose harmony, I feel, is reflected in his music.
>
> Of course, the work of Van Gogh or Picasso or Munch is great art. If it is based on some unhealthy displacement and if they were to have undergone a successful psychoanalytical treatment, they presumably could not have gone on to produce the kind of art for which they were famous (though just possibly they could then have produced a *different* kind of art resting on sublimation rather than on displacement). This is why many artists fear that Freudian psychoanalysis would destroy their creativity. They would feel more comfortable in a Jungian analysis because Jung, as we shall see,[1] sees art rooted in quite different origins.

In both displacement and sublimation, the unconscious is extremely fertile in finding a relationship between the original subject of the repression and the replacement subject. The replacement subject becomes a *symbol* of the original subject, and Freud showed the huge range of symbolism in the lives of each one of us. The symbols are mostly quite unconscious, though our language often shows an awareness, sometimes conscious and obvious, sometimes unconscious and hidden, of the substitution that has taken place. Conscious exam-

1 p. 593 below.

ples abound, for instance, in the iconography of medieval and Renaissance paintings. At some stage, theologians decided to use the lily as a symbol for purity, and the artists then juxtaposed it with portrayals of the Virgin Mary. The symbolism was deliberate and meant to be read by the viewer. The coinage of words like "fatherland" and "motherland" was also conscious and deliberate: the words were intended to express feelings for one's country which are akin to the feelings for one's parents.

Other words and symbols were probably coined unconsciously, and these usually refer to things about which we feel for some reason uncomfortable. The description of wealth as "filthy lucre" supports Freud's theory that money, in its hoarding and spending, is often a symbol for an unresolved infantile attitude to excrement, and St Paul, who seems to have been the first to coin that phrase in his Epistle to Titus (I.11), was almost certainly unaware of that.

When nowadays we readily identify weapons, poles, or towers as phallic objects in certain contexts, or identify rooms and cupboards as representing wombs, we think we are being ever so "Freudian". Perhaps sometimes we forget that Shakespeare, for example, made quite conscious play with such *double entendres*, which were well understood and appreciated by his audiences: many jokes and puns are deliberately based on such word plays. The *double entendre*, significant as it is, is often quite unconscious, manifesting itself in "slips of the tongue" which can betray unconscious wishes or fears. Freud's most popular book was entitled *The Psychopathology of Everyday Life* (1904), in which he showed how slips of the tongue or of memory, or the apparent accidents of everyday life (like losing or misplacing things so that we cannot do things we unconsciously may not want to do, or accidentally leaving something behind in a place you want to visit again) - how all these *can* have far more meaning than perhaps we think.

The final strategy for dealing with repressed material is the one that is used in psychoanalytical treatment of patients who have sought help. We have seen that both the repression and the content of what is repressed are unconscious, and as long as they remain so, there is no way in which a patient can deal with them. The central idea of psychoanalytic treatment is that the patient should be helped to bring back to consciousness - to recall - the painful experiences which he or she has pushed into the unconscious. In psychoanalytic therapy a common situation is as follows.

The patient begins by talking about something that concerns him. At a certain point he will come to the end of his account, and a silence ensues. The analyst does not break the silence and the patient knows he is supposed to express the next thought that occurs to him. Apparently, his mind has "gone blank". Then, at some point, he may say something like, "my next thought seems quite irrelevant to what I have previously been talking about, but it is so-and-so." The theory is that it is not irrelevant; that there *is* a connection, but the connecting thoughts are so uncomfortable that they have travelled through the unconscious until they are sufficiently disguised to re-emerge safely into consciousness. The patient is then prompted, by further association with the ideas expressed before and after the pause, to discover for him what those apparently missing links might be.

When the conscious mind is asleep, the unconscious often has a field day in the formation of dreams. Some dreams are explicit depictions of scenes of fear, of shame, or of unacknowledged wishes, but even in sleep there is a censorship which, if it does not wake one up, creates in the dream some apparently non-sequential associations. In this case, too, the psychoanalyst will try to get the patient to make further associations with the dream content until he discovers the repressed connection. So the analysis of dreams was considered by Freud "the royal road into the unconscious", a very fruitful way into the real content of the psyche, and the book from which this quotation comes, *The Interpretation of Dreams* (1900), was the one with which he first made his name with the general public. His theory reinforced the feeling that goes back to the earliest history of mankind, that dreams are pregnant with significance, and it produced a fresh crop of depiction of dreams in painting and in other art forms.

> We have already seen[2] that dreams were of particular interest to the Romantics, whereas the rationalists of the Enlightenment tended to dismiss them as "hallucinations". After Freud, artists like the Surrealists would once again attempt to depict dreams. In post-Freudian literature, some novelists used the "stream of consciousness" (free association) method, where one thought led to another, apparently non-sequential, thought. Virginia Woolf is particularly associated with that technique, and it is surely not a coincidence that her husband, Leonard Woolf, managed the Hogarth Press which published most of the English translations of Freud.

Of course, this business of association, of delving into repressed connections, will meet with enormous resistance because the repressed material is so painful; the links will be recovered only bit by bit, with the deepest and most painful experiences being recovered last. This is the reason why the classic depth-analysis takes so long, though it may of course not always be necessary to get to the deepest level before a patient can tackle and cope with many manifestations of his neurosis. The theory is that, as the causes of the original repression are re-experienced and "worked through" by the patient as an adult, the power of the infantile trauma to damage adult behaviour will have been destroyed. A patient will still have to confront difficult or unhappy situations, for life is difficult and even tragic, but the ability to cope with them will be reality-based. The link between a difficult situation and its unconscious and non-rational associations will have been brought to light and thereby severed, and as a result the response to the difficult situation will not be distorted by reactions which owe their origin to the unconsciously created symbolical associations with childhood traumata.

As long as these distortions operate, the patient's behaviour is heavily determined by them; only when the distortions have been recognized and dealt with can we talk of the patient being able to act with any genuine freedom and responsibility – and also being able to understand what the genuine external constraints on his freedom are.

> There are philosophical implications here regarding Free Will and Determinism. Freud's implication is that our freedom of action is immeasurably enlarged when we are no longer held captive by our unconscious distortions.

2 p. 325 above.

> In that sense he would have agreed with Hegel's dictum that "Freedom consists in the *knowledge* of *reality*." Of course, we can never be totally free because we will always be subject to objective external restraints.

So the aim of psychoanalysis is for the patient to discover the real content of the psyche, and this content is many-layered. For example, in the case of an obsessional hatred for an employer, the upper layers below the level of consciousness may be the hatred of the father, but the discovery of that will only raise the further question as to the cause of the hatred of the father. A bad marriage may turn out to have as one of its unacknowledged causes that a wealthy husband resents his wife spending money, but when that has been acknowledged, it raises the deeper question of what the spending of money represents that it becomes such an irritant to the husband.

What made Freud most notorious in his lifetime was his idea that the very deepest layer of the psyche was to be found in childhood experiences relating to sex. It is difficult to see why Freud, who was prolific in coining a specialized vocabulary (for instance inventing the word "Superego" to express a conceptual shade that distinguishes it from the commonly understood meaning of the word "conscience") chose the loaded word "sex" to embrace the experiences of stimulation to the sensitive oral and anal, as well as the genital regions.[3] Although these have in common that their gratification brings sensual pleasure while their frustration is a painful experience, they are nevertheless distinct and separate experiences. But because Freud described all three of them as sexual, and because they are very acute in the very first years of life, he spoke about infantile *sexuality*, again making it clear that by this term he meant not only a strong *gender* consciousness in childhood, but also the oral and anal phase. Many of his contemporaries found frank discussion of adult sexuality distasteful enough. The idea that "sexuality" (by which term *they* understood genital sexuality) was already found in infants brought a storm of obloquy upon his head from many of his colleagues, and it would in fact be one of the causes of his breach with Jung (who had vainly suggested to Freud that he should use another word).[4]

Freud described the importance of what a child experiences in connection with its erogenous zones. So he explained, for example, that obsessive eating, drinking or smoking *may* have their root in the first period in a baby's life when it centres its whole existence on oral gratification and during which the region around the mouth is especially sensitive to the pleasure of gratification or the pain of frustration. Where acute frustration takes place, the baby has a traumatic experience whose traces may later manifest themselves, especially in stressful situations, in the obsessive need to pacify or stimulate that region,

3 He did use the word *libido*, which might have served the purpose to embrace all the drives to secure gratification of the various erogenous zones, but he specifically described the *libido* as, "the *sexual* drives which are the foundation of *all* those manifestations of life whose aim is the gratification of the senses" (*Lustgewinn*).

4 It seems to me that Freud was deliberately provocative in his choice of vocabulary, almost as if he were inviting the pillory. So, for example, he talked of "infantile *per*version" to describe the way a small child *di*verts its activities from sucking the breast to sucking the thumb or from a wish to play with excrement to playing with mud and sand. In the normal sense of the word, such transfers of activity could hardly be described as perversions.

either directly or symbolically. Inability to shake off these traces lead, in psychoanalytical vocabulary, to the "oral fixation" of the personality.

When toilet training begins, the child will focus on another ultra-sensitive region, where it is under pressure to perform or to withhold at the wish of its parents, and if, for example, withholding is the child's device for rebelling against parental wishes, or if the inability to perform is punished, the later traces of the situation may be transferred to the compulsive withholding of other things – of money, perhaps, or of information, or of praise. This is known as fixation on the anal level.

There is also the stage when children become acutely aware of the sensations in their genital region, and experiences in connection with that region may likewise leave profound marks on later life. It is to be noted here that these early childhood experiences, though not then related to procreation, already carry a strong association with gender. In this connection Freud named the famous Oedipus Complex, in which a small boy sees his father as a rival who is felt to threaten the boy's possession of his mother, and which is said to arouse in the small boy the wish to eliminate the father. As this wish is felt by the child to be both potent and dangerous, it is repressed, only to manifest itself in later life in attitudes to other males or, for that matter, to other females.[5] Freud believed that every boy experiences these Oedipal feelings. Whether it becomes a *complex* in later life depends on how traumatic the experience of these feelings was at the time. If it does become a complex, it is likely to manifest itself, for example, in the displacement of hostile feelings from the father to other authority figures, as has been shown above.

> The Oedipal situation is likely to be more traumatic if, for example, during that phase the father is actually harsh, unloving, or perhaps actively jealous of the attention his wife now gives to the child. If, on the other hand, the child sees reasons to love the father, the chances are that it will pass through the Oedipal phase without developing a complex in adulthood.

Parents and other adults, in play or in caressing, often consciously or unconsciously pleasure the erogenous zones of their children, but they may at the same time express disapproval and evoke guilt if the children pleasure themselves by thumb-sucking, or by "playing with themselves". By the age of about five, the erogenous zones become physically less sensitive and the tensions related to them less severe: the children enter what Freud called the latency period. But the biological changes during puberty will reawaken tensions and the problems associated with them, and this contributes to the strongly ambivalent feelings that adolescents have towards their parents. Initially, uncertain about their relationships with the opposite sex, adolescents seek security in the company of contemporaries of their own sex, and here is another moment when some of them may become fixated into open or repressed homosexuality. In most cases, the biological attraction of the opposite sex will in due course draw them into heterosexual relationships.

5 There is a corresponding – but not wholly symmetrical – situation where the child is a little girl. This has been called the Electra Complex, though the term is often erroneously ascribed to Freud instead of to Jung. Freud specifically disclaimed it.

The fact that Freud found the aetiology - that is the origin - of so much behaviour in what he called sexuality has had two general cultural effects. In the first place, after the widespread initial hostility, it has contributed to a far freer discussion of sex (in families, schools and the media) and ultimately to permissiveness in that area. It has led on the one hand to a welcome liberation, but on the other to a sex-obsessed culture which is surely far from healthy. We should note, incidentally, that other *avant garde* intellectuals in Freud's own youth had already been publicly breaking all taboos on the discussion of sex and on the open acceptance of sexual adventurism. Many other social factors have, of course, also played a part in that change. Contraception, for example, has obviously contributed to more adventurism, but one might possibly argue that permissive behaviour, especially in the case of women, is today less burdened by guilt than it was in the past.

Secondly, since Freud, the concepts of the happiness and innocence of childhood have retreated a good deal. Much greater attention has been paid to the feelings of children and greater efforts have been made to get them to express themselves rather than to repress their feelings. Many parents have taken this on board, and educational theory and practice has been influenced by it. "Child-centred" education has become much more important, though of course this had been advocated long before Freud, by Rousseau, Pestalozzi, Montessori, Froebel and others.

As it was recognized what harm can be done to children in their formative years, so more action has been taken by governments to protect them: for social workers the rule is now that "the best interests of the child" are paramount, if necessary, even over the interests of parents. (Whether in fact they always *do* act in the best interests of the child is of course open to question.)

The art of children has been given an importance which it had never previously had, and some artists have tried to recapture in their work the naïve vision of childhood.

Nor is it only the art of children that we now approach in a different way. We have seen above that whole schools of art and literature have sprung up that are dedicated to the exploration of the unconscious. Likewise, there has been an appreciation of the qualities of so-called primitive art, which Freud himself had collected. Like the art of children, it seemed to him be a relatively uninhibited expression of what the artists *feel* rather than what they physically *see*; and that quality is always in danger of being eroded when it is tamed by too much rational refinement.

The understanding of the unconscious can, of course, be misused. Some politicians have known instinctively how to express or whip up emotions that we normally repress. Freud himself, in *Group Psychology and the Analysis of the Ego* (1922) explored the special factors that operate in masses, and many advertisers finance specific studies that help them to play on consumer motivations that are scarcely conscious at all.

Freud has also influenced the way in which many people now think about crime and punishment. It is now fairly common for people to think that antisocial behaviour is an illness that needs to be treated; that it is caused by drives in the unconscious which have found no satisfactory sublimation and over which the offenders have little control and that restraint of delinquents, though necessary, should not be essentially punitive in motivation. The role of the psychiatrically trained social worker is to help and not to punish.

It would be a mistake to think that Freud had a wholly negative attitude to repression. He believed that all human beings, and not just neurotics, were forced, in the course of their childhood, to repress their instincts. The clinically neurotic person was one whose experiences were more traumatic, whose conflicts were more acute, and who in later life had not been able to successfully sublimate the repressed material, but had merely displaced it. But Freud did not believe, as is often thought, that repression as such was a bad thing. In fact, he made the point, in *Civilization and its Discontents* (1930) that repression of primitive urges was, in the end, an essential prerequisite for becoming a socialized human being, let alone for building up what we call a civilization. Achievements in almost any area of civilization are the result of urges which had to be repressed but whose energies were then sublimated, or even displaced, into cultural products ranging from the arts to the sciences and from economic to military activity. What Freud gave us was some understanding of the dynamics of our behaviour and of our culture.

Many of his insights had been anticipated by thinkers of the past, by the great classical tragedians, by Shakespeare, and above all by the Romantics who had an acute awareness of the non-rational forces within mankind. Likewise, we have seen that educationalists like Rousseau and Pestalozzi had wanted to liberate childhood from the repressive attitudes of their time. Freud was very ready to acknowledge this, but claimed to have been the first to give some *systematic* explanation of unconscious motivation.

> He would have claimed that his explanations were not only systematic, but also scientific, and this claim has been much contested by most scientists. They would say that the evidence of individual case histories and their interpretations by Freud lack the rigour that scientists require. They also make much of the fact that Freud's account of human nature is based on his experiences with neurotics, and that one cannot draw conclusions from these about human nature in general. These criticisms are, I think, quite valid, and the personal intolerance of Freud and of some of his disciples have done no service to his ideas. All the same, ideas do not have to meet strict scientific criteria to be immensely fruitful, suggestive, valuable and philosophically interesting, and one does not have to accept Freud lock, stock and barrel to show that his theories meet with quite a lot of ordinary, everyday experiences.

It has sometimes been said that, because Freud showed how much of our behaviour was outside our conscious control, he presented a determinist view of mankind, but that was not his position. It is true that many of us are not free and that, if our darker unconscious emotions dominate us, we are, to use religious terminology, "enslaved to sin". The religious believer, however, does not think this enslavement to be inescapable: we can be liberated from the enslavement by faith. For Freud, the role of faith was taken by psychoanalytical insight: to the extent to which we could achieve this, we enlarged our freedom.

A belief in a personal God, however, was regarded by Freud as at best an illusion (*The Future of an Illusion*, 1927) and at worst based on neurotic projections of the unconscious.[6] Since the Age of Reason in particular, religious faith had already been eroded by science, by relativism and by biblical criticism. Freud added another arrow to the atheist's quiver. He was ready to accept that religious belief helped some people to cope better with life, as a crutch helps to support the lame, but he did not think that religions harboured any enriching truths, let alone that being in tune with the religious dimension was actually a condition of psychic health. This was one of the major differences between him and Carl Gustav Jung.

CARL GUSTAV JUNG
1875 to 1962

Jung's work at a psychiatric hospital in Switzerland had drawn him to Freud's work, and from 1907 to 1912 he had been a close collaborator of Freud's, but personal and theoretical differences began to emerge. The publication of Jung's *The Psychology of the Unconscious* in 1913 marked the parting of the ways between Freudian psychoanalysis and what Jung would call analytical psychology. The essential differences between them were Jung's postulation of a collective unconscious, his attitude to religion and to dreams and his downplaying of the purely "sexual" origins of neurosis.

The Collective Unconscious

For Freud, the Unconscious was merely a personal unconscious: it harboured only the (repressed) ideas in an individual's personal history. Jung agreed that there was a personal unconscious, which contains the unacceptable part of oneself. This he called the Shadow - represented in myths, for example, by the Tempter (the Serpent or the Devil). The Shadow, however, is not to be found exclusively in the unconscious; we may be perfectly conscious of that side of our personality which fills us with shame, or which we consciously fight against, or which, for one reason or another, we want to keep private. So a liberal, for example, may be opposed to racism and yet be uncomfortably aware that he also harbours racist feelings. Jung feels that such awareness is positive, because as long as we are aware of the Shadow, we can combat it. People who are driven by their prejudices are generally people who would deny that what drives them *is* a prejudice.

Jung calls the outward appearance we wish to present the *persona*, after the Latin word for a mask.[7] Because the Shadow is that part of ourselves of which society disapproves, we all assume *a persona* in the course of becoming socialized.

6 Freud confined the word "religion" to a belief in a personal God. "Critics persist in calling 'deeply religious' a person who confesses to a sense of Man's insignificance and impotence in the face of the Universe, although it is not this feeling that constitutes the essence of religious emotion, but rather the next step, the reaction to it, which seeks a remedy against this feeling. He who goes no further, he who humbly acquiesces in the insignificant part man plays in the universe, is, on the contrary, irreligious in the truest sense of the word."

7 Masks were worn by actors in ancient Greece. They had two functions: the first was to indicate the character the actor was assuming (the villain's mask looked villainous, the masks of noble characters looked noble). The second was to project sound in an amphitheatre through a megaphone that was built into the mask, and it was this function that is picked up in the Latin word *per-sona* (for sounds). It is an irony that the word "person" now often means the inner part of oneself (as in "be your own person) whereas in its origin it meant the outward mask that concealed the inner part of the actor.

> There may be great discomfort if the *persona* we put on in one social situation is challenged when another social situation intrudes. For example, a boy is often embarrassed when his mother comes to his school. At home he may be very happy to kiss his mother, but at school he may have put on the *persona* of being "cool". That mask would slip if he kisses his mother in the presence of his fellow-pupils. A henpecked husband may find his *persona* as the masterful boss in the office threatened if his wife turns up there.

In some cases the *persona* becomes hugely inflated: we become so much mask that we lose touch with the shadow part of ourself altogether; and because the Shadow is an inescapable part of our inner self, this means that we lose touch with a part of ourself, and that must be damaging. It is obviously a healthier state of affairs if we are conscious of our Shadow: we may be uncomfortably aware of it, but we will be in a better position to deal with it than if we are not even aware of how it affects our actions.

More than that, there are times when the acceptance and integration of the Shadow positively enriches us. Although "masculine"" characteristics predominate in the genetic make-up of most men and "feminine" ones in that of most women, we all have within us a greater or lesser share of the characteristics of the opposite sex. But most men have been taught to suppress the feminine part of themselves (Jung calls it the *anima*), and most women have been forced to deny their masculine side (the *animus*). Such repression locks up much psychic energy. Both men and women would be healthier if they were in touch with, and gave adequate expression to, the qualities which society has tended to allocate exclusively to the opposite sex and which have consequently been pushed into the shadow.

> In that respect there has been great progress in recent years, largely as the result of the feminist movement. Many men have become less "macho", and have allowed themselves to take part in aspects of looking after babies or in household chores that had previously been left entirely to women, whilst many women have developed "leadership qualities" outside the home which had previously been reserved for men.

Like Freud, Jung sometimes compared himself to an archaeologist who dug down to the foundations of our personality. Jung claimed to dig down to much deeper layers than the personal unconscious. Below that lay strata of the Collective Unconscious which we inherit from our most distant ancestors. In *Analytical Psychology* (1953) Jung drew a picture to illustrate the foundations of the human personality. A chain of mountains arises out of the sea; there are mountains and valleys below, on the sea floor; only the peaks of the highest mountains are above sea level. The individual stands on such a high peak. He can see other individuals standing on other peaks, but apparently isolated from each other by the sea which fills the valleys. What we are consciously aware of is only what is on the peaks above the surface of the sea. Below them lie a number of strata which run below sea-level and link up the mountains: they represent the unconscious. At the lowest levels (the sea floor and the two levels above it), the strata link all the mountains, and so represent foundations which are common to all human kind. These common strata represent (from the bottom upwards) all our animal ancestors, our primate ancestors, and the human species. The last of these gives expression to our common humanity.

> There is an interesting correlation here with what we now know about genomes. Astonishingly, humans and fruit-flies share nearly 60% of their genetic material, and of course an even bigger proportion with the primates. The genetic differences between, say, a Eurasian and an African are proportionately minute.

Then we come to the floor of the submarine valleys, which are at various heights, so that from now on the strata link some of the mountains, but not all of them. This level represents the divergence of large groups of human beings from other large groups – it represents large racial or national identities. Above that level are the strata of smaller communities – clans or tribes – they, too, may be separated from each other, the valley floors being at different levels. Then, finally, above sea-level, at the level of consciousness, we draw on family roots and on our own experiences.

The roots of our unconscious go deep into these other strata. All mankind has unconscious memories in common that date back to the beginning of man's existence. They are incorporated in *archetypes*, the name given by Jung to forms of apprehension which exist before consciousness and which have been engraved on the human brain during evolution. They are connected with universal experiences such as birth and death; they are expressed in rituals, such as rites of passage, and in a wealth of symbols, of which Jung thought the most potent is the sun, standing for life, fertility, growth. (In the picture of the strata referred to in the previous paragraph Jung placed at the very bottom, below those I have mentioned, "the central fire", representing the hot core at the centre of the earth, which is the result of the earth having been formed by fragments hurled from the sun.)

At a slightly higher level, archetypes are incorporated in the myths of the most primitive civilizations and in those that are more advanced, like those of ancient Greece or of the ancient Middle East. Myths were not stories that were obviously not true, on the contrary, they conveyed true insights into human nature. Freud had valued myths, too, though he thought that the truths they conveyed generally expressed some kind of neurosis, as for example the myth which gave the name to the Oedipus Complex. The idea of the Mother or of the Father develops from the experience of each one of us as we grow up, and we may then, by way of sublimation or displacement, embody or find this experience in myth. Where Freud saw myths as being shaped by men to express their feelings, for Jung the mythical archetypes had a more autonomous existence. Although in the first instance they were obviously articulated by humans in the distant past, Jung would lay stress on our inheritance rather than on our creation of them.

> The implication is that when a baby is born, its mind is not a *tabula rasa* as Locke, for example, had thought.[8] It is true, of course, that the baby is not aware of any myths when it is born, but its capacity to recognize the myth in due course is like its inborn, if initially latent, capacity to grow teeth as it grows older. Scientists would agree that our *physical* development is programmed by our genetic inheritance. Our mental development *in part* shares this char-

8 See p. 276 above.

acteristic: as we grow up, our understanding naturally unfolds. However, it is debatable whether we are entitled to include the recognition of mythical archetypes in this development. Jung was closer here to Leibniz than he was to Locke.[9] We might argue that there is little or no scientific evidence for the innate recognition of archetypes, and that, at best, Jung's theories about them are to be taken metaphorically and not literally. I think that Jung did take them literally, but that it would not be an unJungian response to the criticism to point to the significance and "truths" that can be embodied in metaphor.

For Jung, if we were in touch with myths, we were for the most part in touch with a creative and health-giving interpretation of life. They also provide us with human archetypes like the Innocent, the Orphan, the Warrior, the Wanderer, the Martyr, the Wise Old Man or Woman, the Magician, the Demon and the Trickster, all of whom express a way of being which we instantly recognize and relate to as representing types of human beings.

The Innocent is the unformed person, not really in touch with everything that life can throw at him. If this type persists into physical maturity, he may be a person like Dostoevsky's Idiot – not an idiot at all in the normal sense of that word, but someone who confronts the world with a kind of innocence.

The Orphan emerges from innocence into a world of disillusion, has a sense of powerlessness and abandonment. Whilst for some people that may correspond to an objectively real situation – the inmate of a concentration camp, for example – we know there are others in whom this view of the world is largely subjective.

The Martyr is willing to make sacrifices, to embrace suffering, to put him or herself unselfishly at the service of others.

The Wanderer adventurously explores the outer and the inner world. He does not meekly accept the social roles expected of him. He corresponds to the "authentic" person in Kierkegaard, Heidegger or Sartre, who does not conform unthinkingly to group opinion or behaviour.[10] He may be a loner.

The Warrior wants to change the world (not necessarily by violence). He is ready to defend what he believes in. He knows what is healthy and what is unhealthy, will promote the former and combat the latter.

I feel that in attributing to the Warrior archetype a feeling for what is healthy, Jung is being somewhat Teutonic. Nietzsche had ascribed this quality to the Superman.[11] Alas, there is no guarantee that the cause for which one fights is a healthy cause.

The Wise Old Man or Woman – a guru figure.

The Magician contributes towards the process of creation, both within himself and in the outside world. He brings into being something that was not there before. He is the archetype of the artist, the inventor, the person with innovative and life-changing ideas. The Devil represents, of course, the malevolent side of us. A milder version of him is the Trickster: the uninhibited, childlike mischief maker, the practical or obscene joker. He breaks rules not, like the

9 See p. 276 above.

10 For Kierkegaard, see p. 414 above; for Heidegger p. 488 above; for Sartre p. 508 above.

11 See p. 473 above.

Wanderer, in a genuine truth-seeking way (the Trickster is often dishonest), but in a mocking, subversive way.

> The names given to some of these archetypes may seem misleading: we have already seen, for example, that the Warrior need not be a soldier type. The reason these names are chosen is because it is in that guise that they generally appear in the myths.

When we see persons who strongly represent one of these archetypes, we have particular attitudes towards them according to our own personality type. We must remember that the dominant archetype in any one individual may, and indeed should, change over time – that he may graduate, for example, from the Warrior to the Wise Old Man. Sometimes, however, we build our *persona* so exclusively on one of these archetypes that we lose touch with the qualities represented in the others. For Jung, psychological health involved a balance of the positive and an acknowledgement of the negative archetypes which are part of our inheritance.

At the next levels up, that of great racial or national groups or of tribal communities, we have seen that there is a divergence in the strata. For example, Germans are rooted in the experiences of past generations of Germans, and this experience is different from that in which Frenchmen are rooted. Here Jung links with the *völkisch* philosophy which stemmed from Herder [12] and would branch out into the excesses of nineteenth- and twentieth-century nationalism. Though Jung himself was Swiss, he identified himself as a member of the wider German nation. He particularly valued German culture and had much sympathy for German *völkisch* ideas. He was not a Nazi, but he did think that the Nazis drew powerfully on the German unconscious, on Germanic myths and on German archetypes like Wotan. This made his relationship with German nationalism after the rise of the Nazis distinctly ambivalent. On the one hand, he believed that acknowledgement rather than rejection of the truths embodied in a nation's myths is essential for spiritual health, while on the other, he had warned against an unbalanced admiration for one archetype at the expense of others. He feared what would happen in Germany if the dark Wotanic side burst through the restraints of a rapidly weakening Christian civilization.

> Jung had always accepted that, valuable as the deeper strata were, they needed to be *transcended* (not destroyed) if civilization is to develop. The deepest layers of Germanic culture were Wotanic and pre-Christian. The Christian layer was above the Wotanic one. As Christianization had taken place as long ago as the ninth century, it, too, was quite a deep layer forming the soil of later German culture. A German Christian could therefore draw on the more positive imaginative and creative side of the *völkisch* stratum and on the almost equally native restraining stratum of Christianity.

It is easy to see that this ambivalence should have led to him being criticized as a Nazi sympathizer. The Nazis also liked what Jung had to say about the Jews. He saw them as people who had no roots in the deeper strata of the societies in which they now lived (and were therefore, by implication, lacking in the spiritual health which such roots could provide). He also thought that Jewish culture lacked vigour, not only because it had no roots in the soil, but also because

12 See pp. 356f above.

it was 3,000 years old. German culture, on the other hand, was not only rooted, but was also relatively young. That, too, gave it a vigour as displayed by "the formidable phenomenon of National Socialism, on which the whole world gazes in astonishment".[13] Freud certainly thought that Jung was, at bottom, antisemitic. It is, however, fairer to say that what Jung had in common with Nazism is that both sprang from the same Romantic *völkisch* roots. Not everything that came from these roots was as perverted as Nazism.

> The Nazis have brought discredit on the whole *völkisch* idea. That should not blind us to the fact that national roots do in fact give a sense of identity to most people. Only a minority do not feel that something would be lacking in them if they could not feel rooted in this way.

Religion

Given that Jung found health-giving truths embodied in myths, it is natural that he should have a very different attitude from Freud to religions. Freud had considered them as illusions,[14] as displacements or at best sublimations of infantile attitudes. Jung, on the other hand, believes that the religious dimensions of life are immensely nourishing to the soul of man.

> One can even find today some bishops who do not believe in the literal truth of, say, the Resurrection, but they would argue that it represents in myth form the notion that you cannot kill the truth by "nailing it to the Cross". It may be persecuted to the very extreme, but, if it is the truth, it will rise again. If a Christian remembers that this, and not an assertion of literal truth, is the point of the Bible, then he need fear nothing that science can throw at it. Science has damaged the literal truth of the Bible in many respects, but it really has nothing to say about the messages conveyed by its myths.

Freud was very interested in the mind, but showed no interest in what others call the spirit. This, however, was very important to Jung. He talked about us needing to find "the god within" – a phrase which would have been totally alien to Freud.[15] Jung was the son of a Protestant pastor, and some of his writings have a strong Christian angle, but he saw values in all religions, and particularly those of the Far East. These, with their notion (expressed in the yin and yang symbol) that dark and light, male and female, creation and destruction, even good and evil complement and need each other and cannot be understood except in relationship to each other, were much closer to Jung s philosophy than the Either Or separation that the Christian religion tends to make between such opposites.

> This sympathetic attitude to religion tends to make ungians the therapists of choice for religious people who fear that a reudian analysis would show up their beliefs as an illusion or as superstitions.

13 Quoted in Anthony Stevens – *Jung* (Oxford 1994). This quotation comes from an article Jung published in Germany, and was of course gleefully received by the Nazis. All the same, we should note that he said "astonishment", not "admiration". For all his failure at the time to condemn Nazism, he more than made up for this after the war, in a work called *After the Catastrophe.*

14 The book in which he discussed religion most fully had the title *The Future of an Illusion* (1927).

15 In some of his writings, Jung equated "the god within" with the "central fire" or with the psychic energy within each individual.

The yin and yang symbol expresses some kind of integration and balance between what appear to be opposites. In the make-up of the healthy individual there should be a balance between the introvert and the extrovert, between the thinking (rational) and the feeling capacities, between sensing (observing) and intuition, between judging (by which he meant organizing our experiences) and perceiving (being open to new experiences, being spontaneous). Even when there are tensions between these opposites, they are creative tensions, and we ought not to allow one of these pairs to become too dominant.

That had also been the teaching of medieval and renaissance alchemy. This had conveyed the intuitive insight that in a healthy human being the four elements (earth, air, fire and water) or the four humours (sanguine, choleric, phlegmatic, and melancholic) are suitably balanced, and Jung was extremely interested in alchemy. Alchemy is nonsense, say the scientists. Not so, said Jung, alchemy may be based on myth – but then Jung respected myth for the truths it conveyed.

Astrology also had a kind of meaning for him. He believed that humans are influenced by the seasons, and that this influence was then mythically projected onto the stars. This, too, had probably happened since the beginning of Man's existence, so that the Collective Unconscious might actually be "star-driven".[16]

Jung was also interested in mandalas. These are concentric and symmetrical geometric diagrams. To Tantric Buddhists, Hindus and some North American Indians, they represent the universe, and are used as instruments of meditation. By contemplating them, worshippers are drawn into the centre of the diagram, and for Jung this represented the quest that a healthy human being should pursue into the centre, the inner depth of his being. It is easy to see that Jung would be accused of nonsensical mysticism by his critics. Just like religion, so also does art draw, not only on the personal, but also on the collective unconscious and on collective insights and wisdom.

> As a result, those endowed with artistic creativity also tend to prefer Jung and avoid Freud. They fear that their artistic activity will dry up once it has been explained by the Freudian analyst as the displacement or sublimation of infantile drives.

Jung is also in tune with all those who value, rather than look down on, "primitive" civilizations. It is not surprising that one of the most influential studies of Jung has been made by Laurens van der Post (*Jung and the Story of Our Time*, 1976) for van der Post himself had a profound interest in the Bushmen, their wisdom and their intensely sensitive awareness of their connectedness with all life, even as it manifests itself in animals and plants. Arguments for ecological awareness have a strong scientific basis, but the philosophical outlook of Jung or van der Post has also made a major contribution towards it. They believed that western civilization is materialistic, impoverished, blinkered and spiritually arid because it has cut itself off from nature and therefore from the deepest roots of being.

16 See Frank McLynn – *Carl Gustav Jung* (London 1996), pp. 491 to 492.

> One might extrapolate here. The sickness of modern western society, Jung might have said, lies in an individualism that pays steadily less attention to the deeper levels of human experience. The level below the individual is the family, and the importance attached to the family is steadily being undermined – first by the shrinking of the extended family to the nuclear one, and then by erosion of the nuclear family itself as cohabitation and single parenthood have become more widespread and accepted. Other lower strata have also been weakened: tribal and regional cohesions have increasingly suffered from the pressure of centralizing nationalism, while nationalism itself is yielding, culturally and politically, under pressure from internationalism – and all this is considered progress.
>
> Doubtlessly these developments are a response to the negative aspects that lie within the successive strata. The family structure *can* be stifling and restrictive; tribalism (as in Afghanistan) and nationalism (as in modern history) *can* lead to narrow and destructive allegiances. There *could* be progress if, while the developments *transcended* the strata in question they still *contained* and *respected* them. Instead, they have often ignored, if not actually destroyed, them. This transcendence, as has been mentioned above, is necessary for the advance of civilization, but we have to respect the "infrastructure" without allowing it to destroy the "superstructure" which civilization has erected upon it.
>
> In this respect, the recent development of regional assemblies in Britain, Germany and Spain gives expression and respect to the roots of the people in those regions. Many people resent the uniformity that the bureaucracy of the European Union is trying to impose on its people; perhaps before long this unease may find expression in a more meaningful "subsidiarity" and in a return to what De Gaulle used to call *L'Europe des Patries.*

Jung saw the development of our species moving from the lower to the higher levels - and it is important to note that the words "lower" and "higher" are used in a geological rather than in a qualitative or judgmental sense. The lower levels support the higher ones; without that support, one might say, the higher levels rest not on rock, but on sand, which can provide no stability.

What goes for the species also goes for the individual. The child functions on a "geologically" lower level than the adult; its feelings and the way it interprets the world are akin to those of the earlier stages of the species. As we grow up, we move from the "primitive" level with its particular ingredient of imaginative "fantasy thinking" to the "directed thinking" of the adult. However, the adult is impoverished to the extent to which, rather than transcending, he denies, represses or cuts himself off from this imaginative phase of his development.

> This notion is now well entrenched in educational thinking. We now value the imaginative life of young children. We know how much it is at risk as the child grows up and its education lays a premium on "directed thinking" (i.e. thinking which is controlled and not free), on disciplined and rational thought, on the discouragement of "daydreaming". So a good education will not promote "learning" at the expense of, or to the exclusion of, the imagination, on the contrary it will try to keep alive and stimulate the imaginative life. This, too, is at bottom, a Romantic idea going back to Rousseau.[17]

17 See p. 340 above.

Dreams

Like Freud, Jung attached great importance to dreams. He agreed with Freud that *some* dreams express unresolved problems of the very recent or of the more remote past, but there were many dreams that he would not explain in this way. Freud thought they were difficult to interpret because they were designed to conceal, disguise or distort. Jung thought the reason for the difficulty lay in the fact that we are really only dimly aware of the deep strata of the Collective Unconscious. True, dreams give expression to our unconscious, but we have seen that, whereas, for Freud, the Unconscious was little more than the home of the individual's unresolved tensions, for Jung it was also the source of the archetypal insights and wisdoms of the *Collective* Unconscious. So we would expect Jung to see in *some* dreams, at any rate, the expression of these wisdoms. He found the symbolism of dreams to be not exclusively a disguise necessitated by the half-awake conscious, but often rather as embodying the insights of ancient myths and symbols. In most ancient myths, dreams are *prophetic.* Many myths show that dreams or oracles are not always properly interpreted: they speak in a hidden or ambiguous language, as, for instance, they spoke to Oedipus. In other myths, dreams are successfully interpreted, as they were, for example, by Joseph in Egypt. Jung, at any rate, held that dreams do not always struggle with problems in the past; they *can* also convey insights and guidance for wise actions in the future.

Perhaps what fits into this future-oriented category of dreams are those which present the *solution* to problems that we could not find during the day.

Modern Man in Search of a Soul

This was the title of a book Jung published in 1933, and it expresses the aspect of therapy that interested him most. For Freud, the origin of every neurosis was, in the last resort, sexual (in the broader sense in which he used that word – see above) and that this needed to be traced back to early childhood experiences. Jung agreed that this was *sometimes* the case, but he did not think that sexual problems were always the root of a neurosis, and he was less interested in childhood experiences than he was in what we now call "the mid-life crisis". This, he thought, afflicted many people who were not in the strict sense "neurotic" at all, and it certainly had very little to do with sexual frustrations, or an inability to sublimate. Certainly there were some middle-aged people who were still fixated in childhood phases of sexuality, and these might be helped by Freud, but the distress for which a patient might seek help could be caused by feelings that had nothing to do with sexual frustrations or the inability to sublimate. It often afflicted people who had been very successful in the first half of their lives: they had been what Freud would have described as competent sublimators. They had been effective in and derived great satisfaction from building a family and a career. Many people achieve this by focusing exclusively on those functions, on those parts of their personality which were necessary to achieve these successes, and they may have neglected to nourish those parts of themselves that did not contribute to them. Very often, they then reached, at about the age of forty (and perhaps even more so on retirement), a philosophical identity crisis. The children have left home, and the care for the children may have been the main thing that kept a marriage going. Now that the children had left, they may realize that the rest of what made marriage meaningful had disappeared. Retirement presents similar problems. In these situations, some people become conscious of the fact that their life now lacked "meaning", and that it was in many respects empty. The cause of this was their having lost touch with important parts of their soul, the part that was to be found, not only in their personal unconscious, but, more significantly, in the Collective Unconscious which contains so many clues to the deeper meaning of life - and, for that matter, of death. The goals that this person has aimed at - success and standing in the material world - are usually the goals that society (what Heidegger had called "*Das Man*" and Sartre "*Les Autres*") has set for him and for which he had been praised. It is now time to detach oneself from conforming to these external goals, to search for what the existentialists call "authenticity", to become an autonomous individual - hence Jung gives the name "individuation" to the process that is now necessary. This implies, among other things, coming to terms with a number of significant but difficult truths: a sense of proportion about one's previous successes and failures, to both of which we may have attached excessive importance, and a more philosophical acceptance of death than we were perhaps capable of at an earlier stage of our lives.[18] It is in these processes that the Jungian therapist can help.

Conclusion

Freud, as has been said in the Introduction, thought of himself as a scientist rather than as a philosopher (although there are many philosophical implications in his theories, as of course there would be in scientific theories also). Jung was much more consciously a philosopher: he wrote that, "it was a great mistake on Freud's part to turn his back on philosophy."[19] There can be no doubt that Jung stands within the tradition of romantic philosophy: his insistence that intuition, religions, myths, and dreams give access to truths that cannot be given by reason; his *völkisch* sympathies; the value he attaches to the mystical insights that can be provided by mandalas; the worship rather than the analysis of nature, and the existentialist prescription that he offers to his patients, all suggest that he was perhaps the last of the romantic philosophers. The tendencies of those thinkers whom we will consider in the next chapter, and who dominated the end of the twentieth century, revert once again to a more analytical and unmetaphysical mode.

18 Perhaps Freud had some feeling for this when, in his middle sixties, he wrote *Beyond the Pleasure Principle* (1920 to 1922). In this book he tentatively developed the concept of Thanatos, the death instinct, as a counterpart of Eros, the life Instinct. He saw Thanatos as an organic instinctual drive, but he saw it also as a destructive and aggressive force directed against the self - a far cry from the mood of Jung's vision of a wise and tranquil preparation for and acceptance of death.

19 *Modern Man in Search of a Soul*, p. 135.

CHAPTER 48

Structuralism and Post-Structuralism

Introduction

In Chapters 41 to 45 we have looked at philosophers whose main interest had been to analyze the meaning of propositions. In addition to this they were concerned with whether how one could verify that a proposition was true. This had been the common pursuit of the American Pragmatists, G.E. Moore, Bertrand Russell, the Wittgenstein of the *Tractatus* and the Logical Positivists. Karl Popper thought you could get nearer to the truth, not so much by Verification as by looking for Falsification. The Wittgenstein of the *Philosophical Investigations* and, following him, the Linguistic Philosophers, were still interested in the meaning of propositions, but more interested in their *use* than in their *truth*. The philosophers we will discuss in this chapter are entirely concerned with how language is used.

Many Structuralists and Post-Structuralists tend to use a fearsome specialist vocabulary and are often extremely difficult to read. Some of them are truly masters of obfuscation, whose pretentiousness has been devastatingly exposed in *Intellectual Impostures* by Alan Sokal and Jean Bricmont (Profile Books, 1998). I owe much of this chapter to one of the very few writers who handles the topic in a lucid manner: John Sturrock in his *Structuralism* (Paladin, 1986), in his own piece on Roland Barthes in *Structuralism and Since* (Oxford University Press, 1979) and in his Introduction as Editor of the essays that are collected in this book. He is kind enough in this Introduction to defend the Structuralists' lack of clarity as having a deliberate philosophical purpose, "They are demonstrating that there is far more to language than lucidity."[1]

FERDINAND DE SAUSSURE
1857 to 1913

The pioneer of what is called Structuralism, Ferdinand de Saussure, was not primarily a philosopher but a technical language specialist, and he might have

1 pp.16/17. I confess that I can make no sense of the Structuralist texts that I have looked at. So I must add that, although Sturrock explains Structuralism so clearly, I may well have misunderstood the finer points, and, if any expert sees errors in my condensed account, I should like to make it clear that they are mine and not Sturrock's.

been rather surprised at the philosophical conclusions that later thinkers would extrapolate from his theories.

Before Saussure's time, linguistic studies had concentrated on studying how languages evolved "diachronistically" through time (say from Latin to Italian or from Anglo-Saxon to English). Saussure set against this the "synchronistic" study of language: how its structure is shaped by society, how this becomes part of the "collective consciousness" to which the individual who is born into that society is heir and which compels him to operate within it and so to think in certain ways.

The careful study of language lays bare its social structure. When we have done this, we can "deconstruct" what is "really" being said in a language. It is not difficult to see how this notion could spread from linguistics to other areas to show how we are shaped by the structures we inherit in society (the area studied in sociology, anthropology and history) or what is "really" being said in the literature (giving rise to a new school of literary criticism). In the course of the expansion into these disciplines, human beings were seen as steadily less free, increasingly "incarcerated" in structures over which they had no control – at least in so far as they have not been deconstructed for the general public by persuasive philosophers.

> In the same way Marx had seen a way out of determinism if Marxists could, by their efforts, dispel the "false consciousness" in which the working classes were trapped, and that psychoanalysts thought they could dissipate the crippling power of unconscious forces by showing the patient exactly how he was imprisoned by them. So we see why many Structuralists were interested in Marxism, in Freudian psychoanalysis, which seeks to lay bare what our behaviour "really" means, or in Jungian analytical psychology, which had laid so much stress on the Collective Unconscious we inherit. All of this we shall look at in later sections of this chapter, but for the moment we need to look at Saussure's analysis of language structure a little more closely.

Saussure developed a special and elaborate vocabulary for describing the elements of a word, which I am simplifying a little. Words can have up to four elements:

The first is the *Signifier*. This is what we see in writing or hear in speech – for example, the actual written or spoken word "forest".

Next comes the *Signified*: the concept or picture of a forest which is evoked in the mind when the word "forest" is read or heard.

The word "*Sign*" is used as a shorthand word which combines the Signifier and the Signified.

Then there is the *Referent* or *Denotation*: the actual forest in the outside world. The Referent, like the Signified, is the same even if the Signifier is different: the Signifier for a forest will be *forêt* in French, *Wald* in German. Saussure described the study of the relationship between Sign, Signifier, and the Signified as *Semantics*.

> It seems to me that Semantics resembles grammar and syntax more than it does philosophy, not even in the narrow sense given to it by Logical Positivism, let alone in the wider sense in which philosophy was traditionally understood.[2] Unlike grammar, and unlike some other philosophies which are

2 See the discussion on p. 553 above.

> concerned primarily with language, like Logical Positivism, a knowledge of *Semantics* does not train one to *use* words more accurately, precisely, "meaningfully" or (in the case of grammar) elegantly. It is a different case with *Semiotics.*

Saussure gave the name *Semiotics* to a further quality a word can have, which he called Connotation. By this he meant the association a word brings to our minds: the forest in Romantic literature is not merely a neutral thing, but carries, consciously or unconsciously, heavy emotional loading (Hänsel and Gretel being lost in the forest; the spookiness of the Grindelwald; the cherished opposite of urbanism). The word "forest" *need* not carry any connotations; but there are many words that are connotational from the start, for instance when a horse is described as a "steed" or as a "nag".

There is one group of Connotations which refers to the function of an object, which Saussure described as *Value* and which he distinguished from *Signification*. The *Signification* of the word "pawn" is a piece of wood on a chessboard shaped in a particular way. The *Value* of the word "pawn" is the understanding of its role on the chessboard and the relationship of the Sign "pawn" with other Signs.

Whereas *Semantics* seems of little interest other than to someone engaged in a particularly narrow form of Linguistics, *Semiotics* will play a key role for anyone concerned with deconstructing not only words, but as the so-called Post-Structuralists will do, anything else that carries a Connotation going beyond Signifier, Signified and Referent. For example, a gesture or a facial expression is seen like a word is seen on the page (Signifier), is neutrally registered in the mind (Signified) and refers to an actual movement (Referent), but the way it is interpreted, either socially or individually – a scowl as representing anger, a shrug as representing indifference – is of interest to the semiotician. The same is true of dress: the semiotician is interested in the statement that a person who is wearing a bow-tie or a low-cut dress is making and the way that statement is received by the society or the individual.

Nor does the connotation always have to be symbolic: whenever we go beyond what we see or hear to draw conclusions, we are looking for connotations. Sherlock Holmes, for example, was a master of deducing from Signs (say, the sight and concept of a footprint) what it might mean beyond the Referent (the actual footprint) – where the person who made the footprint was going, what kind of shoes he was wearing, whether he had a limp, what the weather was like at the time, etc.

Connotations, of course, are not fixed. Beethoven intended the four notes that open the first movement of the Fifth Symphony to connote Fate. Because their rhythm – short, short, short, long – is that of the Morse signal for the letter V, and V stood for Victory, those four notes were used as the signature tune in the BBC's broadcast to occupied Europe to connote resistance and impending victory. The swastika connoted glorious triumphalism for the Nazis but evil for their enemies.

Many connotations are quite conscious and deliberately evoked. Politicians and advertisers know all about it, even if their audiences may not. Anyone who deconstructs them for the general public to make it aware how it is being exploited hopes thereby to undermine the power of the political or commercial message, and there are teachers who see it as an important role of education to train the young in "seeing through" the messages that they receive from society. Connotations give a clue to underlying ideologies, and the deconstruction offered by a semiotician is often subversive in intention. Deconstruction is demystification, and the Post-Structuralist Roland Barthes (1915 to 1980) gave the title *Mythologies* to a book he wrote in 1957.

Connotations often operate at an unconscious level because people tend to take the social structure within which they live for granted. For example, Jane Austen was very conscious of the role or connotation of wealth where eighteenth- century match-making was concerned, but some deconstructionists have claimed that she took the exploitation (of colonies abroad or of agricultural labourers at home) which sourced that wealth so much for granted that, if it is mentioned at all, it is merely *en passant*: it requires the attention of the semioticist to bring out the underlying assumptions of the text.

Films are another kind of "text" that can be deconstructed: a semiotician will bring out, for example, what was simply taken for granted – occasionally by directors, more frequently by the spectators – in many a 1930s Hollywood film in which black characters were usually portrayed as childlike, amusing, unthreatening, not to be taken seriously. It is not difficult to deconstruct the ideology that lay behind such depictions.

Semiotics and Psychoanalysis

Psychoanalysis was bound to be of interest to the Semioticists: it, too, sets out to elicit the "values" of words, gestures, behaviour, dreams and works on the relationship between them and other Signs. Jacques Lacan (1901 to 1981) fused structuralist language theory with Freudian theories of the unconscious; but he enlarged the notion of the Freudian Unconscious by saying that this was not only within us, but also in part outside us, in the sense that we absorb into the Unconscious much of the social framework within which we are born.

Before we consider how Structuralism affected theories of Anthropology, History and Literature, we must have a look at the development in linguistic studies that is associated with Noam Chomsky.

NOAM CHOMSKY
born 1928

Noam Chomsky accepted that part of the linguistic apparatus we inherit is socially conditioned: society trains us in what words mean and what resonances or "connotations" they evoke. But beyond that, Chomsky guessed,[3] our language inheritance has a strictly genetic component. This gives us the *innate* ability to absorb words into a grammatical and syntactical structure. When we are born this appears nonexistent in the same way in which body-hair is nonexistent at birth, but it develops naturally in the same way (though of

3 He admitted that he could not demonstrate this theory. We can no more understand by introspection how these structures of the mind work than we can understand by introspection how the kidneys work, and ethical considerations prevent us from invasive experiments on human beings to find out.

course much earlier) as body-hair develops. Grammar in the widest sense is not something we have to be taught, though in the narrower sense of the niceties of academic grammar it is of course a learnt skill. One of the inborn faculties of the mind is the "tacit knowledge" of language structure,[4] which unfolds with great rapidity and complexity and enables a child's grasp of language to make such astonishing progress in the first few years of life. It also explains the ease with which children can become bilingual, when this becomes so much more difficult for most adults.

However, our language structure also limits us; it decides what we can think and say either easily, not very well, or not at all. Chomsky believes that because language structures are *fairly* precise, they equip us quite well to think scientifically because the structure of science is also precise. The scientific theories we develop through history have certainly not always been accurate, but they have never been completely random, and for Chomsky this fact makes a major contribution to explaining why science has made such notable progress during the history of mankind. Our language structure is better attuned to the structure of the world of science than it is to the structure of the world of ethics or of aesthetics. It simply does not allow us to form concepts which would lead to steady and widely recognized progress in these areas.

Structuralism and Anthropology

CLAUDE LÉVI-STRAUSS
born 1908

Lévi-Strauss specifically applied the approach of Linguistic Structuralism to Anthropology. It, too, should be a synchronic rather than a diachronic study, not concerned with how a social structure *came about* but with how it works *now*, how the different parts of it relate to each other.

I would think that this was not a very new or controversial position: by its nature anthropology tends not to be diachronic, but an examination of what a society is like at the time when the anthropologist studies it. If it goes into the past, it is not to trace sequences or development, but to make comparisons between one society and another. If it were diachronic, it would surely be more like pre-structuralist social history than anthropology.

For the anthropologist the past history of a society is of interest only in the way in which that society uses the past – a notion that will be taken up by structuralist historians, as we shall see in a moment.

Just as Saussure had been interested in the social rather than the individual aspects of language, so the structural anthropologist will study the social structure of, say, kingship without being interested in the policies of an individual king. If an individual king falls foul of his subjects and is overthrown, the question that would interest a structural anthropologist is not so much what errors the king had committed, but what structures in that society upheld a king and what structural sanctions there are if he transgresses too much. This is not to

4 He believes that we also have "tacit knowledge" of other, nonverbal, structures, like, for example, music.

deny that within those structures there may be immense differences. For example, whether the sanctions are formal as in the constitutional arrangements made by the Bill of Rights in 1689, or informal as in the military coups staged by an Assad or a Saddam Husein.

> One might object that such differences *within* the structure are vastly more important than the similarities. The Structuralists would not deny that, they would merely say that it is the general and not the particular that interests them as a subject of study.

In Saussurian terms, the anthropologist should work on the connotations of the Signs (the observable behaviour of a society) and see what role it plays in the "game".[5] When he does that, the synchronicity – that is, the connectedness – of the phenomena he studies cannot escape him: he will see that social, cultural, economic and political practices are all interconnected – each is likely to influence the other. If we make an anthropological study of marriage, for example, we see that its connotations involve notions of kinship (who may marry whom), economic relationships (bride-price etc.), the public nature of the occasion, the clothing and other rituals connected with marriage. None of these are determined by the individuals concerned: like language, they are socially conditioned, and, like grammar in the linguistic field, the structural framework of any society is broadly the same as that of any other society: what differences there are lie within the structure.

> For example, every society has a special recognizable dress for brides to wear, though the actual bridal costumes differ from one society to another. What is called a bride-price in one culture is called a dowry in another: there are really the same, though one sounds a little more sophisticated. To take another example, almost every religion has a priesthood, a system of discipline, rituals, and an attitude towards people outside the religion. In that respect they have a common structure. Again one might point out how important the differences within those structures can be – people have, after all, fought wars about them, for instance about the distribution of power within the structure; the structuralist would make the same reply that we have already noted.
>
> There is also another problem: if the structure of one society is "broadly the same" as that of any other society existing elsewhere or at a different period, can there be such a thing as basic changes in structures, especially over time? Or can a structural anthropologist really dismiss the apparent structural, political and social changes from Imperial Germany to the Weimar Republic, then to the Nazi state and then to the German Federal Republic with the idea that *plus ça change, plus c'est toujours la même chose*? That surely could hardly stand up.

So Lévi-Strauss would be interested in the similarities of authority structures in, say, an African tribe and a modern European state. This, as well as his stress on synchronicity, set him apart from anthropologists like Bronislaw Malinowski (1884 to 1942) who made a distinction between "primitive" and "advanced" societies and who were also interested in the (diachronic) study of how the one developed into the other. (However, Malinowski's stress on the

5 Note that Wittgenstein, in his *Philosophical Investigations*, had used the same metaphor for eliciting what a proposition might mean; see pp. 544ff above.

inter-relationship of various customs and on their "functionality" was very close to Lévi-Strauss's approach).

It is also partly because societies shared structural similarities that their myths show such similar patterns. Like Freud and Jung, Lévi-Strauss believed that art and myths were very significant, and highly "functional", but because he saw myths as either confirmation of, or as "wish-fulfilling" opposition to, the structure of a *society*, he was rather closer to Jung (though he shared none of his mysticism) than to Freud, who had seen them, like dreams or artistic creations, as reflecting individual rather than socially-shaped preoccupations.

Structuralism and Post-Structuralism in History

FERNAND BRAUDEL
1902 to 1985

In 1956, Fernand Braudel succeeded to the editorship of the influential and by then twenty-seven year old French historical journal *Annales: économies, sociétés, civilisations*, and so he became the head of what is known as the *Annales* school of French historians. This school applied to history some of the concepts of Structuralism which we have already seen. History seemed, by definition, to be a diachronic study, examining societies over time, dealing with causes, development and story telling – what Braudel called *l'histoire événementielle.* The *Annales* school distrusted this linear approach because it is usually the product of selecting and imposing on history trends of which people living at the time were often unaware. The trends *they* saw may have been quite different from those perceived by a later generation – and just as selective as they impose their own pattern on the past. We have already seen towards the end of Chapter 38 that some twentieth-century historians had seen that any account of history tells us almost as much about the period in which a historian is writing as it does about the period with which he is dealing. That is why the *Annales* school preferred to avoid the word "History", which carries the implication that it can describe how things actually were. What is available to us is not history in that sense, but only what has been written about the past, namely "Historiography".

> I see an amusing similarity here with Kant's notion of *das Ding an sich*. History appears like the *noumenon* which is not directly accessible to us: it appears to us only in the "phenomenal" form that is mediated for us by the kind of intellectual spectacles we are wearing.[6]

The strength of the *Annales* school lay in its interdisciplinary approach – to study the widest synchronic structure within which the events (*évènements*) of a period take place. When we do that, politics – still the staple of historical writing at the time – are seen to be the most transient and least significant features of a given period. Braudel illustrated this point in his magisterial two-volume *History of the Mediterranean in the Reign of Philip II* (first published in 1949). In this work, the politics of the reign are treated only at the very end. It begins with

6 See p. 366 above.

a discussion of the geography of the region. Together with the climate, this influences the agriculture and raw materials of the area which in turn affect the trade routes and other economic activities. Social structures are formed by these and they involve the ordinary people, not just the political classes. Then there are political structures built on top of the social ones. Technological developments take place in ship-building, industry and armaments, and the intellectual and cultural climate is shaped by the interaction of all these. Religious differences spring up and then, finally, we come to the political events. National structures are newer than both wider regional and narrower local ones. Braudel uses the notion of *longue durée* and *courte durée*: the profoundest influences are those that have been there for the longest period; at the other end of the scale, we have the temporary, short-lived political events which make up the *histoire événementielle.*

Braudel was not a Marxist, but we can see some affinities with Marxism. The oldest and profoundest influences are seen to be the materialist ones: they form the structure of which, in Marxist terms, cultural and political institutions are the superstructure, and the latter cannot be understood without the former.[7] Both Braudel and the Marxists thought that this synchronic approach produced, in the *longue durée,* an interpretation of history's essential meaning.

MICHEL FOUCAULT
1926 to 1984

Can the synchronic view of history claim to be freer than the diachronic from the selection imposed on the past by the historian? Foucault thought not. He held that the historian should refrain from explicit interpretation and content himself with collecting historical material.

> One might ask whether even the collection of material is not bound to be selective, determined by what one is interested in collecting.

Foucault had originally been a Structuralist, but moved into what is called Post-Structuralism as the result of a more radical assertion that all historiography not only *reflects* selectivity, but *uses* that selectivity as an instrument of *control.* Very often, "historiography, together with the documents it rests on, is a conspiracy of the powerful and orthodox against the powerless and eccentric."[8] That is true of the history which is "normative" in any culture. So, for example, a culture that is male-centred or white-centred will, in its history, "privilege" the role of men or of whites and "marginalize" that of women or of blacks. However, there is also a historiography which sets out to counter that conspiracy: "black" history and "feminist" history, for example, are an effort to change the prevailing power relationships.

> Whether they are true or not, such statements surely go beyond the mere collection of materials which Foucault had recommended: the assertion that historiography is a conspiracy (or an attempt to counter it) is of course itself an interpretation.

7 See p. 446 above.

8 The quotation is from Sturrock – *Structuralism, p. 67.*

Jacques Derrida (born 1930) particularly saw it as his function to "de-centre" the readings of cultures, to show that there are many possible centres, all of them coherent within their own context, but none of them granted any privileged position.

Note the similarity with Wittgenstein's theory that there is no point in looking for a truth that exists outside the "language game" that is being played.[9]

Structuralism and Post-Structuralism in Literature

Structuralism in Literature developed out of the theory of Russian Formalism, whose chief exponent was Roman Jakobson (1896 to 1982). The Soviet government disapproved of his work, and in 1933 he went to Czechoslovakia, where he gathered around him a group of linguistic analysts known as the Prague School. In due course he had to emigrate from Czechoslovakia also, and from 1941 to his death he lived in the United States.

The Prague School was initially involved in studying the sounds of words. It was particularly interested in the way Surrealists used words for their sound rather than for their meaning. They managed to make an obscure philosophical point of this, claiming that it showed the surrealist author as willing to be the servant of words rather than as their master; but they eventually moved on to Formalism (shifting from individual words to texts) and from there to Structuralism proper.

Formalism focussed on the general structure of texts (described as *la langue*) to the exclusion of the value of anything that might make the text within structures (described as *la parole*) notable as a work of art, or of any other extraneous considerations like the psychological or social insights the text might have – the relationship it might bear to the personality or life of its author or of some character whom the author had used as a model, or the social and historical setting in which it was written.

One may feel that this approach is a quite unnatural impoverishment of the study of literature. Most of us want to know something about the author and the society in which he lived, not only out of normal human curiosity but also because we feel that it illuminates our understanding and appreciation of the text. That remains true even if we recognize the Deconstructionists' argument (see below) that any such reading will be subjective: even a subjective reading of a work of art is usually life-enhancing, which can hardly be said of the dry approach of the Formalists.

However, their approach is perfectly legitimate, and indeed it has a distinguished ancestry. It is, after all, the kind of analytical process in which, for example, Aristotle had engaged when he had described what he thought "made" a tragedy. All the Formalists were doing was to say what interested *them*. They were not being prescriptive: they did not claim that it was reprehensible if other people were interested in extraneous influences on the text. They were perhaps rather like scientists who describe how atomic power works and are not concerned, *qua* scientists, with ethical questions about how atomic power might be used or abused. They might themselves be involved in such questions, but it would be in their capacity as concerned citizens and not

9 See p. 544 above.

> in their capacity as scientists. (However, one must say that there were some disciples of Formalism – among literary critics and teachers of literature – who unfortunately *did* convey a prescriptive message, to the great impoverishment of their readers.)

The Formalists wanted to identify the devices on which a text relies: the *type* of plot; the *type* of characterization; the uses made of dialogue, rhyme, rhythm and metaphor; and the way in which themes, phrases, images, or characters are repeated to impress themselves on the reader. These structures will vary from one *genre* of literature to another. Works of tragedy follow one kind of pattern, and there are other patterns for detective stories, Mills and Boone romances, or fairy tales. In 1928, for example, a member of the Formalist School, Vladimir Propp, published *The Morphology of the Russian Folk Tale*, in which he examined a hundred folk-tales and identified thirty-one elements (he called them "functions") a large number of which are present in each of them: the hero, the villain, the quest, the rescue, an object of magic etc.

> We can see here a close relationship with the archetypes that Jung had identified in myths, but when Propp had analyzed these elements, he considered that he had finished the task he had set himself. Unlike Jung, the Formalists did not erect upon this analysis an entire philosophy of life – doubtlessly to the approval of people who are sceptical of Jung's philosophical superstructure.

The Prague School paid little attention, initially, to the Connotation of a Text, but later Jakobson and his followers moved from Formalism into Structuralism. In Stucturalism, as we have seen, Connotations will play a significant role and will often yield an understanding of the conscious and unconsious ideology of a text.

The notion that one could pin down the connotations and therefore the ideology underlying any text was called into question by the post-structuralists, whose leading exponents were Michel Foucault, Jacques Derrida and Roland Barthes. An author will choose words for the connotations *he* thinks they have, but he is never in full control of his text. Sometimes he has "blind moments" – when the words control him rather than *vice versa*, perhaps because they are not fully *controlled* by his consciousness, but rather, *well up* from the unconscious.

> Note again the connection with psychoanalysis. Also note that Derrida made the point, in criticism of Lacan, that a psychoanalytical interpretation of the text is also only a subjective interpretation which is brought to the text by the psychoanalytically-inclined critic.

Sometimes the author creates such "blind moments" deliberately, as in the ambiguity or elusiveness of much poetry. Here the author positively invites the reader to make of them what he can.

> This feature is particularly strong since the early part of the twentieth century, with Surrealism, Dadaism and then abstract art. Few artists before the twentieth century would have made such a cult of the "blind moment".

In any case, the author has lost control of *everything* he writes once he has set it down and released it to the general public. The language he has used may have meant one thing to him, but may mean something quite different to the reader, who always brings to the text his own interpretation, which is as valid as the author's - and writers do sometimes acknowledge, in response to comments from their readers, that some possible meanings in their text had "escaped" them. Every text "disseminates" (Derrida's term) a multiplicity of meanings: in Mikhail Bakhtin's phrase, it is "polyphonic". This word at least implies that the different meanings enrich each other like the strands of a polyphonic piece of music. Barthes seems to have been more conscious of the inharmonious clash of readings, which he describes as a "cacophony".

Sometimes the author takes part in this game by making deliberate allusions to or parodies of other texts, but in any case, the author is the reader's construct. This led Roland Barthes to entitle one of his essays *The Death of the Author* (1968).

> We may think that this is going too far, after all, there is a real man or woman, not constructed by the reader, who has written the text. From what we know of Charles Dickens, we know that certain passages in *David Copperfield* are based on his own life, and it is surely therefore not subjective for the reader to bring this knowledge to bear on his understanding of the text. It seems unlikely that a Post-Structuralist could shut out such knowledge when he reads the text, but when he takes it on board, it is not in his capacity as a Post-Structuralist. In that capacity his philosophy tells him that the text is all that matters and the author's life is to be excluded.

So, unlike the Structuralists, the Post-Structuralists did not see a text (or anything else) *anchored* in a synchronic context. The Structuralists had excluded considerations of the life, background or intentions of the author because they had no significant bearing on the structure of the text, which is all they were interested in. The Post-Structuralists also found such considerations irrelevant, but in their case the reason was that whatever might have been the original intentions of the author, the reader will always "de-originate" the text. All structures in the work of an author and all those read into a text by the reader are subjective. Because Post-Structuralism dissolved the solidity of structures in that way, "Deconstruction" is an appropriate alternative name for it.

> We should note, however, that this does not mean that interpretations are invalid. We cannot read a text without trying to interpret it: this is therefore both inevitable and legitimate. All the Deconstructionists urge upon us is to remember that every interpretation is, equally inevitably, *subjective*.

What the reader has seen in the text may be influenced by the critics' commentary upon it - but then the critic is only another subjective reader, and *his* commentaries, too, have no life apart from that which his own readers bring to them.

> Let us suppose that the critic or the reader is a Marxist. He will then bring his Marxist ideology to bear on the interpretation of the text. He will look at the text through, as it were, ideological spectacles. However, the spectacles need not be ideological at all: they may simply reflect his life experiences or his interests. Some people love India; others are repelled by its squalor. If we read a book about the slums of Bombay, for example, one reader may focus on the wretchedness of the slums, while another may find the way in which the people living under those conditions rise above their squalid circumstances most

significant. Some readers are interested in symbolism and so look for symbolical meanings which may pass other readers by.

Barthes was, in any case, opposed to most literary criticism. Just as Foucault had seen historiography as a conspiracy, so Barthes thought that we must "demystify" the ideologies of the critics. He especially criticized the criterion of *clarté* (lucidity) which was so important to French critics. To begin with, only clear-cut notions are susceptible to *clarté,* and Barthes was suspicious of clear-cut notions because they tried to impose structures on an essentially fluid world. More importantly, he was hostile to the criterion because the achievement of *clarté* required a lengthy training, so insistence on it was tantamount to élitism. Elitism was seen by Barthes as a mechanism of social control, and as an egalitarian in his political philosophy he was opposed to it.

Someone with an élitist education will look down on pulp fiction, yet millions of people, who do not have the privilege of wearing élitist spectacles, enjoy pulp fiction: their "reading" of it is as legitimate and as subjective as is that of the educated person.[10]

Whatever one thinks about canons of taste in literature, there are some areas where a so-called élite understanding is objectively sounder than that of an uneducated person. For example, a view based on a poor understanding of science is in every way inferior to a soundly based one. In the arts (and arguably in ethics also) the retort, "that's only your point of view" may carry some more or less grudging philosophical respect, but in science that retort would really be unacceptable.

We can recognize in Post-Structuralism an extreme form of the relativism which we have come across at other times in the history of philosophy. It questions every kind of authority, every social norm, every cultural canon, and every ideology. It also refuses to erect any authority or canon of its own. So we will not be surprised to find some of the post-structuralist idiom among the young anarchists of the French student uprising in 1968. The uprising faded away, but it is difficult not to conclude that the culture and lifestyle of the Western world at the beginning of the twenty-first century are still deeply impregnated with Post-Structuralist attitudes.

10 For a full discussion of the issues involved in this statement, refer back to pp. 298ff.

Bibliography

General Histories

Beginners might give themselves a present of **Bryan Magee** - *The Story of Philosophy,* 250 pp., Dorling Kindersley, 1998. It is a history of philosophy, and, like all Dorling Kindersley books it is lavishly and beautifully illustrated, so the text is quite short. I have not seen a more attractively presented introduction.

Another lucid one-volume survey is **Marvin Perry** - *The Intellectual History of Modern Europe,* 490 pp., Houghton Mifflin pbk, 1999. The title is a little misleading. The introductory sixty pages are about the Classical and the Medieval world because their thought is so often drawn upon by modern thought. When we come to the modern world (Renaissance onwards) there are only a few pages on each important thinker, but it's one of the best summaries I know.

A delightfully written book is the first volume of a projected History of Philosophy by **Anthony Gottlieb** - *The Dream of Reason,* 460 pp., Penguin pkb 2001. This volume covers the period from the Ancient Greeks to the Renaissance. His engagement with the Greek philosophers stimulates ours. For the thought of Antiquity it is the best and most readable introduction I know, but he devotes only sixty pages to the Middle Ages. These include a dozen pages of a fresh and sparkling introduction, but then become very cursory: just a few scattered remarks about Aquinas, for example. For the Greeks it is the best and most readable introduction I know.

An astonishing tour de force is **Peter Watson** - *A Terrible Beauty,* "A History of the People and Ideas that Shaped the Modern Mind". The text of 772 pages begins with Freud and ends with Stephen Hawking. The text includes aperçus of every significant European and American thinker of the twentieth century - philosophers, scientists, economists, sociologists, literary figures, film makers etc.

By far the most readable and enjoyable accounts for general readers of philosophies between the time of the Ancient Greeks and the French Revolution are the relevant chapters in **Durant** - *The Story of Civilization.* This is a monumental 32 volume enterprise undertaken by the American Will Durant, joined from volume 20 onwards by his wife Annie, and published between 1935 and 1967 by Simon and Schuster.

This followed the success of **Will Durant**'s earlier (1927) *The Story of Philosophy,* 530 pp. in Washington Square Press pbk edition of 1953. Subtitled "The Lives and Opinions of the World's Greatest Philosophers from Plato to John Dewey". The preface makes it clear that the book concerns itself mostly with the effect that philosophy can have on ordinary life and that it makes the minimum reference to the more abstract aspects of pure philosophy - metaphysics, epistemology and similar areas. So the Durants quite brilliantly go in for what the French call *haute vulgarisation.*

For beginners, I would recommend two books by **Nigel Warburton** (who teaches at the Open University). *Philosophy: The Basics* (170 pp., Routledge pbk,

2nd edn. 1995) is not a history, but a very clear and well-set out discussion of the main issues in philosophy. In the same vein, but in historical sequence, he has also written *Philosopy: the Classics* (215 pp., Routledge pbk 1998). This summarizes, in between ten and twenty pages, one key work from each of twenty philosophers. There is nothing between Aristotle and Descartes, and Hegel is left out – never mind, the rest is very good.

If you are looking for one-volume histories, probably the best known is still **Bertrand Russell** - *History of Western Philosophy*, 1946, 900 pp. It is readable, but thin. I find it rather disappointing, and of course it does not deal with post World War Two philosophy.

In my opinion the most stimulating one-volume general history of philosophy for beginners is: **Richard Tarnas** - *The Passion of the Western Mind*, 500 pp., Pimlico pbk 1996. It does not try to cover everything, but it is very lucid (especially in the first half; it becomes more difficult in the second) and suggestive about what it does cover. Especially good on the philosophical implications of the progress of science and astronomy at various stages of history. He finishes with a fascinating personal thirty page epilogue about the possible future of philosophy.

A general caveat about histories of philosophy: the earlier chapters are almost always much easier to read than the later ones. Though there are some difficult philosophers before the nineteenth century, there is no doubt that philosophy from the nineteenth century onwards generally becomes much more difficult; it becomes much harder to write lucidly about, and very few writers manage it!

There now follows a list of books which are altogether tougher: The most magisterial is the nine-volume ***History of Philosophy* by Frederick Coplestone, S.J.** - 4,500 pp. in all, covering the period from the Ancient Greeks to Sartre, which he started in 1946 and finished in 1974 and which is published in three tomes of three volumes each by Image Books (pbk), a division of Doubleday (New York). This is not only very detailed and in places very hard going, but it is also a critical history, in that Father Coplestone includes a discussion of the strengths and weaknesses of each philospher - and occasionally one is aware that these commentaries are written from a Jesuit point of view. Nevertheless, I would say it is an indispensable secondary work for anyone who really wants to follow the subject up in depth.

D.W. Hamlyn - *Pelican History of Western Philosophy*, 1987, 345 pp. Good, but quite difficult.

D. Scott-Kakures and others - *History of Philosophy*, Harper Collins pbk, 1993, 430 pp. This is a course textbook in a series called "HarperCollins College Outlines", intended "to supplement major textbooks". The chapters are very selective, dealing with only a small range of the topics covered by each philosopher. It is not an easy book, because it concentrates on some of the most difficult technical arguments, whereas other general histories of philosophy tend to state the conclusions without paying close attention to the arguments which lead to them. The book, therefore, requires concentrated and careful reading.

Roger Scruton - *Modern Philosophy: an Introduction and Survey*, 1994, Mandarin pbk, 600 pp. A thematic rather than historical treatment. Don't be misled by the title or the blurb, I don't consider this an "introduction" at all. It is very difficult for any newcomer to the subject, and I also find it very arid – just the sort of book that makes some people wonder what is the point of studying philosophy at all if it is so remote from the kind of philosophical issues laymen care about.

John Shand - *Philosophy and Philosophers,* 1994, Penguin, 350 pp. A freshly thought-out presentation. Requires close reading, but rewarding. Don't be too put off by his occasional use of algebraic symbols when concrete examples might have done just as well.

Bryan Magee - *The Great Philosophers,* 1987, 345 pp., OUP. Scripts of expository discussions Magee had on television with leading authorities on each of the great philosophers.

Bryan Magee - *Men of Ideas: Some Creators of Contemporary Philosophy,* 1978, 275 pp., OUP. Same format as above. This time the discussions are with the living philosophers themselves.

Bryan Magee - *Confessions of a Philosopher,* 1997, 500 pp., Weidenfeld & Nicolson. A brilliant book. Magee is the most lucid writer on philosophy I know. The book is an intellectual autobiography, and he treats philosophers more or less in the order in which he came to grips with them. So it is not a chronological account of the history of philosophy. I find his own responses to these philosophers wonderfully clean and true; only the last chapter is not always easy to understand.

OUP's *History of Western Philosophy*. Each between 200 and 250 pp. long, and very clear:

1. **Terence Irwin** - *Classical Thought*
2. **David Luscombe** - *Medieval Philosophy*
3. **Brian Copenhaver and Charles Schmitt** - *Renaissance Philosophy* (360 pp.)
4. **John Cottingham** - *The Rationalists*
5. **R.S. Woolhouse** - *The Empiricists*
6. **John Skorupski** - *English Language Philosophy, 1750 to 1945*
7. **Robert C. Solomon** - *Continental Philosophy since 1750*
8. **Thomas Baldwin** - *Philosophy in English since 1945.*

Histories of Political Philosophy

G.H.Sabine - *History of Political Theory,* 1937, 774 pp., Harrap. A masterpiece. There are several later editions.

Masters of Political Thought, 1947 to 1959, Harrap. Three volumes of about 370 pp each. Extensive extracts with commentaries:
Vol. I, ed. **M.B. Foster** - *Plato to Machiavelli*
Vol.II, ed. **W.T.Jones** - *Machiavelli to Bentham*
Vol. III, ed. **L.W. Lancaster** - *Hegel to Dewey*

C.L.Wayper - *Political Thought, 1954,* 300 pp., English University Press.

In the Teach Yourself Series. Treatment is not chronological, but by types of political thought. ed. **David Thompson** - *Political Ideas,* 1966, 200 pp., Pelican Originally a series of radio talks. Chronological.

Theology

Karen Armstrong - *A History of God,* 1993, 500 pp., Mandarin pbk.

Karen Armstrong - *The Battle for God*, 2001, 440 pp., CollinsHarper, pbk.
Paul Johnson - *A History of Christianity*, 1976, 550 pp., Penguin.

Aesthetics

Monroe C. Beardsley - *Aesthetics from Classical Greece to the Present*, 1966, 400 pp., University of Alabama Press.
Anne Sheppard - *Aesthetics*, 170 pp., 1987, OUP.

Ethics

A.C.Ewing - *Ethics*, 1953, 180 pp., *Teach Yourself Books*, English University Press.
P.H.Nowell-Smith - *Ethics*, 1954, 325 pp., Pelican.
Alasdair McIntyre - *A Short History of Ethics*, 1967, 270 pp., Routledge.
Mary Midgley - *The Ethical Primate*, 1994, 190 pp., Routledge. A powerful and readable attack on "reductionism" in ethics.
Mary Midgley - *Animals and Why They Matter*, 1983, 158 pp., University of Georgia, pbk. Very well written, and goes far wider in philosophical analysis of obligations than the title would suggest.

Reference Books

ed. J.O. Urmson and Jonathan Rée - *The Concise Encyclopaedia of Western Philosophy and Philosophers*, 1960, 330 pp., Unwin Hyman, pbk.
Diané Collinson - *Fifty Major Philosophers*, 1987, 170 pp., Croome Helm, pbk.
Dan Cohn-Sherbrook - *Fifty Key Jewish Thinkers*, 1997, 130 pp., Routledge, pbk.
John Lechte - *Fifty Key Contemporary Thinkers* - from Structuralism to Post-Modernity, 1994, 250 pp., Routledge, pbk. Many of these fifty are not exacty household names. They are very difficult thinkers, and Lechte's text is only occasionally lucid. This book confines itself to Western Philosophy, but if you want an introduction to Asian and Islamic Philosopy: **Ian P.McGreal** has edited *Great Thinkers of the Eastern World*, 500 pp., Harper Collins, pbk, 1995.
Rom Harré's *One Thousand Years of Philosophy*, 350 pp, Blackwell, pbk, 2000. About a third of this book deals with the philosophies of Asia and the Islamic world.

Short Books on Individual Philosophers

There are two excellent series, each of which presents one philosopher in about 100 to 150 pp. Not all of these are in print yet, though most of them are:

<u>Past Masters (OUP):</u>

Socrates (Bernard Williams)
Plato (R.M.Hare)
Aristotle (Jonathan Barnes)
Augustine (Henry Chadwick)
Aquinas (Anthony Kenny)
Machiavelli (Quentin Skinner)
Francis Bacon (Anthony Quinton)
Montaigne (Peter Burke)

Descartes (Tom Sorrell)
Pascal (Alban Krailsheimer)
Spinoza (Roger Scruton)
Montesquieu (Judith Shklar)
Diderot (Peter France)
Leibnitz (G. MacDonald Ross)
Locke (John Dunn)
Berkeley (J.O.Urmson)
Hume (A.J.Ayer)
Burke (C.B.Macpherson)
Rousseau (Robert Wokler)
Kant (Roger Scruton)
Hegel (Peter Singer)
Kierkegaard (Patrick Gardiner)
Bentham (John Dinwiddy)
J.S.Mill (William Thomas)
Marx (Peter Singer)
Bergson (Leszek Kolakowski)
Russell (John G. Slater)

A Very Short Introduction to ... OUP, about 160 pp. each (some of these are reprints of the Past Master Series listed above):

Ancient Philosophy (Julia Annas)
Aristotle (Jonathan Barnes)
Augustine (Henry Chadwick)
Continental Philosophy (Simon Critchley)
Darwin (Jonathan Howard)
Descartes (Tom Sorrell)
Freud (Anthony Storr)
Heidegger (Michael Inwood)
Hume (A.J.Ayer)
Jung (Anthony Stevens)
Marx (Peter Singer)
Nietzsche (Michael Tanner)
Socrates (C.C.W.Taylor)
Wittgenstein (A.C.Grayling)

Fontana Modern Masters:

Nietzsche (J.P. Stern)
Sartre (Arthur C. Danto)
Heidegger (George Steiner)
Popper (Bryan Magee)
Wittgenstein (David Pears)
Chomsky (John Lyons)
Berlin (John Gray)

Phoenix paperbacks:

Phoenix (a subsidiary of Orion and Weidenfeld) is in the process of publishing a series called "The Great Philosophers". Each booklet is only about 50 pages long, and tends to concentrate on one or two ideas of the thinker in question in such a way as to bring out, often in the words of the philosopher himself, his particular method of arguing. Most of them are very clearly written, though some of them are more difficult than others. The booklets which have so far appeared are on:

Democritus (Paul Cartledge)
Socrates (Anthony Gottlieb)
Plato (Bernard Williams)
Aristotle (Kenneth McLeigh)
Descartes (John Cottingham)
Pascal (Ben Rogers)
Spinoza (Roger Scruton)
Locke (Michael Ayres)
Berkely (David Berman)
Hume (Anthony Quinton)
Voltaire (John Gray)
Kant (Ralph Walker)
Schopenhauer (Michael Tanner)
Hegel (Raymond Plant)
Marx (Terry Eagleton)
Nietzsche (Ronald Hayman)
Ayer (Oswald Hanfling)
Wittgenstein (P.M.S.Hacker)
Popper (Frederic Raphael)
Collingwood (Aaron Ridley)
Turing (Andrew Hodges)
Russell (Ray Monk)
Heidegger (Jonathan Ree)
Derrida (Christopher Johnson)

Various other Books Recommended

A vigorous and vivid attack on Socrates and Plato in: **I.F. Stone** - *The Trial of Socrates*, 1988, 250 pp., Picador pbk. And a magisterial one on Plato, Hegel, and Marx in: **Karl Popper** - *The Open Society and its Enemies*, two vols., 1945, 750 pp. in all, Routledge, pbk.
A.J. Ayer - *Voltaire*, 1986, 175 pp., Fontana, pbk.

Also excellent on Voltaire:

Peter Gay - *Voltaire's Politics*, 1959, 400 pp., Vintage. pbk, New York.
Roy Porter - *Enlightenment: Britain and the Creation of the Modern World*, 2000, 480 pp. of text, Penguin. pbk. This book protests against the identification of the Enlightenment largely with the French *philosophes*, and argues convincingly that it had its roots in England, and flourished abundantly there from the Glorious to the French Revolution.
Terry Pinkard - *Hegel: a Biography*, 2000. 780 pp. (*ca.* 100 pp. of which are notes etc.), CUP. Ten interesting chapters on biographical material and social and political background. The philosophical material is mercifully separated into five other chapters, and these are pretty impenetrable.

A large and powerful book on Schopenhauer: **Bryan Magee** - *The Philosophy of Schopenhauer*, 450 pp., revised edition OUP, pbk, 1997. Schopenhauer is

Magee's favourite philosopher. Even Magee, a master of clear exposition, cannot make some of Schopenhauer's more difficult ideas easily digestible, but, bearing this in mind, this is still a lucid account of an immensely stimulating philosopher.
Robert C. Solomon and Kathleen M. Higgins - *What Nietzsche Really Said*, 270 pp, Schocken, 2000
Louis Menand – *The Metaphysical Club*, 2001, 550 pp., Flamingo, pbk. This book interweaves the biographies and thoughts of four American philosophers – C.S. Peirce, William James, John Dewey and Oliver Wendell Holmes. It won the prestigious Pulitzer Prize for History in 2002.
Richard Noll - *The Jung Cult*, 390 pp., Fontana, pbk, 1996.

In Peter Halban (Weidenfeld & Nicolson) series on Jewish Thinkers:
Buber (Pamela Vermes).
Three excellent works on Existentialism:
John Macquarrie - *Existentialism*, 1973, 250 pp., Penguin.
Nathan A.Scott - *Mirror of Man in Existentialism*, 1969, 250pp., Collins.
J.H.Blackham - *Six Existentialist Thinkers*, 1952, 180 pp., Routledge.

Covering Existentialism, Structuralism and other aspects of French thought, there is **Eric Matthews** - *Twentieth Century French Thought*, 1996, 275 pp., Oxford University Press.

The only moderately readable book I have come across on Structuralism:
John Sturrock - *Structuralism*, 1986, 190 pp., Paladin.

Sturrock had also edited *Structuralism and Since*, 1979, 190 pp., OUP, pbk. I found the only reasonably comprehensible parts to be the chapters written by Sturrock himself - the Introduction and the chapter on Roland Barthes. The chapters, written by others, on Lévi-Strauss, Foucault, Lacan, and Derrida seemed to me impenetrable.

Some Biographies:

P.N.Furbank - *Diderot*, 1992, 500 pp, Minerva, pbk.
Hugo Ott - *Martin Heidegger: A Political Life*, 1994, 400 pp, Fontana, pbk.
Ray Monk - *Ludwig Wittgenstein*, 1990, 660 pp, Vintage, pbk. (Quite superb!)
Allan Janik and Stephen Toulmin - *Wittgenstein's Vienna*, 1973, 270 pp., Elephant, pbk. In parts very difficult, but stimulating in tracing the influence on Wittgenstein's thought of the cultural climate of Vienna in Wittgenstein's time.
David Edmonds & John Eidinow - *Wittgenstein's Poker*, 2001, 260 pp. Faber & Faber. A delightfully readable book centred on what was at stake on the occasion when Wittgenstein threatened Popper with a poker.
Ray Monk - *Bertrand Russell: The Spirit of Solitude*, 700 pp, Vintage pbk, 1996. Vivid picture of the man and his personal life, but as an account of his philosophy, it is not a patch on the Wittgenstein book, as it only occupies a relatively small part of the book and is less successful in making Russell's difficult early philosophy understandable to the average reader. The book ends in 1921. The second volume, *The Ghost of Madness, 1921 to 1970*, is even thinner in philosophical material - not surprisingly, as Russell's creative contributions to philosophy after 1921 were minimal.
Michael Ignatieff - *Isaiah Berlin: A Life*, 300 pp., Chatto & Windus, 1998.

Ben Rogers - *A.J. Ayer: A Life*, 360 pp., Chatto & Windus, 1999.

Some Novels

Robert M. Pirsig - *Zen and the Art of Motorcycle Maintenance,* 1974, 400 pp., Corgi, pbk. An account of a journey across America in which physical as well as philosophical heights are painfully scaled by the principal character. He is in search of the meaning of "Quality", and that leads him to explore great areas of the history of philosophy. The blurb rightly describes it as "an explosive detective story of high ideas". The sequel, *Lila: An Inquiry into Morals* (Bantam Press, 1991, 420 pp.) covers some of the same ground and isn't quite so good, but still has a lot of stimulating ideas.

Bruce Duffy - *The World as I Found It*, 546 pp., Penguin, pbk., 1990. A very enjoyable fictional triple biography of Wittgenstein, Bertrand Russell, and G.E. Moore and the relationship between them. Duffy takes some very slight liberties with facts, but gives a vivid picture of the three men (and of course avoids the grittier parts of their philosophies).

Jostein Gaarder - *Sophie's World*, 436 pp, Phoenix, pbk., 1995. Written by a Norwegian school teacher and intended for teenagers, this is a novel about a fourteen-year old girl learning about philosophy. There is an extraneous and confusing mystery plot which is supposed to have some bearing on the wilder aspects of Romantic philosophy and which I found exceedingly tiresome, but the body of the book is a remarkably clear account of the *basic* history and problems of philosophy. If you can stand the arch and patronizing tone, it is excellent for beginners of every age.

Index[1]

1 In the Index the word "and" before a page number does not necessarily mean that they directly refer to each other. Often it refers to the *context* in which there is a mention of the name or concept in question, or a wide-ranging discussion in which I make comparisons or point out contrasts.

Bold type indicates the main treatment and the letters **fff** indicate a long section dedicated to the name or concept in question.